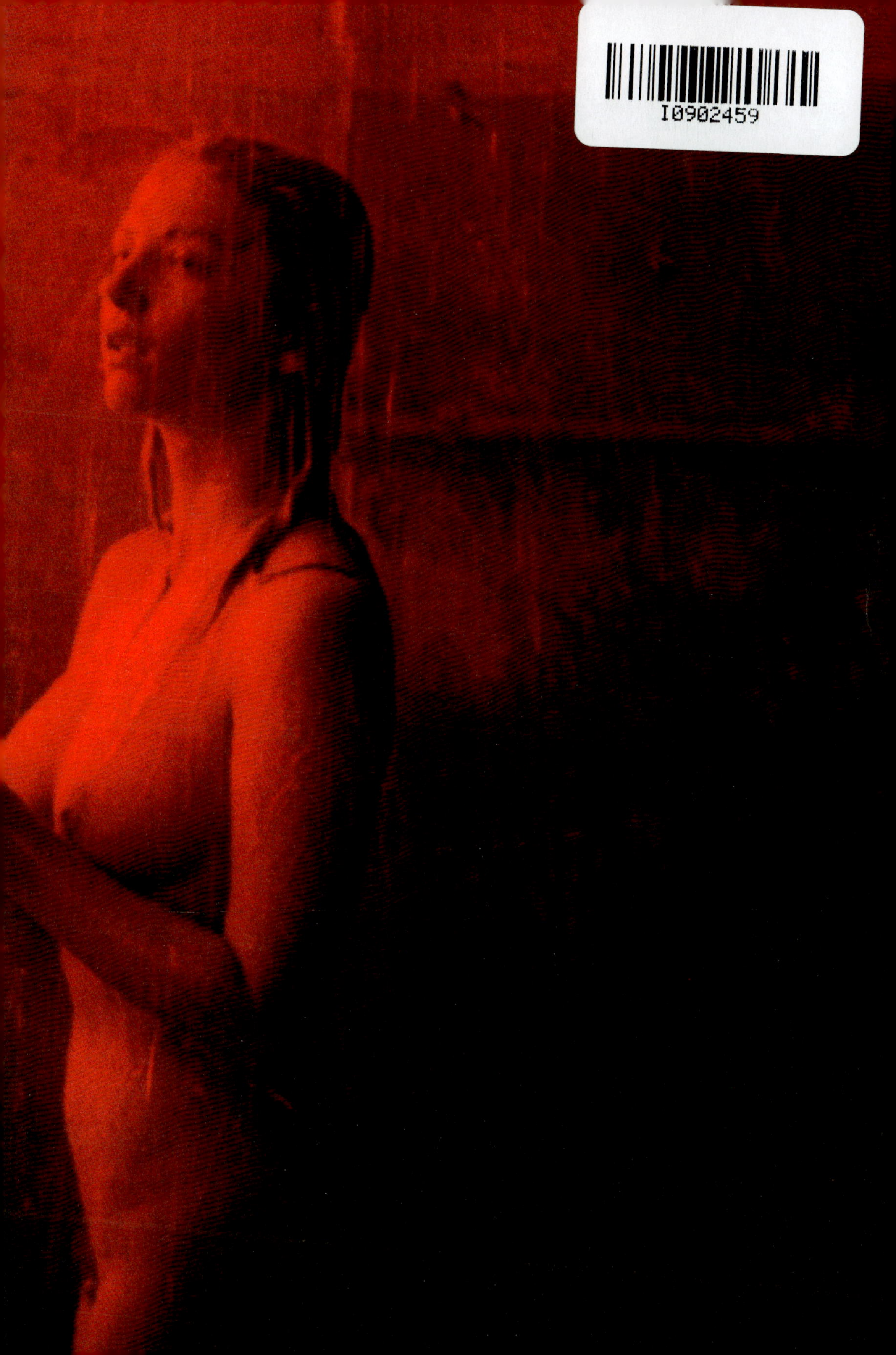

FRONT COVER

Milja Vujanović in *Early Works*, 1968.

BACK COVER

Marko Nikolić and Milja Vujanović in *Early Works*, 1968.

FRONT MATTER

Milja Vujanović in *Early Works*, 1968.

PHOTOS: ANDREJ POPOVIĆ.

ISBN 978-3-95679-520-6

shadow citizens
želimir žilnik

PUBLISHED ON THE OCCASION OF THE EXHIBITION
Shadow Citizens—Želimir Žilnik
19.04–17.06 2018
CURATED BY What, How & for Whom/WHW and presented by the Edith-Russ-Haus for Media Art, Oldenburg

PUBLISHED BY
Edith-Russ-Haus for Media Art
and Sternberg Press

EDITORS
What, How & for Whom/WHW [Ivet Ćurlin • Ana Dević • Nataša Ilić • Sabina Sabolović]

CONTRIBUTORS
Boris Buden • Greg de Cuir Jr • Ana Janevski • Dijana Jelača • Edit Molnár • Bert Rebhandl •
Marcel Schwierin • What, How & for Whom/WHW • Želimir Žilnik

MANAGING EDITOR
Milica Vlajković

PROJECT COORDINATION
Ulrich Kreienbrink • Edit Molnár

TRANSLATIONS
Miljenka Buljević [QUOTATIONS] • Barbara Hess • Bert Rebhandl • Michael Stoeber [FILM DESCRIPTIONS] •
Michael Wolfson

COPYEDITING
Jaclyn Arndt [ENGLISH] • Martin Conrads [GERMAN] • Birgit Eusterschulte [GERMAN]

PRODUCTION
Edith-Russ-Haus for Media Art

GRAPHIC DESIGN
Dejan Kršić

PHOTO EDITING
Skaner Studio • Marija Matijašec

PRINTING & BINDING
Skaner Studio, Croatia

FUNDED BY

KULTURSTIFTUNG DES BUNDES

Niedersächsisches Ministerium für Wissenschaft und Kultur

EWE | STIFTUNG

German Federal Cultural Foundation

ISBN 978-3-95679-520-6

The Deutsche Nationalbibliothek lists this publication in the Deutsche Nationalbibliografie; detailed bibliographic data is available online at https://dnb.dnb.de.

EDITH RUSS HAUS for Media Art

shadow citizens

želimir žilnik

OLDENBURG • BERLIN • NOVI SAD • ZAGREB

Sternberg Press

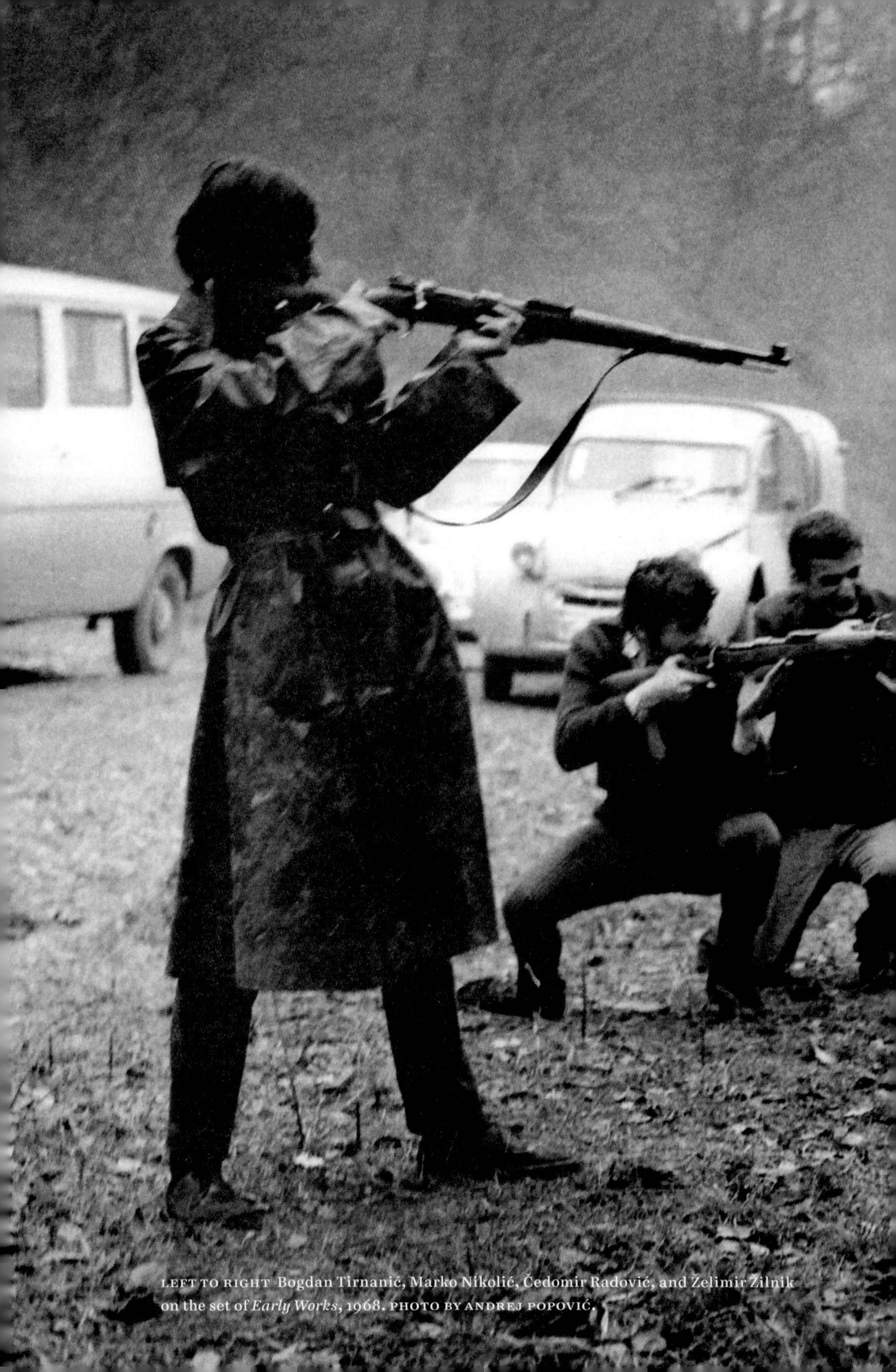

LEFT TO RIGHT Bogdan Tirnanić, Marko Nikolić, Čedomir Radović, and Želimir Žilnik on the set of *Early Works*, 1968. PHOTO BY ANDREJ POPOVIĆ.

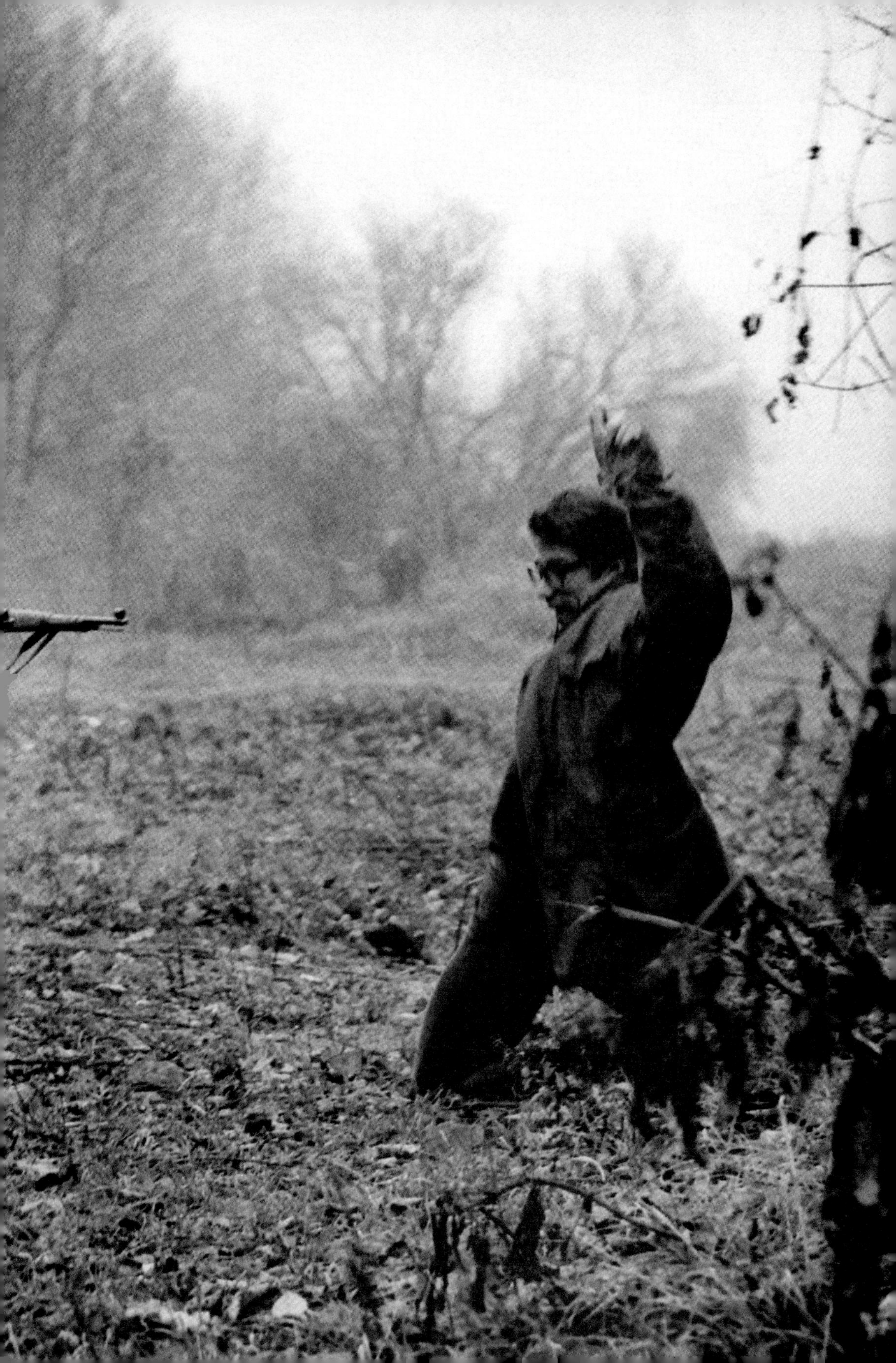

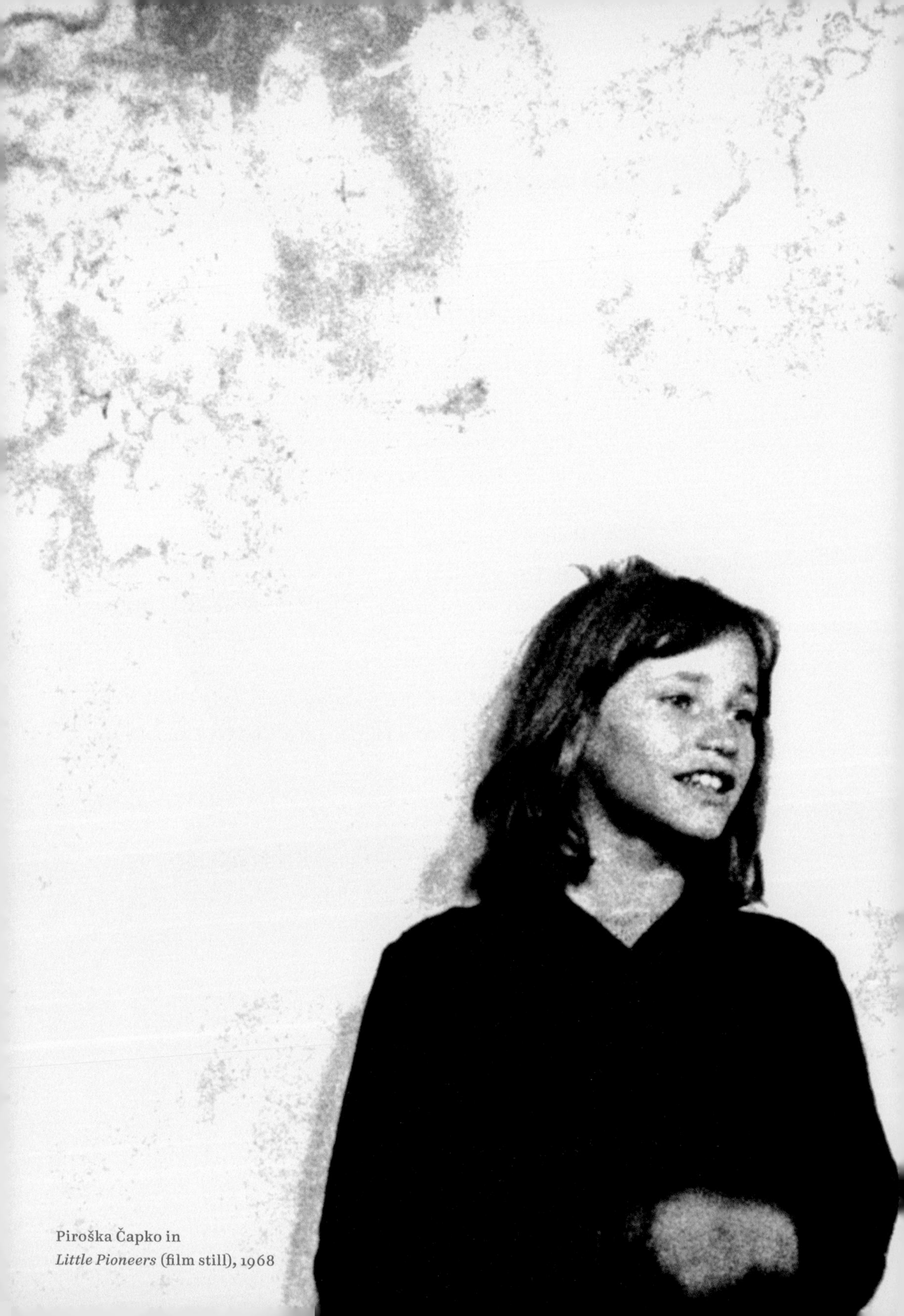

Piroška Čapko in
Little Pioneers (film still), 1968

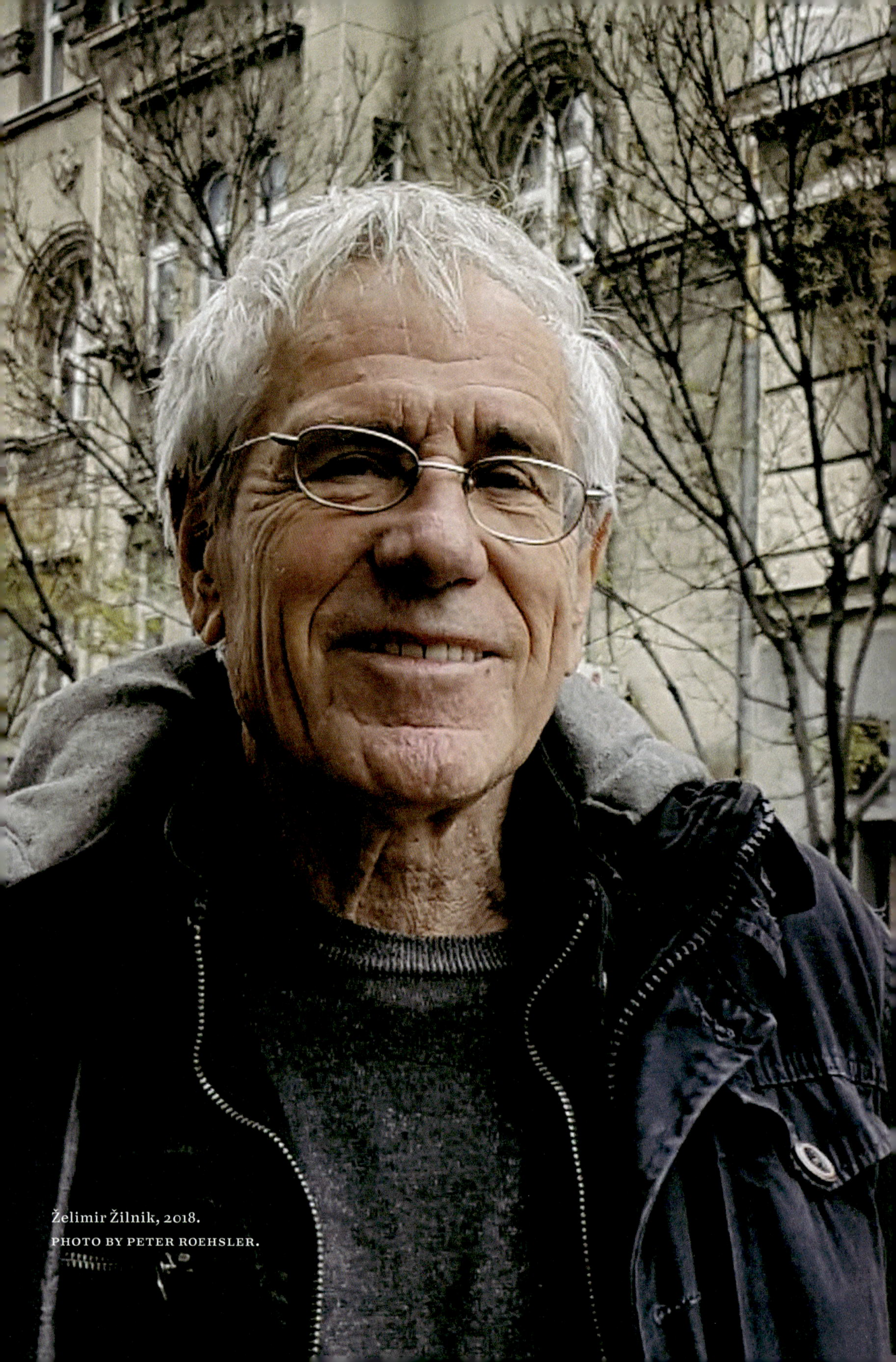

Želimir Žilnik, 2018.
PHOTO BY PETER ROEHSLER.

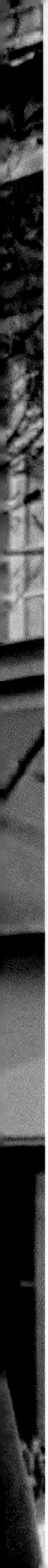

I make movies because we're still not in communism. I make movies to warn about how many things we still need to do in order to get there. I am not interested in art film. When it comes to documentary film, we really don't have time to talk about art. The documentary film is, primarily, a possibility given to a man, a woman, or a child to impart in one breath the pain that sits in one's stomach, and which obviously is not only their own private thing. This "possibility," this is actually the sensitivity of silver bromide to light, and nearly all the rest I leave up to the personalities that my documentaries are concerned with.

—Želimir Žilnik, interview, "Art Film Does Not Interest Me," *Susret,* April 5, 1968.

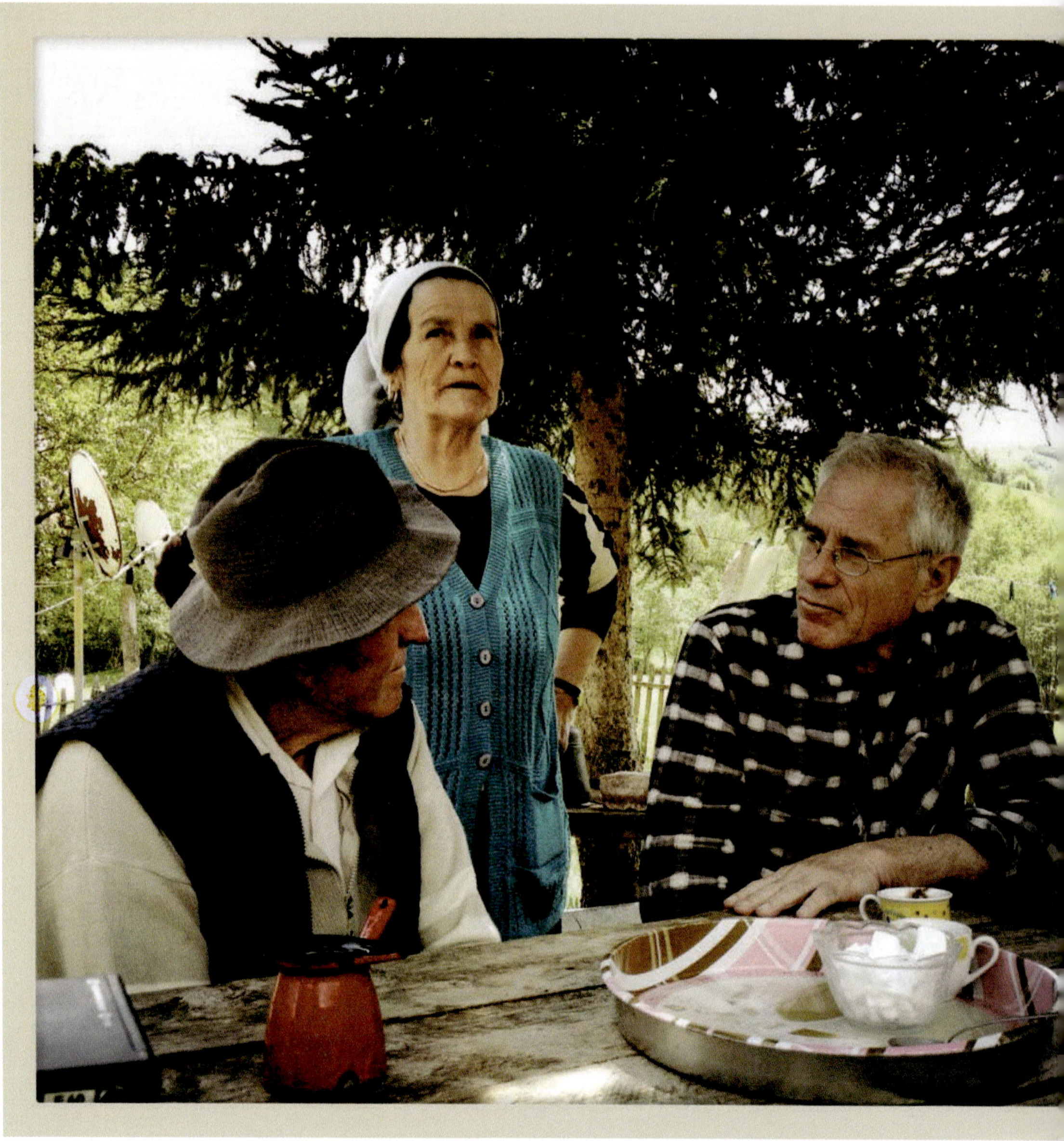

Logbook_Serbistan (on-set photo), 2014.
PHOTO BY ORFEAS SKUTELIS.

EDIT MOLNÁR
&
MARCEL
SCHWIERIN

A Radical, Pragmatic Humanist

During the first stages of our planning for an exhibition of Želimir Žilnik's work, we were faced with the realization that Žilnik's oeuvre is certainly well known in the film world, but almost not at all in a fine art context. However, his artistic methods of social intervention and participatory dialogue with his protagonists, along with his combination of the fictional and the documentary, are crucial strategies in contemporary art. Žilnik developed these methods as early as the 1960s and has continued to use them with unique determination over the ensuing decades. In other words: especially from the perspective of fine art, there is much to discover in Žilnik's practice.

We find three central moments to be particularly defining for his work.

The first is his profound and personally lived humanism. Žilnik likes people. He does not shy away from those who have been shut out by society or who have notions about human coexistence that are completely different from his own. He not only makes his protagonists the heroes of their own stories but also turns them into creative narrators, thus breaking with the classic power imbalance between the people behind and in front of the camera. This artistic approach, which is already alluded to in his first films, like *A Newsreel on Village Youth, in Winter* (1967) and *The Unemployed* (1968), came to fruition in the *Kenedi* trilogy (2003–07). Questions concerning the representation of protagonist-collaborators and their share of autonomy in the work's creation is presently being intensely discussed in the art world and forms the foundation for numerous contemporary artistic approaches. Žilnik was far ahead of his time in this regard.

As friendly as Žilnik is to people, he is just as harsh in his critique of the social conditions that exclude his protagonists. Žilnik has worked under many different political systems and has constantly come into conflict with them. He never allows himself to be fenced in, neither through threats nor through promises. It seems as if the classic bourgeois fear of decline and exclusion is completely alien to him. This relentless critique of political systems from the perspective of the disadvantaged and exploited is the second defining element of his practice.

Žilnik owes his intellectual freedom to a third central quality he possesses: a special artistic pragmatism. He never predefines his filmic methodology but responds flexibly to each challenge that confronts him. When it became impossible for him to produce films for cinema in Yugoslavia or West Germany, after falling out of favor with the decision makers in each country, he turned to television. When he was unable to hire actress Hanna Schygulla to perform in his film *Paradise. An Imperialist Tragicomedy* (1976), he decided it would instead star his costume designer, Gisela Siebauer. When he had only a three-figure budget, as was the case for his satirical masterpiece *Tito among the Serbs for the Second Time* (1994), he made a forty-five-minute film for a sum that would not even have sufficed as petty cash in a commercial film production. Such a filmmaker cannot be blackmailed with the threat common to every system—that is, that his means of production will simply be confiscated. He just continues working.

A further defining aspect of Žilnik's approach to filmmaking is that he did not train at a film school where students learn to work with professional budgets; rather, he came up through the amateur film scene, where one had to learn how to make the most of minimal means. The particular economy of his productions is perhaps why he was also immune to the siren call of the mainstream film industry, which promised talented filmmakers wealth, fame, and an exciting existence if only they subjected themselves to its rules and regulations. The course of Žilnik's career has been accordingly unusual—from winning the Berlinale's Golden Bear award, to his appearance at the International Short Film Festival Oberhausen as a groundbreaking underground star, to becoming a television director and his present-day work as an independent documentary filmmaker.

Transferring this unique film oeuvre to the "white cube" of the exhibition space was no easy task. With the Zagreb-based collective What, How & for Whom/WHW as guest curators, we were able to gain the extraordinary expertise of four curators in the field of Yugoslavian art and film who are able to contextualize and rethink Žilnik's work in the contemporary art sphere. For the exhibition at the Edith-Russ-Haus, WHW developed an experimental, almost analytical, format. While only some of the filmmaker's central works were shown in full, as projections or on monitors, most of his films were exhibited in excerpts organized around diverse themes from his oeuvre. These excerpts appeared on discarded office computer monitors attached to used construction-site fences. The monitor cables came up against the fences' coarse concrete bases, which were still dirty with paint and plaster. This seemingly improvised format was nevertheless meticulously conceived, and it required a particular generosity on the part of the artist—an artist who does not view his work as a personal achievement and as his personal property, but rather as a mutual utopian effort put forth by all the participants in their making, on behalf of another possible world. ★

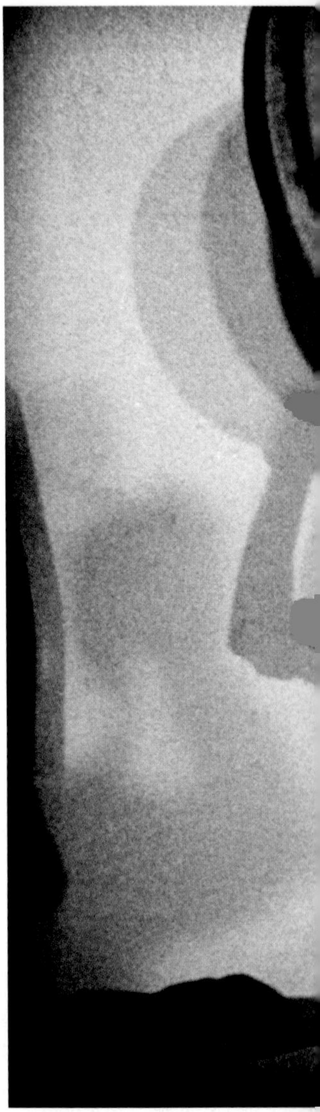

TRANSLATED FROM GERMAN BY MICHAEL WOLFSON

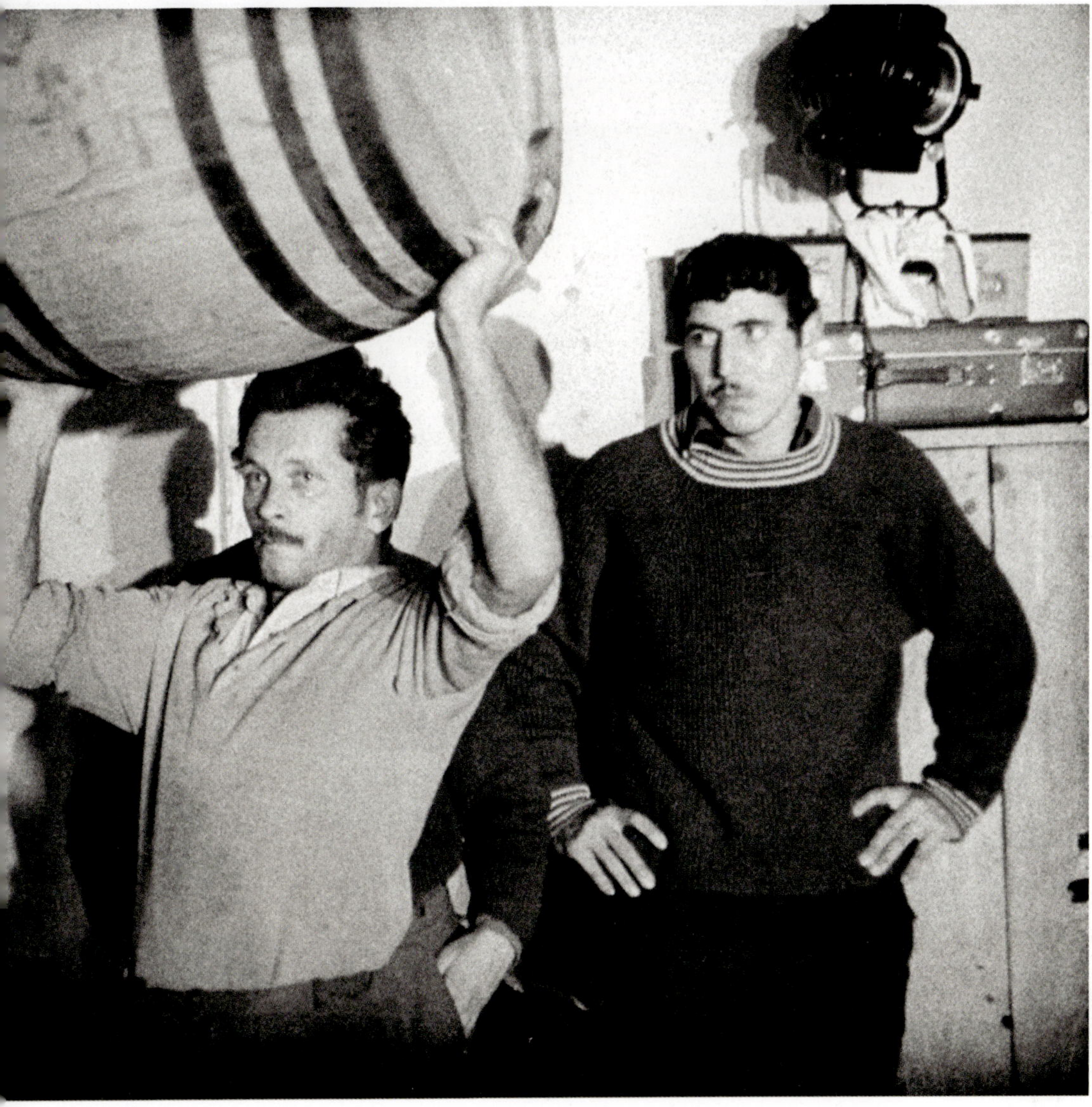

The Unemployed (film still), 1968

I want to tell you this: mostly my films were screened at the time they were made. They had good success even abroad. In the meantime, I made a bunch of TV films. But since here [in Yugoslavia] there are no things that are of normal size, we give everything the flavor of scandal, banning, enmity. We're working hard against ourselves. As if we need dissidents. Instead of being proud for being the only socialist country without dissidents, there are forces that permanently push for something to be banned. Of course, there was a political campaign in this country against critical film. [...] But you can see such comical situations occurring every ten years. All the films from the period of Black Wave had mostly very good success in international festivals. [...] Even the critics who wrote positively about these [new] films are 90 percent the same as the ones who wrote positively about those [earlier] films. And with very similar argumentation. It is a very simple formula by which films from one country become internationally interesting. They become interesting when they speak of the important issues of that country, but also when the issues presented in the film overlap with the stereotypical images of that country that are out in the world. Being a country interesting for social crises and a confusion that we emanate, the films by Boro Drašković or young [Emir] Kusturica articulated well in an authentic way some of those images about the current moment in Yugoslavia.

—Želimir Žilink, interview, "The Director Bored with Black Wave: We Don't Need Dissidents," *Polet*, January 17, 1986.

Žilnik has always been an engaged essayist but never a pamphletist. He has never marked his own position as heroic in any sense. He has never positioned himself above the failure of the society and dominant ideologies to either improve the subject or to discipline the subject. His films, therefore, do not provide some righteous point of view but explore his own beliefs and assumptions in the most critical way.

—Branislav Dimitrijević, "Behind Scepticism Lies the Fire of a Revolutionary!," in *For an Idea – Against the Status Quo: Analysis and Systematization of Želimir Žilnik's Artistic Practice* (Novi Sad: New Media Center_kuda.org, Playground produkcija, 2009), 148.

The implementation of self-management in culture enabled the organizational models of co-production, in which the crew would organize themselves into a film work collective, and invest their "creative labour" while the production house would invest the technical equipment. Our contracts would state something like: "Želimir Žilnik is entering this production by investing 60% of his director's fee that will only be paid if the movie brings in profit..." This way, the "actual" money invested in the film by the production house would be smaller and the risk would fall on the crew, who were working for free. Contracts would also stipulate how the profits, if there were any, would be shared, and also when the film would become profitable.

Avala Film had a policy to produce two feature films of debuting directors each year. In 1968, as I was the author who had won the Grand Prix Oberhausen for my documentary *The Unemployed,* and a silver medal of Belgrade for my short film *Little Pioneers,* it was my turn. As my idea for a film, *Early Works,* seemed too unfeasible, I was asked to take the risky road and I managed to make Neoplanta the co-producer, knowing that this would give me more freedom as an author.

—Želimir Žilnik, in conversation with Dubravka Sekulić, Gal Kirn, and Žiga Testen, in *Surfing the Black: Yugoslav Black Wave Cinema and Its Transgressive Moments,* ed. Gal Kirn, Dubravka Sekulić, and Žiga Testen (Maastricht: Jan van Eyck Academie, 2012), 63.

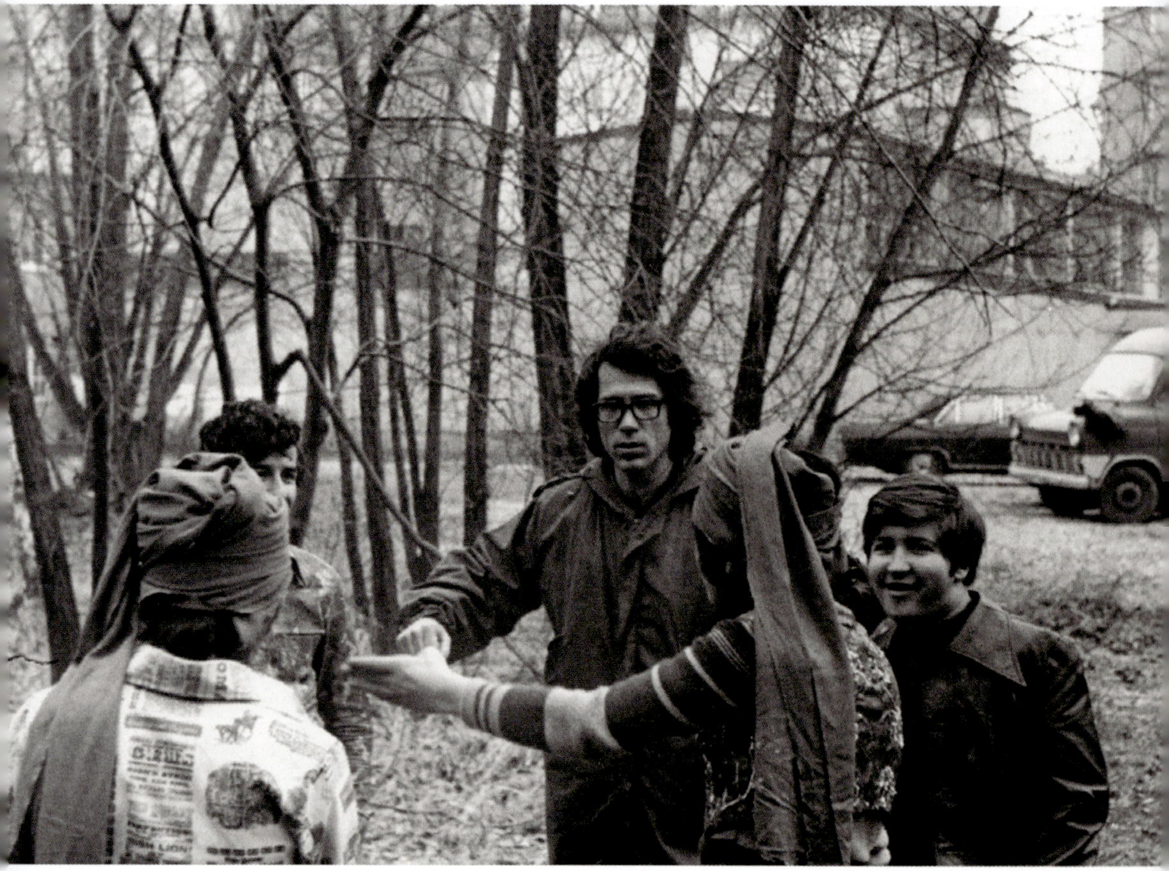

Paradise. An Imperialist Tragicomedy (on-set photo), 1975.
PHOTO BY ANDREJ POPOVIĆ.

WHAT, HOW & FOR WHOM / WHW

Želimir Žilnik — Shadow Citizens

The book *Shadow Citizens* expands upon the exhibition of the same name held at the Edith-Russ-Haus for Media Art in 2018, which for the first time offered insight into the radical film praxis and extensive oeuvre of filmmaker Želimir Žilnik (b. 1942, based in Novi Sad, Serbia) within the exhibition context. From his beginnings in the lively amateur film scene of Yugoslavia in the 1960s, Žilnik has gone on to make more than fifty films, including a number of feature films and TV productions, often in the genre of docudrama. He received international recognition early on, winning the Golden Bear for Best Film at the 1969 Berlin International Film Festival for *Early Works* (1969). In the 1970s, his films encountered political opposition, and he left Yugoslavia for Germany, where he realized several independent films including some of the earliest films dealing with the topic of *Gastarbeiter*, or guest workers. In the 1980s, after leaving Germany—due to his films once again facing political opposition and censorship—and returning to Yugoslavia, Žilnik made numerous TV and feature films through which he portrays early symptoms of the country's growing social conflicts, continuing in the 1990s with films dealing with the maladies of the postsocialist transition as well as questions of migration.

Many of Žilnik's films have prophetically announced real-world events that mirror topics tackled in his work, such as the dissolution of Yugoslavia, its economic transition from socialism to a neoliberal order, the annihilation of workers' rights, and wider social erosion related to labor and migration. The title *Shadow Citizens* reflects Žilnik's lifelong focus on invisible, suppressed, and under- and misrepresented members of society and relates to themes that run through the director's filmography, such as questions of shadow economies, borders, migration, labor, terrorism, revolutionary fatigue, clashes of parallel modernisms, and more. As a concept, "shadow citizens" is related to a form of political engagement toward "amateur politics"—the imaginative and subversive nonnormative knowledge and alternative sensibilities that always lie dormant in a society and occasionally visibly push back against "politics as usual." According to urban theorist Andy Merrifield, amateur and professional politics are in fact political divisions that can be reclaimed and moved like tectonic plates.[01] Courageous amateurism is prominent in Žilnik's films, both as a concept and as a method. The notion of shadow citizens, conceived as different minorities that are increasingly becoming majorities everywhere, runs through Žilnik's oeuvre, where it is taken up as a possibility to imagine a new concept of citizenship that pushes current limits and borders. Different facets of the potentials of shadow citizens and the pressures of the amateur undercurrent in emancipatory politics and artistic production tackled in Žilnik's films also shed light on contemporary social and political urgencies.

Essays commissioned for this book situate Žilnik's body of work in broad social, cultural, and artistic contexts while focusing on more specific, often neglected, points of his practice related to gender,

01 Andy Merrifield, *The Amateur: The Pleasures of Doing What You Love* (London: Verso, 2017).

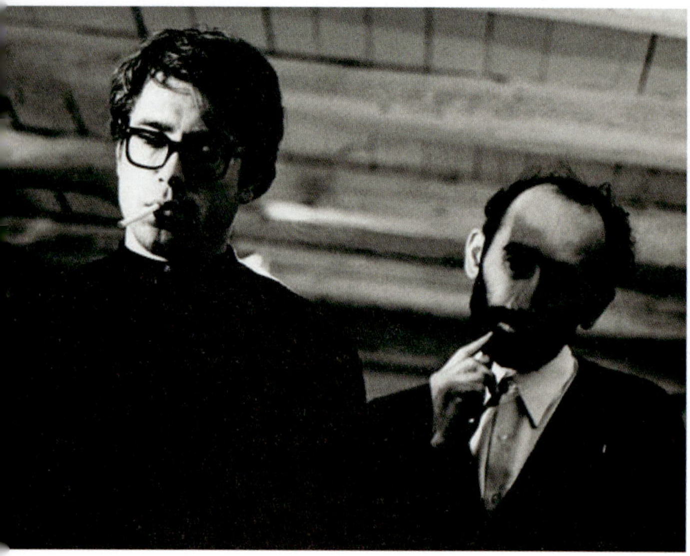 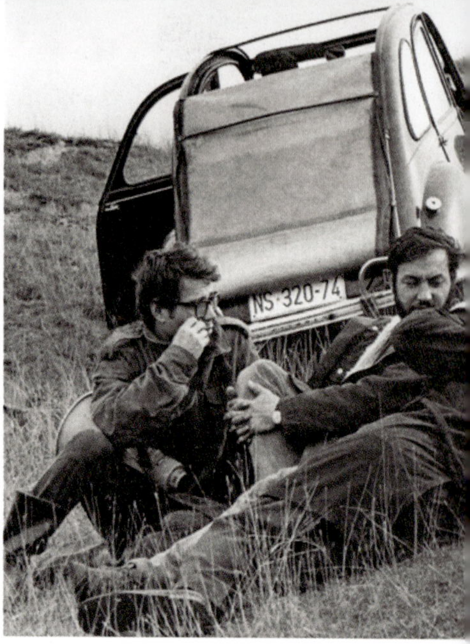

racial, pop cultural, and political issues, shedding light both on particularities of Socialist Yugoslavia and on its relevance in the wretched present moment of a world whose future is threatened by the relentless reproduction of capital.

Early Works (on-set photos), 1968. PHOTOS BY ANDREJ POPOVIĆ. LEFT: Želimir Žilnik and Branko Vučićević (cowriter). RIGHT: Želimir Žilnik, Karpo Godina, and the crew.

Bert Rebhandl introduces Žilnik's oeuvre in relation to international currents of experimental and documentary filmmaking and explicates the political tenets of the ethics Žilnik practices in his documentary approach. Ana Janevski focuses on the abundant performative practices in his films, their structural meanings, and their relations to forms of popular culture. Dijana Jelača discusses the politics of gender and sexuality in relation to Žilnik's attitude toward the intersecting political domains of class, identity, and gender in the specific cultural and political times and places in which his films were made. Greg de Cuir Jr looks into the legacy of the Non-Aligned Movement and how it pertains to Žilnik's approach to his protagonists, including both its blind spots and its emancipatory promises. Boris Buden's essay, originally published in *Afterall* magazine in 2010, analyzes Žilnik's film praxis in relation to the so-called Black Wave films and considers the ideological background of the cultural debates around them in the late 1960s from today's perspective.

The exhibition and the book *Shadow Citizens* rely on the research and writing of numerous colleagues. Particularly precious are the continuous research and publishing efforts of the Novi Sad–based organization kuda.org. Through their project *For an Idea – Against the Status Quo: An Analysis and Systematization of Želimir Žilnik's Artistic Practice*, they laid immense groundwork and created an essential resource for anyone interested in Žilnik's practice.[02] The project both provides access to archival information and original materials and gathers together the insightful voices of many researchers in the first extensive monograph on Žilnik's work, published in 2009.

02 Želimir Žilnik's website (https://www.zilnikzelimir.net) was initially launched in 2009 on the occasion of the project *For an Idea – Against the Status Quo*. The site was extensively updated for the exhibition *Shadow Citizens* at the Edith-Russ-Haus for Media Art, Oldenburg, April 19–June 17, 2018.

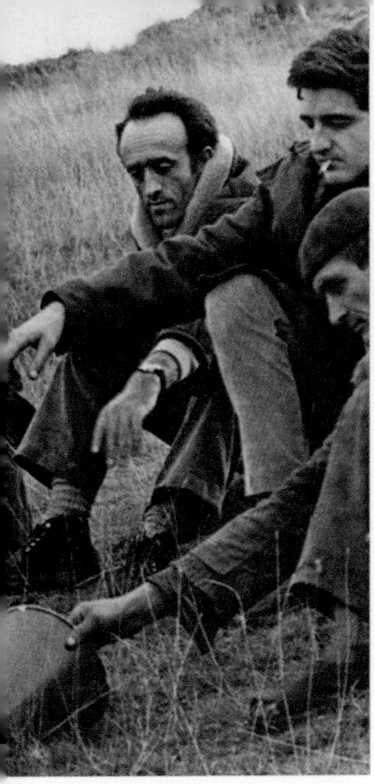

kuda.org's work on Žilnik continued through the book *An Introduction to the Past,* realized by Boris Buden and published by kuda.org in 2013, which stands as a crucial political and theoretical contribution to the understanding of Žilnik's work within the Yugoslav context.

The research organized by Gal Kirn and Dubravka Sekulić and presented in the book *Surfing the Black: Yugoslav Black Wave Cinema and Its Transgressive Moments,* which was published by the Jan van Eyck Academie in 2012, was also a source we constantly went back to. Additionally, the magazine *Afterall* issued an important special section on Žilnik in 2010, and we are thankful for the permission to reprint Buden's text from it. We also want to acknowledge the years of research and writing on Žilnik by Buden, Branko Dimitrijević, Pavle Levi, and Jurij Meden, whose texts are crucial to our understanding of Žilnik's work. We have tried to make all these important voices present through extended quotes placed throughout the book. This volume also includes a number of quotes by Žilnik himself, taken from numerous interviews given over more than five decades.

Much of the abovementioned research on Žilnik was carried out under circumstances of official institutional ignorance toward such critical and experimental practices. This is something that many similar initiatives operating in the territory of former Yugoslavia have experienced. After the breakup of Yugoslavia, most cultural institutions displayed either amnesia or open animosity toward the progressive voices that had arisen during the socialist era, which were clearly critical of the new nationalist regimes that ruled during the harsh and corrupted decades of new nation-state building. Many initiatives have and continue to support each other in their efforts, sharing both the claim that post-Yugoslav generations have a right to be interested in this period and in experimental practices, as well as the political perspective from which we look back at the preceding era. This is why it is worth mentioning that part of the research on this history was done within the collaborative project *Political Practices of (Post-)Yugoslav Art,* organized by Prelom kolektiv (Belgrade), kuda.org (Novi Sad), SCCA/pro.ba (Sarajevo), and WHW (Zagreb), which from 2006 to 2010 looked into numerous cases of joint and neglected history. Of course, over time a lot of this type of work gets picked up by institutional structures, but the groundwork laid by independent initiatives is rarely acknowledged and often ends up framed without sufficient political and critical clarity.

Both the exhibition and book *Shadow Citizens* would not have been possible without the constant and generous support of Sarita Matijević, Žilnik's partner and producer, who not only patiently provided us with access to Žilnik's films and all the documentary material around them, but also shared her deep knowledge about these secondary sources and their authors, which goes far beyond facts and data.

Our deepest gratitude goes to Želimir Žilnik, whose passion for storytelling and political clarity never fails to inspire us. ★

Already in the 1960s, the official politics exhibited, in my opinion, baseless fear in relation to the critical, socialist, youth mood, which was articulated in youth press of limited circulation, in artistic experiments—from film to poetry, in the fields of sociology and philosophy. For me, that fear was baseless and it led to devastating results: to the reactionary trend, not artistic but political, that was first hinted at by suggestions that everyone should stick their noses only in the history of their own regions and nation. And it was later widened by "absolute regional sovereignty" in the economic and cadre policies, and by "limited Yugoslav sovereignty" in all these fields.

Leaders began to speak on behalf of Serbian, Croatian, and other working classes, so everything followed that logic: in order for local interest to be more strongly stressed, it had to be supported by "local whining," and then the bickering about who steals from whom began. And it's understandable that everything has to end in what is at the core of all tribes: both Dušan [Mihajlović] and Trpimir [Macan] stole, the Turks gouged beautiful eyes out, they all smashed arms and legs. The people were lying in heavy chains being suffocated by moldy stones. Serpent tongues bit and scorpions stung.

And our socialist state, instead of spreading literacy, creating new jobs, prescribing health and sexual education, our sad socialist state roars and wails over that "historical tragedy" of our peoples and nationalities, forgetting that all those peoples and nationalities had exactly that destiny: to be oppressed and frittered away by the powerful, and that socialism was invented for precisely that reason—to give people freedom and workers jobs and power.

—Želimir Žilnik, "Stories from the Lives of the People," *Nedjeljna Dalmacija*, May 17, 1987.

As Žilnik recently summed up, the biggest difference between the official ideology under socialism and what happens to be a "post-ideological" discourse of the "transitional" politics in states such as Serbia is that whilst today it is impossible to intellectually, artistically and politically challenge a dominant stance in an open discussion with politicians in power, in the SFRY [Socialist Federal Republic of Yugoslavia] in the 1960s, for example, it was common to have substantial arguments with main ideologists or decision-makers in cultural policy.

—Branislav Dimitrijević, "Concrete Analysis of Concrete Situations: Marxist Education According to Želimir Žilnik," *Afterall*, Autumn/Winter 2010, 52.

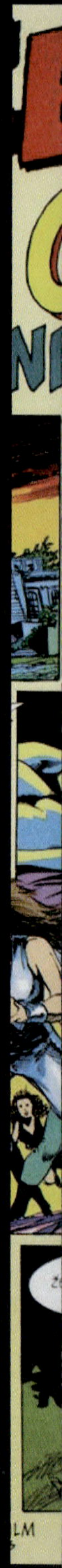

IN THE PRESS:
An interview with Želimir Žilnik in the magazine *Reporter*, September 5, 1986

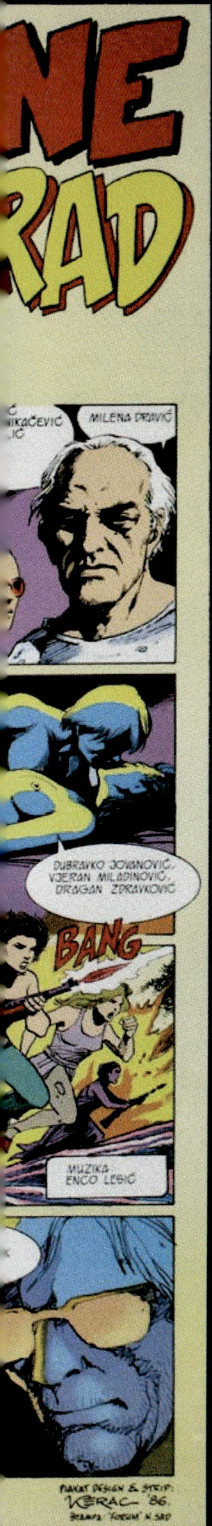

Intervju:
ŽELIMIR ŽILNIK

DA LI JE DOMAĆI FILM OGLUPAVIO?

Ja tvrdim da je bilo godina, ne kada je domaci film bio bolji nego što je danas, nego kada je govorio o važnijim stvarima i kada je u poredenju sa ostalim domenima kulture bio zanimljiviji i pametniji

Žilnik, on the contrary, approaches social problems in a simple, concrete and humane manner, which is after all the only working recipe for solving anything; conditioned, of course, by the spirit of solidarity and no other interest serving as motivation. This ability to familiarise and become one with the most marginal and diverse of environments has been Žilnik's trump card since the very beginning of his career as a filmmaker. Consequently his films fulfil Chris Marker's legendary utopia that true films about the workers will have to be made by the workers themselves, just as films about penguins will become conclusive only when penguins learn how to use a camera. Žilnik is not afraid to travel to the South Pole in a T-shirt and join the penguins; on top of that, his films not only convey this ability, but share with us the inspiring experience and knowledge gained from taking on these challenges.

—Jurij Meden, "Želimir Žilnik's Kenedi Trilogy," in *For an Idea – Against the Status Quo: Analysis and Systematization of Želimir Žilnik's Artistic Practice* (Novi Sad: New Media Center_kuda.org, Playground produkcija, 2009), 185.

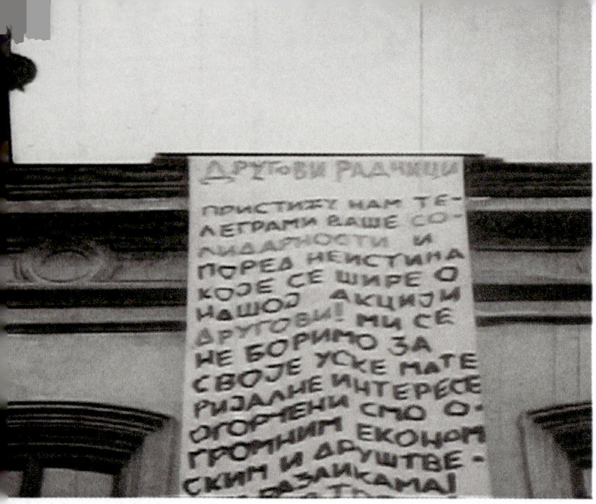

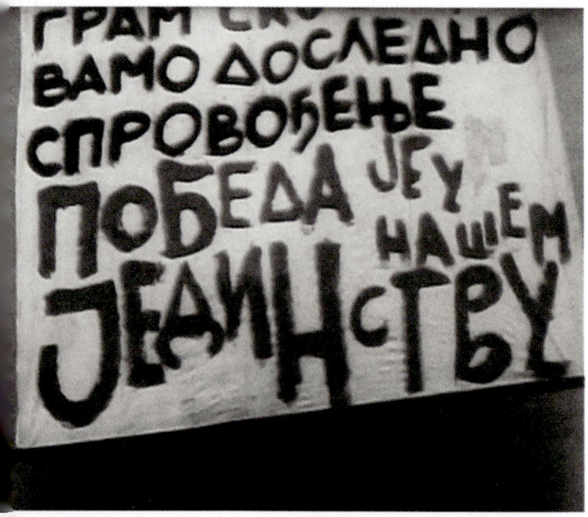

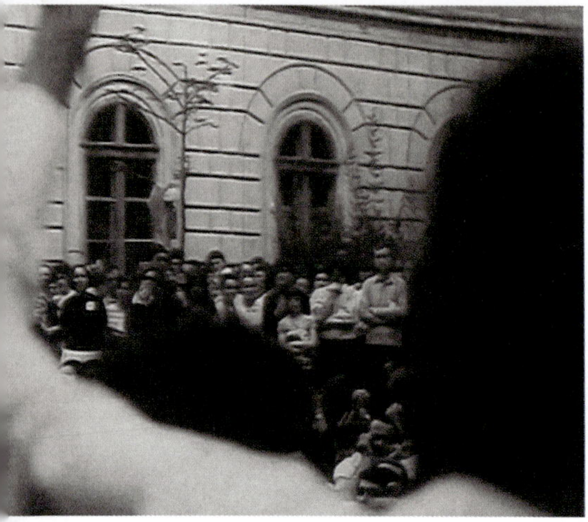

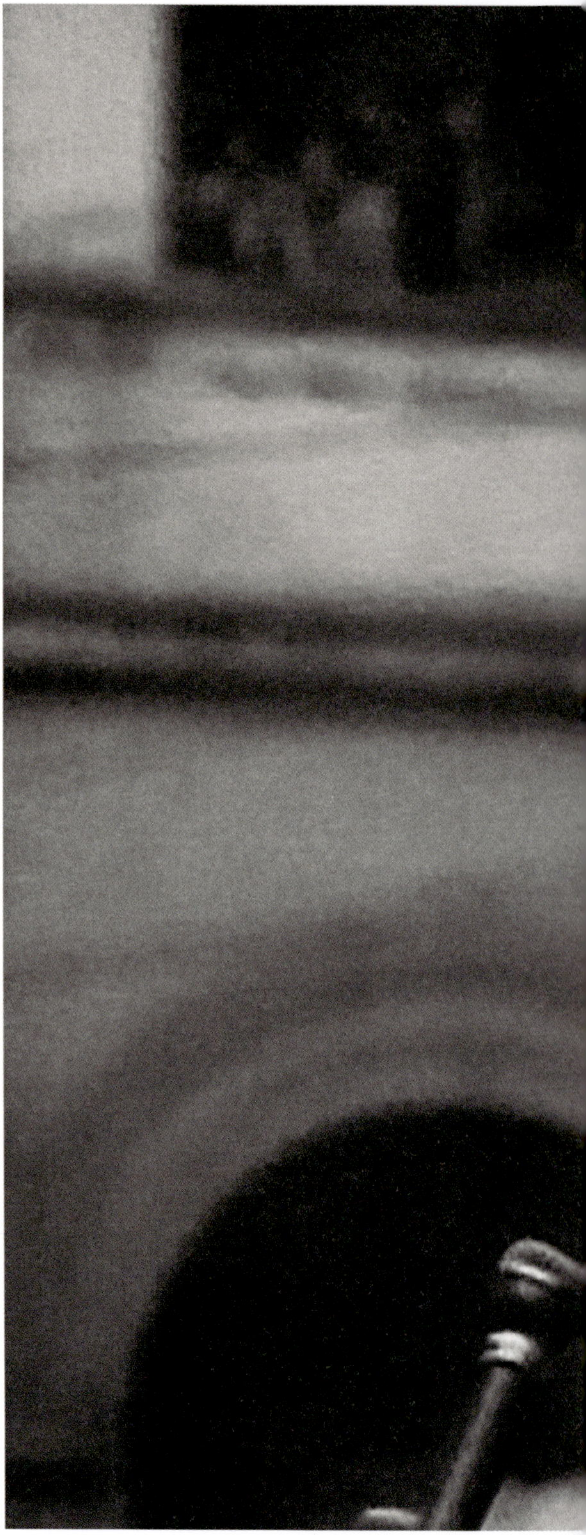

June Turmoil (film stills), 1969.
RIGHT: Stevo Žigon.

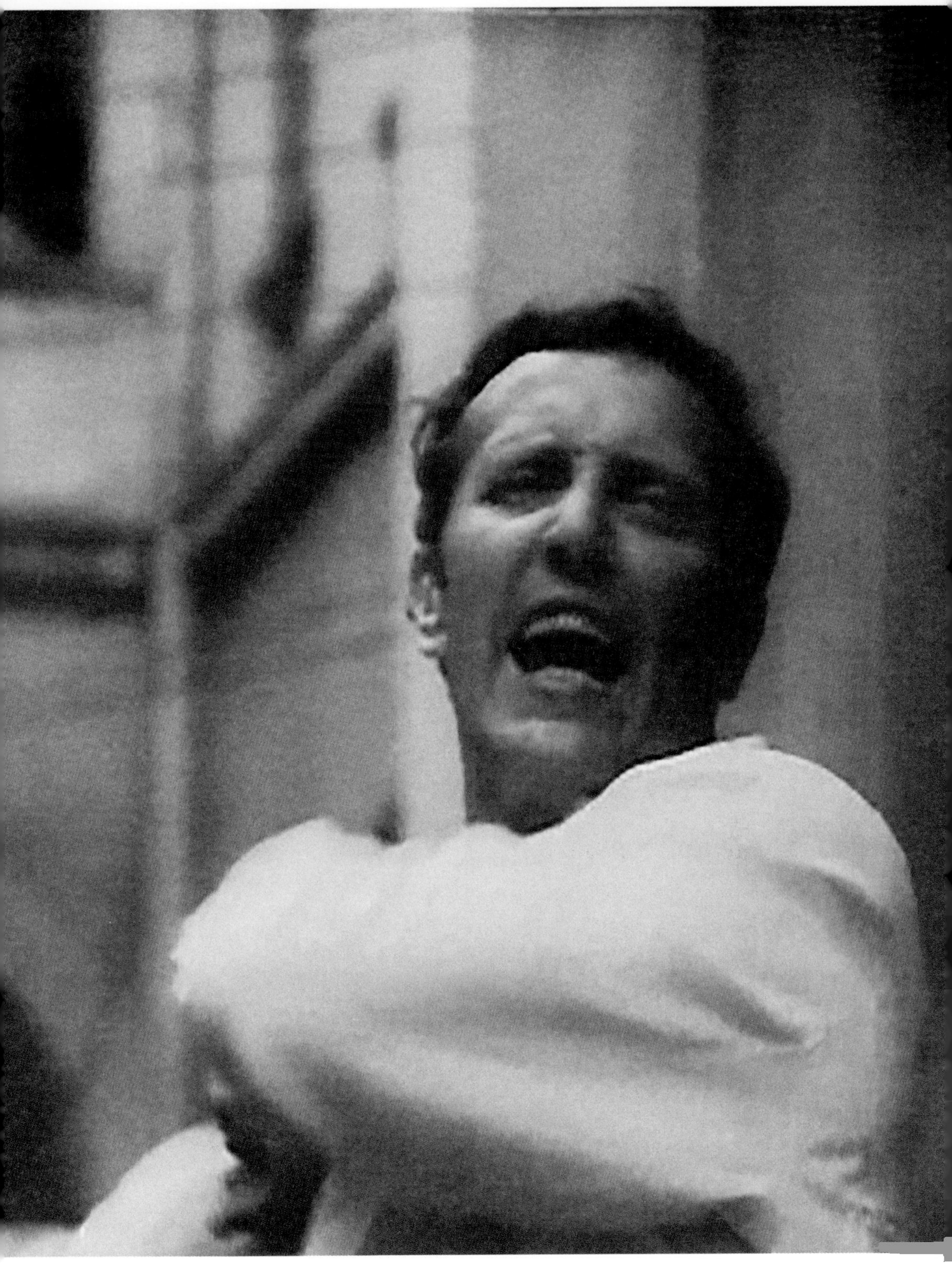

LEFT TO RIGHT Želimir Žilnik, Dušan Ninkov, Branko Vučićević, and Karpo Godina (kneeling) on the set of *Early Works*, 1968. PHOTO BY ANDREJ POPOVIĆ.

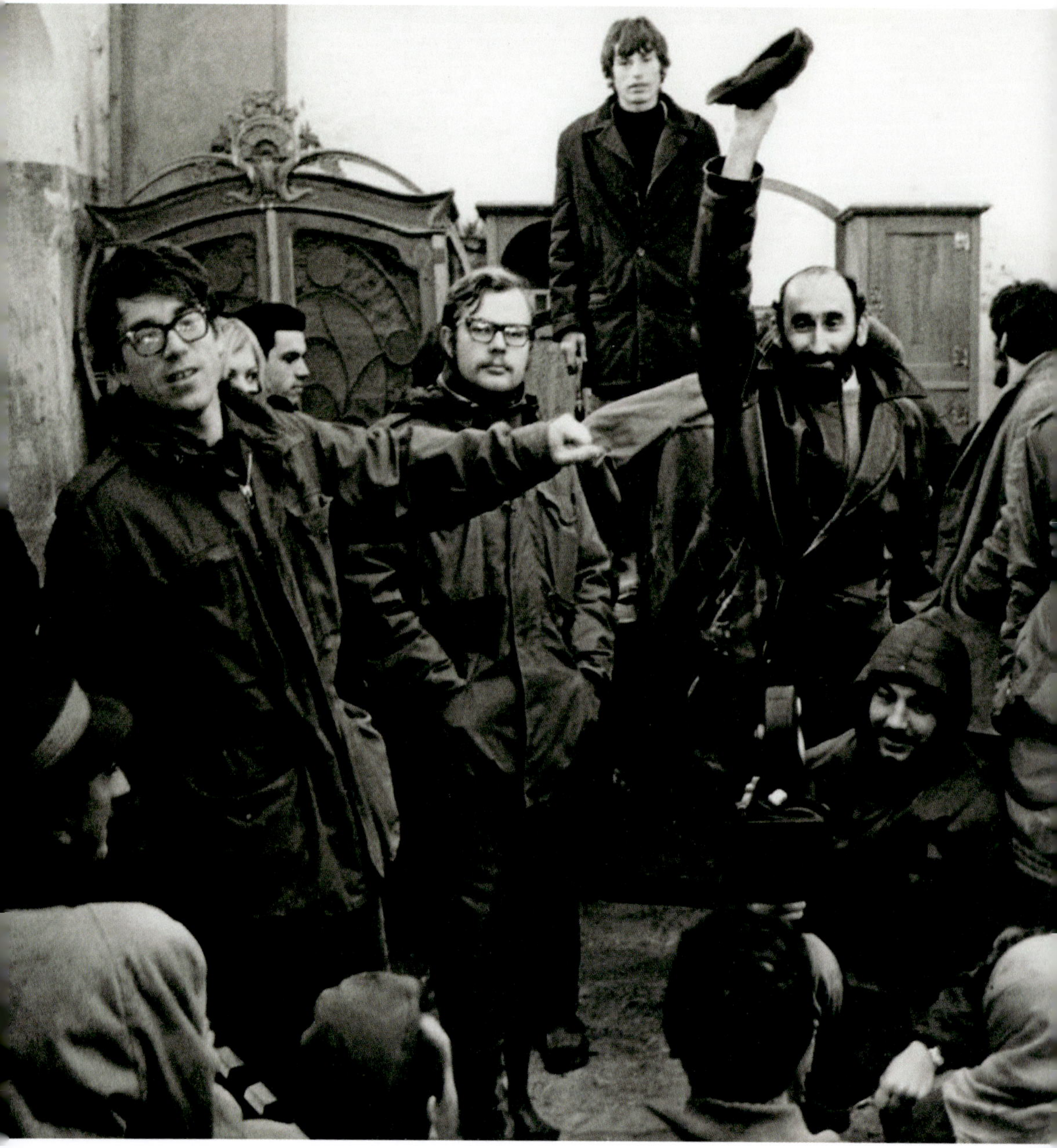

ŽELIMIR ŽILNIK & WHW
In Conversation

APRIL 2018

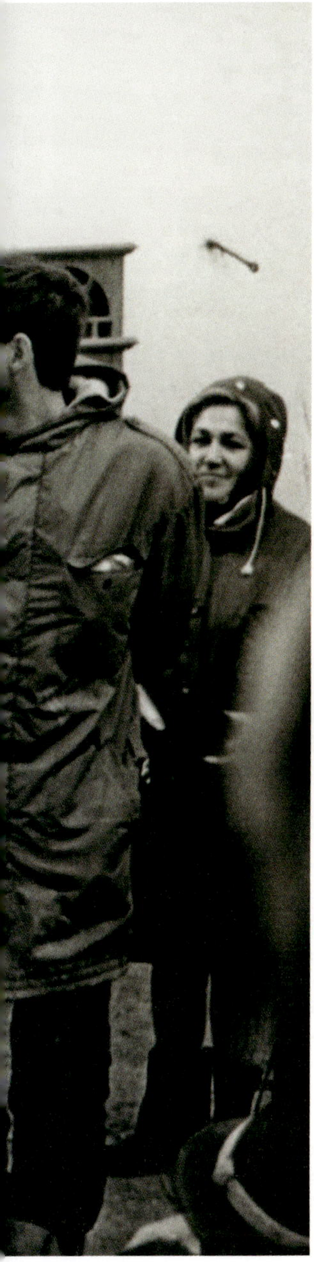

WHW: Since we are trying to touch upon the entirety of your work and engagement through the exhibition *Shadow Citizens,* let's start from the beginning. How did you become interested in movies?

ŽŽ: At the time when my generation was growing up in the mid-1950s, watching films was an obsession, like gadgets for today's digital generation. At that time, the cinema was the only window open into the world. There were ten times more cinemas than there are today, and the repertoire was very rich. In one cinema they showed cowboy sagas by Howard Hawks, John Ford, Fred Zinnemann; in another cinema they showed dramas, Italian beauties, palaces, and the Mediterranean—Vittorio De Sica, Federico Fellini, Luchino Visconti, Michelangelo Antonioni. By the end of the '50s, more realistic films emerged with which we identifed: François Truffaut, Jean-Luc Godard, Louis Malle, and others.

When I finished high school, I was invited to be the editor of programs at a youth cultural center in Novi Sad called the Youth Tribune. This place was as interesting as the cinema. It hosted experimental independent theater groups. We were exhibiting the latest visual trends. The film department exposed us to experimental films. I met filmmakers who were ten years older than me—Dušan Makavejev, Živojin Pavlović, Marko Babac, Mihovil Pansini, Vladimir Petek, Ivan Martinac, and so on. They had not been involved with professional film studios yet. Films were shot on 16 mm and 8 mm in cinema clubs. Participants in philosophical and sociological debates were people who would in a couple of years establish the Korčula Summer School and *Praxis* magazine: Rudi Supek, Gajo Petrović, Taras Kermauner, Veljko Rus, Danko Grlić, Zagorka Golubović, Nebojša Popov, Milan Kangrga, and others. Simultaneously with my work at the Youth Tribune, I went to law school. There was no faculty of fine arts in Novi Sad, and these studies and completion of the law program helped me to cope and defend myself when I had problems with censorship and with court procedures in the years to come.

WHW: What beyond the Youth Tribune and the cinema clubs influenced you?

ŽŽ: From my earliest days, I used to spend a lot of time at the theater. My uncle Milenko Šuvaković was a theater director and the art director of the most important Yugoslav theater festival, Sterijino pozorje. I visited the rehearsals, went to workshops where costumes and sets were made, and I also met many actors. Then, at the production house Avala Film in Belgrade, I became an assistant director upon Dušan Makavejev's invitation. Apart from local films, Avala Film also worked on big coproductions. For example, in collaboration with Artur Brauner's German production house, CCC Film, costumes, props, and huge set designs were made at Avala Film for *Die Nibelungen,* in the mid-1960s, which was the most expensive postwar German film at the time.

I learned there what a complex job a feature film is; that the preparation is essential as well as the coordination of the team and the willingness of the director to make decisions, yet to be open to listening to his associates. I witnessed very awkward situations, conflicts, bullying, nervous breakdowns, and the loss of a lot of time and money—when unprepared bosses shouted at the crew and made demands, and did not know what they were saying. I learned then to focus my energy and time into preparation, into the choice of actor-interpreters and crew.

WHW: One notices a certain fascination with manual work in your oeuvre. You have shot horseshoeing, dough kneading, working in mines, and the like for a long time and with much love.

ŽŽ: We live in a time of virtual jobs, but fifty years ago we all defined ourselves according to what we were doing. Craftsmen not only served people but also were the most respected people in a village. When you needed to find out some information, you would be sent to to a barber's shop; people gathered there, so he knew most. Craftsmen built cities, or rebuilt them after invaders had passed through. Novi Sad, where I live, was appointed the status of a city in 1749 by Empress Maria Theresa of the Habsburg monarchy. Before that, on the southern bank of the Danube, the huge Petrovaradin Fortress had been built, on the border with the Ottoman Empire. Novi Sad was then given its official Latin name, Neoplanta (New Garden); it was built as a center for craftsmen, vegetable growers, and administrators who served the needs of the fortress staff. Every couple of years, the soldiers were replaced or killed. The streets of Novi Sad had names like Shoemakers' Street, Saddlers' Street, Carpenters' Street. If peace lasted, they would build schools, marketplaces and fairs, brothels and theaters.

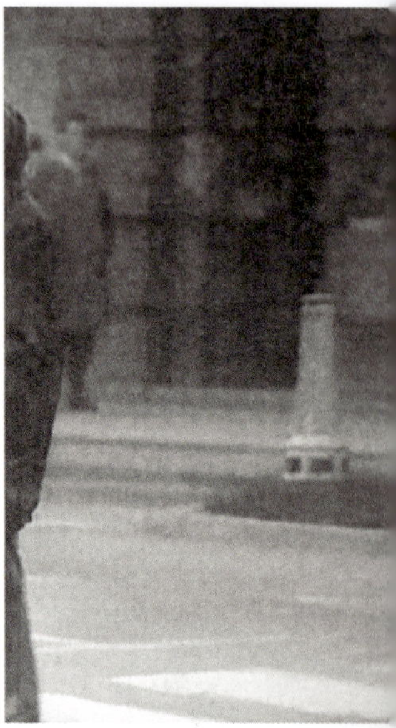

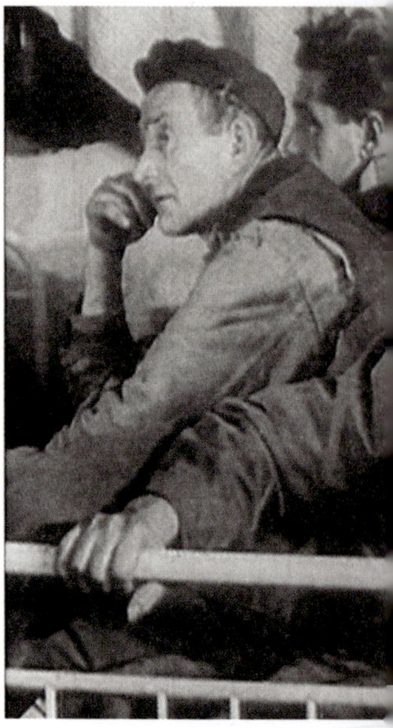

Half a century ago, working on film also required various knowledge of machines, electricity, optics, and chemicals. When I started working in the professional 35 mm format, the camera required a cameraman with seven or eight assistants. One would put negative into the camera, take it out, pack it, and send it to the laboratory. Another one was needed for sharpening—taking care of the sharpness of the shot. A third one for "panning"—camera movements left and right, up and down. Four men were needed to set the rails for the camera, because it weighed 250 to 300 kilograms (this is the Arri Blimp 300). The cameraman, who was the head of that division, was called the director of photography. He mingled around the actors and sets with a light meter, measuring how the reflectors illuminated the faces. He made corrections. Shouted to his assistants telling them which lens to fit on the camera. He did not touch the camera. There were five or six electricians working on lighting, and they followed the directions of the director of photography.

WHW: Let us continue with the topic of work. Already in 1968, you made *The Unemployed*. Why were you interested in the

The Unemployed (film stills), 1968

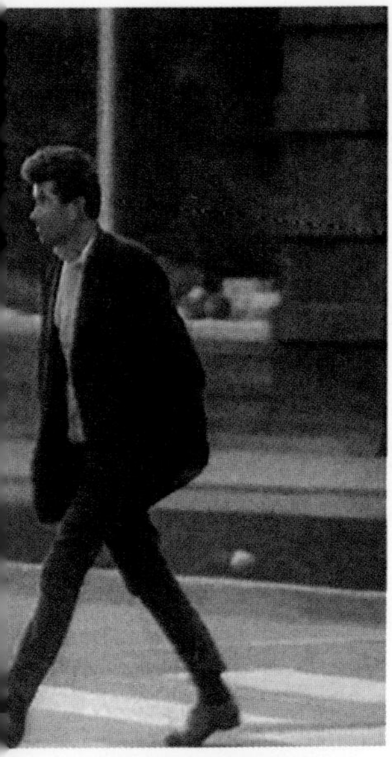

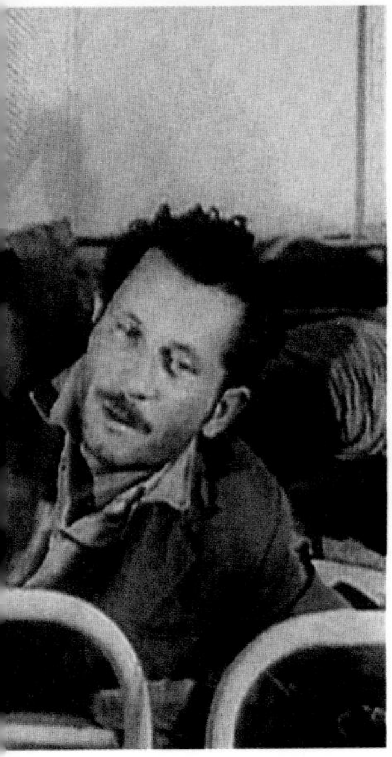

topic of the unemployed so early in your career, and was it connected later with the many stories you told about guest workers, refugees, and so on?

žž: From the mid-1960s onward, it seemed to us that the cultural policy was rather relaxed, that dogmatic party apparatchiks were less influential. Filmmakers, visual artists, and other such types of makers were not employed; theirs was an independent status, and they were paid under authorship contracts. This provided a chance for film projects to be done as joint investments of a team of authors and a film studio that possessed incredibly expensive technology—laboratory, cameras, sound, and lighting. Financial parameters of the investment would be calculated, and the authors and the team would be "coproducers" and co-owners of the film. So both the risk and responsibility were shared. Some of the most important Yugoslav films were made following this model of coproduction, which was called a "film working community."

The "liberal moment" of Yugoslav socialism was epitomized in the proclamation of the new program of the League of Communists from those years: "Nothing that has been created should be so sacred to us that it cannot be transcended and superseded by something still freer, more progressive, and more human." At the same time, factories were being modernized, and companies started doing business with the newly liberated countries of Asia and Africa, but also with the West, which called into question the "state-orchestrated general employment and prices." Adaptation to market conditions was demanded. Trained professionals were employed. The egalitarian principle that the "working class is in line with progress" ceased to exist. In those years, agreements were signed with Germany and Austria under which they took in tens of thousands of Yugoslav workers in an organized manner based on needs for the reconstruction of infrastructure and to work in factories in the West.

I often passed by the Novi Sad Employment Center, and for days I watched the assembled unhappy workers, who said they were made redundant in their companies and now were waiting for the Germans to hire them. And indeed, the representatives of the trade unions from Germany and the medical commission arrived, too. They talked with people, assigned them to work posts. They organized their transport, accommodation, worker status, and employment. It was not just a situation of novelty and hope, but for many it meant stressful changes in rhetoric and memory, because there were a fair number of them who remembered the Second World War. There was little news and explanation in the media about this "new phase of our development." Like most projects, we did *The Unemployed* to hear the whole story from the people who were confronted with an unknown and dramatic situation.

WHW: Later on you dealt often with the topic of guest workers, including in the television productions of the 1980s. Do you

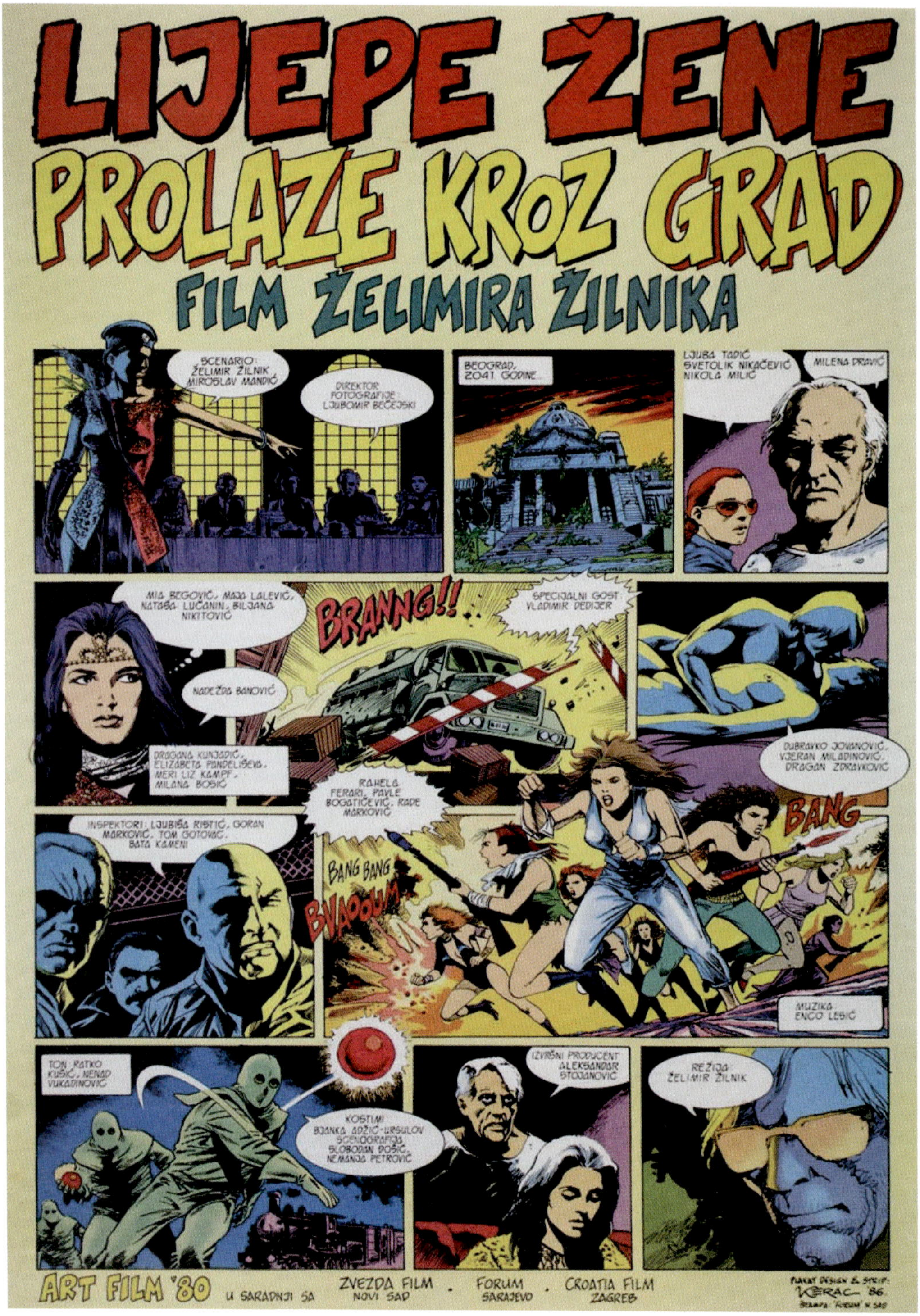

Pretty Women Walking through the City (poster), 1986. DESIGNED BY BRANISLAV KERAC.

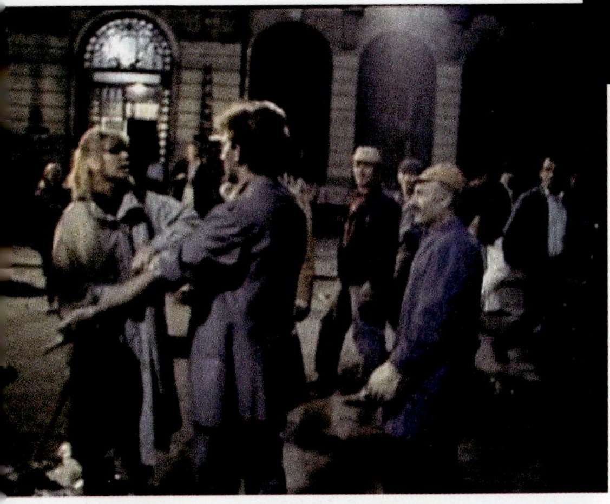

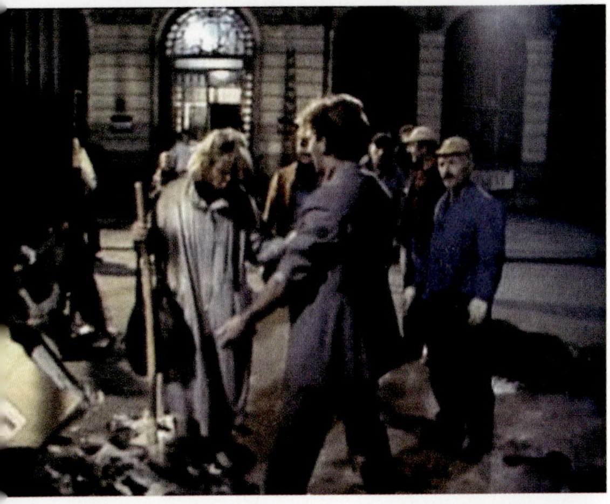

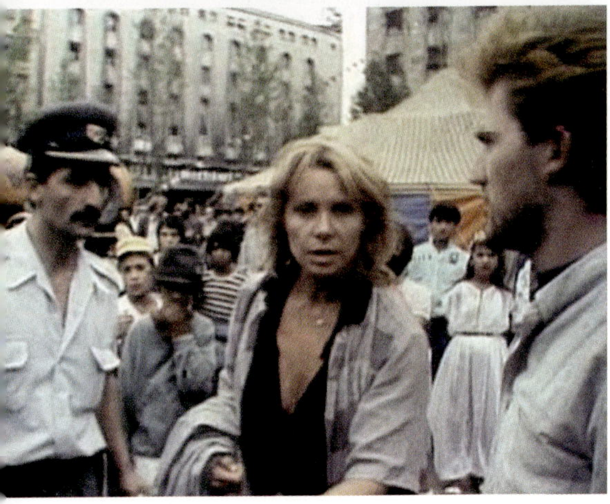

Snežana Nikšić in *Good Morning Belgrade* (film stills), 1985

Good Morning Belgrade

Yugoslavia • 1985 • 70 min. • 16 mm • Betacam

At the center of this docudrama are the events and tensions that occur during the shooting of a feature film about the Belgrade of a speculative future. The director of the film sets up unrealistic expectations of the producer. The producer engages workers of the city utility services as extras and to help her with set design. These people work for waterworks, sewer systems, and sanitation units. In this drama, we are immersed in their lives and the problems they face while trying to keep Belgrade a functioning city. By overstepping the budget of the film, the producer breaks the law, and during a court trial where the crew members are in the witness stand, we follow the drama of how a film is made.

Although this is not mentioned explicitly in the film, the science fiction film that the director is making is in fact Žilnik's *Pretty Women Walking through the City* (1986); *Good Morning Belgrade* is its companion piece and a commentary on the working conditions in film production at the time. Both films—*Good Morning Belgrade*, made as a docudrama for television, and *Pretty Women*, made as a feature film intended for cinemas—were produced so that the budget of one supported the making of the other. This was a rather standard procedure at the time, as republic TV stations had high demand for a constant influx of new programming, and therefore had flexibility in commissioning new works and distributing the funds. At today's rates, the budget procured for a TV film would be approximately €150,000, and as such required radical thriftiness—for example, there was one cameraman working both the movie and Beta video cameras for both films. *Good Morning Belgrade* was filmed during the day and *Pretty Women* during the night. A fortunate circumstance was that the architect Bogdan Bogdanović was the mayor of Belgrade at the time, and he agreed to give access to the civic services. ●

think that you may have anticipated what the film industry is going through today, where an increasing number of respected directors are doing television or Internet series, which are often more brave than mainstream films?

ŽŽ: When I was in Munich in the 1970s asking around for producers, I noticed that filmmakers and teams were communicating through television without any fear. I went to Telepool, Tochtergesellschaft Bayerishe Rundfunk, and several other companies whose addresses and telephone numbers I had. They used to buy ten to fifteen Yugoslav films annually. As I was waiting for the director Siegfried Magold to see me, I heard that there were directors and producers of German and French films coming to see him to discuss coproductions. The director received me warmly, said he appreciated my short films and *Early Works* (1969), and asked me what I had that was new. I explained that I would like to work on a couple of documentaries with guest workers as protagonists. He referred me to Filmverlag der Autoren, which was a kind of film working community where Alexander Kluge, Werner Herzog, Edgar Reitz, and Rainer Werner Fassbinder worked on their films at that time. I had already met these filmmakers at festivals. I learned that if I were to do a feature film, I could send the project to Telepool and they would decide whether they would come on as coproducer, and also that once I finished my short film, I should offer it to them, so it could be bought for television. At that time in Yugoslavia, film production was oriented toward cinema distributors, both in the country and abroad, and new films (part of the so-called Black Wave), which I myself worked on, were very rarely shown on television.

Several years after my return home, I had in mind the Western European practice of creating for television, so I contacted Television Novi Sad. The main reason I did this, however, was the fact that I saw that all the other production doors were closed to me. Television had two extraordinary advantages: technology—from the laboratory to the studios, cameras, and lighting—everything was in-house. And most of the technicians were permanently employed and available. Another advantage was that when a film or a show was made, the audience was secured. In the late 1970s, when I started offering and realizing projects for the Novi Sad and Belgrade television houses, feature films that we had shot for drama departments were shown at eight in the evening and were seen on the Yugoslav Radio-Television network by four to five million people. It was then that I faced a very difficult problem: How was I to keep dealing with destinies and topics that interested me and still be watched not only by people who appreciated such an approach but also by families with three or four generations living in one household? The answer was found in a hybrid genre: docudrama.

And we managed to do several titles that were really innovative, critical, and outside the mainstream, which we would not have been able to do in the film industry—*Brooklyn–Gusinje* (1988), *Hot*

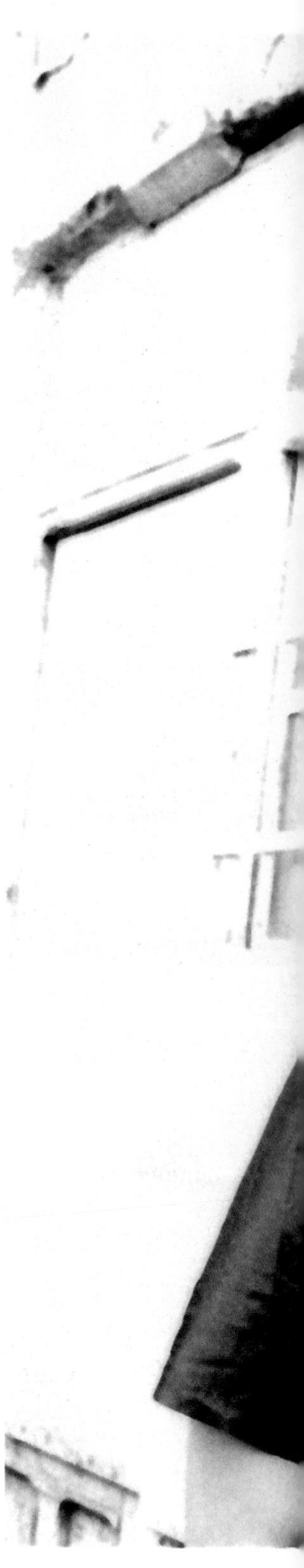

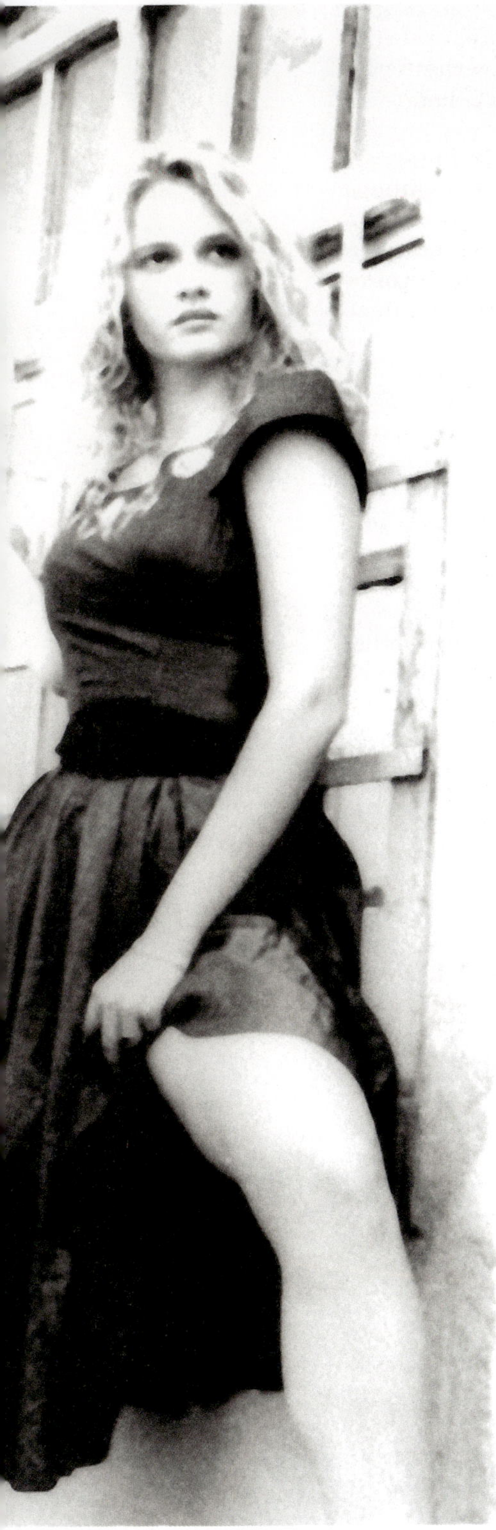

Pretty Women Walking through the City

Yugoslavia • 1986 • 100 min. • 35 mm • color

Belgrade in 2041 is an abandoned and devastated city covered in garbage. A couple of old men live there: a former journalist with his daughter, an ex-politician with his wife, and a former policeman who guards a boarding house where eight girls live. The old men bring up the girls in the spirit of the traditions of the former Yugoslav nations, which is a risky business because Southern Europe is being ravaged by a group that forbids any sort of remembering of the past.

While the "good guys" in the movie are played by established Yugoslav actors, or in many cases by nonprofessional actors, the "bad guys," referred to as the inspectors of Southern Europe, are played by artist Tomislav Gotovac, theater director Ljubiša Ristić, and movie director Goran Marković. Yugoslav partisan fighter, politician, human rights activist, and historian Vladimir Dedijer, expelled from the Communist Party of Yugoslavia in 1954, also appears in the film, playing a 127-year-old version of himself.

The story starts at the moment when the former journalist and the other remaining survivors start an action to revive Belgrade in order to mark the hundredth anniversary of July 4, 1941, the people's uprising against Yugoslavia's German occupiers in the Second World War. The main character recounts the events of his youth, in the 1990s, when hatred and destruction prevailed and brought about the war and dissolution of the country. Upon the movie's premiere at the 1986 Pula Film Festival, the media reported that it was clear from the film that Žilnik had lost connection to both reason and reality. Alas, the future in fact proved Žilnik right. ●

Natalija Lučanin on the set of *Pretty Women Walking through the City*, 1985

Paychecks (1987), *Pretty Women Walking through the City* (1986), *Oldtimer* (1989), and others.

WHW: We are curious about your attitude toward female characters. For example, in *Vera and Eržika* (1981), we have two women fighting for their rights. You portray them with great tenderness and affection. Your films also have scenes like the one with the patriarchal father of a Roma family who wants to marry off his daughter against her will, and she escapes and tries to cope. There are also stories about female friendships in your films. But in *Early Works,* you kill the main character, Jugoslava.

ŽŽ: There are fewer female characters in my films than I wanted. I wanted to have more of them because they fight in their lives on several fronts: they must eliminate the combination of male inferiority and aggressiveness; a husband's frustration and neglect of children; being thrown out of the house; their sons becoming criminals; and alcoholism and domestic violence. In addition to all this, they have to feign seduction, and according to the current Balkan fashion, they also must be harem divas. Mission impossible.

For example, for *Logbook_Serbistan* (2015), we were looking for female characters because they had been through the trauma of war, famine, and threats of rape. But the male refugees would not let the women be in front of the camera. One agreed, provided the woman always held her child in her arms.

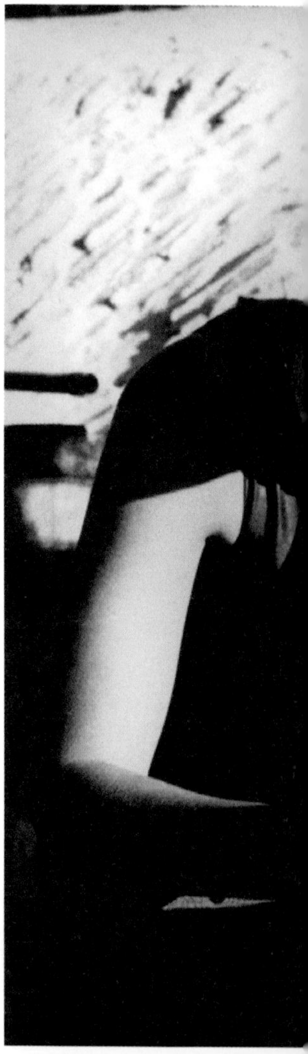

As far as *Early Works* is concerned, the protagonists were portrayed using a specific language, where visual and rhetorical symbols were used, with lots of proclamations and citations. The characters were outlined as a sketch and in a schematic manner. Only the main heroine had enough space to reflect the conundrums of what it means to be a "girl in socialism," and the hypocrisy of the proclaimed freedom of speech and socialist slogans. She has to wade through the mud of male unfulfilled ambition and power. *Early Works* was shot in the autumn of 1968, after the tank intervention in Prague, against Alexander Dubček's "socialism with a human face." That film was a question mark. Could the current state of socialism be repaired, or would it disappear in the flames that took Yugoslavia away?

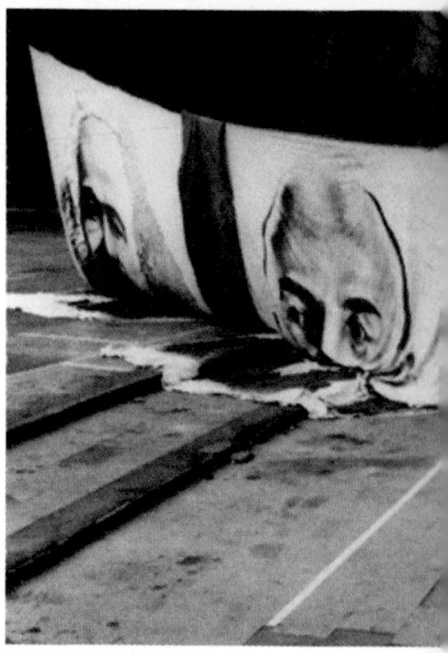

WHW: It seems to us that your political position has had incredible consistency throughout all your films.

ŽŽ: I cannot say anything about that. In my political position or attitude, I endeavor to maintain a kind of independence that matters to me. Without compromise, I will not put up with anything that I find to to be dull, rotten, and suspicious. Here I am ready for what is called a "sacrifice" in bourgeois life; that is, I am willing to give up or lose my position, or to be removed by someone somewhere, which does not seem such a bad consequence to me. It depends on one's

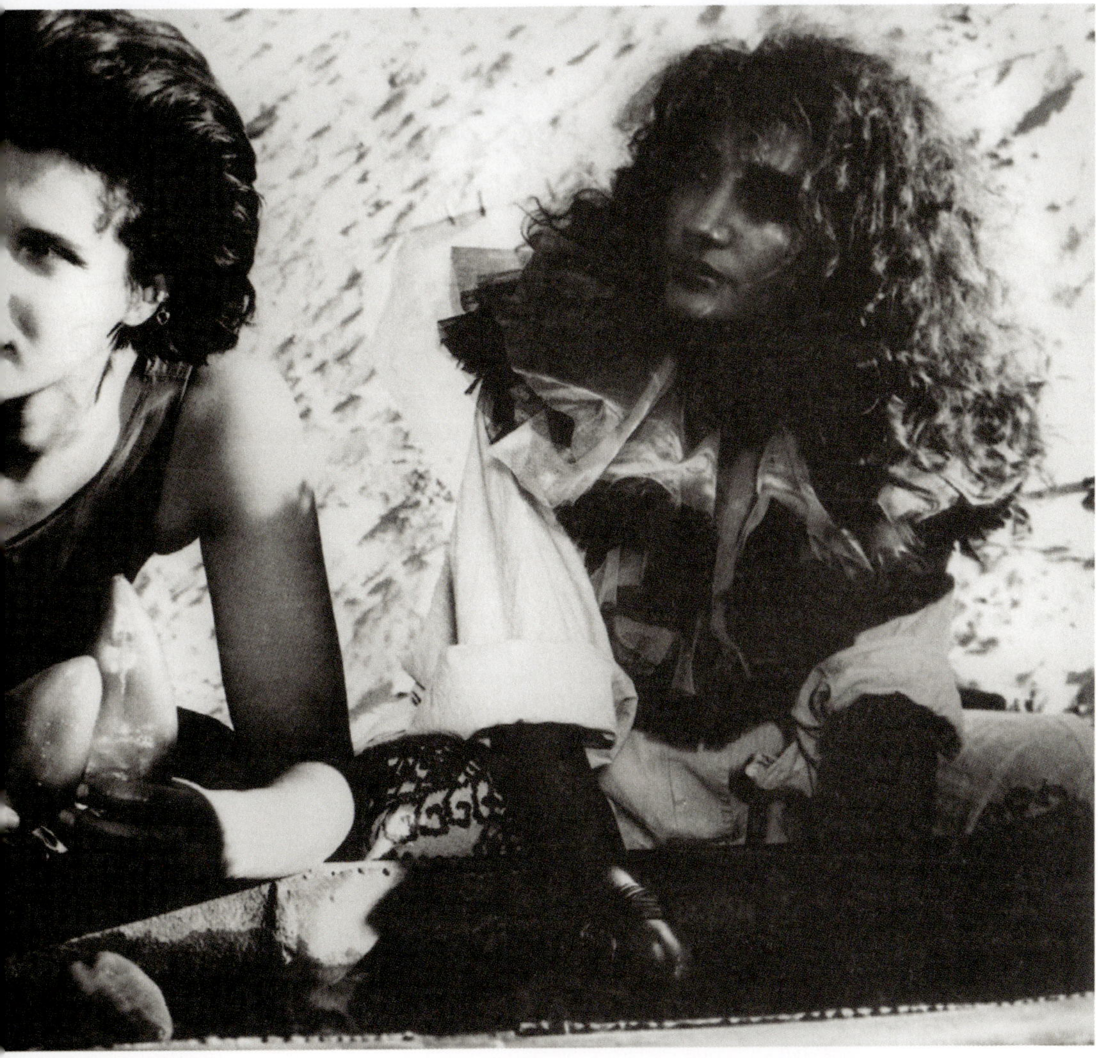

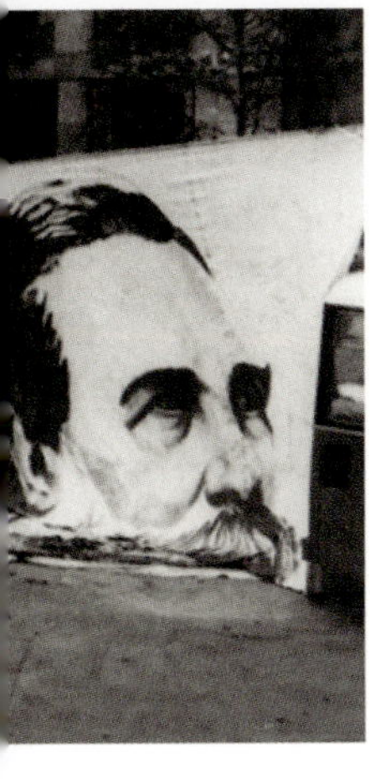

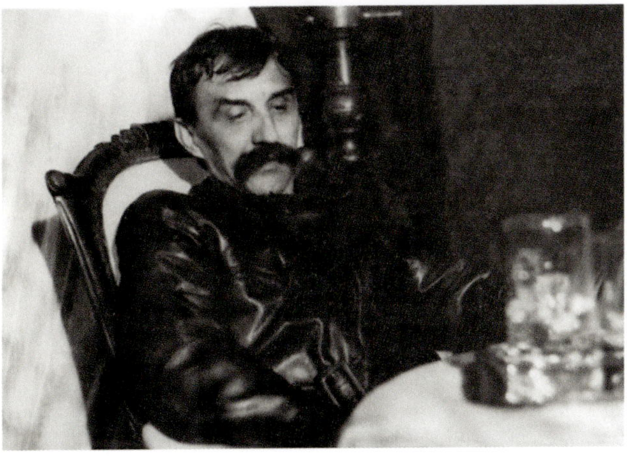

Pretty Women Walking through the City (film stills), 1986

BOTTOM RIGHT
Theater director Ljubiša Ristić

character, and everyone's is different. Some fantastically intelligent and fine people have a need to follow authority. I've had several such friends. They are not bad people; they just feel safer when they are under someone's authority. And I feel as if I were chained under that authority. It is completely individual, and there is no answer to this. I would even find stating some political credo to be absurd. Look at the films—maybe I have somehow taken a position that some people like, and in many situations I took a stance that many people did not like. I've spent most of my life as a man regarded as an eccentric who is always doing some kind of loser stuff. Even those television dramas and films that you consider today to be good were sincerely despised by many of my colleagues.

WHW: You wrote a manifesto that accompanied *Black Film* (1971), and at the 1971 International Short Film Festival Oberhausen, you even showed the movie with the manifesto written over it. How does the manifesto sound to you today?

ŽŽ: It sounds pretty OK to me. If I used the same methodology to analyze the present situation, I would find today's situation to be drastically more inhumane in terms of social difference and basic human rights than it was back then. In ex-Yugoslav countries, there are millions of unemployed people, without any prospects for themselves or for their children. Pension funds have been looted. Factories have been seized in which workers invested their incomes to expand the production and technological innovation, as we did in the film working communities. The new "democratic national-capitalist" authorities do not acknowledge all this. Today's corruption is several dozen times more brutal. Affiliation to the ruling party is more important for promotion in life than it used to be in socialism. The space for culture in the media has been reduced, as has advocacy for workers' rights.

Client-friendly sponsorship of cultural institutions, including support for films, eliminates works that criticize, which is worse than before. The facts show that in the last twenty-five years of "freedom and democracy," there have been no better and more critical films than *When I Am Dead and Gone* (1967) and *The Ambush* (1969) by Živojin Pavlović; *Love Affair, or the Case of the Missing Switchboard Operator* (1967) and *W.R.: Mysteries of the Organism* (1971) by Dušan Makavejev; *The Feast* (1967) and *The Trek* (1968) by Đorđe Kadijević; *Handcuffs* (1969) by Krsto Papić; *Sunday* (1969) by Lordan Zafranović; *The Living Truth* (1972) by Tomislav Radić, and so on.

WHW: Can you tell us something about the figure or position of the dissident? From today's sadly widespread anti-socialist and anti-communist perspective, it is as if this label has been attached to many positions that have not actually had dissident content. Were you seen as a dissident, too?

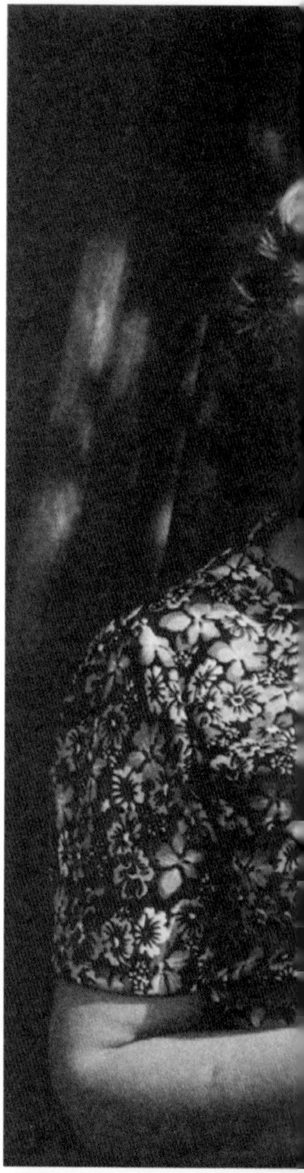

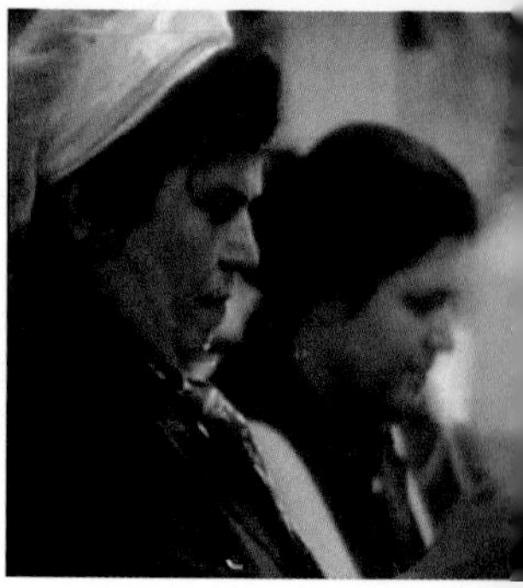

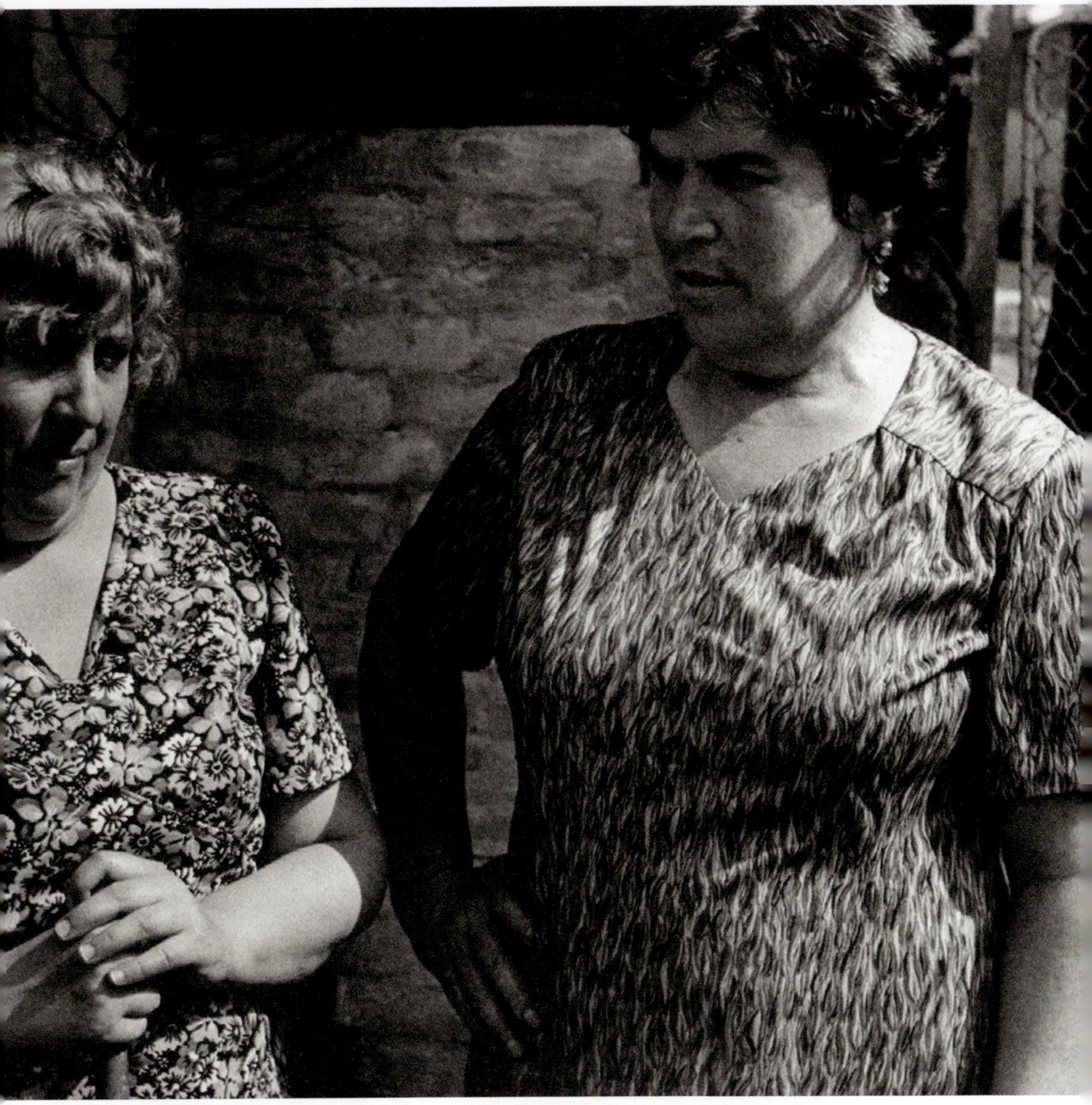

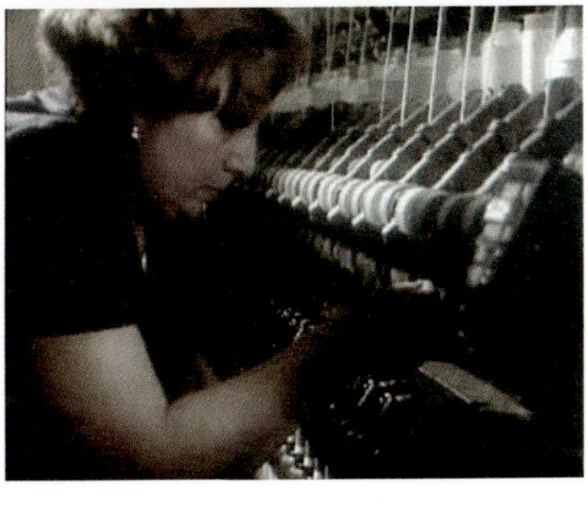

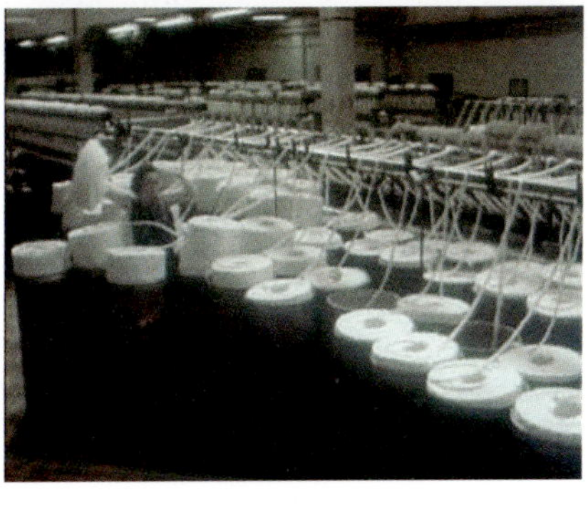

Eržebet Jakab and Vera Miladinović on the set of *Vera and Eržika*, 1981. PHOTO BY VLADIMIR ČERVENKA.

BOTTOM
Vera and Eržika (film stills), 1981

žž: Of those who say they had a critical attitude in the time of socialism, two-thirds are complete liars. Some of them were even placed high up in the bodies of cultural repression, as part of various commissions. My colleagues and I did not call ourselves dissidents. "Dissident" is a term from so-called prison camp socialism, where these artists were forced out of the country, such as Aleksandr Solzhenitsyn, for example. Or they were imprisoned. We had our passports with us in the early 1970s when several of us, all film directors, went abroad. I had the impression that the neo-dogmatic group had nothing against us leaving. On the contrary, it was as if they were expecting us to perform some sort of "enemy activity," so they could arrest us. When we returned, Dušan Makavejev, Aleksandar Petrović, and some writers and painters and I—we were not given the status of dissidents, but were considered "unsuitable," because of our "conceptual errors."

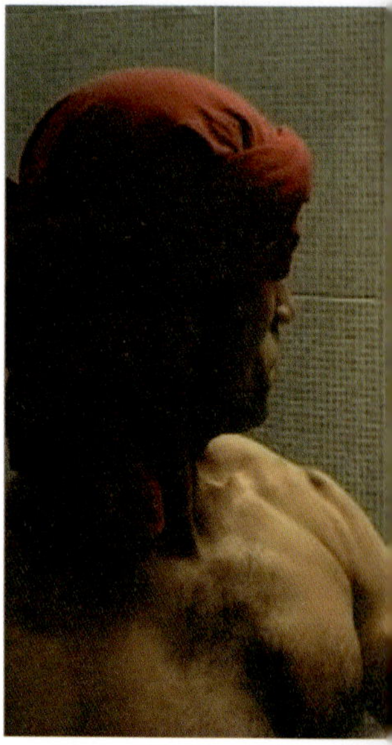

Kenedi Hasani on the set of *Kenedi Is Getting Married*, 2007. PHOTO BY MIODRAG MILOŠEVIĆ.

When I arrived in Germany as a guest worker, I could not say that I was a banned artist in Yugoslavia, because no one would have believed it. In those years, Yugoslavia produced films that received awards at the biggest festivals and that appeared on television in many countries. I was asked by the director Alexander Kluge, an important representative of the German independent film movement, to provide him with Yugoslavia's policy on stimulating film production. He had heard that this policy had been greatly successful. We translated it in a week, and significant parts influenced the development of Germany's new policy on film.

WHW: What do you think of our exhibition title, *Shadow Citizens*, as a suggestion for a through line that connects your work?

žž: The lives and fates of people who live off their work are constantly threaded through my movies. People in this category live in precarious conditions, without security and privileges, and they can rely only on themselves and the people closest to them. What is most important when you make a film based on those stories is that you work with people with nothing to lose. They are the people who should be given a medium through which they can express themselves in some way, by communicating their own attitudes or their feeling of being forgotten. When working with them, you are working with the oppressed and poor people who are least afraid of endangering their status in any way. They have this position of freedom.

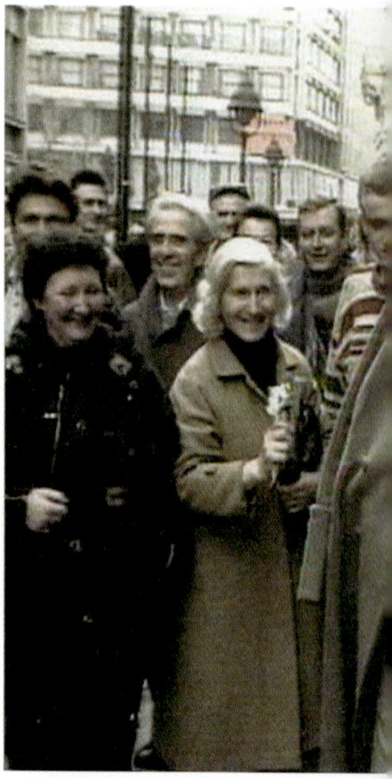

Dragoljub Ljubičić in *Tito among the Serbs for the Second Time* (film still), 1994

I will give you an example from when I worked in Austria on a new film a year ago. The producer raised the funds to make a film about migrants who had received documents and were preparing for a longer stay in Austria and about how they were "becoming EU citizens." With my associate Jasmina Janković, who is a court interpreter, we visited asylum centers to find people who wanted to participate in the film. The loudest ones approached us first, with their agendas: some wanted to form separate ethnic clubs, and they wanted us to promote them. Others changed their political favorites

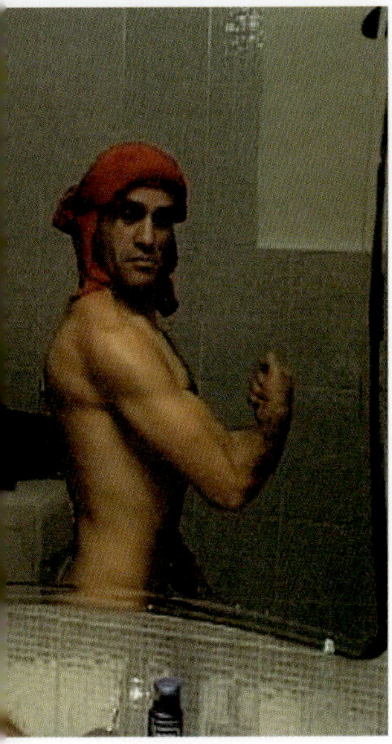

every couple of days—in late 2016, Syrian President Bashar al-Assad was declared a defeated party. But those who declared themselves as his opponents began to praise Iran and Russia in early 2017, while Assad was their "legitimate president." When they heard I was from Serbia, they suggested we speak in the Russian language. I realized that we were wasting our time in the labyrinths of geopolitics between Donald Trump, Recep Tayyip Erdoğan, and Vladimir Putin.

But then we started talking to those who were going through the real administrative labyrinths so they could learn German, present their trades or professions, and get residence permits. Men and women told us stories that were new, stories that described the relations and tensions that had not been present either in the war at home or on the road, such as misunderstandings in the family between authoritarian fathers and children or between relatives who found it difficult to grasp language lessons. The older men felt uncomfortable being taught and evaluated by women. On the other hand, there were young people who found friends and integrated faster; they wanted to live alone, away from their families, in "freedom," as they said. Then girls and women told us about situations they had not expected. For example, that the parents of a young refugee would not allow their son to marry a woman whom he had met as a refugee seeking asylum, because she was "unclean"—she had been through hell and back—and they coerced him to marry a bride he did not know, who was "a virgin," and whom they would bring in illegally.

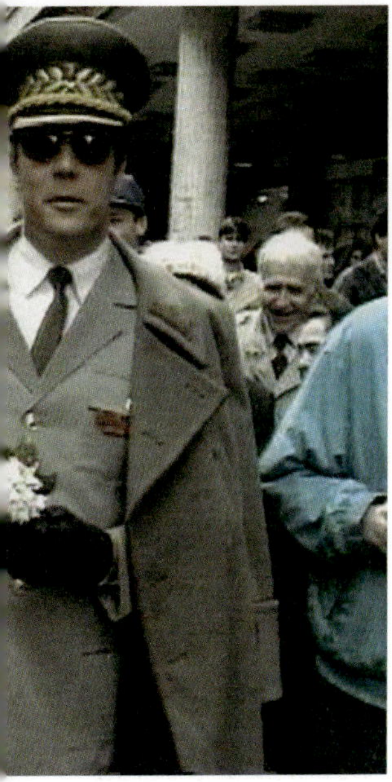

Based on these stories and with the help of those who wanted to take part in the film, we drew up a concept and a shooting schedule. We edited the film a couple of months ago. I told the team and the producer that the first viewers should be the people in the film and those of us who gathered them, because if any of us have any objections to the final edit, we have to correct them. If we accept the film that we have been working on, experience tells me that others will accept it too, and maybe it will travel around the world.

WHW: Would you agree with us if we said that you constantly choose to stay "in the shadow"?

ŽŽ: It's not simply a matter of choice—it is the real position I am in. I come from a country that has a small marginal market and where a marginal language is spoken. For example, regardless of my rather comprehensive film oeuvre, I cannot answer the simplest question that is being asked in America. They say there: "Do not bother us with all these many titles. Make a list only of films that earned $15 million and more." My answer is: "I do not have such a film." This is my real position. I do not want to say that it does not suit me. It does, because it allows me to do what really interests me. ★

Žilnik's production in Germany was not characterised by the exploitation of his socialist experience (as it happened with many dissident writers and artists who left their countries of origin) but by shifting his interest to analysing relations between the ideological discourse and social practice in liberal capitalism.

—Branislav Dimitrijević, "Behind Scepticism Lies the Fire of a Revolutionary!," in *For an Idea – Against the Status Quo: Analysis and Systematization of Želimir Žilnik's Artistic Practice* (Novi Sad: New Media Center_kuda.org, Playground produkcija, 2009), 145–46.

Paradise. An Imperialist Tragicomedy speaks about the fact that part of the anti-terrorist pursuit in Germany is simply provoked by the establishment in order to keep tension in society, which is more compactly organized when the enemy is front and center. The story is based on a true event that happened to a right-wing MP from Berlin, who was kidnapped and held by terrorists for fifteen days. And when he finally managed to get out, or was released, he had a huge career—he was elected by a great majority of voters because he had proved that he had been able to easily deal with leftists, he wrote feuilletons in papers all over. [...] So, this kidnapping worked for him in a brilliant way as a marketing tool. The film *Paradise* tells a story of a venture capitalist company dealing with shady jobs, from illegal imports and exploitation of the workforce to financial speculation. So this venture capitalist company organizes kidnappings of its own bosses so they can appear later in the public as martyrs. I had an impression that, first, we're making the film about certain topics that are very present in the life of Germany, and second, some things, particularly guest workers [*Gastarbeiter*], and so on, which are still on the agenda, we discussed very openly at that time. I think that not only are guest workers being exploited, but they represent an incredible internal market—a whole enormous internal colony that great imperialist states have in their pockets.

Those were the theses of the film, plus this situation with the anti-terrorist agenda, which I felt was like a search for the enemy. And when the film was finished, one situation occurred that for me was a routine situation with those ideological campaigns. [...] I took the film to some people I knew in German television, which regularly bought our socially critical films (laughs). And, so, in those big German television stations, it happened that I showed the film. All the doors suddenly closed one by one. And those friends of mine—editors, even the big bosses—said: "Please take this thing out of the building right away, and nobody can know it was ever here." So that any traces of the film being screened were literally being erased ... There we touched—maybe by not being aware enough of the seriousness of the situation in Germany in 1975–76—we touched some of their taboos, to which they reacted, so to speak, in the same way we reacted here. Even more hysterically than the reactions to the series of "Black Films" were in our country.

—Želimir Žilnik, interview (untitled), *Reporter*, August 1986.

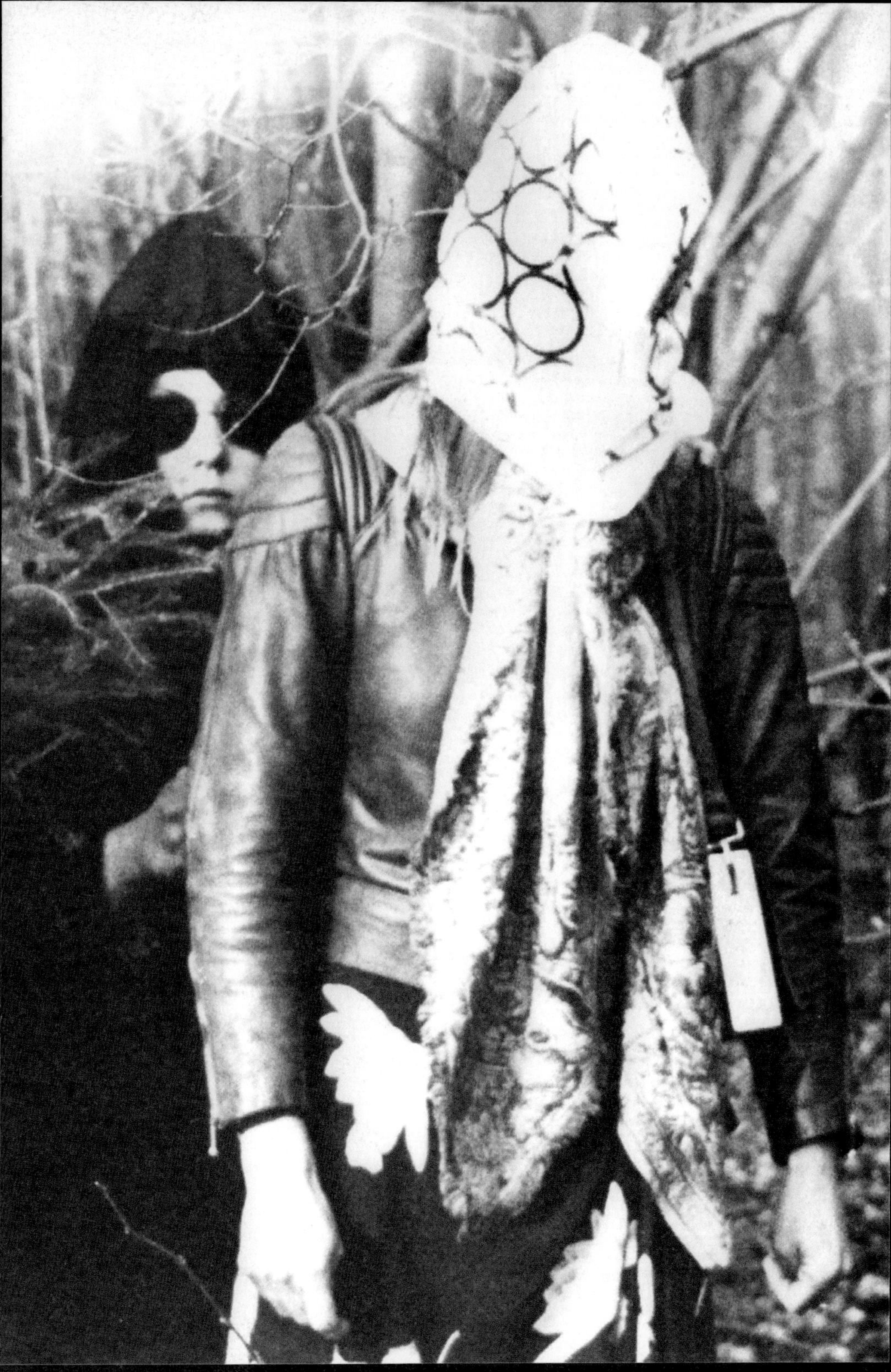

Amelie Ohlbrecht and Gisela Siebauer in *Paradise. An Imperialist Tragicomedy* (film still), 1976

Luka Bauer (back) and Franja Handrla (front) on the set of *Black Film*, 1971.
PHOTO BY ANDREJ POPOVIĆ.

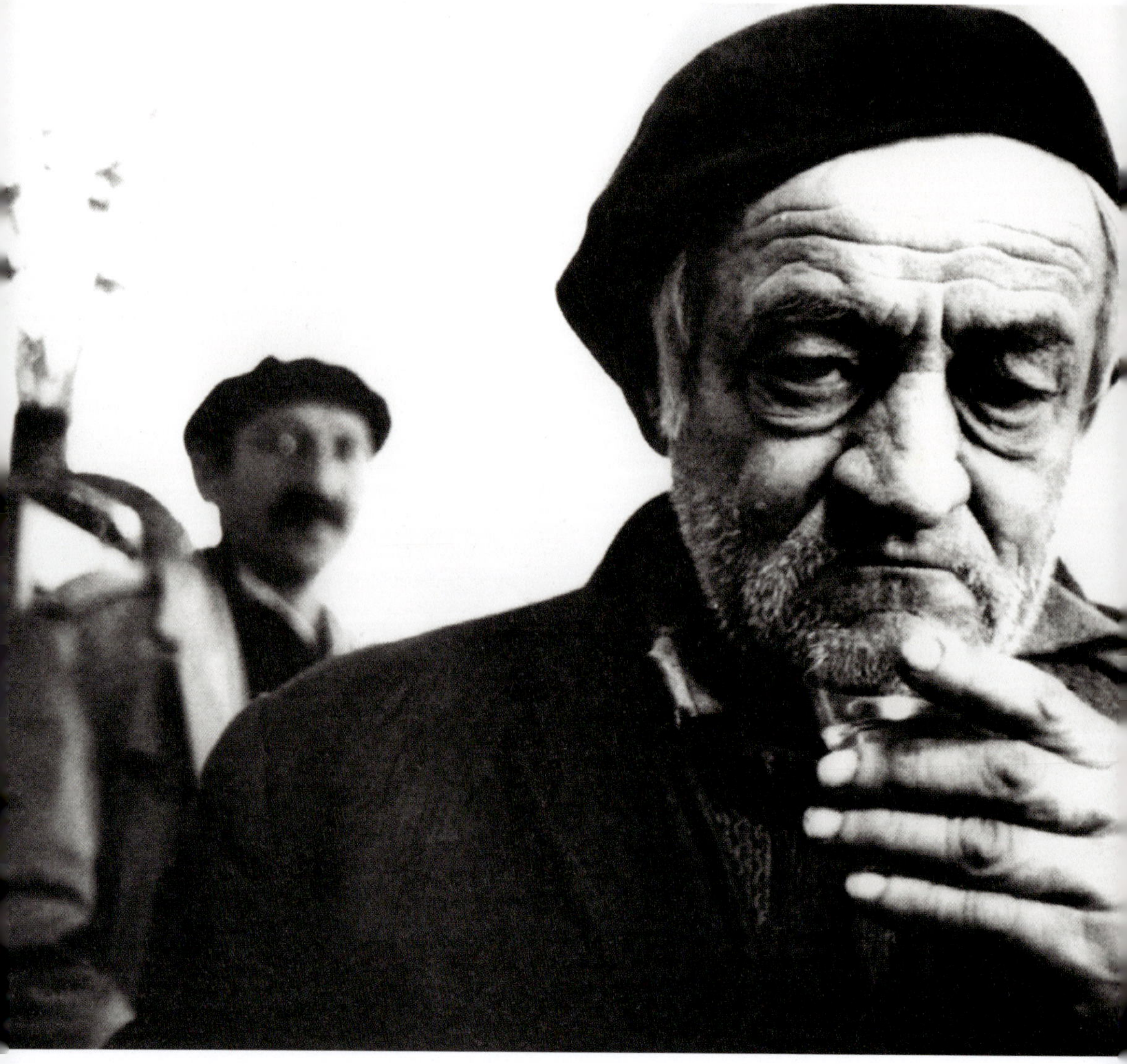

BERT REBHANDL

The Borders of Paradise: Želimir Žilnik between Artistic Strategies and Political Systems

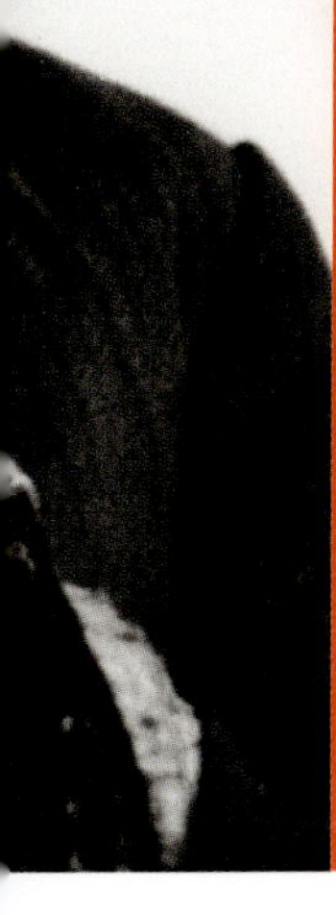

The last word in Želimir Žilnik's film *Marble Ass* (1995)—"men"—is uttered with exasperation and disgust. But there is still, after many bad experiences with men, a sense of longing in the voice of Merlin, a queer woman who lives as a trans sex worker on the fringes of post-Yugoslavian society in Belgrade. As in many other languages, the Serbian word for "man," *čovek,* is the same term that signifies the whole human race. And by the end of *Marble Ass,* there is reason to believe that it has even more layers: mankind or humanity certainly has issues with men (especially tough guys, men prone to demonstrations of masculinity, men fighting wars for their supposed nation). But Merlin is an example of different possibilities for men. A man can actually be a woman, sexually or emotionally or gender stereotypically, a man can be a warrior or a saint, a man can be his own other by putting out to dickheads. There is something intrinsically dialectical about the word "men" at the end of *Marble Ass,* and the film itself is equally made of contradictions, which add up to something original on its own level.

The foundational contradiction sublated by Žilnik in *Marble Ass* is of course between reality and fiction. To put it simply: the fictions of Želimir Žilnik have always been strongly permeated by the realities of his eventful life and the times he came to tell about, more so than the works of other filmmakers who react to their experiences by telling stories directly about them. Žilnik tells stories with his experiences, with his interventions and reflections. His career stretches over half a decade and several systems: the Non-Aligned Yugoslavia, a socialist federal state with a charismatic leader in Marshal Tito and an elite in every regional system from Macedonia to Slovenia, national television being one of them; the post-1968 and pre-1977 Federal Republic of Germany—that is, West Germany—a democracy besieged by leftist terrorism and the temptation to fight it with methods of *Ausnahmezustand* [state of emergency] (Germany received Žilnik as a guest worker, whereas he conceived of himself as a dissident intellectual in exile); the failing state of Yugoslavia, disintegrating violently into its previously federated parts (and smaller parts of the parts) after 1991; and eventually the European Union in its period of Eastern enlargement, with Southeast Europe (a.k.a. the Balkans) in a strategically important and vulnerable position on the outskirts of an increasingly disputed "unified space" of freedoms, which by the definitions of territoriality and "rule-based order" have to be declined or granted to people from outside the EU according to increasingly contested laws such as the Geneva Conventions.

By historical chance, Žilnik, a man born in a Gestapo-run concentration camp in occupied Serbia in 1942, when the Nazis were at the peak of their expansion, became the quintessential European filmmaker from a position just outside the European Union. His political and aesthetic strategies have always been informed by the new waves of the postwar societies of Italy (1940s and '50s; in essence: Neo-Realism, with its turn toward the common people), France (1960s; in essence: Nouvelle Vague, with its several iterations of a cinema informed by pop and mass culture and high modernism at the same time), and Germany (1970s; in essence: Neuer Deutscher Film, with its double-bind between romanticism and experimentalism). But Žilnik's approach to filmmaking instead increasingly came to be taken over by a pragmatism that arose from encounters with the subjects of his films. People like Merlin, Franja Handrla (from his early *Black Film*, 1971), Bora Joksimović (*The Comedy and Tragedy of Bora Joksimović*, 1977), and the Kosovarian Rom Kenedi Hasani (of the *Kenedi* trilogy, 2003–07) are some of the most notable examples of typical Žilnik subjects. When looking back on this exceptional career, one sees many surprising continuities spanning the epochal disruptions that punctuate the director's work. His approach is often playful, but always based on a simple premise: he wants to see history from the viewpoint of "beneath."

We can start with Franja Handrla, a homeless man who became the subject of Žilnik's *Black Film* in the early 1970s. "I sleep badly. I eat badly. In my life there is no comfort," he states. "Nobody gives anything to me." That is, this is the case before he meets Žilnik, who decides to take six homeless people into his home, an apartment of not even fifty square meters. The filmmaker's wife sleeps on a mattress in the living room. Žilnik abruptly wakes her and sends her to sleep in the children's room. He wants to help the poor, but he also wants to make a film. The men bring an "awful stench" into the apartment, but also a challenge for society. How can a system claiming to be a workers' state neglect people like Franja so thoroughly? Žilnik speaks as a lawyer (he studied law before turning to film), as an intellectual, and as an artist.

The next morning, he takes to the streets to ask people what could and should be done about people like Franja. His seemingly spontaneous act is conceptual at the same time: in a socialist society, there are supposedly no gaps to give rise to civil action like Žilnik's, because every possible issue is already taken care of. In *Black Film*, Žilnik points to a blind spot: "bare life" (a term developed by political theory to describe life outside institutionalization and investiture) has been registered only by an artist. The apartment, tiny as it may seem, marks Žilnik as a privileged subject in Yugoslavia. With the outrageous performativity of *Black Film*, he literally puts not only his privilege, but his very existence as a professional, at risk.

The roots of his engagement are easily recognizable in the feature film *Early Works* (1969). Žilnik's generation was a generation of change. Living in a socialist society, Žilnik found the crucial experience of 1968 not in Paris but in the Prague Spring and its repression. The reform movement in Czechoslovakia also had a strong artistic faction, with filmmakers like Věra Chytilová and Evald Schorm at the aesthetic (utopian) forefront of the progressive movement. Yugoslavia went through it with its own trajectory of liberalization and eventual tightening of the ideological grip. The young people who in *Early Works* go into the countryside to build communism under

Black Film (film stills), 1971

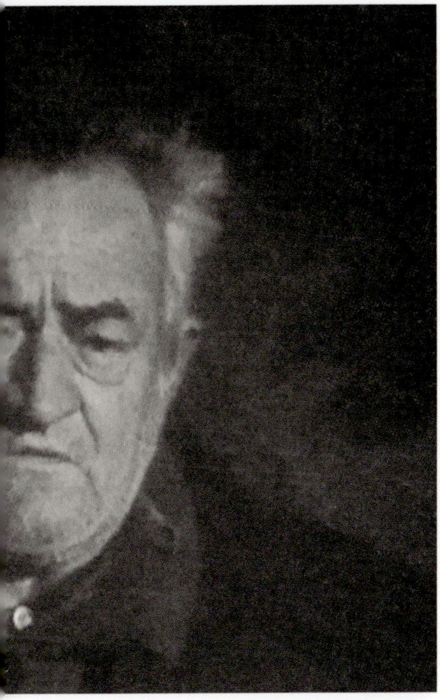

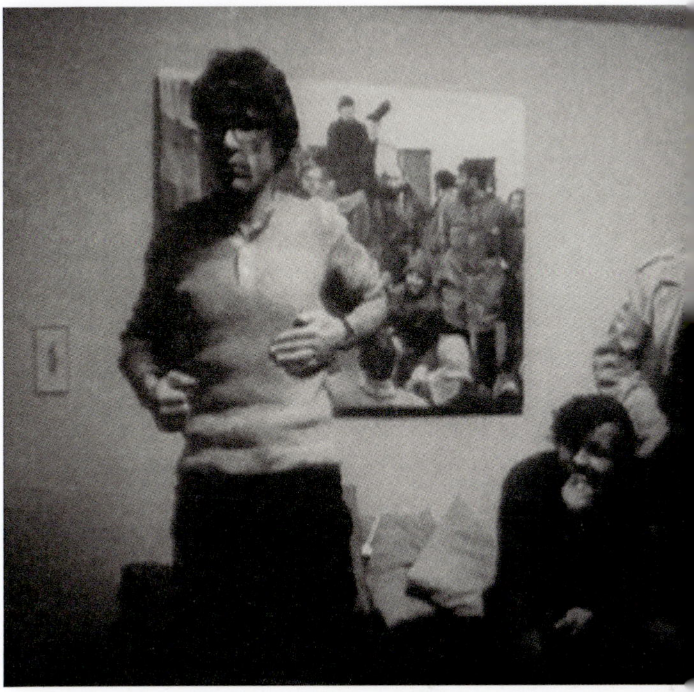

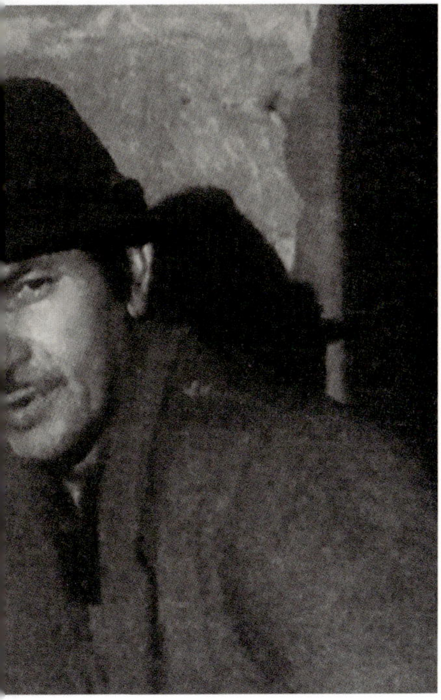

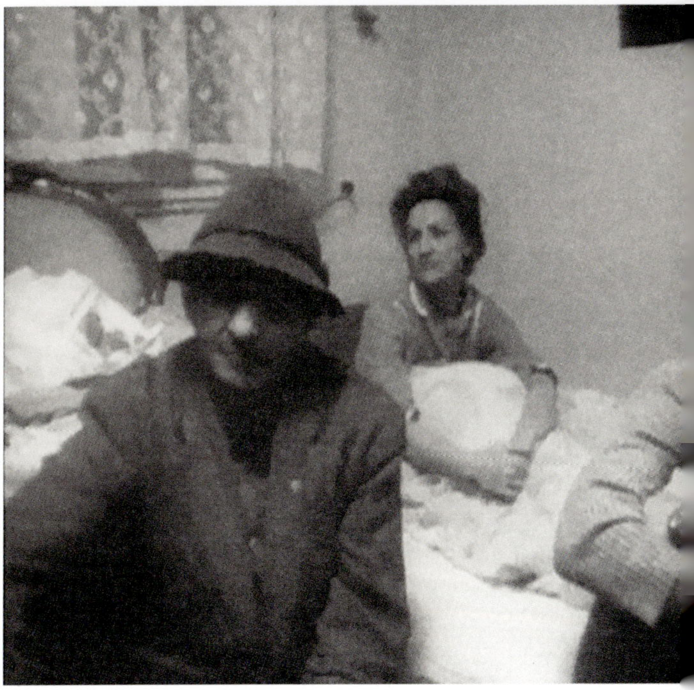

TOP LEFT Franja Handrla
BOTTOM LEFT Cveta Vuletić

TOP RIGHT Želimir Žilnik
BOTTOM RIGHT Cveta Vuletić and Ivana Branovački

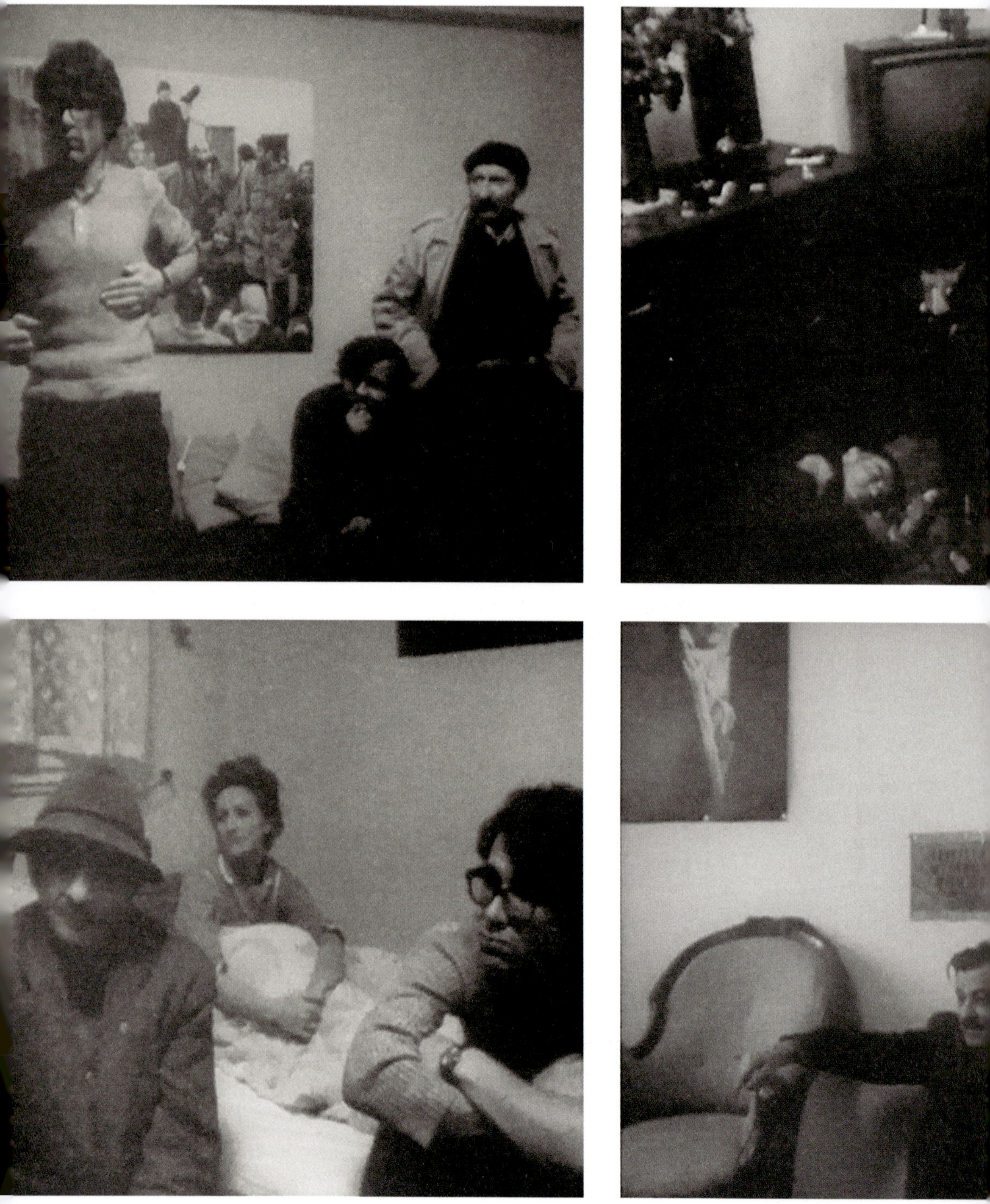

Black Film (film stills), 1971

TOP LEFT Želimir Žilnik and Luka Bauer
BOTTOM LEFT Cveta Vuletić, Ivana Branovački, and Želimir Žilnik
BOTTOM RIGHT Milorad Živančev, Ivana Branovački, and Maša Žilnik

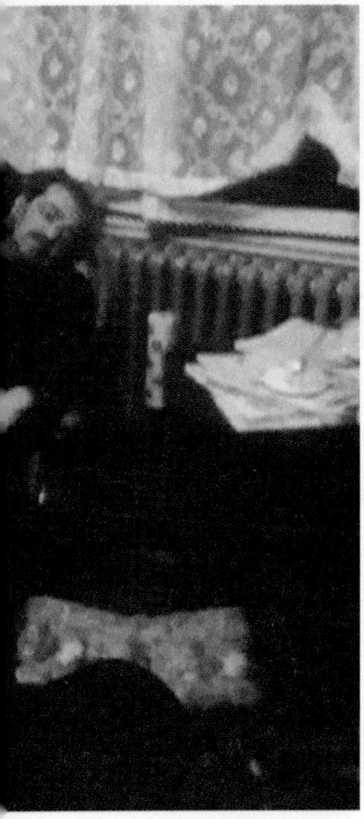

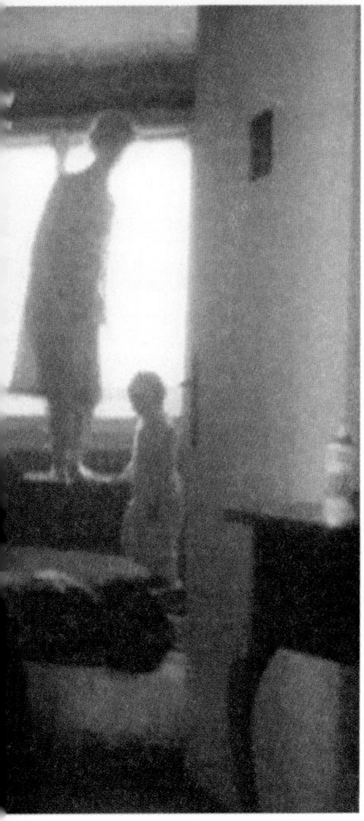

the conditions of backward rurality conceive of themselves as the typical heroes of Soviet propaganda movies and the political trends of Maoism. But their experience shatters their conceptions: notions of progress literally get stuck in the muddy streets. The protagonists' clothing and style would not look out of place in a pre-1968 Jean-Luc Godard movie like *La Chinoise* (1967), but in France the avant-garde never reached regions as *profonde* as the villages Žilnik went to during the making of *Early Works.*

Operating within the system of national (in Yugoslavia, federal and regional) television, Žilnik enjoyed the freedoms of a period of reform-oriented, audiovisual nation-building spanning Central and Western Europe. Broadcasters like ORF (Österreichischer Rundfunk) in Austria and RAI (Radiotelevisione italiana) in Italy at that time were institutions of criticality and didacticism, frequently with the premise of entertainment. That was exactly what Žilnik could relate to.

His short film *Uprising in Jazak* (1973) is an excellent example of his strategy of subversion by affirmation: in many ways, it looks like a propaganda film about the partisan war against fascism between 1941 and 1945. The people of the village Jazak (halfway between Novi Sad and Mitrovica, in the region of Vojvodina) recollect their contributions to the resistance against the occupation ("Schnapps for the wounded," "We took the oath in 1941"). This people's war was the founding myth of Socialist Yugoslavia, so Žilnik was completely in line with official historiography. But the enthusiasm of the people seems to go a little bit too far. The playful directing (sometimes literally collecting memories from people lined up at their doors along a street with a camera on a motor vehicle) causes the testimonials to merge into small reenactments. At the end of the film, people talk about how they welcomed the Red Army with the *Kozara* dance, and Žilnik films a Ferguson tractor "dancing" exuberantly. At a time when cultural bureaucracy was turning sour, this enthusiasm rubbed censors the wrong way. Žilnik was considered unreliable. He ran into difficulties with his next project, *Freedom or Cartoons* (1972), which was never finished, and decided to leave the country and start making films in Germany.

The major topic for this second half of Žilnik's career surfaced at the very beginning of his time in Germany: migration and the resulting multilingual, multilayered society it begets. In the short documentary *Inventory* (1975), he presents the population of a tenement building at Metzstrasse 11 in Munich. The camera was fixed in a position on the stairway, and then all the people living in the building were asked to come down the stairs, one after the other, and give a brief introduction, either in broken German or in their respective mother tongue, about their status of residence (in the country for how many years?), work or education, and social situation ("Für mich schlecht" [Bad for me], says the wife of one Genaro). Only two women speak German as their first language; one says she lives in the building for the cheap rent. The last word goes to the janitor, who has lived

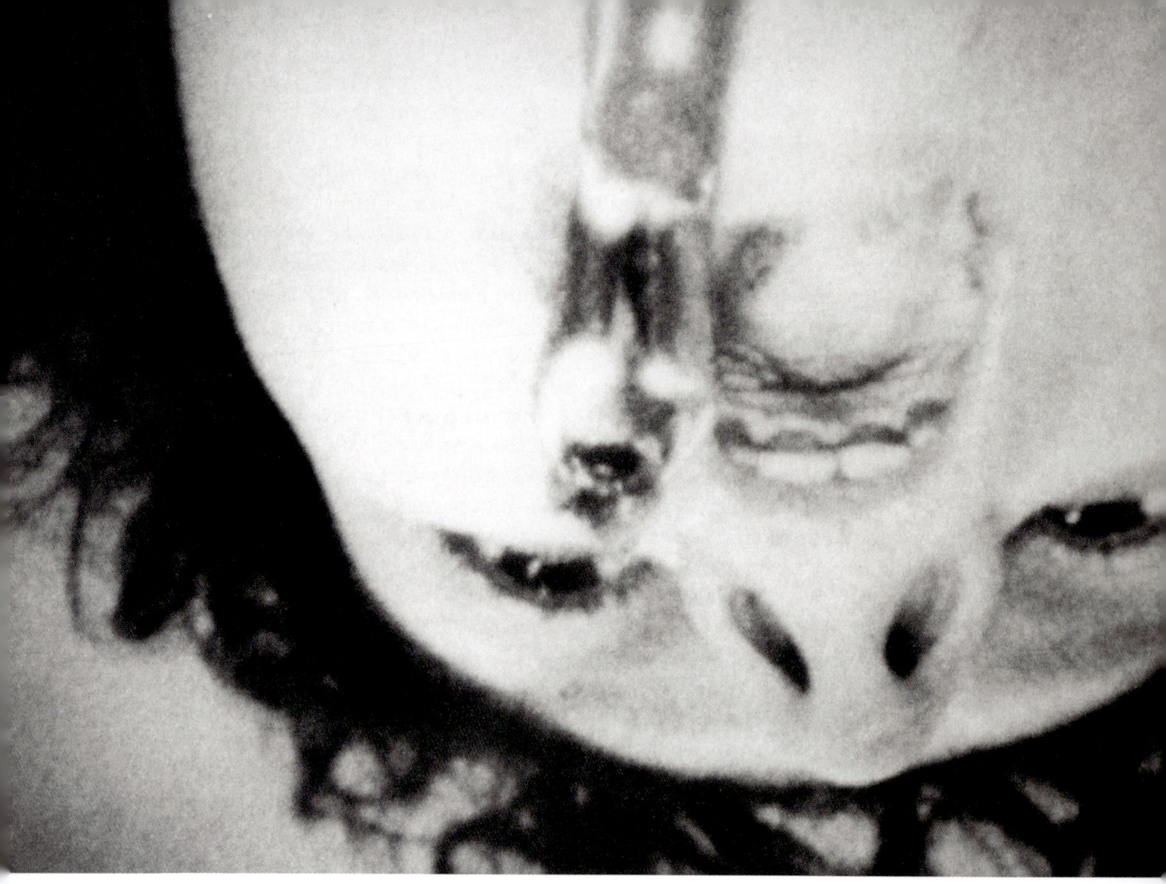

in the building for forty years: “Ich bin mit allen Hauseinwohnern zufrieden” (I am content with all the inhabitants).

The film presents a segment of the German society of the early 1970s that slowly became recognized by Neuer Deutscher Film. Rainer Werner Fassbinder’s *Ali: Fear Eats the Soul* came out in 1973, and its influence is apparent in Žilnik’s work of the period. But, as usual, Žilnik gives his politics a different spin: while Fassbinder was heading toward his version of American-influenced genre cinema, Žilnik persisted with his ambition to subvert notions of genre.

In Bavaria, he connected to an alternative scene of political engagement and communal living. The folk band Sparifankal sang the tune of the times: “Des land is nimma sche zum Lebm” (This country is not offering a good life anymore). The one-hour *Paradise. An Imperialist Tragicomedy* (1976) is Žilnik’s central work from the German period. His approach at that time was militant and playful at the same time. Even today on his website he claims that the contemporary event he drew on for the film’s central narrative was “fake.” But the kidnapping of the conservative politician Peter Lorenz in Berlin in February 1975 was not staged, as Žilnik claims, but an actual act by the Bewegung 2. Juni (a movement whose name refers to the death of student Benno Ohnesorg in 1967, which sparked the protests and revolutionary ambitions of 1968 in Germany). In *Paradise*, the

Paradise. An Imperialist Tragicomedy (film stills), 1976

TOP Gisela Siebauer

BOTTOM LEFT ON THE OPPOSITE PAGE Michael Straleck (facing camera)

Paradise. An Imperialist Tragicomedy

West Germany • 1976 • 90 min. • 16 mm • color

A multinational company owned by Mrs. Judit Angst is facing financial difficulties. She decides to hire a group of young anarchists to fake her kidnapping. After a couple of weeks spent in confinement, she will be able to justify the downfall of her company before the people, and at the same time it will also build her status as an opponent of destruction and chaos. A direct inspiration for the film was the kidnapping of Peter Lorenz, a center-right politician from West Berlin, in 1975. Lorenz spent five days in the captivity of the terrorist group Bewegung 2. Juni (2 June Movement), from which he was released after the government met the kidnappers' demands. The case was subsequently exploited for the benefit of his election bid to become the mayor of Berlin.

The film was planned as a big production with a 250,000 DM budget, and Žilnik had already extensively scouted various locations in Munich and was negotiating the participation of prominent actors such as Hanna Schygulla and Rainer Werner Fassbinder. The atmosphere in the city was tense due to concerns around terrorism and the growing prominence of the Rote Armee Fraktion (Red Army Faction). Because of the political dynamics at the time, Bavarian television withdrew its support for the film. As a result, Žilnik lost both his funding and the producer who facilitated the TV collaboration, so he decided to do the film in a more low-key manner. His production budget shrank to 60,000 DM, which came from some previously confirmed sponsors, and he moved forward with a team of people who were enthusiastic about making the movie happen—such as, for example, his costume designer, Gisela Siebauer, who agreed to play the leading female role. During the editing process, done at Filmverlag der Autoren, colleagues were already warning Žilnik that the film would get him into trouble.

Paradise premiered at Werkstattkino in Munich. Although the audience was enthusiastic, Žilnik learned that the police came the day after and asked that the film be removed from the cinema's repertoire. To evaluate the response his film might receive upon wider release, Žilnik decided to show it to a committee of prominent film critics who worked for the broadcaster ARD in Frankfurt. After watching the film, they advised him not to show it to anyone. Upon Žilnik's return to Munich, he was almost immediately visited by the police. They couldn't find anything to link him to terrorism, but saw receipts that showed that some of the film's collaborators had been paid in cash. Claiming this amounted to tax fraud, they arrested Žilnik and his cameraman, Andrej Popović, and took them to police headquarters at midnight. Žilnik called Alexander Kluge, who at the time was the president of the Directors Association, and also a lawyer to help them out. Kluge negotiated that the police would drop charges and release Žilnik and Popović from jail, on the condition they would leave the country. They had twelve hours to pack before the police escorted them to the Austrian border. They were never officially registered as expelled or banned from returning. ●

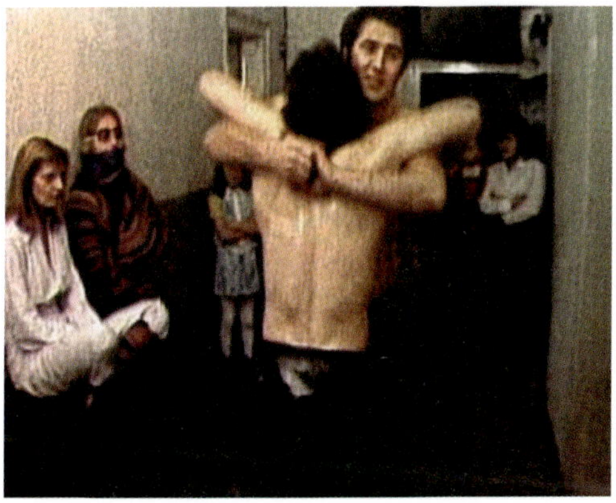

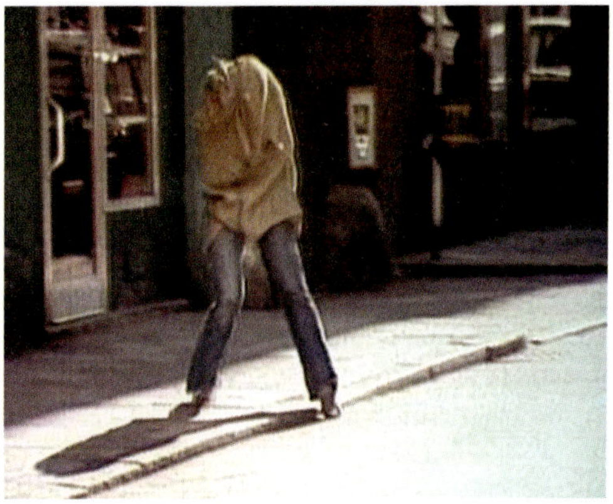

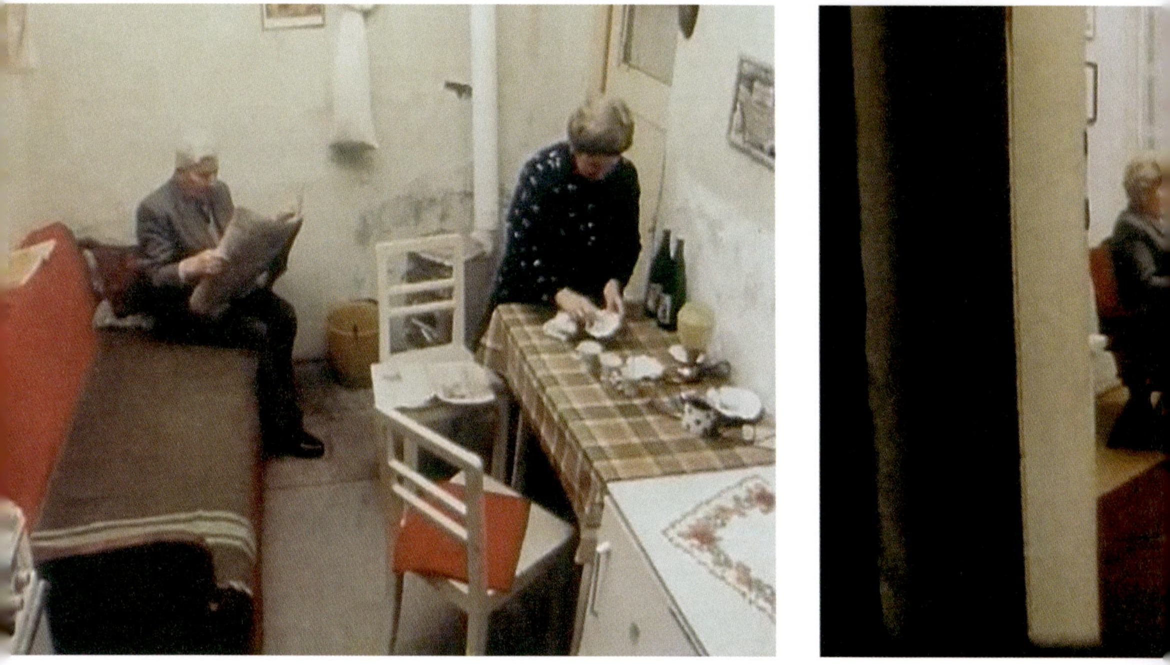

The Comedy and Tragedy of Bora Joksimović (film stills), 1977

kidnapping Žilnik recounts is indeed fake: a woman named Angst ("fear," in English) stages an abduction in order to cause her company to go bankrupt from the resulting uncertainty—and make an illegal profit from the stunt. She has to get in touch with radical elements, and accordingly the film gets more radical by the minute. *Paradise* looks very much like a collective endeavor, a film full of conflicting ideas and strategies, a happening in cinematic form, and at the same a subverted thriller in the fashion of Godard's adaptations of pulp crime material (think *Made in U.S.A.*, 1966). At the core of the analysis of Germany's political economy of the period is again the impact of worker migrations on the local capitalist system, this time in a polemical scene that hints at the selection procedures of a different period in German history.

In 1977, Žilnik was already back in Yugoslavia and working again in television. His portrait *The Comedy and Tragedy of Bora Joksimović*, about a retired theater employee, is very much a paradigm for the way he would come to work with protagonists in the future. Bora's work responsibilities did not include anything remotely artistic; he was a stoker. But secretly he always wrote scripts and scenarios for teleplays. Žilnik takes two of these stories and adapts them, but not in the orthodox manner of "realizing" the written material. Rather, he looks for the stories Joksimović came up with within the life of their author. One story is a comedy, the other a tragedy, and both are strongly informed by sexual fantasies. It might appear as if Žilnik is poking fun at Bora's amateurish plots. But the opposite is true: Bora is the first in a long series of characters that serve as typical Žilnik antiheroes, who are simultaneously his mediums and

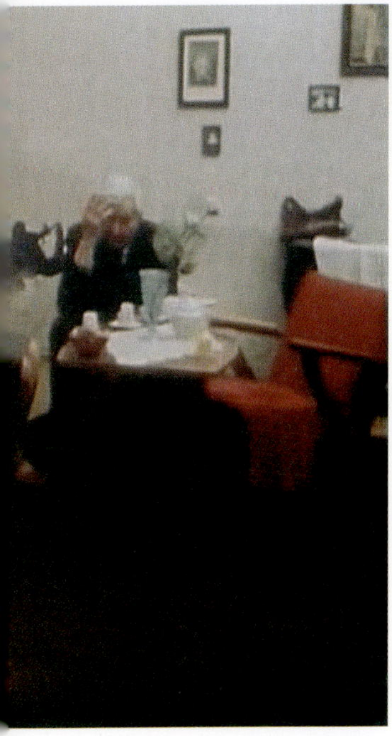

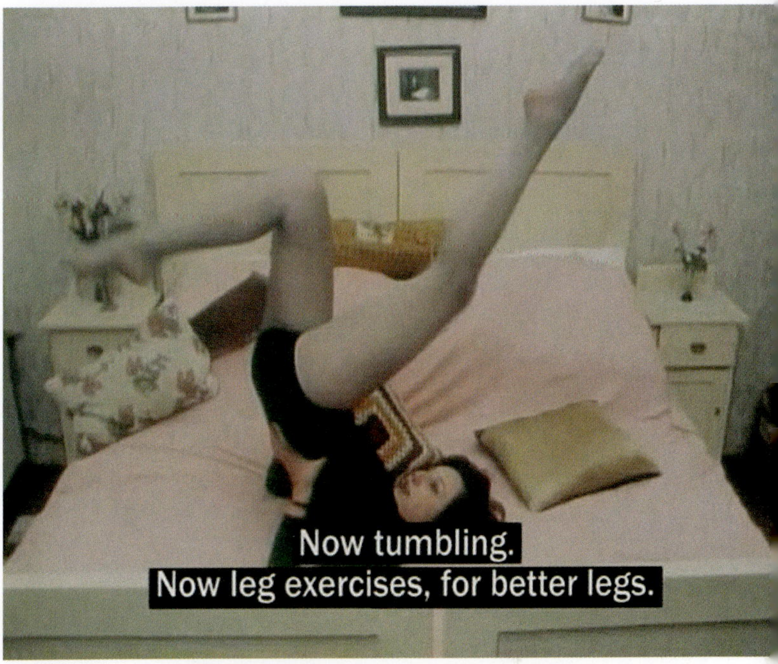

somehow stand-ins for the societies he tries to decipher through outcasts and oddballs.

A good example of Žilnik's television work of the late 1980s is *Brooklyn–Gusinje* (1988), produced by TV Beograd. It is more or less a conventional TV feature, with lead actress Ivana Žigon playing a character with her own first name. Ivana gets "discovered" in a little sweatshop in Novi Pazar by Seljo, who is searching for a waitress for his café. He is from Gusinje, a town in Montenegro near the Albanian border. It proves to be a significant relocation for a young woman, and Žilnik highlights this fact by including a short stop on the trip: Seljo and Ivana enter a classroom, and on the school map Seljo points out where they are going—far away. The locals in Gusinje are Albanians, so Ivana has to learn their "language." She also meets a young man who is there on holiday from Brooklyn in the United States. Škeljzen would like to drive around in a Pontiac, but all that's available to lease is a Volkswagen Polo. He is one of many migrants to come into Žilnik's works, a predecessor especially of Kenedi. *Brooklyn – Gusinje* is not exactly a docudrama, but documentary work is at the core of the project. Žilnik introduces the female protagonist into a world he unfolds according to her experiences. The film's anthropological dimension (most prominent in a sort of speech a man gives about the duties of women and men) is also highlighted by the irony of Škeljzen and his older brother Bećir being strangers in their own world. *Brooklyn – Gusinje* is public broadcasting in its essence: it confronts the general Yugoslav audience with one of its "tribes" and highlights the varieties of peoples that make up the country by putting a "regular gal" in the midst of a group of regional natives.

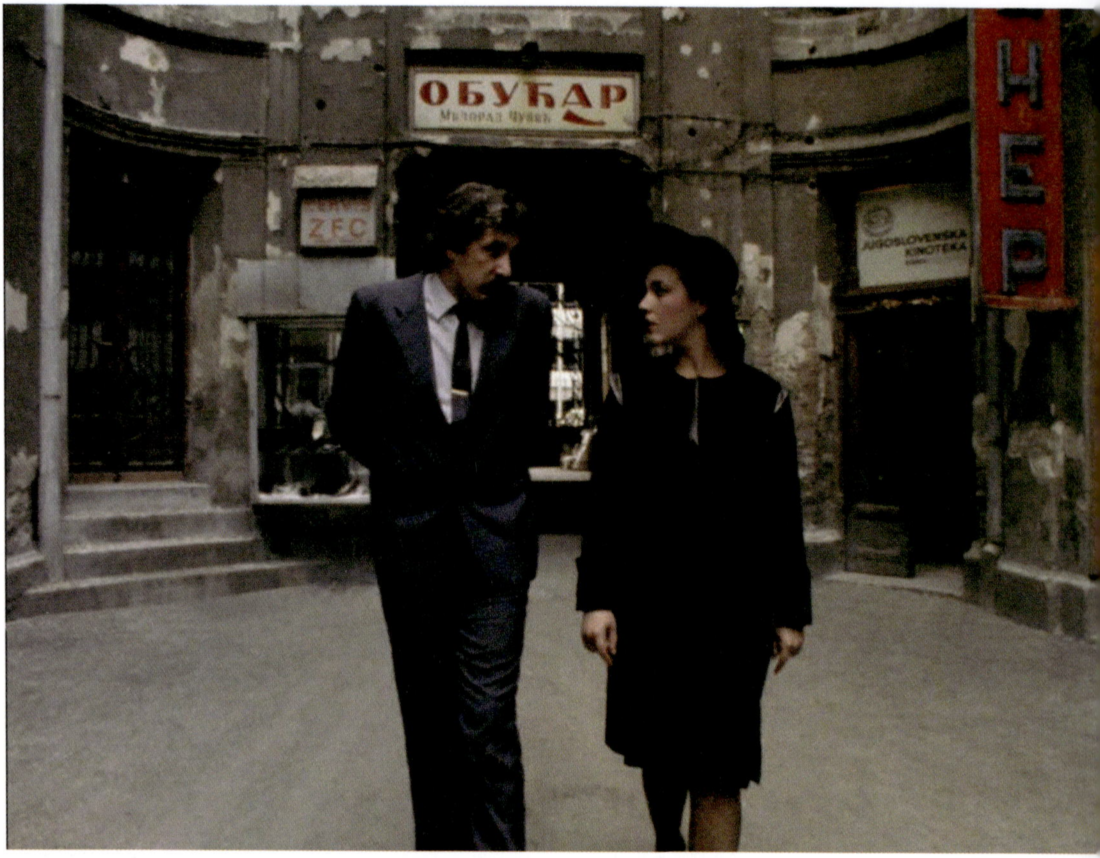

Bećir Uljević and Lidija Stevanović in *Brooklyn–Gusinje* (film still), 1988

At the same time, any possible mythology of nativeness in Gusinje has already been tainted by emigration and its repercussions on the local economic and social spheres. While Yugoslavia was always an exporting country in terms of its workforce, during the socialist period it was also much more open to outside influences than the closed societies of the Eastern bloc.

Žilnik has come to negotiate the internal nationalisms of Yugoslavia with the developing essentialisms of neoliberal globalism. It makes sense that one of his most famous protagonists is a man who is Roma, the one nationality in Europe that is essentially a transnationality. Kenedi is from the city of Mitrovica, in what today is independent Kosovo (at the time it was part of Serbia). Žilnik met him in Belgrade as he was accompanying a Roma family deported from Germany on their way into uncertainty in Serbia. Kenedi is a character very much to Žilnik's taste: a hustler, a man constantly busy running things or organizing people to facilitate something that might include a small profit for himself. For a documentary filmmaker, someone like Kenedi is an ideal medium. His dominion is interference, and that is very much what Žilnik is about as well: he is not there to simply observe; he is there to become engaged, to show reality from the viewpoint of a friend. Solidarity and friendship are core tenets of Žilnik's later engaged documentaries. He never aims to be the invisible fly on the wall common to strictly observational cinema (the most famous example being Frederick Wiseman), but he also refrains from engaging too heavily (as in the narrated, subjective documentaries of Nick Broomfield and the like).

Žilnik's most impressive feat is always finding those trickster protagonists who are not only themselves but also act as proper anchor characters, moderating and experiencing at the same time. Even in collective situations, as when he joined a workers' fight in Serbia in *The Old School of Capitalism* (2009), or in his road movie depicting the adventures of a retired Italian man bride shopping in the post-1989 landscapes of Eastern Europe (*Wanderlust*, 1998), he employs characters as much as he observes or directs them. Žilnik's method is probably most poignant in *Tito among the Serbs for the Second Time* (1994), because in this political comedy about a history that won't go away, the filmmaker blatantly reveals the concept of performativity that informs his documentary work: a man who looks like legendary state leader Josip Broz Tito appears in public spaces of post-Yugoslavia and causes all kinds of reactions. It is entirely justified to draw a line from here back to *Black Film*, in which Žilnik himself is the man in the main square asking painful questions in a playful way.

Žilnik's oeuvre took a different approach in the long run, which may also be ascribed to the systems he worked in: public television gave leeway to idiosyncratic ways of working, but from 1970 to 1990 did not require its makers to become protagonists in their own works. So Žilnik for the most part remained behind the camera but nevertheless became a highly recognizable subject of his genre: his humor, his revolutionary wit, and his deep compassion is mirrored in the people he picks to be the characters of his films. The modes of identification between director and protagonist mirror the modes of engagement for the potential audiences. In this manner, Žilnik and his immense body of work have become something like an integrative figure for cinema's foundational contradictions: reality and second reality and the position of the observer inside or outside either of those are in fact not opposing aspects but rather layers of the same reality. Even with nearly fifty titles, his body of work continues to be underrated. But there is growing recognition that not many filmmakers have earned a greater right to speak about "men," in the widest sense of this loaded term, than Želimir Žilnik. ★

Bert Rebhandl studied German literature, theology, and philosophy in Vienna and Berlin. He works as a freelance journalist, author, and translator in Berlin and is a film critic for *Frankfurter Allgemeine Zeitung*, *Der Standard* (Vienna), and *tip* (Berlin), among other publications. Rebhandl is coeditor of the quarterly magazine *CARGO Film Medien Kultur* (www.cargo-film.de). He has published books on Orson Welles, the western, *Seinfeld*, and most recently *The Third Man*. His personal website (BRO198.net) features other film-related writings.

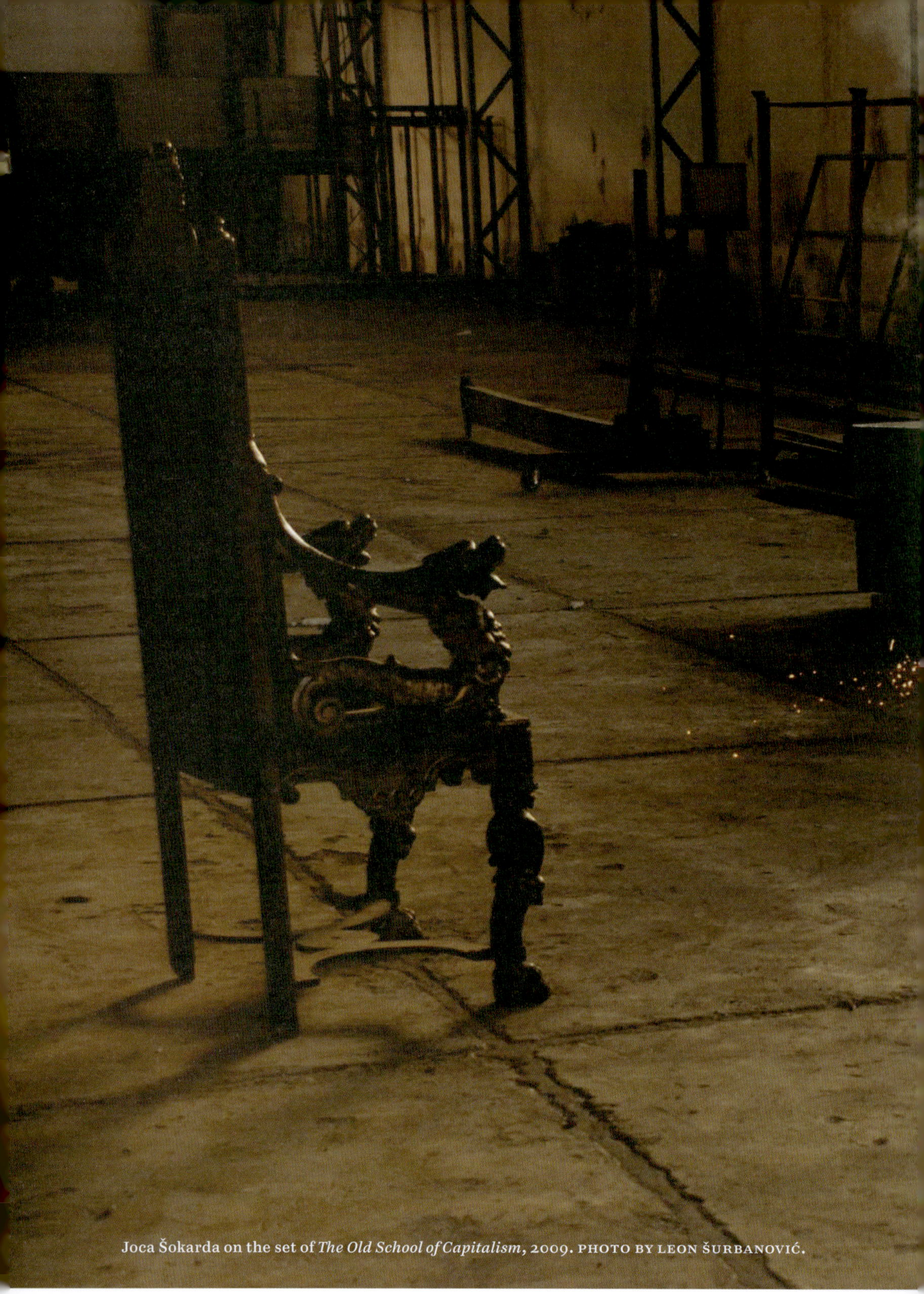

Joca Šokarda on the set of *The Old School of Capitalism*, 2009. PHOTO BY LEON ŠURBANOVIĆ.

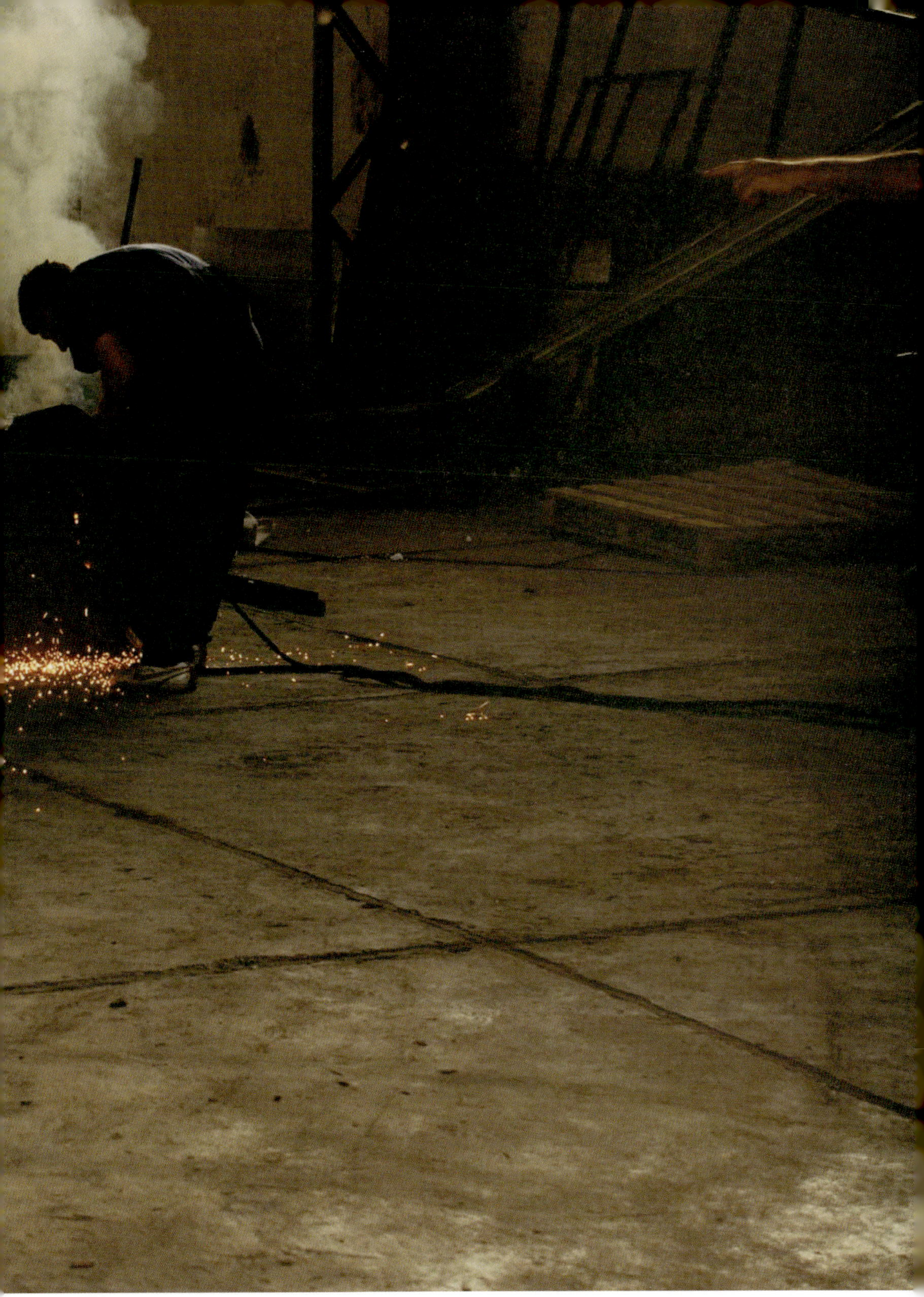

However, in today's post–Cold War, "postideological" world, Marxists are few and far between. Amidst a historical reality distinguished by an all but total discrediting of the "utopia" of communist internationalism and a forceful onset of the supposedly much more "natural," particularist forms of identity politics—the most rampant among which are various ethnic essentialisms—one of the few remaining of the torch of Marxist Cinema is Želimir Žilnik. This in not so because his work has maintained the unaltered course of a radical aesthetico-political program, outlined back in the 1960s. Didactic cine-Marxism (of the kind once made famous by the Dziga Vertov Group) was, to begin with, never a trait of Žilink's filmmaking. His cinema today still successfully functions as a form of praxis simply because it remains committed, as passionately as it was four decades ago, to a total demystification of the processes of production in all their manifestations: film production and sociopolitical activity alike. When the dynamics of the production are made explicit, ideological delusions—be they Stalinist, liberal-democratic, or ethnonationalist—are more easily debunked. The notions of identity and community are thereby also, inevitably, submitted to critical reevaluation.

—Pavle Levi, in Pavle Levi and Želimir Žilnik, "Europe's Internal Exiles: Sound, Image, and Performance of Identity in Želimir Žilnik's Films," in *Ethnic Europe: Mobility, Identity, and Conflict in Globalized World*, ed. Roland Hsu (Stanford, CA: Stanford University Press, 2010), 114 –15.

The routine cultural logic, in which the work of many artists who worked in socialist Yugoslavia was often presented, follows a simple formula: there was the official ideological mantra which created dogmatic, opportunistic culture; and, there was the rebellious opposition to this cultural numbness, displayed in the form of "dissident" political and artistic action. Both positions are mostly presented as seamless and without any internal contradictions: on the one hand we had political opportunism, hunger for power, ideological servitude, cultural uniformity, etc., whereas on the other there is a *man* (the dissident figure is almost always male) who suffers in such circumstances, a man who relentlessly achieves a creative distance from these circumstances, but a man who is a public figure and not some clandestine renegade. Some of the most "official" cultural products of the Socialist Federal Republic of Yugoslavia (SFRY) were insisting on "artistic autonomy" and on creating a certain political and aesthetic distance from the direct visibility of ideology, and the example of Yugoslav modernist art, especially the flourishing trend of abstract painting and sculpture in the 1960s and 1970s. On the other hand, some artists who were identified as "dissident" were an integral part of the SFRY cultural policy. Their projects were, in one way or the other, financed through official channels (as there were no other channels through which ambitious cultural projects could be produced), so that it was these projects that represented [the] SFRY internationally as an open and free-thinking country, etc.

Želimir Žilnik had a very unique position within this ideological dichotomy.

—Branislav Dimitrijević, "Behind Scepticism Lies the Fire of a Revolutionary!," in *For an Idea – Against the Status Quo: Analysis and Systematization of Želimir Žilnik's Artistic Practice* (Novi Sad: New Media Center_kuda.org, Playground produkcija, 2009), 136–37.

Upon release the film was on the one hand critically acclaimed by the newly developing international film scene and on the other hand accompanied by uproar and scandals locally. It was a lucky coincidence that at the time there was great interest in the Yugoslav film production coming from the international audience. For example German TV would in that year buy 10—perhaps even 15—movies from the region to be screened on their channels.

My film got noticed by a German film critic from [the broadcaster] ARD who decided to buy it and it was this single purchase that paid off the whole investment in the film. The production cost us approximately 3,500 DEM and all the profit above that amount became our fee.

—Želimir Žilnik, in conversation with Dubravka Sekulić, Gal Kirn, and Žiga Testen, in *Surfing the Black: Yugoslav Black Wave Cinema and Its Transgressive Moments,* ed. Gal Kirn, Dubravka Sekulić, and Žiga Testen (Maastricht: Jan van Eyck Academie, 2012), 67.

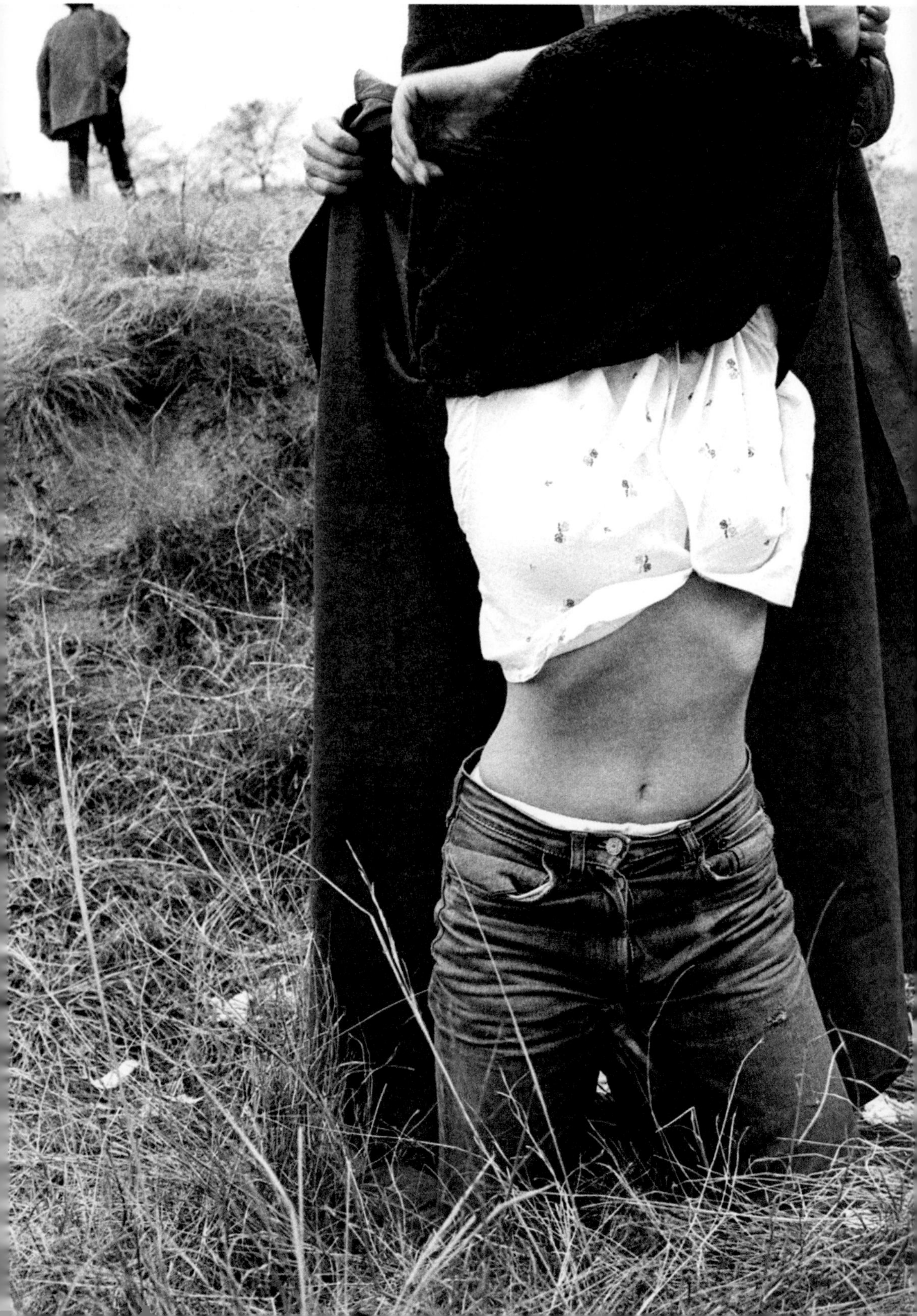

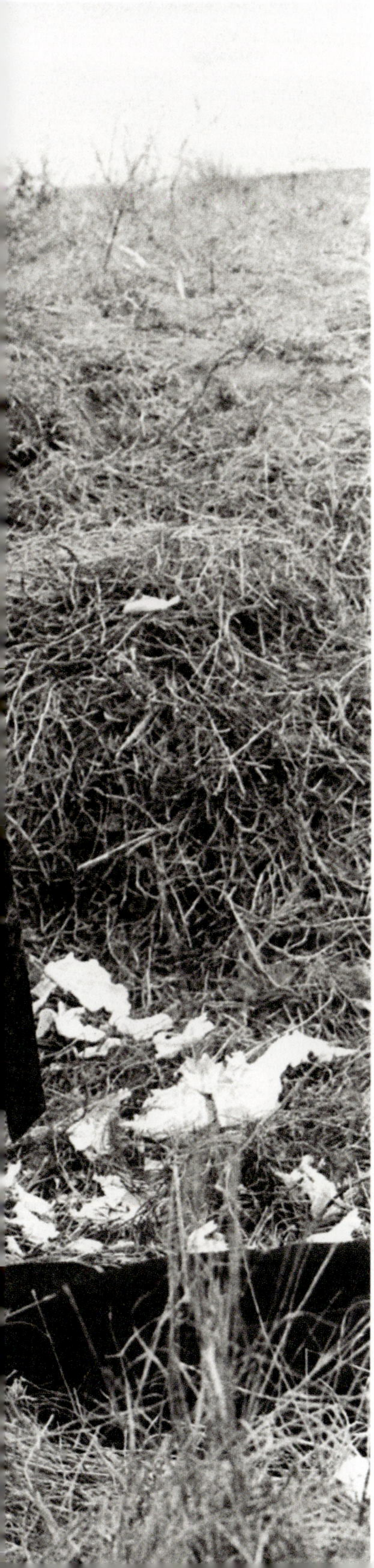

Milja Vujanović on the set of *Early Works*, 1968. PHOTO BY ANDREJ POPOVIĆ.

Early Works

Yugoslavia • 1969 • 87 min. • 35 mm • black & white

In an allegorical manner, *Early Works* recounts the story of young people who took part in student demonstrations in June 1968 in Belgrade, and, as its opening credits state, it includes "additional dialogue by Karl Marx & Friedrich Engels." Three young men and a girl, Jugoslava, defy the petit-bourgeois routine of everyday life. Wishing to "change the world," inspired by the writings of the young Marx, they go to the countryside and to factories to "wake up people's consciousness" and to encourage them to fight for emancipation and a life worth living. In the countryside, they face traditionalism and squalor, but they show their own limits, weaknesses, incapacities, and jealousy. They get arrested. Frustrated because the planned revolution has not been realized, the three young men decide to eliminate Jugoslava, who is the witness of their impotence. They shoot her, cover her with the Communist Party flag, and burn her body. A dark pillar of smoke rising into the sky is the only thing that remains of the intended revolution.

This was Žilnik's first feature film, produced by the biggest production house in Yugoslavia, Avala Film in Belgrade, and coproduced by Neoplanta Film in Novi Sad. The film passed the censorship commission in early March 1969 and premiered in Belgrade, Zagreb, Ljubljana, and Skopje. After three months of successful screening in cinemas throughout Yugoslavia, extensive polemics in the media, and the film's acceptance as an official selection of the Berlin International Film Festival, Žilnik was summoned to the office of the director of Avala Film. The night before, the film had been screened at the presidential residency. The screening was interrupted, and President Josip Broz Tito allegedly asked, "What do these lunatics want?" At Avala Film, Žilnik was asked to sign a statement that the film was still in the editing stage. He refused, arguing that both the professional and general public would see through it as a lie. That same day, all copies of the film were confiscated and the "Decision on the temporary ban on public screening of *Early Works*" was issued. Court proceedings started just a few days later. Since he had a law degree, Žilnik defended himself and the film in court. The accusations were dismissed and the film was shown at the Berlin International Film Festival a week later, where it won the Golden Bear for Best Film and an Award for Young Generation. That same summer, the film won several awards at Pula Film Festival.

The film stirred up much controversy among Yugoslavia's political establishment, particularly due to symbolic, but also fairly explicit, reflections on the invasion of Czechoslovakia by Soviet tanks in August 1968, as well as due to portraying the manipulation and persecution of the student activists who organized protests in Belgrade in June 1968. As a consequence, the Party Committee in Novi Sad organized an ideological campaign that proclaimed the movie to be anarchistic. Žilnik was criticized as being "under the influence of [Leon] Trotsky and Rudi Dutschke" and was expelled from the Communist Party of Yugoslavia. The film was withdrawn from domestic movie distribution, but at the same time, the official state exporter, Yugoslavia Film, distributed it in more than thirty countries around the world. The next time *Early Works* was to be shown in Yugoslavia was nearly twenty years later, in 1987, on state television.

The debate surrounding *Early Works* was huge across all parts of Yugoslavia and in various media, from daily newspapers to popular and specialized magazines. Many of the articles also published Žilnik's closing arguments of his court defense:

> The prosecutor is trying to prove the political offense of the film *Early Works*. He is mystifying the content of the film and its protagonists, and is trying to present it as a document about a particular event, and then claiming that the event did not take place as it was presented. The prosecutor does not even understand the medium of the feature film at all. He does not realize that the only possible offense of the film is its artistic failure. But if it really is a bad film, it is not for the prosecutor to prove it.
>
> However, all the prosecutor's actions—a motion for a temporary ban, an unsupported argument, his refusal of evidence, etc.—these are no longer things from an artistic film, these are things from our real life, these are the political acts that we should seriously think about. By these political acts, the prosecutor really is deeply depreciating, I would not say all the contemporary settings of social relations, as he claims *Early Works* does—I would be even more specific: by acting in such a political manner, the prosecutor is severely depreciating the progressive, anti-dogmatic, self-management principles of

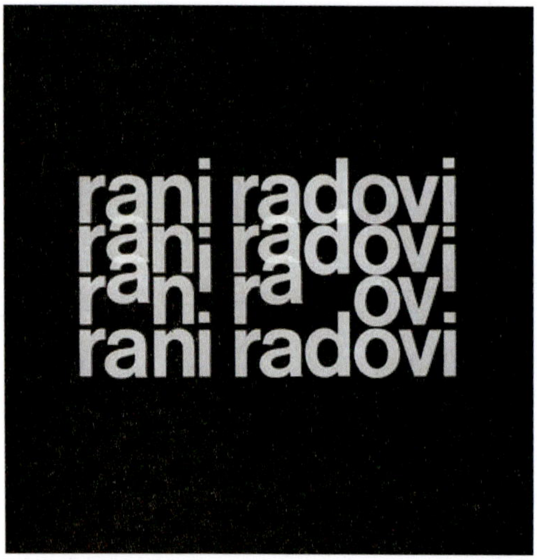

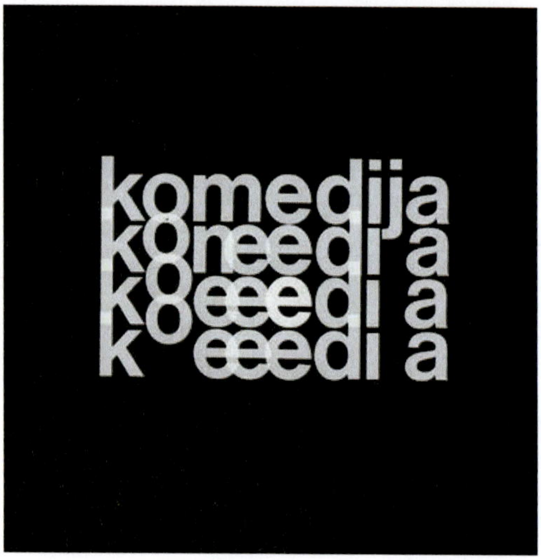

Early Works (opening titles), 1969. DESIGNED BY SLOBODAN MAŠIĆ.

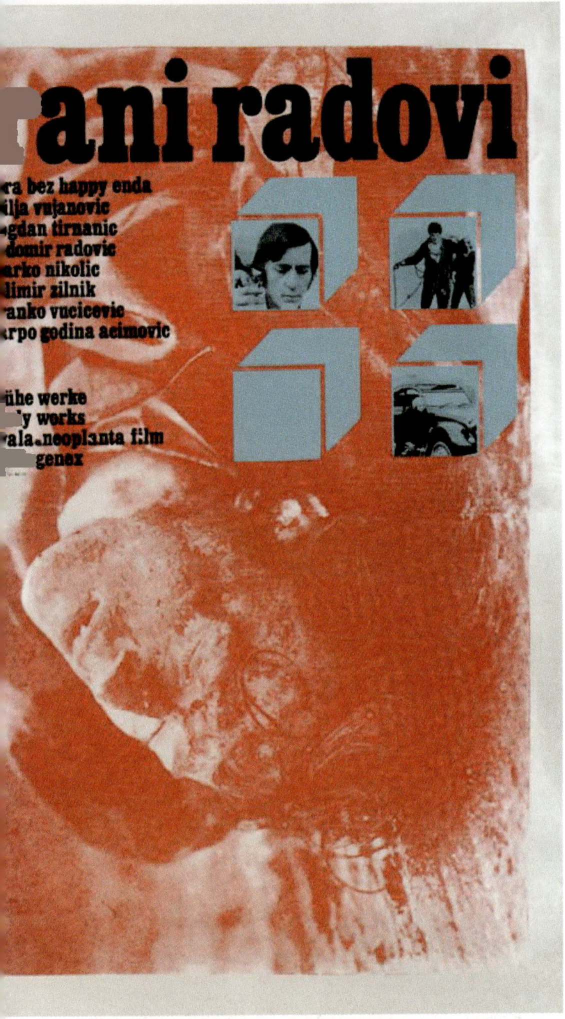

Early Works (poster), 1969.
DESIGNED BY SLOBODAN MAŠIĆ.

social relations. By acting in this way, he is glorifying, supporting, and developing other types of "modern principles" of social relations: bureaucratic, dogmatic, anti-self-managing. With his actions, he is trying to prove the following in real life and not in an art film: that confusion and irresponsibility rule the authorities who practice self-management in this country; that "we are not yet ready for self-management"; that the social authorities comprising professionals and politicians do not worry about social interest, and that, instead of them, only the state authorities should be in charge of the social interest. This is what the prosecutor is trying to say by banning the film four months after it has been part of the regular cinema repertoire, and after it has been approved and evaluated by the competent bodies of self-management and social authorities.

Furthermore, the prosecutor is trying to prove that irresponsibility prevails in the information media of this country, that there is incompetence, and that "things should be put in order here, too." He doubts the value of the principles of freedom and responsibility of the press. He ignores the fact that the film has been rated by fifteen news media, three of them bodies of the Socialist Alliance of Working People of Yugoslavia, and two bodies of the Youth Alliance. He believes that state control should be established over these media. Thirdly, the prosecutor doubts the international reputation of Yugoslavia. He claims that when, in his opinion, a bad Yugoslav film appears abroad, the world will immediately identify this film with Yugoslavia and its politics, and that we will consequently suffer. The prosecutor obviously does not know the scope of film and does not understand how his dogmatic political behavior not based on real arguments is far more dangerous for the reputation of our country than any film. ●

FOLLOWING PAGES
Early Works (on-set photos), 1968.
PHOTOS BY ANDREJ POPOVIĆ.

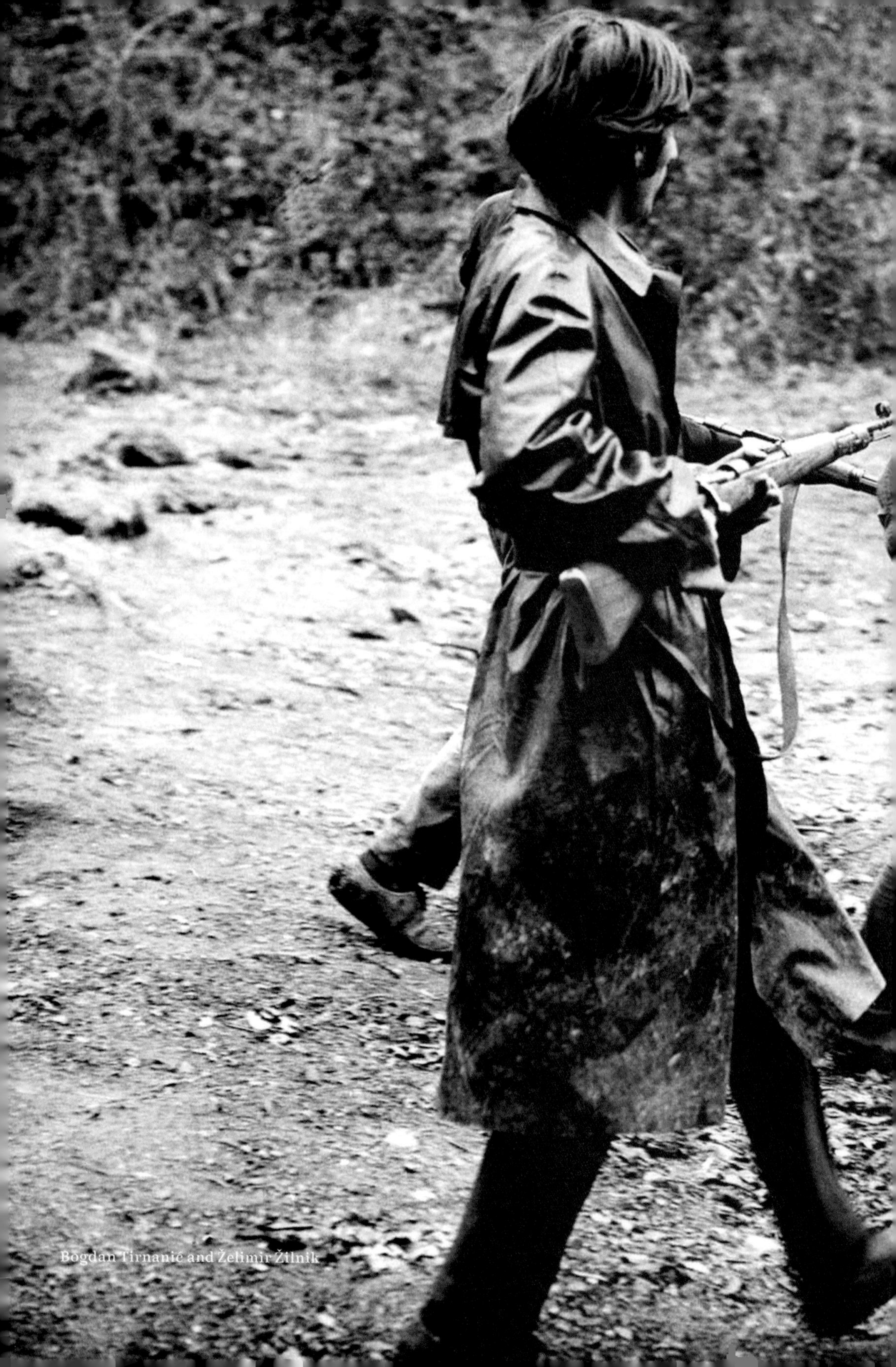

Bogdan Tirnanić and Želimir Žilnik

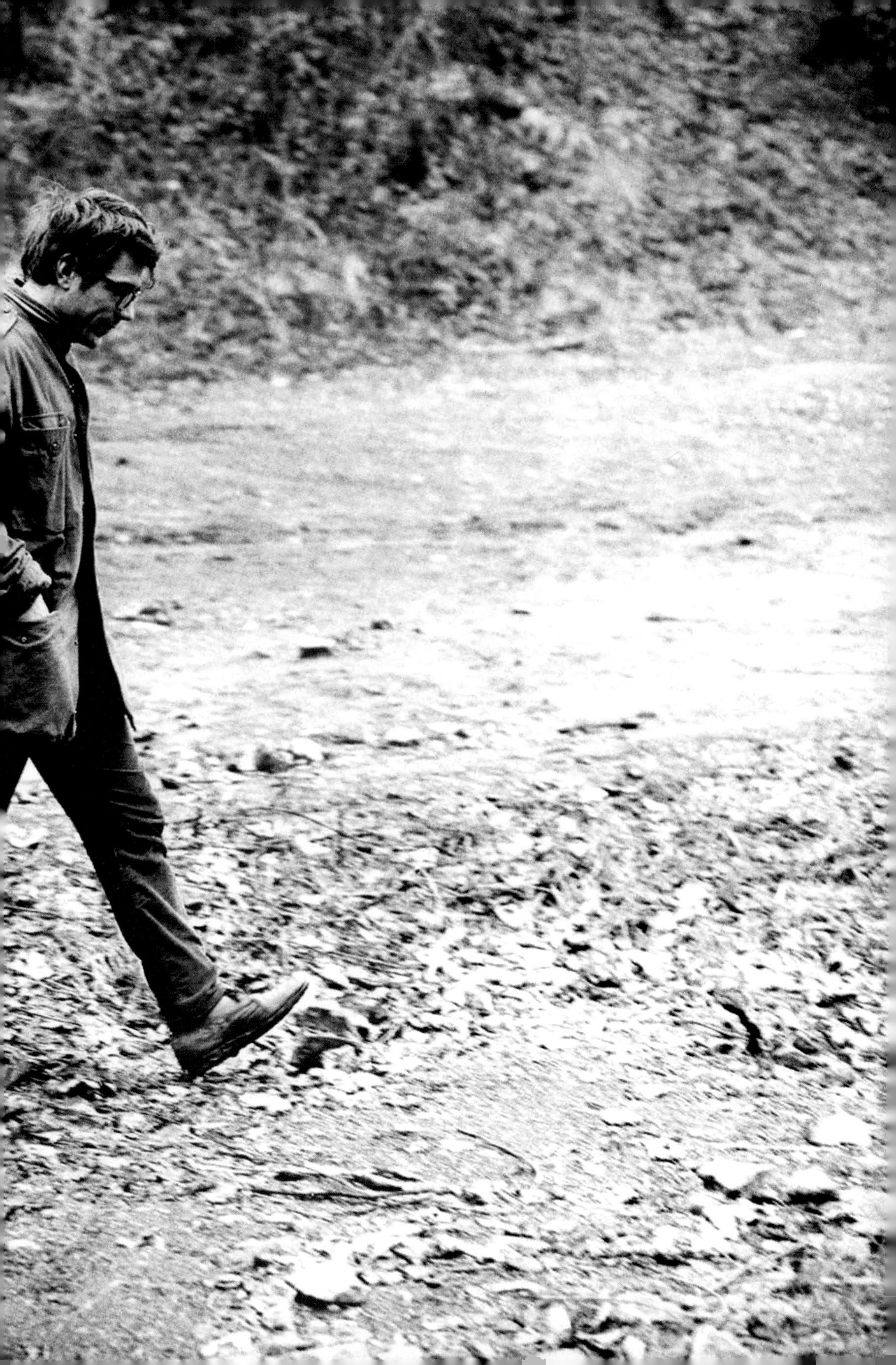

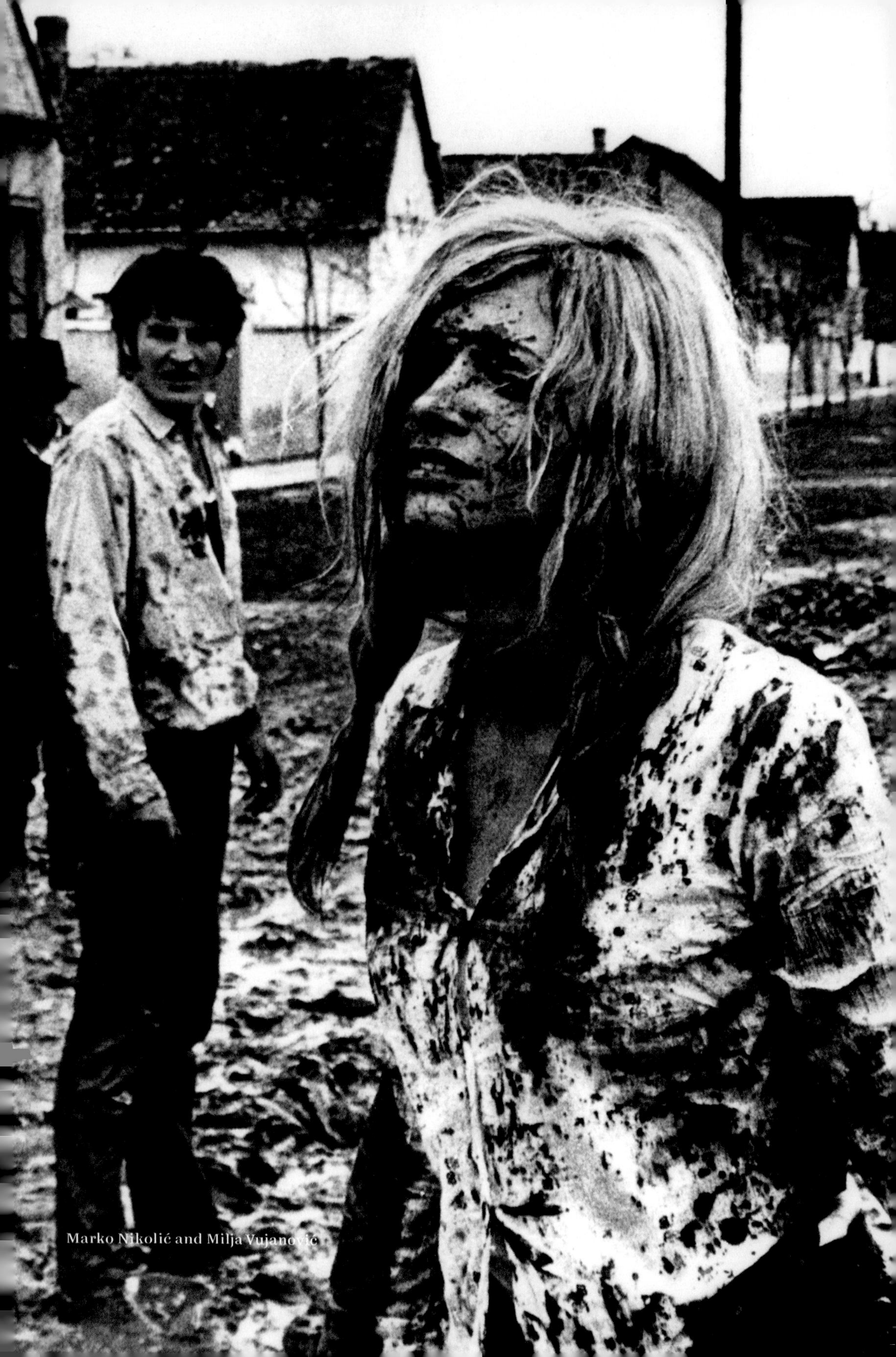

Marko Nikolić and Milja Vujanović

BORIS BUDEN

Shoot It Black! An Introduction to Želimir Žilnik

It's not easy facing up when your whole world is black.
—The Rolling Stones, "Paint It Black," 1966

It is usually said that Želimir Žilnik is one of the most prominent directors of the Black Wave, a tendency in Yugoslav film that emerged in the wake of the political and economic liberalization of the country in the 1960s and '70s, and presents the best that Yugoslavia had produced culturally in its short-lived history.[01] But what does it actually mean to be a protagonist in this cultural story from the Communist past? To what does "black" concretely refer in the famous phrase the "Black Wave"? Let us start with this simple question.

The newspaper article from 1969 in which the notion of the Black Wave was first introduced opens from a curious perspective.[02] The author looks at the reality of Yugoslavia from the future of several decades on—thus from today's present—and argues that this future will not be able to find "our true picture." That is, the authentic picture of Yugoslav society of that time is not in the "yellowed yearbooks of the contemporary daily press," for "this informative level stored in the archives and computer brains will fade into oblivion," but instead in the art made at the time. The future, as he states, will not believe those who had directly witnessed the actual reality but rather the "condensed and suggestive artistic story and picture that this reality produced."[03] In his view, this is why the future will have a black picture of Yugoslav society of the 1960s and '70s—because Yugoslav art, and above all Yugoslav film, painted this society black.

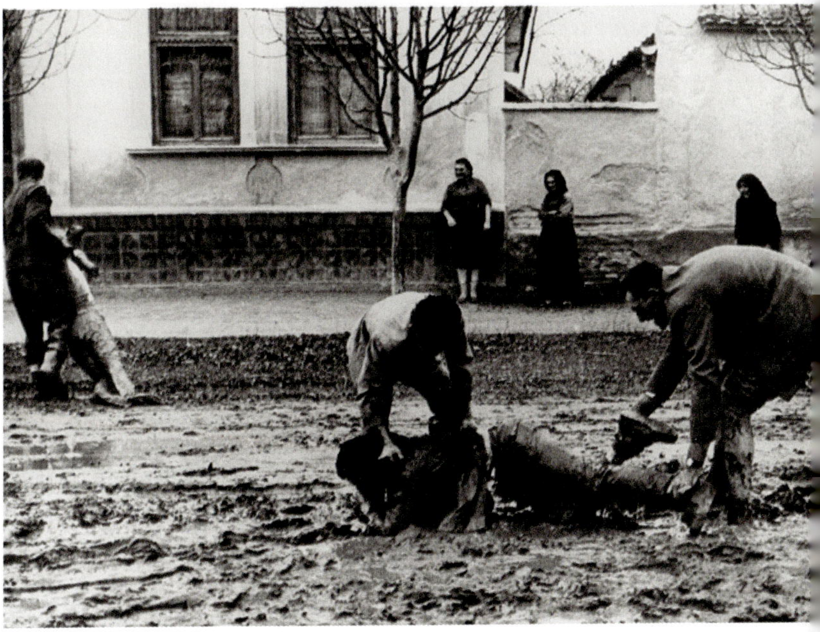

Early Works (on-set photo), 1968. PHOTO BY ANDREJ POPOVIĆ.

01 Inspired by Italian Neorealism and various new waves in European cinema, the authors of Black Wave rejected the norms and ideals of an optimistic, self-congratulatory official culture and openly exposed the dark side of socialist society—above all its ideologically hidden capitalist truth that emerged with the implementation of the market economy and its devastating social consequences like unemployment, massive migrations of workers both within the country and abroad, poverty, crime, etc. The most prominent directors along with Žilnik were: Živojin Pavlović, Bato Čengić, Dušan Makavejev, and Aleksandar Petrović.

02 Vladimir Jovičić, "'Crni val' u našem filmu," *Borba*, Belgrade, August 3, 1969, 17–24. All translations the author's.

03 Jovičić, "Crni val," 17.

Isn't it interesting? In a society ruled by Communists one would expect the voice of the Party to be at the same time the voice of the history itself—which *Borba*, the newspaper where this article appeared, undoubtedly was[04]—and not to tremble before this history helplessly expecting its final judgment. "What will the future think of us?" This is not the question of those who are supposed to know the course of history and legitimize their rule precisely from this very future. Moreover, no law of historical materialism, no Marxist concept, however undogmatic and creatively enlightened, would endow art, that superstructural phenomenon, with the power to give the only "true picture" of society and even to be the last word of history itself. And yet this is the logic on which the argument against the Black Wave filmmakers relies. *Borba*'s critic accuses them of betrayal. But betrayal of what? Not, primarily, of reality: they are not so much blamed for having unfaithfully represented reality in their films—for painting it more black than it really is—but rather their real "crime" consists in misrepresenting the society they belong to. So when the critic uses the notion of a "true picture of our society," it is not so much the "truth" that is at stake here—that is, a realistic representation of social life—but "the picture of the society" that he is actually concerned about. He complains that society, in the Black Wave films, "dresses in rags before taking pictures of itself." But by that he obviously doesn't mean that it should take off its clothes and expose itself in full nakedness, as it really is.

This apparently slight shift in accentuation from "truth" to "picture" has far-reaching consequences. The real conflict between the critic and the "traitors" doesn't take place where we usually project it from our postcommunist perspective: between Communist ideology on one side and the autonomy of art on the other. The case of Yugoslav "Black Wave" is definitely not that of ideologically stubborn communist apparatchiks who try to impose the dogma of (Socialist) Realism on freedom-loving artists. Moreover, it is not even the socialist cause that the critic insists upon: the well-known discourse on the social function of art, of its programmatic role in building a new society, of its educational duties, for instance, in boosting optimism. A classical discourse of Socialist Realism is totally absent from this polemical text.[05] Rather, he argues that the problem with the pessimism of which he, and through his voice the Party itself, accuses the Black Wave filmmakers is not that it spreads defeatism and so disarms the progressive forces of society, but rather that it spreads an unflattering picture of Yugoslav society. This is what the whole drama is about: how the society represents itself to the Other, both the Other abroad and the Other of posterity. Specifically, the authors of "Black Films" are blamed for "clownishly presenting the nation and the society for the sake of a cheap and ephemeral mundane fame." In the eyes of the critic they are guilty of submission to the fashionable taste of the international market.

In support of his criticism, he naturally calls on authorities. However, these are not Marx, Engels, or Lenin, nor any of the Yugoslav

04 For this reason I do not mention the name of the author of this particular article explicitly in this text. His personality is of secondary importance, since his personal and public opinion at that time was immediately identified as the opinion of the Party itself.

05 Indeed, the author explicitly distances himself from any concept of an "educational" function of art. For him it is "didactically old-fashioned to ascribe any functional attribute to art." The idea that a work of art should deliver some sort of message he also puts aside as Zhdanovism, the party doctrine on Soviet arts and culture developed by the Central Committee Secretary Andrei Zhdanov in 1946. Moreover, he openly writes that he would have some understanding for the "blackness" of Yugoslav film only if it would stay within the "art for art's sake" concept of art. Jovičić, "Crni val," 9.

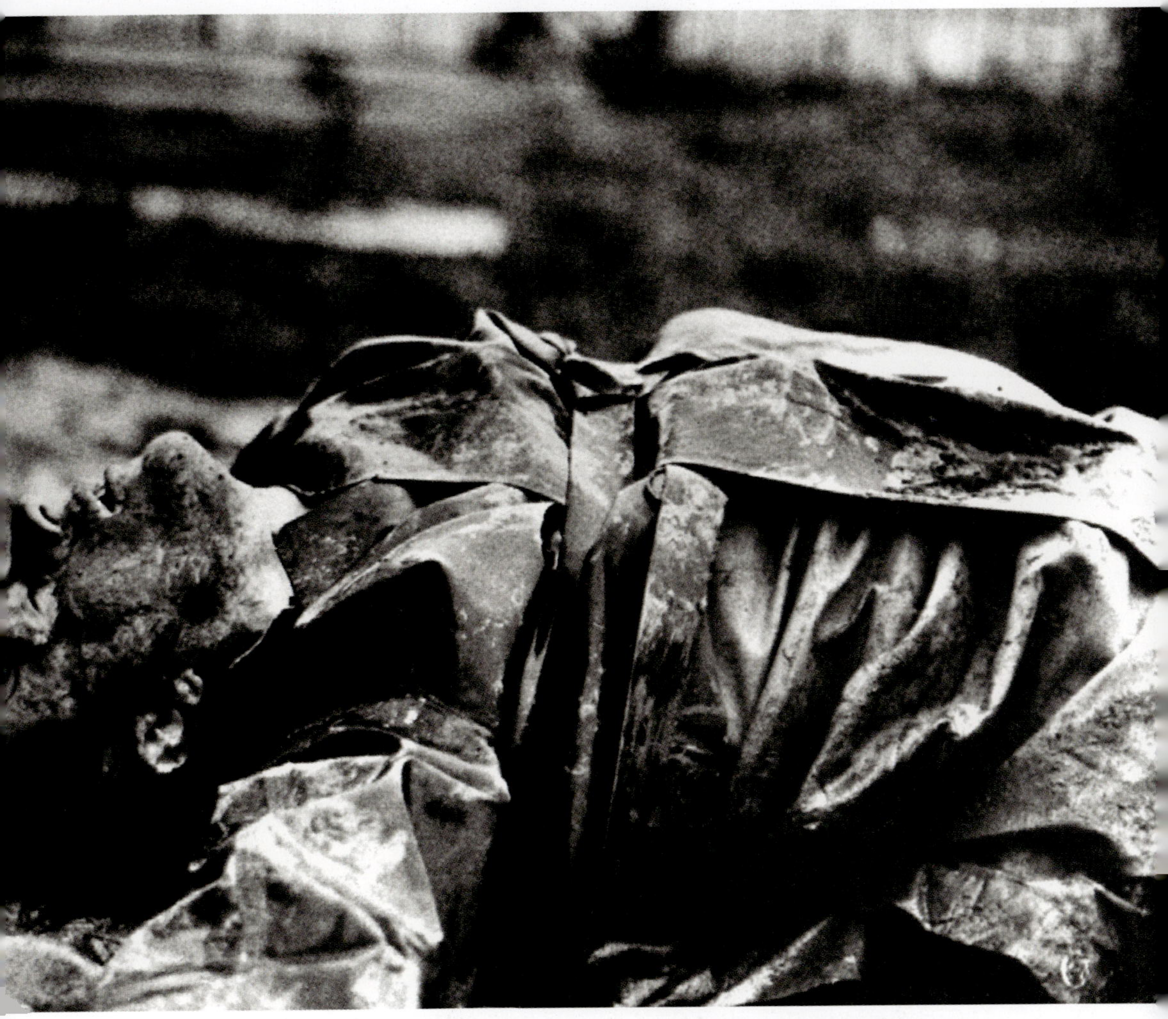

Early Works (on-set photo), 1968. PHOTO BY ANDREJ POPOVIĆ.

Marxists or leading Party intellectuals. It is instead Bosley Crowther, legendary film critic for the *New York Times* and at that time art director of Columbia Pictures, who is quoted from an interview he gave at that time to a Yugoslav magazine:

> You Yugoslavs [...] you are so vital [...] you know how to look at women, you can laugh from the heart, you are open, there is an original joy of life in you. Why then are your films so bitter, so dark? What is the truth? You as I have seen you, or you as you present yourselves in the films? [...] Or is this all in your film a temporary fashion of pessimism which, with a certain delay, comes to your authors from abroad?[06]

Thus we have the official position of the Party on cultural issues at the time drawing its arguments from an identification with a Western-Orientalist gaze that imagined Yugoslavia as an exotic realm of authentic enjoyment of life and natural vitality.

06 Jovičić, "Crni val," 20.

But the question of representation becomes even more dramatic from the perspective of the future, or in relation to posterity. Again, at stake is the picture of the society that will survive it in works of art, or as *Borba*'s critic writes, "a picture of us that is going to be bequeathed" to the future. He insists that we shouldn't be indifferent to this "sort of recognition," for if the art is now painting this picture black, the future too will have a black picture of us.

Writing from a contemporary perspective, this all is to suggest that we must necessarily abandon our postcommunist perspective if we really want to understand what that "blackness" ascribed to a great deal of Yugoslav film production at the end of the 1960s really was about. Not only because of all those unbearable clichés about the communist past (whose real ideological effect is not so much in blackening the utopia of the past but rather in brightening the actual one about liberal democracy and capitalism as the only exit solution of world history), but because there is one more, even better reason: the notion of the Black Wave was coined from this postcommunist perspective itself.

Black Wave is obviously a concept forged in struggle, and it implicates a certain instrumentalization of art in that struggle. But what struggle? Not the one for a better—for instance, a just, classless, in short, communist—society. Here we are definitely not dealing with a story about art being (unjustly) caught in a social struggle. From the point of view of the critic who introduced the slogan "Black Wave," the social struggle was already over, or more precisely, the social cause of the struggle had become obsolete. However, the struggle went on, but in another form, on another battlefield, and for another cause. Now it was the struggle for recognition that was fought exclusively on the field of culture. What was at stake in this struggle was now *identity*.

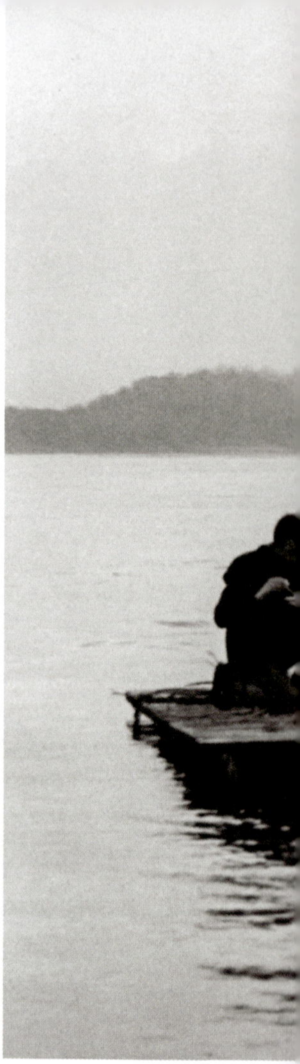

Early Works (on-set photos), 1968. PHOTOS BY ANDREJ POPOVIĆ.

TOP, LEFT TO RIGHT Čedomir Radović, Bogdan Tirnanić, Milja Vujanović, and Marko Nikolić.

BOTTOM, LEFT TO RIGHT Bogdan Tirnanić, Milja Vujanović, Marko Nikolić, and Čedomir Radović.

It sounds paradoxical, but the position from which the voice of the Party announced its *j'accuse* against the Black Wave filmmakers was the position of an already dead society—a society that had exhausted all its utopian potential and had reached the limits of its further expansion in terms of social justice and an overall social prosperity. It was a society that was facing its historical end, a society with no future whatsoever. It literally didn't see itself in the future, or, better, it saw only an alienated picture of itself there, a picture that had been already appropriated by art, by the Black Wave films. This is why our understanding of the Black Wave cannot be reduced to a postcommunist cliché about art struggling with society for its freedom. On the contrary, it is about a society struggling with art for the "true" picture of itself, a society in the final struggle for its cultural survival. In launching this struggle in 1969, the communist critics of the Black Wave precisely proved to be postcommunists long before all those democrats who would replace them later. They knew very well that they were no longer in command of history, but were still able to anticipate its development. Moreover, by occupying

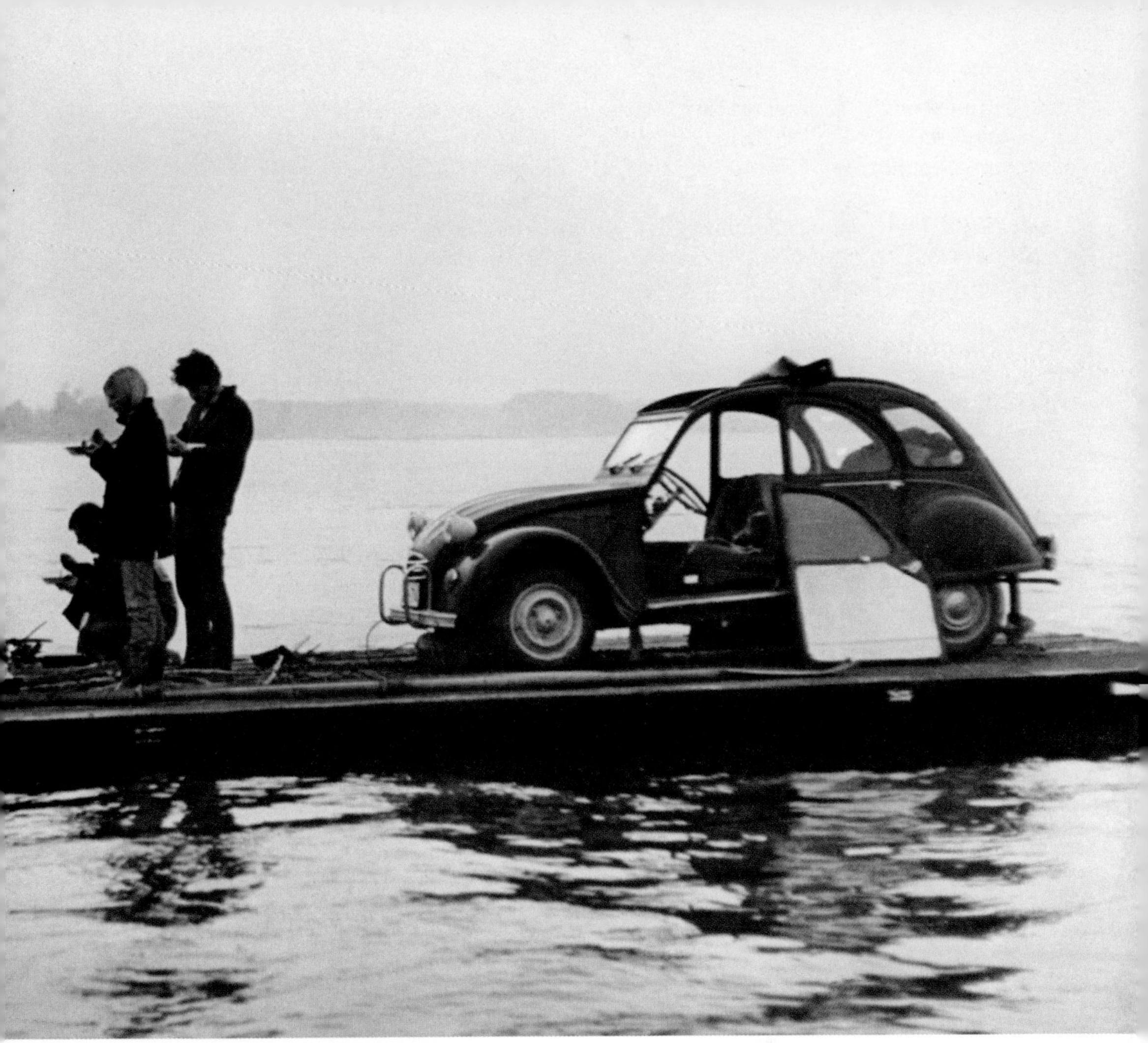

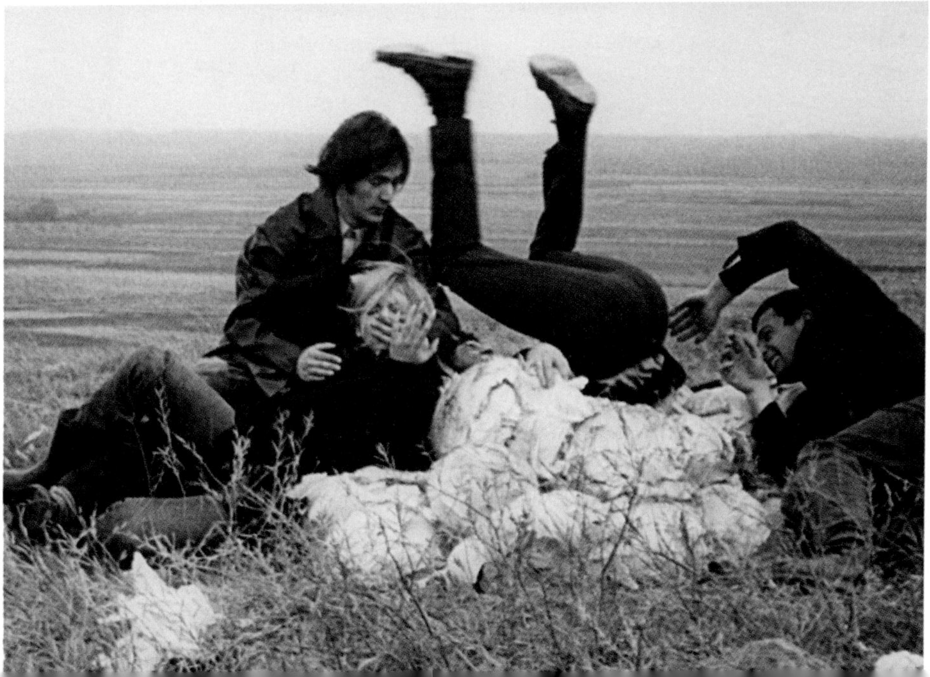

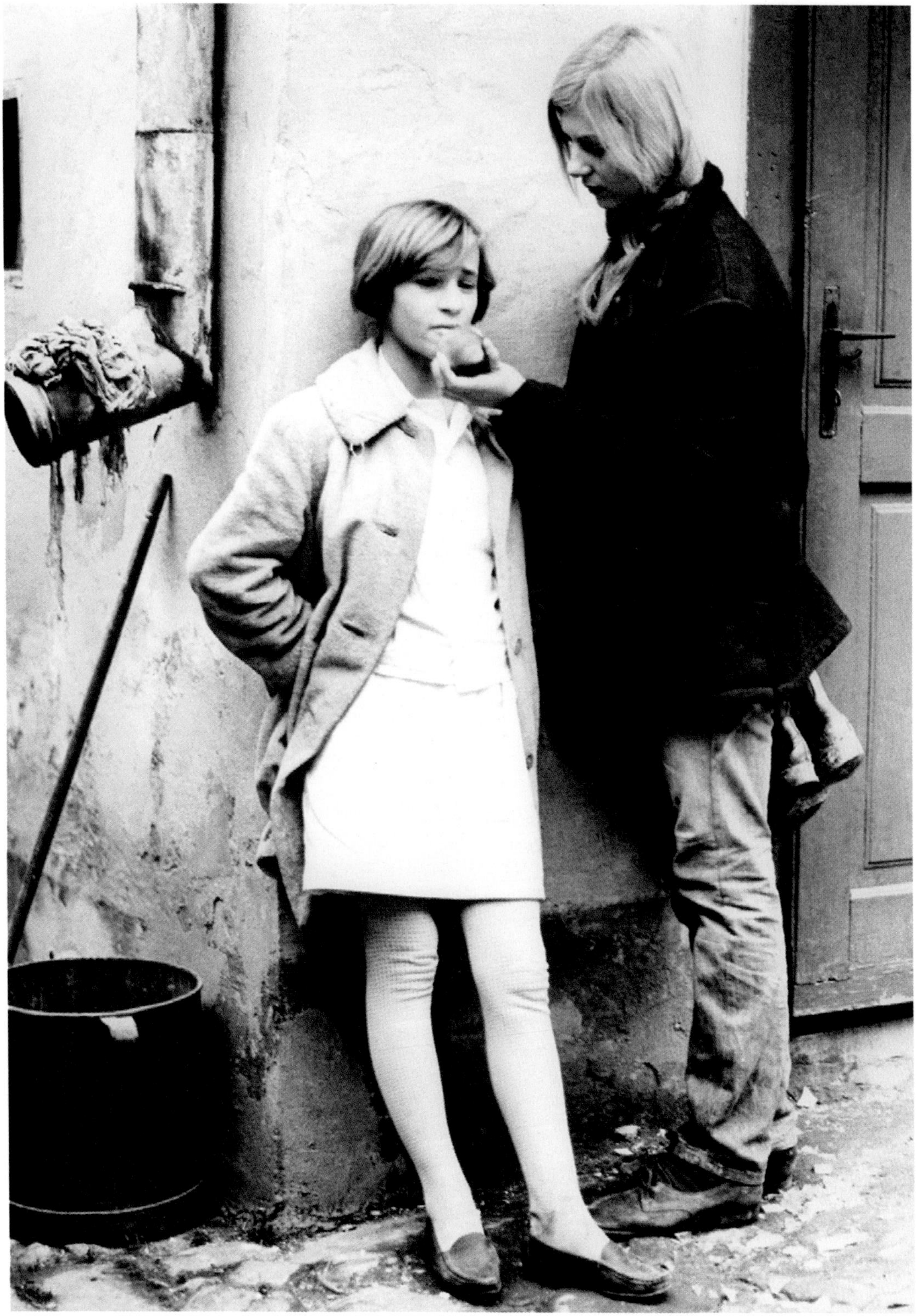

Piroška Čapko and Milja Vujanović on the set of *Early Works*, 1968. PHOTO BY ANDREJ POPOVIĆ.

themselves exclusively with the question of cultural representations, they had already accomplished that notorious cultural turn that would be later ascribed to postmodernism as one of its main features. Yugoslav communists of that time already looked at the society they were in charge of from the point of view of its cultural afterlife.

Of course, politically the Party was still identified with its historical mission—to radically change the society for the better—and still saw itself as being able to achieve this goal. But this, to use Lacanian terms, existed only on the imaginary level of their identification. In short, this was how Yugoslav communists identified with the ideal picture of themselves, with their ideal-ego. However, at the same time, but on a symbolical level, they identified with the gaze of the history itself—i.e., with their ego-ideal—in which they saw the society they had built surviving only in a cultural translation that fully escapes their control. They ruled society, but only in an imaginary realm. Symbolically, they had already lost it, they had surrendered society to culture. For them, in 1969, the challenge was no longer to build a new, better society, but rather to properly represent the dead one. Thus, a true picture of social reality still seemed to be possible, but only in an anticipated cultural retrospective. This also marks a move within Realism itself: from its socially prospective dimension (the concept of Socialist Realism deployed in the service of society as a utopian project) to a culturally retrospective Realism. The latter is no less ideologically dogmatic than the former. The name of the dogma now is cultural memory—the only form in which social experience is still available to us today, in retrospect of course. The Party knew this in 1969.

Now, we could probably answer the introductory question: To what does "black" refer in the notion of the Black Wave of Yugoslav cinema? It refers primarily to the end of society, to the experience of the abyss that opens up at this end, to that bottomless contingency one encounters after a social experiment—or, better, after the human experimentation with the social has been historically exhausted. It is the blackness that has absorbed all the utopian light that had hitherto clearly illuminated society's path to the future. In its subjective dimension, it is the darkness of the fear we are filled with when we face, existentially, the terminality of society—that is, when we become aware of the possibility of its total absence, in short, a social fear in its ontological dimension.[07] This is best expressed in the words of one of the most famous actors of the Yugoslav Black Wave, Bekim Fehmiu, who acted in European and Hollywood productions as well. In *Borba*'s article, Fehmiu is quoted as saying: "We have never lived better and yet, everything is black before our eyes."[08]

However, to calm this fear and to pacify this ambivalence, a fetish was introduced: the fetish of cultural identity that also implied, within the political concept of sovereignty, national identity. At that time—the end of the 1960s and the beginning of the '70s in Yugoslavia—there was a major shift in the way the Communist Party

07
In terms of Heideggerian *Angst* that makes a subject experience society's being-toward-death.

08
Bekim Fehmiu, quoted in Jovičić, "Crni val," 20.

legitimized its rule. The narrative of class struggle was essentially abandoned. The Party stopped conceiving of itself as the vanguard of a universal history that would lead it to its classless end, communism. Instead it began to legitimate its rule within the history of a particular nation by identifying itself as its political elite, which, after having finally accomplished the goal of national liberation and achieved full national sovereignty, was leading the (nationally framed) society into progress under the given historical conditions of a socialist, regulated market economy and open participation in international *Realpolitik* and global capitalism. In short: the communist leaders of this era did not aim to adapt society to the communist utopia. Rather, they adapted the communist utopia to a society that had fully identified itself with its nation. Of course, this fundamentally changes the situation on the so-called cultural front. The communists were no longer fighting in the trenches against the traditional bourgeois culture that was devoted to creating essentialist identities of the Yugoslav nations—Serbs, Croats, Slovenes, Bosnians, Macedonians, Montenegrins, Albanians, etc. Rather, they made a nonaggression pact with it—"you leave politics to us, we leave national culture to you" (with a few clearly defined exceptions)—and so even strengthened their identitarian, that is, national, legitimation. To stay in the saddle they had to remount a fresh horse of identity politics, and were now riding it blindly into the catastrophe of the 1990s.[09]

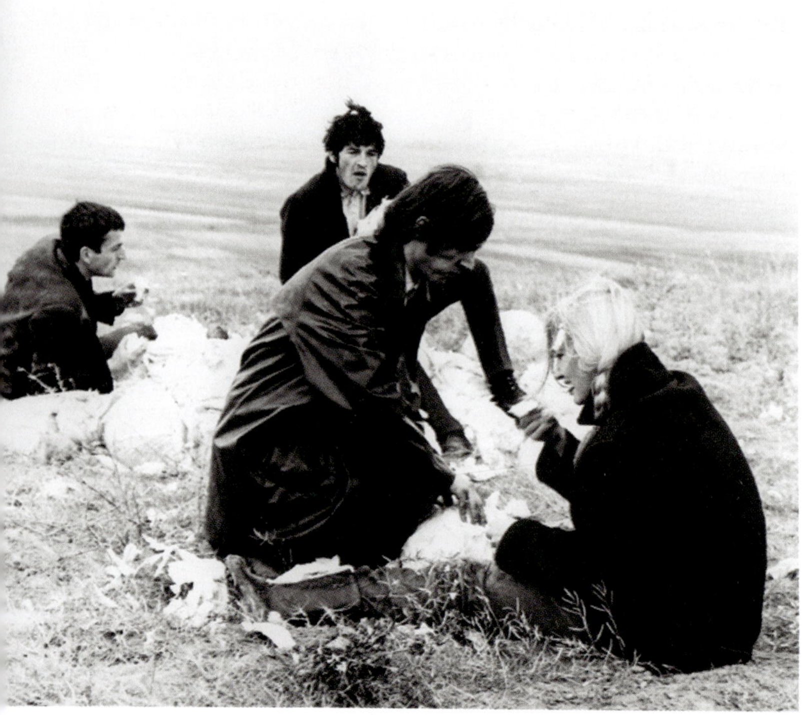

LEFT TO RIGHT Čedomir Radović, Marko Nikolić, Bogdan Tirnanić, and Milja Vujanović on the set of *Early Works*, 1968. PHOTO BY ANDREJ POPOVIĆ.

09
With the new constitution of 1974, multiculturalism became the official ideology of the Yugoslav state. The discourse on social justice didn't simply disappear from Yugoslav politics. It was translated into the new language of identity politics, which dominated the political public—not, however, as an intra-social cause but rather as an inter-national one. The question of an (un)just redistribution is now posed not in relation of one class of society to another, but rather in relation of one republic—one nation—of Yugoslav (con)federation to another. This is clearly a postsocialist turn, as defined by Nancy Fraser in her *Justice Interruptus: Critical Reflections on the "Postsocialist" Condition* (London: Routledge, 1997), 2: it demonstrates a shift away "from a socialist political imaginary, in which the central problem of justice is redistribution, to a 'postsocialist' political imaginary, in which the central problem of justice is recognition."

Milja Vujanović and Marko Nikolić on the set of *Early Works*, 1968. PHOTO BY ANDREJ POPOVIĆ.

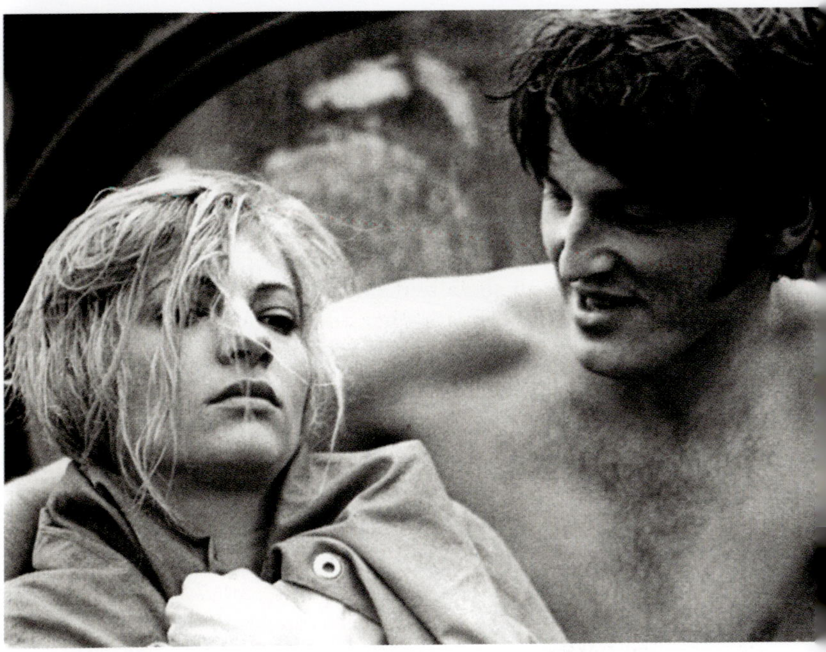

To sum it up: identity or, in a slightly broader sense, cultural identification, was what from then on was able to offer a perspective of a life after the end of society. No wonder almost all grasped for it. But not all indeed. Some preferred not to.

The most prominent among those who entered the darkness at the end of society with their eyes—and the lenses of their cameras—wide open was and still is Želimir Žilnik, whose entire filmic opus, extending over almost half a century, represents the most radical and consistent expression of its "blackness."

Moreover, Žilnik is the only one of the Black Wave filmmakers who explicitly responded to the official accusation: "You are blaming me for making black films. So be it, then." In 1971, he shot a documentary that he titled literally *Black Film*.[10] Žilnik picked up six homeless people from the street and brought them to his home, not only to share the warmth of a middle-class apartment (it was January), but also to actively participate in making a film about their problems. (This would become typical of Žilnik's documentary drama: allowing his amateur actors, whom the film story is about, to consciously participate in its making, or, in other words, to play themselves.)[11] The next day on the streets of Novi Sad, he used his camera to inquire about how to solve the problem of homeless people in the city. Neither the passersby nor the officials have an answer to this question. The filmmaker himself doesn't have it either, for "these stinky people," as he calls them in the film, cannot stay in his flat forever. So, finally, after telling them that no solution to this problem has been found and that he is running out of tape, Žilnik asks those people to leave his home.

10 *Black Film* was featured in the film program of documenta 12 (2007), curated by Alexander Horwath.

11 "I do not hide from the people I am shooting the fact that I am making a film. On the contrary. I help them to recognise their own situation and to express their position to it as efficiently as they can, and they help me to create a film about them in the best possible way." Žilnik, interview, *Dnevnik*, Novi Sad, April 14, 1968. Quoted in Dominika Prejdová, "Socially Engaged Cinema According to Želimir Žilnik," in *For an Idea — Against the Status Quo: Analysis and Systematization of Želimir Žilnik's Artistic Practice*. (Novi Sad: New Media Center_kuda.org, Playground produkcija, 2009), 164.

Again: what is black in this "Black Film"? The reality it depicts? The failure of communists to solve social problems? The notorious gap between a utopian promise and reality? No! It is the film itself, the very idea of art, especially film art, claiming power to change social reality—this is what is really black in *Black Film*. In fact, it begins with the author saying to the camera: "I used to make these films two years ago, but such people [the homeless] are still here."

The film is a radically honest self-reflexive critique of the idea and practice of so-called socially engaged cinema. Žilnik openly considers *Black Film* as being his own tomb. In a manifesto published on the occasion of the 1971 film festival where the film premiered, he calls the whole festival a "graveyard."[12] Black here refers to the "misery of an abstract humanism"[13] and to the "socially engaged film that has become a ruling fashion in our bourgeois cinematography";[14] it refers to its false avant-gardism, social demagogy, and left-wing phraseology; to its abuse of a socially declassed people for the purposes of film; to the filmmakers' exploitation of social misery, etc.[15] But what is even more important is that black doesn't refer at all to a "lack of freedom," which is usually presented from today's postcommunist perspective as the worst "blackness" of the communist past. Already in 1971, Žilnik explicitly stated: "They left us our freedom, we were liberated, but ineffective."[16] Black refers to a chasm that no freedom can bridge, a chasm that will survive the fall of communism.

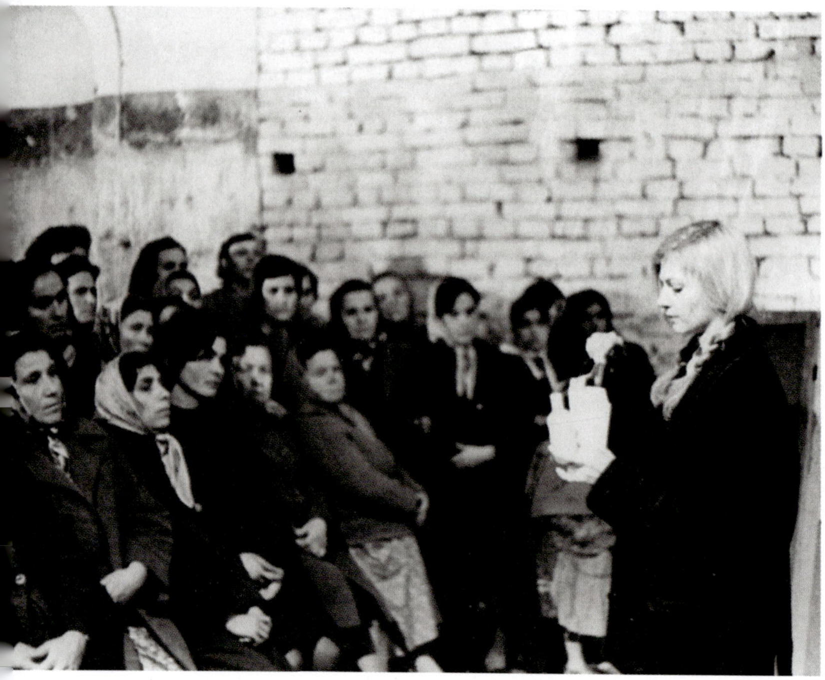

Extras and Milja Vujanović on the set of *Early Works*, 1968.
PHOTO BY ANDREJ POPOVIĆ.

12
Želimir Žilnik, "This Festival Is a Graveyard," in *XVII. Westdeutsche Kurzfilmtage Oberhausen*, ed. Will Wehling (Oberhausen: Westdeutsche Kurzfilmtage Oberhausen, 1971).

13
Želimir Žilnik, quoted in Heinz Klunker, "Soziale Experimente," in Wehling, *XVII. Westdeutsche Kurzfilmtage Oberhausen*, 23.

14
Žilnik, "This Festival Is a Graveyard." 24.

15
Želimir Žilnik, quoted in Klunker, "Soziale Experimente," 23.

16
Žilnik, quoted in Klunker, "Soziale Experimente," 23. Reporting from the festival in Belgrade, the same German critic, Heinz Klunker, criticizes Žilnik for seeing the situation "too darkly" and for underestimating the freedom that filmmakers in Yugoslavia have been granted, a freedom that Žilnik, as Klunker writes, "equates with pure complacency." Heinz Klunker, "Leute, Filme und Politik in Belgrad," *Deutsches Allgemeine Sonntagsblatt*, Hamburg, March 28, 1971.

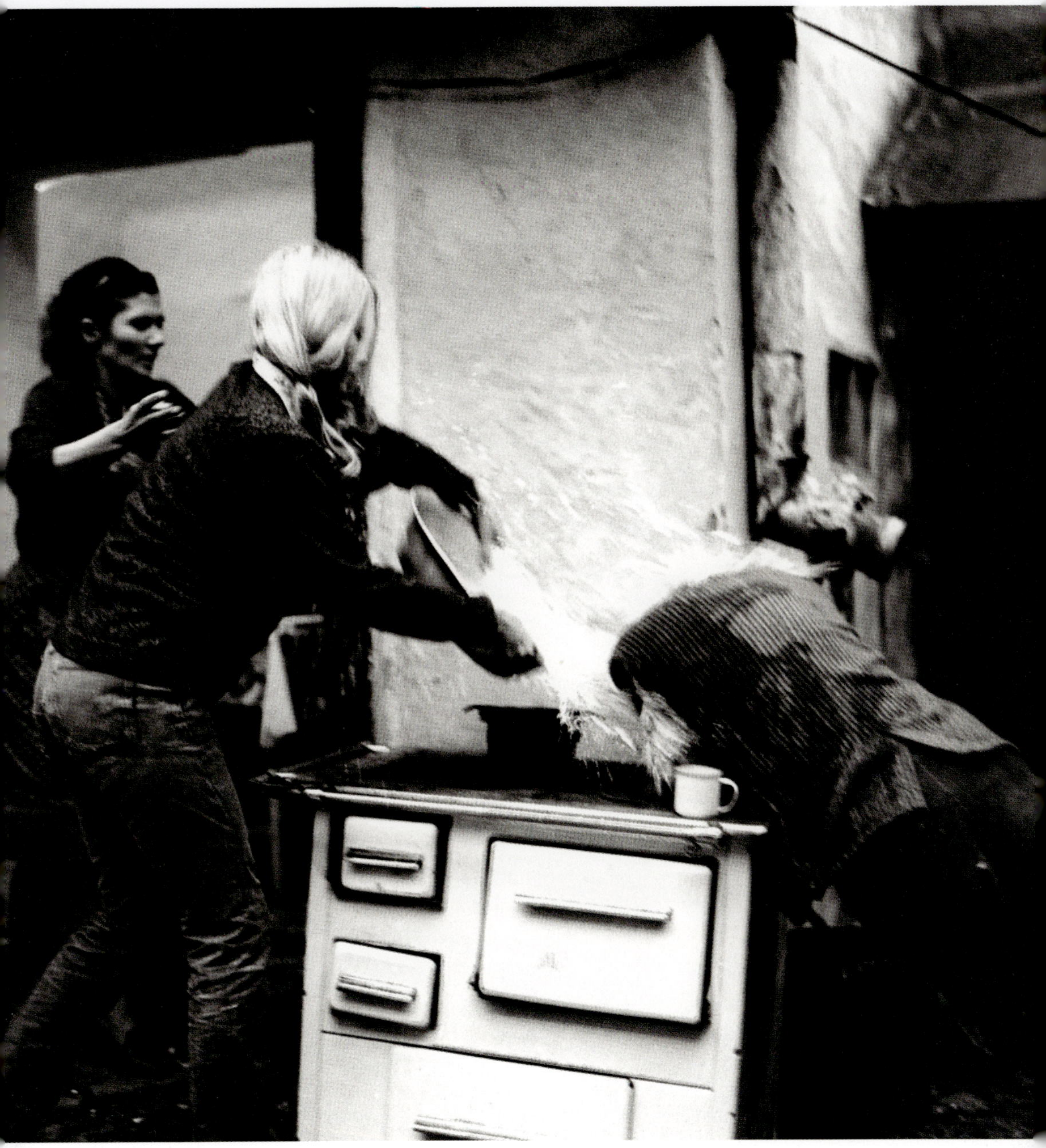

LEFT TO RIGHT Želmira Žujović, Milja Vujanović, and Slobodan Aligrudić on the set of *Early Works*, 1968. PHOTO BY ANDREJ POPOVIĆ.

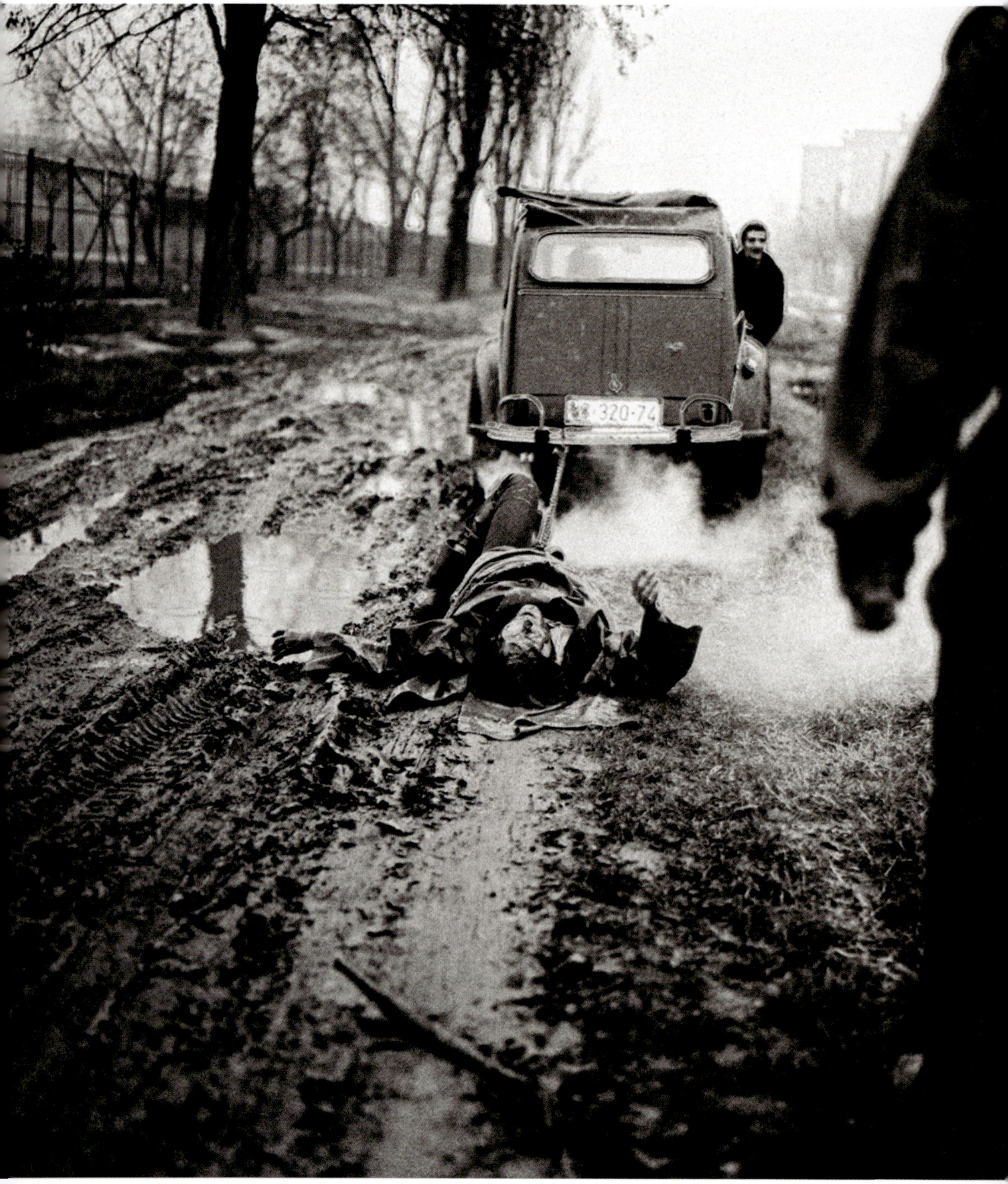

Bogdan Tirnanić (on ground) and Čedomir Radović on the set of *Early Works*, 1968.
PHOTO BY ANDREJ POPOVIĆ.

17
Žilnik, "This Festival Is a Graveyard," 24.

For Žilnik, a film, and in a broader sense, culture, however liberated from totalitarian oppression, will never provide a remedy for social misery. For him the emancipatory promise of culture is a bluff. In his mocking the authors of the socially engaged films from 1971 who search "for the most picturesque wretch that is prepared to convincingly suffer,"[17] he already makes fun of the liberal inclusivism that twenty years later would impose its normative dogmatism on the cultural producers of the new (and old) democracies. We know that picture very well: one discovers somewhere on the fringes of society the victims of exclusion, those poor subaltern creatures with no face and no voice. But luckily there is an artist around to help them show their faces and make their voices heard. How nice: what a bad society has excluded, a good art can include again. For, as one believes, what has been socially marginalized can always be made culturally central, that is, brought to light—to the transparency of the public sphere—from the dark fringes of society. The rest is a democratic routine: a benevolent civil society, sympathetic to the suffering of the poor and excluded, makes a political case of the social darkness; and as soon as the party politics is involved, a political solution searched for and finally found, a low is changed, a democracy is reborn, now more inclusive than ever before.

Not with me, answers Želimir Žilnik, already in 1971. He, who has been working his entire life with different kinds of so-called marginalized people—from street children, unemployed and homeless people, to transvestites, illegal migrants, Roma, etc.—knows well what their "blackness" is about. It is about where the society as society is absent and about what politics, however democratic, cannot represent: a "blackness," which is rapidly swallowing that light we have historically gathered around. ★

Boris Buden is a writer and cultural critic based in Berlin. He received his PhD in cultural theory from Humboldt University of Berlin. In the 1990s, he was editor of the Zagreb-based magazine *Arkzin*. His essays and articles span the topics of philosophy, politics, and cultural and art criticism. He has participated in various conferences and art projects in Western and Eastern Europe, Asia, and the United States, including documenta 11 in Kassel. Buden is a permanent fellow of the European Institute for Progressive Cultural Policies in Vienna. He taught cultural theory in the Faculty of Art and Design at Bauhaus University, Weimar. Buden is the coeditor and author of several books, including *Der Schacht von Babel* (2004), *Zone des Übergangs* (2009), and *Transition to Nowhere* (2019).

THIS IS A LIGHTLY EDITED VERSION OF A TEXT ORIGINALLY PUBLISHED IN: *Afterall: A Journal of Art, Context and Enquiry* (University of Chicago Press), vol. 25, Autumn/Winter 2010, 38–47.

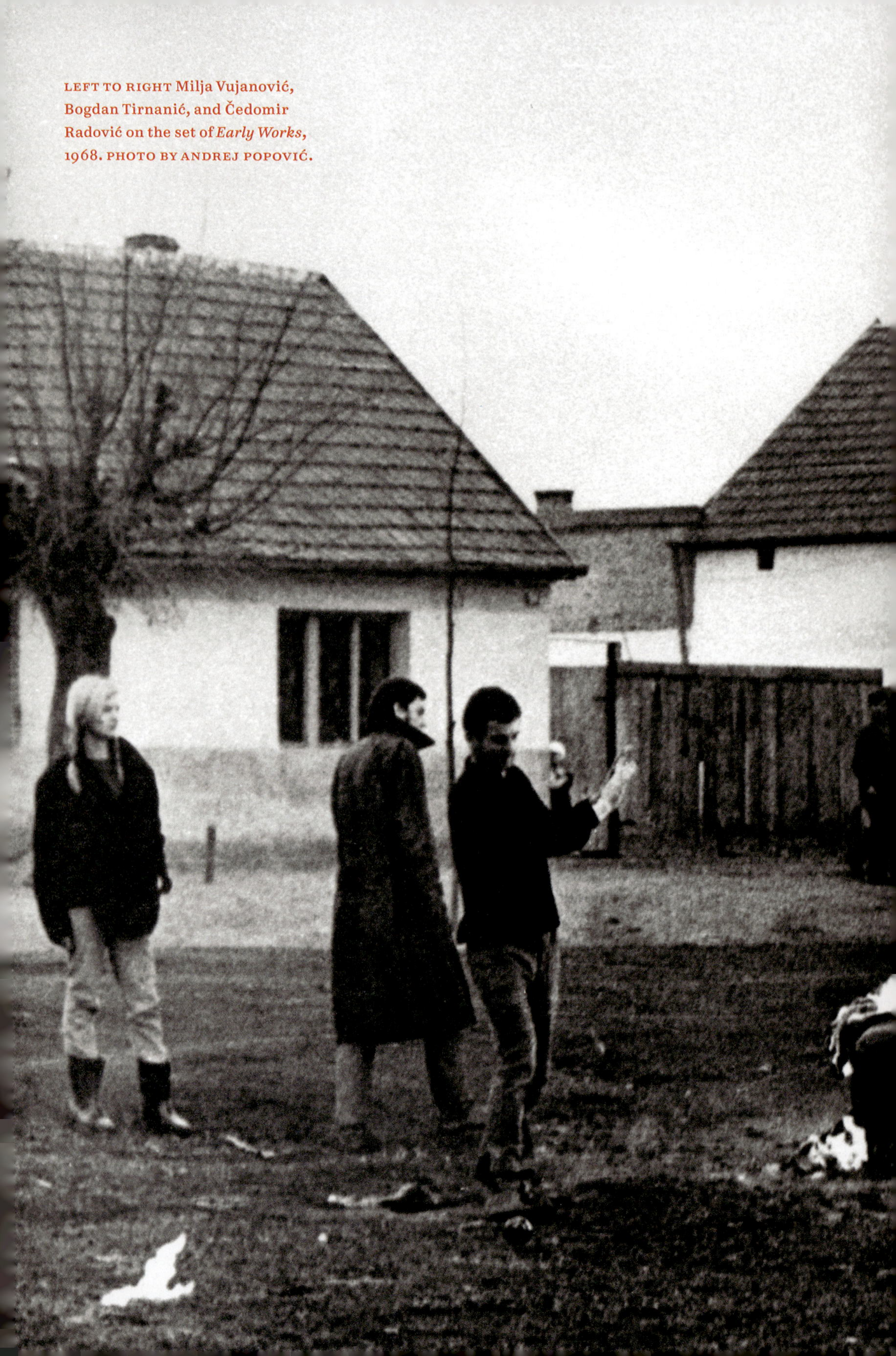

LEFT TO RIGHT Milja Vujanović, Bogdan Tirnanić, and Čedomir Radović on the set of *Early Works*, 1968. PHOTO BY ANDREJ POPOVIĆ.

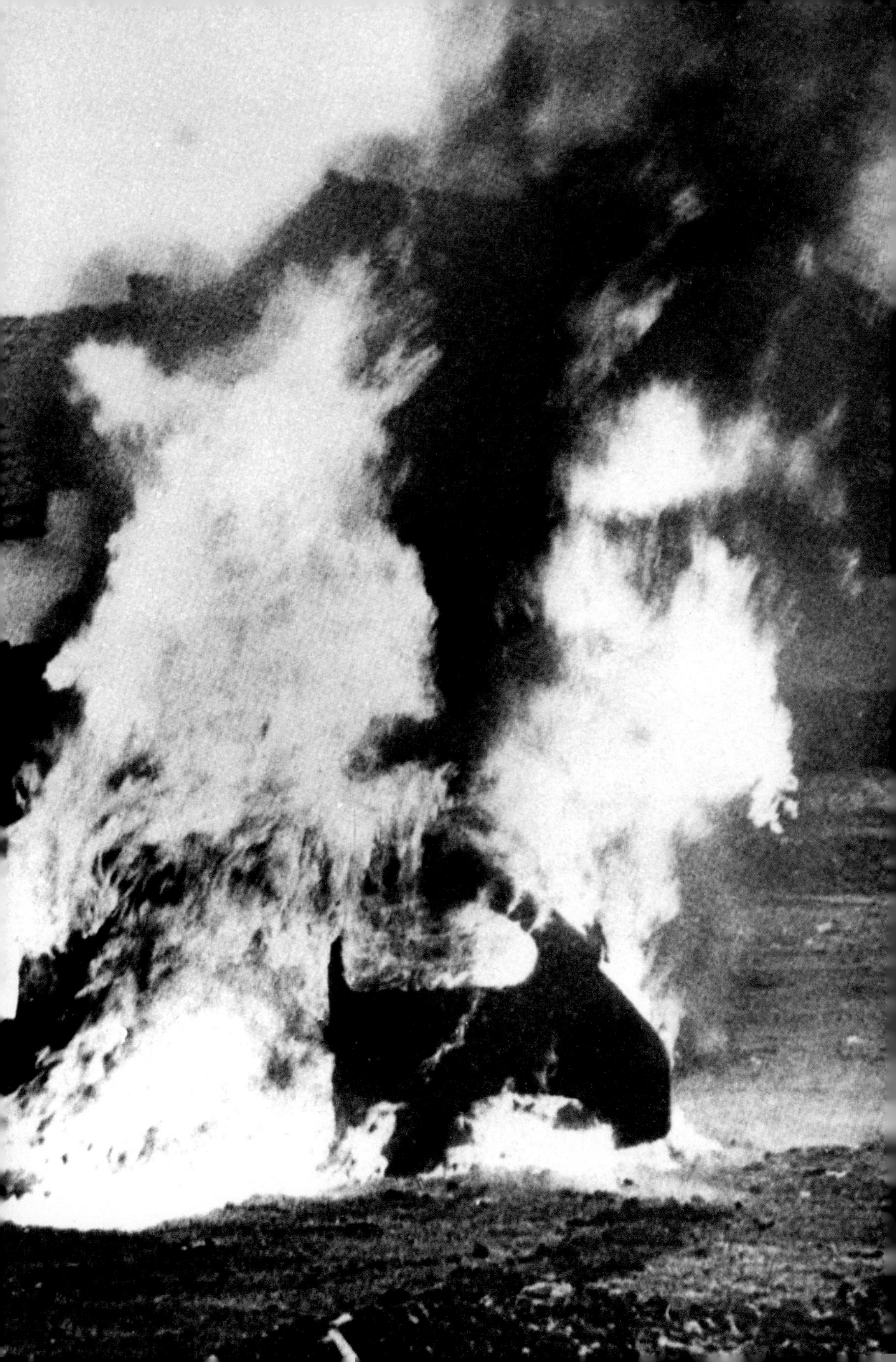

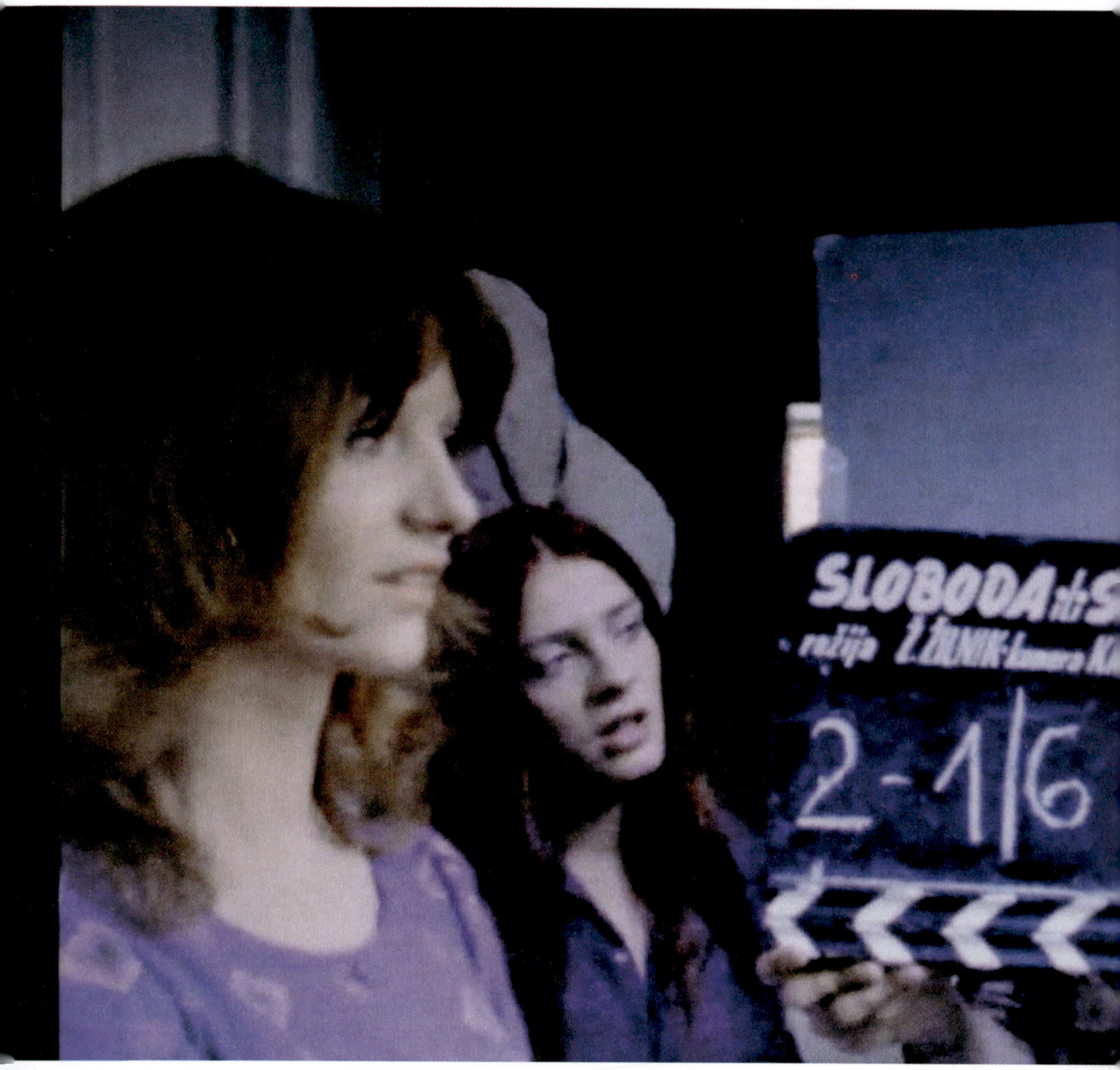

LEFT TO RIGHT Milja Vujanović, Dragana Đurić, Branko Vučićević, and Alenka Zdešar on the set of *Freedom or Cartoons*, 1971. PHOTO BY KARPO GODINA.

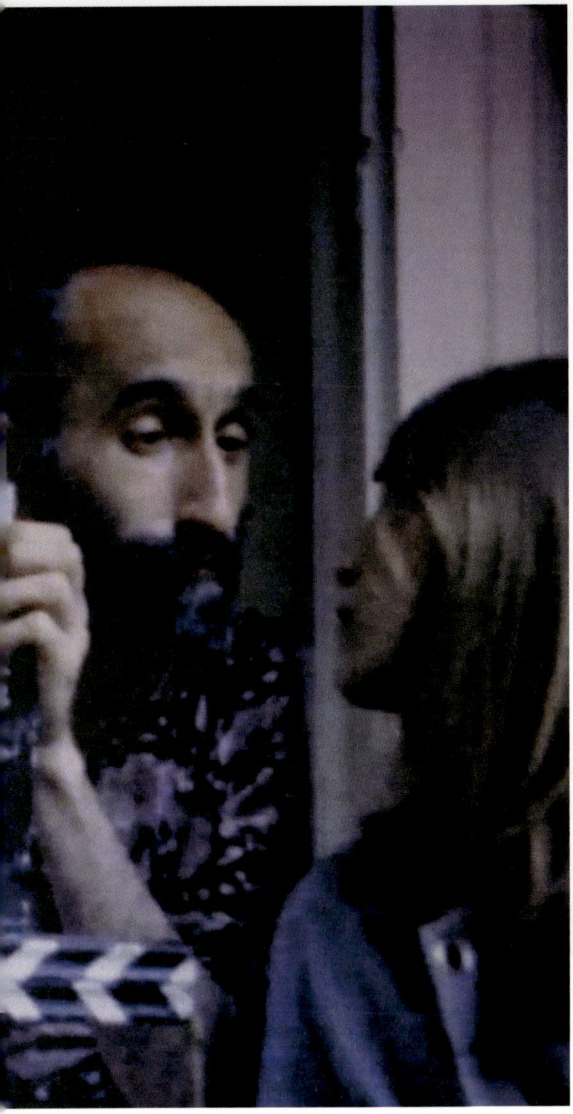

Freedom or Cartoons

Yugoslavia • 1972 • unfinished • 35 mm • color

Through the story of Svetozar, a successful independent salesman from Vojvodina, and the children he had out of wedlock in several cities in Yugoslavia (Zagreb, Belgrade, Ljubljana, and Skopje), *Freedom or Cartoons* recounted turbulent political events of the summer of 1971. The film incorporated documentary footage of events in Zagreb, capturing a wave of national awakening and the arrival of young politicians as the leaders of the students' organization; the pro-Mao student demonstrations in Ljubljana; and, in Belgrade, the inflammatory debates for and against the changes to the Yugoslav Constitution.

After heated public debates surrounding Žilnik's *Early Works*, released in 1969, and Dušan Makavejev's *W.R.: Mysteries of the Organism*, released in 1971, as well as attacks on both films for their anarchism and supposed anti-communism, the director of the production house Neoplanta Film, Svetozar Udovički, was removed from his position. The new director requested that Žilnik remove from *Freedom or Cartoons* the footage of the events in Zagreb and Ljubljana, which at that time were under police investigation, as well as the "parts with unacceptable political allusions." Although the premiere was expected to take place at Pula Film Festival, after Žilnik refused to make these cuts, the film was stopped in its editing process in 1972 and never finished. Recently part of a non-edited film negative was found, the sound of which has been lost, and Žilnik is now looking into the possibility of making a reconstructed version. ●

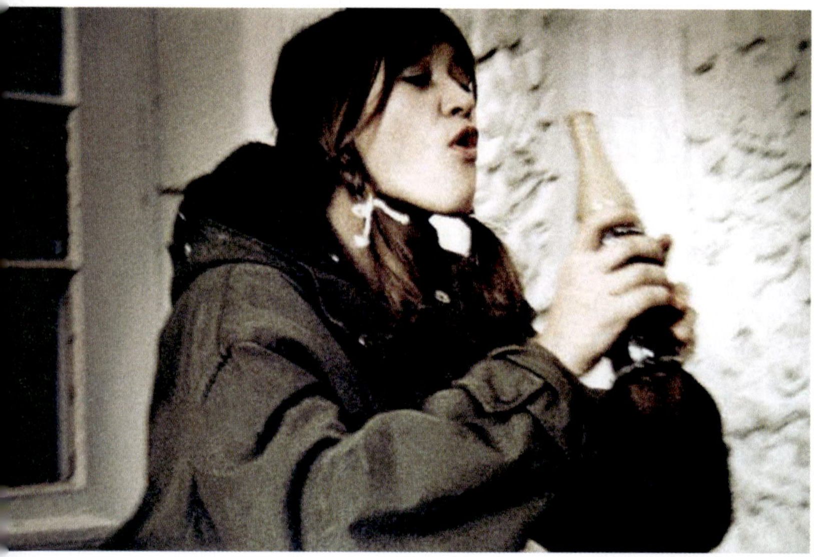

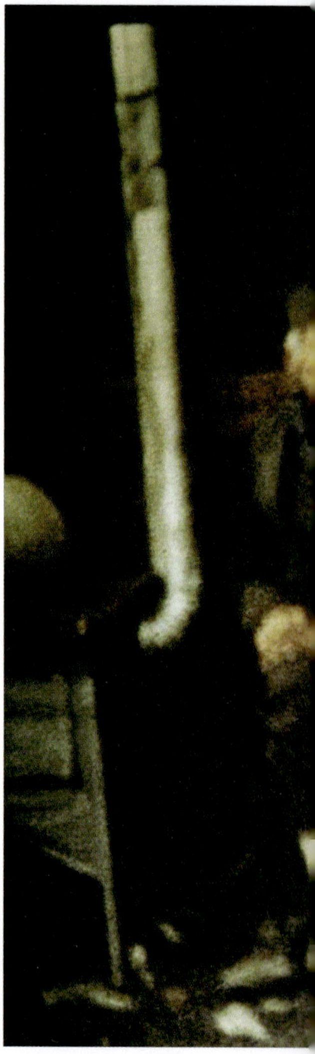

Freedom or Cartoons (on-set photos), 1971.
PHOTOS BY ANDREJ POPOVIĆ.
TOP LEFT Alenka Zdešar.
TOP RIGHT Alenka Zdešar and Dragana Đurić.
BOTTOM Alenka Zdešar.

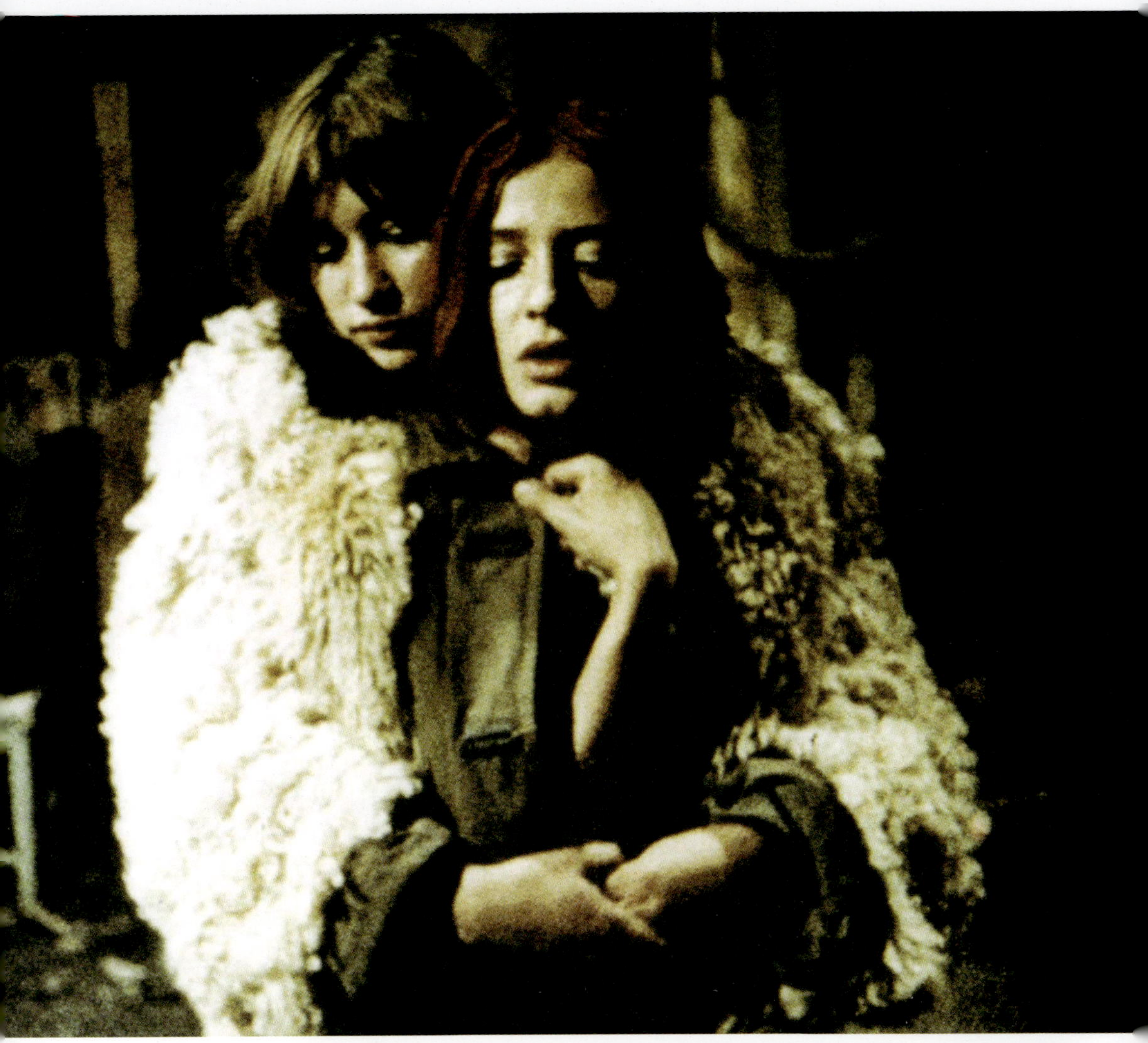

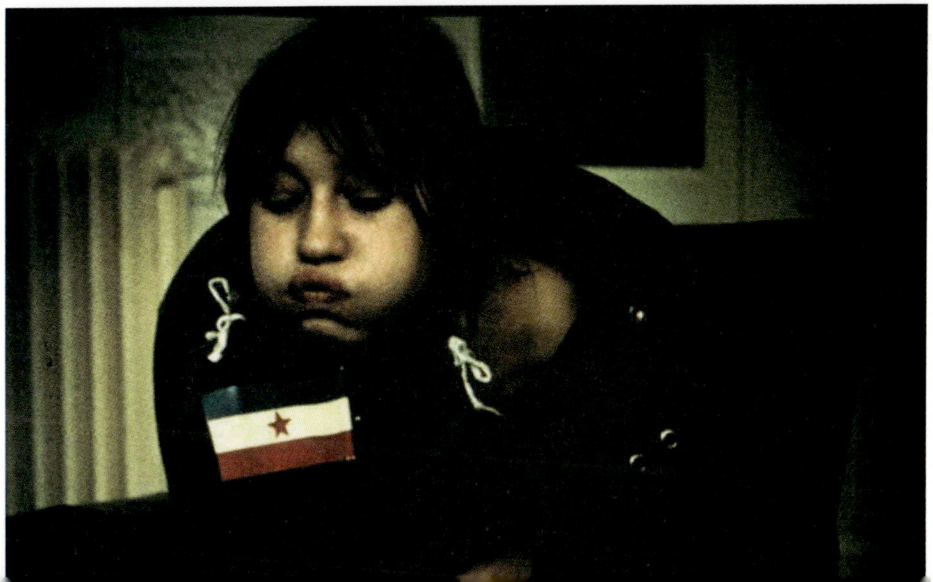

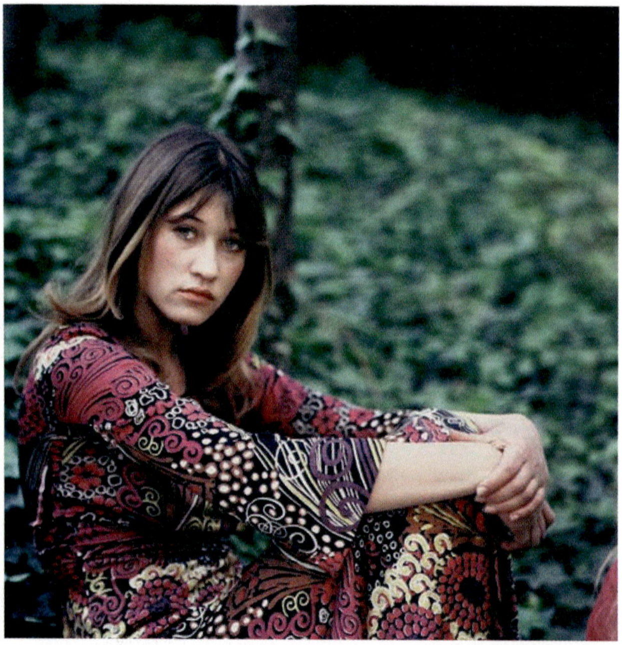

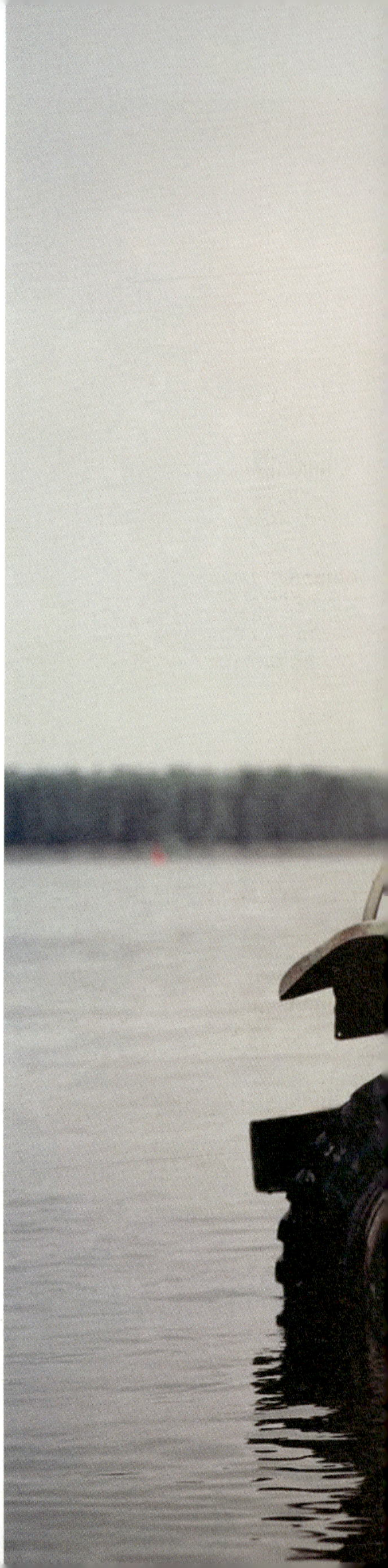

Freedom or Cartoons (on-set photos), 1971.
PHOTOS BY ANDREJ POPOVIĆ.
LEFT Alenka Zdešar.
RIGHT Čedomir Radović and Dragana Đurić.

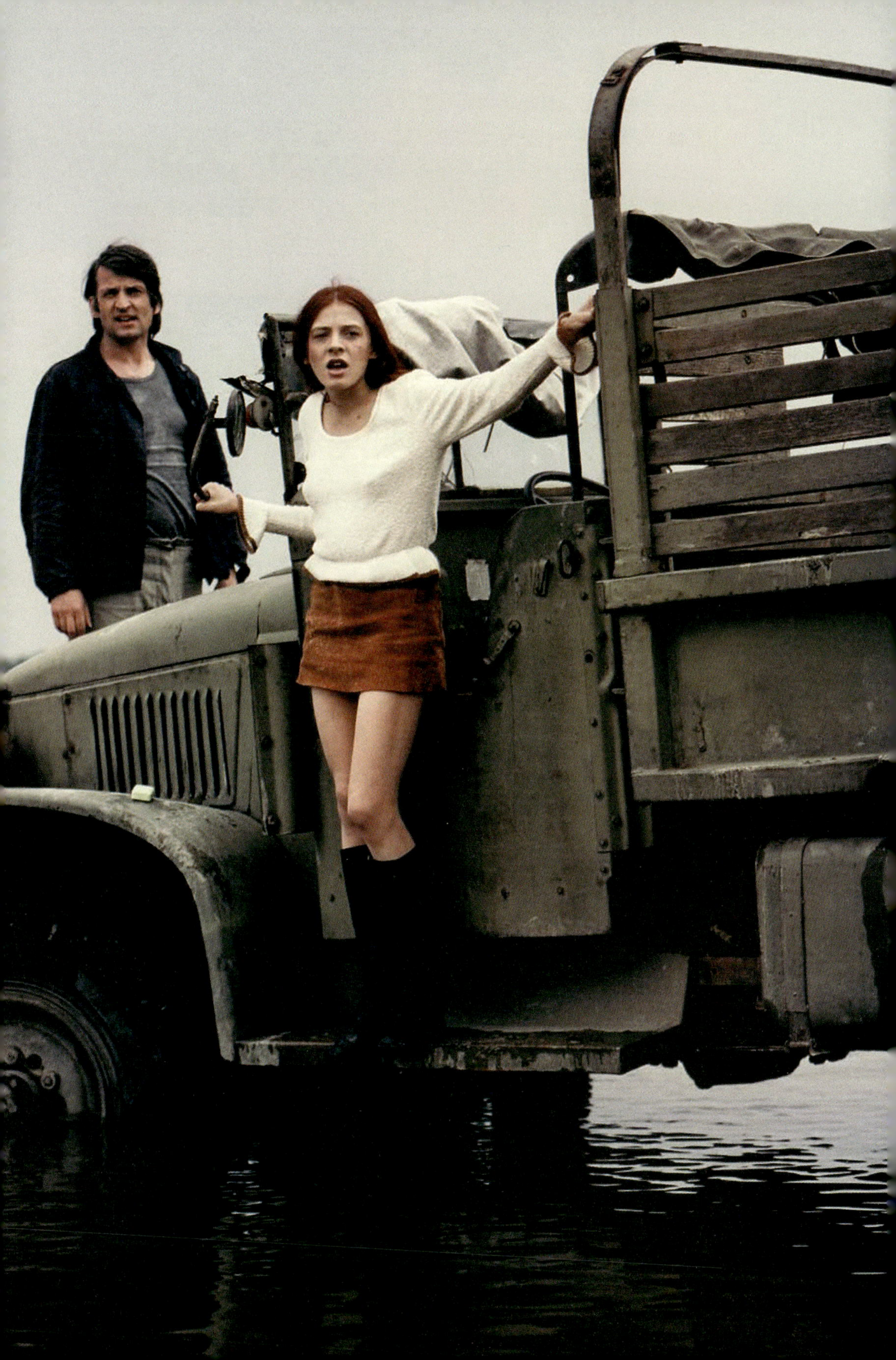

Žilnik has always managed to point to a blind spot of ideology, or to some highly controversial symptom of the impotence of an ideology appearing as operating in accordance [with] its declared principles.

—Branislav Dimitrijević, "Behind Scepticism Lies the Fire of a Revolutionary!," in *For an Idea – Against the Status Quo: Analysis and Systematization of Želimir Žilnik's Artistic Practice* (Novi Sad: New Media Center_kuda.org, Playground produkcija, 2009), 145.

Each film made by Želimir Žilnik is an exercise in creating a new and authentic human collective; an attempt in inserting this collective as deeply as possible into the existing social fabric. This is, ultimately, why these films are at the same time fictional and documentary, and why they can hardly be otherwise: their protagonists are always playacting, regardless of whether they are portraying themselves (through documentary reenactments) or someone else (as characters defined within the framework of acted fiction). Žilnik's cinematographic subjects are the laborers and operatives of a (permanently) approaching film commune.

—Pavle Levi, in Pavle Levi and Želimir Žilnik, "Europe's Internal Exiles: Sound, Image, and Performance of Identity in Želimir Žilnik's films," in *Ethnic Europe: Mobility, Identity, and Conflict in a Globalized World*, ed. Roland Hsu (Stanford, CA: Stanford University Press, 2010), 122.

One moment we're talking about warriors and war victories, and already in the next these people are accused of being members of the paramilitary, of being new profiteers. Some people are at one point in the parliament and at another victims of the gang wars in Belgrade. We have the criminalization of the entire scene, the crush of the whole system of values, while a new system has not been established. These groups of people are on the one hand on the margins and on the other in a situation where they can feel the pulse of society.

When I talked to prostitutes and transvestites while making this film [*Marble Ass*], I learned that in some periods, they spent two or three months [living] in a Hyatt, driving around in super luxury cars. They were in that part of society that feels safe. It's the same with warriors. There are documents in newspapers that show that many of the so-called solo players [self-enlisted soldiers] who followed the "call of the nation" were actually connected to the Ministry of Internal Affairs and the police, social organizations, municipalities. They went to war in an organized manner. I want to say that the film we made is not far from the main current of that life that we all endure. And that life itself is an enormous effort of walking the tightrope between war and peace: from the fact that we're in one moment enemies and then in the next friends with the whole world, through the fear about where we'll go once the bombing starts, to the present euphoria caused by seeing our footballers playing internationally.

—Želimir Žilnik, interview, "Contributions for a Biography," *Ekran 2000*, no. 2, 1995.

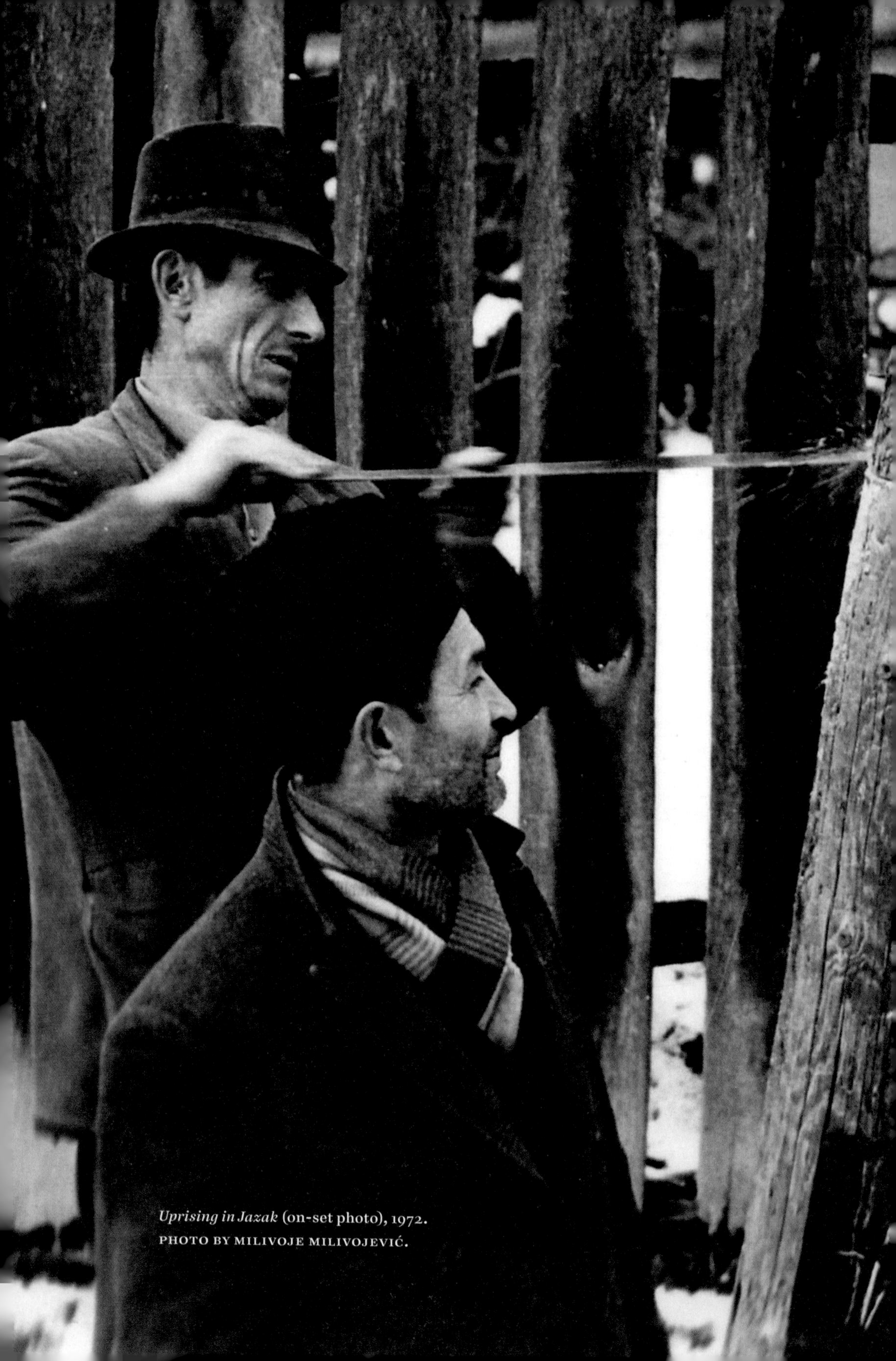

Uprising in Jazak (on-set photo), 1972.
PHOTO BY MILIVOJE MILIVOJEVIĆ.

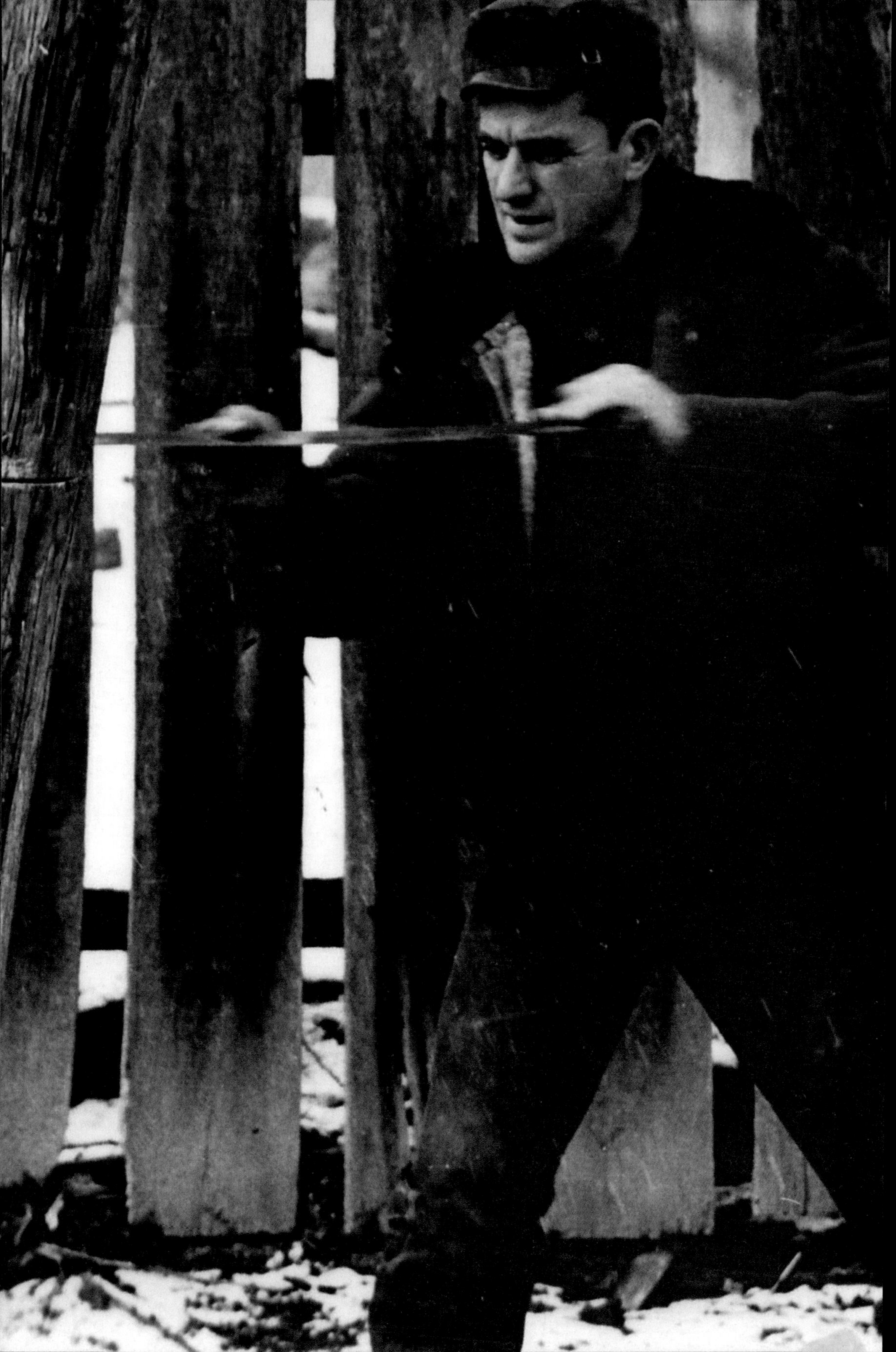

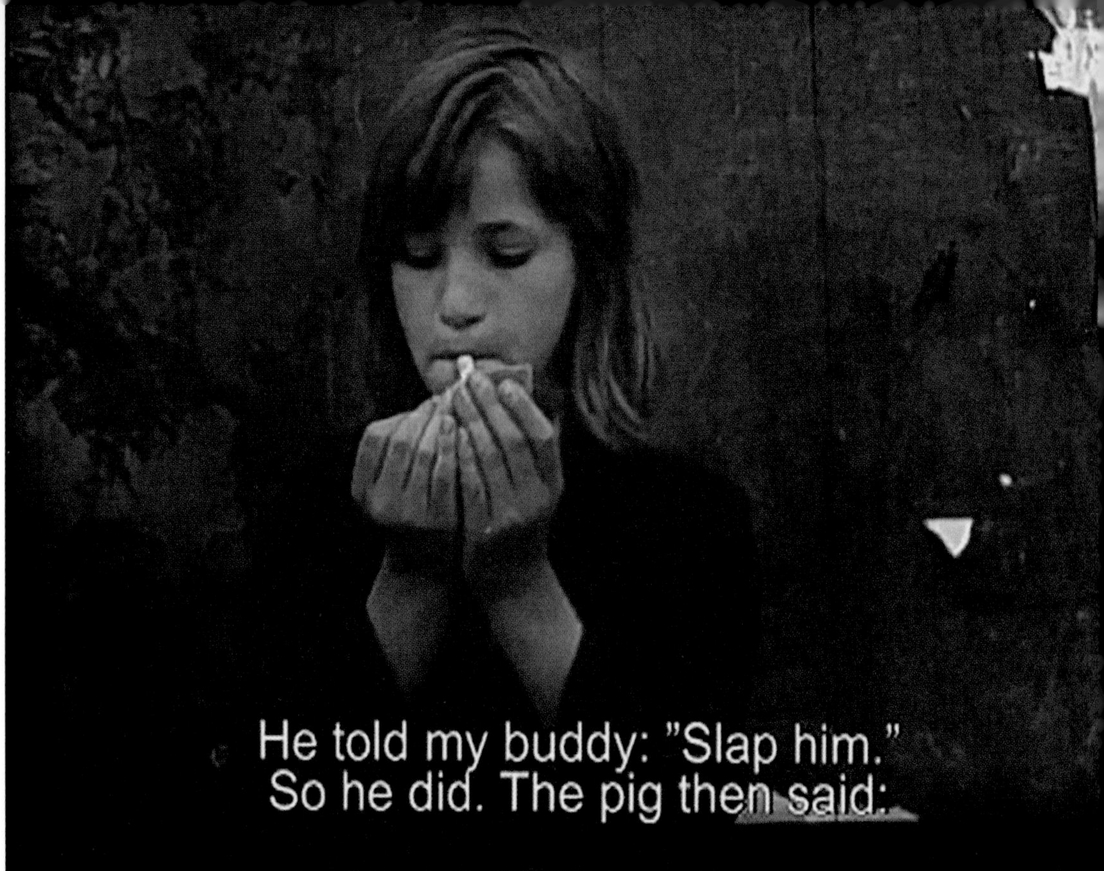
He told my buddy: "Slap him."
So he did. The pig then said:

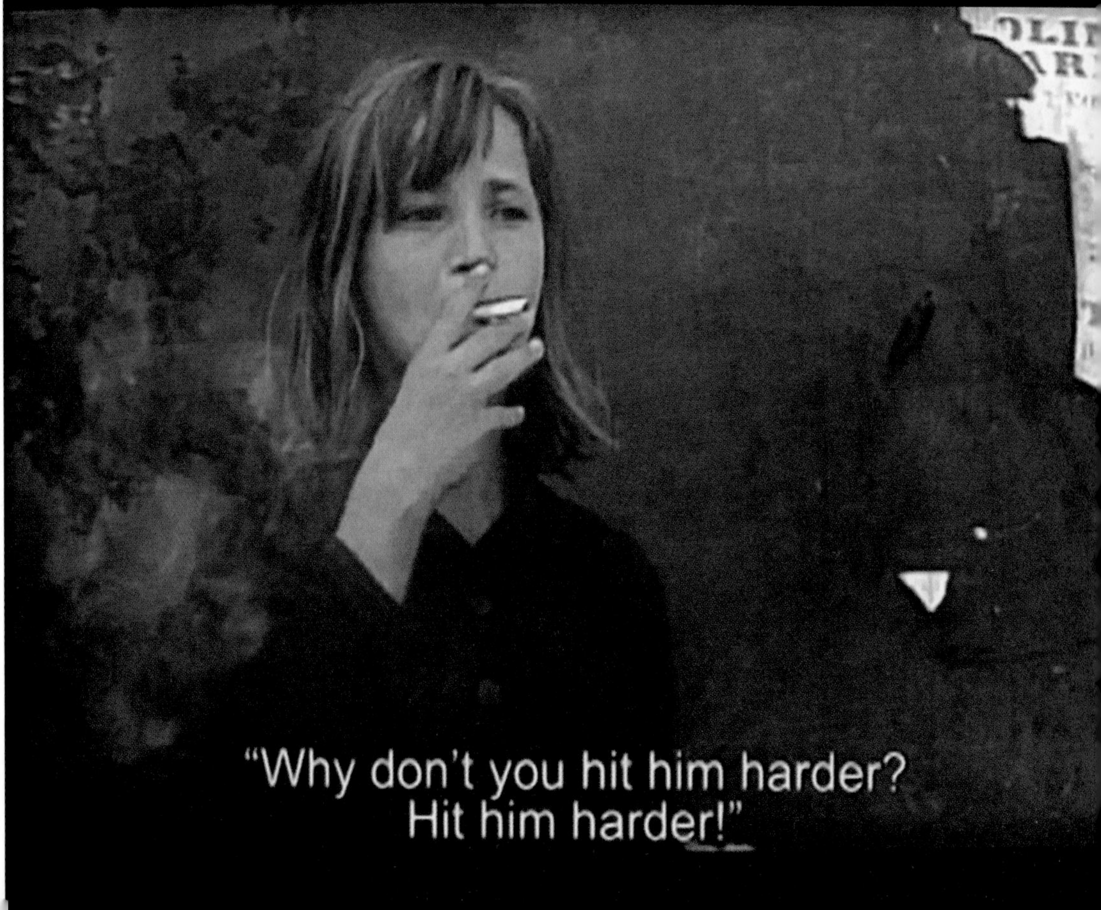
"Why don't you hit him harder?
Hit him harder!"

DIJANA JELAČA

Double Binds: The Politics of Gender and Sexuality in the Films of Želimir Žilnik

Since his earliest works, Želimir Žilnik has been a consistently provocative explorer of the politics of gender and sexuality. A more standard, epochal approach to Žilnik's work might separate the films he made during the so-called New Yugoslav Film movement (which lasted for about a decade, approximately 1962 to 1972) from the rest of his oeuvre, or perhaps such an approach would create a differentiation between the films he made during his Yugoslav and post-Yugoslav periods. This essay, by contrast, will illustrate how Žilnik's work reflects, across historical, social, geographical, and cultural epochs, a consistent and keen cinematic attention to the intersecting political domains of class, identity, gender performativity, and performance. To wit, one of Žilnik's frequent points of interest is the political dimensions of gender and sexuality, particularly as they intersect with the contingent social and cultural issues of the specific locales and times in which the director's films were made.

Žilnik's early documentary short *Little Pioneers* (1968) announces what will turn out to be the director's lifelong interest in social outcasts—individuals and groups on society's margins, systemically discriminated against and often rendered entirely invisible. In this short, Žilnik gives visibility and voice to poor and homeless children, most of them Roma. As the camera shows the children, some of them disabled, running through abandoned, decrepit houses, the voice-over narration gives us the children's often shocking testimonials about their everyday life, from the petty crimes they engage in to the police violence they are frequently subjected to. That the film is called *Little Pioneers* is an overt and provocative political intervention in and of itself: the phrase is the first verse of a popular children's song about Yugoslavia's children as little pioneers who are honorable, decent, healthy, and obedient—proper soldiers of the socialist state. The children in Žilnik's documentary are on the opposite end of the spectrum from Yugoslavia's socialist youth idolized in the children's song. By juxtaposing the song and its overt implications about Yugoslav youth with stark images of the poverty, neglect, and grittiness experienced and embodied by the children in the film, Žilnik provocatively and insightfully calls attention to what is otherwise rendered invisible or willfully ignored by the official ideology of Yugoslavia, a society whose citizens, and particularly its children, are conceived as unwaveringly honorable and exemplary.

But the film does not stop at the shocking positioning of the rough street children as being worlds apart from the dominant image of Yugoslavia's children as innocent and hard-working pioneers. As the children's testimonials unfold, an unmistakable pattern emerges: stories of unwanted sexual advances and looming threats of sexual violence that the girls frequently experience in encounters with adult men are described by some of them through voice-over in detailed and startlingly matter-of-fact terms. In fact, the short's final few minutes (separated from the rest of the film by the intertitle "The

Little Pioneers (film stills), 1968

Next Episode") are dedicated solely to this topic: first, a young man tells us that he often has sex with girls, and that sometimes the girls are willing participants, and sometimes not. He asserts that some of them need to be forced to have sex with him, and he does so by applying "a few slaps and things like that." As he talks, the camera pans over a few other young men socializing, talking, and laughing. The young man's testimonial is abruptly interrupted by a shot of a young girl seen in profile, who tells the story of being offered money by a stranger in exchange for sex. She accepts the offer only after she is able to negotiate double the amount. Her story is likewise interrupted, by another girl who speaks about a sexual assault she experienced when a man held her at knifepoint in an attempt to rape her. Here, interestingly, Žilnik inserts himself into the film: as the harrowing account is heard in voice-over, we see the director facing the girl and giving the camera the "action" cue (FIG. 1).

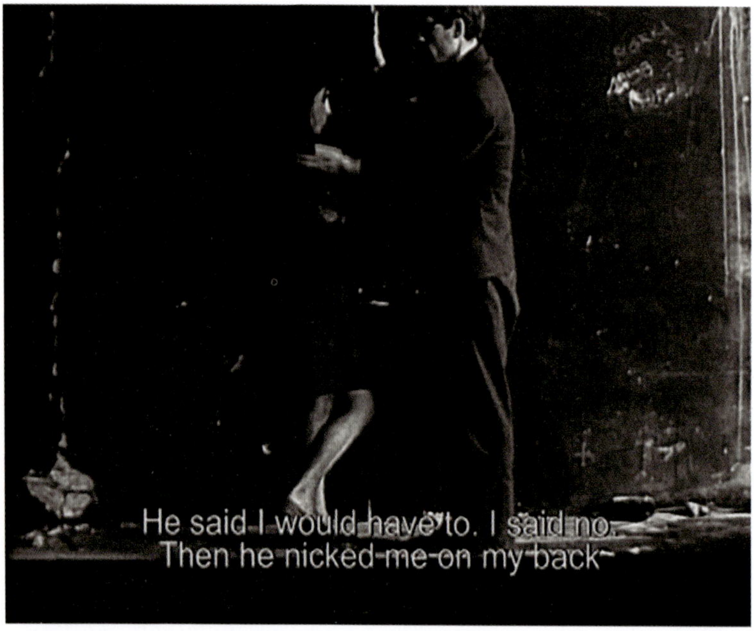

FIGURE 1: The filmmaker and his subject. *Little Pioneers* (film still), 1968.

By putting himself into his own film—in fact, by showing himself direct it—at this key moment, Žilnik calls attention to the camera's presence, and his own: an adult man filming a young girl who is recounting details of a traumatic assault by another man. In rendering himself and his directing visible here, Žilnik acknowledges the power imbalances, particularly in relation to gender and age, that frame the politics of representation in the film. After the shot, the screen turns to black while the voice-over continues: the girl describes being warned by the man who assaulted her to not tell anyone about it. She answered back that she would tell no one dumber than him, but that she would instead tell her story to someone smarter. Here again, the presence of the storytelling apparatus—the camera, the filmmaker, and the film crew—is directly pointed to, interrupting a seamless depiction of a testimonial that would otherwise aim to render the presence of said mechanism invisible. After that, we see the action cue in front of the girl's face once more, as her voice-over tells us that the man who assaulted her now threatens to kill her, "but has not put that into action yet." Her story ends on this unnerving note of a threat hanging in the air. The film's final frame shows another girl, who informs us that she is not yet eighteen and has not yet had sex with men, but thinks "it is a nice thing." This ending note serves as another counterpoint that further layers the narrative of girlhood, sexuality, and agency, complicating it by refusing to depict the girls solely through the framework of violence, victimhood, precarity, and threat. Nevertheless, their girlhood is unquestionably vulnerable. Even within the already precarious population of the poor homeless children, there are further degrees of vulnerability, and girls appear to be at the bottom of the hierarchy. They are in a double bind: vulnerable not only because they are poor and therefore socially ostracized but also because they are girls.

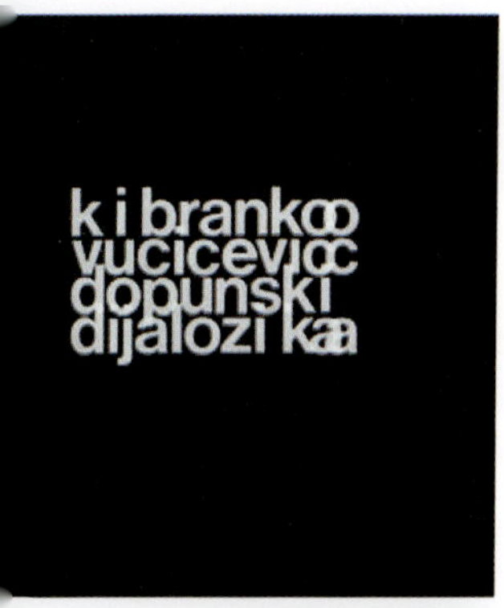

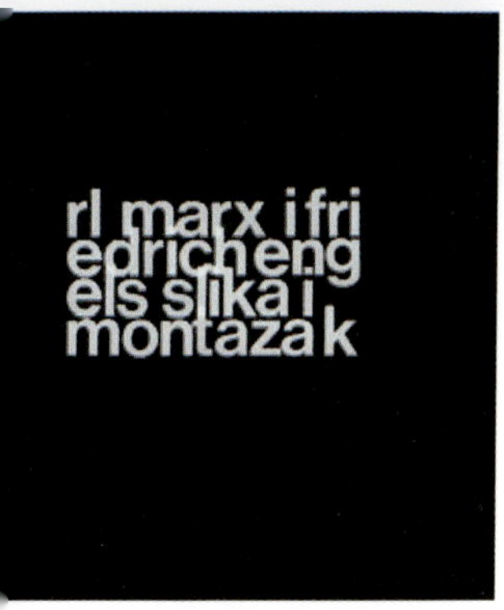

Credits for Karl Marx and Friedrich Engels in the opening titles of *Early Works*, 1969. TITLES DESIGNED BY SLOBODAN MAŠIĆ.

Drawing an intertextual link between his films, and between documentary and fiction, one of the girls who appears in *Little Pioneers*, Piroška "Pirika" Čapko, appears in Žilnik's feature narrative debut, *Early Works* (1969), as a younger sister of the female protagonist, Jugoslava. In the spirit of Žilnik's organic collaboration with nonprofessional actors across the documentary-narrative spectrum, Čapko went on to become the director's subject in more recent works as well: in 2013, for the documentary *Pirika on Film*, as well as in 2018, for the documentary *Among the People: Life & Acting*. The latter, commissioned for Žilnik's exhibition at the Edith-Russ-Haus for Media Art, aptly titled *Shadow Citizens*, sees Žilnik return to many participants of his earlier films, who revisit the stories of their collaborations with the director.

In Žilnik's now legendary *Early Works*, gender politics arises yet again as an important subtext and, I contend, a crucial aspect of the social critique that the film lays out. One of the earliest lines that Jugoslava, a young woman from a poor working-class background, utters is: "I get why my father beats my mom. He's all beaten up after work." In other words, at home the father perpetuates the violence he endures in the outside world due to his lack of agency as a social actor. In these early scenes, we often see Jugoslava's father drunkenly digging up a toilet in muddy ground. Precarious social conditions that precipitate and perpetuate gendered and domestic violence are therefore immediately put front and center, and overtly serve as an important motivating factor for Jugoslava to take up a revolutionary cause with her three male companions. The four youth often quote or read directly from Karl Marx and Friedrich Engels's *Communist Manifesto* and Marx's *Capital* (indeed, Marx and Engels are credited as contributors to the film's screenplay, alongside Žilnik and Branko Vučićević), in what the intertitles deem "political theater." But this theater is not a performance separate from everyday life; rather, it becomes a performance of politics *in* everyday life.

After Jugoslava's father returns from work drunk one day, a physical altercation ensues between him, his wife, and Jugoslava. This prompts Jugoslava to declare that "feudalism reigns in this house," and she announces to her family that they are seeing her for the last time. Just before she leaves home, she stops in front of the house to give her younger sister (the aforementioned girl who appears in *Little Pioneers*) a bite out of an apple (FIG. 2)—a symbolic gesture that acknowledges the older sister's effort to pass on knowledge, as well as strength and resilience, to the younger sister who stays behind. Precarious girlhood is yet again given critical attention and, for Jugoslava, serves as a key trigger that moves her to political action.

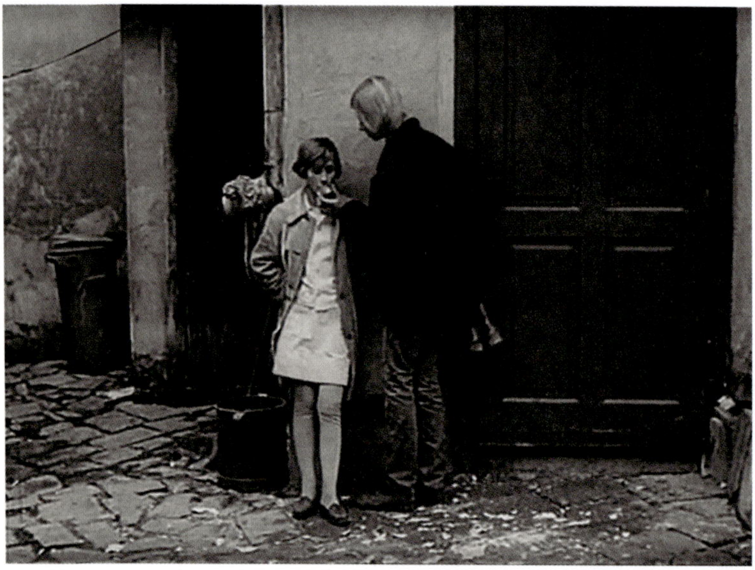

FIGURE 2: Jugoslava (Milja Vujanović) gives her younger sister (Pirika Čapko) a bite of her apple. *Early Works* (film still), 1969.

Together with her male companions, Jugoslava embarks on a tour of Serbia's rural areas to propagate a socialist revolution. Her relationship with her male friends is frequently punctuated by sexual tension, but also permeated by an encroaching threat of violence toward her. For instance, after her first sexual encounter with one of the men, she teases him for not being able to immediately have sex again, which prompts him to point a gun at her as we hear the sound of (for the moment, imaginary) gunfire. This mock shooting foreshadows the looming gendered violence that will dramatically materialize by the film's end.

In one striking scene, during which the group is bringing their revolutionary ideas to the countryside, Jugoslava is seen holding a workshop for village women to educate them on the best methods of contraception (FIG. 3). The women, all nonprofessional actors, pose various questions, from the consequences of abstinence on health to which contraceptive method is proven most effective. In her talk, Jugoslava cites the revolutionary thoughts of the leftist feminist icon Clara Zetkin, namely that revolutions cannot happen "until the man of the family stops behaving like a lord, an aristocrat and an owner, while a woman is exploited like a proletarian. Women can be freed from submission *only* through changing the structure of employment and through the disintegration of the monogamous family." Here Jugoslava brings forth a very pointed critique of real existing socialism: while the proletariat is nominally put in charge and on equal footing in socialist systems, women continue to be oppressed subjects under the autocratic rule of men due to ongoing patriarchal gender dynamics. As a result, a true revolution cannot happen without disposing of this gender hierarchy—a disposal that, importantly, includes the monogamous family. Furthermore, a woman's right to not bear children, nor be saddled with unwanted reproductive and domestic labor, should be recognized as a legitimate demand. That Jugoslava is here addressing a group located at the very bottom of the social hierarchy—uneducated rural women—makes her critique all the more poignant. These women, like the poor girls in *Little Pioneers,* experience precarity as a double bind. Gender and class intersect once again to provide critical insight into the unequal distribution of social agency in Socialist Yugoslavia. This scene is, somewhat humorously, followed by male voices exclaiming, "Long live the 8th of March, International Women's Day!," a widely celebrated holiday in Yugoslavia during which women's rights were often only nominally acknowledged.

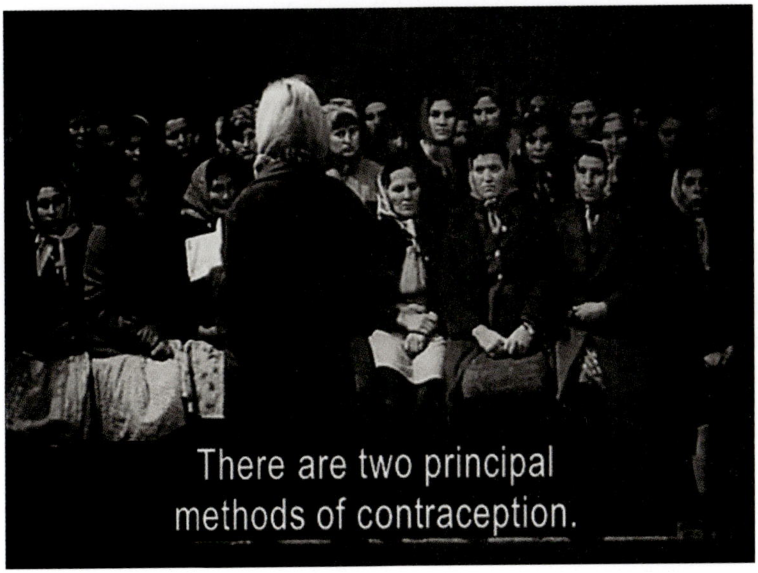

FIGURE 3: Jugoslava (Milja Vujanović) addresses a group of rural women. *Early Works* (film still), 1969.

In her speech to the women, Jugoslava adds that "a technological revolution, one that we are marching towards," will finally lead to women's full emancipation. Echoing this claim about technology in a later scene, Jugoslava somewhat bitterly proclaims, "My mother would be more liberated by the washing machine than by a right to vote." Throughout the film, lighter satirical moments are often abruptly punctuated by scenes of brutal violence, such as when a group of villagers, apparently fed up by the young revolutionaries' preaching, assault Jugoslava and her friends. The sustained attack sees Jugoslava particularly targeted, with two villagers dragging her off to the side and ripping off her clothes. This is where the scene suddenly ends, with a strong implication of sexual assault. That assault appears to foreshadow the film's end: the four youths' failed revolution culminates in all their guerilla military "training" throughout the film now being directed at Jugoslava's body. Amid increasing disillusionment with their revolutionary cause, and growing tensions between Jugoslava and her male companions, Jugoslava leaves the group and returns home. The three men, however, show up at her house, take her to a field, tear off her clothes, shoot her, and burn her body. The only apparent outcome of their revolutionary cause seems to be a near ritualistic sacrifice of the woman, both because of her perceived betrayal of the cause and also because, yet again, accumulated social frustrations are ultimately most dramatically taken out on a woman's body. *Early Works,* as a powerful indictment of Yugoslavia's "half-way revolution," offers an illuminating study of the (failed) revolution's gender politics by exposing the double bind that ostensibly propagates equality among the sexes while upholding the primacy of patriarchy. Jugoslava's death at the end of the film therefore pointedly embodies the words she speaks earlier in the film: no socialist revolution can succeed if patriarchy itself is not relinquished.

It should be noted that throughout Žilnik's oeuvre, his keen interest in women's social agency (or lack thereof) is most frequently focused on working-class and poor women, from the aforementioned *Little Pioneers* and *Early Works* to his documentary *The Women Are Coming* (1972), which follows a group of women *Gastarbeiter* working in Germany who are traveling home to their families in Yugoslavia for their vacation. Other important examples include *Vera and Eržika* (1981), a TV movie about two longtime textile factory workers (one of the most common professions for working-class women in Yugoslavia), and the TV series *Hot Paychecks* (1987), which focuses on, among other things, the everyday life of cleaning ladies. Another significant instance of the director's interest in working-class communities is his TV movie *Brooklyn – Gusinje* (1988), which follows the experience of the young waitress Ivana, who is a newcomer to a small town on the Yugoslav-Albanian border. Ivana becomes close to a young man, Škeljzen, who is originally from the area but now lives in Brooklyn in the United States. Like many of Žilnik's works, the film deals with economic migration, both domestic (Ivana leaves her tailoring job in Prizren for a higher paying job as a waitress in Gusinje) and international (many locals of Gusinje, like Škeljzen, seek to move abroad in search of better opportunities). As a free-spirited and somewhat naive young woman, Ivana often needs to be schooled in local traditions, but at the same time her naivete does not get in the way of a pointed critique of patriarchy—for instance, in a scene in which she visits an Albanian household, that of some of Škeljzen's relatives, and asks her male host what women in their family do. Upon

01
Dijana Jelača, *Dislocated Screen Memory: Narrating Trauma in Post-Yugoslav Cinema* (New York: Palgrave Macmillan, 2016), 116.

02
EDITORS' NOTE: Grammatically, Merlinka is the female form of Merlin. However, this form is uncommon in Serbo-Croatian and is mostly used to refer to Marilyn Monroe. The protagonist of the film *Marble Ass* is referred to both as Merlin and Merlinka.

03
J. Jack Halberstam, *In a Queer Time and Place: Transgender Bodies, Subcultural Lives* (New York: NYU Press, 2005).

04
Jelača, *Dislocated Screen Memory*, 118.

hearing a long list of women's "obligations" comprising housework and child-rearing, Ivana responds, "What do you men do, then?" Ivana and her friend and fellow waitress Goca are headstrong and independent young women who increasingly realize that they do not fit well in conservative patriarchal environments. When Goca has second thoughts about marrying a local man, the two women flee her wedding and are helped by a kind stranger—a deaf man who utters the film's most overtly feminist message: "Women need to have the same rights that men have, so that men aren't the only ones privileged." A frequent backdrop to Žilnik's treatment of gender politics is a more general working-class milieu, fraught interethnic borderlands, and transnational movements of people, particularly for economic reasons.

When it comes to queer topics and non-heteronormative approaches to gender and sexuality, Žilnik's film *Marble Ass* (1995), about trans sex workers living in the midst, but also on the margins, of Serbia's nationalist warmongering fervor of the 1990s, offers an extremely provocative treatment of the politics of gender and sexuality, here specifically articulated in relation to the imagined heteronormative "health" of the collective ethnonational(ist) body as such. As I have argued elsewhere, *Marble Ass* provides a poignant oppositional gaze and a subversive statement about "the way in which some bodies are too inappropriate to be interpellated into an ethno-nationalist discourse: two transvestite prostitutes that exist on the margins of society are literally too queer, their lives and uses of both time and place too far removed from convention to be hailed into a collective ethno-national subjectivity constituted as 'healthy' through the violence it performs."[01] The film is a unique instance of regional queer and trans cinema, as it was made in close collaboration with its trans protagonists, Merlinka[02] and Sanela, who are both nonprofessional actors playing a version of themselves in the film. Like most of Žilnik's other nondocumentary work, *Marble Ass* plays more like a docudrama than a straightforward narrative film, and this adds to its provocative edge, where fact and fiction are never firmly set apart.

The film is unique because it is, still today, perhaps the only regional (post-Yugoslavia) film that is not merely "queer themed," where such films typically articulate the "plight" of local LGBTQ populations through the lens of heterosexual, cisgender filmmakers and actors, as is the case with *Fine Dead Girls* (2002) and *Go West* (2005), for instance. *Marble Ass* instead provides an unrelentingly consistent vision of what queer theorist Jack Halberstam has, in a different context, theorized as a queer time and place.[03] The film does so by putting front and center "the otherwise marginalized vision of queer temporality and spatiality"[04] and by refusing to channel the trans protagonists' experiences through anything other than this lens of queer temporality and spatiality. Moreover, "the film insists that queer bodies cannot be fully interpellated into an ideology of normative, violent ethno-national body, and thus the two transvestite protagonists exist in their own seemingly parallel universe, albeit one that is nevertheless constituted by its proximity to the normative and violent nationalism that envelops the wartime reality around them."[05] Here, the politics of embodied experience again blurs fact and fiction, since the trans protagonists in the film are not cis actors playing trans characters but rather are individuals whose experiences outside the boundaries of the film very much mirror what goes on in the film. This shared reality was tragically brought further into focus in 2003, when one of the protagonists, Vjeran Miladinović Merlinka, was brutally murdered.[06]

I will conclude this discussion of Žilnik's ongoing and always keenly engaged interest in the political dimension of gender by turning to the documentary *One Woman – One Century* (2011), in which the director's subject is Dragica Vitolović Srzentić (FIG. 4), a woman who, at the time of the documentary's making, was nearly one hundred years old. Vitolović Srzentić was a socialist revolutionary in the 1930s

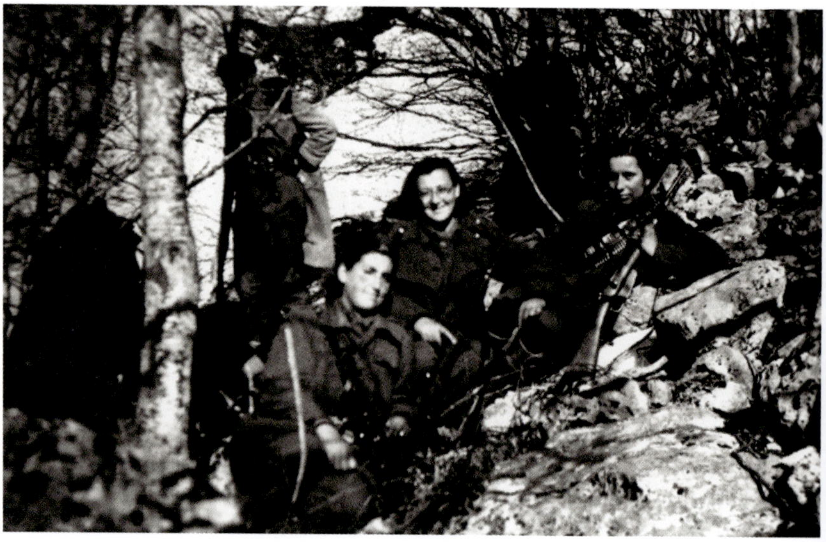

FIGURE 4: Dragica Vitolović Srzentić with her female squad during the Second World War. *One Woman – One Century* (film still), 2011.

and, among other things, a contributor to the progressive women's magazine *Žena danas* (Woman today, 1936). She also participated in the revolutionary anti-fascist fights of the Second World War, known as the People's Liberation Struggle, or NOB, and, after the war, became the person who delivered President Josip Broz Tito's "historic no" to Joseph Stalin in 1948, marking the (in)famous moment the two leaders parted ways, triggering Yugoslavia's emancipation from USSR and the development of its own unique form of market socialism. As Vitolović Srzentić recounts her century-long story in the documentary, the footage of her is frequently intercut with block letters that slowly spell out the names of prominent men who were her contemporaries, close friends, and/or collaborators: from her family members—her brother Viktor Vitolović and husband Vojo Srzentić—to well-known figures of Yugoslav socialism such

05 Jelača, *Dislocated Screen Memory*, 118–19.

06 Merlinka was Žilnik's long-term collaborator, and before *Marble Ass* appeared in *Good Morning Belgrade* (1985) and *Pretty Women Walking through the City* (1986).

07
Karl Marx, quoted in Pavle Levi, *Jolted Images: Unbound Analytic* (Amsterdam: Amsterdam University Press, 2017), 87.

08
Levi, *Jolted Images*, 87. Emphasis in the original.

09
Levi, *Jolted Images*, 87.

as Otokar Keršovani, Miroslav Krleža, Veselin Masleša, Moše Pijade, Jaša Prodanović, Bora Prodanović, and Tito himself. All these are male names firmly inscribed in Yugoslavia's history, while Vitolović Srzentić's has remained fairly obscure. Through Žilnik's documentary, an intervention is therefore staged: it is not that these male names interrupt Vitolović Srzentić's story; on the contrary, it is her story that interrupts the largely male-dominated history of Socialist Yugoslavia and the revolutionary anti-fascist struggle of the Second World War, as a woman's name and lived experience is inserted into it. *One Woman – One Century* illustrates how attention to the gendered dynamics of historical events, large and small, has permeated the entirety of Žilnik's rich and diverse filmmaking career.

Reappropriating Marx's famous pronouncement that "the philosophers have only interpreted the world, in various ways; the point, however, is to change it,"[07] the film scholar Pavle Levi posits that "Žilnik is, essentially, a version of Karl Marx's *11th Thesis on Feuerbach*, set in the realm of film practice: *the filmmakers have only* reproduced (represented) *the world, in various ways; the point, however, is to* produce *it*."[08] This conclusion is based on Levi's following poignant assertion:

> [Žilnik is] a firm believer that the camera's duty is not simply to depict existing reality, but rather to strive to generate within it that which is to be depicted; to induce a variety of desired as well as unexpected movements, torsions, and ruptures in the social fabric (filming as a negation of the status quo), and to inspire the forging of some novel, often improvised and only temporary, communal bonds among the people who are being filmed (emancipation catalyzed by image-making).[09]

With respect to any theme and social issue they tackle, gender and sexuality included, Želimir Žilnik's films are never calculated political pronouncements but rather collaborative encounters and frequently spontaneous performances of new social possibilities that illuminate something heretofore invisible about existing conditions. ★

Dijana Jelača is a film scholar who teaches in the Film Department at Brooklyn College and at the Feirstein Graduate School of Cinema, New York. Her areas of inquiry include feminist film studies, transnational cinema, posthuman approaches to gender and sexuality, and South Slavic film cultures. Jelača's most recent publication is the textbook *Film Feminisms: A Global Introduction* (Routledge, 2019, with Kristin Lené Hole). She is also the author of *Dislocated Screen Memory: Narrating Trauma in Post-Yugoslav Cinema* (Palgrave, 2016) and coeditor of *The Routledge Companion to Cinema and Gender* (Routledge, 2017), *The Cultural Life of Capitalism in Yugoslavia* (Palgrave, 2017), and *The Future of (Post)Socialism* (SUNY Press, 2018). Jelača's essays have appeared in *Camera Obscura*, *Signs*, *Feminist Media Studies*, *Jump Cut*, and elsewhere.

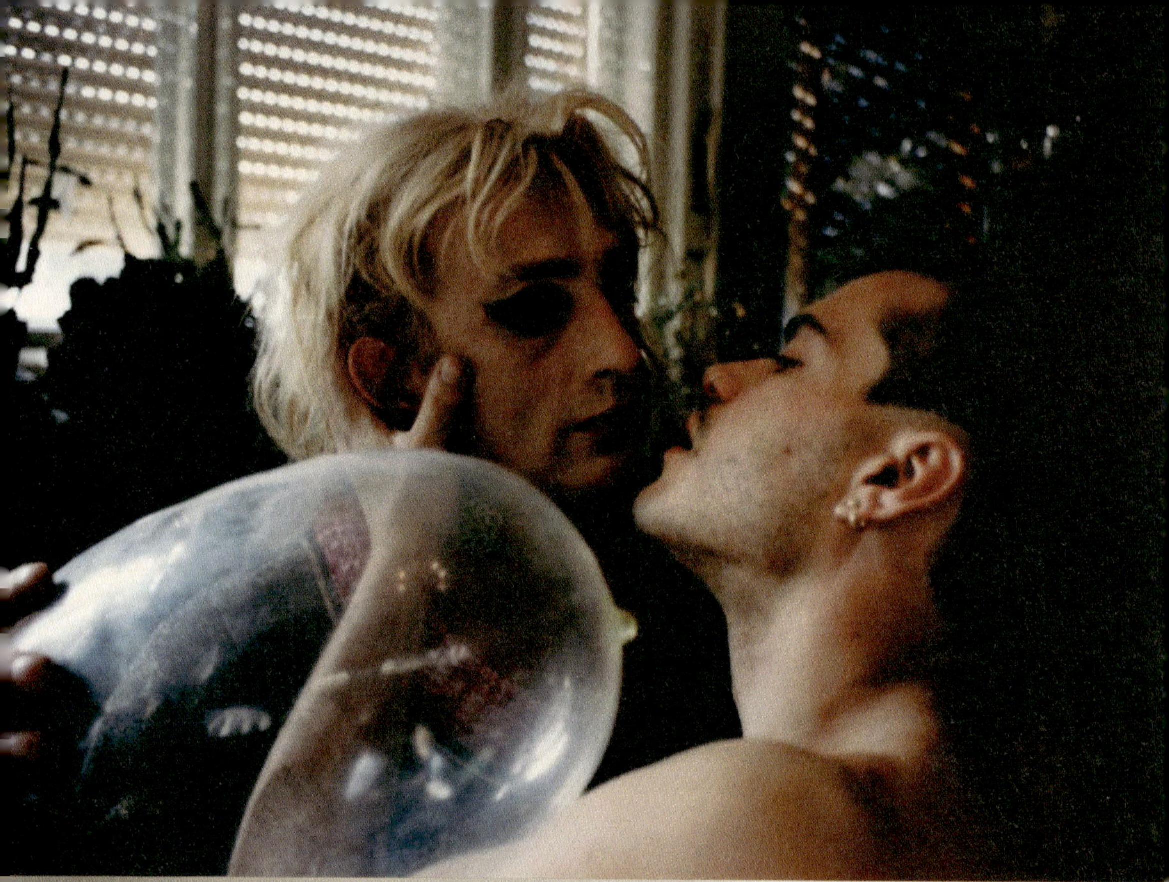

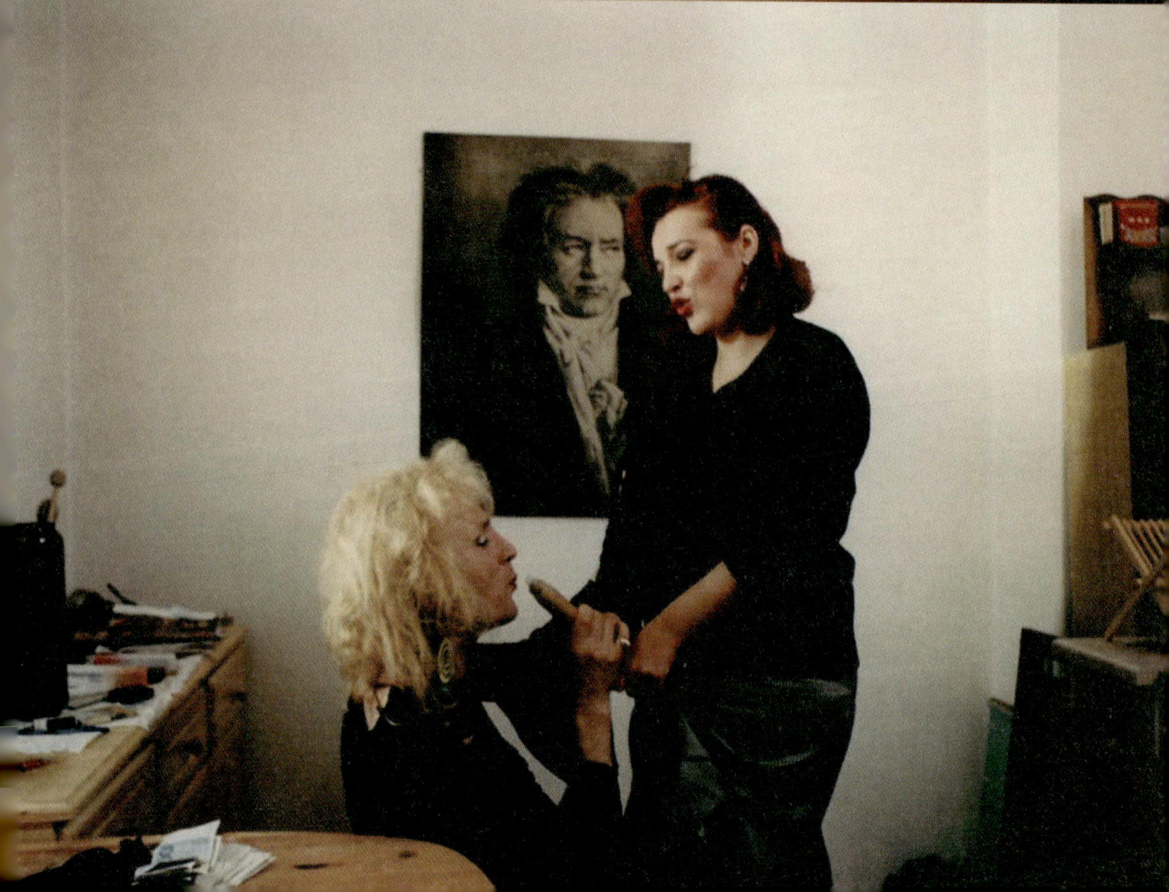

Marble Ass

Federal Republic of Yugoslavia • 1995 • 87 min. • Betacam to 35 mm • color

Merlin has been helping to pacify the Balkans by turning tricks with countless Serbian men. She acts as a lightning rod that shelters Belgrade—calming violent nighthawks, swanky big spenders, miserable loners, and horny young studs, and taking on the charge that would otherwise befall little girls, unprotected mothers, and helpless old women. Combined with guns, this unbridled energy would otherwise eventually lead to bloodshed. Merlin cools the boiling blood of violent man and enriches it with love. Džoni (Johnny) returns from war and arrives home in Belgrade. His motives are apparently similar to Merlin's—he also wants to cool boiling blood, but he does it by letting it out through holes in the human body, which he makes with bullets and knives. *Marble Ass* is a treatise on the different methods of resolving conflicts, as resorted to by Merlin and Džoni.

The semi-fictional character of Merlin is played by actor Vjeran Miladinović, who also appears in a few of Žilnik's previous movies, and with whom a chance encounter prompted the making of this film. She was the one who introduced Žilnik to Belgrade's trans bars and hangouts, where Žilnik realized that, in the midst of the war, this felt like the most normal and levelheaded community. The movie was funded by the earnings of *Tito among the Serbs for the Second Time* (1994). It was very successful, receiving the Teddy Award at the 1995 Berlin International Film Festival and shown in numerous LGBT film festivals around the world. ●

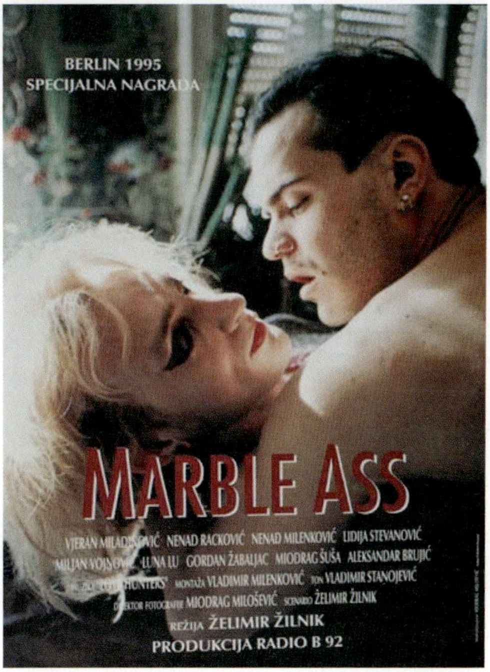

Marble Ass (poster), 1995.
DESIGNED BY MIODRAG MILOŠEVIĆ.

LEFT
Marble Ass (on-set photos), 1995.
PHOTOS BY MIODRAG MILOŠEVIĆ.
TOP Vjeran Miladinović and Nenad Racković.
BOTTOM Vjeran Miladinović and Lidija Stevanović.

Black Film shows the self-justifying and self-serving position of humanistic compassion, characteristic of left-wing liberals, to be fundamentally misleading.

—Branislav Dimitrijević, "Concrete Analysis of Concrete Situations: Marxist Education According to Želimir Žilnik," *Afterall*, Autumn/Winter 2010, 55.

A director who also does screenplay—and I'm such a case—experiences his film as a kind of giving birth. And when giving birth, even when bad sides are visible, they try to hide them—but man can't run away from himself. I started making films a long time ago, and I realized that it is the only art in which life enters directly, in pieces. So everything I have done has never attempted to follow mainstream aesthetics; for me it was incidental. Rather, I have always tried to put on film what I found important in my life at the moment when the film was made. Everything I have done, either documentary or feature, was something of a happening when it was being made. That is the thing I find challenging, and not the mere imitation of reality through "the realization of the text."

—Želimir Žilnik, interview (untitled), *Reporter*, August 1986.

Žilnik's cinema [...] resides in the process, the series of relations, which constitute the making of a film and which are here conceived as already a direct and worthy intervention into the social sphere. In this type of cinema, the act of filming is at least as important as the (finished) film. Deprived of the aura of a privileged creative activity, art/film practice thus becomes a situation of common labor. In a sense, Žilnik's films may be thought of as chronicles left by a group of workers—the director, the cast, the crew—of their attempted exercises in grassroots social and cultural productivity. They are "films-as-documents" of their own production, which is conceived as first and foremost an end unto itself: a dereified collective engagement in "sensuous human activity."

In Žilnik's case (even more so than in the case of other New Film authors, [Dušan] Makavejev included), "cinema-as-praxis" decidedly casts filmmaking as a mode of play. Each new project functions as yet another installment of an experimental social game. As issue is introduced, a situation is established, and the process of filming is set in motion. The making of a film functions simultaneously as 1) an incentive to resolve issues at hand; 2) an exercise in giving birth to a new subcultural cell/formation; and 3) a reflection on what, if anything, will have been accomplished in or through the production process. Thus, even if by the time the filming has come to an end the issues that are being dealt with have not yet been successfully settled, the making of the film will still have constituted a worthy exercise in social activism.

—Pavle Levi, in Pavle Levi and Želimir Žilnik, "Europe's Internal Exiles: Sound, Image, and Performance of Identity in Želimir Žilnik's Films," in *Ethnic Europe: Mobility, Identity, and Conflict in Globalized World*, ed. Roland Hsu (Stanford, CA: Stanford University Press, 2010), 117.

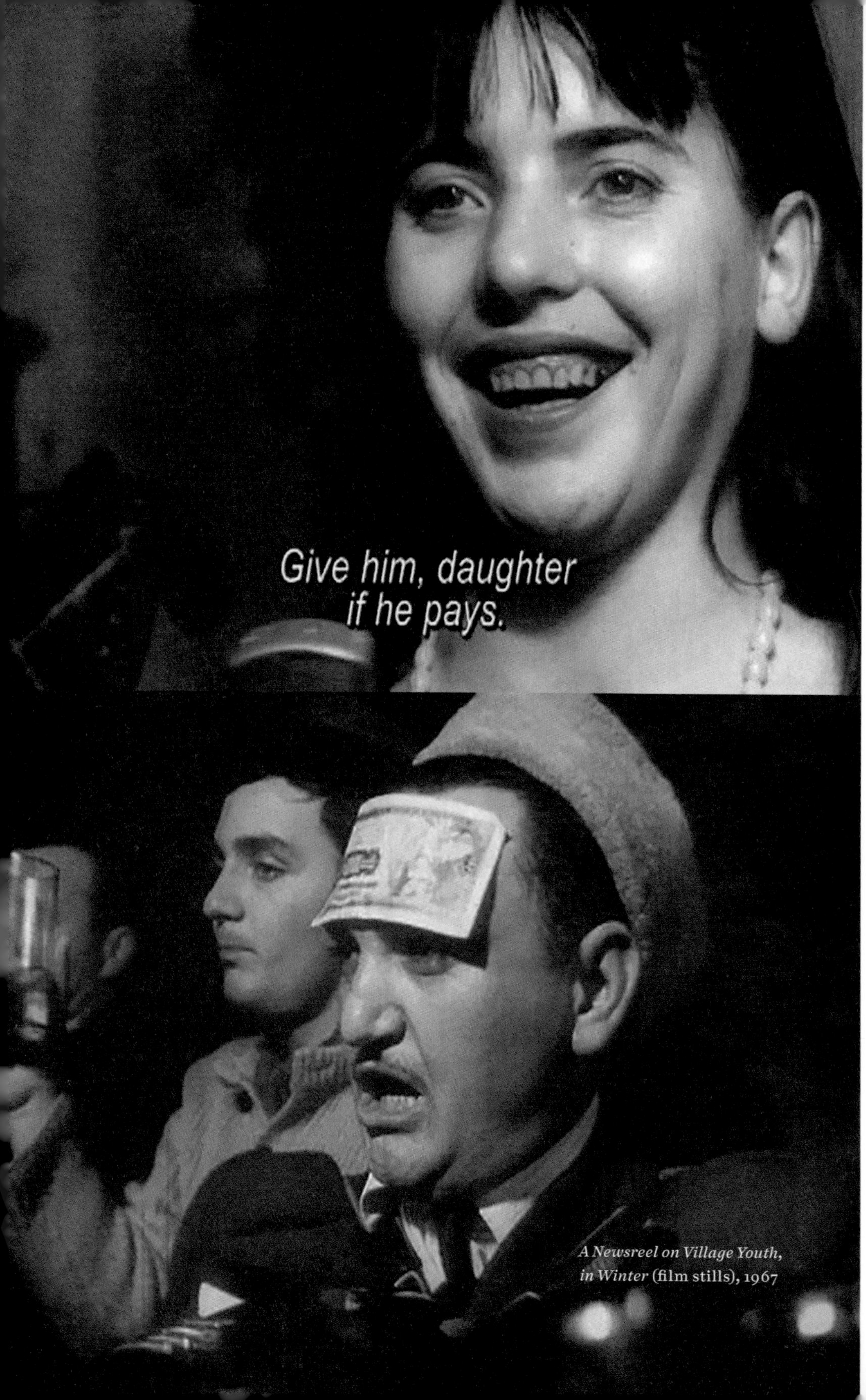

A Newsreel on Village Youth, in Winter (film stills), 1967

ANA JANEVSKI

The Dancing Paradox: On Movement, Dance, and Bodies in Želimir Žilnik's Films

The camera pans up from the bottom right of the frame, capturing the faces and poses of a cross-generational crowd, either leaning against the wall or forming a front row. While most of them are confronting the camera, smiling or being serious, some of the participants direct their gaze off-frame, slightly balancing their bodies. The music in the background, an experimental rock tune, reveals that the scene takes place in a dance hall. The camera zooms in on the frontman of the band, who sings, "Hey Jelo Jeleno / don't tread the mown hay" (*Oj Jelo Jelena / ne gazi seno košeno*). Then the camera focuses on a group of young people dancing, surrounded by a crowd. Their bodies move and contort frenetically to the rhythm of the music. If we were to isolate this scene, it would show an average group of young people dancing to rock music sometime during the 1960s. Once again, the camera goes back to the singer and then back to the dance floor, zooming in on the legs of the dancers, twisting and bending. Suddenly, an imperceptible moment—the rock theme gradually shifts into a folk tune and the contemporary choreography turns into a popular folk dance: *kolo*.[01]

This is one of the scenes of Želimir Žilnik's early film *A Newsreel on Village Youth, in Winter* (1967). Filmed in villages near Novi Sad, the film focuses on the leisure time of young people in the countryside, or, as the opening title suggests: "Cultural and entertainment life in Vojvodina." The film reveals some of Žilnik's best-known innovations and experimentations, starting with its "fictional documentarism or documentarist fictionalism,"[02] which involves working with nonprofessional actors, the direct relation of the protagonists to the camera-eye, and a lack of distinction between the "acted" and the "spontaneous." The protagonists featured in Žilnik's films are not only amateur actors but also outcasts—invisible, suppressed, and under- and misrepresented members of society, or, as the title of this book and the exhibition that preceded it eloquently puts it, "shadow citizens." Žilnik shows them without prejudice or judgment. As noted in a review of *A Newsreel on Village Youth, in Winter* at the time:

> He approaches his subjects in an open manner, without preconceived conclusions, and despite its authentic creepiness, the film manages to surprise us with the fact that we were hitherto not aware that nearby there was such an oasis of despair and spiritual misery where young men from a wealthy part of the country spend their free time smashing beer bottles with their hard heads.[03]

Postwar Yugoslavia drew upon emancipatory socialism, an ideology in which the future is ostensibly in the hands of the young generation. Since the very beginning of his career, Žilnik has pointed to the contradictions and omissions of the Yugoslav socialist system and its official discourse. His disclosing of futile, prosaic, and unsophisticated ways of spending leisure time can thus be read as an almost subversive act.[04]

01 *Kolo* ("circle" or "wheel") is a South Slavic traditional dance performed among groups of people who hold each other's hands, ideally in a circle (hence the name).

02 Branislav Dimitrijević, "Behind Scepticism Lies the Fire of a Revolutionary!," ZilnikZelimir.net, n.d., https://www.zilnikzelimir.net/essay/behind-scepticism-lies-fire-revolutionary-1.

03 Bogdan Tirnanić, "Njihov prvi film (ili šta su pokazali debitanti 14. festivala)," *Filmnovosti*, March 29, 1967. All translations from Serbo-Croatian are the author's, unless otherwise noted.

04 The film was selected for the 14th Debutant

I would like to focus on some aspects of Žilnik's films that so far haven't been discussed in the many evaluations of his oeuvre, namely his approaches and analyses of movement, speech, music, and the composition of bodies in relation to the contradictory, complex, and multifaceted aspects of the Yugoslav socialist system and its social dynamics.

Žilnik is interested in youth culture and in the generational change that happened in the 1960s, when the younger generation without direct experience of anti-fascist struggle came onto the scene. Hence in *A Newsreel on Village Youth, in Winter*, the older generation complains that today there is no discipline and young people do whatever they want. It was also a time when the influence of popular genres from the West (particularly American and Western European popular music) was strongly linked to the country's opening to the West and the ensuing effect on established local cultural production. The rock tune mentioned at the start of this essay is a distinctive local variation of the Western pop music idiom. The intertwining and overlapping of local legacy and foreign influence is a particularly interesting example of a hybrid creation poignant with symbolism. The bodies dancing to a rock tune are an affirmation of social transformation, a point of convergence of modernization within a traditional form of socialization. The socialist cultural policy insisted on the modernization of mass culture, while socialist folklore was an ideological category used by the authorities to showcase modernization, acting as a deceptive facade portraying a happy and prosperous rural life, which also helped to disguise the poor reality of peasant life. Furthermore, socialist folklore was seen as "a primary tool employed in the building process of a supranational identity."[05]

Žilnik is not focused on the repertoire of amateur ensembles or established singers; instead, he turns toward the people and their stories that are usually forgotten and marginalized. In *A Newsreel on Village Youth, in Winter*, he observes how these two moments, rock and folklore, are embodied in everyday life and in vernacular culture. The double nature of the dancing youth in Vojvodina doesn't stand so much for a duality or clash of the urban and the rural as much as for the parallel coexistence of the two, where one doesn't exclude the other, both in ordinary life as well as in politics and pop cultural activities in Yugoslavia.

Miroslav Krleža, a Croatian writer and prominent intellectual figure in Socialist Yugoslavia, claimed, while reflecting on the modernization of Yugoslavia in 1979, that Josip Broz Tito's socialism had contributed to the cultural prosperity and development of the Yugoslav nation over the previous thirty years more than the last 150 years combined. "Hence," he added, "this rhythm of cultural development is so far incomparable." However, he also believed that Yugoslavia wouldn't be able to cross into the third millennium without emancipating itself from nationalist myths: "The Party has been overcome by the peasant uprising, and it succeeded in orienting the masses, but

Film Festival in Belgrade in 1967. It was not shown in the official competition but as part of the informative section, as the jury was not able to accept "the aspect of our life we were not familiar with, while Žilnik in his film surprised us with its complexity and defeat[s] us with its own existence." Tirnanić, "Njihov prvi film."

05 Ana Hofman, "Questioning Socialist Folklorization: The Beltinci Folklore Festival in the Slovenian Borderland of Prekmurje," in *Audiovisual Media and Identity Issues in Southeastern Europe*, ed. Eckehard Pistrick, Nicola Scaldaferri, and Gretel Schworer (Newcastle upon Tyne, UK: Cambridge Scholars, 2011), 238.

A Newsreel on Village Youth, in Winter (film still), 1967

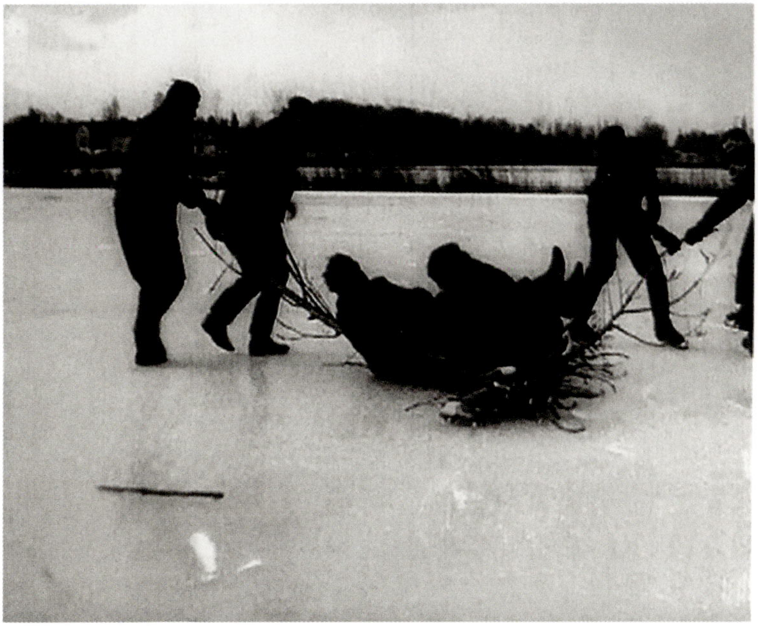

unfortunately its symbol is *kozaračko kolo*, when instead we should be moving forward. *Kozaračko kolo* should be left to history."[06]

Žilnik, by contrast, doesn't seem to hold a stance as assertive as Krleža's. He instead merely observes the symptoms of the impotence of the party ideology. The dancing youth in *A Newsreel on Village Youth, in Winter* pose a challenge to the ideological task of producing a fixed, static concept and interpretation of socialist culture. The young men and women embodying both rock and *kolo* represent the paradox present not only in socialist cultural policy but more generally in socialist society at large. This paradox recurs as an important feature throughout Žilnik's ouevre. In that regard, the art historian Branislav Dimitrijević writes in his analysis of Žilnik's work:

> Among its various meanings, a paradox can be defined as an apparently true statement, or group of statements, that leads to a contradiction or a situation which defies intuition; or it can be an apparent contradiction that actually expresses a non-dual truth. In the notion of the paradox there is an effective means to deconstruct not only any static argument, but also an exercise in which there is no simple refutation of one of the relevant points of view, but a synthesis or combination of the opposing assertions.[07]

Paradox is also present in Žilnik's relation to dominant ideology. After being expelled from the Party for his anarcho-liberal views, Žilnik continued to deal with the complexity of Marxism in a socialist Yugoslavia, himself remaining a leftist.[08] His intention was not to critique socialist reality but to bring a critical enrichment to the

06
Miroslav Krleža, quoted in Damir Pilić, "Tito očima Krleže," unpublished manuscript. The *Kozaračko kolo* is a traditional dance (see footnote 01).

07
Dimitrijević, "Behind Scepticism Lies the Fire of a Revolutionary!"

08
"The tragedy of the Communist Union is that the most important party functions are occupied by people with evident family complexes who are trying to be bigger Catholics than the Pope," pronounced Žilnik when expelled from the Communist Party after a dispute over the Neoplanta Film production house. Quoted in Boris Buden, *Uvod u prošlost*, ed. Kuda.org (Novi Sad: New Media Center_kuda.org, 2013), 88, https://kuda.org/sites/default/files/Uvod%20u%20proslost_web.pdf.

social discourse.[09] As an acute observer as he is, Žilnik noticed that motion, body dynamics, and pop culture contained this criticality.

In conceiving of an "anthropology of the body" to begin unpacking Žilnik's approach to the human form and its movement, Michel Foucault's notion of "biopower" provides a useful tool. Biopower focuses on the body as the site of subjugation, highlighting how individuals are implicated in their own oppression through their participation in daily bodily practices and habits. Power, according to Foucault, is not imposed from above but rather comes from below. That is, we are all "vehicles of power," because power is "embedded in discourses and norms that are part of the minute practices, habits, and interactions of our everyday lives."[10] Thus, power is everywhere: it is "exercised from innumerable points, in the interplay of non-egalitarian and mobile relations."[11] Bodily disciplinary techniques, which organize time, space, and daily practices in a society, are institutionalized in schools, prisons, hospitals, and workshops and also individually internalized through self-regulating behavior. In choosing "shadow citizens" as his protagonists, Žilnik focuses on "undisciplined bodies," or the part of the population that is not institutionalized or self-regulating—often dancing, singing, moving, and exercising on their own.

In *Little Pioneers* (1968),[12] Žilnik shows neglected children who are taking care of themselves and are involved in pickpocketing, begging, and other illegal activities. These children are the exact

09
Dimitrijević, "Behind Scepticism Lies the Fire of a Revolutionary!"

10
Jen Pylypa, "Power and Bodily Practice: Applying the Work of Foucault to an Anthropology of the Body," *Arizona Anthropologist* 13 (1998): 23.

11
Michael Foucault, *The History of Sexuality*, vol. 1, *The Will to Knowledge* (London: Penguin, 1976), 94.

12
For a description of this film, see Dijana Jelača's essay in this volume (p. 89).

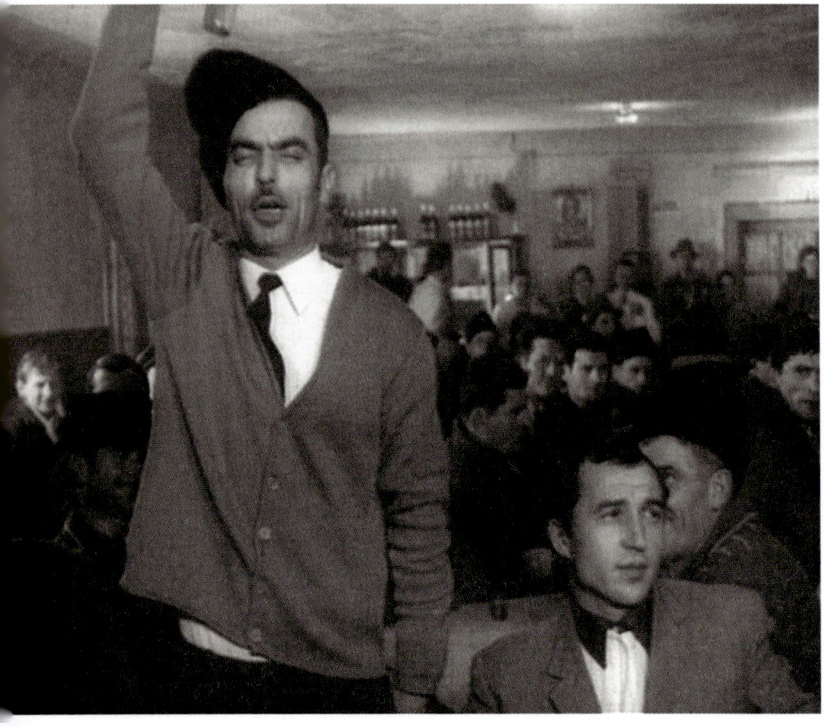

A Newsreel on Village Youth, in Winter (film stills), 1967

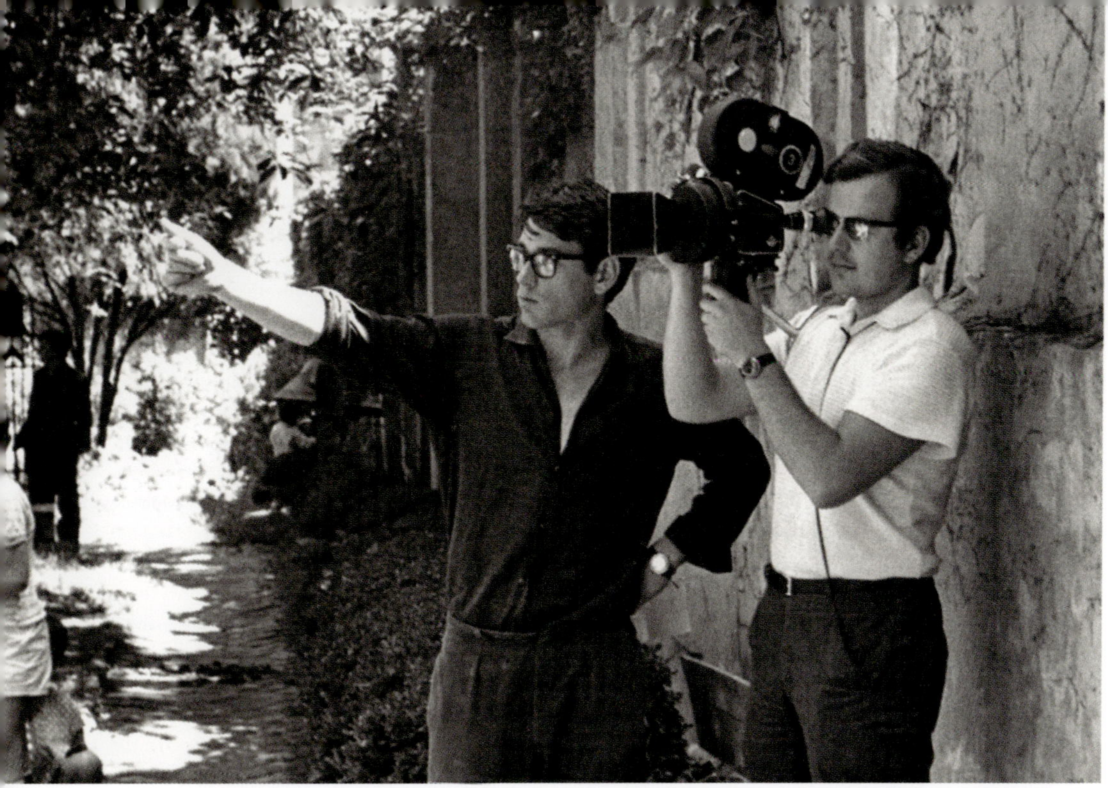

Želimir Žilnik and Dušan Ninkov on the set of *Little Pioneers*, 1967. PHOTO BY ANDREJ POPOVIĆ.

opposite of the happy and carefree image of the "young socialist pioneers" put forward by the Yugoslav government. Žilnik's film has no pedagogical or moralizing attitude to speak of. One of the initial scenes of the film shows a young girl leaning against a dilapidated wall and singing. The lyrics of the song—about a young woman abandoned before her wedding—are in opposition with her young age. The camera follows the children in their daily adventures while their voice-overs narrate situations of pickpocketing, prostitution, and abuse. Žilnik shows them always in motion, mainly in neglected parts of the city, in a group, singing, wailing, screaming, whispering, producing sound with any kind of found object, smoking, throwing stones. Once again we are brought to a dance hall. Instead of music, here we hear one of the young protagonists recounting his adventures while a group of nearby young people contort their bodies in recognizable rock movements. In the midst of these progressive Yugoslav youth engaging in dancing, the "little pioneers" are smoking and talking, dancing and rhythmically banging their hands on the stage. With *Little Pioneers*, Žilnik thus captures another social paradox of the time as well as the contradictory nature of the official cultural policy. Following its screening at the fifteenth Yugoslav Documentary and Short Film Festival, the film once more triggered several film critics to write about Žilnik's talent of shining a light on the most obscure and hidden parts of Yugoslav society. In the filmmaker's own words: "In my films I am dealing with serious social issues, not in a pseudo-engaged way, but rather in a polyvalent manner. I think that a pathos-filled approach to a subject can never be sincere. That's why I consider it important to have a

13
Želimir Žilnik, quoted in "Nova filmska nada," *Filmske novosti*, September 1967.

humorist stance toward life."[13] He cites his admiration of the films of the Czech director Miloš Forman and his apparent "light" motives, which hide a darkness that viewers can either uncover or not, as inspiration for his own approach to filmmaking. This darkness is perhaps a presumptive quality of Žilnik's *Black Film* (1971) and of the idea of "blackness" that accompanied him and his peers from the 1970s onward following accusations that their films portrayed Yugoslav society as black and negative.[14]

For Žilnik, documentary film and culture do not provide a remedy from social misery. He doubts the emancipatory power of culture. Toward the end of *Little Pioneers*, the children begin insulting each other, in a rather vulgar and adult way, while in the background a young boy smashes into a cardboard box, and a girl, who previously recounted her sexualized encounters with older men, dances and moves her body sensually. They are both disconnected from the group and from each other, yet they create a unity. Žilnik doesn't film the vitality or energy of young bodies; rather, he shows them as symptoms of the realities born of the impotence of the socialist ideology, while everyday life continues in all its darkness. Žilnik, who started his film practice in the amateur cine clubs of Novi Sad, describes how a do-it-yourself approach contributed to his ability to tackle such subversive subjects in his work: "Very early on I was forced to use all the methods of movement of amateur film. This environment of amateur film enabled me to rid myself of administrative labyrinths, which were the only way to acquire money to make a film. It was a form of freedom."[15] Courageous amateurism is prominent in Žilnik's films, both as a concept and as a method, and

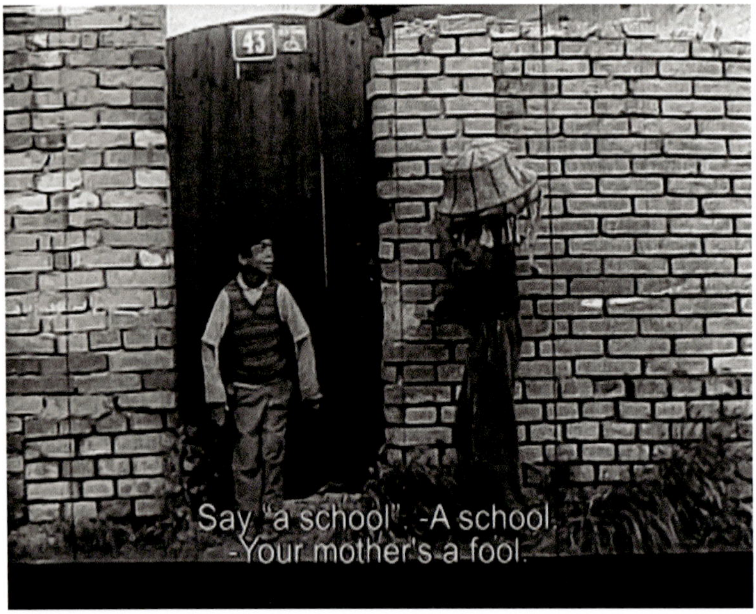

Little Pioneers (film still), 1968

14
Žilnik together with other filmmakers, including Dušan Makavejev and Živojin Pavlović, in their films openly criticized the alienation of the socialist man, pointing to class and social contradictions in Socialist Yugoslavia at the time. As a consequence of an ideological campaign led by the cultural-political establishment, these films became known as the Black Wave. The article that introduced the term "Black Wave" was published in the newspaper *Borba* in 1969. A journalist stated that the Black Wave in Yugoslav film presents "a systematic distortion of the present," in which everything is viewed through a monochromatic lens. Its themes are "obscure and present improper visions and images of violence, moral degeneracy, misery, lasciviousness and triviality." Vladimir Jovičić, "'Crni val' u našem filmu," *Borba* Belgrade, August 3, 1969.

15
Želimir Žilnik, quoted in Stevan Vuković, "Notes on Paradigms in Experimental Film in Socialist Yugoslavia," in *This Is All Film!*

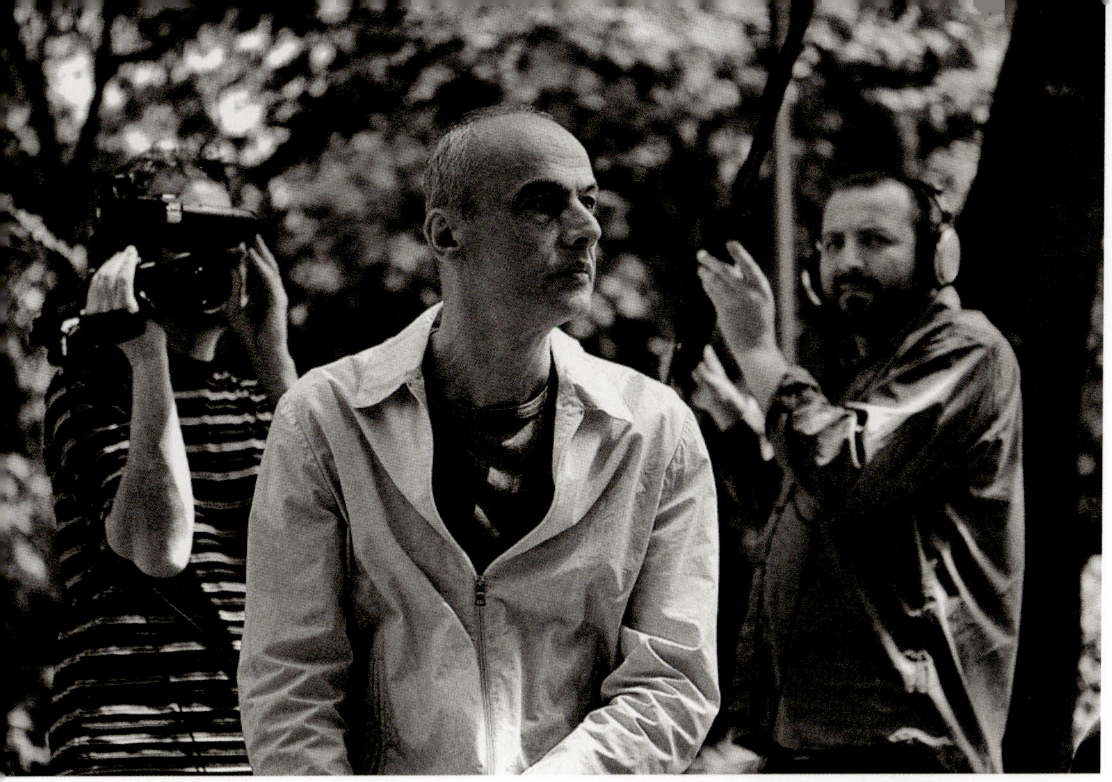

LEFT TO RIGHT Miodrag Milošević, Branimir Stojanović Trša, and Dragan Kolarov on the set of *The Old School of Capitalism*, 2009. PHOTO BY LEON ŠURBANOVIĆ.

Experimental Film in Yugoslavia, 1951–1991, ed. Bojana Piškur, Ana Janevski, Jurij Meden, and Stevan Vuković (Ljubljana: Moderna Galerija, 2010), 53.

16
What, How & for Whom/WHW, "Želimir Žilnik, Shadow Citizens," ZilnikZelimir.net, 2018, https://www.zilnikzelimir.net/project/zelimir-zilnik-shadow-citizens.

the *Shadow Citizens* exhibition at the Edith-Russ-Haus for Media Art specifically elaborated on "different facets of the potentials of shadow citizens as well as the pressures of the amateur undercurrent in emancipatory politics and artistic production."[16]

In the 1970s, Žilnik left Yugoslavia for Germany, where he realized several films that examine local politics, capturing in particular a moment of rising terrorism and the sociopolitical position of immigrant workers. He soon, however, had to leave Germany due to political opposition, and returned to Yugoslavia where he next made a series of both television and feature films. While in his early films Žilnik deals with the complex interplay of ideology, movement, music, and practice, in his films from the 1980s he detects the early symptoms of the country's growing social conflicts through the figure of the *Gastarbeiter*. The anthropologists Tanja Petrović and Ana Hofman describe the social situation of such guest workers in Yugoslavia and elsewhere in the mid-twentieth century:

> The culturalized image of a *gastarbeiter* as a bizarre, grotesque individual whose cultural taste is characterized by kitsch and eclecticism, who does not fit in the acceptable cultural norms of either the society he or she left nor of the one she or he came to, dominates both popular culture and academic discussion, while the harsh life and hard work of migrants, anxieties resulting from their separation from their children

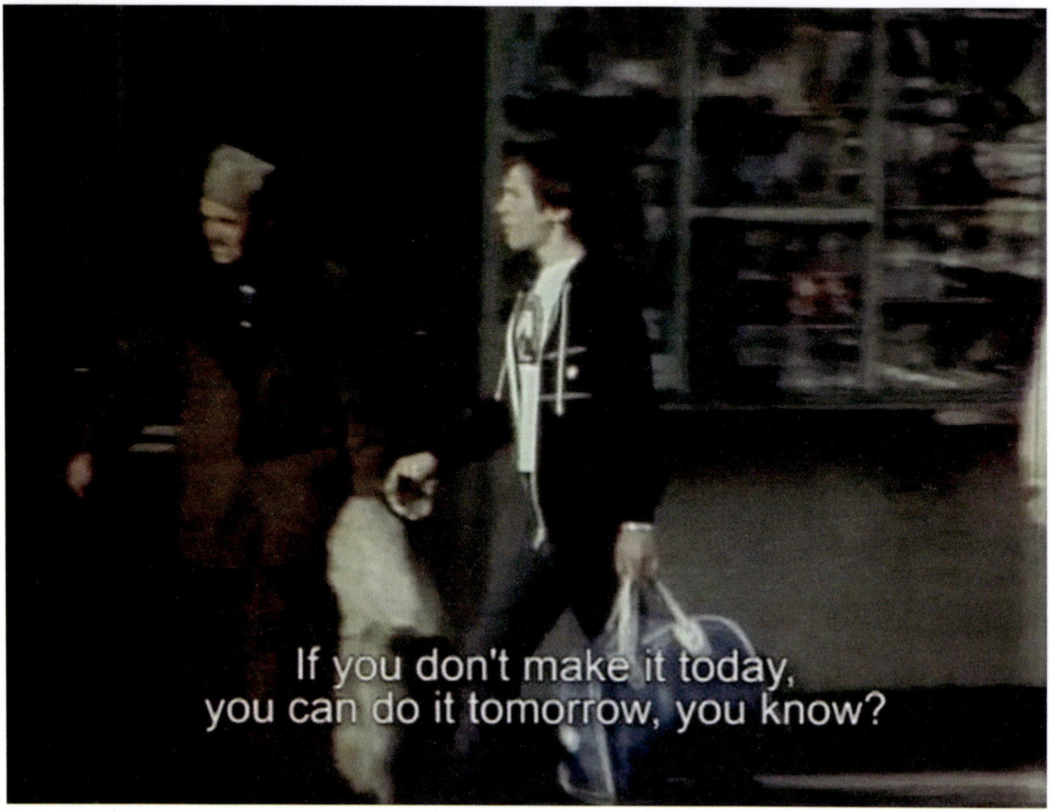

and families, and other existential and psychological aspects of their work and life remain only rarely addressed in their complexity.[17]

Young people were, once again, at the center of Žilnik's interest during this era. The TV film *The First Trimester of Pavle Hromiš* (1983) offers a touching and acute overview of the titular teenager, who returns to Yugoslavia while his parents stay in Germany to work, as it follows his integration into the Yugoslav society of the 1980s. The main character is fifteen-year-old Pavle Hromiš, who, after spending the past eleven years with his family in Germany, comes back to Yugoslavia to live with his grandmother in a village near Novi Sad. Žilnik documents another generational conflict, this time between grandmother and grandson, following which Pavle decides to instead live in a boarding house while he attends secondary school.

At school he meets new friends who share a similar experience. Pavle and his friends are lost between two identities. Their confessions to the camera detailing comparisons between the different countries they have lived in are very moving and vivid. One teenager talks about how Austrians don't respect Turks and Yugoslavs, and another boy explains he had to leave a history class in Russia after he refused the idea that the Red Army liberated Yugoslavia. Their stories are also

17
Tanja Petrović and Ana Hofman, "Rethinking Class in Socialist Yugoslavia: Labor, Body, and Moral Economy," in *The Cultural Life of Capitalist Yugoslavia*, ed. Dijana Jelača, Maša Kolanović, and Danijela Lugarić (Baskingstoke, UK: Palgrave Macmillan, 2017), 71.

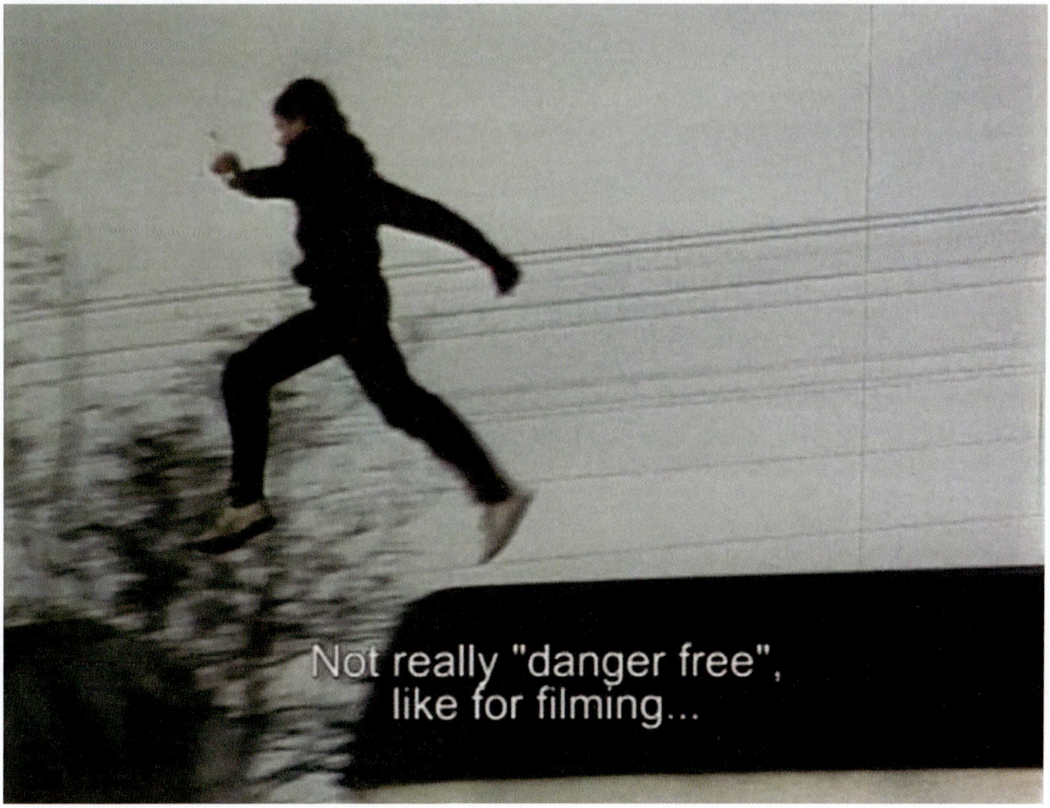

LEFT AND RIGHT
The First Trimester of Pavle Hromiš (film stills), 1983

surprising. A girl claims in Dutch that the people in the Netherlands seem more respectful and altruistic than they do in Yugoslavia. Different stories alternate with Pavle's narration about his limited possibilities to succeed in an important profession in Germany and how his most likely path there is that of a manual worker. His voice-over accompanies a scene of him and his classmates exercising and training in some type of martial art. They are all in constant movement, whether their bodies are shown being trained in a gymnastic class at school or running, twisting, curling, or resting on the roof of a building or on a quay along the river. In other moments of the film, Žilnik captures Pavle alone in motion, racing or jumping from one train car to the other, as in an action movie. Once again, the kinetic metaphor stands for unstable social dynamics.

Žilnik likewise remains attentive to the prevalence and role of pop culture, as, for example, when the group is preparing for a school play and a girl sings a folk song. Her mates quickly begin to boo her. Yugoslav culture during the 1980s was, in some respects, progressive and westernized, and thus no longer accepting of any folk elements. This inclination is also present in the conversation Pavle and his friends have around music, covering disco, funk, and heavy metal, among other genres, and bands like Depeche Mode and Simple Minds, while at the same time Žilnik shows the underground music scene in Novi Sad through scenes of a concert featuring alternative and new wave bands such as Obojeni Program and Boye.

The teenagers of *The First Trimester of Pavle Hromiš* are lost between two socioeconomic systems, a fact made explicit through an animated discussion among the students about the pros and cons of socialism and capitalism. Most of the students still consider socialism to be a more fair and secure system (not everyone's main preoccupation is money); yet if Yugoslav socialism is based on the leadership of its youth, the moment any of the youth start to doubt it, the system shows its first signs of weakness. Eventually, Pavle is attracted by the military life, as it gives him order and security to combat the uncertainty present in his personal life. The final scene of the film features the everyday military ritual of making one's bed and putting on standard-issue clothing; Žilnik soundtracks this new alignment into soldier life with a post-punk tune by Gang of Four. While the body is eventually disciplined, punk and Yugoslav socialism continue to coexist in yet another paradox, until the system's final dissolution.

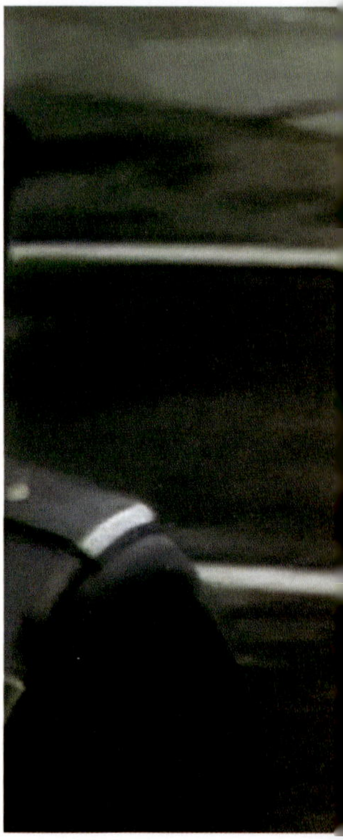

The good life was so elusive
Handouts, they got me down
I had to regain my confidence
So I got into camouflage
The girls they love to see you shoot
I love a man in a uniform[18] ★

Ana Janevski is currently Curator in the Department of Media and Performance Art at the Museum of Modern Art, New York. Most recently, she co-organized the exhibition *Judson Dance Theater: The Work Is Never Done* (with Thomas Lax and Martha Joseph) in 2018–19. She has collaborated with many choreographers and artists, such as Anne Teresa De Keersmaeker, Jérôme Bel, Yvonne Rainer, Rabih Mroué, Boris Charmatz and Musée de la danse, Simone Forti, Martha Rosler, Ralph Lemon, and Trajal Harrell, among others. From 2007 to 2011, she held the position of Curator at the Museum of Modern Art in Warsaw, where she curated, among many other projects, the large-scale exhibition *As Soon as I Open My Eyes I See a Film*, on the topic of Yugoslav experimental film and art from the 1960s and '70s. She also edited an accompanying book of the same title. In 2010, Janevski cocurated the first extensive show about experimental film in Yugoslavia, *This Is All Film! Experimental Film in Yugoslavia 1951–1991*, at the Museum of Modern Art in Ljubljana.

18
Gang of Four, "I Love a Man in Uniform," *Songs of the Free*, EMI, 1982. Gang of Four played in Zagreb at the Music Biennial in 1981. See "Entertainment: Gang of Four, live in Zagreb, 1981," *Dangerous Minds*, August 20, 2014, https://dangerousminds.net/comments/entertainment_gang_of_four_live_in_zagreb_1981.

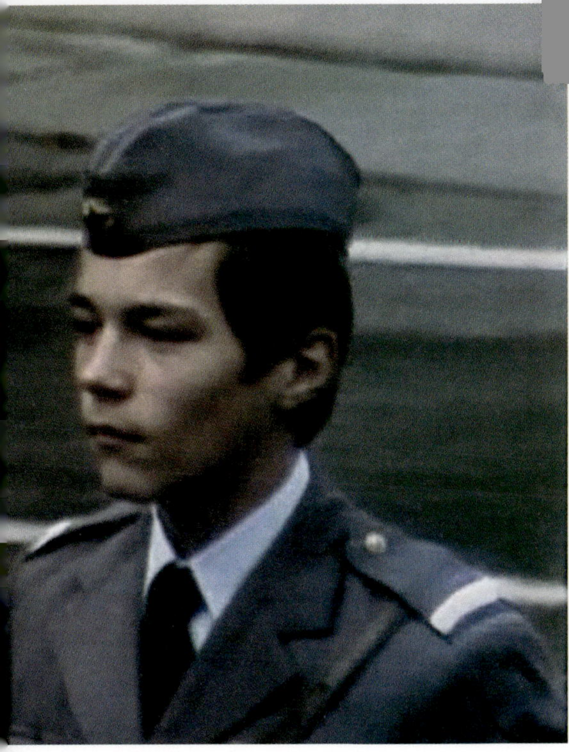

Vladimir Sinko in *The First Trimester of Pavle Hromiš* (film still), 1983

The Gastarbeiter Opera

Yugoslavia • 1977 • theater play

The first project Žilnik undertook after his return to Yugoslavia from West Germany was this theater play, staged at the Experimental Scene of the Serbian National Theatre in Novi Sad. It is a singing play in five scenes, following several women from rural areas in Yugoslavia as they travel to West Germany as *Gastarbeiter* (guest workers). They encounter new working conditions, a new culture, and a new language. While the younger women are able to adjust, the older ones experience shock and conflict. After a period of time, the entire group decides to return home to Yugoslavia. At the border, before entering the country, the main protagonist dies.

The play was both a critical and popular success. It was performed over eighty times and won awards at several festivals. However, a few months after the premiere, the West German cultural attaché to Yugoslavia wrote a formal complaint, as he realized after seeing the play that it featured the Nazi anthem "Horst Wessel Lied," and he understood this as an anti-German provocation. He requested the removal of the play from the theater's repertoire. In response, the theater sent an audio recording that made it clear that the song in question was in fact a Bertolt Brecht quote in which the playwright mocks the Nazi song, and the lines are changed to "das Kalb marshiert" (a calf marches). As a result of this dispute, several German newspapers wrote about the play and a report was also broadcast on German television. •

Jugoslawischer Kulturreport (II): „Gastarbeiter-Oper" von Zelimir Zilnik in Novi Sad – eine politisch-theatralische Revue

Drei Frauen ziehen aus, das Glück zu finde

Von Heinz Klunker

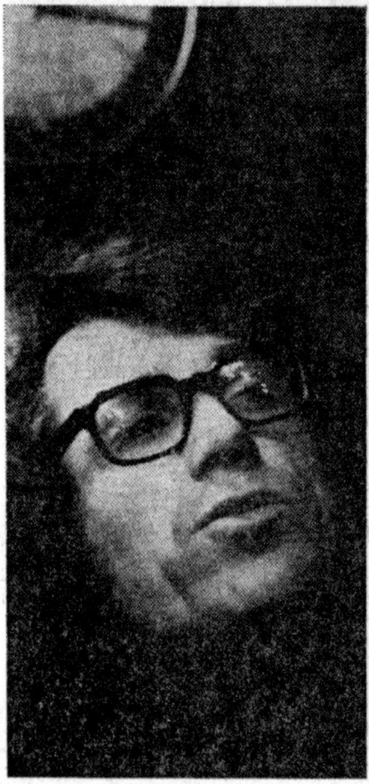

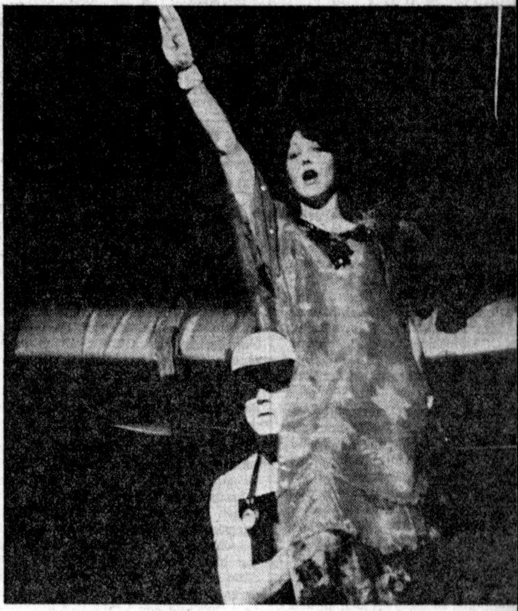

PARTEINAHME FÜR FRAUEN: Szene aus der „Gastarbeiter-Oper" in Novi Sad; links: Regisseur Zilnik

Fotos: Zolta

Kyrillisch nimmt sich der Titel zwar fremd aus, aber ins Lateinische übertragen enthüllt er seine deutsche Herkunft: *Gastarbeiter-Opera*. Er bezeichnet ein theatralisches Ereignis, das in Novi Sad, etwa 80 Kilometer nördlich von Belgrad, nach der Premiere am 24. Januar erst einmal eine Schrecksekunde auslöste. Sie dauerte, genährt vom Vorwurf des Anarchismus gegen den Autor in einer lokalen Kritik, fast 14 Tage. Dann rauschte es im jugoslawischen Blätterwald zwischen Ljubljana und Belgrad, Zagreb und Sarajevo, und das Rauschen verhieß einen künstlerischen, aber auch einen politischen Erfolg. Das kulturelle Klima ist noch wechselhaft, schlägt erst allmählich ins sonnige Tauwetter um; vor einem Jahr jedenfalls wäre dieses Stück kaum schon möglich gewesen.

Die Gastarbeiter-Problematik, ein öffentlich umstrittenes Thema in der Bundesrepublik, zumal in der Rezession, rührt in Jugoslawien an die Existenz von Staat und Gesellschaft. Scham und schlechtes Gewissen belasten eine offene Diskussion, deren Nutzen freilich niemand nachweisen kann. Da ist einerseits das ökonomische Plus, das sich im Unterhalt für Tausende von Familien niederschlägt und dem Staat nebenher noch wertvolle Devisen einbringt; dem steht andererseits der Exodus großer Teile der arbeitsfähigen und -willigen Bevölkerung gegenüber, verbunden mit der Entfremdung von Familie und Heimat, geprägt von der Enttäuschung über einen Staat, der ihnen Arbeitsplatz und Auskommen nicht gewähren kann. Diese moralische Herausforderung an die jugoslawische Gesellschaft hat ihren Ausdruck bereits in Literatur und Film, besonders im kritischen Kurzfilm, gefunden. Die Kehrseite der Gastarbeiter-Medaille konnten wir in Filmen wie *Sonderzüge* oder *Bei der Mahlzeit*, die bei uns im Fernsehen gezeigt wurden, kennenlernen.

Man geht von zwölf Millionen Gastarbeitern in Europa aus, wobei der Begriff, der mit dem Status dieser Bürger zweiter Klasse fortwährend kollidiert, nur noch ironisch gebraucht werden kann. Das tut auch Zelimir Zilnik, Autor und Regisseur der *Gastarbeiter-Oper*, der die ausländischen Arbeiter, seine Landsleute und Türken, Griechen oder Italiener, mit den Goldgräbern vergleicht, die einmal in den Wilden Westen zogen: „Es sind die positiven Helden unserer Zeit. Für einen landlosen Bauern, der von Anatolien aufbricht und in Hamburg ankommt, ist das ein Abenteuer, vergleichbar mit Kolumbus, der nach dem Westen ging, um Indien zu erreichen."

Zilnik und seinem Komponisten Pedja Vranesevic kam es nicht auf eine Story an, sondern auf Situationen, denen sie Menschen aussetzen, die aus einem ihnen vertrauten Milieu gerissen wurden. Sie haben eine Art Schuldgefühl, wie Kinder vor ihren Eltern, Schüler vor ihren Lehrern; ihnen fehlen die Möglichkeiten, sich sprachlich differenziert auszudrücken, sie sprechen reduziert, in Chiffren. Ihre auf die Häufung von Verben und Substantive eingeschmolzene Prosa schlägt in Pop-Verse um, wenn sie mit Vorgesetzten reden.

Aber da sind wir bereits bei der Struktur des unkonventionellen Stückes. Es beginnt naturalistisch in einer Baracke, einer Art Nachtasyl, das drei Frauen zusammengeführt hat: Eine hat ihren Mann verloren, die andere ist ohne Job und die dritte auf Abenteuer aus. Ihre Gespräche sind bitter, ironisch und von schwarzem Humor getönt. Sie malen sich eine Zukunft aus, angesichts derer die Gegenwart noch unerträglicher wird, und beschließen, ins Ausland zu gehen. Der Schritt in die schillernde Konsumwelt setzt die Frauen unerwarteten Verwandlungen aus. Sie probieren nicht nur neue Kleider, sondern auch neues Verhalten. Dem Schwarzweißfilm des Eingangsbildes folgt nun der Farbfilm mit rührend komischen Wirkungen. Wieder ein Schnitt: Die drei Frauen geraten ins unerbittliche Räderwerk der modernen Industrie, wo Befehl herrscht und Gehorsam — Chaplins *Moderne Zeiten* sind da nicht weit. Unseren Heldinnen gelingt die Anpassung nicht, sie werden von der Arbeit gejagt, streunen herum und überdenken ihre Lage. Als sie auf ein zerstrittenes „Kapitalistenpaar" treffen, schlagen sie sich auf die Seite der Frau, solidarisieren sie sich gemeinsam gegen den Patriarchen. Der letzte Akt zeigt die Frauen, westlich ummontiert, bei der Heimreise an der Grenze. Eine Vision vom Müll-Europa wird konfrontiert mit pervertierter Folklore, die ihres volkstümlichen Charakters gänzlich entkleidet wurde — leere Euphorie in fremder Sprache. Entfremdet nun auch von der Heimat, endet das bitterböse Stück mit einem Aufschrei, der an Polanskis *Rosemary's Baby* erinnert: Wächst da ein Kind im Bauch oder ein Geschwür? Kein großes Gesangsfinale, kein Happy-End.

Dieser Stoff geht ganz in theatralischen Formen auf, am roten Faden einer eingängigen Musik-Collage aufgereiht — das dokumentarische Theater der Eingangsszene schlägt um in zeremonielles Theater bei der Westankunft, die Rockshow der Maschinenwelt wird abgelöst vom Melodrama im allgemeinen Katzenjammer, und endlich wird jene auf den Schlager gekommene Folklore parodiert. Die Musik, so vergnüglich sie immer sein mag, schärft die Inhalte, kommentiert die Haltungen und Situationen. Das Stück vermittelt über Emotionen und Aggressionen soziale und ökonomische Einsichten, die beim Publikum offensichtlich ankommen.

Zelimir Zilnik, der selbst in Novi Sad lebt, dem Mittelpunkt der buntgemischten Vojvodina, hat sein Engagement für die Unterdrückten und Aufbegehrenden, wie es bereits in Kurzfilmen (etwa *Studentenstreik*, *Der schwarze Film* oder *Aufstand in Jasak* — alle mit Preisen bedacht) und in seinem mit dem Berliner Goldenen Bären ausgezeichneten Spielfilm *Frühe Werke* zum Ausdruck drängte, nun auf die Bühne übertragen. Hinter Polemik und Satire, Parodie und Ironie erkennt man eine entschiedene Parteinahme für die Frauen, die nicht nur als Arbeitskräfte, sondern auch als Frauen ausgebeutet werden. Sie haben ein menschliches Angesicht und reagieren irritierend menschlich; die Männer, sie sind die Bosse, dürfen nur Symbole sein, Plakate der Herrschaft. In diesem Sinne ist Zilniks *Gastarbeiter-Oper* fast ein feministisches Stück, und in diesem Sinne ist wohl auch der provinzielle Anarchismus-Verdacht gemeint. Es wäre interessant, die Produktion aus Novi Sad als Gastspiel dort zu sehen, wo die Gastarbeiter ihre zugleich gewünschte und bloß geduldete Gastrolle spielen — in der Bundesrepublik etwa.

IN THE PRESS

An article on *Gastarbeiter Opera*, in the newspaper *Deutsches Allgemeines Sonntagsblatt*, March 6, 1977

I made my first film via the "risk it method." I assembled the entire crew with people who were willing to work without being paid upfront. Films considered as a "safe" investment had to have a finished script and a plan of shooting to get into actual production and budget would be allocated. I didn't have a budget, I also didn't and couldn't have a detailed script, so I had decided to play it by ear.

—Želimir Žilnik, in conversation with Dubravka Sekulić, Gal Kirn, and Žiga Testen, in *Surfing the Black: Yugoslav Black Wave Cinema and Its Transgressive Moments*, ed. Gal Kirn, Dubravka Sekulić, and Žiga Testen (Maastricht: Jan van Eyck Academie, 2012), 67.

Žilnik did not limit his approach to a certain humanistic empathy toward the underprivileged but explored the unpredictability of the political and the social role of this group. There is no sentimentalism in his approach yet there is an understanding for a certain *creativity-from-below* (as opposed from *modernisation-from-above* which was the tendency of the cultural policy) which Žilnik observes and later incorporates in his films, especially in those made for TV in the 1980s.

—Branislav Dimitrijević, "Behind Scepticism Lies the Fire of a Revolutionary!," in *For an Idea – Against the Status Quo: Analysis and Systematization of Želimir Žilnik's Artistic Practice* (Novi Sad: New Media Center_kuda.org, Playground produkcija, 2009), 144–45.

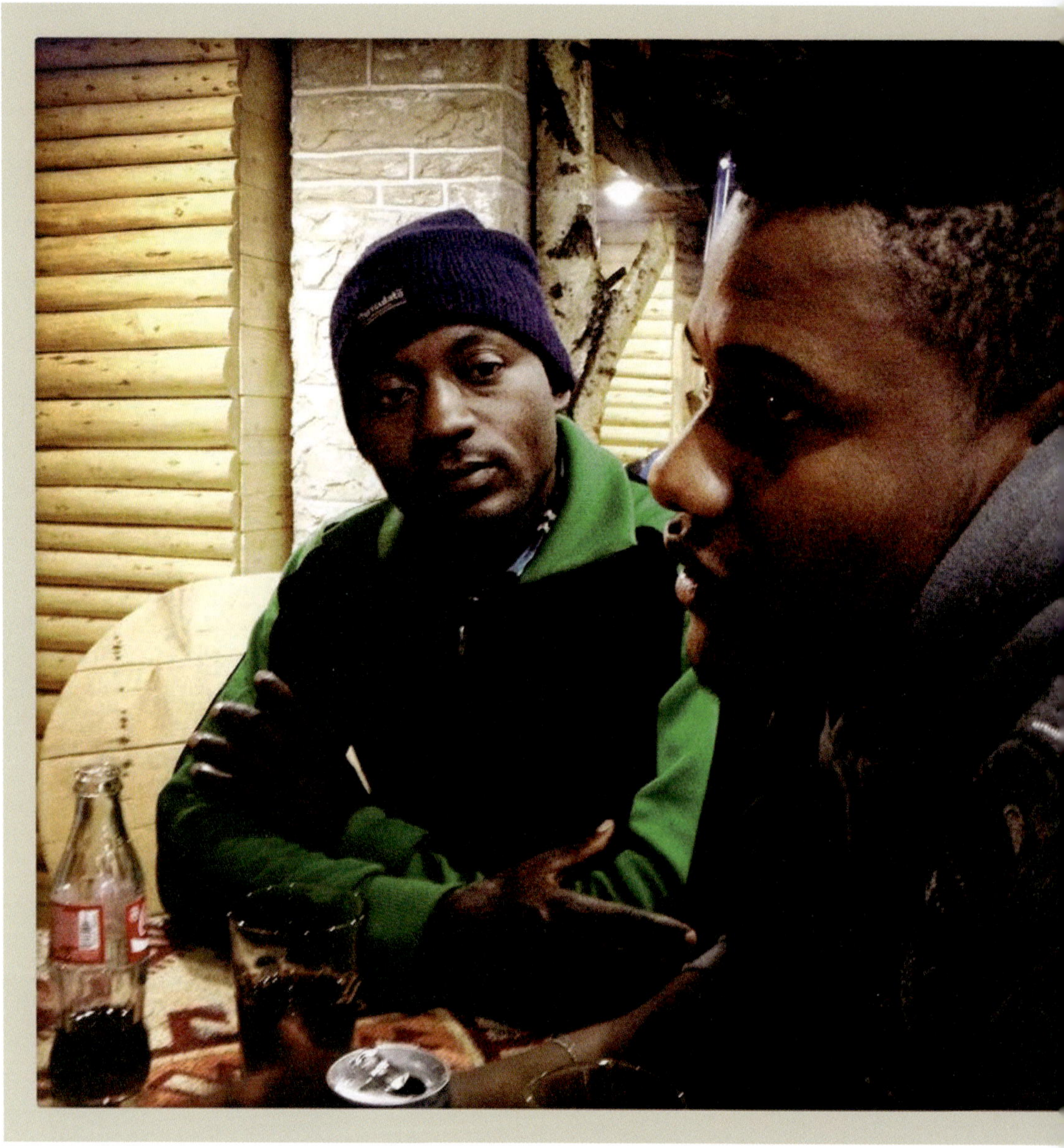

Stanley Akumbe (left) and unnamed castmate on the set of *Logbook_Serbistan* (on-set photo), 2014. PHOTO BY ORFEAS SKUTELIS.

GREG DE CUIR JR

Black Soil

Prescript

Carbon has often been referred to as the king of the elements. It is a nonmetallic element, part of group 14 of the periodic table, atomic number 6, with a melting point of 3,550°C (6,420°F) and a boiling point of 4,827°C (8,721°F). In 1961, the isotope carbon-12 was selected to replace oxygen as the standard relative against which the atomic weights of all the other elements are measured. Like any good leader should, carbon stands as an instructive model to its peers, ruling by a right ascribed to it collectively in a manner that uplifts the community it both serves and is a part of.

Carbon is king because it forms more compounds than all the other elements combined. Furthermore, it is the second most abundant element in the human body by mass (about 18.5 percent), after oxygen. Indeed, carbon is one of the few elements known since antiquity. In the nineteenth century, most of the known carbon compounds were considered to have originated in living organisms. However, elemental carbon exists in several forms, each of which has its own physical characteristics and its own particular applications.

There is about 60 percent carbon in the substance humus. Humus is nonliving, finely divided organic matter in soil, derived from microbial decomposition of plant and animal substances. Though a nonliving substance, it grants life. As it decomposes, its components transform into forms usable by plants. As such, it is valued by farmers and gardeners. Humus ranges in color from brown to black. One might venture the hypothesis that the darker the color, the more nutritious and valuable the humus, but this would be a position that needs further scientific substantiation.[01]

Chernozem contains a high percentage of humus, anywhere from 4 to 16 percent, which makes chernozem a very fertile grassland soil that can produce high agricultural yields. In the nineteenth century, legends of the fabled fertility of chernozem and the ease of cultivating it were widespread. It was described as a peculiar soil, and today it still remains something of a wonder, even if we can elaborate its qualities and values with scientific facts.

There are only two chernozem belts in the world, and one of them is the Eurasian Steppe. Research into this storied natural substance began during a formative stage of soil science, with most attributing the identification and classification of chernozem to the Russian geologist and geographer Vasily Dokuchaev in 1883. Dokuchaev considered soil to be "a natural body having its own genesis and its own history of development, a body with complex and multiform processes taking place within it."[02] Indeed, Dokuchaev is commonly regarded as the father of soil science, in no small part due to his visionary and anthropomorphizing conception of soil. But there was another scientist who preceded Dokuchaev and whose thesis laid the foundation for these subsequent findings.

01 Data on carbon and humus derived from www.britannica.com.

02 N.A. Krasilnikov, "Soil Microorganisms and Higher Plants," 1958, Soil & Health Library, https://soilandhealth.org/wp-content/uploads/01aglibrary/010112.krasilnikov.pdf.

The Austrian subject Franz Josef Ruprecht was invited to Russia in the early nineteenth century and offered a position as a botanical curator. The Eurasian Steppe soon captured his attention, and with it the fantastic soil that is characteristic of it. In 1866, Ruprecht wrote an influential article titled "Geo-Botanical Researches into the Chernozem." It is significant for its pioneering measures, as well as for introducing the term "geo-botanical." The title of this article also evidences the fact that the term "chernozem" was already in circulation, perhaps even long before Ruprecht mobilized it. It would have been commonly spoken by peasants, farmers, and any others who worked the land and were shaped by intimate proximity to it—for the Russian compound "chernozem" simply means "black soil," or what we might more metaphorically and inductively call "black earth."

★

The opening shot of *Logbook_Serbistan* (2015) depicts rushing floodwaters carrying away sediment and other detritus. The setting is the Southeast European floods of 2014, caused by the heaviest recorded rains in the region in 120 years. In particular, the setting is the Republic of Serbia, with two men who seem to be travelers standing over the rushing waters and watching in amazement.

The Non-Aligned Movement was formally established in 1961 in Belgrade, then part of the Socialist Republic of Serbia, within the Socialist Federal Republic of Yugoslavia. The states that belonged to this movement were not aligned on a geopolitical scale with either of the two dominant powers that then existed: the United States of America and the Union of Soviet Socialist Republics. One might call the Non-Aligned Movement a de facto conference linking together the Global South, and therefore consolidating a majority of peoples of color in the world. African countries were founding members of the Non-Aligned Movement, and all except two African nations are currently members. President Josip Broz Tito of Yugoslavia had always felt a certain affinity to Africa. As a bona fide political renegade, rarely was Tito invited on official state visits to either the US or the USSR. However, he was invited to numerous African nations, traveled extensively on the continent, and always had the red carpet rolled out for him. Among the original principles of the Non-Aligned Movement were mutual respect, equality, and peaceful coexistence. Though the principles remain the same today, they are not always put into practice, particularly in the territory of former Yugoslavia, not to mention the rest of Europe.

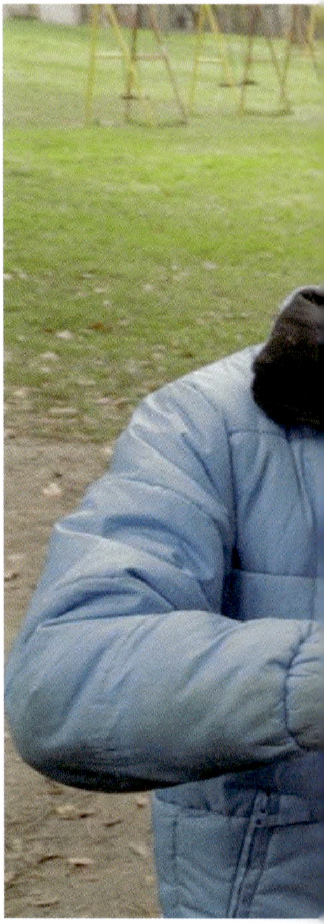

Logbook_Serbistan (film still), 2015

The artist Želimir Žilnik was also forged in the early 1960s, coming of age at a moment when Yugoslavia was ascending. In practical terms, this meant he was afforded the leisure to study law while also working as the chief organizer of the cultural center Youth Tribune in his hometown of Novi Sad. And while he was engaged in these parallel activities, he showed an interest in the art of cinema, got involved in Kino Klub Novi Sad, and began making

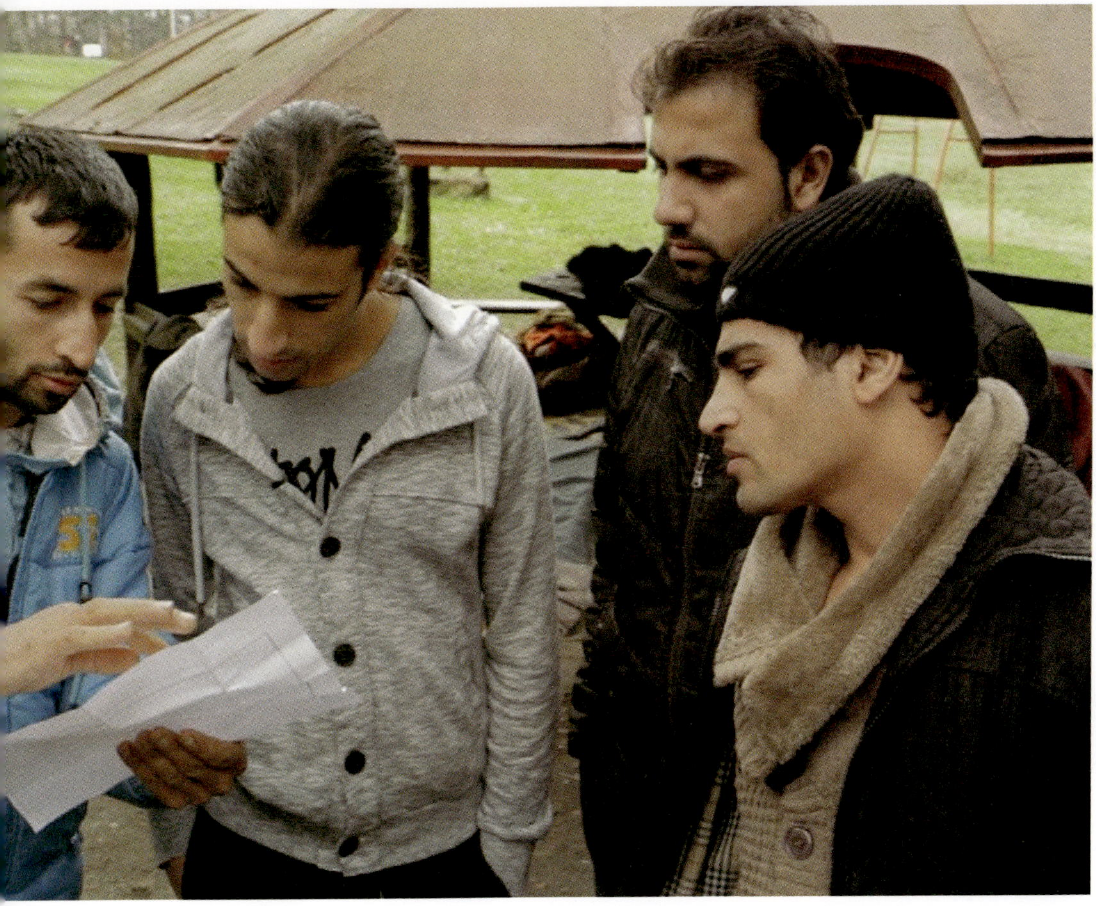

nonprofessional, nonconformist short films, which soon led to an opportunity to make professional films. One of the added bonuses of the Non-Aligned Movement was a freer flow of international citizens to and from Socialist Yugoslavia, which brought with it a freer flow of ideas and cultures. It was not uncommon for Žilnik to rub shoulders with students from all over Africa and other Non-Aligned countries as well. Therefore, his disposition was seeded by political ideals that valued the "other," that in fact thrived on close contact and cross-cultural networks of support and exchange. This cultural value was also at the core of Socialist Yugoslav identity, just as it was central to the earlier values of the region that predated the two twentieth-century Yugoslavias, spanning the nineteenth century and stretching back even further, through the Hapsburg and Ottoman Empires all the way to the sixth century, when various Slavic tribes migrated onto the Pannonian Plain, which was a province of the Roman Empire at the time of the birth of Christ and named after Pan, the god of nature.

The two men standing on the bridge over troubled waters in *Logbook_Serbistan* are two African migrants trying to come to terms with what the floods mean for the prospects of living in Serbia, both for them and the citizens of the state. This visual symbolism might be read as insensitive, with migrant flows into Europe often cruelly defined as waves or swarms or surges—all reminiscent of biblical-scale calamities. But Žilnik upends this punitive symbolism and uses it instead as a pathway to something that has concerned him throughout his career: collective labor. Even more specifically, cross-cultural transnational labor. The next section in the film is an extended wordless sequence that depicts the work done to salvage homes ruined in the floods and to clear out debris so that reconstruction can begin. One of the African men on the bridge, Lee, who becomes one of the protagonists we follow closely throughout the film, can be seen participating in the labor along with his coworkers, among them Serbians and migrants from Africa and the Middle East.

We might pause here on this early sequence and savor the vision it offers. It evokes the golden age of the Non-Aligned Movement, also the heyday of the mythologizing of collective labor. We also see a snapshot of how a modern Europe can and perhaps must work: various races, ethnicities, nations, and faiths bonding together to build a new and more humane society, a better society built on the mutual affordances that were agreed to more than half a century earlier in Belgrade when non-alignment as political practice was first consolidated. This sequence might be one of the more utopic that Žilnik has ever created. But like many of the sequences in his oeuvre, it is handled with not a trace of exaggeration, either aesthetic or emotional. The sequence instead becomes a matter of fact, of rational conclusion. This is how the world should work—maybe even this is how the world did work at one point. Certainly, this is how Žilnik's world worked—for a brief spell. His cinema operates this way because he carries the pieces of his former world and all that it stood for within him. That world may have failed him on more than one occasion, but he is an artist who never lost his faith. Perhaps this is in fact what makes him an artist in the first place.

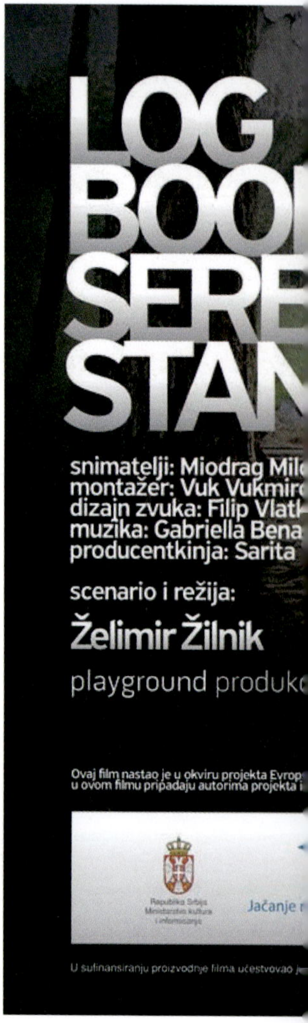

Logbook_Serbistan (poster), 2015. DESIGNED BY NIKOLA BERBAKOV.

There has been no shortage of works of art, including films and videos, dealing with the migrant situation in Europe in the last five years. Some of these works win awards and other forms of cultural capital for their makers. Some of them have large budgets and attractive effects that call attention either to the brilliance of the creator or the sturdiness of their engaged stance. Few, however, can make a film like *Logbook_Serbistan*, in which migrants as points of focus are treated as participants in the transgression of the border between fiction and documentary, which is also a transgression of hegemonic principles, and a transgression of the myth of the single genius auteur. The generosity that characterizes Žilnik's work is evident in the way he portrays both the travelers passing through the Balkan corridor and those they encounter along the way. Žilnik's relation to his subjects, and his relation to the ethical trappings of genre, can be seen in the closing sequence of the film, in which we also see the benevolent hand of the director.

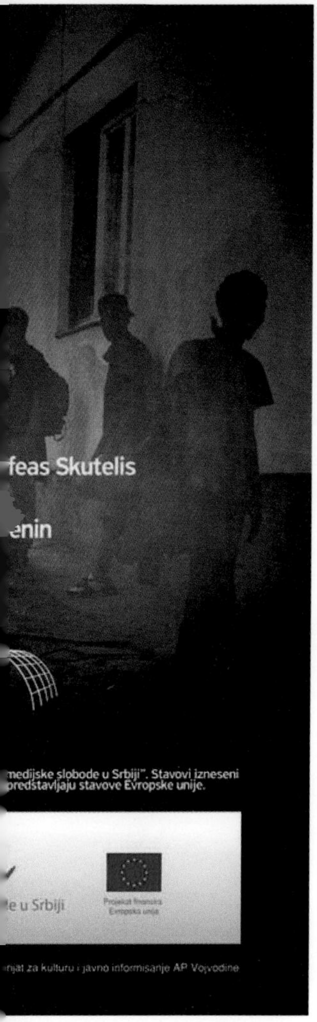

Plenty of ink has been spilled on the ethics of documentary intersecting with its interventionist capacities. The debate as to whether directors should step from behind the camera to insert themselves into the lives of their subjects—usually while at a crossroads, when good deeds are in short supply, and thus fracturing the seamless representation that is being constructed—is still relevant and unresolved. For Žilnik, as the old saying goes, this is where the rubber meets the road. He has always intervened. This is a moral position that is a luxury to be debated by those who do not put themselves on the frontlines, for whom the work is of more importance than the human material used. Žilnik approaches from the opposite direction. Near the conclusion of *Logbook_Serbistan,* when Lee and his traveling partner, Stanley, have come close to the Hungarian border—that is, the border of the European Union, which is the final destination for most—they come across a group of Middle Eastern migrants taking shelter in an abandoned building. They have been walking the treacherous Balkan route for days, and one of them has injured feet that will carry him no further. It is a difficult sight and also the climax of the film in some ways. After the two protagonists offer a few words of encouragement, a member of the production crew reaches into the frame to pass over an ointment to help heal the injured traveler's feet. This minor gesture has epic proportions for the politics of the film and its final effect, its embedded argument. It is a moment that comes with very little fanfare, not played for dramatic or reflexive effect. But it is one of the more consequential gestures in contemporary European cinema. This is the hand that Žilnik should be remembered by. Maybe it is even his own.

The film ends on an image of Stanley walking off into the distance, toward the Hungarian border and into an unknown future in the European Union. The television film *Black and White* (1990) opens with the inverse: a man from Africa, Reuben, is hitchhiking on a freeway on his way into Serbia, in particular to Novi Sad, where he was once a student and where he left behind a girlfriend. A direct result of the Non-Aligned Movement was that a large number of students from the Global South moved to Yugoslavia to study. Reuben is one example of such a student, and here Žilnik is interested in investigating how he is reintegrated into a society that he once knew but that in the final years of the 1980s, when he was last in Serbia, was transitioning into something else.

Black and White includes a scene where Reuben visits a Roma family and engages in a conversation about their background. They mention they have roots in Egypt and that President Gamal Abdel Nasser once asked President Tito if all Egyptians could be returned to their land of origin. Tito's response was no, because, as the family in the film states, the Roma are his finest and best people. Whether the anecdote is true, and whether Tito actualized this level of respect, is questionable. But the story is telling, as exaggeration often can be. There is a legend, a myth, a tradition of cross-cultural tolerance that was upheld in Yugoslavia, particularly the region Novi Sad is located within. People felt this ideology, relied on it, and even used it as moral and emotional support. Imagine a European country today in which the minorities genuinely feel that those in charge would never give them up, that they are the salt of that particular piece of earth, and that they will always have a home within the national borders in question. The irony of the situation is that the territory of former Yugoslavia, which once held a rich ethnic mélange, is now more bereft than other European nations that never before experienced such a movement of peoples and rebalancing of national demographics. There is an economic rationale to this social restructuring to be sure, and also political shifts, but as we look back with hindsight we can already hold up Socialist Yugoslavia as exemplary of the best collection of nations and ethnicities.

Again, something biblical can be sensed in this brief parable about Egypt, lost tribes, and the desire to reclaim people, to urge people to come home. In *Black and White,* people are not rooted. Reuben is constantly traveling. Likewise, Reuben's Serbian friend Saša has returned home to Novi Sad from London, but finds himself on the road again by the end of the film. Saša's father, Steve, abandons his home and spends most of his time on a *salaš*, or ranch, trying to reclaim a sense of who he is. Milena, Reuben's girlfriend, is banned from leaving home after her father discovers she is in a relationship with an African man. The homeless musician that Reuben and Saša meet sleeping under Steve's window also lives an itinerant lifestyle.

Salt was an extremely significant substance in biblical times, a symbol that surpassed most others. Salt fertilized soil, and it was also used as currency. The idea of people as "the salt of the earth" can be traced back to the Gospel of Matthew in the New Testament, the thirteenth verse of the fifth chapter, which has been translated as: "You are the salt of the earth, but if the salt has lost its flavor, with what will it be salted? It is then good for nothing, but to be cast out and trodden under the feet of men." That can be taken as a warning. Lose not the flavor, the variety, the beautiful differences in men and women, otherwise something elemental, something essential, has been forsaken. This is the subtextual message that Reuben's presence in Novi Sad carries, which is the message of Žilnik's film, which stands as a cautionary tale for the region and beyond, just like the verses from the Book of Revelation that Saša's friend cites to him and Reuben.

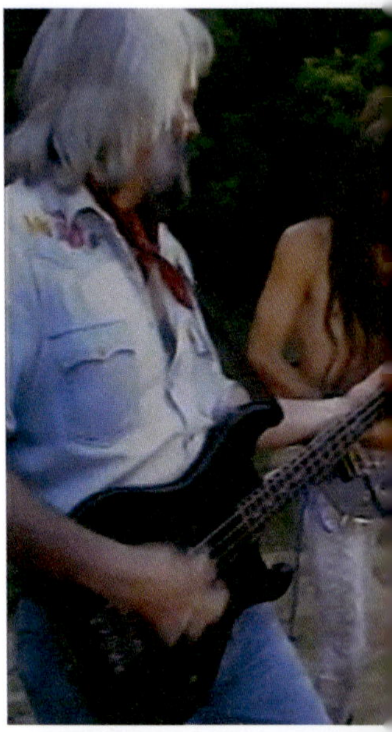

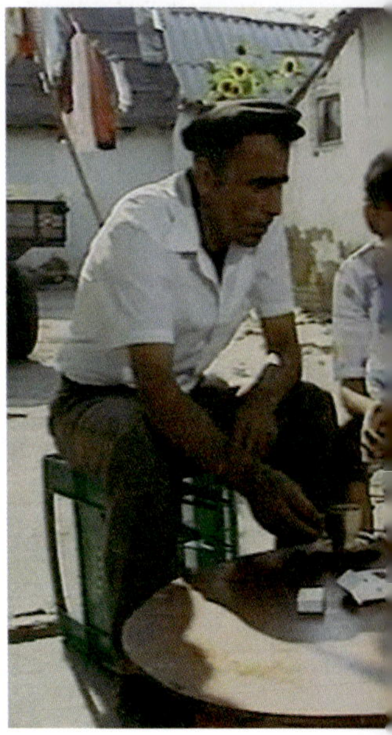

Black and White (film stills), 1990.

TOP Vladimir Janković-Džet (left) and bandmates.

BOTTOM Reuben Oyeyle.

In addition to the implicit argument for cultural exchange and close contact for the betterment of society, Žilnik makes a genre pastiche out of *Black and White.* The film opens and closes on the road and its characters are always in transit, and so the genre of the road movie is evoked, in which characters must follow a predetermined path but never actually reach their destination. The film also contains elements of the romantic melodrama, with forbidden love at the core and what seems like the entire world set against the two lovers. There is also the western, with remote settings away from

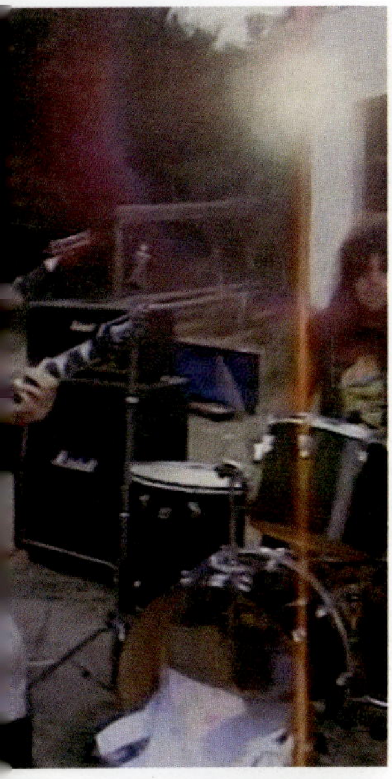

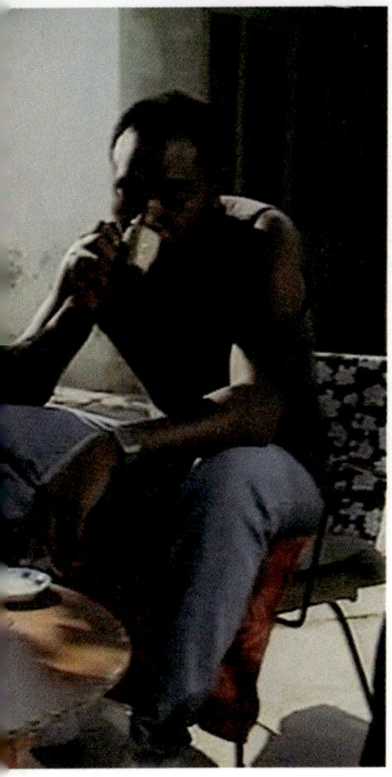

urban locales, horses, farms, and shootouts. The music of the film can also be seen as a pastiche or mélange. There are the African rhythms melded with African American spirituals that Reuben and his comrades play. There is the heavy metal that Steve and his band are involved with, and the rock music of his youth. And there is the iconic strains of Ennio Morricone and his scores for Sergio Leone's famous westerns. All of this creates a world in which cultures intermingle and thrive off of one another.

Saša's aforementioned friend, who turns religious after a life of sin, speaks about the end times, the last days, and the fires that follow. Later in the film, Reuben teaches the homeless musician the song "When the Saints Go Marching In." It is an old spiritual, as well as a biblical reference to the Apocalypse, with stars falling from the sky and the moon turning red with blood. These are not-so-coded warnings for the characters in the film, whose world is spinning out of control due to corruption, intolerance, and other deadly evils. This is not the famous, friendly Novi Sad but rather a region possessed by a sort of fever. If we follow the song "Paranoid," the structuring motif of the film, then we might get a better sense of the affliction sweeping the area. Steve and his makeshift band constantly rehearse this song by the group Black Sabbath. The lyrics speak to an unsatisfied feeling, about the need to pacify, about being blind to true happiness, and about it being too late to enjoy life. Black Sabbath's name recalls the title of Žilnik's film, but, once again, it also conjures biblical notions. The Sabbath is a day of religious observance, and also a day to refrain from work. However, when choosing it for their name, the band likely had in mind the secondary definition: a midnight meeting held by witches. This is the devil worship that Saša's friend fears, that he feels is indicative of the last days—and he is not far off in his prediction, as Novi Sad indeed proves to be an untenable proposition for all the characters in the film.

Black and White is very similar to *Logbook_Serbistan* in the way that borders are treated, in the way that internationalism is prioritized. Borders need to be crossed, though the prospects of finding happiness on the other side are dimmed in *Black and White*. *Logbook_Serbistan* offers the idea that the borders you cross en route, unexpectedly, might lead to more hospitable conditions than the ones demarcating your final destination. Internationalist outlooks are a source of paranoia in *Black and White*. When Saša tells his father that he can work as a DJ in London, Steve laughs in response and tells him he is crazy. When Reuben explains the value of his university degree to Saša, and that he can work anywhere, particularly because he speaks multiple languages, Saša laughs it off and tells him he is crazy. People are paranoid about the borders they cross—but they know they must cross them or wither away where they stand. The migrants in *Logbook_Serbistan* are much more idealistic about the borders they cross, despite the fact they face police repression, hate, and minimal opportunities at their destinations. Their belief that there is something better on the other side is what keeps them going.

Žilnik has always carefully noted this quality in travelers, rendering them in moving images accordingly. The internationalist stance of his cinema is indissociable from a humanist stance. Not black or white, but black *and* white.

In the city of Munich in Germany, there is a borough formed out of two districts: Au and Haidhausen. This borough was originally an area with accommodations for trade workers and day laborers. The Franzosenviertel, or French Quarter, is located in Au-Haidhausen, which receives its Gallic signification for the many streets named after the locations of victories in the Franco-Prussian War of the nineteenth century. This neighborhood is where the address Metzstrasse 11 can be found.

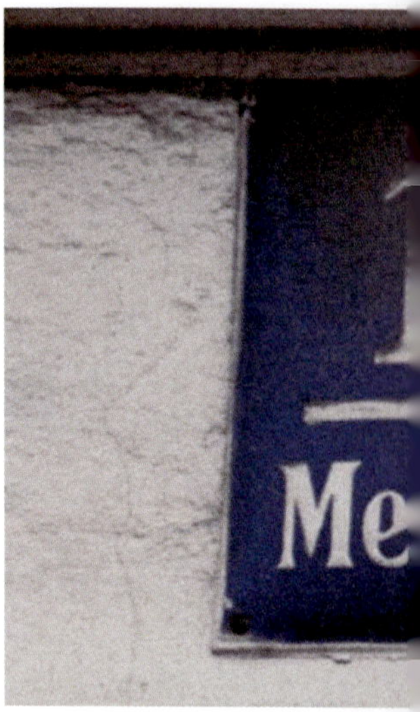

The film *Inventory* (1975) is just that: a cataloging of the occupants of the apartment building at Metzstrasse 11. It is a short, structural, minimalist documentary experiment for which Žilnik placed his 16 mm camera at the bottom of a staircase in a fixed position and allowed all the residents of the building to flow downstairs, pause, introduce themselves and their living conditions, and then continue walking down the next flight of stairs. This cataloging is significant because most of the building's occupants are *Gastarbeiter*, or guest workers, who have come from all over Europe to contribute to the West German gross domestic product and to earn some money to send to extended families back home.[03] There are Italians, Greeks, Turks, and Yugoslavs. They come from the south or southeast of Europe, and many of them speak of not earning much money or of having a hard time adjusting to life in West Germany. We might view this situation as the inverse of the Non-Aligned Movement, where there is no mutual respect or meaningful cultural exchange, only the hunt for capital.

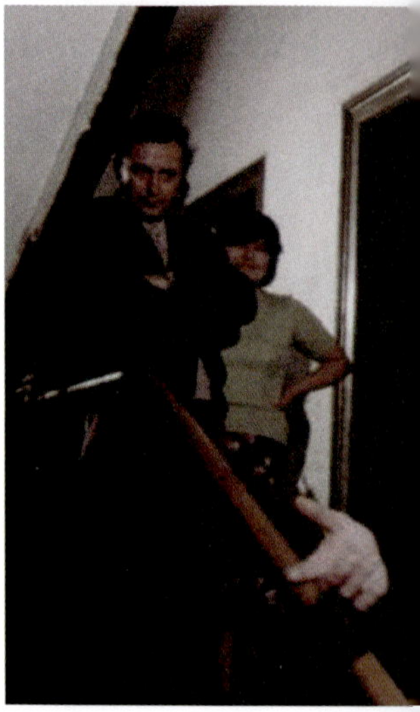

Elsewhere I have written that Žilnik uses his camera like a scalpel rather than a paintbrush, to excise and examine rather than to decorate. This aesthetic of social analysis can be seen clearly in *Inventory*. On the surface the film has a cold, surgical quality, heightened by the stringent formal position the camera assumes. But the accumulated effect of the film is a warm and very human argument for upward social mobility, for better working and living conditions, for the emancipation of the international working class.

We should note that the workers Žilnik trains his camera-eye on are usually considered European "others" or minorities and are often charged with being a drain on affluent, developed society and its resources. Žilnik has always sided with the marginalized, with those living on the outskirts as outcasts. Like President Tito told President Nasser, these are the best people, and he would not forsake them. Žilnik is also demonstrating here his solidarity and affinity for the full cultural spectrum of the world, for the cohabitation of those with different backgrounds, different experiences, and different worldviews. He knows that this elemental compound forms the salt,

03
The only exception are two young German-speaking women, one of whom introduces herself as an office secretary living in the building because she does not earn much and the apartment is inexpensive.

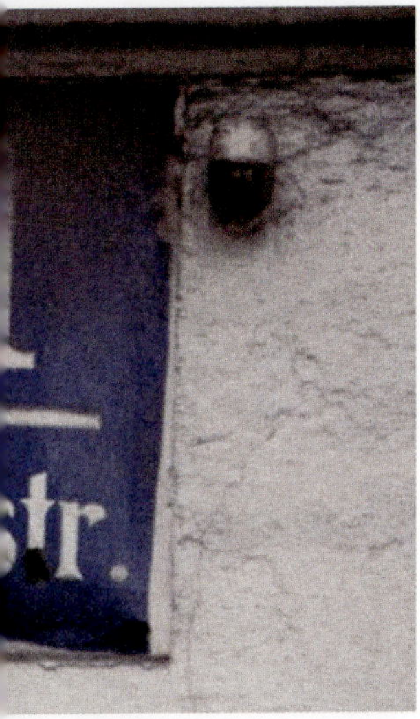

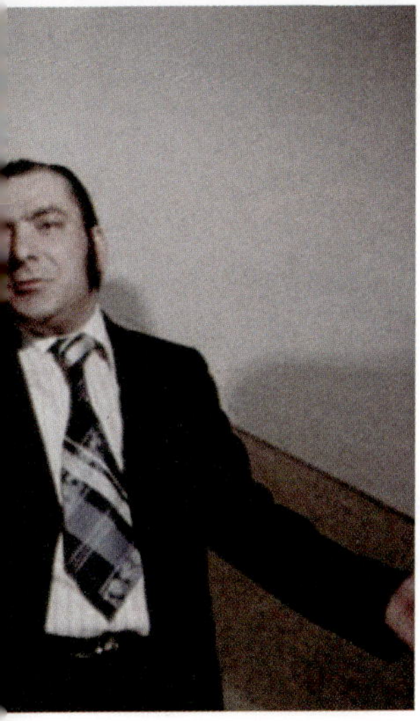

Inventory (film stills), 1975

the seasoning of the earth, and that anything less is a dangerous experiment in unnatural social engineering.

Inventory is also exemplary of Žilnik's internationalist artistic method, as someone who takes his camera across borders to aid and participate in liberation struggles. Žilnik shot a number of films in West Germany that soon put him into direct conflict with the state. These were ruthlessly critical films, always designed to uncover injustice—no different than the types of films he made in Socialist Yugoslavia before and post-Socialist Yugoslavia after. One can imagine that a film like *Inventory* could actually be made every few years, as a renewed attempt to take stock of the way we treat our neighbors, the way the economy works or does not work for those in the most precarious situations, and how people live when they cross borders in search of a decent existence.

The history and nexus of what has been called structuralist-materialist film has been drawn with tight borders around Western Europe and North America. Scant room in the canon is allocated to films that are non-aligned in relation to these cine-powers. The canon serves at the leisure of these powers, and it has often served as a weapon. The formal rigor of *Inventory* derives a great deal of its power from an adherence to a structuralist aesthetic. Jean-Luc Godard once called tracking shots a question of morality. For Žilnik, the placement of the camera and allowing the world to flow around and through it is the chief moral concern. Instead of tracking, he allows the people to create the movement in relation to the apparatus. In structural film, the camera often assumes an amoral stance, or an apolitical field of vision. Here Žilnik politicizes the experimental, because he knows that taking inventory is something more than an inert taking of stock. People's lives are at stake, and their integral qualities should be preserved, and so the camera must bear witness. However, Žilnik's is an interventionist cinema, not a neutral one. He picks his spots with care and orchestrates accordingly. The structuralism he evokes and analyzes is the structure of society, the structure of a building, the architecture of social relations. Form follows function, and the material he works with is the human subject, the souls of all types of folks. The old directors of the classical period were fond of saying that there is nothing more beautiful and mysterious, nothing so consequential, as pointing a camera at a human face. They were right, but they often only looked for a certain type of face, representing a certain type of experience, serving a certain type of viewer. Žilnik, in opposition, takes inventory of the full range of faces that in their variety and combinable nature constitute the beauty and wonder of the world. There is no world without these faces. And the director who does not open their eyes to them, who does not open the world to them, is no director.

Metzstrasse in the twenty-first century, more than forty years after Žilnik's film was shot, is full of trendy cafés and restaurants. It is just another increasingly expensive neighborhood in an increasingly

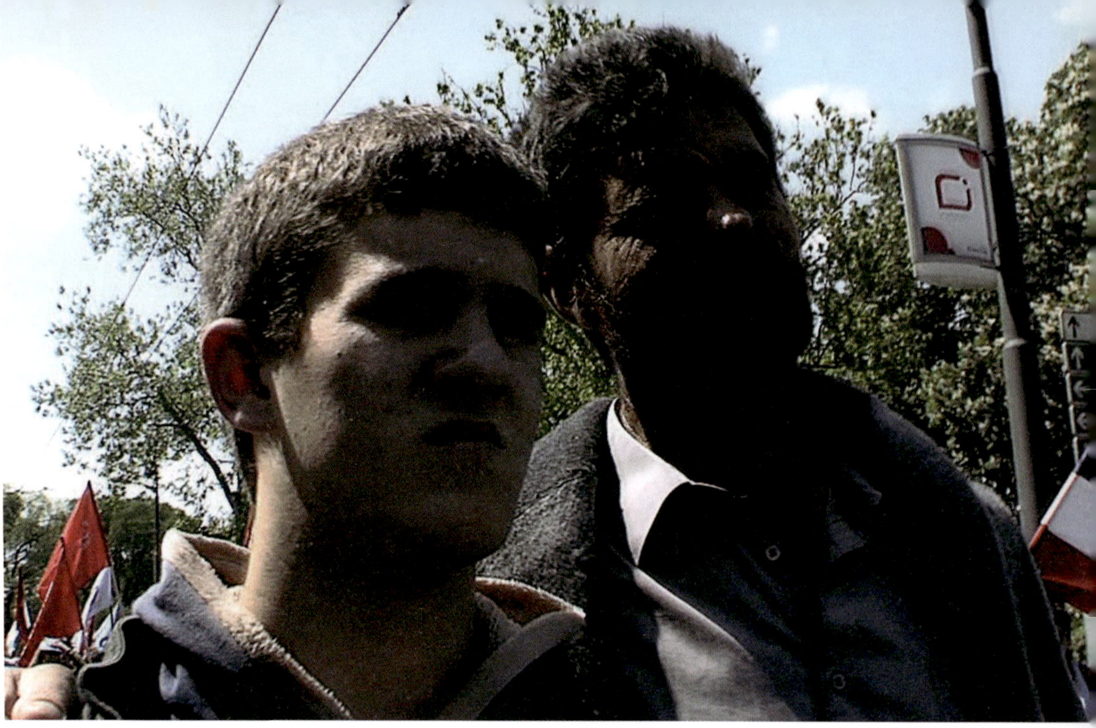

expensive Munich. It would be hard to imagine *Gastarbeiter* living there now. Max-Weber-Platz is right around the corner from Metzstrasse. The founding father of the discipline of sociology once wrote: "Modern capitalism has as little use for *liberum arbitrium* persons as laborers as it has for the businessman fully without scruples in the running of his company."[04] True indeed, but postmodern capitalism is a different beast.

★

Postscript

Vojvodina is an autonomous province in the north of the Republic of Serbia. The province measures 21,506 km², which is more than the area of either Montenegro or the Republic of Slovenia. Out of this land, 75 percent is cultivable, measuring 1,628,000 hectares. In fact, Vojvodina has the most fertile land in Europe. This is because of the heavy presence of chernozem that spans the plain.[05]

Because of this uncommonly fertile soil, Vojvodina has attracted immigrants throughout its history. Indeed, by its position and geographical structure, Vojvodina is a natural bridge between Central Europe, the Balkan Peninsula, and the Middle East. As a result, and by its national structure, Vojvodina represents a special ethnic phenomenon, perhaps unlike any other in the history of the continent. In the 2002 census, 2,031,992 people were recorded as residing in Vojvodina. For over 150 years, no ethnic entity has been in the majority, and only in recent decades have Serbs emerged as one in the province—and this happened only through the influx of refugees, as a byproduct of war and intolerance.

04
Max Weber, *The Protestant Ethic and the Spirit of Capitalism*, trans. Stephen Kalberg (1905; Chicago: Fitzroy Dearborn, 2001), 20.

05
Dragomir Jankov, *Vojvodina, the Ruination of a Region: Data and Facts* (Novi Sad: Vojvodina Club, 2005).

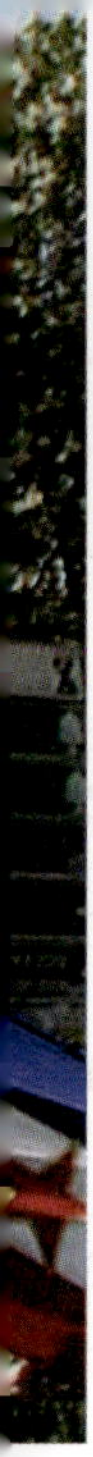

Zoran Paroški and Milan Paroški in *The Old School of Capitalism* (film still), 2009

For centuries in Vojvodina, official languages included Serbian, German, Croatian, Hungarian, Romanian, and Ruthenian, among others. It is said that the vitality of Vojvodina lies in its openness to an inclusive environment, where ethnicities and religions meld together as a polyvalent norm. This ingrained mentality of tolerance and the valuation of difference was achieved by many years of cohabitation. But it is not just that; it is something else, perhaps something indefinable on an elemental level, that makes Vojvodina the unique place it is.

It is likewise believed that Vojvodina represents a political concept rather than a geographical one. That concept might be considered a prototype for the principles of non-alignment, indeed as a prototype for the various Yugoslavias that have existed; yet they have all fallen, and Vojvodina still stands. This latent political potential might be symbolized by the name given to Vojvodina's capital city: Novi Sad, or Neuestadt, or Neoplanta, or New Seed.

Every botanist knows that "a species can live and reproduce far from its place of origin."[06] Anthropologists know the same. Sociologists know that, in some cases, peoples and nations must thrive far from their roots. And political scientists know that those unique cases and their rationales are the locomotives of history. Artists should and must know that this spiritual and physical movement of peoples and cultures is a strength, an opportunity to shape the world for the better, and a method for truly knowing your fellow human beings, which means truly accepting them for who they are, and maybe even standing up for them when no one else will. We might venture the hypothesis that the specific political concept that infuses the spirit of Vojvodina allows the autonomous province to cultivate artists who exhibit a correlating political consciousness. Europe would do well with more of these aesthetic phenotypes and the works they create. If only they grew as easily and abundantly as plant life on the Eurasian Steppe.

> These bodies always have their own particular origin; they always and everywhere are the result of the totality of activity of the bedrock, the living and inanimate organisms (plant as well as animal), climate, the age of the country, and the topography of the surroundings.
> —Vasily Dokuchaev[07] ★

06
Anastasia A. Fedotova, "The Origins of the Russian Chernozem (Black Earth): Franz Joseph Ruprecht's 'Geo-botanical Researches into the Chernozem' of 1866," *Environment and History* 16, no. 3 (August 2010): 271–93.

07
Vasily Dokuchaev, *Collected Works*, vol. 2 (Moscow-Leningrad, 1949), 260.

Greg de Cuir Jr has organized programs at the National Gallery of Art, Washington, DC; Institute of Contemporary Arts, London; National Museum of African American History and Culture, Washington, DC; Palais des Beaux-Arts, Brussels; Los Angeles Filmforum; Locarno Film Festival; Flaherty Film Seminar, New York; International Short Film Festival Oberhausen; Museum of Modern Art in Warsaw; Museum of Contemporary Art Vojvodina, Novi Sad; and Alternative Film/Video, Belgrade, among other institutions. De Cuir is Managing Editor of the journal *NECSUS* and Editor of the book series Eastern European Screen Cultures, both published by Amsterdam University Press. His writing has been commissioned by the Centre Pompidou in Paris and Institute of Contemporary Arts in London and featured in *Cineaste*, *Jump Cut*, *Millennium Film Journal*, *ARTMargins*, and other publications.

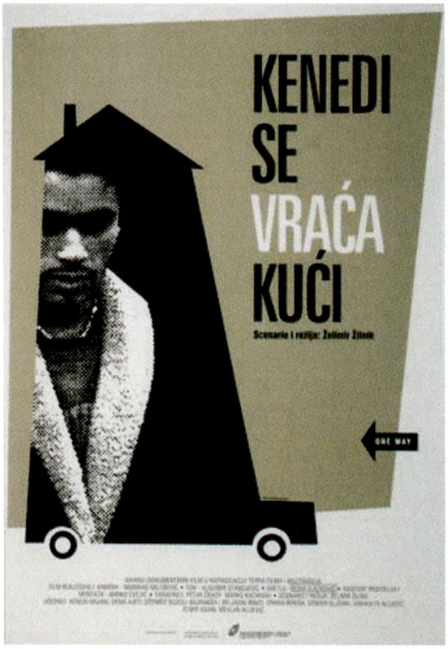

Kenedi Goes Back Home

Serbia and Montenegro • 2003 • 75 min. • DV to 35 mm

This is a story of Yugoslavs who left the country during the war and spent over ten years in Western Europe as refugees or in asylum. In the second half of 2002, the European Union sent many of these people back to Serbia and Montenegro together with their families, believing there was no longer any reason for their stay. Procedures for their return were usually very strict. Families were gathered during the night, transported to the airport, and sent to Belgrade on the first flight. To make things more dramatic, the majority of children born in Western European countries could speak and write the other language better than their mother tongue. As these families often had to sell everything they owned when leaving, they faced a situation back home where normal life was practically impossible.

Kenedi Goes Back Home follows two friends, Kenedi and Denis, as well as the Ibinci family from Kostolac, during the first couple days after arriving at Belgrade Airport. We see them trying to find accommodation and searching for friends and other family members. Kenedi goes to Kosovska Mitrovica, where his family used to have a house, to which he now does not have access. The film focuses on the position of the Roma people as the most vulnerable part of the returned population.

The making of this film began with research into the situation of children who were born or grew up in Germany and were now being forcibly deported back to Serbia. Žilnik filmed the kids as they sent regards to their former classmates, and when shown in public discussions and forums, this footage stirred public outrage. Žilnik was contacted by the German authorities and it came to light that the German government had given monetary support for each family to the Serbian government, but it never made its way to the deported families to assist their return. Consequently, Žilnik was not allowed at the airport to film the returnees, and by sending out a casting call for someone who spoke German, Serbian, and Romani, he met Kenedi, who could pretend he was at the airport to wait for relatives.

At the same time, Žilnik was contacted by the German Green Party, which sent five parliament members to Serbia to look into the embezzlement of the support funds for the refugees. When they visited expelled families and saw the dire situations in which they were living, the delegation asked Žilnik if he could put together a feature-length film to

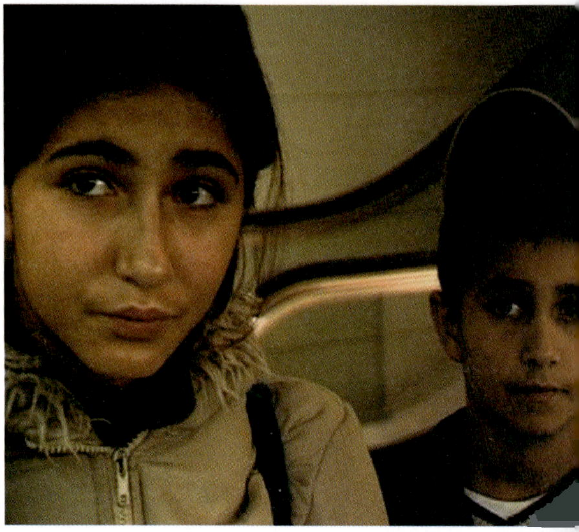

TOP LEFT *Kenedi Goes Back Home* (poster), 2003
TOP RIGHT Denis Ajeti and Kenedi Hasani in *Kenedi Goes Back Home* (film stills), 2003
BOTTOM LEFT AND RIGHT
Kenedi Goes Back Home (film stills), 2003

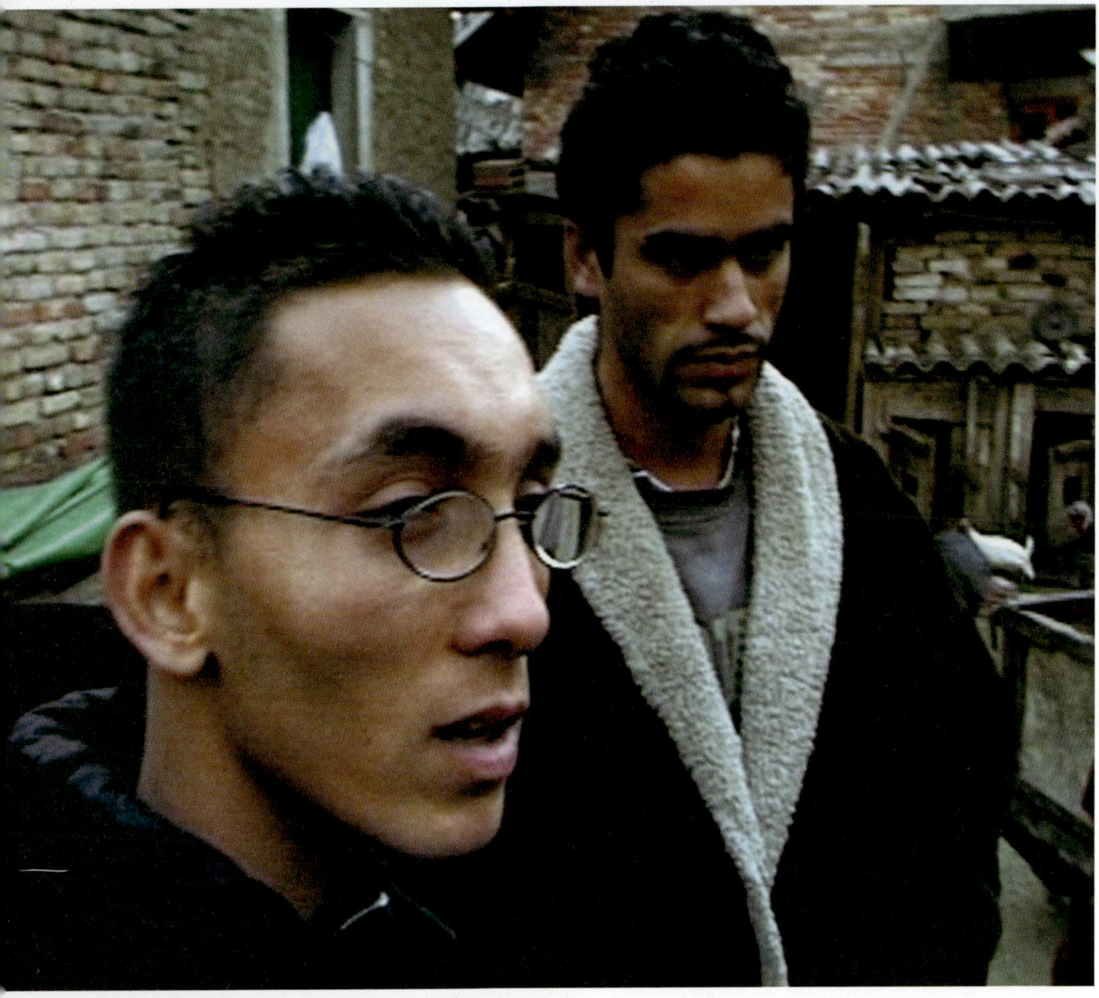

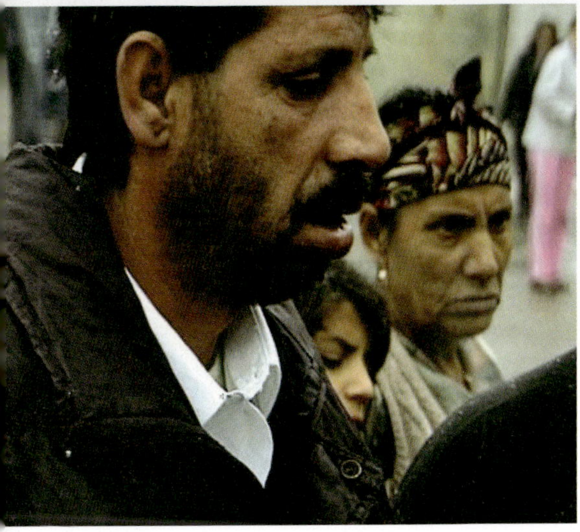

show at public cinemas in Germany. The Green Party held the opinion that good students and pupils should not be expelled from the country, as Germany needed educated workers. They paid for the production house Terra Film to produce a 35 mm print, and the film went on tour in North Rhine-Westphalia, Hessen, and Berlin. It stirred a lot of debate in the cities where it was screened, and even led to decisions in certain cities to stop the deportation of young people. The film was also shown in regional parliaments and at the European Parliament, as well as discussed at the Asylpolitisches Forum Deutschland. Žilnik went on to make two more films with Kenedi. ●

Žilnik's experimental attitude was an attempt to go beyond simple contradictions (usually manifested in the dichotomy between what was "official" and what was "dissident") and, following the logic set out by the "materialist dialectic"—to use this inverted term as it was originally used by Engels, which seems more appropriate than the "dialectic materialism" perverted by Stalinism—to locate symptomal opposites in material practices through which they may be set in motion and not left in their idealist contradictions.

—Branislav Dimitrijević, "Concrete Analysis of Concrete Situations: Marxist Education According to Želimir Žilnik," *Afterall*, Autumn/Winter 2010, 51.

žž: I think that the basic characteristic of that so-called public engagement you're talking about is in fact being chameleon-like. People sail under false colors, they present their earlier work under false pretenses, and keep on working on, driving this unfortunate people of ours insane. I'm sick when I see the people who, until recently, until two years ago, carried the flag of nationalism and whom we can consider to be the main culprits of spreading hatred and fascism, how they're attempting to make fools of us all, as if we didn't know that the beast being released from the cage is their fault too. In our public sphere, as has been common in the past decades, there's a lot of bragging and little referring to one's own work. I think that what is called our alleged public sphere is a big circus, and of course a horror similar to the circus and the horror of the official fascism.

[INTERVIEWER]: Don't you see an option you might possibly join?

žž: Well, what I see is, for example, the human rights movement. Anyway, I don't deal with anything else but human rights. In films, in TV programs—the experience of being hindered, again, in any way. Everything I've done was either not socialist enough, or not Serbian enough, or not Non-Aligned enough, or too Non-Aligned ...

—Želimir Žilnik, interview, "These Are Only Old Movies," *Nezavisni vojvođanski građanski list*, January 15, 1993.

The Old School of Capitalism (poster), 2009. DESIGNED BY ANDREJ DOLINKA.

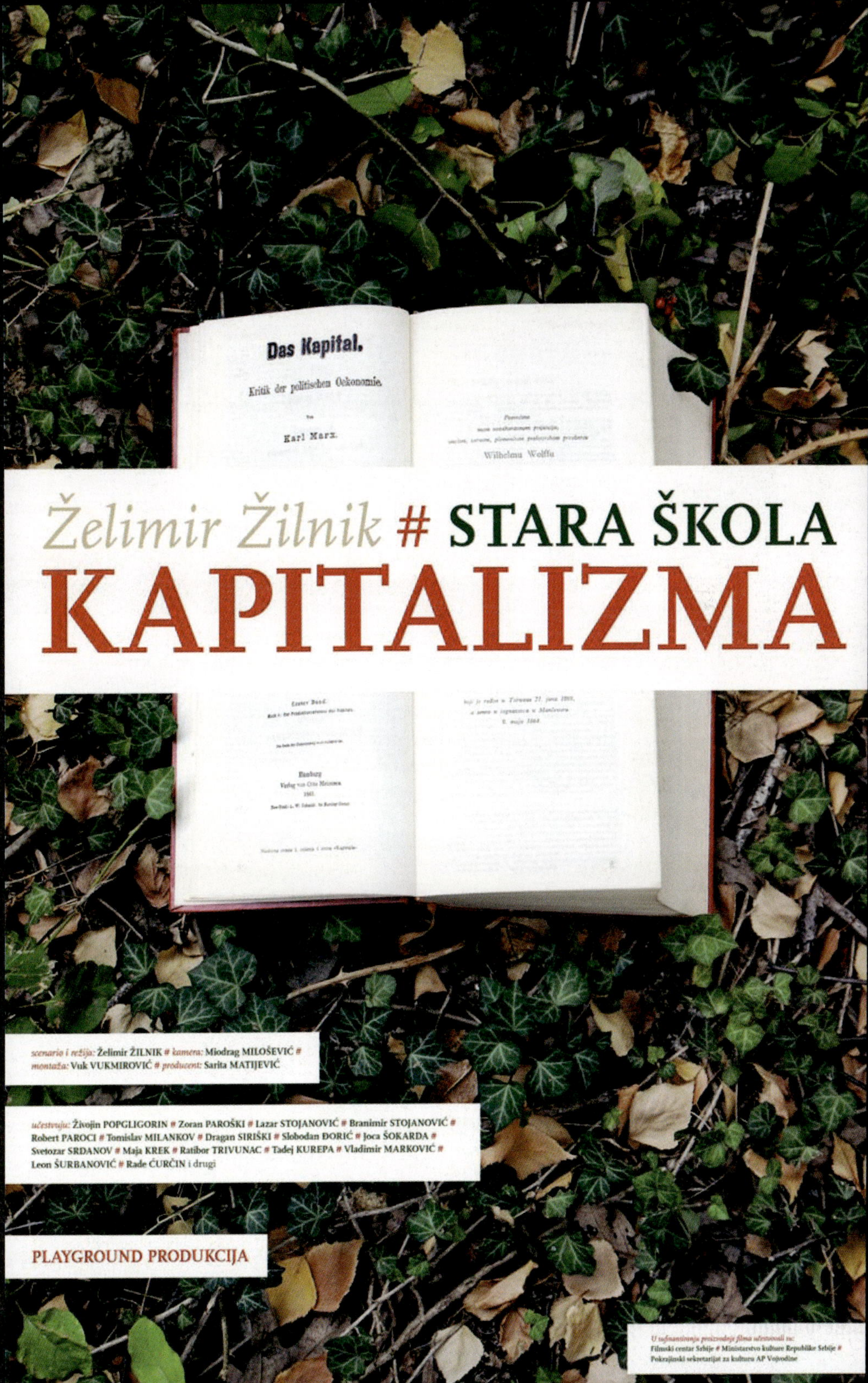
Das Kapital.
Kritik der politischen Oekonomie.
Karl Marx.
Wilhelm Wolff
Želimir Žilnik # STARA ŠKOLA
KAPITALIZMA
scenario i režija: Želimir ŽILNIK # kamera: Miodrag MILOŠEVIĆ #
montaža: Vuk VUKMIROVIĆ # producent: Sarita MATIJEVIĆ
učestvuju: Živojin POPGLIGORIN # Zoran PAROŠKI # Lazar STOJANOVIĆ # Branimir STOJANOVIĆ #
Robert PAROCI # Tomislav MILANKOV # Dragan SIRIŠKI # Slobodan ĐORIĆ # Joca ŠOKARDA #
Svetozar SRDANOV # Maja KREK # Ratibor TRIVUNAC # Tadej KUREPA # Vladimir MARKOVIĆ #
Leon ŠURBANOVIĆ # Rade ĆURČIN i drugi
PLAYGROUND PRODUKCIJA
U sufinansiranju proizvodnje filma učestvovali su:
Filmski centar Srbije # Ministarstvo kulture Republike Srbije #
Pokrajinski sekretarijat za kulturu AP Vojvodine

Biography

—

Želimir Žilnik

Želimir Žilnik (born 1942; living and working in Novi Sad, Serbia) has written and directed numerous feature and documentary films. From the very beginning, his films have focused on contemporary issues, featuring social, political, and economic assessments of everyday life (*A Newsreel on Village Youth, in Winter*, 1967; *Little Pioneers*, 1968; *The Unemployed*, 1968; *June Turmoil*, 1969; *Black Film*, 1971; *Uprising in Jazak*, 1973).

The student demonstrations of 1968 and the turmoil that followed the occupation of Czechoslovakia are at the center of Žilnik's first feature film, *Early Works* (1969), which was awarded the Golden Bear at the Berlin International Film Festival (Berlinale) and four prizes at Pula Film Festival that same year.

After facing problems with censorship in Yugoslavia during work on his second feature film, *Freedom or Cartoons* (1972, produced by Neoplanta Film, not completed), Žilnik spent the mid-1970s in Germany, where he independently made seven documentaries and one feature film, *Paradise. An Imperialist Tragicomedy* (1976). These films were among the first ever to touch on the foreign workforce, or *Gastarbeiter*, in West Germany, and they continue to be shown to this day at various retrospectives and symposia.

Following his return to Yugoslavia at the end of the 1970s, he directed a substantial series of television films and docudramas for TV Belgrade and TV Novi Sad (*The Illness and Recovery of Buda Brakus*, 1980; *Vera and Eržika*, 1981; *Dragoljub and Bogdan: Electricity*, 1982; *The First Trimester of Pavle Hromiš*, 1983; *Stanimir Descending*, 1984; *Good Morning Belgrade*, 1985; *Hot Paychecks*, 1987; *Brooklyn–Gusinje*, 1988; *Oldtimer*, 1989; *Black and White*, 1990; and others).

By the end of the 1980s, Žilnik was making films through a cooperative production structure of television and cinema, each work foreshadowing the growing tensions and looming political and social changes that were to affect the country (*The Second Generation*, 1984; *Pretty Women Walking through the City*, 1986; *The Way Steel Was Tempered*, 1988).

Turning to independent film and media production in the 1990s, he went on to make a series of feature and documentary films revolving around the cataclysmic events in the Balkans (*Tito among the Serbs for the Second Time*, 1994; *Marble Ass*, 1995; *Throwing Off the Yolks of Bondage*, 1996; *Wanderlust*, 1998). In 1995, *Marble Ass* won the prestigious Teddy Award at the Berlinale.

The breakdown of the system of values in post-transitional Central and Eastern European countries and the problems concerning refugees and migration in the new circumstances of an extended Europe became the focus of Žilnik's most recent films, from *Fortress Europe* (2000), to *Logbook_Serbistan* (2015), to *The Most Beautiful Country in the World* (2018).

Films by Želimir Žilnik have won numerous awards at national and international film festivals. Recently, his work has been the subject of major career film retrospectives at the Centre Pompidou, Paris, 2019; Cinemateca Argentina, Buenos Aires, 2018; Mar del Plata International Film Festival, 2017; Anthology Film Archives, New York, and Harvard Film Archive, Cambridge, Massachusetts, 2017; Ankara International Film Festival, 2016; Doclisboa, 2015; Arsenal, Berlin, 2015; Cinusp, São Paulo, 2014; Thessaloniki International Film Festival, 2014, and more.

Since 2010, his work has also been featured in the programs of art galleries, museums, and art institutes around the world, including documenta, Kassel; Venice Biennale; Institute of Contemporary Arts, London; mumok–Museum Moderner Kunst Foundation Ludwig Wien; Barcelona Museum of Contemporary Art; MACBA–Museo Universitario Arte Contemporaneo, Mexico City; and Museo Nacional Centro de Arte Reina Sofia, Madrid.

Most recently, in 2018–19, Žilnik's films and video installations have been featured in the programs of the Museum of Modern Art, New York; Renaissance Society, Chicago; National Gallery of Art, Washington, DC; Flaherty Seminar, New York, Edith-Russ-Haus for Media Art, Oldenburg; Lentos Art Museum, Linz; MMK–Museum für Moderne Kunst Frankfurt; German Historical Museum, Berlin; Arsenal–Institute for Film and Video Art, Berlin; and Galleria Nazionale d'Arte Moderna e Contemporanea, Rome, among others.

Alongside his ceaseless filmmaking and production work, Žilnik has been active in educational areas: since 1997 he has been a mentor and executive producer in many international workshops, in both Europe and the United States. ●

Dragana Đurić and Alenka Zdešar
on the set of *Freedom or Cartoons*, 1971.
PHOTO BY ANDREJ POPOVIĆ.

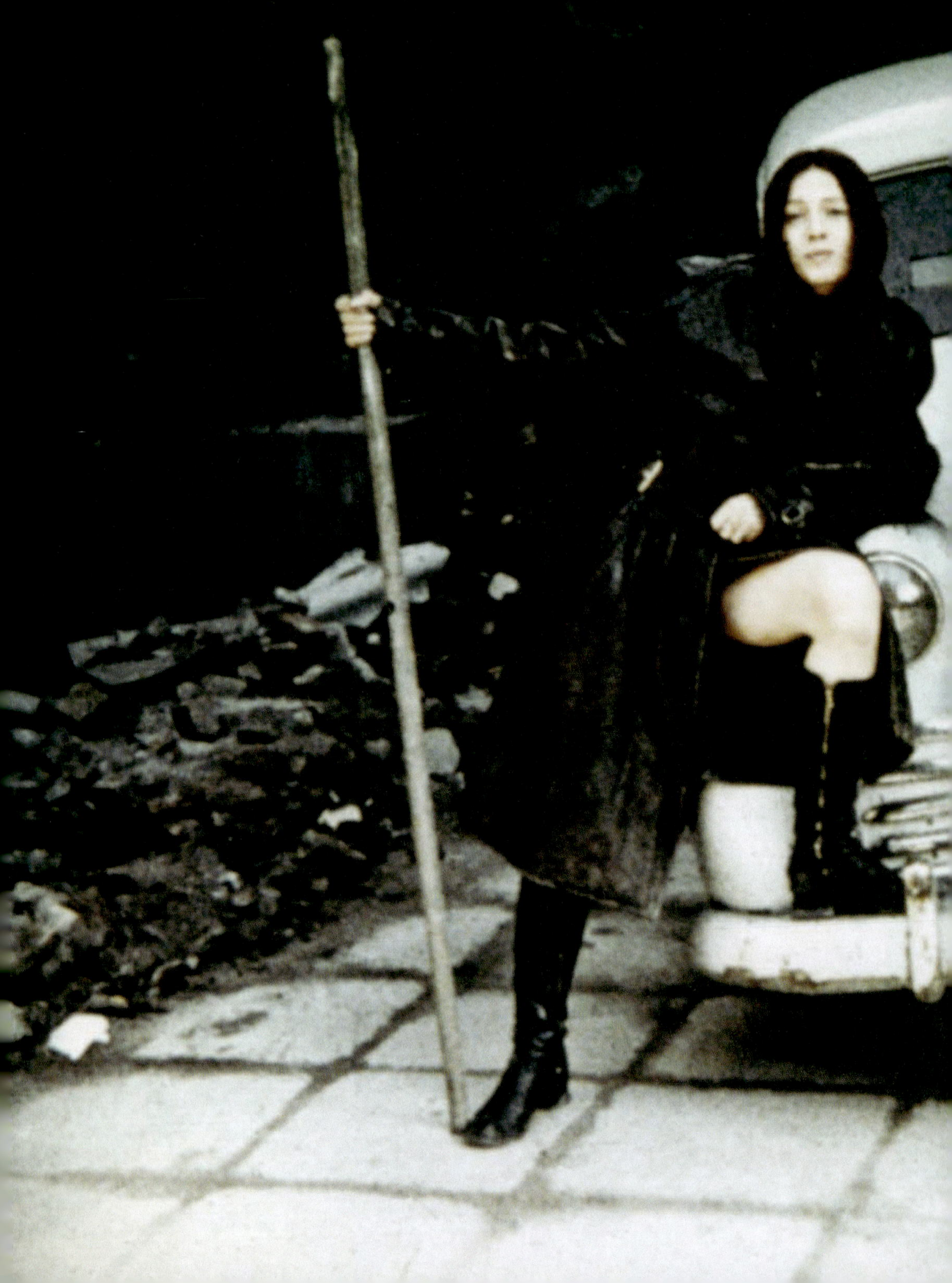

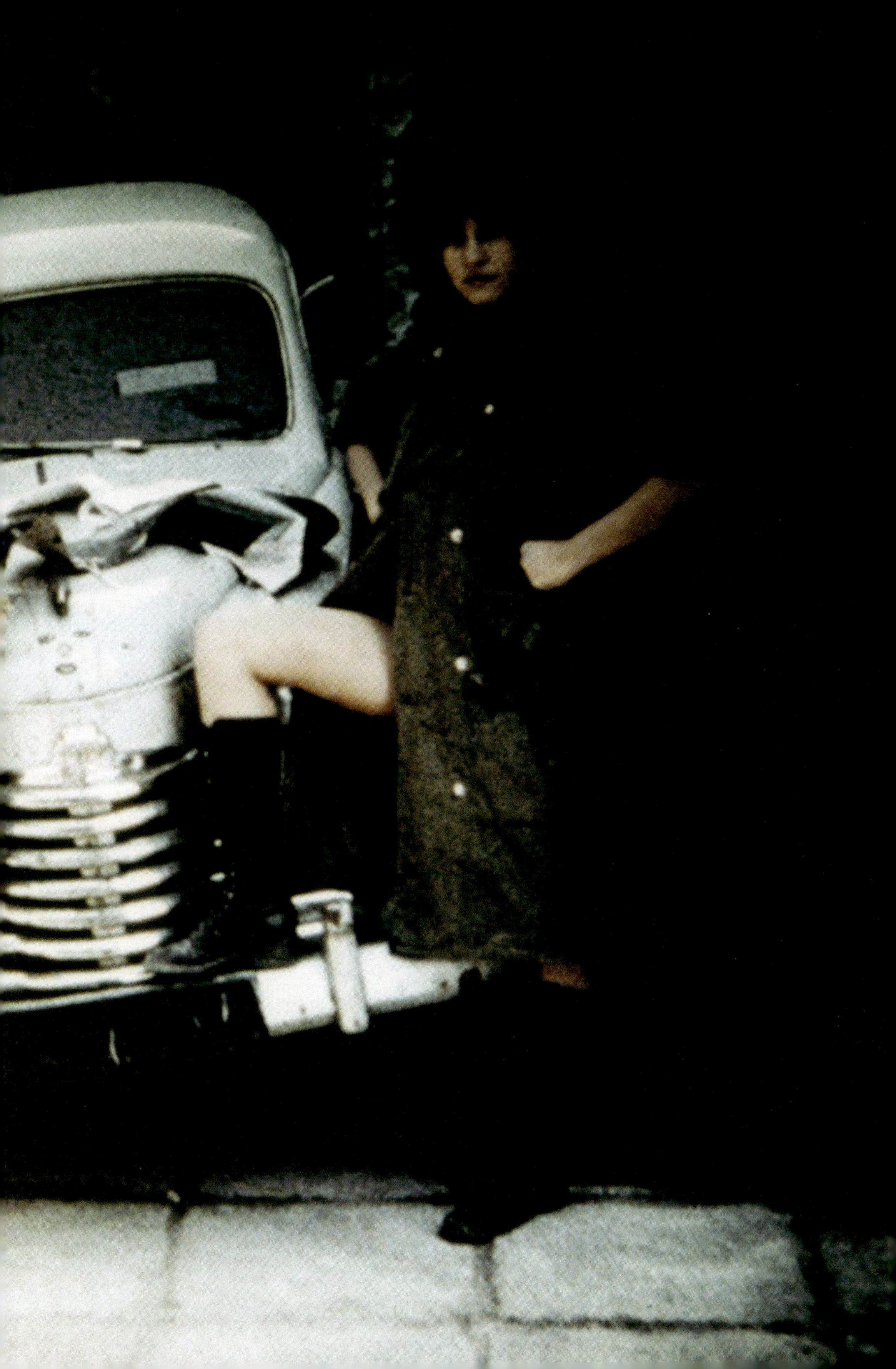

Around 1965 when I started collaborating with Avala Film the Yugoslavian system was in a process of trying to prove its distinction against the Soviet Union. The organizational structure of self-management, which until then existed only in the industrial field, was just introduced into the cultural policies. The system of self-management was extremely successful in the process of the reconstruction and industrialization of the country and this success gave us a critical energy.

Workers, who were part of that system, really felt [like] the co-owners of the factories; they believed they could really influence decisions made by directors. But we, filmmakers, were actually part of the free market since we were not employed. We were more outside of the system than in the system. We saw that all the benefits of the system—a permanent safe job, good pensions, [a right to] housing, [including that] workers would be given a flat in a new housing compound and a permanent tenancy—were diminishing the revolutionary potential of the workers and transforming them into socialist *kleinburgers*. The transformation of the country from year to year we had been witnessing was huge. And this is what we drew inspiration from.

—Želimir Žilnik, in conversation with Dubravka Sekulić, Gal Kirn, and Žiga Testen, in *Surfing the Black: Yugoslav Black Wave Cinema and Its Transgressive Moments*, ed. Gal Kirn, Dubravka Sekulić, and Žiga Testen (Maastricht: Jan van Eyck Academie, 2012), 60–62.

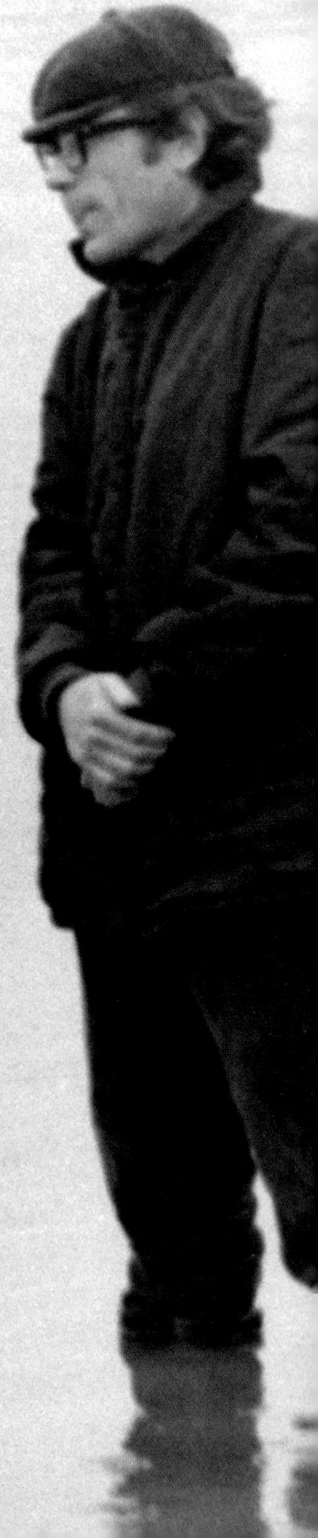

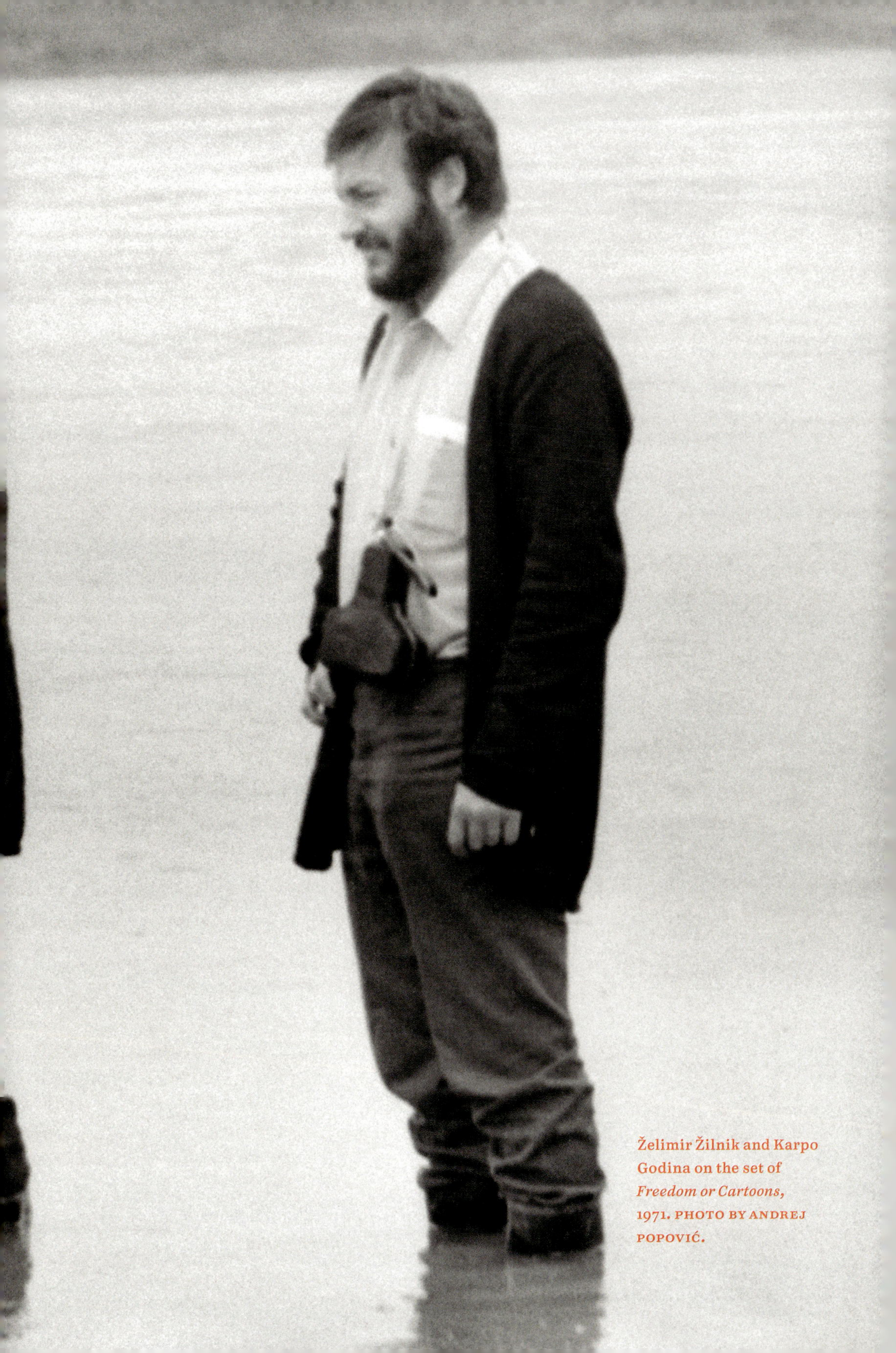

Želimir Žilnik and Karpo Godina on the set of *Freedom or Cartoons*, 1971. PHOTO BY ANDREJ POPOVIĆ.

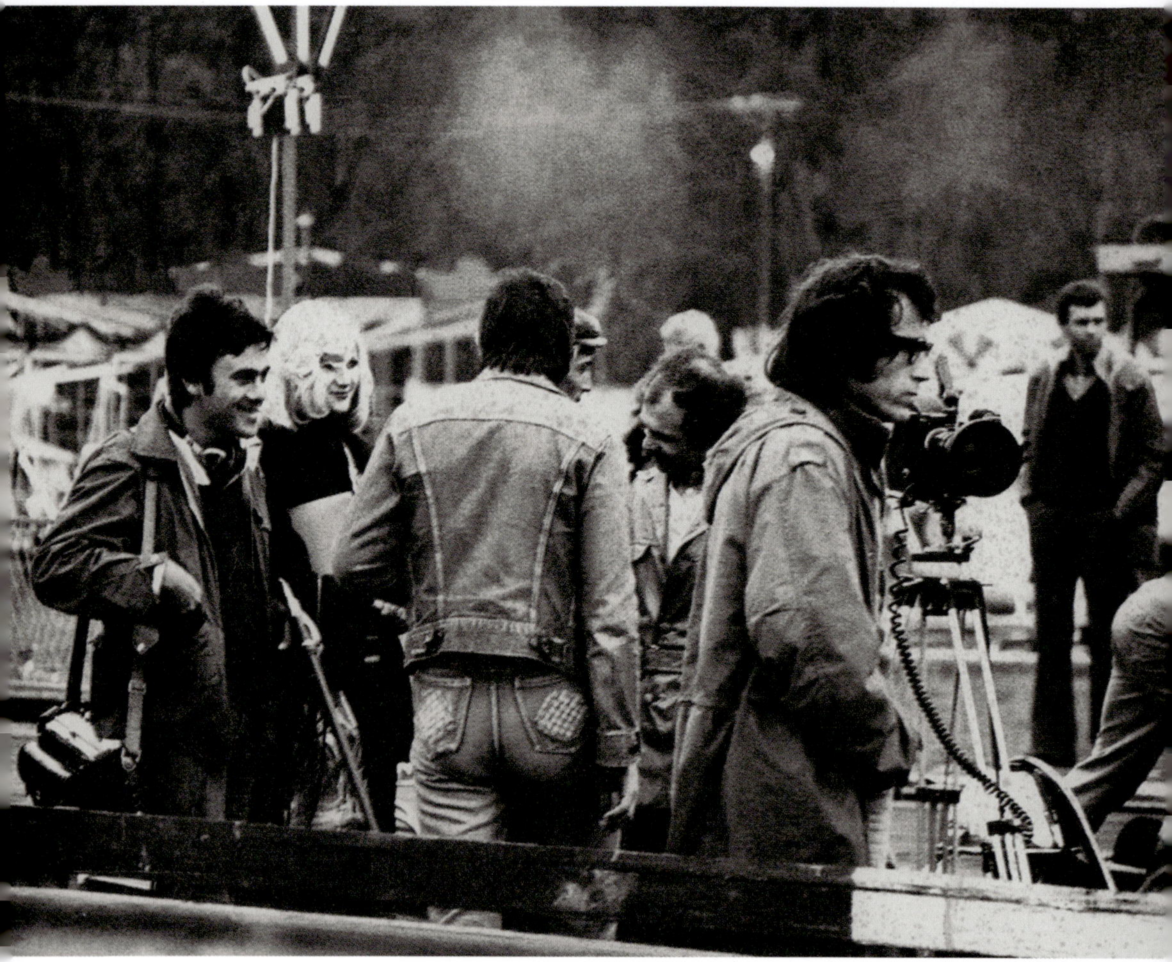

LEFT TO RIGHT Aleksandar Mitrović, Ljubomir Bečejski, and Želimir Žilnik on the set of *Market People*, 1977. PHOTO BY VLADIMIR ČERVENKA.

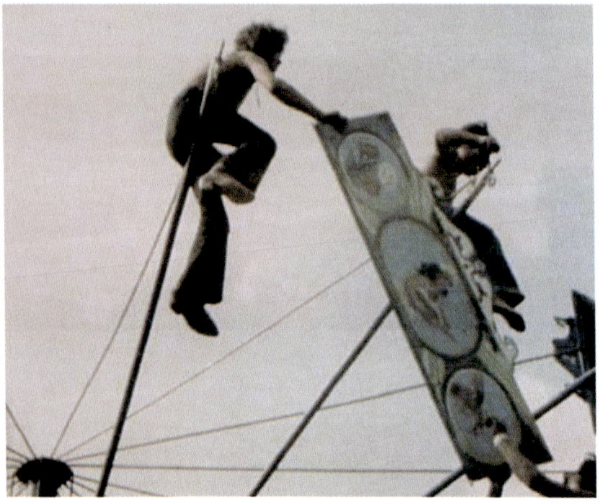

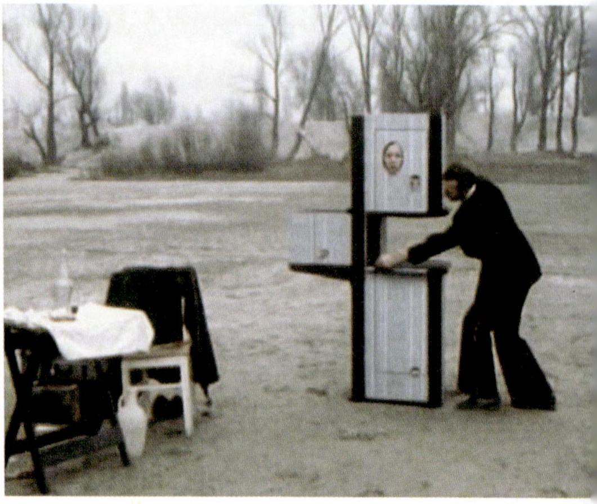

Market People (film stills), 1977

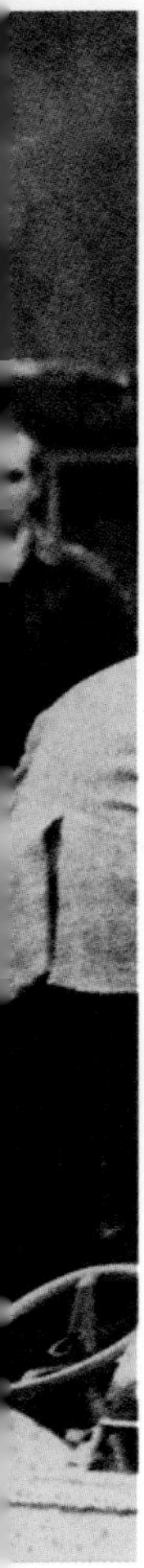

The television is a priori free of the mystifications of film work. Here [in Yugoslavia], a part of film mystification exists because people rub off on film. Each brick moved in a film has fivefold greater significance and cost. Spending on television is big—labor is valued more realistically. When we talk about film, we talk about the market, price, goods, turnover, while out of thirty-something films produced annually, only two, three, earn back a portion of the investment. If there were any economic thinking , the rest of the producers would have to go bankrupt. The law on a market this small should be: financial modesty, collaboration with television, and extraordinary investments only after possible commercial effects have been expertly verified. While here, dozens of filmmakers are sitting waiting for Hollywood spectacles!

Television is closer to a normal relation to life. [...] TV Novi Sad has fifty great cameras, thirty filmcutting boards, and that's a technical foundation a hundred or a thousand times stronger than the one camera at Neoplanta, around which there are hundreds of mystifications. Television has become the art of the widest masses, and it has also begun to deal with popular culture. When I had an opportunity to participate in television, I did it with an awareness of its possibilities, and I tried to participate in some aspects of that power. A man feels normal working on television. He knows that everything that is normal and good has already been broadcast on TV, and the very fact that he himself speaks means that he is an integrated man. Television has the possibility to constantly investigate the fundamental value of our society: diversity.

—Želimir Žilnik, interview, "Getting a Film Made Is Getting a Mandate," *TV Novosti*, May 14, 1982.

Filmography

1967
Žurnal o omladini na selu, zimi
A Newsreel on Village Youth, in Winter
15 min.
35 mm
Neoplanta Film

1968
Pioniri maleni mi smo vojska prava, svakog dana ničemo ko zelena trava
Little Pioneers
18 min.
35 mm
Neoplanta Film

Nezaposleni ljudi
The Unemployed
13 min.
35 mm
Neoplanta Film

1969
Lipanjska gibanja
June Turmoil
10 min.
35 mm
Neoplanta Film

Rani radovi
Early Works
87 min.
35 mm
Avala Film • Neoplanta Film

1971
Crni film
Black Film
14 min.
16 mm ➡ 35 mm
Neoplanta Film

1972
Žene dolaze
The Women Are Coming
12 min.
16 mm
Neoplanta Film

Sloboda ili strip
Freedom or Cartoons
unfinished
35 mm & 16 mm
Neoplanta Film

1973
Ustanak u Jasku
Uprising in Jazak
18 min.
35 mm
Panfilm

1974
Antrag
Request
10 min.
16 mm ➡ 35 mm
Vlada Majic Filmproduktion KG

Öffentliche Hinrichtung
Public Execution
9 min.
35 mm
Vlada Majic Filmproduktion KG

1975
Ich weiß nicht, was soll es bedeuten
I Do Not Know What That Should Mean
9 min.
35 mm
Vlada Majic Filmproduktion KG

Abschied
Farewell
9 min.
16 mm
Vlada Majic Filmproduktion KG

Inventur – Metzstraße 11
Inventory
9 min.
16 mm
Alligator Film

Unter Denkmalschutz
Under the Protection of the State
11 min.
16 mm
Alligator Film

Hausordnung
House Orders
12 min.
35 mm
Vlada Majic Filmproduktion KG

1976
Paradies. Eine imperialistische Tragikomödie
Paradise. An Imperialist Tragicomedy
90 min.
16 mm
Alligator Film

1977
Placmajstori
Market People
29 min.
16 mm
TV Novi Sad

Komedija i tragedija Bore Joksimovića
The Comedy and Tragedy of Bora Joksimović
30 min.
16 mm
TV Novi Sad

1978
Naše zvezde sa ekrana duševna su naša hrana
Stars of 45 Turning in Your Mind
10 min.
35 mm
TV Novi Sad

Sedam mađarskih balada
Seven Hungarian Ballads
30 min.
16 mm
TV Novi Sad

1979
Dobrovoljci
Volunteers
30 min.
16 mm
TV Novi Sad

1980
Bolest i ozdravljenje Bude Brakusa
The Illness and Recovery of Buda Brakus
98 min.
16 mm
TV Novi Sad

1981
Vera i Eržika
Vera and Eržika
75 min.
16 mm
TV Novi Sad

1982
Dragoljub i Bogdan: struja
Dragoljub and Bogdan: Electricity
85 min.
16 mm
TV Beograd

1983
Prvo tromesečje Pavla Hromiša
The First Trimester of Pavle Hromiš
87 min.
16 mm
TV Novi Sad

1984
Druga generacija
The Second Generation
87 min.
16 mm ➡ 35 mm
Art film • TV Novi Sad

Stanimir silazi u grad
Stanimir Descending
75 min.
16 mm
TV Beograd

1985
Beograde dobro jutro
Good Morning Belgrade
57 min.
16 mm
TV Beograd

1986
Lijepe žene prolaze kroz grad
Pretty Women Walking through the City
103 min.
35 mm
Art Film

Posrnule ovčice
Stumbling Sheep
46 min.
Betacam
TV Novi Sad

1987
Vruće plate
Hot Paychecks
103 min.
Betacam
TV Novi Sad

1988
Bruklin – Gusinje
Brooklyn – Gusinje
87 min.
16 mm
TV Beograd

Tako se kalio čelik
The Way Steel Was Tempered
101 min.
35 mm
Terra Film

1989
Stara mašina
Oldtimer
81 min.
16 mm
TV Ljubljana

1990
Crno i belo
Black and White
58 min.
Betacam
TV Novi Sad

1993
Silos Dunav, Vukovar
Silo Danube, Vukovar
1 min.
35 mm
Terra Film

1994
Tito po drugi put među Srbima
Tito among the Serbs for the Second Time
43 min.
Betacam
B92

1995
Marble Ass
84 min.
Betacam ➡ 35 mm
B92

1996
Do jaja
Throwing Off the Yolks of Bondage
12 min.
Betacam
B92

1997
Za Ellu
For Ella
10 min.
Betacam
Terra film

1998
Kud plovi ovaj brod
Wanderlust
91 min.
Betacam ➡ 35 mm
Teresianum b.t. • VP Kregar • Terra Film • Kvadrat • TV Crna Gora

2000
Trđava Evropa
Fortress Europe
80 min.
Betacam
Low Budget Production • RTV Slovenia

Cosmo Girls
27 min.
Betacam
Teresianum b.t.

2002
EXIT ujutru
EXIT in the Morning
12 min.
Betacam
Terra Film • Radio 021

2003
Kenedi se vraća kući
Kenedi Goes Back Home
75 min.
DV ➡ 35 mm
Terra Film • Multiradio

2005
Evropa preko plota
Europe Next Door
61 min.
DV
Terra Film

Gde je dve godine bio Kenedi
Kenedi, Lost and Found
26 min.
DV
Terra Film

2006
Dunavska sapunska opera
Soap in Danube Opera
70 min.
DV
Terra Film

2007
Kenedi se ženi
Kenedi Is Getting Married
80 min.
DV ➡ 35 mm
Terra Film • Jet Company VKTV

2009
Stara škola kapitalizma
The Old School of Capitalism
122 min.
DV & HD ➡ 35 mm
Playground produkcija

2011
Jedna žena – jedan vek
One Woman – One Century
110 min.
HD
Playground produkcija

2013
Pirika na filmu
Pirika on Film
54 min.
HD
Playground produkcija

2014
Naš čovek u Gabonu
Our Man in Gabon
66 min.
HD
Žilnik produkcija

2015
Destinacija_Serbistan
Logbook_Serbistan
94 min.
HD ➡ DCP
Playground produkcija

2018
Among the People: Life & Acting
83 min.
HD
Žilnik produkcija, Edith-Russ-Haus for Media Art

The Most Beautiful Country in the World
101 min.
HD ➡ DCP
nanookfilm • Tramal Films • Factum • RTV Vojvodina

2019
Où en êtes-vous, Želimir Žilnik?
Where Do You Stand Today, Želimir Žilnik?
20 min.
HD ➡ DCP
Playground produkcija • Centre Pompidou

EDITORS' NOTE: The English film titles listed here are the international distribution titles.

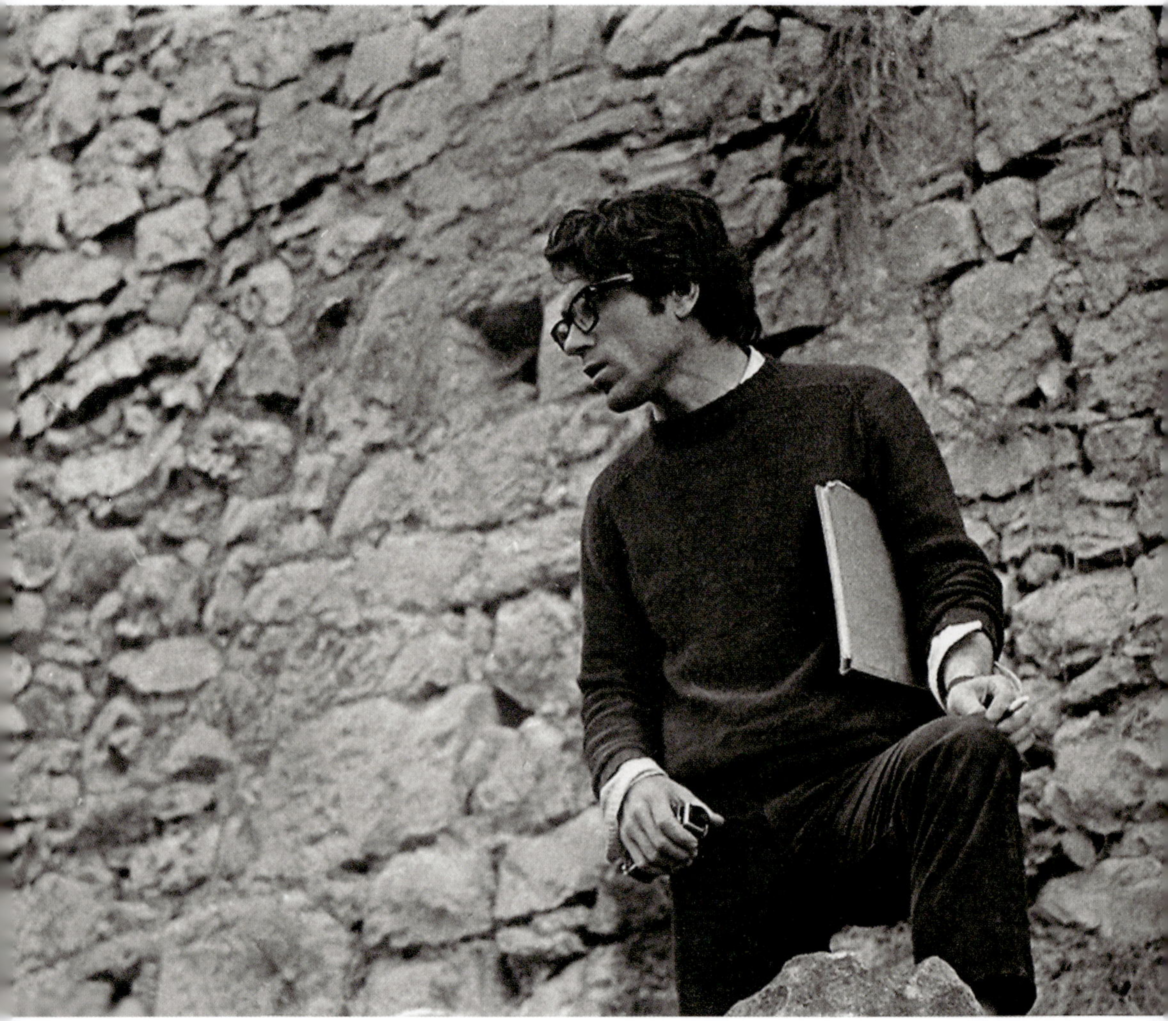

Želimir Žilnik on the set of *Freedom or Cartoons*, 1971.
PHOTO BY ANDREJ POPOVIĆ.

Those authorities of ours, which we usually find incompetent, were utterly successful in one thing—the endeavor to spill the blood of the nationalities [that comprised] the region of former Yugoslavia. In my opinion, it was manufactured hatred, and the process began years before the war broke out. We were undergoing the horrors of late fascism, when nation-states were created in a war effort headed by the [various] tribes' elders. The fact is that, only when I come to Croatia can I speak the language that you understand, just like you understand my films. These nations have so much in common that even that love and that hatred resemble some family fights, which can be very brutal.

—Želimir Žilnik, interview, "From Early Works to Late Wars," *Zarez*, April 7, 2000.

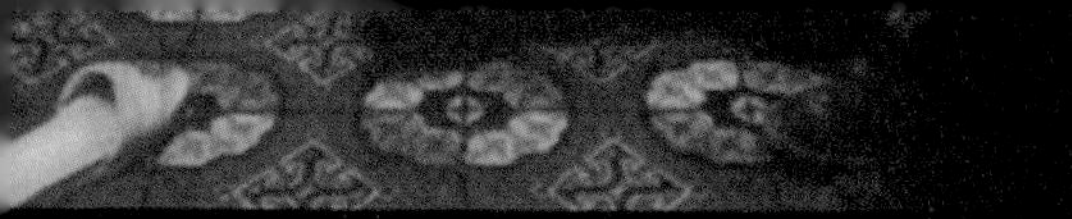

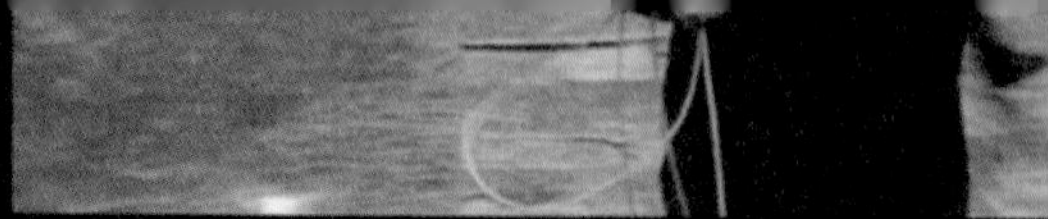

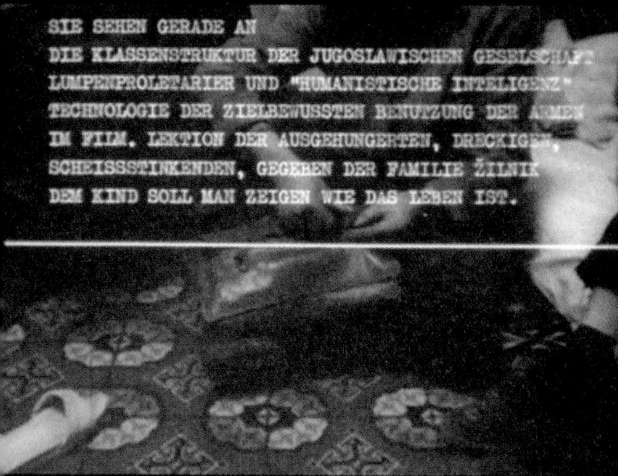

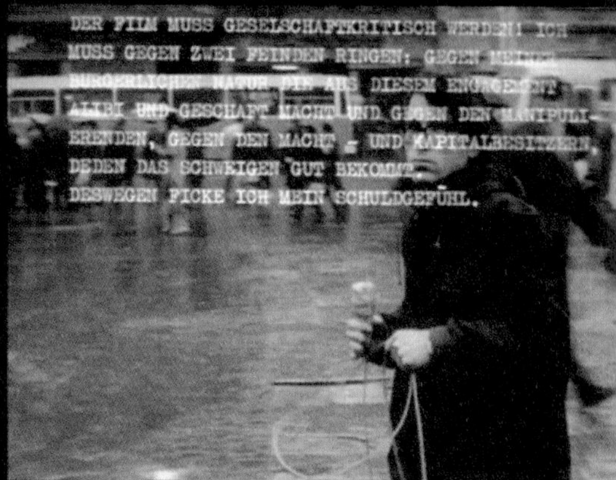

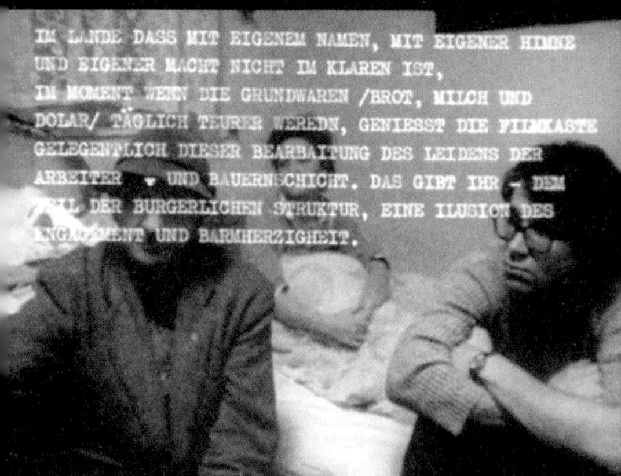

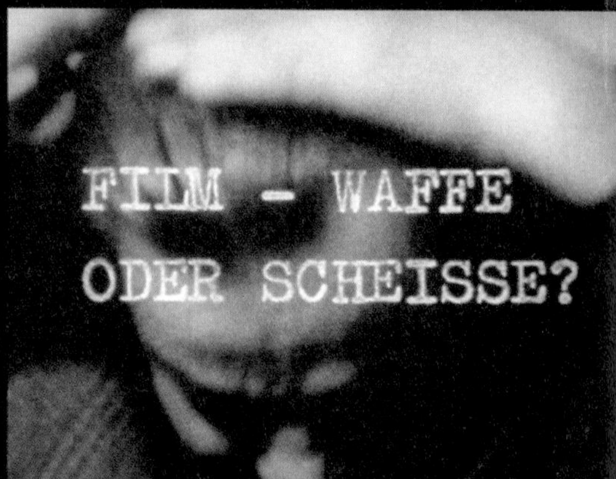

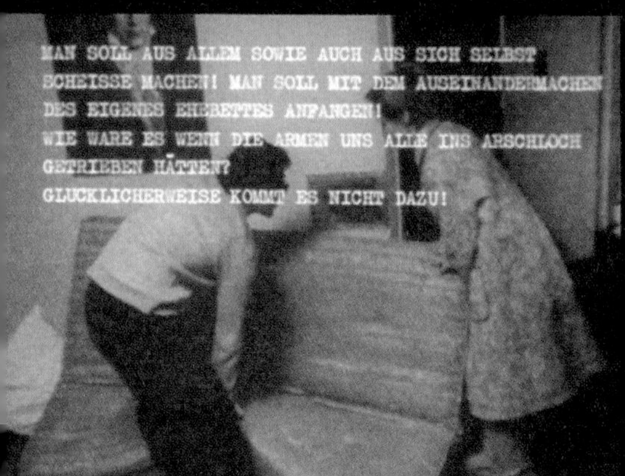

DER FILM MUSS GESELSCHAFTKRITISCH WERDEN! ICH MUSS GEGEN ZWEI FEINDEN RINGEN: GEGEN MEINER BURGERLICHEN NATUR DIE AUS DIESEM ENGAGEMENT ALIBI UND GESCHAFT MACHT UND GEGEN DEN MANIPULI-ERENDEN, GEGEN DEN MACHT - UND KAPITALBESITZERN, DEDEN DAS SCHWEIGEN GUT BEKOMMT.
DESWEGEN FICKE ICH MEIN SCHULDGEFÜHL.

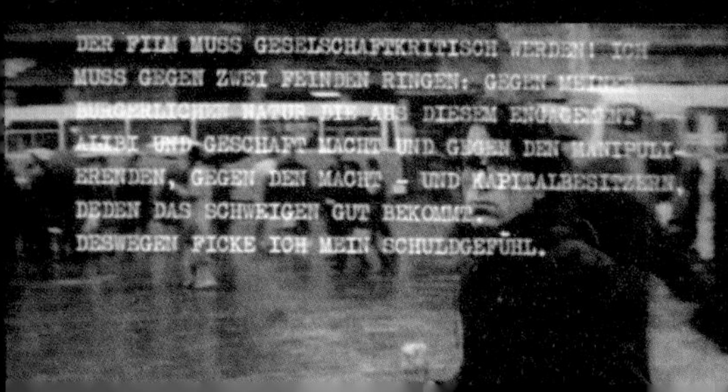

DER FILM MUSS GESELSCHAFTKRITISCH WERDEN! ICH MUSS GEGEN ZWEI FEINDEN RINGEN: GEGEN MEINER BURGERLICHEN NATUR DIE AUS DIESEM ENGAGEMENT ALIBI UND GESCHAFT MACHT UND GEGEN DEN MANIPULI-ERENDEN, GEGEN DEN MACHT - UND KAPITALBESITZERN, DEDEN DAS SCHWEIGEN GUT BEKOMMT.
DESWEGEN FICKE ICH MEIN SCHULDGEFÜHL.

Black Film Manifesto

1 You are observing the class structure of Yugoslav society. The lumpenproletariat and "humanist intelligentsia." Instrumentalized exploitation of the poor for filmic purposes. A lesson to family Žilnik regarding the hungry, the dirty, and the stinky. The child needs to be shown what life really is.

2 In the country that is not quite sure in its name, anthem, or government, at the moment when basic needs (bread, milk, and dollars) are becoming increasingly expensive, the film caste is narcissistically enjoying the "elaboration" of the workers' and peasants' suffering. This enables them, as constitutive elements of the part of civic structure that manipulates society, an illusion of engagement and compassion.

3 Everybody should be screwed, including oneself. Starting with scattering one's own marital bed! How would we feel if the wretches really started putting it up our asses? Luckily that is not going to happen.

4 I still need to make socially engaged films though. Because I am confronting two enemies—Firstly, my petit bourgeois nature that transforms my engagement into an alibi and a business opportunity, and secondly, the powerful manipulators and structures of power who would only benefit from my silence. This is why I say "fuck you" to my feeling of guilt.

5 FILM—WEAPON OR BULLSHIT?

6 Look again at point 4.

In 1971, Žilnik was invited to the International Short Film Festival Oberhausen, but was unable to attend. Instead of addressing the audience and media in person, he wrote a manifesto (originally in Serbo-Croatian), whose German translation was printed onto the film itself. This copy was shown only at Oberhausen and the film was never screened elsewhere in this form, until the 2018 exhibition at the Edith-Russ-Haus. Film stills printed here are from this very copy. The English text is a translation from the Serbo-Croatian.

LEFT
Black Film (film stills), 1971

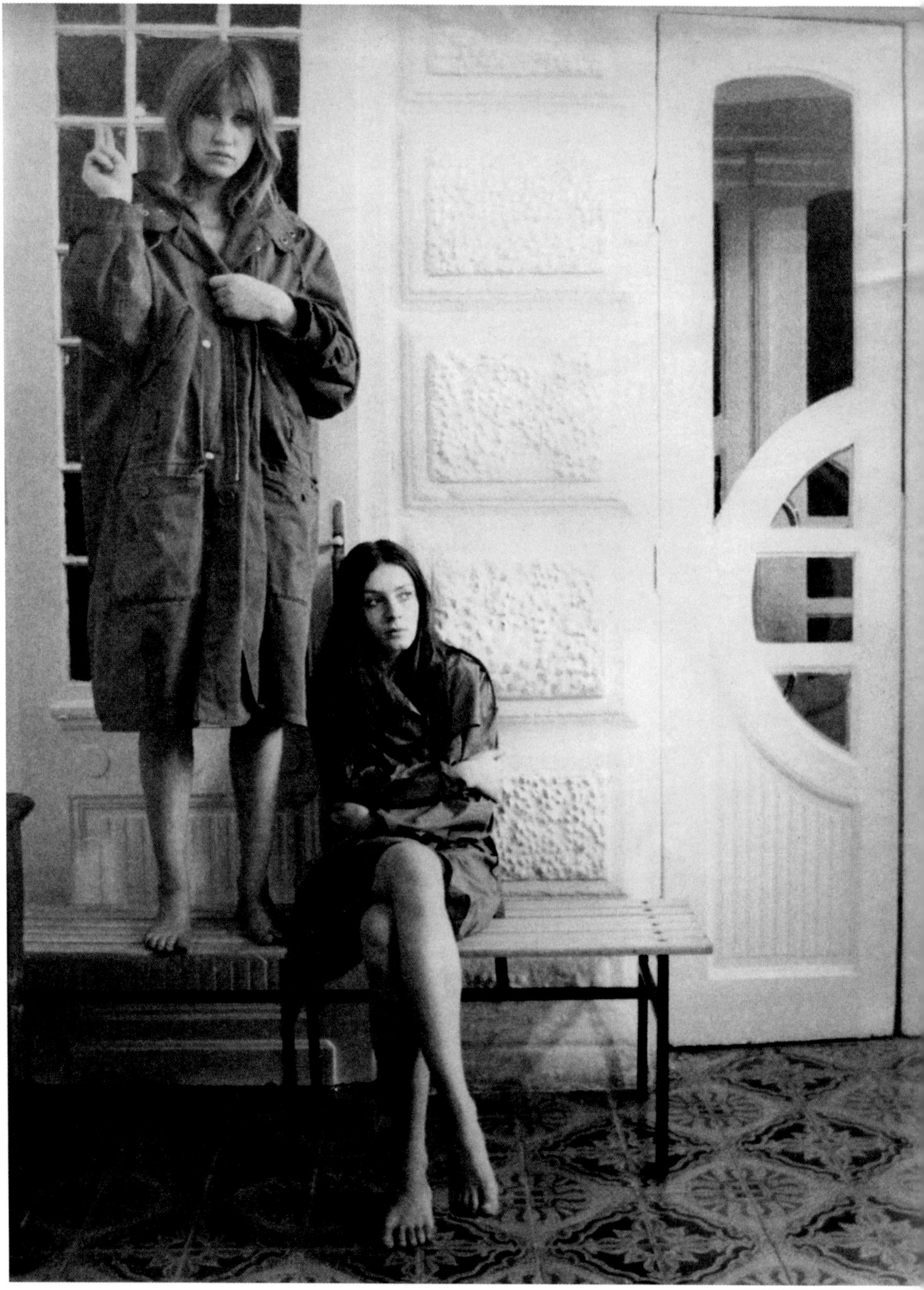

Edit Molnár is a curator currently based in Germany. She earned her MA in Art History and Art Theory from Eötvös Lóránd University, Budapest. From 2000 to 2005, she was Director of the Studio Gallery, Budapest, the nonprofit exhibition space of the Studio of Young Artists Association; from 2005 to 2007, she worked as a curator at Műcsarnok | Kunsthalle, Budapest; and from 2007 to 2009, she was Director of the Cairo-based independent nonprofit institution the Contemporary Image Collective. Since 2015, she has been Co-director, together with Marcel Schwierin, of the Edith-Russ-Haus for Media Art in Oldenburg.

Marcel Schwierin is a curator, filmmaker, and co-founder of the Werkleitz Biennial in Halle, the experimental film database cinovid, and the Arab Shorts film festival in Cairo. His films include *The Images* (experimental, 1994) and *Eternal Beauty* (feature-length documentary, 2003). He has regularly curated for the Werkleitz Biennial, the Goethe-Institut, and the International Short Film Festival Oberhausen, among others. From 2010 to 2015, he was Curator of Film and Video for transmediale in Berlin. Since 2015, he has been Co-director, together with Edit Molnár, of the Edith-Russ-Haus for Media Art in Oldenburg.

What, How & for Whom / WHW is a curatorial collective that formed in 1999 in Zagreb. Its members are curators Ivet Ćurlin, Ana Dević, Nataša Ilić, and Sabina Sabolović and designer and publicist Dejan Kršić. WHW organizes a range of production, exhibition, and publishing projects and since 2003 has directed the city-owned Gallery Nova in Zagreb. Since its first exhibition, titled *What, How & for Whom, on the occasion of the 152nd anniversary of the Communist Manifesto,* which took place in Zagreb in 2000, WHW has curated numerous international projects. These include, most recently, *Everything we see could also be otherwise (My sweet little lamb)*, cocurated with Kathrin Rhomberg and held at various locations in Zagreb in 2016–17; and the 2nd Industrial Art Biennial: *On the Shoulders of Fallen Giants,* held across Croatia at different venues in the cities of Rijeka, Pula, Labin, Raša, and Vodnjan in 2018. Also in 2018, WHW launched a new international study program for emerging artists called WHW Akademija, based in Zagreb. In March 2019, three members of WHW—Ivet Ćurlin, Nataša Ilić, and Sabina Sabolović—were appointed as Artistic Directors of Kunsthalle Wien. WHW as a collective continues working in Zagreb, where activities are coordinated by Ana Dević. ★

Alenka Zdešar and Dragana Đurić on the set of *Freedom or Cartoons*, 1971. PHOTO BY ANDREJ POPOVIĆ.

Bans and lawsuits, those petty rebukes, they are not only surgical operations that throw books or films into the garbage, and that's it. On the contrary. Bans and lawsuits, they are incentives—that's a concept, that's a road sign for a practice that attempts to not be sued or banned. It is trite and well known that if critical thinking is on trial, the same procedure richly manures the field where careerism, spinelessness, and slothfulness will shoot up like weeds. The aesthetics of a shut mouth is fly glue. Even the smallest repression will find advocates who, allegedly scared by it, make justifications for all their possible gutless passions. So, if there really were films made by foes, soon enough we'll get the final answer on what kind of film is made by "a friend."

—Želimir Žilnik, interview, "Film Cannot Stand Head Transplantation," *Telegram*, September 15, 1972.

Already from the moment of refeudalization of the state in the mid-1970s, when the local elites began grabbing as much as they could along with establishing their own criteria, it was evident what was in store. Strings were tightening, tensions were rising, and there were two possible outcomes: either a wave of opening, democratization, and freedom, or something that can only end like this, in national elitocracies cutting each other's throats. It was clear to me, but that film, *Pretty Women Walking through the City,* **was relatively unsuccessful. It was probably rumored: Žilnik went nuts! He went soft in the head! … And now when this horrible wound has opened, when what happened happened, when hundreds of thousands of dead bodies and millions of displaced people are behind us, when we witness awful destruction—things are becoming clearer. This mutual destruction could not be created only by politicians.**

—Želimir Žilnik, interview, "Contributions for a Biography," *Ekran 2000,* no. 2, 1995.

Early Works

Photo Essay from *ROK* Magazine

Frühe Werke

Foto-Essay aus dem Magazin *ROK*

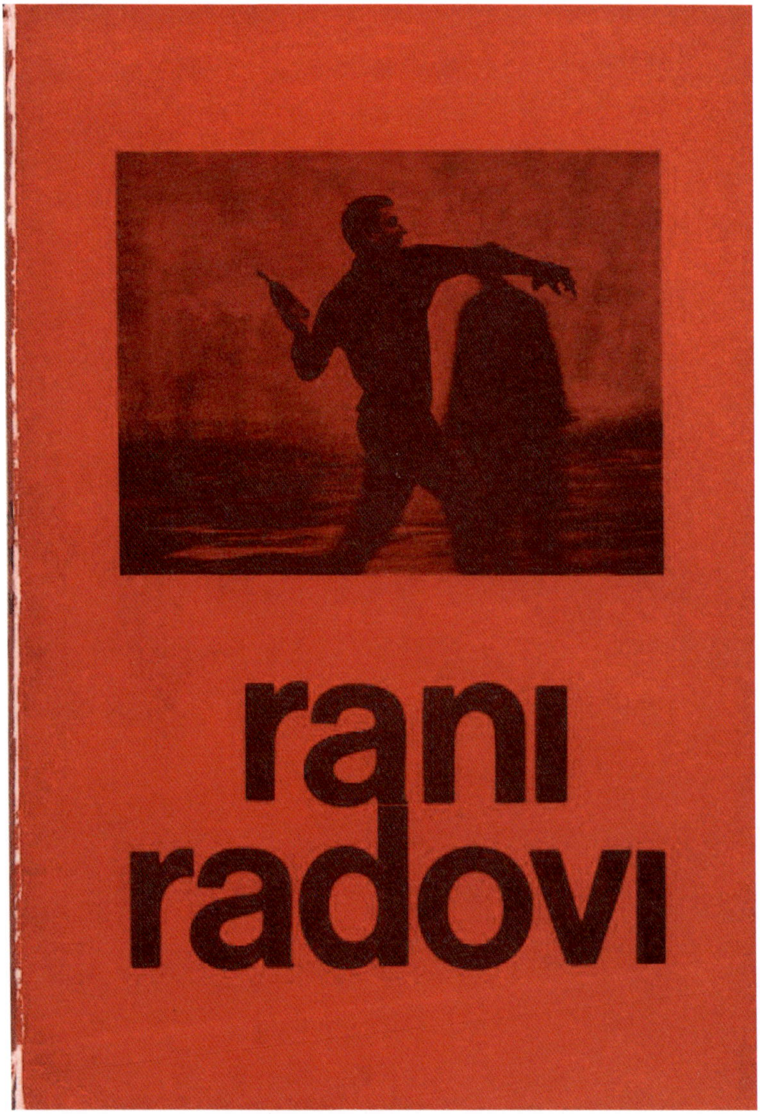

PAGES 152 TO 168
Facsimile reproduction of a photo essay originally published in *ROK—Magazine for Literature, Art and Aesthetic Inquiry into Reality*, vol 3. Belgrade, December 1969. EDITED BY BORA ĆOSIĆ, DESIGNED BY BRANKO VUČIĆEVIĆ.

SEITEN 152 BIS 168
Reproduktion eines Foto-Essays aus dem *ROK-Magazin für Literatur, Kunst und ästhetische Erforschung der Wirklichkeit*, Nr. 3, Belgrad, Dezember 1969. HERAUSGEBER: BORA ĆOSIĆ; GESTALTUNG: BRANKO VUČIĆEVIĆ.

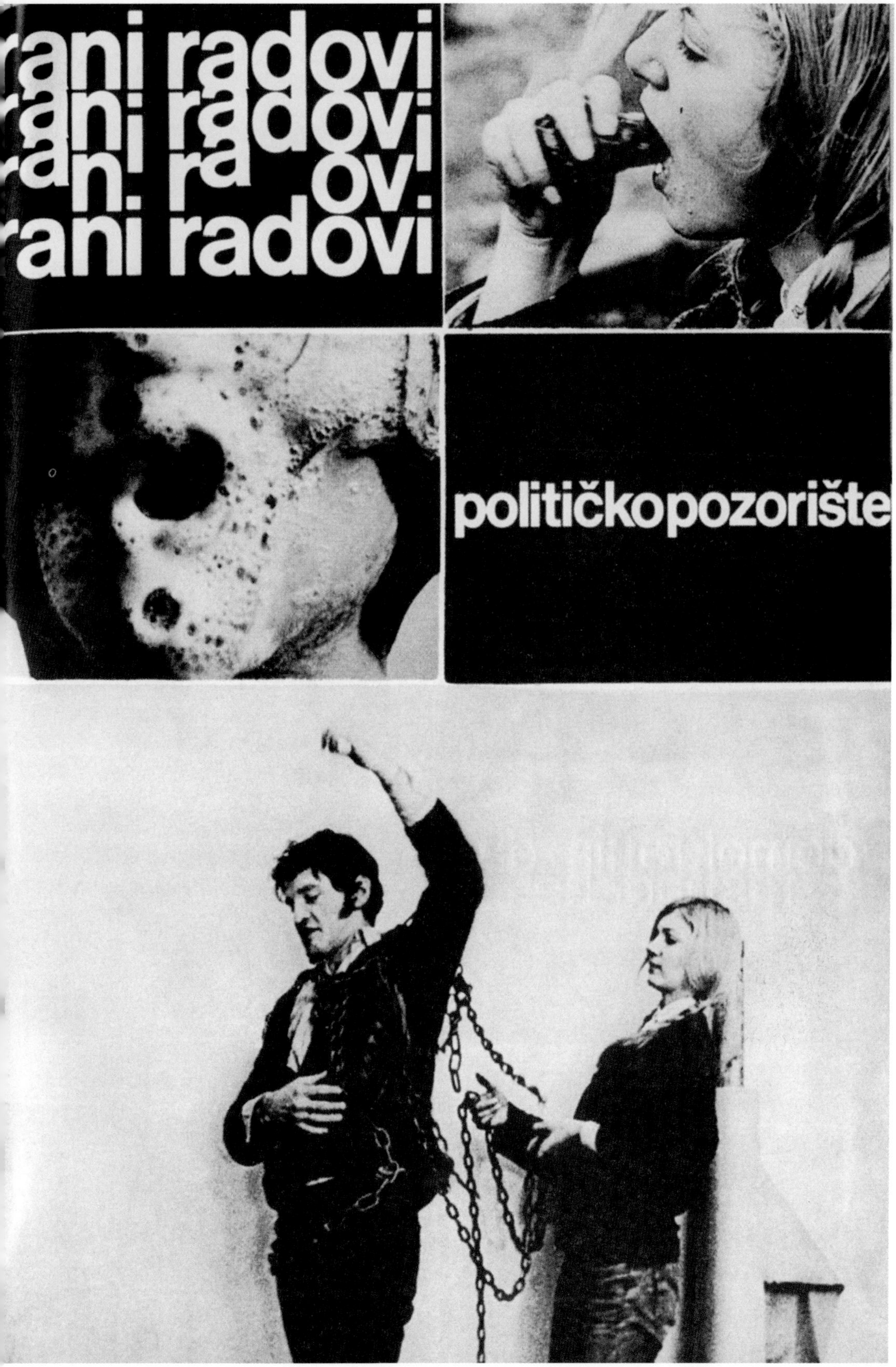
rani radovi
rani radovi
ran ra ovi
rani radovi
političkopozorište

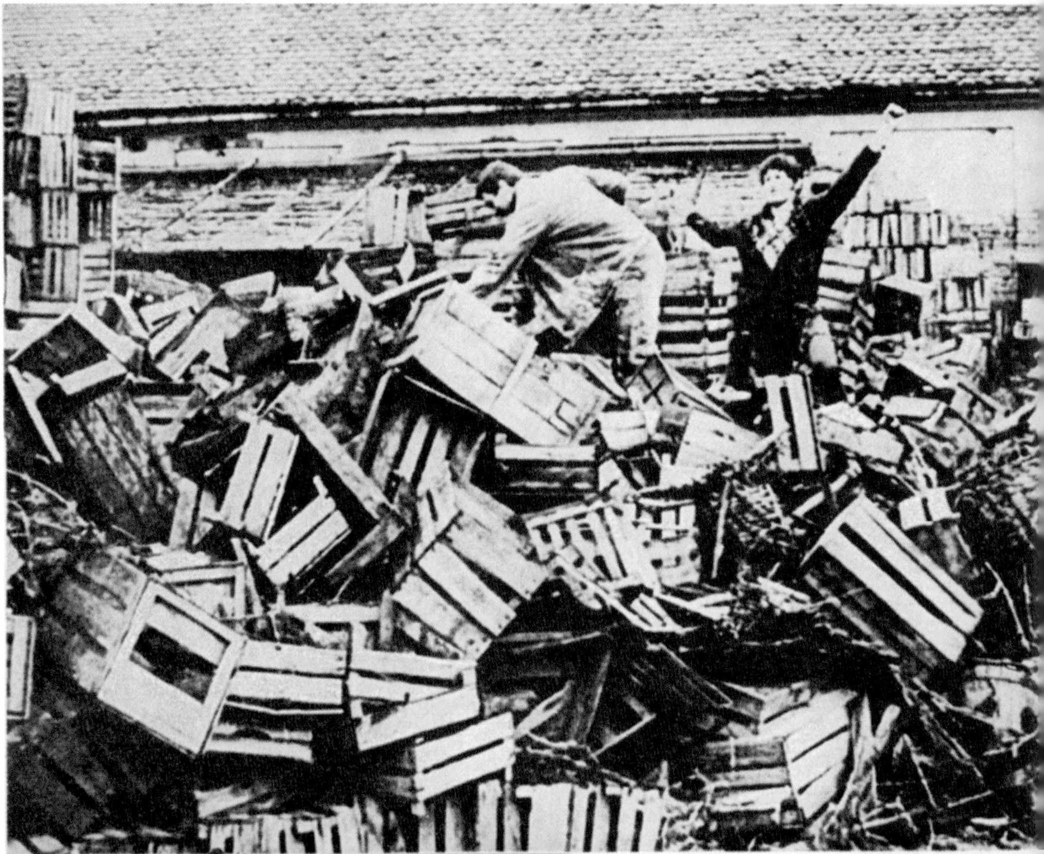

demokratija · da
raspad · ne

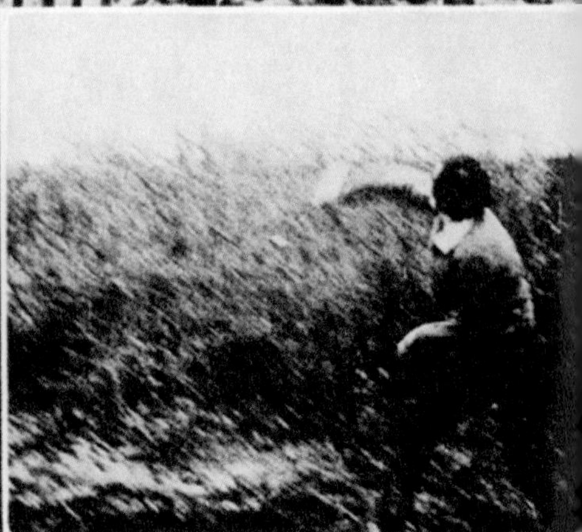

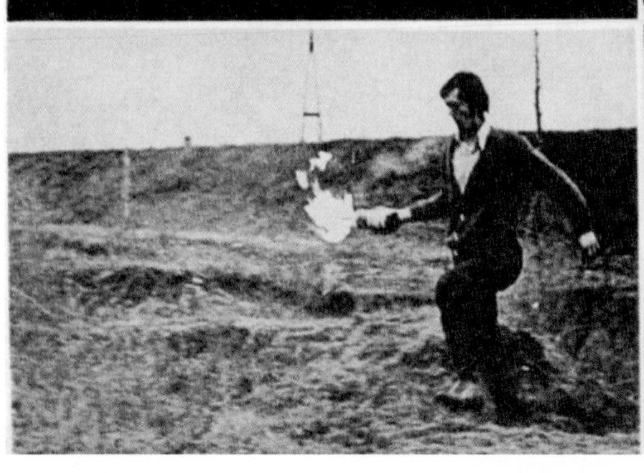

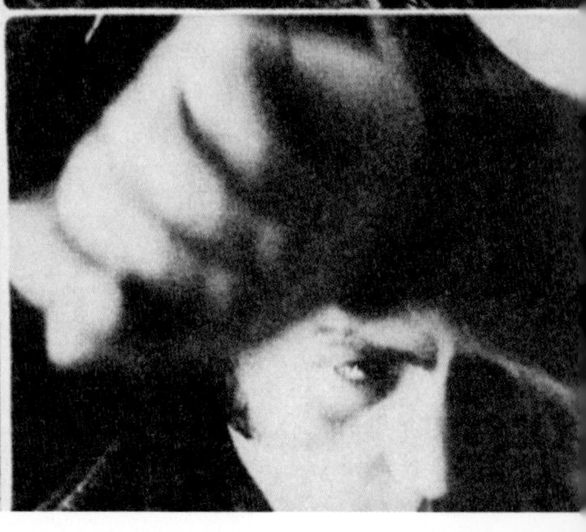

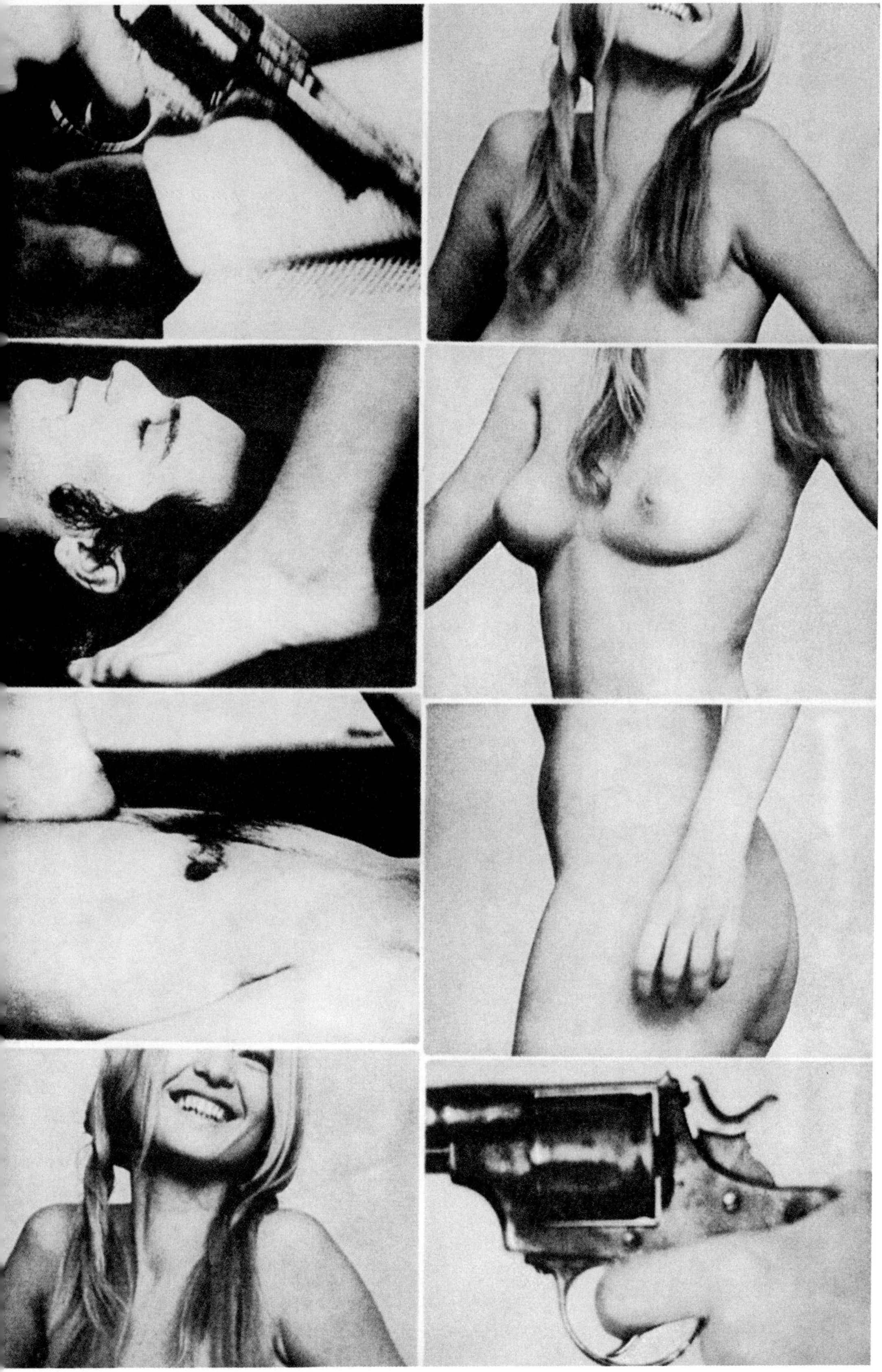

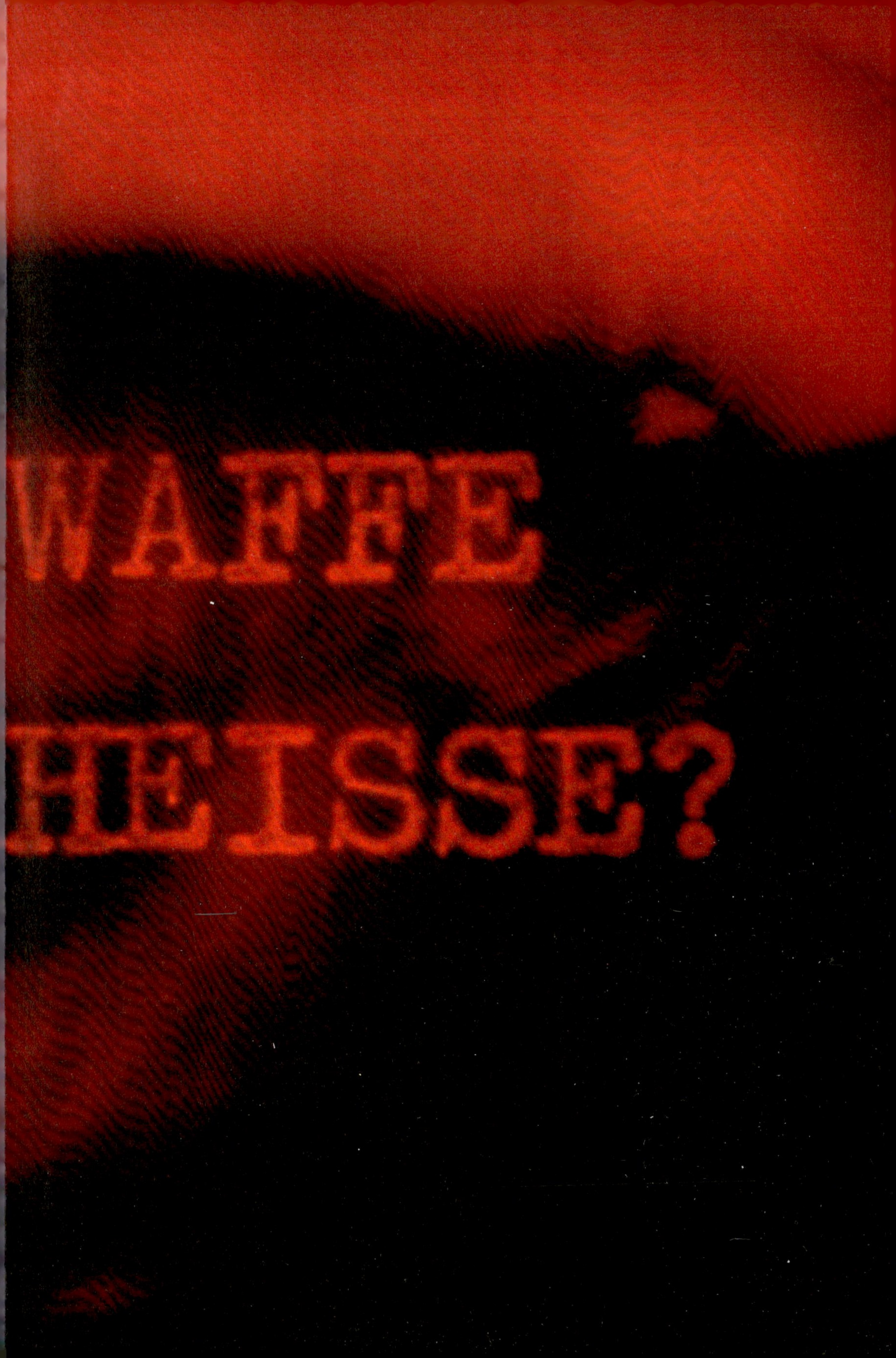
WAFFE
HEISSE?

VORDERSEITE

Marko Nikolić und Milja Vujanović bei den Dreharbeiten zu *Frühe Werke*, 1968.

RÜCKSEITE

Milja Vujanović bei den Dreharbeiten zu *Frühe Werke*, 1968.

FOTOS: ANDREJ POPOVIĆ.

VORSATZ

Der schwarze Film (Standbild), 1971

ISBN 978-3-95679-520-6

shadow citizens
želimir žilnik

DIESE PUBLIKATION ERSCHEINT ANLÄSSLICH DER AUSSTELLUNG
Shadow Citizens—Želimir Žilnik
19.04.–17.06. 2018
KURATIERT VON
What, How & for Whom/WHW für das Edith-Russ-Haus für Medienkunst

VERÖFFENTLICHT VON
Edith-Russ-Haus für Medienkunst und Sternberg Press

HERAUSGEBERINNEN
What, How & for Whom/WHW [Ivet Ćurlin • Ana Dević • Nataša Ilić • Sabina Sabolović]

BEITRÄGE VON
Boris Buden • Greg de Cuir Jr • Ana Janevski • Dijana Jelača • Edit Molnár • Bert Rebhandl • Marcel Schwierin • What, How & for Whom/WHW • Želimir Žilnik

EDITORISCHE KOORDINATION
Milica Vlajković

PROJEKTKOORDINATION
Ulrich Kreienbrink • Edit Molnár

ÜBERSETZUNGEN
Miljenka Buljević [ZITATE] • Barbara Hess • Bert Rebhandl • Michael Stoeber [FILMBESCHREIBUNGEN] • Michael Wolfson

LEKTORAT UND KORREKTORAT
Jaclyn Arndt [ENGLISCH] • Martin Conrads [DEUTSCH] • Birgit Eusterschulte [DEUTSCH]

PRODUKTION
Edith-Russ-Haus für Medienkunst

GRAFISCHE GESTALTUNG
Dejan Kršić

BILDBEARBEITUNG
Skaner Studio • Marija Matijašec

DRUCK UND BINDUNG
Skaner Studio, Kroatien

GEFÖRDERT VON

KULTURSTIFTUNG DES BUNDES

Niedersächsisches Ministerium für Wissenschaft und Kultur

EWE STIFTUNG

ISBN 978-3-95679-520-6

Die Deutsche Nationalbibliothek verzeichnet diese Publikation in der Deutschen Nationalbibliografie; detaillierte bibliografische Daten sind im Internet über http://dnb.dnb.de abrufbar.

EDITH RUSS HAUS für Medienkunst

shadow citizens

želimir žilnik

OLDENBURG • BERLIN • NOVI SAD • ZAGREB

Sternberg Press

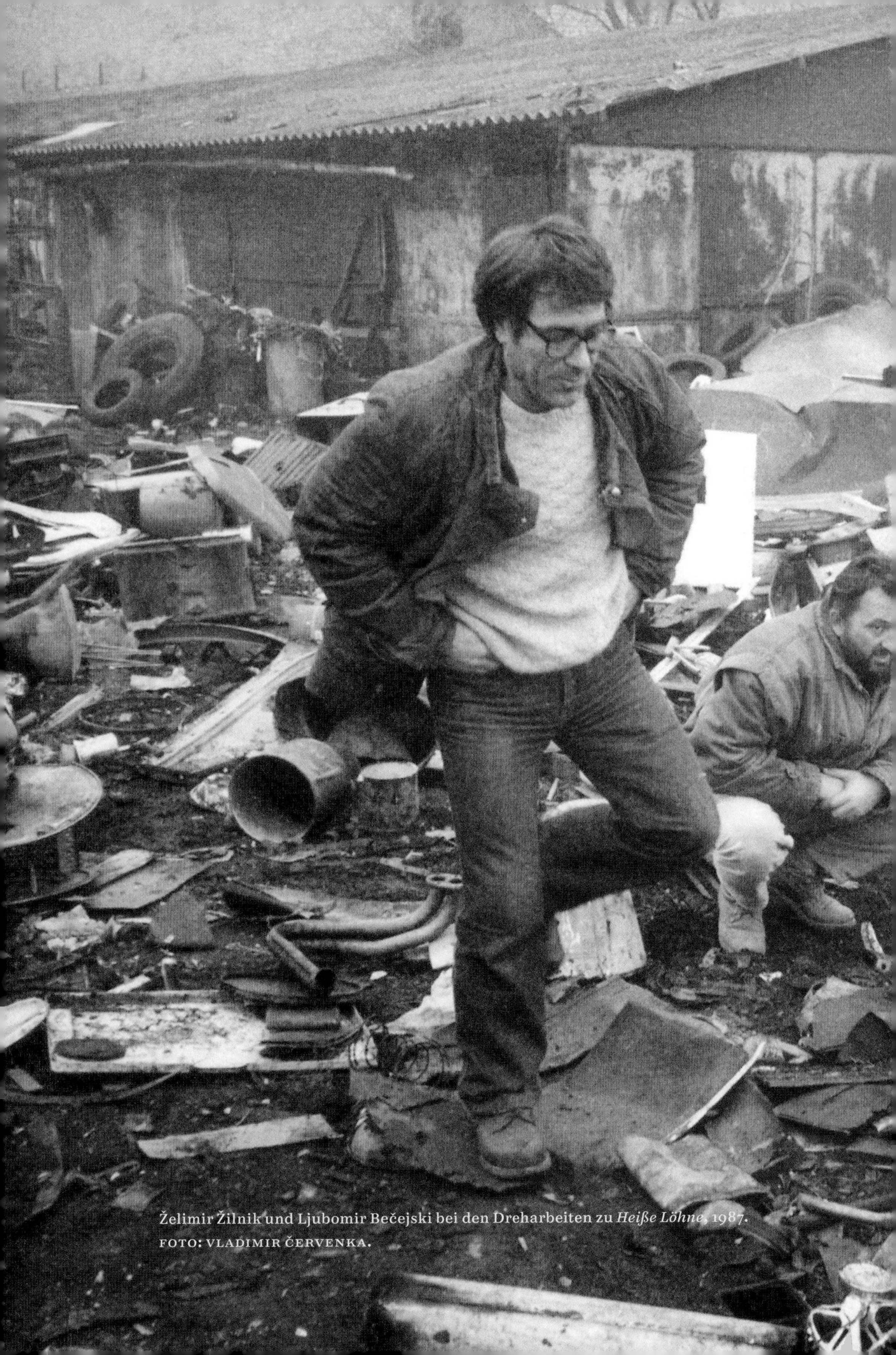

Želimir Žilnik und Ljubomir Bečejski bei den Dreharbeiten zu *Heiße Löhne*, 1987.
FOTO: VLADIMIR ČERVENKA.

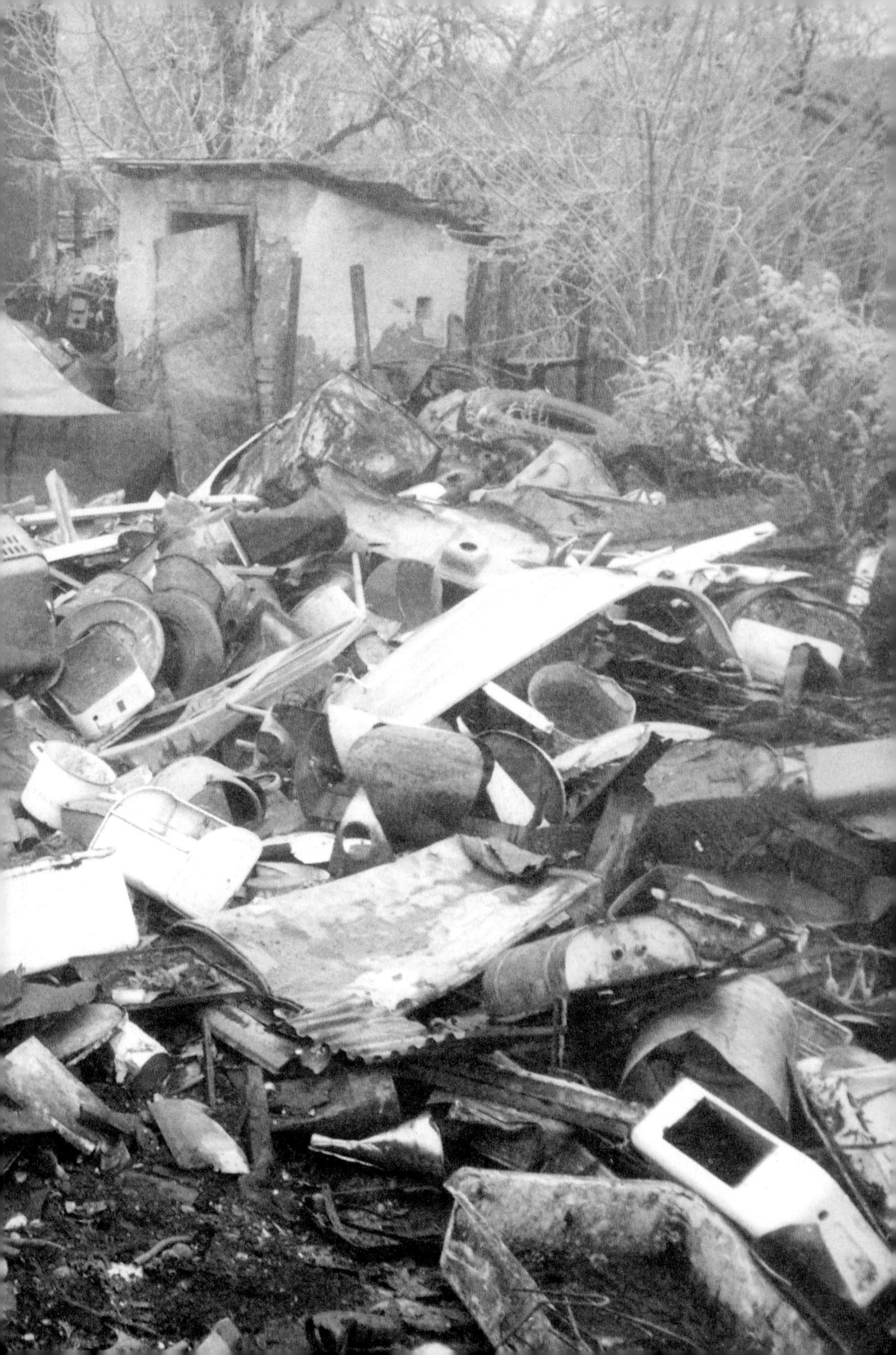

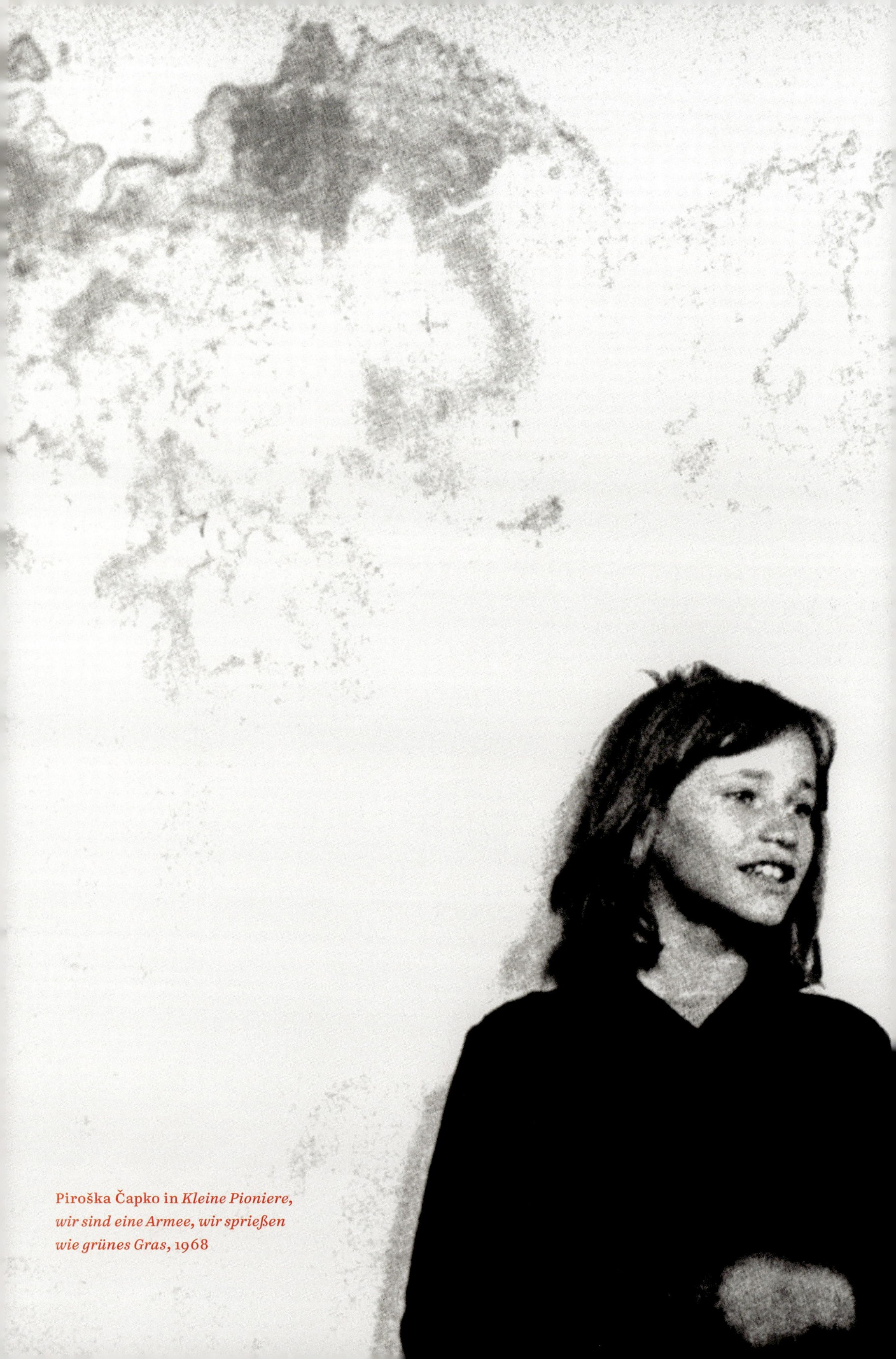

Piroška Čapko in *Kleine Pioniere, wir sind eine Armee, wir sprießen wie grünes Gras*, 1968

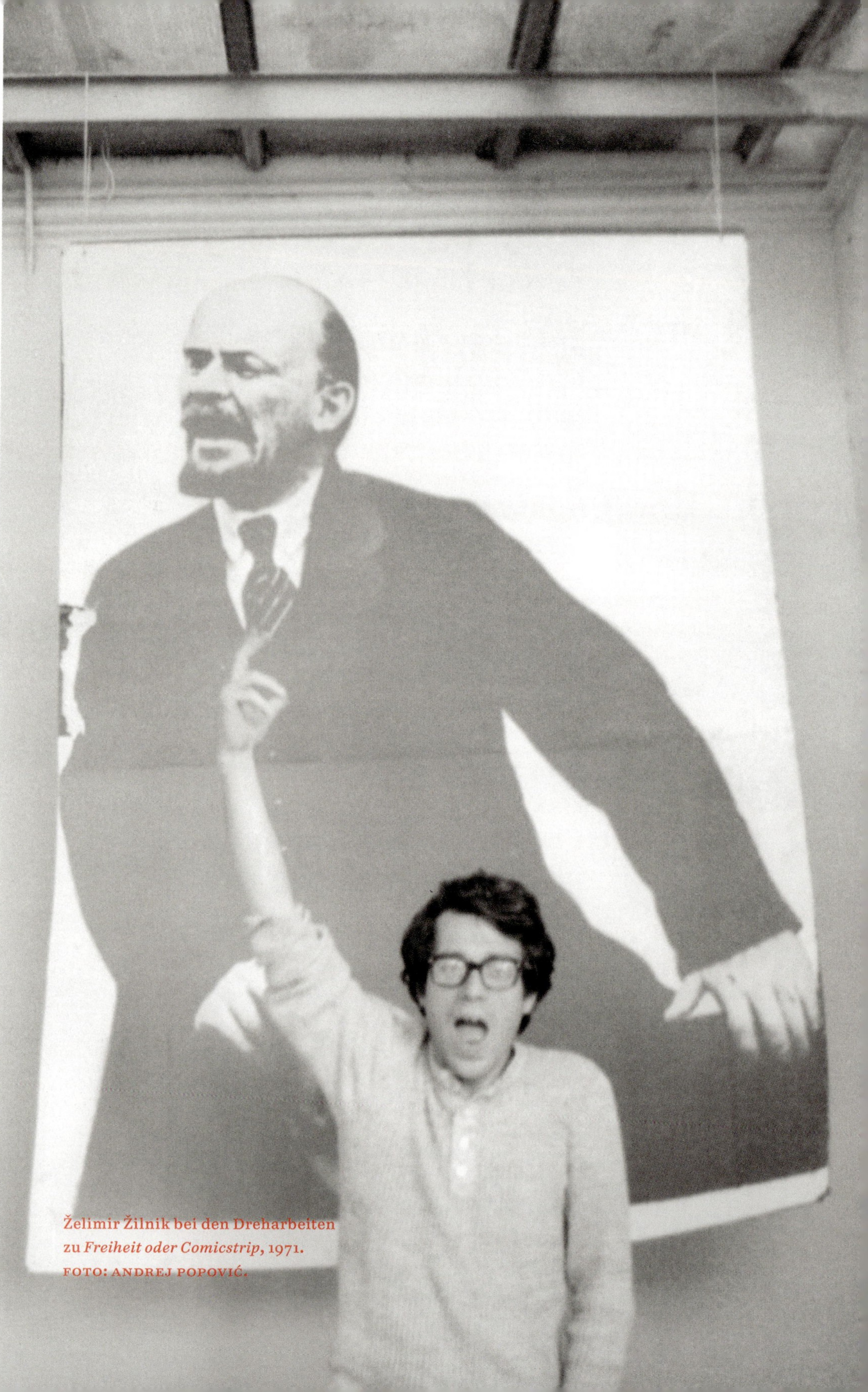

Želimir Žilnik bei den Dreharbeiten zu *Freiheit oder Comicstrip*, 1971.
FOTO: ANDREJ POPOVIĆ.

Ich mache Filme, weil wir immer noch nicht im Kommunismus leben. Ich mache Filme, um anzumahnen, wie viele Dinge wir noch tun müssen, um dorthin zu kommen. Der Kunstfilm interessiert mich nicht. Wenn es um den Dokumentarfilm geht, haben wir wirklich keine Zeit, um über Kunst zu sprechen. Der Dokumentarfilm ist in erster Linie eine Möglichkeit, die ein Mann, eine Frau oder ein Kind bekommt, um in einem Atemzug die Bauchschmerzen zu vermitteln, die sie haben und die offenkundig nicht nur ihre Privatangelegenheit sind. Diese „Möglichkeit", das ist eigentlich die Lichtempfindlichkeit des Silberbromids, und den Rest überlasse ich fast ausschließlich den Persönlichkeiten, mit denen sich meine Dokumentarfilme beschäftigen.

—Želimir Žilnik, Interview, „Art Film Does Not Interest Me", in: *Susret*, 5. April 1968

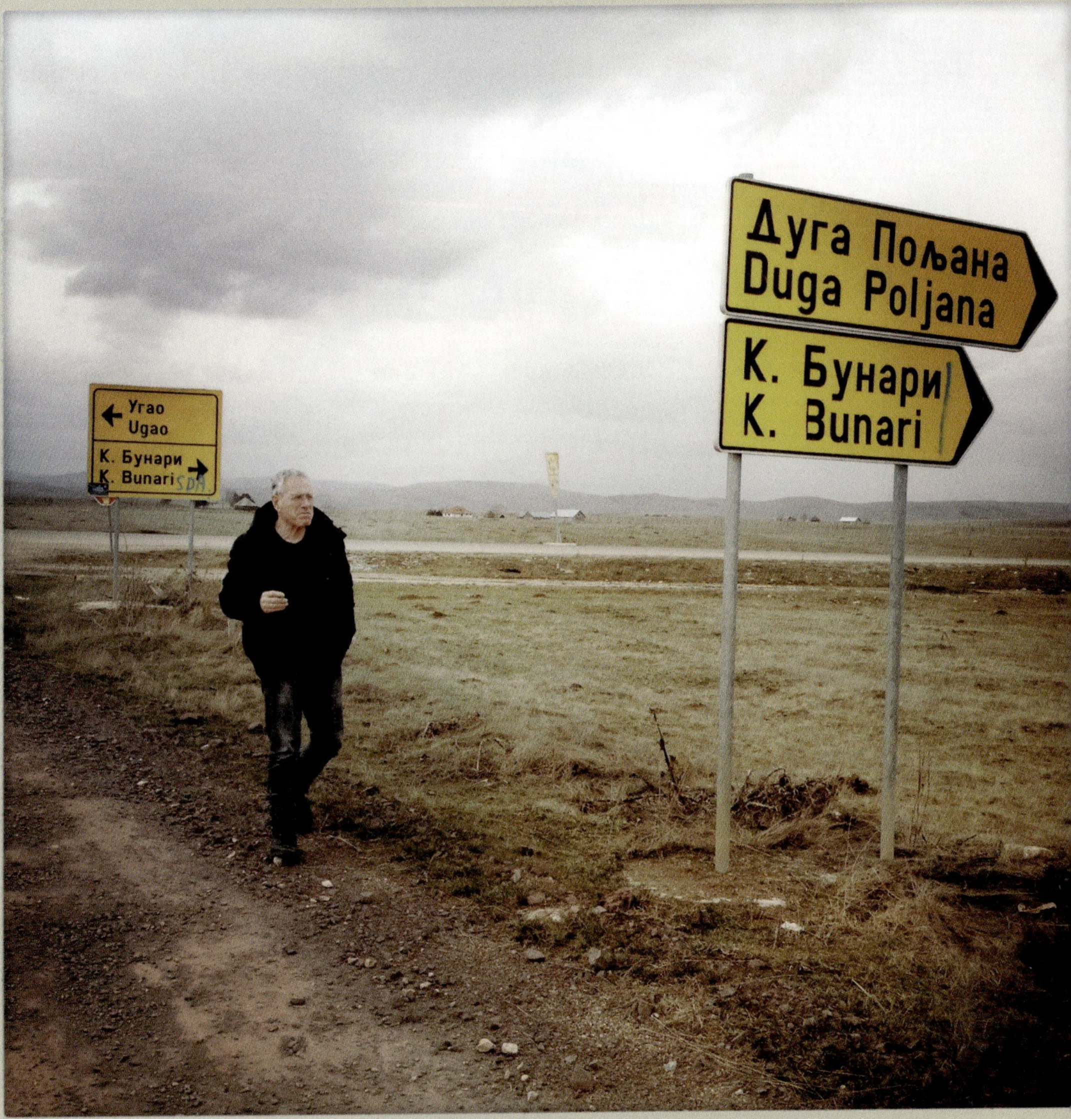

Želimir Žilnik bei den Dreharbeiten zu *Destination_Serbistan*, 2014.
FOTO: ORFEAS SKUTELIS.

EDIT MOLNÁR
&
MARCEL
SCHWIERIN

Ein radikal-pragmatischer Humanist

Am Anfang der Idee zu einer Ausstellung mit Želimir Žilnik stand für uns die Überlegung, dass das Œuvre Žilniks zwar durchaus bekannt in der Filmwelt ist, sehr wenig jedoch im Kontext der Bildenden Künste. Seine künstlerischen Methoden der sozialen Intervention, des partizipativen Dialogs mit seinen Protagonistinnen und Protagonisten und der Mischung von fiktionalen und dokumentarischen Momenten sind jedoch Strategien, die in der zeitgenössischen Kunst von zentraler Bedeutung sind. Žilnik hat sie bereits in den 1960er Jahren entwickelt und mit einer einzigartigen Konsistenz über Jahrzehnte weiterentwickelt. Mit anderen Worten: Es gibt gerade aus der Perspektive der Bildenden Kunst sehr viel in Žilniks Praxis zu entdecken.

Dabei scheinen uns besonders drei zentrale Momente prägend für sein Werk zu sein:

Da ist zunächst sein tiefer, auch persönlich gelebter Humanismus. Žilnik mag Menschen. Er hat weder Berührungsängste gegenüber denen, die von der Gesellschaft ausgegrenzt werden, noch vor denen, die völlig andere Ideen von menschlichem Zusammenleben haben. Er macht seine Protagonisten nicht nur zu den Helden ihrer eigenen Geschichten, sondern lässt sie selbst zu gestaltenden Erzählern werden und bricht so das klassische Machtgefälle zwischen Menschen vor und Menschen hinter der Kamera. Diese künstlerische Herangehensweise, die sich bereits in seinen ersten Filmen wie *Chronik der Landjugend im Winter* von 1967 und *Die Arbeitslosen* von 1968 andeutet, kam in der *Kenedi*-Trilogie (2003–2007) zur Vollendung. Heute wird die Frage der Repräsentation von Protagonisten und ihr Anteil am Werk in der Bildenden Kunst intensiv diskutiert und ist Grundlage für viele künstlerische Ansätze. Žilnik war hier seiner Zeit weit voraus. Das ist das erste prägende Element seiner Arbeit.

So freundlich Žilnik zu den Menschen ist, so harsch ist er gegenüber den gesellschaftlichen Verhältnissen, die seine Protagonisten ausgrenzen. Žilnik hat in vielen verschiedenen politischen Systemen gearbeitet und immer ist er mit ihnen in Konflikt geraten. Er ließ sich niemals einhegen, weder durch Drohungen noch durch Versprechungen. Es scheint, als sei ihm die klassische Angst des Bürgertums vor Abstieg und Ausgrenzung völlig fremd. Diese unerbittliche Kritik an den politischen Systemen aus der Perspektive der Benachteiligten und Ausgebeuteten ist das zweite prägende Element seiner Arbeit.

Seine geistige Freiheit verdankt er auch einem weiteren Moment, einem besonderen, künstlerischen Pragmatismus. Žilnik hat sich nie in seiner filmischen Methodik festgelegt, sondern auf jede Herausforderung flexibel reagiert. Wenn er keine Kinofilme mehr produzieren konnte, weil er es sich sowohl in Jugoslawien als auch in Westdeutschland mit den Entscheidern verscherzt hatte, dann machte er eben Fernsehfilme. Wenn er nicht Hanna Schygulla als Darstellerin haben konnte, wurde seine Kostümbildnerin Gisela

Siebauer zum Star des Films *Paradies. Eine imperialistische Tragikomödie.* Hatte er nur ein dreistelliges Budget, wie für sein satirisches Meisterwerk *Tito zum zweiten Mal unter den Serben,* dann drehte er einen 45-minütigen Film mit Mitteln, die für eine kommerzielle Filmproduktion nicht mal die sprichwörtliche Portokasse gefüllt hätten. Einen solchen Filmemacher kann man nicht mit der in jedem System gängigen Drohung erpressen, dass man ihm die Produktionsmittel wegnehmen werde. Er macht einfach immer weiter. Das ist das dritte zentrale Element seiner Arbeit.

Für seine Haltung zum Filmemachen war auch prägend, dass er nicht von einer Filmschule kam, in der Studierende lernen, mit professionellen Budgets zu arbeiten, sondern aus der Amateurfilmszene, in der man lernen muss, mit minimalen Mitteln auszukommen. Vielleicht war er deshalb auch immun gegen die sirenenartigen Verlockungen der Filmindustrie, die den Talentierten Geld, Ruhm und ein aufregendes Leben versprechen, wenn sie sich nur ihren Gesetzen unterwerfen. Entsprechend ungewöhnlich war der Verlauf seiner Karriere: vom Gewinner des Goldenen Bären der Berlinale über den prägenden Undergroundstar der Oberhausener Kurzfilmtage bis hin zum Fernsehspielregisseur und unabhängigen Dokumentarfilmer, der er heute ist.

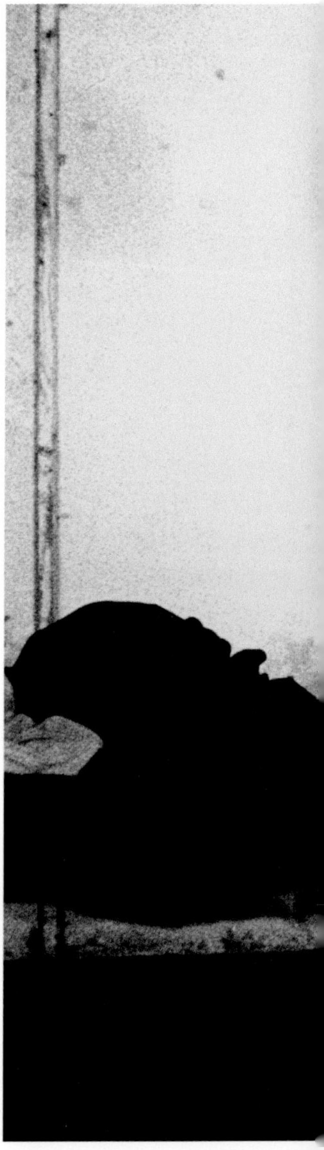

Dieses einzigartige filmische Werk in den „White Cube" des Ausstellungsraumes zu transferieren, war keine leichte Aufgabe. Mit dem Kollektiv WHW aus Zagreb haben wir vier Kuratorinnen gewinnen können, die den „anderen" Blick der Kunstwelt auf Žilniks Œuvre mitbringen, gleichzeitig aber herausragende Kennerinnen der jugoslawischen Kultur- und Filmszene sind. Für die Ausstellung im Edith-Russ-Haus haben sie ein experimentelles, geradezu analytisches Format entwickelt. Während nur einige zentrale Arbeiten in voller Länge als Projektionen oder auf Bildschirmen gezeigt wurden, war der größere Teil der Werke in Ausschnitten zu sehen, die verschiedenen Themen in Žilniks Œuvre zugeordnet waren. Diese Ausschnitte liefen auf ausrangierten Büromonitoren, die an gebrauchten Bauzäunen befestigt waren. Die Kabel der Monitore trafen auf die groben, noch mit Putz und Farbe verdreckten Betonsockel der Zäune. Dieses sorgfältig konzeptionierte, aber in der Anmutung improvisierte Format bedurfte einer besonderen Großzügigkeit des Autors – eines Autors, der sein Werk nicht als seine persönliche Leistung und als seinen persönlichen Besitz betrachtet, sondern als eine gemeinsame, utopische Anstrengung aller Beteiligten für eine andere Welt. ★

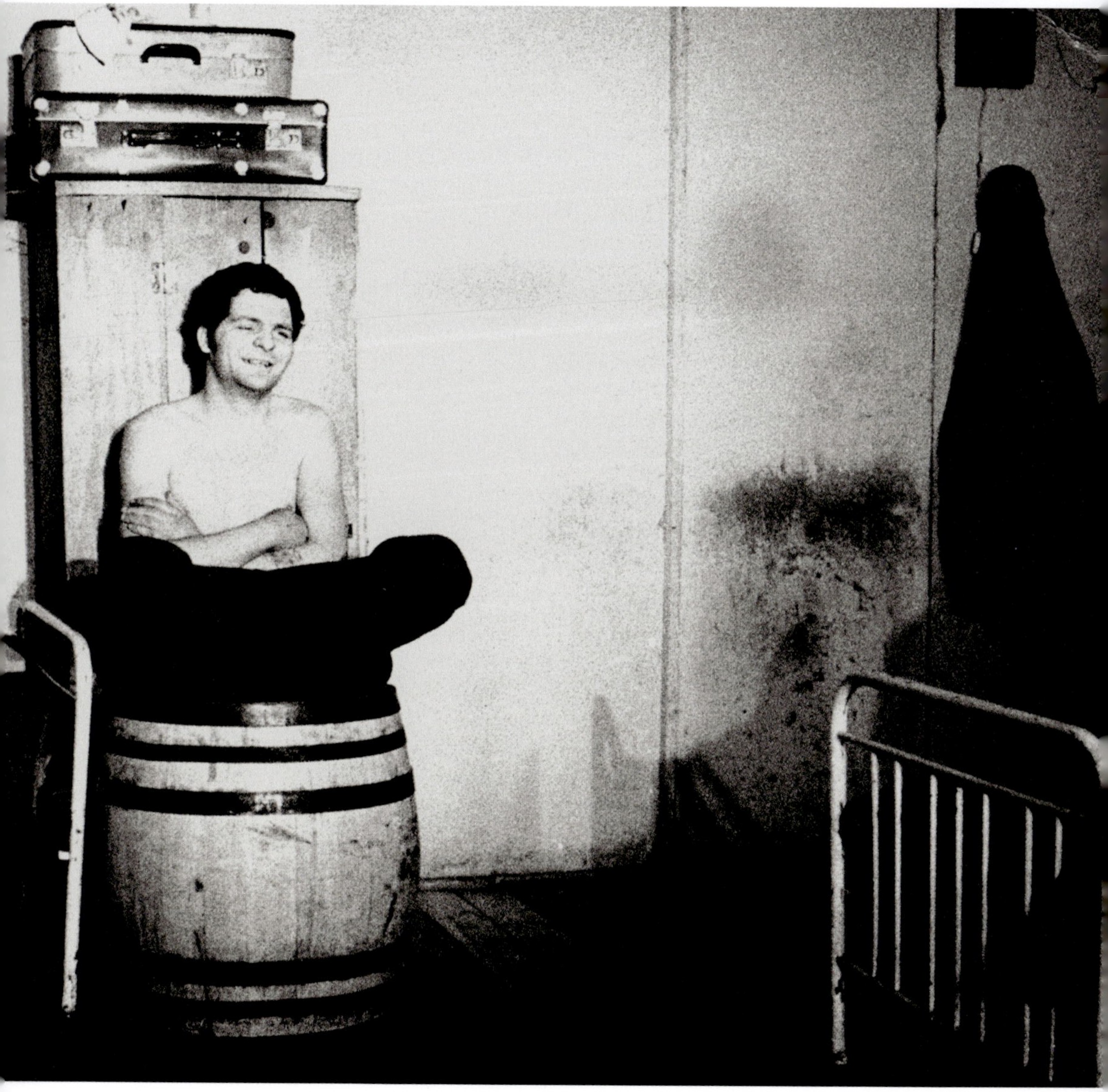

Die Arbeitslosen (Standbild), 1968

Žilnik war immer ein engagierter Essayist, aber er hat nie Pamphlete verfasst. Er hat seine eigene Position nie in irgendeiner Weise als heroisch dargestellt. Er hat nie behauptet, über das Scheitern der Gesellschaft und der vorherrschenden Ideologien erhaben zu sein, um das gesellschaftliche Subjekt zu verbessern oder zu disziplinieren. Deshalb vermitteln seine Filme keine selbstgerechten Standpunkte, sondern erforschen so kritisch wie möglich seine eigenen Glaubensvorstellungen und Annahmen.

—Branislav Dimitrijević, „Behind Scepticism Lies the Fire of a Revolutionary!“, in: *For an Idea – Against the Status Quo: Analysis and Systematization of Želimir Žilnik's Artistic Practice* (Novi Sad: New Media Center_kuda.org, Playground produkcija 2009), S. 148.

Ich möchte Ihnen etwas erzählen: Meine Filme wurden meistens in der Zeit gezeigt, in der sie gemacht wurden. Sie waren sogar im Ausland erfolgreich. Zwischendurch habe ich mehrere Fernsehfilme gemacht. Aber weil es hier [in Jugoslawien] nichts in normaler Größe gibt, bekommt bei uns alles einen Beigeschmack von Skandal, Verbot, Feindseligkeit. Wir arbeiten hart gegen uns selbst. Als ob wir Dissidenten bräuchten. Anstatt stolz darauf zu sein, dass wir das einzige sozialistische Land ohne Dissidenten sind, gibt es Kräfte, die ständig darauf drängen, dass etwas verboten wird. Selbstverständlich gab es in diesem Land eine politische Kampagne gegen den kritischen Film. [...] Aber solche komischen Situationen erleben wir alle zehn Jahre. Die Filme aus der Zeit der Schwarzen Welle waren auf internationalen Festivals meistens sehr erfolgreich. [...] Kritiker, die positiv über diese [neuen] Filme geschrieben haben, sind zu neunzig Prozent dieselben, die positiv über die [früheren] Filme geschrieben haben. Und mit sehr ähnlichen Argumenten. Es gibt eine ganz einfache Formel, nach der die Filme eines Landes international interessant werden. Sie werden interessant, wenn sie etwas über die wichtigen Fragen dieses Landes sagen, aber auch, wenn die Fragen, die in diesem Film vorgestellt werden, sich mit den klischeehaften Bildern dieses Landes überlagern, die draußen in der Welt im Umlauf sind. Weil wir ein Land sind, das wegen seiner gesellschaftlichen Krisen und des Durcheinanders, das wir ausstrahlen, interessant ist, haben die Filme von Boro Drašković oder die des jungen [Emir] Kusturica in manchen Bildern auf authentische Weise treffende Aussagen zur aktuellen Lage in Jugoslawien gemacht.

—Želimir Žilnik, Interview, „The Director Bored with Black Wave: We Don't Need Dissidents“, in: *Polet*, 17. Januar 1986

Die Einführung der Selbstverwaltung im Kulturbereich ermöglichte das Organisationsmodell der Koproduktion, bei der sich die Crew als Filmarbeitskollektiv organisierte und ihre „schöpferische Arbeit" investierte, während der Produktion in die technische Ausrüstung investierte. Unsere Verträge lauteten dann ungefähr folgendermaßen: „Želimir Žilnik beteiligt sich an dieser Produktion, indem er 60% seines Honorars als Regisseur investiert, die nur bezahlt werden, wenn der Film einen Gewinn erwirtschaftet …" Auf diese Weise war der „effektive" Betrag, den die Produktion in den Film investierte, geringer und das Risiko fiel auf die Crew zurück, die gratis arbeitete. In den Verträgen wurde auch vereinbart, wie der Gewinn, sofern es ihn gab, aufgeteilt würde, und ab wann ein Film profitabel war.

Avala Film hatte eine Richtlinie, jedes Jahr zwei Spielfilme von debütierenden Regisseure zu produzieren. 1968 war ich an der Reihe, weil ich als Autor für meinen Dokumentarfilm *Die Arbeitslosen* den Großen Preis der Internationalen Kurzfilmtage Oberhausen und für meinen Kurzfilm *Kleine Pioniere* in Belgrad eine Silbermedaille bekommen hatte. Da meine Idee für einen Film, *Frühe Werke,* nicht praktikabel genug erschien, wurde ich aufgefordert, einen riskanten Weg einzuschlagen, und es gelang mir, Neoplanta als Koproduzenten zu gewinnen, weil ich wusste, dass mir das als Autor mehr Freiheit geben würde.

—Želimir Žilnik im Gespräch mit Dubravka Sekulić, Gal Kirn und Žiga Testen, in: Gal Kirn, Dubravka Sekulić und Žiga Testen (Hg.), *Surfing the Black: Yugoslav Black Wave Cinema and Its Transgressive Moments* (Maastricht: Jan

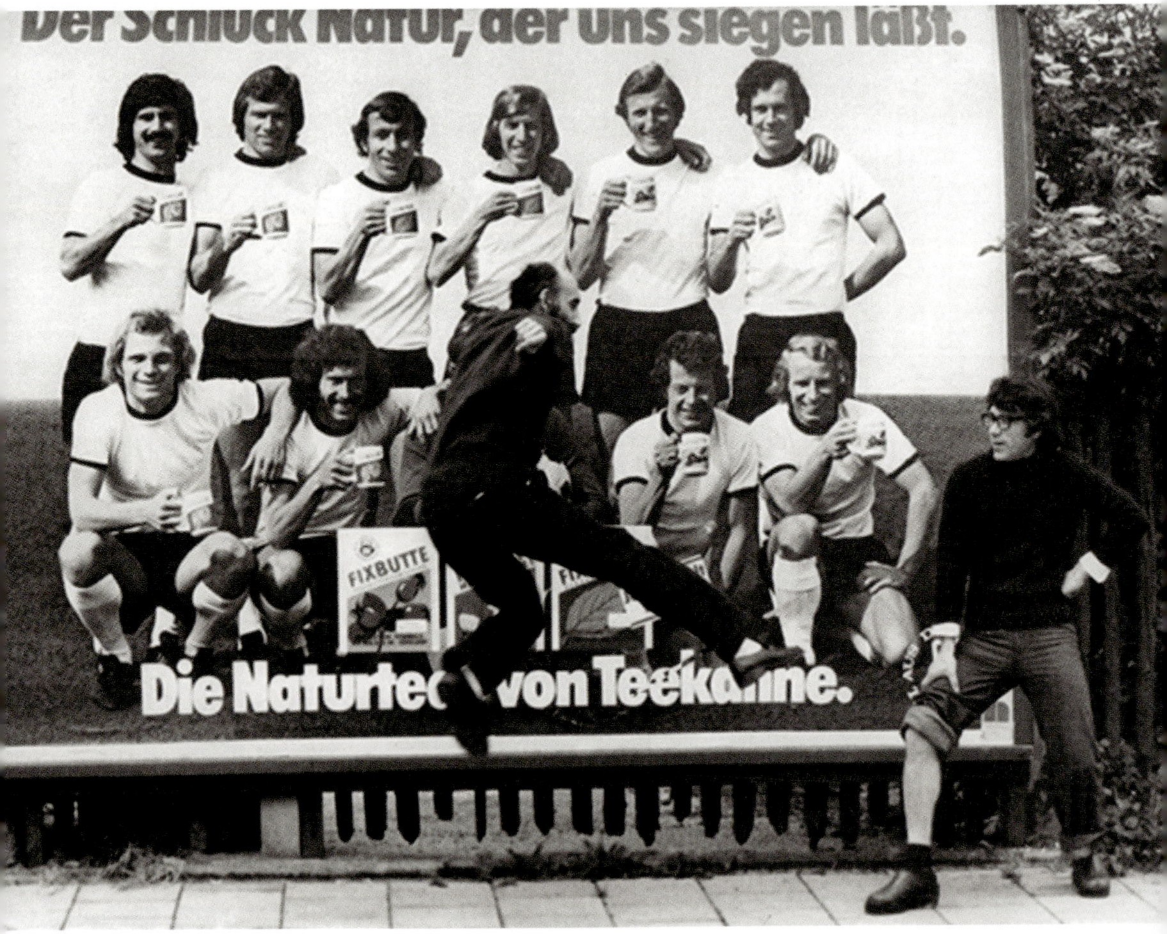

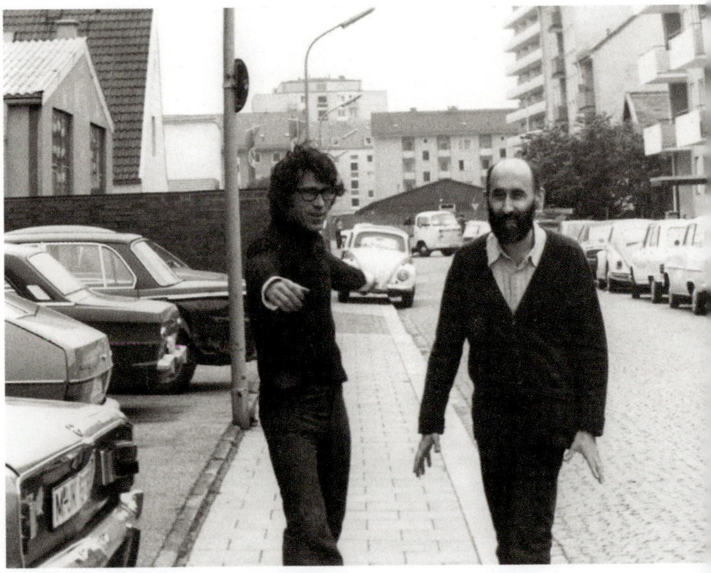

Želimir Žilnik und Branko Vučićević in München, 1974.
FOTOS: ANDREJ POPOVIĆ.

WHAT, HOW & FOR WHOM / WHW

Želimir Žilnik — Schattenbürger

Das Buch *Shadow Citizens* ist eine Erweiterung der gleichnamigen Ausstellung, die 2018 am Edith-Russ-Haus für Medienkunst stattfand; dabei wurde – erstmals im Rahmen eines Ausstellungsformates – ein Einblick in die radikale filmische Praxis und das umfangreiche Werk des Filmemachers Želimir Žilnik (geb. 1942, lebt in Novi Sad, Serbien) geboten. Seit seinen Anfängen in der lebendigen jugoslawischen Amateurfilmszene der 1960er Jahre realisierte Žilnik über fünfzig Filme, darunter mehrere Spielfilme und Fernsehproduktionen, oft im Genre des Dokudramas. Er fand früh internationale Anerkennung; schon 1969 erhielt er für *Frühe Werke* (1969) auf der Berlinale einen Goldenen Bären für den besten Film. In den 1970er Jahren stießen Žilniks Filme auf politischen Widerstand; er verließ daraufhin Jugoslawien und ging nach Westdeutschland, wo er mehrere unabhängige Filme realisierte, darunter einige der ersten, die sich mit dem Thema der sogenannten „Gastarbeiter" beschäftigten. Nachdem seine Filme auch in Westdeutschland politischem Druck und Zensurmaßnahmen ausgesetzt waren, kehrte er in den 1980er Jahren nach Jugoslawien zurück. Dort entstanden zahlreiche Fernseh- und Spielfilme, in denen er frühe Symptome der wachsenden gesellschaftlichen Konflikte des Landes aufzeigte. In den 1990er Jahren beschäftigten sich seine Filme mit den Problemen der postsozialistischen Transition und mit Fragen der Migration.

Viele von Žilniks Filmen haben auf geradezu prophetische Weise Ereignisse in der realen Welt angekündigt – Ereignisse, welche die in seinem Werk behandelten Themen widerspiegeln: sei es die Auflösung Jugoslawiens, dessen ökonomische Transition vom Sozialismus zu einer neoliberalen Ordnung, die Abschaffung von Rechten der Werktätigen oder eine weitreichende gesellschaftliche Erosion, die mit Arbeitsbedingungen und Migration zusammenhängt. Der Titel *Shadow Citizens* reflektiert Žilniks lebenslange Beschäftigung mit den unsichtbaren, unterdrückten, unzureichend oder falsch dargestellten Mitgliedern der Gesellschaft, und er verweist auf Themen, die sich durch die gesamte Filmografie des Regisseurs hindurchziehen, wie etwa Fragen der Schattenökonomie, Grenzen, Migration, Arbeit, Terrorismus, Revolutionsmüdigkeit und Konflikte zwischen parallelen Modernen. Als konzeptueller Begriff deutet „Shadow Citizens" auf eine Form des politischen Engagements für eine „Amateurpolitik" – auf fantasievolles und subversives nichtnormatives Wissen und auf die alternativen Sensibilitäten, die immer in einer Gesellschaft schlummern und manchmal sichtbaren Widerstand gegen die gewöhnliche Politik leisten. Dem Urbanisten Andy Merrifield zufolge sind amateurhafte und professionelle Politik tatsächlich politische Bereiche, die zurückerobert und wie tektonische Platten in Bewegung versetzt werden können.[01] Žilniks Filme sind – konzeptuell wie methodisch – von einer mutigen Amateurhaftigkeit getragen. Das Konzept der Schattenbürgerinnen und -bürger, verstanden als unterschiedliche Minderheiten, die überall zunehmend zu Mehrheiten werden, zieht sich durch Žilniks Werk hindurch. Es wird als eine Möglichkeit aufgegriffen, eine neue Vorstellung von Bürgerschaftlichkeit zu entwickeln, die gegenwärtige Beschränkungen und Grenzen

01 Andy Merrifield, *The Amateur: The Pleasures of Doing What You Love*, London: Verso 2017.

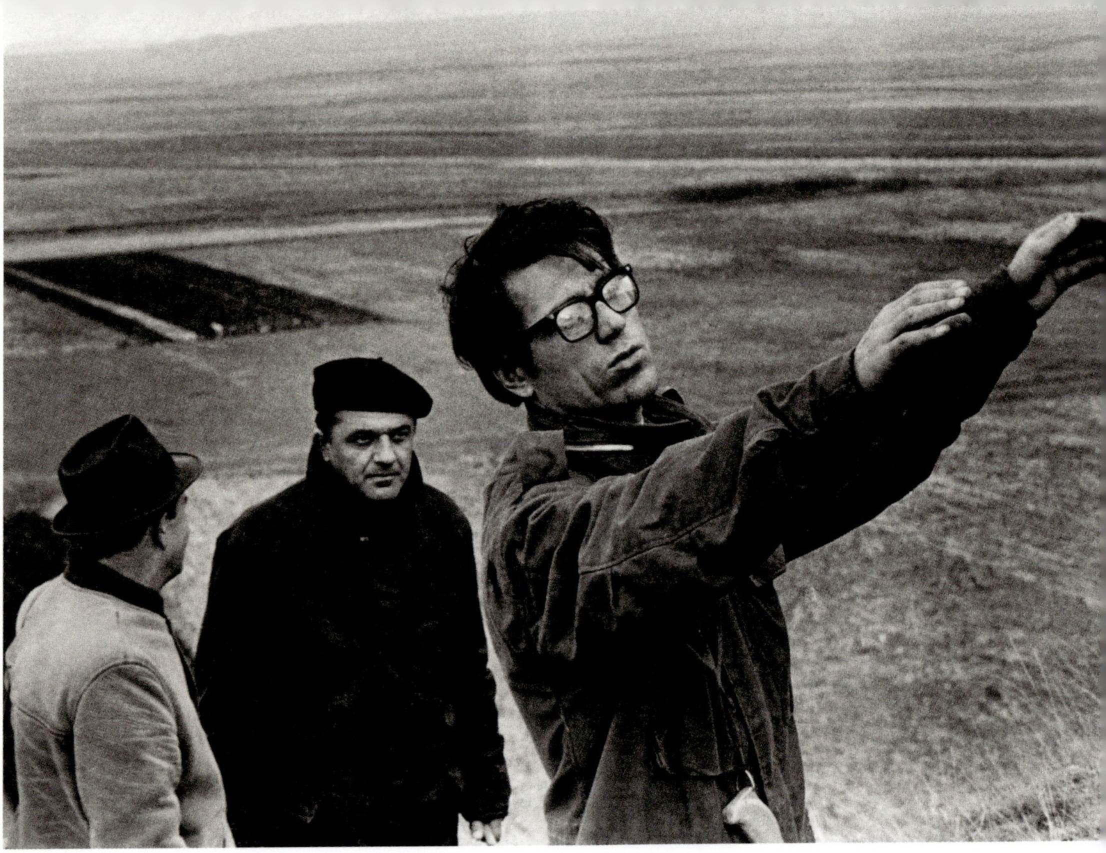

Frühe Werke (Produktionsfoto), 1968.
FOTO: ANDREJ POPOVIĆ.

erweitert. Die verschiedenen Facetten der Potenziale von Schattenbürgern und der Druck der Unterströmungen von Amateuren in der emanzipatorischen Politik und künstlerischen Produktion, von denen Žilniks Filme handeln, geben auch Aufschlüsse über aktuelle gesellschaftliche und politische Dringlichkeiten.

Die Essays, die für dieses Buch entstanden sind, verorten Žilniks Werk in umfassenderen gesellschaftlichen, kulturellen und künstlerischen Kontexten und konzentrieren sich zugleich auf bestimmte, oft übersehene Aspekte seiner Praxis, die sich mit genderspezifischen, ethnischen, popkulturellen und politischen Fragen beschäftigen. Sie erhellen die Besonderheiten des sozialistischen Jugoslawiens ebenso wie seine Bedeutung für die klägliche Gegenwart einer Welt, deren Zukunft aufgrund der erbarmungslosen Reproduktion des Kapitals gefährdet ist.

Bert Rebhandl setzt Žilniks Werk in Beziehung zu internationalen Strömungen des Experimental- und Dokumentarfilms und erläutert die politischen Grundsätze der Ethik, die Žilnik in seiner dokumentarischen Herangehensweise praktiziert. Ana Janevski beschäftigt sich mit den zahlreichen performativen Praktiken in seinen Filmen, ihren strukturellen Bedeutungen und ihren Beziehungen zu Formen der Populärkultur. Dijana Jelača diskutiert die Politik von Gender und Sexualität im Hinblick auf Žilniks Einstellung zu den sich überschneidenden politischen Bereichen von Klasse, Identität

und Gender und vor dem Hintergrund der kulturellen und politischen Rahmenbedingungen, unter denen seine Filme entstanden. Greg de Cuir Jr betrachtet das Erbe der blockfreien Bewegung, einschließlich ihrer blinden Flecke und Emanzipationsversprechen, und untersucht, wie diese mit Žilniks Herangehensweise an seine Protagonistinnen und Protagonisten zusammenhängen. Der Essay von Boris Buden, der zuerst 2010 in der Zeitschrift *Afterall* erschien, analysiert Žilniks filmische Praxis im Verhältnis zu den Filmen der sogenannten Schwarzen Welle und erforscht aus heutiger Sicht den ideologischen Hintergrund der kulturellen Debatten, die in den 1960er Jahren über sie geführt wurden.

Die Ausstellung und das Buch *Shadow Citizens* beruhen auf der Forschungsarbeit und den Veröffentlichungen vieler Kolleginnen und Kollegen. Besonders wertvoll ist die kontinuierliche Forschungs- und Publikationstätigkeit der in Novi Sad ansässigen Organisation kuda.org. Mit ihrem Projekt *For an Idea – Against the Status Quo: An Analysis and Systematization of Želimir Žilnik's Artistic Practice* hat sie wichtige Grundlagen gelegt und eine unverzichtbare Ressource für alle geschaffen, die sich für Žilniks Praxis interessieren.[02] Das Projekt bietet Zugang zu Archivinformationen und Originalmaterialien und versammelt zudem die aufschlussreichen Beiträge zahlreicher Forscherinnen und Forscher, die 2009 in der ersten umfangreichen Publikation zu Žilniks Werk erschienen. 2013 setzte kuda.org die Arbeit über Žilnik mit dem Buch *An Introduction to the Past* fort, das von Boris Buden realisiert wurde und einen entscheidenden politischen und theoretischen Beitrag zum Verständnis von Žilniks Werk im jugoslawischen Kontext geleistet hat.

Eine weitere Quelle, auf die wir immer wieder zurückgegriffen haben, waren die Recherchen von Gal Kirn und Dubravka Sekulić; diese wurden in dem Buch *Surfing the Black: Yugoslav Black Wave Cinema and Its Transgressive Moments* vorgelegt, das 2012 von der Jan van Eyck Academie veröffentlicht wurde. Darüber hinaus erschien in der Zeitschrift *Afterall* 2010 ein wichtiger Sonderteil über Žilnik, und wir danken für die Erlaubnis, den dort publizierten Text von Boris Buden hier wieder abdrucken zu dürfen. Unsere Anerkennung gilt auch der jahrelangen Forschungs- und Publikationstätigkeit von Buden, Branko Dimitrijević, Pavle Levi und Jurij Meden, deren Texte für unser Verständnis von Žilniks Werk von grundlegender Bedeutung waren. Wir haben versucht, diesen wichtigen Stimmen durch ausführliche Zitate, die sich durch das gesamte Buch hindurchziehen, eine Präsenz zu geben.

Darüber hinaus enthält der vorliegende Band einige Zitate von Žilnik selbst, die wir seinen zahlreichen Interviews aus mehr als fünf Jahrzehnten entnommen haben.

Viele dieser Forschungsarbeiten über Žilnik sind unter den Bedingungen der Ignoranz offizieller Institutionen gegenüber solchen kritischen und experimentellen Praktiken entstanden – eine Erfah-

02
Želimir Žilniks Website (https://www.zilnikzelimir.net) entstand ursprünglich 2009 anlässlich des Projekts *For an Idea – Against the Status Quo*. Diese Website wurde im Rahmen der Ausstellung *Shadow Citizens* am Edith-Russ-Haus für Medienkunst, Oldenburg, 19. April – 17. Juni 2018, umfassend aktualisiert.

rung, die zahlreiche ähnliche Initiativen gemacht haben, die auf dem Gebiet Ex-Jugoslawiens arbeiten. Nach dem Zerfall Jugoslawiens zeigten die meisten Kulturinstitutionen entweder Amnesie oder offene Feindseligkeit gegenüber den progressiven Stimmen, die in der Zeit des Sozialismus aufgekommen waren und die den neuen nationalistischen Regimes, die in den harten, von Korruption geprägten Dekaden der Entstehung neuer Nationalstaaten regierten, eindeutig kritisch gegenüberstanden. Viele dieser Initiativen unterstützen einander bis heute in ihren Bemühungen; gemeinsam erheben sie den Anspruch, dass die postjugoslawischen Generationen das Recht haben, sich für diese Zeit und für experimentelle Praktiken zu interessieren, und sie teilen die politische Perspektive, von der aus wir auf die vorige Epoche zurückblicken. Daher gilt es zu erwähnen, dass die Erforschung dieser Geschichte zum Teil im Rahmen des Kooperationsprojekts *Political Practices of (Post-) Yugoslav Art* stattfand, das von Prelom kolektiv (Belgrad), kuda.org (Novi Sad), SCCA/pro.ba (Sarajevo) und WHW (Zagreb) organisiert wurde – ein Kooperationsprojekt, das von 2006 bis 2010 zahlreiche Beispiele einer gemeinsamen, vernachlässigten Geschichte in den Blick nahm. Solche Arbeiten werden mit der Zeit selbstverständlich oft von institutionellen Strukturen aufgegriffen, doch die von unabhängigen Initiativen geschaffenen Grundlagen werden nur selten anerkannt und schließlich oftmals ohne ausreichende politische und kritische Deutlichkeit vereinnahmt.

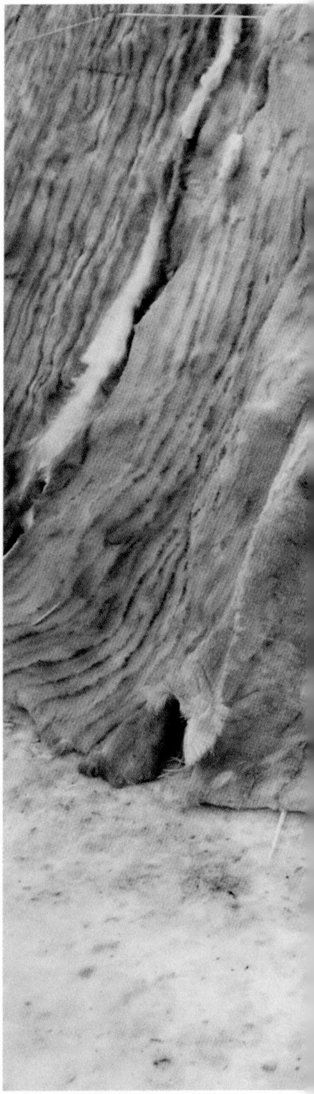

Die Ausstellung und das Buch *Shadow Citizens* wären nicht möglich gewesen ohne die kontinuierliche, großzügige Unterstützung von Sarita Matijević, Žilniks Partnerin und Produzentin, die uns nicht nur geduldig den Zugang zu Žilniks Filmen und allen dazugehörigen Dokumenten ermöglichte, sondern auch ihr weit über Daten und Fakten hinausgehendes, vertieftes Wissen über diese Sekundärquellen und ihre Autorinnen und Autoren mit uns teilte.

Unser größter Dank gilt Želimir Žilnik, dessen Leidenschaft für das Geschichtenerzählen und für politische Klarheit uns unablässig inspiriert. ★

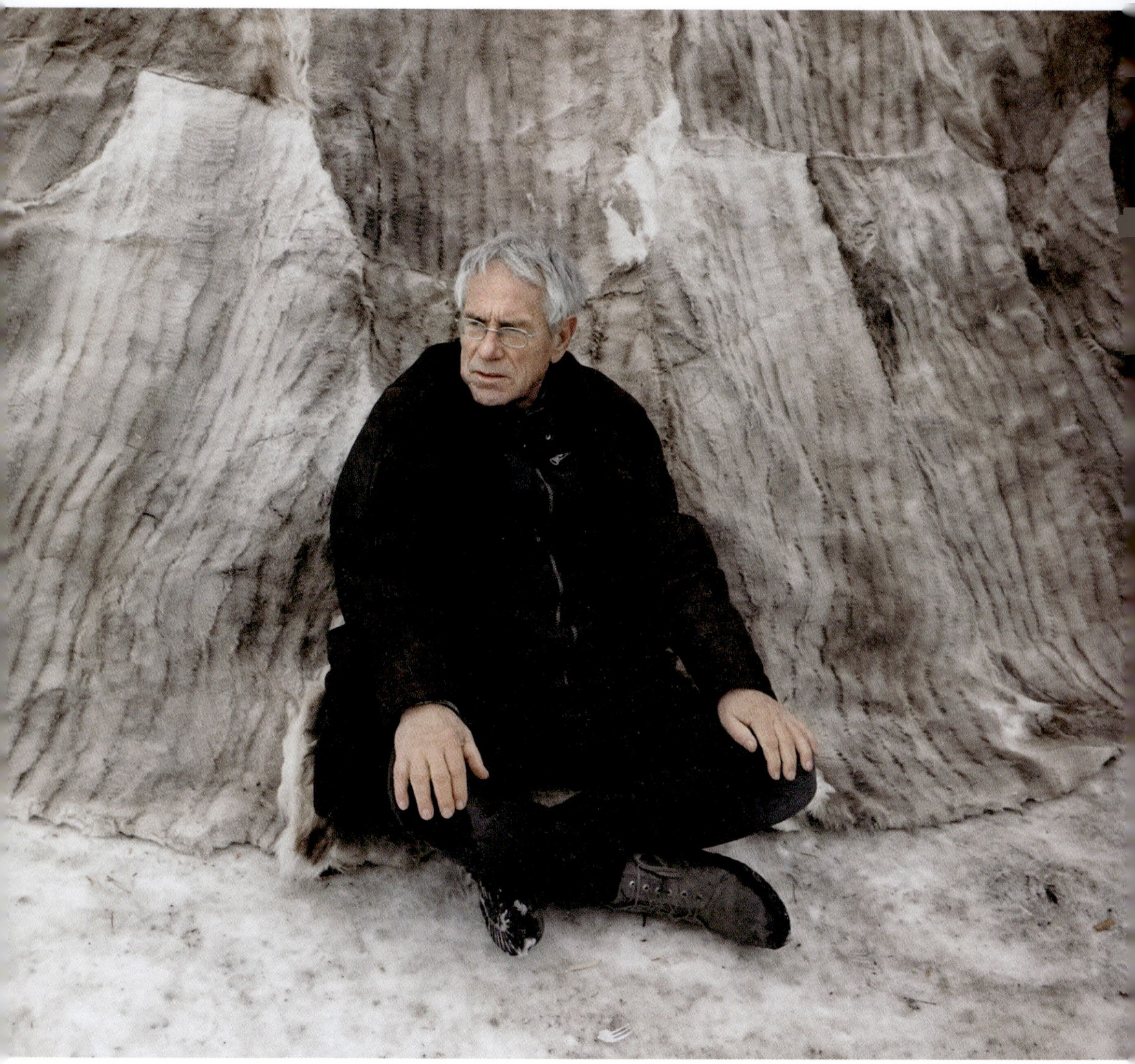

Želimir Žilnik, 2017. FOTO: KARPO GODINA.

Die offizielle Politik zeigte schon in den 1960er Jahren eine aus meiner Sicht unbegründete Angst vor der kritischen, sozialistischen Stimmung der Jugend, die in Jugendzeitschriften mit geringer Auflage und in künstlerischen Experimenten zum Ausdruck kam – vom Film bis zur Lyrik, in der Soziologie und Philosophie. Für mich war diese Angst unbegründet, und sie hatte verheerende Auswirkungen: die nicht künstlerische, sondern politisch reaktionäre Tendenz, die sich zuerst darin andeutete, dass es hieß, alle sollten ihre Nase nur in die Geschichte ihrer eigenen Region und Nation stecken. Und das wurde später durch die „absolute regionale Souveränität“ in der Wirtschafts- und Kaderpolitik und mit der „begrenzten jugoslawischen Staatsgewalt“ auf all diesen Gebieten erweitert.

Die politischen Führer fingen an, im Namen von serbischen, kroatischen und anderen Arbeiterklassen zu sprechen, und dann folgte alles dieser Logik: Um lokale Interessen stärker betonen zu können, mussten sie durch „lokales Quengeln“ unterstützt werden, und dann begann die Streiterei darüber, wer wen bestiehlt. Und es ist nachvollziehbar, dass alles mit dem zentralen Problem aller Stämme enden muss: Sowohl Dušan [Mihajlović] als auch Trpimir [Macan] haben gestohlen, die Osmanen haben schöne Augen ausgestochen, alle haben Arme und Beine zerschlagen. Die Menschen lagen in schweren Ketten und wurden von modernden Steinen erstickt. Schlangen bissen und Skorpione stachen.

Und anstatt die Bildung zu fördern, neue Arbeitsplätze zu schaffen, Gesundheits- und Sexualerziehung anzuordnen, brüllt und jammert unser sozialistischer Staat, unser trauriger sozialistischer Staat über die „historische Tragödie“ unserer Völker und Nationalitäten und vergisst dabei, dass all diese Völker und Nationalitäten genau dieses Schicksal hatten: von den Mächtigen unterdrückt und verbraucht zu werden, und dass der Sozialismus aus eben diesem Grund erfunden worden ist – um den Menschen Freiheit und den Werktätigen Arbeit und Macht zu geben.

—Želimir Žilnik, „Stories from the Lives of the People“, in: *Nedjeljna Dalmacija*, 17. Mai 1987

Wie Žilnik es kürzlich auf den Punkt brachte, besteht der größte Unterschied zwischen der offiziellen Ideologie des Sozialismus und dem „postideologischen“ Diskurs einer Politik des „Übergangs“ in Staaten wie Serbien darin, dass es heutzutage unmöglich ist, in einer offenen Diskussion mit führenden Politikerinnen und Politikern einen dominanten Standpunkt intellektuell, künstlerisch und politisch zu hinterfragen. Dagegen war es in der SFRJ in den 1960er Jahren beispielsweise üblich, mit einflussreichen Ideologen oder kulturpolitischen Entscheidungsträgern grundlegende Debatten zu führen.

—Branislav Dimitrijević, „Concrete Analysis of Concrete Situations: Marxist Education According to Želimir Žilnik“, in: *Afterall*, Herbst/Winter 2010, S. 52

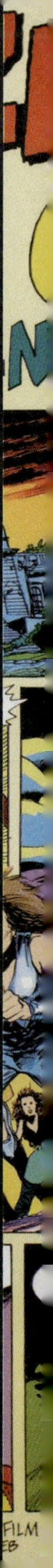

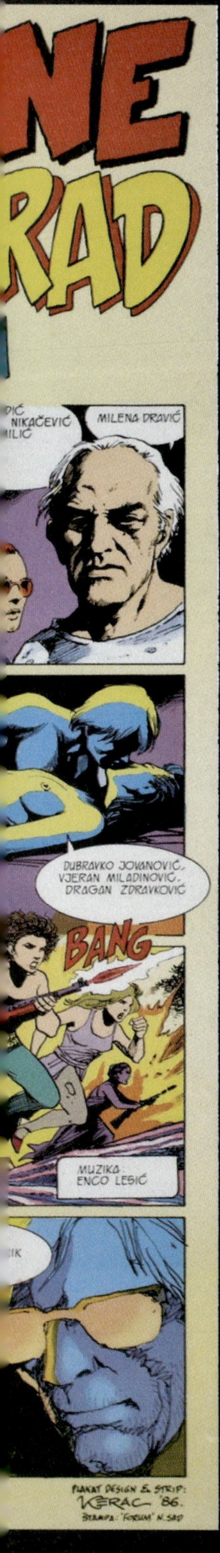

Intervju:
ŽELIMIR ŽILNIK

DA LI JE DOMAĆI FILM OGLUPAVIO?

Ja tvrdim da je bilo godina, ne kada je domaci film bio bolji nego što je danas, nego kada je govorio o važnijim stvarima i kada je u poređenju sa ostalim domenima kulture bio zanimljiviji i pametniji

Žilnik hingegen nähert sich gesellschaftlichen Problemen auf eine einfache, konkrete und menschliche Weise; das ist letztlich das einzige Rezept, mit dem sich Probleme lösen lassen, und es beruht selbstverständlich auf dem Geist der Solidarität und ist nicht durch andere Interessen motiviert. Žilniks Fähigkeit, sich mit den randständigsten und unterschiedlichsten Umgebungen vertraut zu machen und mit ihnen eins zu werden, war seit den Anfängen seiner Laufbahn als Filmemacher seine Trumpfkarte. So erfüllt sich in seinen Filmen Chris Markers legendäre Utopie, dass wahrhaftige Filme über Werktätige von diesen selbst gemacht werden müssen, so wie Filme über Pinguine erst dann aussagekräftig sein werden, wenn Pinguine lernen, wie man mit der Kamera umgeht. Žilnik hat keine Angst, im T-Shirt zum Südpol zu reisen und sich den Pinguinen anzuschließen; überdies vermitteln seine Filme nicht nur diese Fähigkeit, sondern lassen uns auch an den inspirierenden Erfahrungen und Kenntnissen teilhaben, die er gewonnen hat, während er sich diesen Herausforderungen stellte.

—Jurij Meden, „Želimir Žilnik's Kenedi Trilogy", in: *For an Idea–Against the Status Quo: Analysis and Systematization of Želimir Žilnik's Artistic Practice* (Novi Sad: New Media Center_kuda.org, Playground produkcija 2009), S. 185.

AUS DER PRESSE: Ein Gespräch mit Želimir Žilnik im Magazin *Reporter*, 5. September 1986.

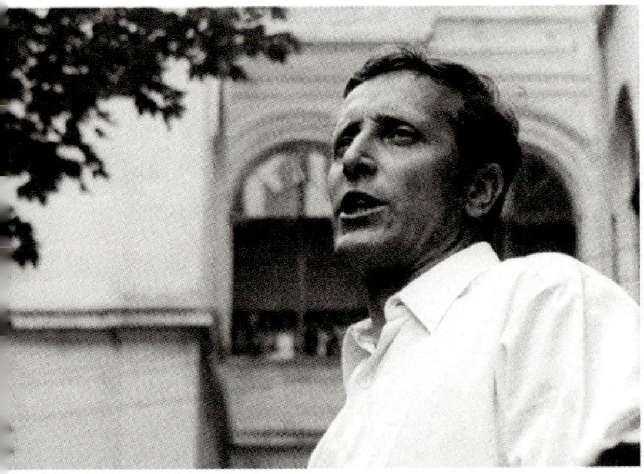

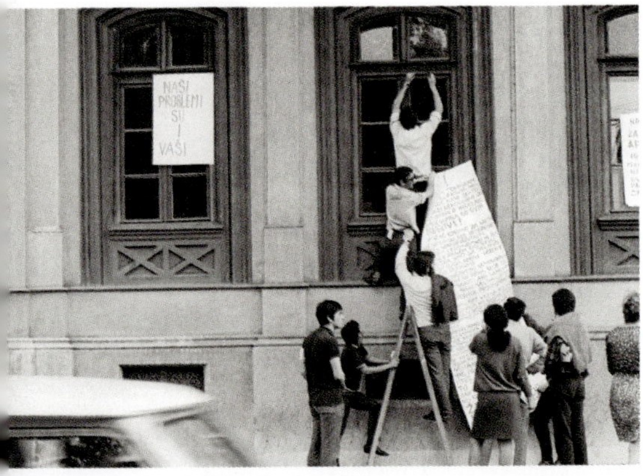

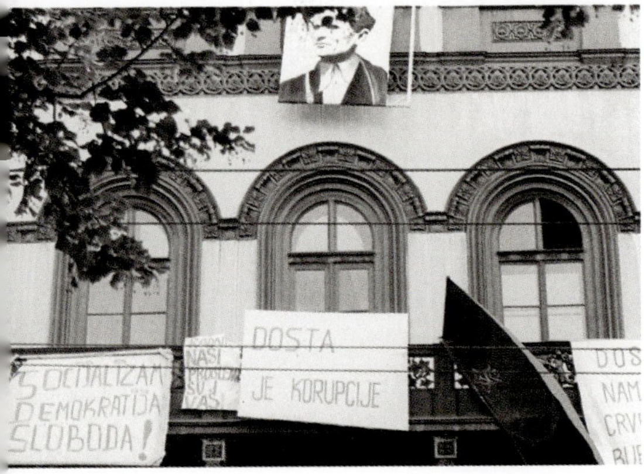

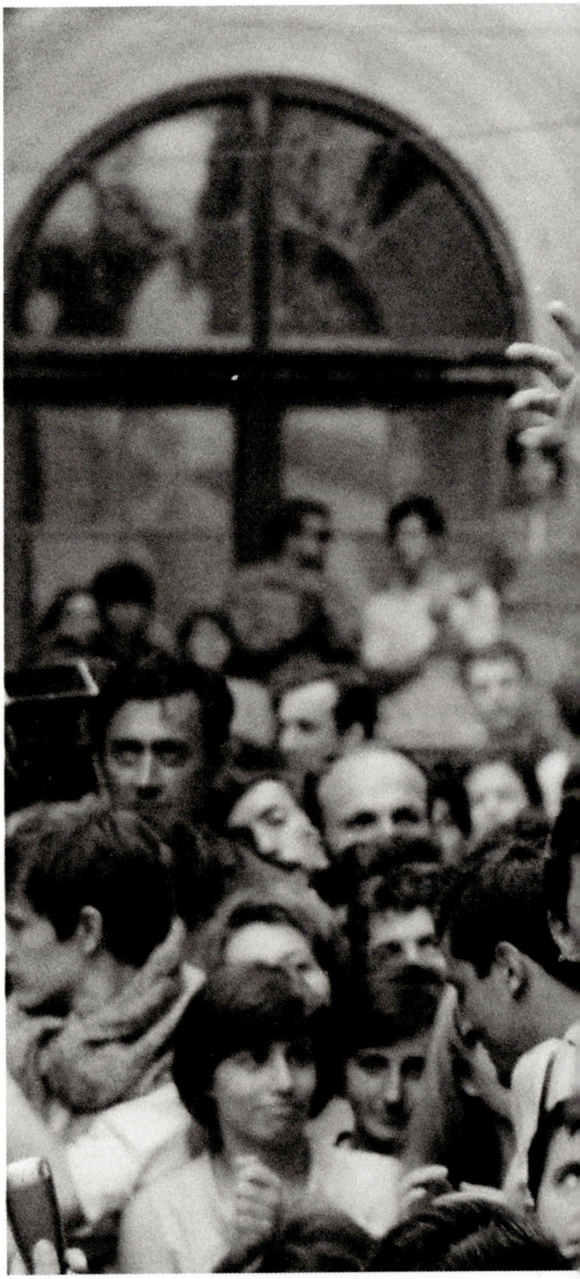

Der Studentenstreik (Standbilder), 1969
Foto oben links: Stevo Žigon

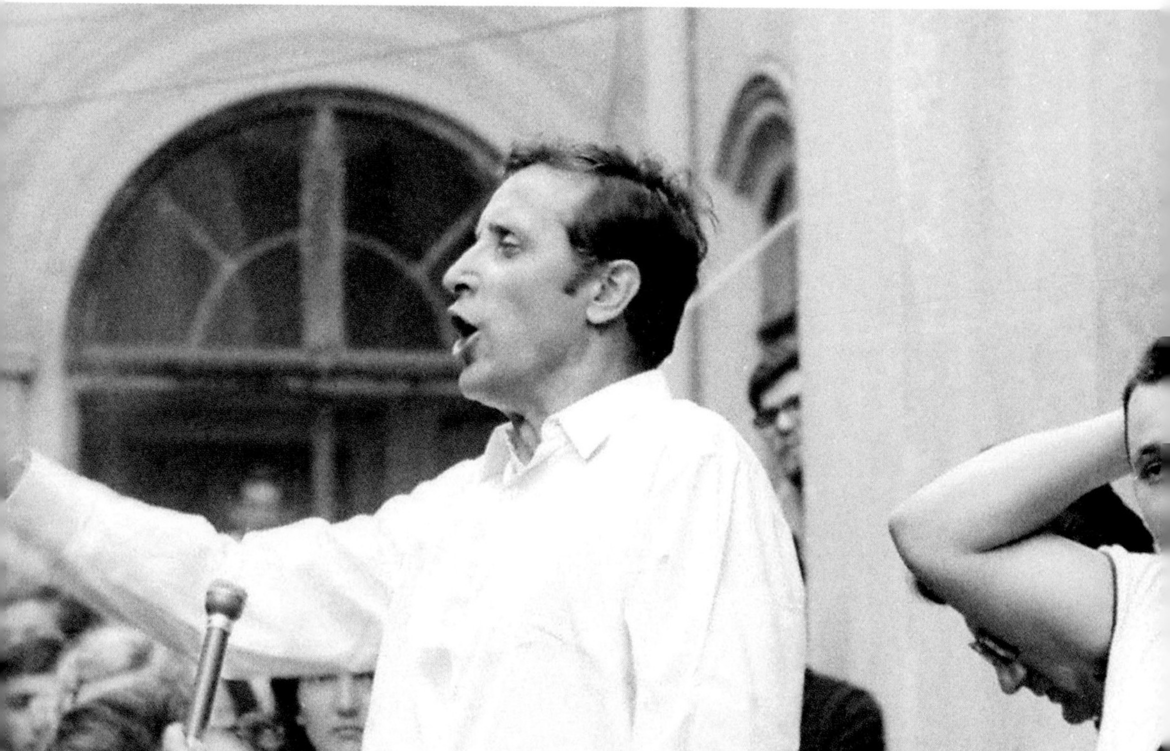

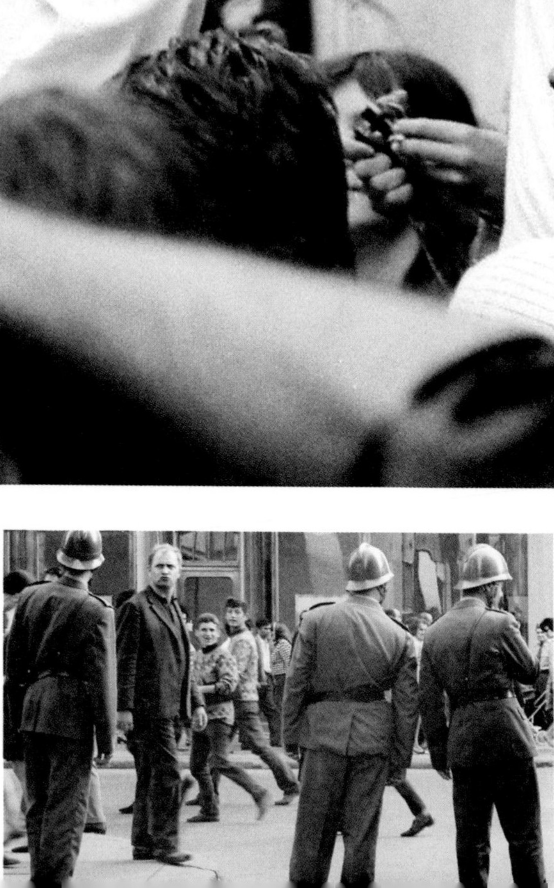

Želimir Žilnik bei den Dreharbeiten zu *Frühe Werke*, 1968.
FOTO: ANDREJ POPOVIĆ.

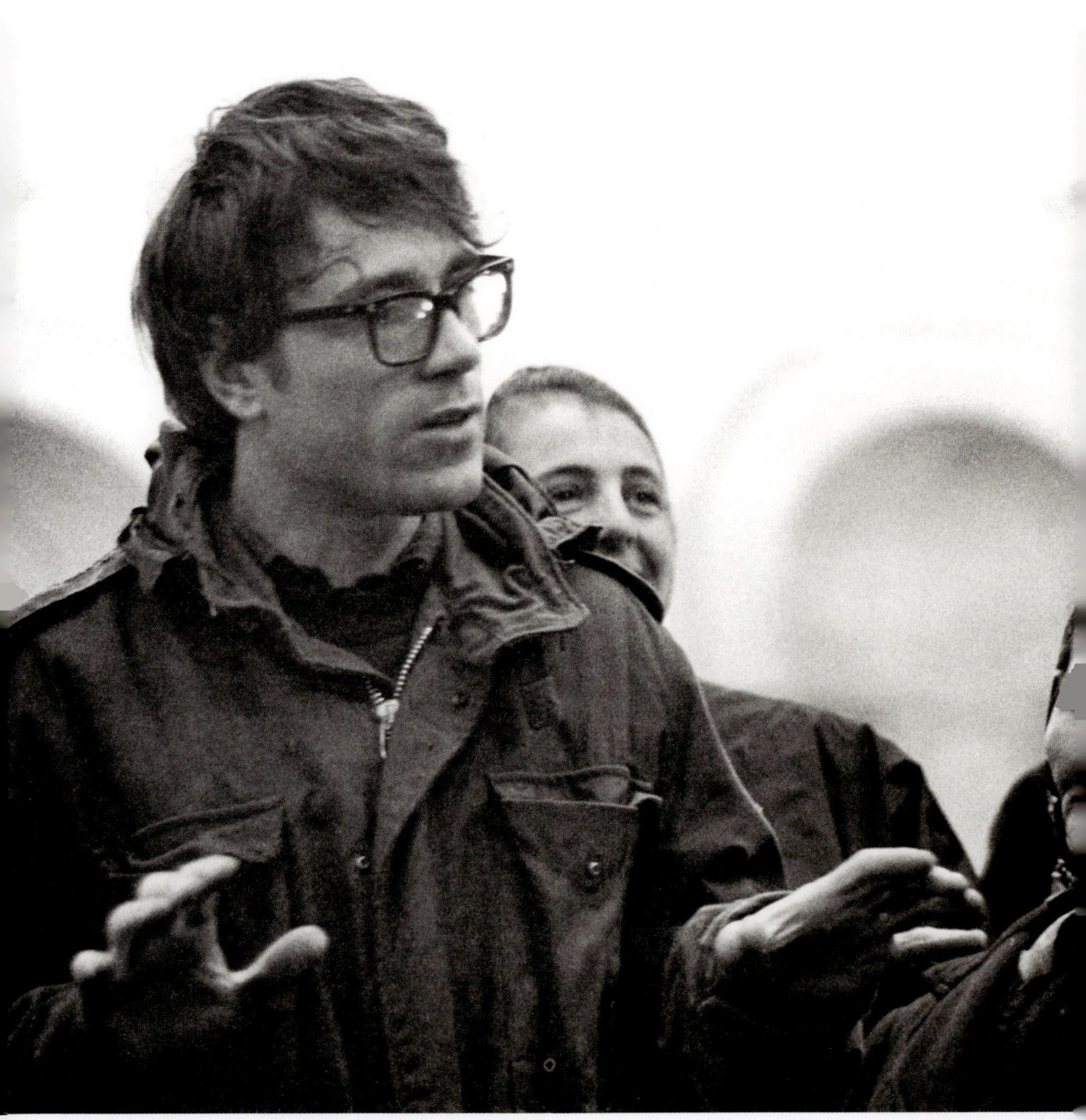

Želimir Žilnik im Gespräch mit WHW

APRIL 2018

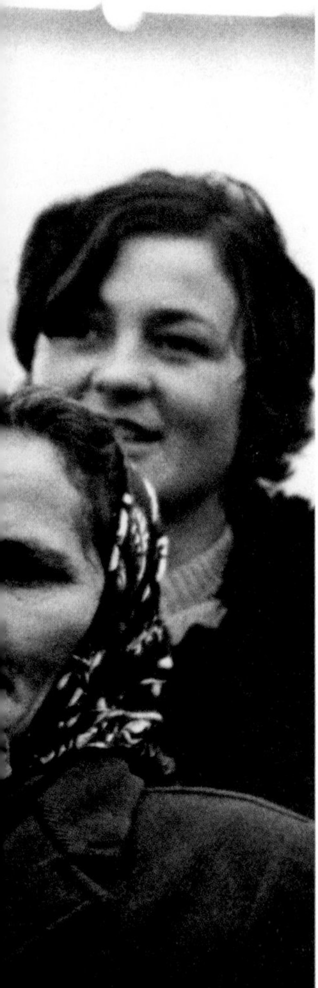

WHW: Da es uns in der Ausstellung *Shadow Citizens* um den gesamten Zusammenhang deines Werkes und Engagements geht, beginnen wir am besten ganz am Anfang. Wie ist es zu deinem Interesse am Film gekommen?

ŽELIMIR ŽILNIK: Für meine Generation, die Mitte der 1950er Jahre aufwuchs, war das Kino eine Obsession. Filme schauen war so wichtig, wie es Gadgets für die heutige, digitale Generation sind. Das Kino war zu dieser Zeit das einzige Fenster, das zur Welt hin offenstand. Es gab zehnmal mehr Kinos als heute, und das Repertoire war sehr reichhaltig. In einem Kino zeigten sie Cowboy-Sagas von Howard Hawks, John Ford, Fred Zinnemann; in einem anderen konnte man Dramen, italienische Schönheiten, Paläste und das Mittelmeer sehen – Vittorio De Sica, Federico Fellini, Luchino Visconti, Michelangelo Antonioni. Ende der 1950er Jahre tauchten realistischere Filme auf, mit denen wir uns identifizierten: François Truffaut, Jean-Luc Godard, Louis Malle und andere.

Nach meinem Schulabschluss wurde ich eingeladen, in einem Jugendkulturzentrum in Novi Sad namens Tribüne der Jugend das Programm zu machen. Es zeigte hauptsächlich experimentelle, unabhängige Theatergruppen. Wir zeigten die neuesten visuellen Entwicklungen. Die Filmabteilung brachte uns mit experimentellem Kino in Kontakt. Ich traf auf Filmemacher, die zehn Jahre älter waren als ich – Dušan Makavejev, Živojin Pavlović, Marko Babac, Mihovil Pansini, Vladimir Petek, Ivan Martinac, und so weiter. Sie waren damals noch nicht mit professionellen Filmstudios verbunden. Filme wurden auf 16 mm und 8 mm im Zusammenhang von Filmclubs gedreht. Leute beteiligten sich an philosophischen und soziologischen Debatten, einige Jahre später entstanden daraus die Korčula-Sommerschule und das Magazin *Praxis*: Rudi Supek, Gajo Petrović, Taras Kermauner, Veljko Rus, Danko Grlić, Zagorka Golubović, Nebojša Popov, Milan Kangrga und andere. Neben meiner Arbeit im Jugendzentrum studierte ich Rechtswissenschaften. Es gab in Novi Sad keine Kunstfakultät, aber das Studium und der Abschluss der Rechtswissenschaften halfen mir in den Jahren darauf, wenn ich Probleme mit der Zensur hatte oder es mit Gerichtsverfahren zu tun bekam.

WHW: Woher kamen neben der Tribüne der Jugend und den Filmclubs weitere Einflüsse?

ŽŽ: Von meiner frühesten Kindheit an habe ich viel Zeit im Theater verbracht. Mein Onkel Milenko Šuvaković war Theaterdirektor und der Intendant des wichtigsten jugoslawischen Theaterfestivals, Sterijino pozorje. Ich besuchte die Proben, ging in die Werkstätten für Kostüm- und Bühnenbild, und ich traf auch viele Schauspielerinnen und Schauspieler. Dann wurde ich bei der Produktionsfirma Avala Film in Belgrad auf Einladung von Dušan Makavejev Regieassistent. Avala Film war sowohl mit einheimischen Filmen befasst als auch mit großen, internationalen Koproduktionen. Zum Beispiel *Die*

Nibelungen, der Mitte der 1960er Jahre gedreht wurde, und der zu dieser Zeit die größte deutsche Nachkriegsproduktion war. Avala Film arbeitete dabei mit CCC-Film, der Filmproduktionsfirma von Artur Brauner, zusammen und stellte für die Dreharbeiten Kostüme, Requisiten und aufwendige Kulissen her.

Ich habe damals gelernt, was für eine komplexe Angelegenheit ein Spielfilm ist; dass die Vorbereitung ebenso entscheidend ist wie die Abstimmung mit dem ganzen Team und die Entscheidungsfreudigkeit des Regisseurs, der zugleich aber auch seine Mitarbeiterinnen und Mitarbeiter hört. Es gab höchst heikle Situationen: Konflikte, Schikanen, Nervenzusammenbrüche. Zeit und Geld gingen verloren, wenn schlecht vorbereitete Chefs das Team anschrien und Dinge verlangten, ohne auch nur eine Ahnung zu haben, worum es wirklich ging. Ich habe damals gelernt, meine Energie und meine Konzentration auf die Vorbereitung zu verwenden, auf die Auswahl der Darstellerinnen und Darsteller und des Teams.

WHW: Man kann eine gewisse Faszination für Handwerk in deinem Werk erkennen. Pferde werden beschlagen, Teig wird geknetet, man sieht aber auch die Arbeit in einem Bergwerk, alles wird mit viel Geduld und Liebe gezeigt.

ŽŽ: Wir leben in einer Zeit virtueller Jobs. Aber vor fünfzig Jahren haben wir uns alle durch das definiert, was wir getan haben. Handwerker waren nicht nur für die Menschen da, sie waren die angesehensten Leute in einem Dorf. Wenn jemand etwas in Erfahrung bringen musste, schickte man ihn zum Barbier, denn bei ihm kamen die Leute zusammen, deswegen wusste er am meisten.

Handwerker bauten Städte oder bauten sie wieder auf, wenn Eindringlinge sie verwüstet hatten. Novi Sad, wo ich lebe, bekam 1749 von der Habsburger Kaiserin Maria Theresia den Status einer Stadt verliehen. Davor hatte man am südlichen Donauufer die riesige Festung Petrovaradin errichtet. Sie markierte die Grenze zum Osmanischen Reich. Novi Sad bekam dann seinen offiziellen lateinischen Namen Neoplanta (Neuer Garten). Die Stadt wurde als Zentrum für Handwerker, Gemüsebauern und Verwaltungskräfte für die Festung gebaut. Alle paar Jahre wurden die Soldaten ersetzt, wenn sie nicht getötet worden waren. Die Straßen von Novi Sad trugen Namen wie Schuhmacherstraße, Sattlerstraße, Zimmerleutestraße. Wenn einmal ein wenig länger Frieden war, bauten sie Schulen, Marktplätze und Messen, Bordelle und Theater.

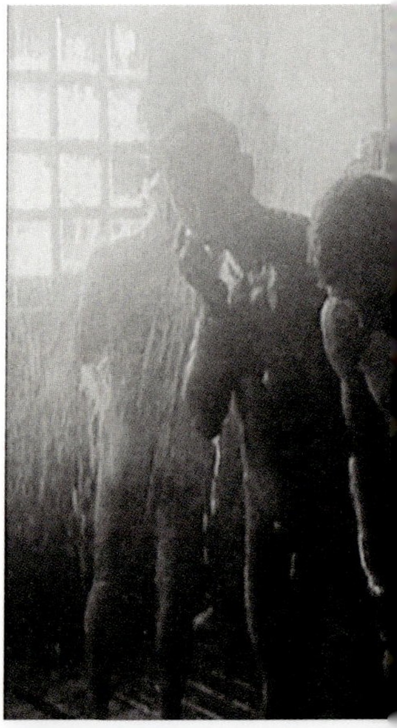

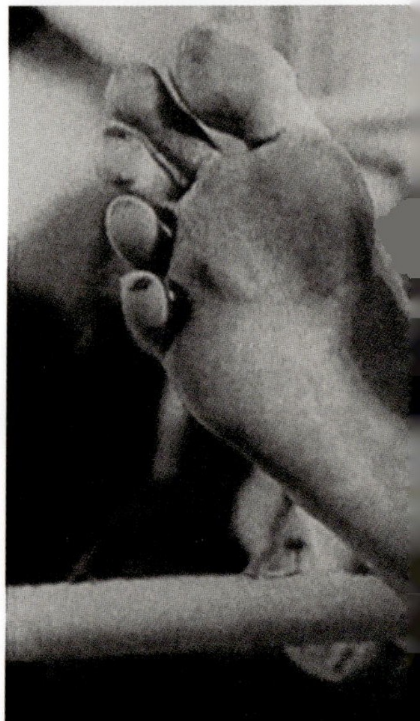

Die Arbeitslosen (Standbilder), 1968

Vor fünfzig Jahren musste man für die Arbeit an einem Film auch wissen, wie Maschinen und Geräte funktionieren. Man musste sich mit Elektrizität, Optik und Chemie auskennen. Als ich mit dem 35-mm-Filmformat zu arbeiten begann, benötigte ein Kameramann sieben oder acht Assistenten. Einer war dafür zuständig, das Negativ in die Kamera einzulegen, später wieder herauszunehmen, es zu verpacken und in die Entwicklung zu schicken. Jemand anderer war

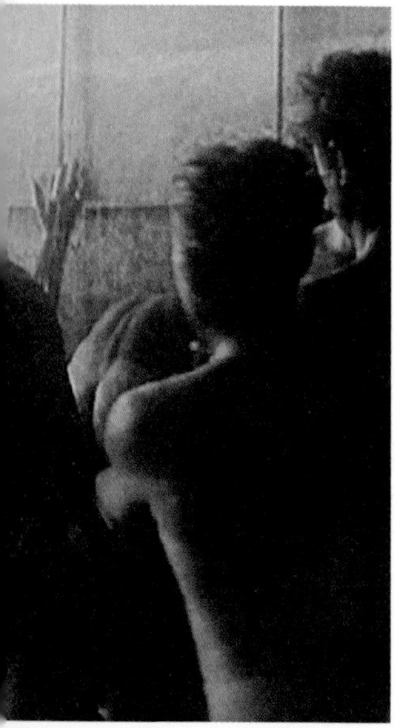

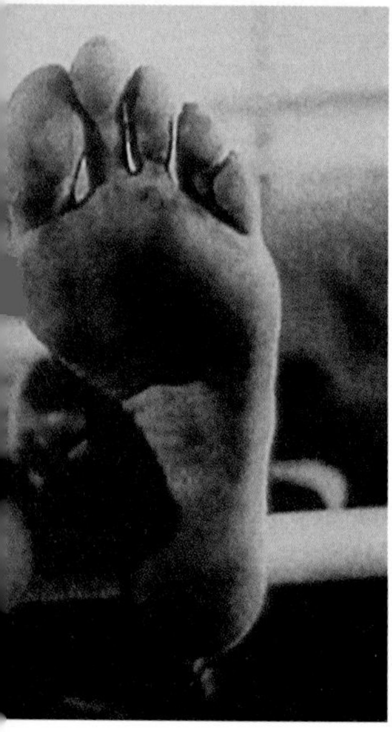

für das Ziehen der Schärfe zuständig – er musste dafür sorgen, dass das Bild an den richtigen Stellen scharf war. Ein dritter kümmerte sich um das panning – also um Bewegungen der Kamera nach rechts oder nach links, nach oben oder nach unten. Vier Männer wurden gebraucht, um die Schienen für die Kamera zu verlegen, denn sie wog 250 oder 300 Kilogramm (wir sprechen von der Arri Blimp 300). Den Kameramann, der dieser Abteilung vorstand, nannte man Bildregisseur [director of photography]. Er war mit seinem Lichtmesser ständig in der Nähe der Schauspielerinnen und Schauspieler und maß, wie stark die Reflektoren die Gesichter ausleuchteten. Dann veranlasste er die erforderlichen Korrekturen. Er rief den Assistenten zu, welche Optiken sie verwenden sollten. Er selbst rührte die Kamera nicht an. Fünf oder sechs Elektriker, die den Anweisungen des Bildregisseurs folgten, arbeiteten an der Beleuchtung.

WHW: Machen wir mit dem Thema Arbeit weiter. Schon 1967 hast du den Film *Die Arbeitslosen* gemacht. Warum hast du dich schon so früh in deiner Karriere für das Thema Arbeitslosigkeit interessiert, und hat sich das auf die vielen Geschichten ausgewirkt, die du später über Gastarbeiter, Flüchtlinge und so weiter erzählt hast?

ŽŽ: Von Mitte der 1960er an hatten wir den Eindruck, dass die Kulturpolitik eher entspannt war. Dogmatische Parteifunktionäre hatten nicht mehr so viel Einfluss. Filmemacher, Künstler und andere in ähnlicher Form Produzierende waren nicht angestellt. Sie hatten den Status von Unabhängigen und sie wurden auf Grundlage von Autorenverträgen bezahlt. Dieser Umstand machte es möglich, dass Filmprojekte in partnerschaftlichem Einvernehmen zwischen einem Team von Autoren und einem Filmstudio realisiert werden konnten. Das Studio verfügte über die Technologie, alle diese unglaublich teuren Geräte, es gab Labore, Kameras, Tonequipment und Beleuchtung. Man kalkulierte die finanziellen Parameter der Investition, und die Autoren wurden zu Koproduzenten und Miteigentümern des Films. Risiko und Verantwortung wurden im gleichen Maß geteilt. Einige der wichtigsten jugoslawischen Filme wurden unter diesem Koproduktionsmodell hergestellt. Wir sprachen von Filmarbeitsverbänden.

Der liberale Moment des jugoslawischen Sozialismus fand seinen Inbegriff in der Proklamation des neuen Programms der Kommunistischen Liga dieser Zeit: „Nichts, das geschaffen wurde, darf uns so unantastbar sein, als dass es nicht in Frage gestellt werden und seinen Platz noch fortschrittlicheren, freieren und menschlicheren Lösungsmöglichkeiten überlassen könnte." Gleichzeitig wurden Fabriken modernisiert, und die Betriebe machten Geschäfte mit den jüngst befreiten Ländern in Asien und Afrika, aber auch mit dem Westen. Die staatlich orchestrierte Vollbeschäftigung und Preisbildung wurden hinterfragt. Man forderte die Anpassung an Marktbedingungen. Man beschäftigte ausgebildete Fachkräfte. Das egalitäre Prinzip, dass die Arbeiterklasse im Einklang mit dem Fortschritt ist,

Guten Morgen, Belgrad (Beograde dobro jutro)

Jugoslawien • 1985 • 70 min. • 16 mm • Betacam, Farbfilm

Im Mittelpunkt dieses Dokudramas stehen die Ereignisse und Spannungen, die sich während des Drehs eines Spielfilms ereignen, in dem Belgrad in einer fernen Zukunft gezeigt wird. Der Regisseur dieses Films baut dabei auf die völlig unrealistischen Erwartungen seiner Produzentin, die Arbeiterinnen und Arbeiter der Stadt einstellt, um bei der Filmausstattung zu helfen. Sie arbeiten bei den Wasserwerken, bei der Kanalisation und der Wasseraufbereitung. Das Filmdrama zieht uns in ihr Leben und in die Probleme hinein, die sie dabei haben, Belgrad als Stadt funktionsfähig zu halten. Indem sie das Budget des Films überzieht, kommt die Produzentin mit dem Gesetz in Konflikt. In der darauffolgenden Gerichtsverhandlung treten die Crewmitglieder als Zeugen auf, und wir erleben in diesem Drama, wie ein Film gemacht wird.

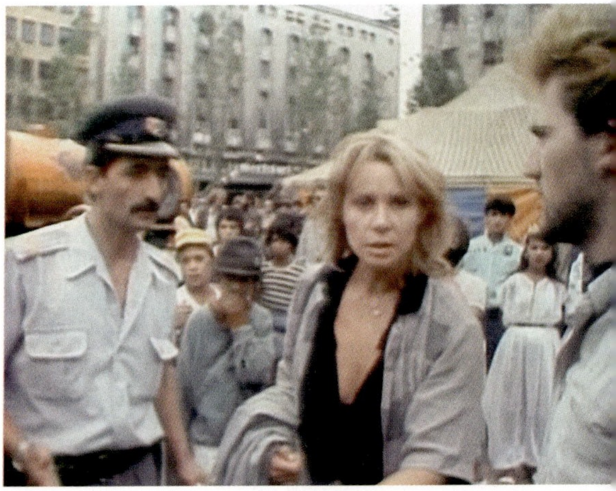

Obgleich das in dem Film nicht explizit erwähnt wird, handelt es sich bei dem Science-Fiction-Film, den der Regisseur dreht, um Žilniks *Schöne Frauen gehen durch die Stadt* (1986). *Guten Morgen, Belgrad* begleitet diesen Film als eigenes Werk und dokumentiert die Arbeitsbedingungen bei einer Filmproduktion in jener Zeit. Beide Filme – *Guten Morgen, Belgrad*, der als Dokudrama für das Fernsehen hergestellt wurde und *Schöne Frauen*, der als Spielfilm für die Kinos konzipiert war – wurden so produziert, dass das Budget des einen Films auch die Herstellung des anderen gewährleistete. Das war zu der Zeit ein durchaus übliches Verfahren, da die Fernsehstationen der Republik für ihre Programmgestaltung eine hohe Nachfrage nach immer neuen Filmen hatten und daher auch die Mittel besaßen, um neue Werke in Auftrag zu geben. In heutiger Währung betrug das Budget für einen Fernsehfilm in etwa 150 000 Euro, sodass man ungeheuer sparsam sein musste. Es gab nur einen Kameramann für beide Filme und ausschließlich Betacam-Kameras. *Guten Morgen, Belgrad* wurde am Tag gedreht und *Schöne Frauen* in der Nacht. Als glücklicher Umstand für die Produktion stellte sich heraus, dass der Architekt Bogdan Bogdanović zu der Zeit Bürgermeister von Belgrad war und sein Einverständnis dazu gab, den öffentlichen Dienst in Anspruch zu nehmen. •

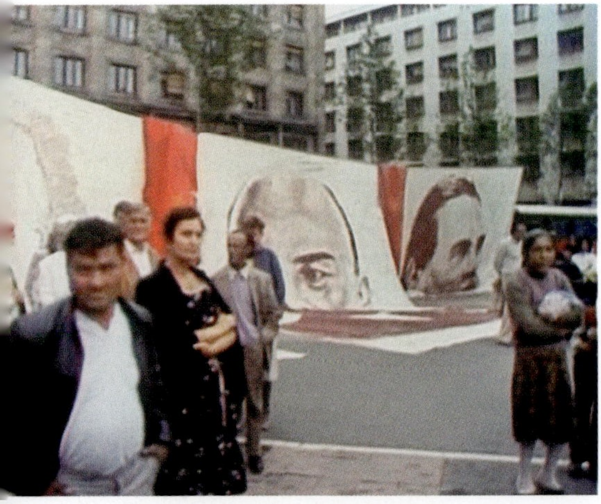

Guten Morgen, Belgrad (Standbilder), 1985
Foto oben rechts: Snežana Nikšić

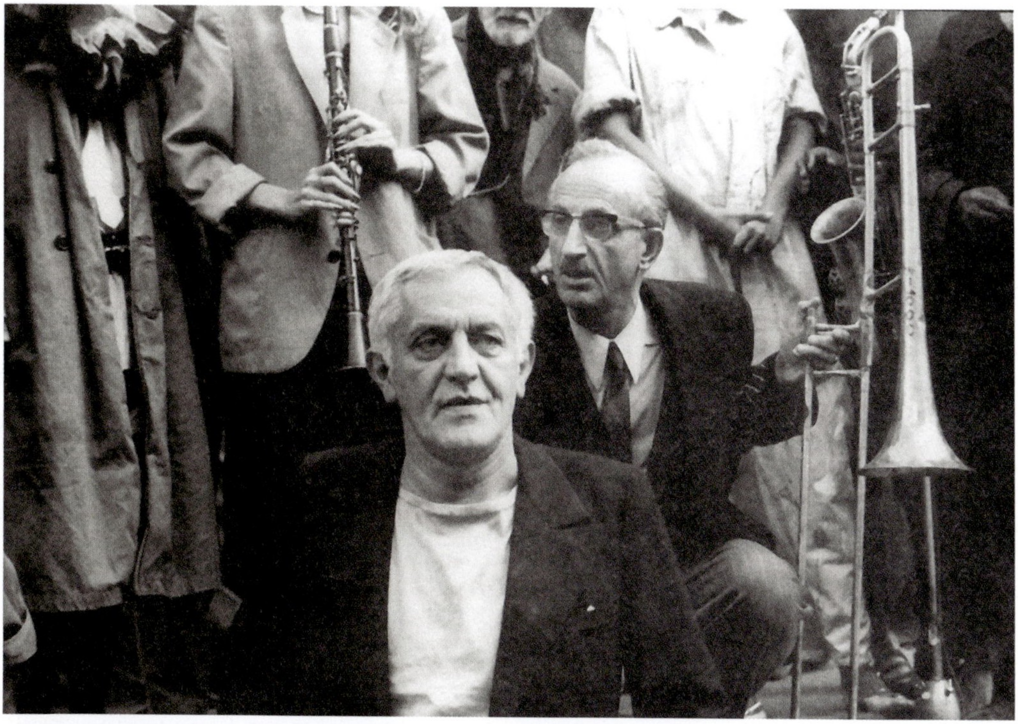

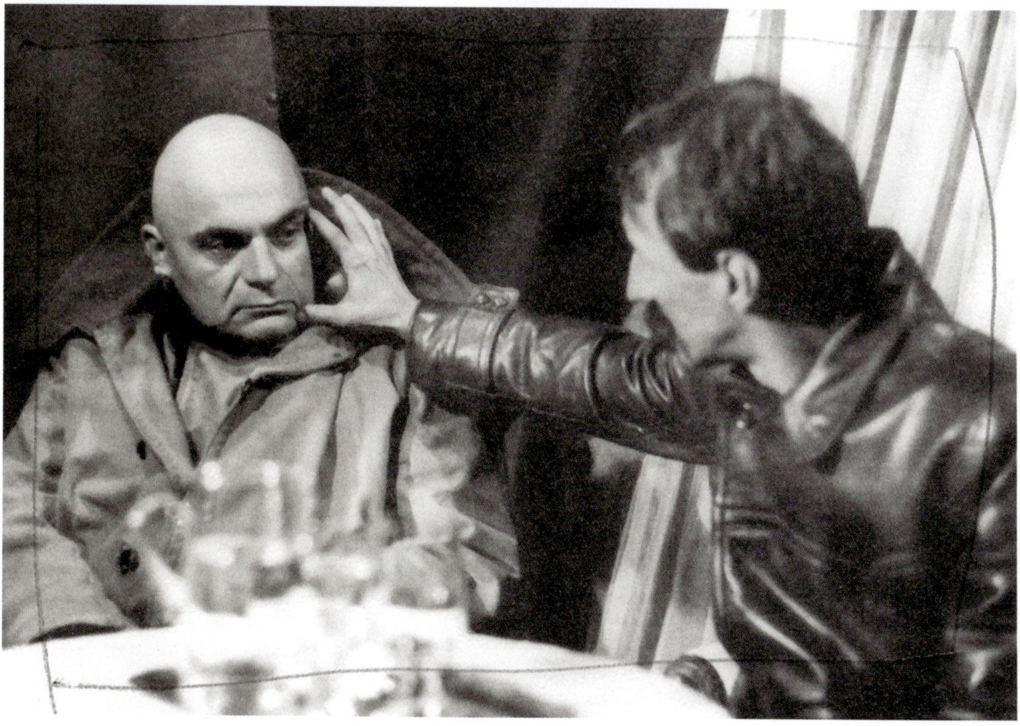

Schöne Frauen gehen durch die Stadt (Produktionsfotos), 1985
Foto oben: Ljuba Tadić und Nikola Milić. Foto unten: Tomislav Gotovac und Ljubiša Ristić

glaubte niemand mehr. Man schloss in diesen Jahren Verträge mit Deutschland und Österreich über die organisierte Aufnahme Tausender jugoslawischer Arbeiterinnen und Arbeiter, die im Westen für den Wiederaufbau der Infrastruktur oder ganz einfach aufgrund eines Mangels an Arbeitskräften benötigt wurden.

Ich kam oft bei der Arbeitsbehörde Novi Sad vorbei und beobachtete tagelang die versammelten, unglücklichen Arbeiterinnen und Arbeiter. Sie waren aus ihren Betrieben entlassen worden und warteten nun darauf, von den Deutschen angeheuert zu werden. Und tatsächlich kamen aus Deutschland Vertreter von Gewerkschaften als auch Ärzte. Sie sprachen mit den Leuten und teilten Arbeitsplätze zu. Sie organisierten Reise, Unterkunft, Arbeitsgenehmigung und Anstellung. Das bedeutete nicht nur Hoffnung und neue Lebensumstände, sondern belastende Veränderungen. Viele mussten ihre Rhetorik, ja sogar ihre Erinnerungen anpassen, denn sie hatten ihre Erinnerungen an die Deutschen ja aus dem Zweiten Weltkrieg. In den Medien wurde wenig über diese neue Phase unserer Entwicklung geschrieben. Wir machten *Die Arbeitslosen*, um ausführlicher von Menschen zu hören, die mit einer unerwarteten und dramatischen Entwicklung konfrontiert waren. Im Grunde so wie es auch bei meinen meisten anderen Projekten war.

WHW: Du hast dich später immer wieder mit dem Thema Gastarbeit beschäftigt, nicht zuletzt in Fernsehproduktionen der 1980er Jahre. Hast du damals vielleicht vorweggenommen, was man heute in der Filmindustrie beobachten kann, dass nämlich viele angesehene Regisseure und Regisseurinnen Serien für das Fernsehen oder das Internet machen? Vieles davon ist deutlich wagemutiger als Mainstreamfilme.

ŽŽ: Als ich in München in den 1970er Jahren nach Produzenten suchte, fiel mir auf, dass Filmemacher und Teams ohne Bedenken mit dem Fernsehen arbeiteten. Ich ging zu Telepool, einer Tochtergesellschaft des Bayerischen Rundfunks, und zu einigen anderen Firmen, von denen ich Adressen und Telefonnummern hatte. Sie kauften für gewöhnlich zehn bis fünfzehn jugoslawische Filme im Jahr. Ich wartete also auf einen Termin bei Siegfried Magold, deren Direktor, und bekam dabei mit, dass Regisseure und Produzenten aus Deutschland und Frankreich angekündigt waren, um mit ihm über Koproduktionen zu sprechen. Magold hieß mich freundlich willkommen. Er sagte, dass ihm meine Kurzfilme und *Frühe Werke* (1969) gefielen, und wollte wissen, was ich Neues vorhätte. Ich erzählte ihm, dass ich ein paar Dokumentationen mit Gastarbeiterinnen und Gastarbeitern machen wollte. Er verwies mich auf den Filmverlag der Autoren, eine Art Arbeitsgemeinschaft für Filmemacher, in der Alexander Kluge, Edgar Reitz und Rainer Werner Fassbinder damals an Filmen arbeiteten. Ich kannte sie schon von Festivals. Ich erfuhr Folgendes: Wenn ich einen Spielfilm machen wollte, dann konnte ich das Projekt an Telepool schicken, die dann entscheiden würden, ob sie als Koproduzenten einstiegen. Und

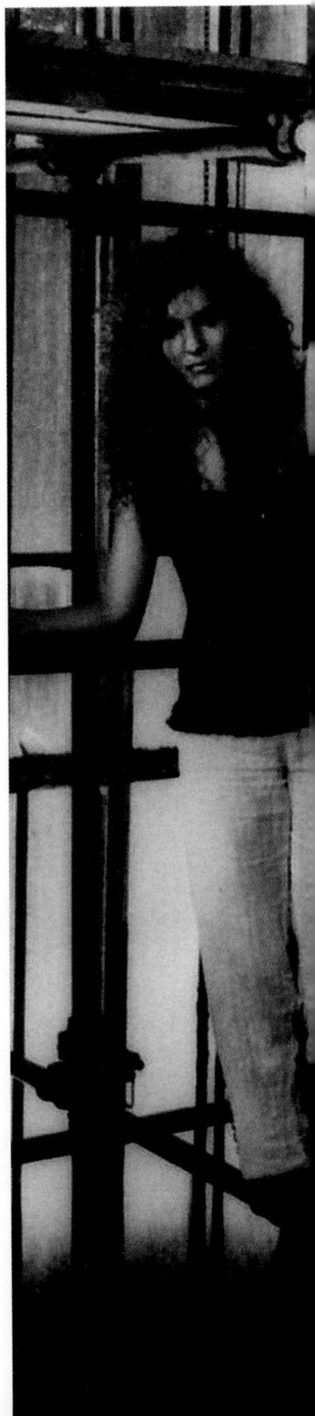

Schöne Frauen gehen durch die Stadt (Produktionsfoto 1985

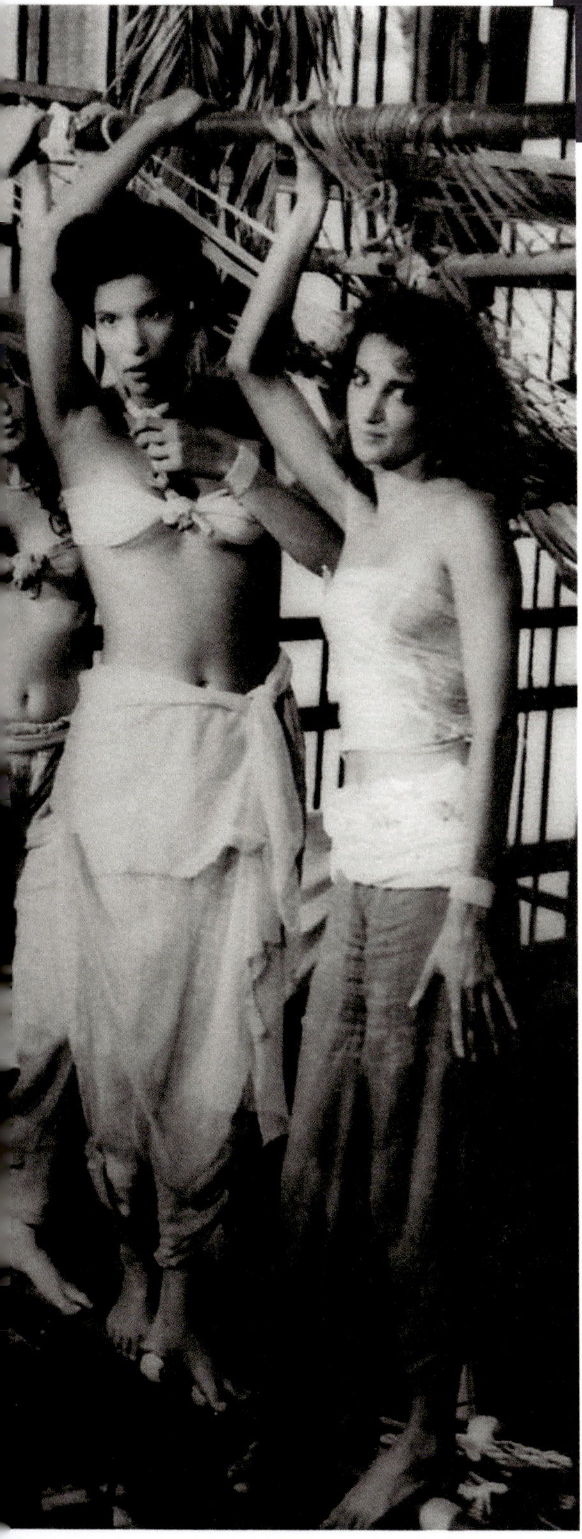

Schöne Frauen gehen durch die Stadt (Lijepe žene prolaze kroz grad)

Jugoslawien • 1986 • 100 min. • 35 mm • Farbfilm

Belgrad im Jahre 2041 ist eine verlassene und verwüstete Stadt, die im Müll versinkt. Dort leben ein paar alte Menschen: ein ehemaliger Journalist und seine Tochter, ein Ex-Politiker und seine Frau sowie ein ehemaliger Polizist, der eine Pension bewacht, in der acht junge Frauen wohnen. Die alten Männer erziehen diese jungen Frauen im Geist des früheren Jugoslawiens und seiner Traditionen. Das ist ein riskantes Unternehmen, wird Südosteuropa doch von einer Bande heimgesucht, die jede Form der Erinnerung an die Vergangenheit verbietet.

Während in dem Film anerkannte jugoslawische Schauspieler, oder in vielen Fällen auch Amateure, die „Guten" darstellen, werden die „Bösen" als Inspekteure Südosteuropas von dem Künstler Tomislav Gotovac, dem Theaterleiter Ljubiša Ristić und dem Filmregisseur Goran Marković dargestellt. Der jugoslawische Partisan, Politiker, Menschenrechtsaktivist und Historiker Vladimir Dedijer, der 1954 aus der Kommunistischen Partei Jugoslawiens ausgestoßen wurde, tritt in dem Film ebenfalls auf. Er spielt eine 127 Jahre alte Version seiner selbst.

Die Geschichte fängt in dem Augenblick an, als der ehemalige Journalist und die anderen verbliebenen Überlebenden sich anschicken, Belgrad wieder zum Leben zu erwecken, um dort den hundertsten Jahrestag des 4. Juli 1942 zu feiern, als sich mitten im Zweiten Weltkrieg das jugoslawische Volk gegen seine deutschen Besatzer erhob. Der Hauptdarsteller des Films berichtet von den Ereignissen in seiner Jugend in den 1990er Jahren, als überall Hass und Zerstörung herrschten, die schließlich zum Krieg und zur Auflösung des Landes führten. Als der Film beim Filmfestival von Pula zum ersten Mal gezeigt wurde, meinten die Medien, nun habe Žilnik endgültig jede Verbindung sowohl zur Wirklichkeit als auch zu seinem Verstand verloren. Aber leider hat ihm die Zukunft Recht gegeben. ●

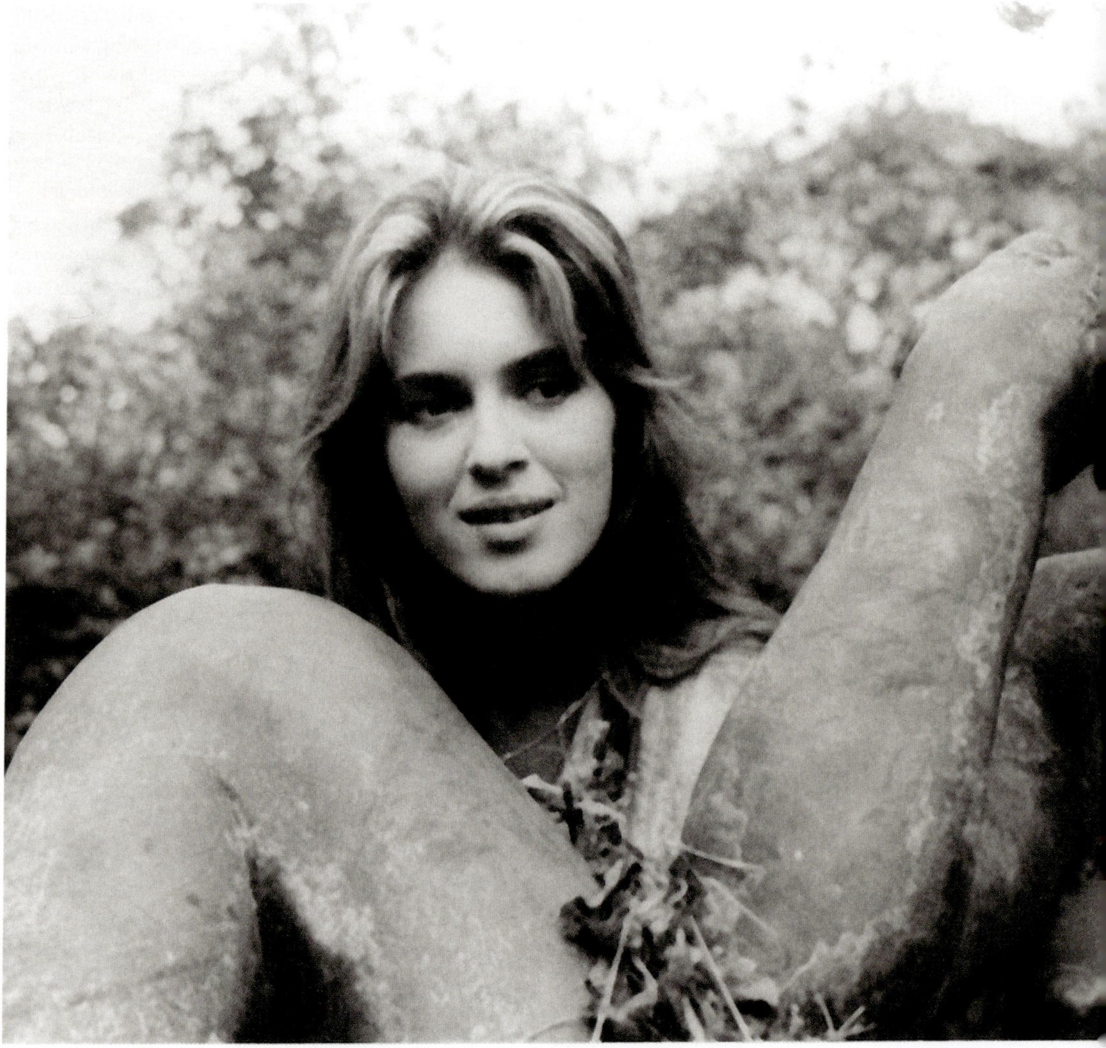

Schöne Frauen gehen durch die Stadt (Produktionsfotos), 1986
Foto oben: Nataša Banović
Foto unten links: Ljuba Tadić und Svetislav Nikačević
Foto unten rechts: Milena Dravić und Želimir Žilnik

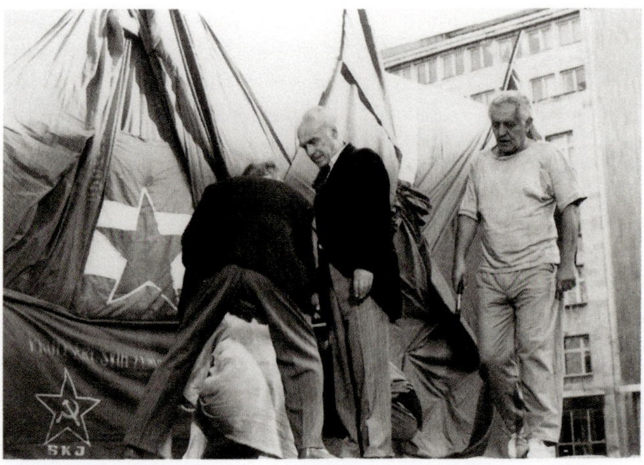

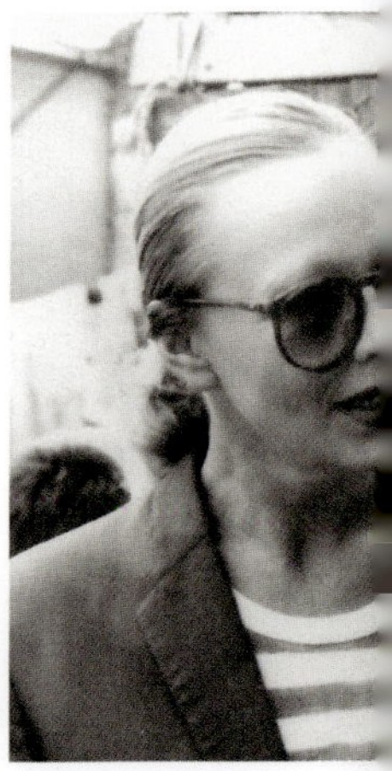

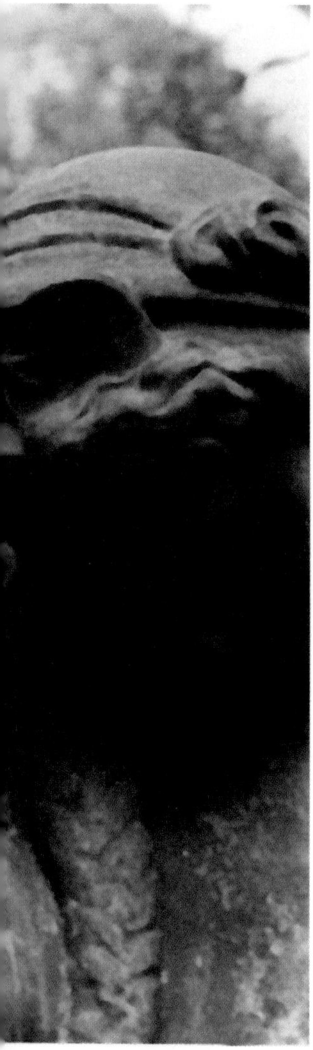

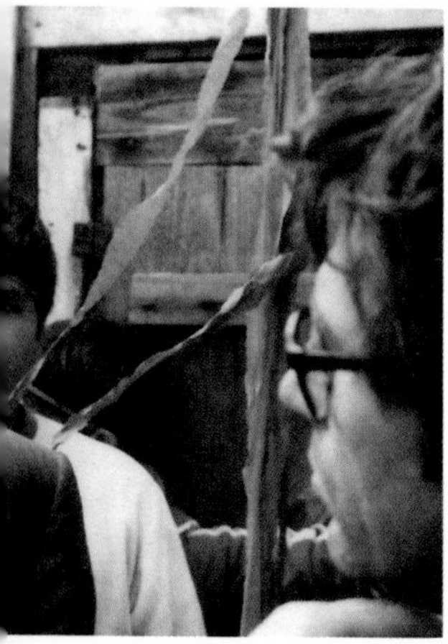

sobald ich meinen Kurzfilm fertig hätte, sollte ich ihn Telepool zum Kauf für eine Fernsehausstrahlung anbieten. In Jugoslawien war die Filmproduktion damals auf Kinoauswertung ausgerichtet, sowohl auf nationale als auch auf internationale. Neue Filme, die Teil der sogenannten Schwarzen Welle waren, zu der ich selbst gehörte, wurden sehr selten im Fernsehen gezeigt.

Einige Jahre nach meiner Rückkehr hatte ich diese westeuropäische Fernsehpraxis immer noch im Kopf, und so wandte ich mich an Radio Novi Sad. Der Hauptgrund war allerdings, dass für mich zu diesem Zeitpunkt alle anderen Türen verschlossen waren. Fernsehen hatte zwei herausragende Vorteile: die Technologie war im Haus – Labore, Studios, Kameras, Beleuchtung, es war alles da. Und die Techniker waren angestellt und standen zur Verfügung. Ein weiterer Vorteil war, dass ein Film, den man für das Fernsehen gemacht hatte, ein sicheres Publikum hatte. In den späteren 1970er Jahren, als ich begann, bei den Fernsehanstalten in Novi Sad Projekte anzubieten und zu realisieren, wurden Filme, die wir für die Abteilung Fernsehdrama gemacht hatten, um acht Uhr abends ausgestrahlt und im Jugoslawischen Radio- und Fernsehverbund (JRT) von vier bis fünf Millionen Menschen gesehen. Damals wurde ich mit einem schwierigen Problem konfrontiert: Ich wollte mich weiterhin mit Schicksalen und Themen befassen, die mich interessierten, aber ich musste nun nicht nur an Menschen denken, die einen solchen Zugang zu schätzen wussten, sondern auch an Haushalte, in denen drei, manchmal vier Generationen unter einem Dach lebten. Die Antwort fand sich in einem hybriden Genre: Dokudrama.

Und es gelang uns, einige wirklich innovative, kritische Filme außerhalb des Mainstreams zu machen, die in der Filmindustrie nicht möglich gewesen wären – *Brooklyn-Gusinje* (1988), *Heiße Löhne* (1987), *Schöne Frauen gehen durch die Stadt* (1986), *Oldtimer* (1989) und andere.

WHW: Wir würden gern mehr über deine Frauenfiguren wissen. In *Vera und Eržika* (1981) haben wir es beispielsweise mit zwei Frauen zu tun, die für ihre Rechte kämpfen. Du zeigst diese Frauen mit großer Zuneigung und Zärtlichkeit. Es gibt in deinen Filmen auch Szenen, wie die mit der Tochter einer Roma-Familie. Der Vater, ein echter Patriarch, will sie gegen ihren Willen verheiraten. Sie läuft davon und versucht, sich durchzuschlagen. Es gibt auch Geschichten von Frauenfreundschaften in deinen Filmen. In *Frühe Werke* lässt du allerdings Jugoslava sterben.

ŽŽ: In meinen Filmen gibt es nicht ganz so viele weibliche Figuren, wie ich es gern hätte. Ich hätte gern mehr gehabt, weil Frauen in ihrem Leben an verschiedenen Fronten kämpfen: Sie müssen die Kombination aus männlichem Minderwertigkeitskomplex und männlicher Aggressivität in Schach halten, den Missmut eines Ehemanns aushalten und seine Vernachlässigung der Kinder; manche

werden aus dem Haus geworfen; manchmal werden die Söhne kriminell; dazu kommen Alkoholismus und häusliche Gewalt. Zu allem Überfluss sollen sie auch noch verführerisch sein und Haremdivas. So will es die Sitte auf dem Balkan. Ein aussichtsloses Unterfangen.

Für *Destination_Serbistan* (2015) haben wir beispielsweise nach Frauen gesucht, weil sie alles durchgemacht hatten: Krieg, Hunger und die Gefahr der Vergewaltigung. Aber die männlichen Flüchtlinge ließen die Frauen nicht vor die Kamera. Einer stimmte schließlich zu, jedoch unter der Bedingung, dass die Frau bei den Aufnahmen immer ihr Kind auf dem Arm tragen sollte.

In *Frühe Werke* wurden die Protagonistinnen und Protagonisten in einer spezifischen Sprache dargestellt; wir verwendeten visuelle und rhetorische Symbole, mit einer Menge Proklamationen und Zitaten. Die Figuren waren als Skizzen und in schematischer Weise konzipiert. Nur die Hauptfigur hatte genug Raum, um die Tücken zu reflektieren, mit denen es ein Mädchen im Sozialismus zu tun bekam – und die Heuchlerei einer behaupteten Redefreiheit und der sozialistischen Slogans. Sie muss durch den Morast unerfüllter männlicher Ambition und Macht. *Frühe Werke* wurde im Herbst 1968 gedreht, nachdem die Panzer in Prag eingerollt waren und Alexander Dubčeks „Sozialismus mit menschlichem Gesicht" den Garaus gemacht hatten. Der Film stellte ein Fragezeichen dar. Konnte man den damaligen jugoslawischen Staat reparieren oder würde er in den Flammen aufgehen, die später dann tatsächlich Jugoslawien auslöschten?

WHW: Es wirkt auf uns, als hätte deine politische Position sich über all diese Filme hinweg gar nicht groß verändern müssen. Sie ist geradezu unglaublich konsistent.

ŽŽ: Dazu kann ich nichts sagen. Bei meiner politischen Position oder Haltung versuche ich, eine gewisse Unabhängigkeit zu bewahren. Das zählt für mich. Wenn ich etwas dumpf, faul oder verdächtig finde, lasse ich das nicht gelten. Da bin ich kompromisslos. Da bin ich auch zu einem Opfer bereit, wie man das im bürgerlichen Leben nennt. Das heißt, ich lasse mich auf das Risiko ein, meine Stelle aufzugeben oder zu verlieren, oder aus einer Stelle entfernt zu werden. Das scheint mir nicht das Allerschlimmste zu sein. Das hängt natürlich sehr vom Charakter ab, jeder ist da anders. Manche Leute sind außergewöhnlich intelligent und sehr in Ordnung, verlangen aber nach einer Autorität. Ich wiederum fühle mich durch eine solche Autorität angekettet. Das ist eine gänzlich individuelle Angelegenheit, und ich weiß auf diese Unterschiede auch keine Antwort. Für mich ist es sogar absurd, ein politisches Credo zu äußern. Schaut euch die Filme an – vielleicht habe ich da irgendwie eine Position eingenommen, die Leuten gefällt. In vielen Situationen habe ich eine Position eingenommen, die die Leute nicht mögen. Ich verbrachte die längste Zeit meines Lebens als Mann, der als Exzentriker betrachtet wurde, der sich mit Verliererangelegenheiten abgibt. Selbst

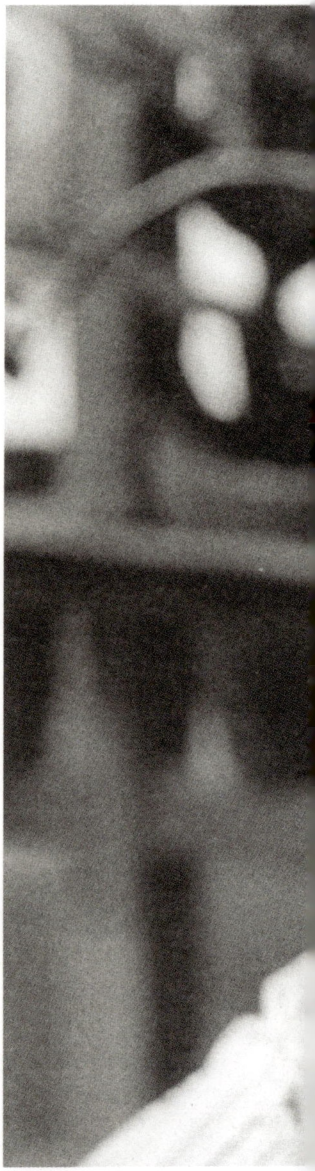

Foto oben:
Eržebet Jakab in *Vera und Eržika* (Standbild), 1981

Fotos unten:
Vera und Eržika (Standbilder), 1981

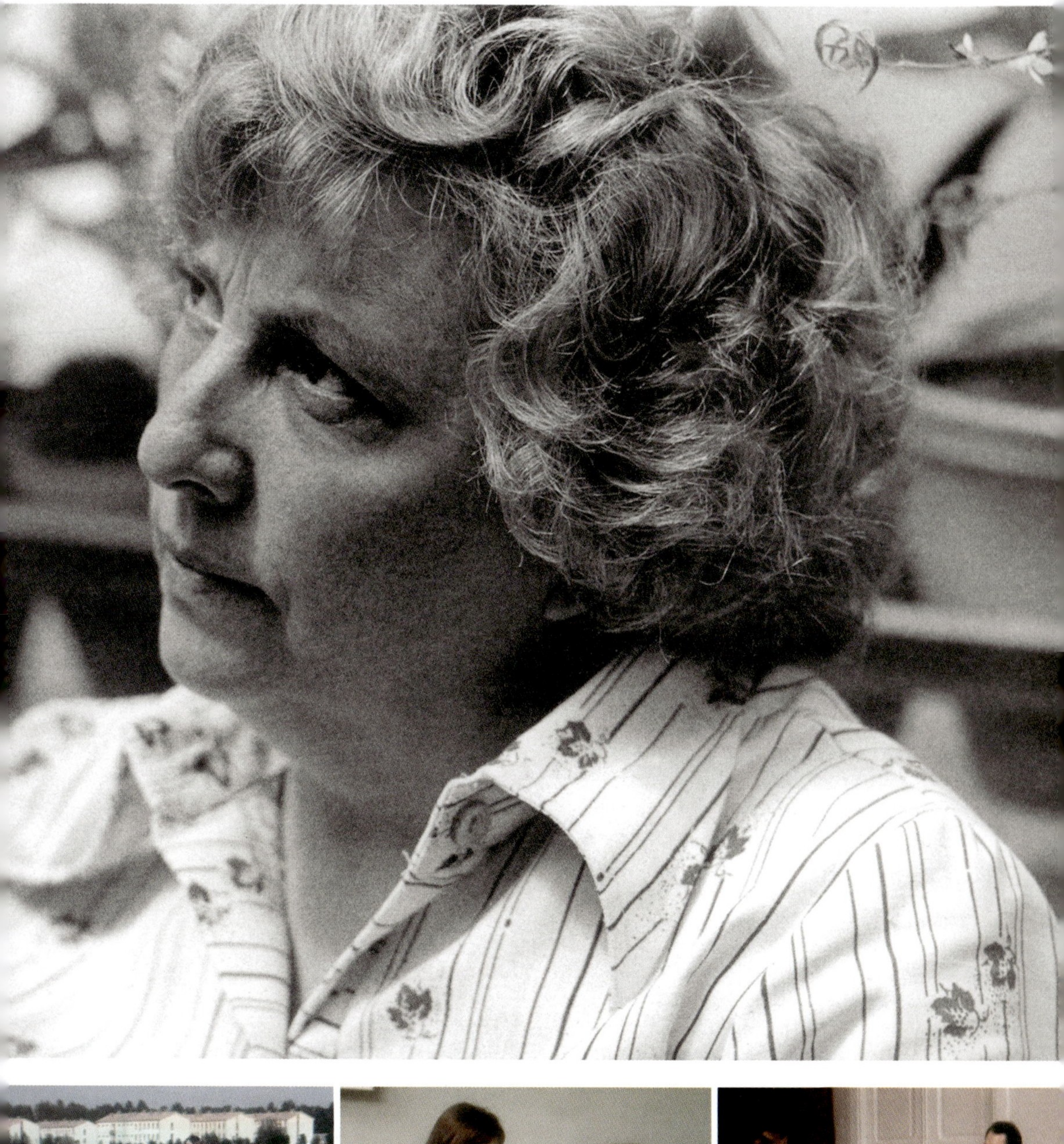

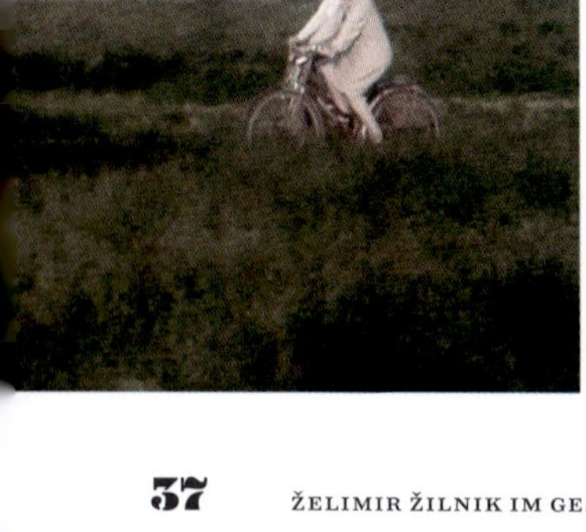

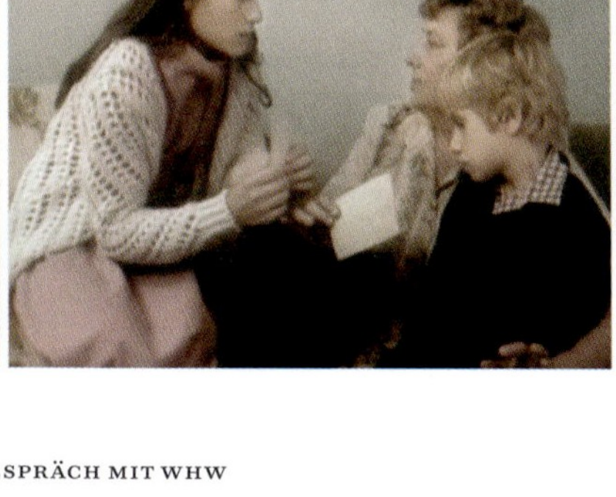

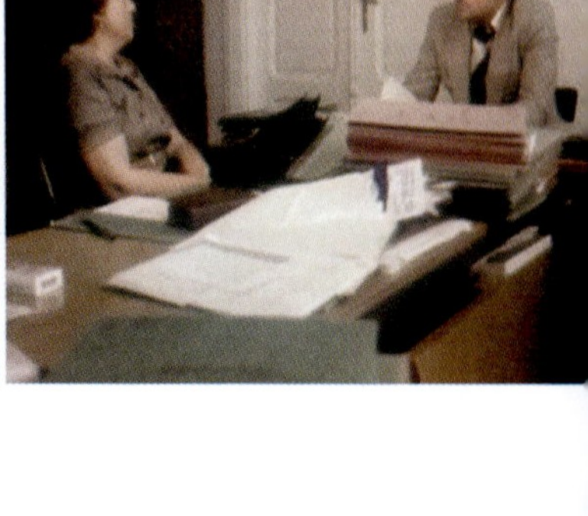

diese Fernsehdramen und Filme, die euch heute gefallen, wurden von vielen meiner Kollegen gründlich verachtet.

WHW: Du hast zu *Der schwarze Film* 1971 ein Manifest geschrieben und bei den Kurzfilmtagen in Oberhausen hast du den Film sogar so gezeigt, dass das Manifest über die Filmbilder projiziert wurde. Wie hört sich das Manifest heute für dich an?

ŽŽ: Ich finde es immer noch sehr in Ordnung. Wenn ich die gegenwärtige Situation mit den gleichen Methoden analysieren würde, käme mir diese wohl deutlich unmenschlicher vor: Die sozialen Unterschiede sind drastisch gewachsen, grundlegende Menschenrechte werden stärker verletzt. In den Ländern Ex-Jugoslawiens sind Millionen Menschen ohne Arbeit, ohne irgendwelche Aussichten für sich oder ihre Kinder. Pensionskassen wurden geplündert. Fabriken, in die Arbeiter und Arbeiterinnen ihre Einkommen investiert hatten, um die Produktion und technische Innovation voranzubringen, wurden einfach in Beschlag genommen. Wir haben uns mit unseren Filmen in solchen Arbeitergemeinschaften engagiert. Die neuen demokratischen, national-kapitalistischen Autoritäten gehen da einfach darüber hinweg. Die heutige Korruption ist ein Vielfaches brutaler. Wer es heute im Leben zu etwas bringen will, für den sind Verbindungen zur herrschenden Partei noch viel wichtiger als im Kommunismus. Der Raum für Kultur in den Medien wurde eingeschränkt ebenso wie das Eintreten für die Rechte der Arbeitnehmer.

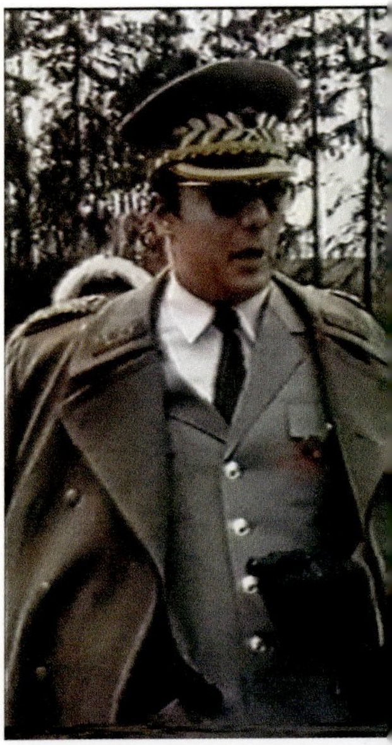

Dragoljub Ljubičić in *Tito zum zweiten Mal unter den Serben* (Standbild), 1994

Kulturelle Institutionen werden nur gefördert, solange sie den Geldgebern genehm sind. Das gilt auch für die Filmförderung. Kritische Arbeiten fallen damit weg, das ist viel schlimmer als früher. In den letzten fünfundzwanzig Jahren Freiheit und Demokratie gab es keine besseren oder kritischeren Filme als *When I am Dead and Gone* (1967) und *The Ambush* (1969) von Živojin Pavlović, *Love Affair, or the Case of Missing Switchboard Operator* (1967) und *W.R.: Mysteries of the Organism* (1971) von Dušan Makavejev, *The Feast* (1967) und *The Trek* (1968) von Đorđe Kadijević, *The Handcuffs* (1969) von Krsto Papić, *Sunday* (1969) von Lordan Zafranović, *The Living Truth* (1972) von Tomislav Radić und so weiter.

WHW: Kannst du uns etwas über die Figur oder die Position des Dissidenten sagen? Aus einer heutigen, leider weit verbreiteten anti-sozialistischen oder anti-kommunistischen Perspektive wird diese Bezeichnung vielen Positionen zugeschrieben, die eigentlich keinen dissidenten Inhalt haben. Wurdest du auch als Dissident betrachtet?

ŽŽ: Heute behaupten viele, sie wären während des Sozialismus kritisch eingestellt gewesen. Das ist in zwei Dritteln der Fälle eine Lüge. Manche waren sogar ziemlich weit oben in den Apparaten der kulturellen Repression und Teil verschiedener Kommissionen. Meine Kollegen und ich, wir nannten uns nicht Dissidenten. Dissident ist ein Begriff aus dem sogenannten Lagersozialismus, der Künstler

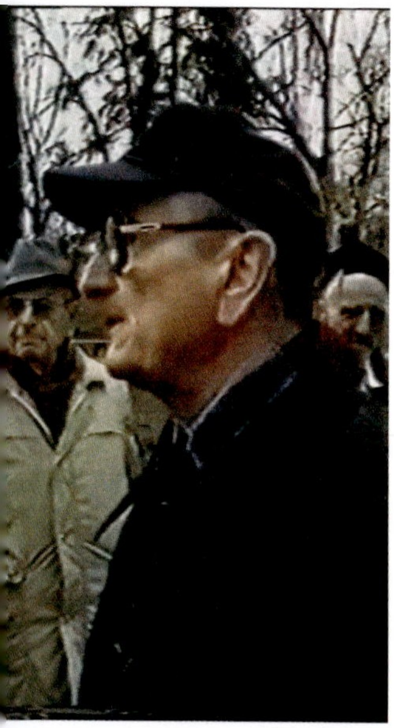

zur Ausreise zwang, zum Beispiel Alexander Solschenizyn. Oder sie wurden in Straflagern inhaftiert. Wir hatten unsere Reisepässe bei uns, als eine Reihe von uns in den frühen 1970er Jahren ins Ausland ging. Ich hatte damals den Eindruck, dass unser Weggehen den neodogmatischen Gruppen nur recht war. Sie warteten förmlich darauf, dass wir eine feindliche Aktivität begehen würden, damit sie einen Anlass bekamen, uns zu verhaften. Als wir zurückkamen – Dušan Makavejev, Aleksandar Petrović, einige Schriftsteller und Maler, und ich –, wurden wir nicht als Dissidenten bezeichnet, sondern wir galten als unbrauchbar, wegen unserer fehlerhaften Einstellung.

Als ich als Gastarbeiter nach Deutschland kam, konnte ich nicht darauf pochen, dass ich in Jugoslawien ein verbotener Künstler war. Niemand hätte das geglaubt. In diesen Jahren brachte Jugoslawien Filme heraus, die auf den größten Festivals ausgezeichnet wurden und die in vielen Ländern im Fernsehen liefen. Der Regisseur Alexander Kluge, damals ein wichtiger Repräsentant des unabhängigen deutschen Films, fragte mich nach der jugoslawischen Politik, die hinter der Belebung der Filmproduktion steckte. Er hatte gehört, dass diese Politik sehr erfolgreich war. Wir übersetzten das innerhalb einer Woche, und maßgebliche Teile beeinflussten die Entwicklung einer neuen deutschen Filmpolitik.

WHW: Was hältst du von unserem Ausstellungstitel *Shadow Citizens*? Findest du darin etwas, was sich auf dein ganzes Werk beziehen lässt?

ŽŽ: Das Leben und die Geschicke von Menschen, die von ihrer Arbeit leben: das zieht sich durch alle meine Filme. Menschen in dieser Kategorie leben in prekären Umständen, ohne Sicherheit und Privilegien, und sie haben nur sich selbst und ihr engstes Umfeld. Sie können sonst auf niemand zählen. Wenn man einen Film über diese Geschichten macht, ist das Wichtigste, dass diese Menschen nichts zu verlieren haben. Sie sind die Menschen, denen man ein Medium geben muss, durch das sie sich in irgendeiner Form ausdrücken können. Sie können ihre Einstellungen kommunizieren. Sie können darauf aufmerksam machen, dass sie überall übersehen werden. Wenn man mit ihnen arbeitet, arbeitet man mit Unterdrückten und Armen, die keine Angst davor haben, ihren Status in irgendeiner Form zu gefährden. Das ist ihre Position der Freiheit.

Ich gebe ein Beispiel aus Österreich, wo ich vor einem Jahr gearbeitet habe. Der Produzent besorgte eine Finanzierung für einen Film über Migrantinnen und Migranten, die Dokumente erhalten hatten und sich auf einen längeren Aufenthalt in Österreich einrichteten und dabei waren, EU-Bürger und -Bürgerinnen zu werden. Mit meiner Kollegin Jasmina Janković, die Gerichtsdolmetscherin ist, besuchte ich Asylzentren, um Menschen zu finden, die bei dem Film mitmachen würden. Die Lautesten kamen zuerst zu uns, sie hatten alle etwas im Sinn: einige wollten getrennte ethnische Clubs gründen, und wir sollten dafür Werbung machen. Andere wechselten alle

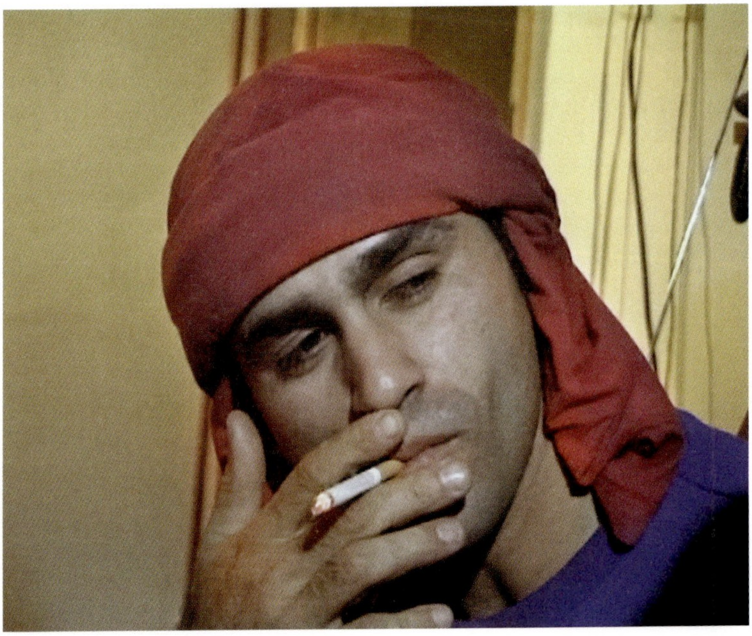

Kenedi Hasani in *Kenedi heiratet* (Standbild), 2007

paar Tage ihre politischen Favoriten – Ende 2016 galt der syrische Präsident Assad als geschlagen. Aber die, die sich als seine Gegner bezeichneten, verteidigten Anfang 2017 schon den Iran und Russland, und Assad war nun plötzlich ihr legitimer Präsident. Als sie hörten, dass ich aus Serbien komme, wollten sie mit mir auf Russisch reden. Ich begriff, dass wir in diesem geopolitischen Labyrinth zwischen Trump, Erdoğan und Putin unsere Zeit verschwendeten.

Dann aber begannen wir mit denen zu sprechen, die durch die Mühlen der Bürokratie gingen. Sie versuchten, Deutsch zu lernen, ihre Berufe und Gewerbe anerkennen zu lassen und Aufenthaltsgenehmigungen zu bekommen. Männer und Frauen erzählten uns Geschichten, die wir davor noch nicht gehört hatten. Sie beschrieben Beziehungen und Spannungen, die sie weder im Krieg daheim noch unterwegs gekannt hatten. Zum Beispiel gab es Schwierigkeiten zwischen autoritären Vätern und ihren Kindern, andere berichteten von den Problemen beim Lernen der Sprache. Die älteren Männer fühlten sich unwohl, wenn sie von Frauen unterrichtet und bewertet wurden. Umgekehrt gab es junge Leute, die Freunde fanden und sich rasch integrierten; sie wollten allein leben, ohne ihre Familien, in Freiheit, wie sie sagten. Dann erzählten uns Mädchen und Frauen von Situationen, mit denen sie nicht gerechnet hatten. Zum Beispiel, dass die Eltern einem jungen Geflüchteten nicht erlauben wollten, eine Frau zu heiraten, die er im Zuge seines Asylgesuchs kennengelernt hatte. Sie hielten sie für unrein – sie war durch die Hölle gegangen – und sie zwangen ihn, eine Braut zu nehmen, die er nicht kannte, eine Jungfrau, die illegal nach Österreich gebracht werden sollte.

Auf Grundlage dieser Geschichten und mit der Hilfe derer, die bei dem Film mitmachen wollten, entwarfen wir ein Konzept und einen Drehplan. Vor ein paar Monaten haben wir den Schnitt abgeschlossen. Ich sagte zum Team und zum Produzenten, dass die Leute im Film ihn zuerst sehen sollten, und die von uns, die diese Leute gefunden hatten. Denn wenn es aus dieser Gruppe Einwände gegen die Schnittfassung gibt, dann müssen wir sie verändern. Wenn wir mit dem Film, den wir gemacht haben, einverstanden sind, dann wird er meiner Erfahrung nach auch darüber hinaus Zustimmung finden und kann sich vielleicht auf eine Reise durch die Welt machen.

WHW: Wir haben den Eindruck, dass du dich dafür entschieden hast, immer im Schatten zu bleiben. Siehst du das auch so?

ŽŽ: Das ist nicht nur eine Frage der Wahl – das ist einfach die Position, in der ich bin. Ich komme aus einem Land, das einen kleinen, marginalen Markt hat, und in dem man eine marginale Sprache spricht. Ich habe zweifellos ein umfangreiches Werk, aber ich kann zum Beispiel nicht einmal die einfachste Frage aus Amerika beantworten. Dort heißt es nämlich: „Das sind viel zu viele Titel. Nennen Sie uns nur die, die mehr als 15 Millionen Dollar eingespielt haben." Da muss ich sagen: „Solche Filme habe ich nicht." Das ist meine wahre Position. Ich will nicht sagen, dass mir das nicht passt. Es passt mir, denn es erlaubt mir, das zu machen, was mich wirklich interessiert. ★

Erschienen in englischer und serbischer Sprache unter
www.zilnikzelimir.net/index.php/essay/interview-zelimir-zilnik-april-2018.

ÜBERSETZUNG AUS DEM ENGLISCHEN VON BERT REBHANDL.

Žilniks Arbeit in der Bundesrepublik Deutschland war (im Unterschied zu vielen dissidenten Autoren und Künstlern, die ihr Herkunftsland verließen) nicht von der Ausbeutung seiner sozialistischen Erfahrung geprägt; vielmehr verlagerte er sein Interesse darauf, die Beziehungen zwischen dem ideologischen Diskurs und der gesellschaftlichen Praxis im liberalen Kapitalismus zu analysieren.

—Branislav Dimitrijević, „Behind Scepticism Lies the Fire of a Revolutionary!", in: *For an Idea – Against the Status Quo: Analysis and Systematization of Želimir Žilnik's Artistic Practice* (Novi Sad: New Media Center_kuda.org, Playground produkcija 2009), S. 145 f.

Žilniks Verteidigung von *Frühe Werke* vor Gericht 1969 ist ein gutes Beispiel für seine Widerlegung aller Argumente, die gegen ihn vorgebracht wurden; wenige Wochen vor der Premiere auf der Berlinale war dem Film vorgeworfen worden, dass er einen heftigen Angriff auf die „gesellschaftliche und politische Ethik" darstelle. Žilniks Verteidigung umfasste sechs Punkte, in denen er die Anschuldigungen des Staatsanwalts zurückwies und ihn darauf aufmerksam machte, dass das im Film Gezeigte offenkundig mit der offiziellen Politik in Einklang stand; denn diese hatte inzwischen auf viele Vorfälle reagiert, die im Film kritisiert wurden. Dazu gehörte die sowjetische Intervention in der Tschechoslowakei, die ungleiche Behandlung der albanischen Minderheit in der SFRJ, die Politik der Kollektivierung, die verbreitete Arbeitslosigkeit und so fort. Indem Žilnik – durch die Äußerungen der Protagonistinnen und Protagonisten in ihren artifiziellen (paradoxen) Gesprächen – Marx zitierte, reflektierte er die Forderungen der damaligen Studentenbewegungen, die in einem sozialistischen Land einen ausgesprochen paradoxen Charakter hatten. In seiner Verteidigungsrede vor Gericht schloss Žilnik mit den Worten:

> „Alle Widerstandsbewegungen der Welt sind, unabhängig von ihrem Erfolg, von den Ideen der ‚Klassiker des Marxismus' inspiriert. Diese Tatsache spricht für die Vitalität dieser Ideen. Es ist unmöglich, die Ideen der Klassiker nur einigen offiziellen Kräften vorzubehalten. Der Film zeigt, dass diese Ideen Tendenzen inspirieren können, die in ihrem konkreten Realitätsbezug dilettantisch und unangemessen wirken und so auf die ewige Diskrepanz zwischen Denken und Handeln hinweisen."

—Branislav Dimitrijević, „Behind Scepticism Lies the Fire of a Revolutionary!", in: *For an Idea – Against the Status Quo: Analysis and Systematization of Želimir Žilnik's Artistic Practice* (Novi Sad: New Media Center_kuda.org, Playground produkcija 2009), S. 140 f.

Paradies. Eine imperialistische Tragikomödie spricht über die Tatsache, dass die Verfolgung von Terroristen in Deutschland zum Teil einfach vom Establishment in Gang gesetzt wird, um die Gesellschaft in Anspannung zu halten, weil sie kompakter organisiert ist, wenn der Feind an vorderster Front steht. Die Geschichte beruht auf einem realen Ereignis, das einem rechtsgerichteten Berliner Abgeordneten passiert ist; er wurde gekidnappt und zwei Wochen lang von Terroristen festgehalten. Und nachdem er es schließlich geschafft hatte, zu entkommen, oder vielleicht wurde er auch freigelassen, hat er eine große Karriere gemacht – er wurde mit großer Stimmenmehrheit gewählt, weil er bewiesen hatte, dass er imstande war, mit den Linken problemlos umzugehen; er schrieb in allen Feuilletons darüber … Diese Entführung funktionierte für ihn also als ein wunderbares Marketing-Instrument.* Der Film *Paradies* erzählt die Geschichte einer Risikokapitalgesellschaft, die in dunkle Geschäfte verwickelt war, von illegalen Importen und der Ausbeutung von Arbeitskräften bis zur Finanzspekulation. Diese Risikokapitalgesellschaft organisiert also Entführungen ihrer eigenen Bosse, damit diese später in der Öffentlichkeit als Märtyrer auftreten können. Ich hatte den Eindruck, dass wir den Film erstens über bestimmte Themen machen, die im Leben in Deutschland sehr präsent sind, und zweitens haben wir einige Dinge, die immer noch auf der Agenda stehen, wie vor allem etwa die Gastarbeiter, damals sehr offen diskutiert. Ich denke, dass Gastarbeiter nicht nur ausgebeutet werden, sondern einen unglaublichen Binnenmarkt darstellen – eine riesige interne Kolonie, die die großen imperialistischen Staaten in der Tasche haben.

Das waren die Thesen des Films, und dazu kam der Umstand der antiterroristischen Agenda, die ich wie eine Suche nach dem Feind wahrgenommen habe. Und als der Film fertig war, kam es zu einer Situation, die für mich bei diesen ideologischen Kampagnen eine Standardsituation war […]. Ich zeigte den Film einigen Leuten beim deutschen Fernsehen, die ich kannte; das deutsche Fernsehen hat unsere sozialkritischen Filme regelmäßig gekauft [lacht]. Und so kam es, dass ich den Film diesen großen deutschen Sendern zeigte. Und plötzlich schloss sich eine Tür nach der anderen. Und diese Freunde von mir – Redakteure und selbst die großen Vorgesetzten – sagten: „Bitte entferne das sofort aus diesem Gebäude, und niemand darf erfahren, dass es jemals hier war." Was dazu führte, dass alle Spuren der Vorführung dieses Films buchstäblich ausgelöscht wurden … Wir hatten damit – vielleicht, weil uns der Ernst der Lage in Deutschland 1975/76 nicht ausreichend bewusst war – einige ihrer Tabus berührt, worauf sie gewissermaßen genauso reagierten, wie wir hier. Sogar noch hysterischer, als es die Reaktionen auf die Filme der „Schwarzen Welle" in unserem Land gewesen waren.

—Želimir Žilnik, unbetiteltes Interview, in: *Reporter*, August 1986

* ANMERKUNG DER HERAUSGEBERINNEN: Žilnik bezieht sich hier auf die Entführung von Peter Lorenz. Der Text von Bert Rebhandl in diesem Band weist auf Schwierigkeiten hinsichtlich Žilniks Interpretation dieser Ereignisse hin. Für eine historisch fundierte Darstellung der Entführung von Peter Lorenz siehe: Matthias Dahlke, „‚Nur eingeschränkte Krisenbereitschaft'. Die staatliche Reaktion auf die Entführung des CDU-Politikers Peter Lorenz 1975", in: *Vierteljahrshefte für Zeitgeschichte* 55 (Heft 4), 2007, S. 641 ff.

Cveta Vuletić in
Der schwarze Film (Standbild),
1971

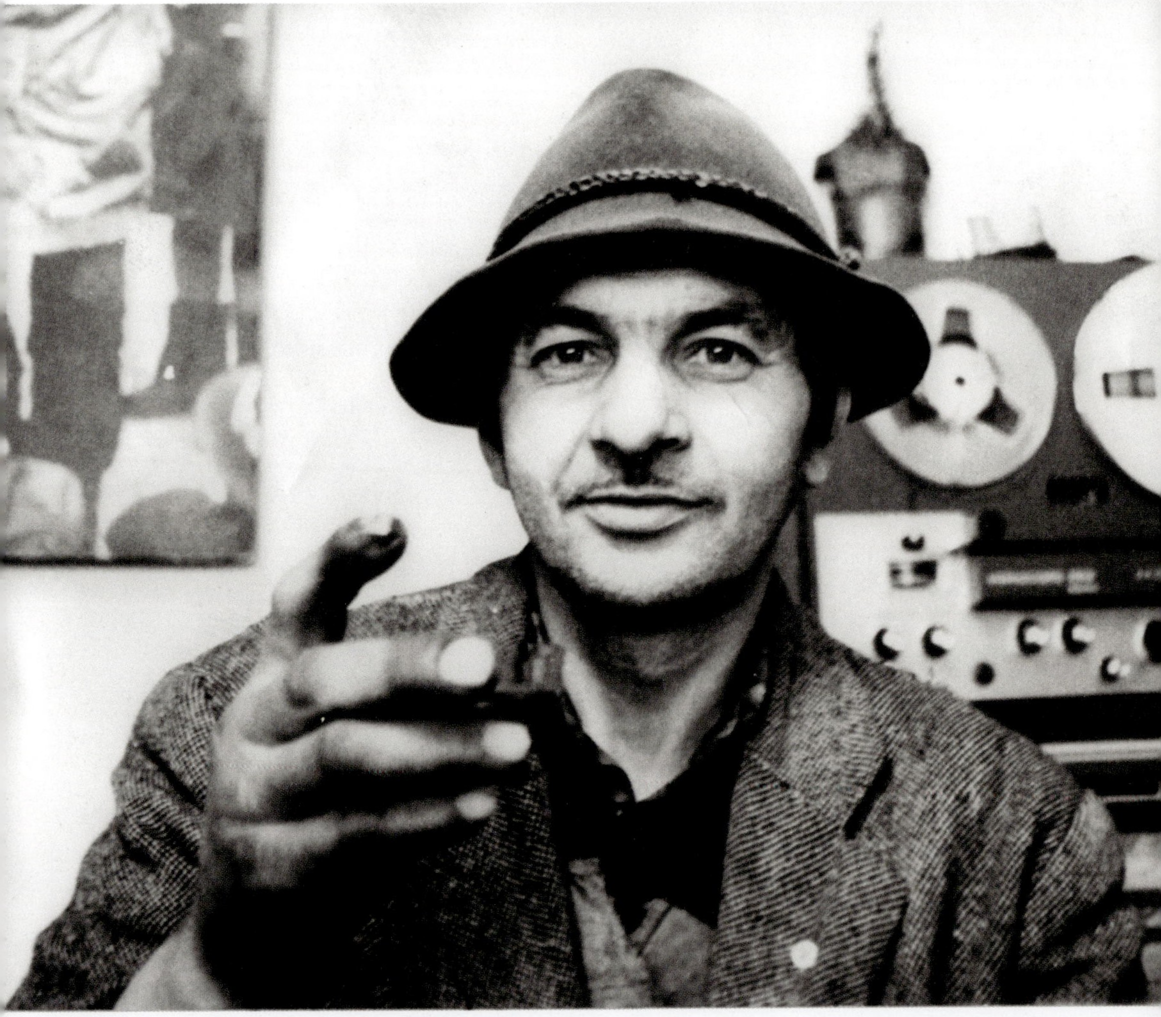

BERT
REBHANDL

Die Grenzen des Paradieses. Želimir Žilnik zwischen künstlerischen Strategien und politischen Systemen

„Männer!" Das ist, in einem Tonfall, aus dem Erbitterung und Ekel herauszuhören sind, das letzte Wort in Želimir Žilniks Film *Marble Ass* (1995). Aber auch nach zahlreichen schlechten Erfahrungen mit Männern ist aus der Stimme von Merlin, einer queeren Frau, die als Trans-Sexarbeiterin an den Rändern der postjugoslawischen Gesellschaft in Belgrad lebt, immer noch auch ein Begehren zu vernehmen. Wie in vielen anderen Sprachen ist auch das serbische Wort für Mann (*čovek*) zugleich der Begriff, der für die ganze menschliche Gattung steht. Und am Ende von *Marble Ass* hat der Begriff sogar noch weitere Bedeutungsschichten: Die Menschheit hat sicherlich mit den Männern etwas aufzulösen und auszutragen (vor allem mit harten Kerlen, mit Typen, die mit ihrer Männlichkeit protzen, mit Männern, die für ihre vermeintlichen Nationen in Kriege ziehen). Aber Merlin ist ein Beispiel für andere Möglichkeiten des Männlichen. Ein Mann kann auch eine Frau sein, sexuell oder emotional oder genderstereotypisch, ein Mann kann ein Krieger sein oder eine Heilige, ein Mann kann sein eigener Anderer sein, indem er sich von Schwanzgesteuerten nehmen lässt. Dem Wort Männer, wie es am Ende von *Marble Ass* zu vernehmen ist, eignet eine gewisse Dialektik. Und der Film selbst beruht auch auf Widersprüchen. Sie heben sich auf höchst originelle Weise auf.

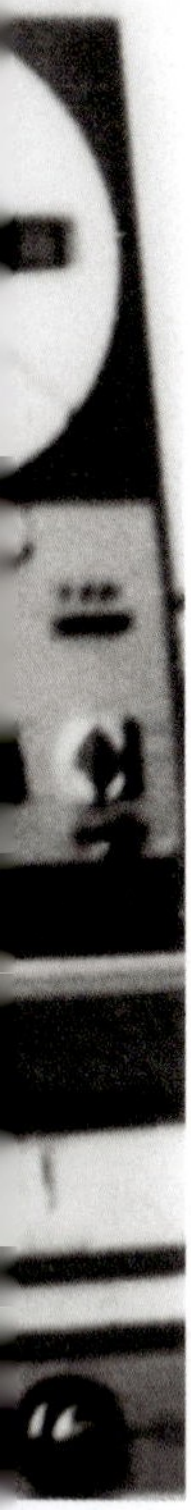

Die grundlegende Aufhebung, die Žilnik in *Marble Ass* bewerkstelligt, ist natürlich die eines Widerspruchs zwischen Realität und Fiktion. Auf einen einfachen Nenner gebracht: Die Fiktionen von Žilnik waren immer schon sehr stark von den Wirklichkeiten seines ereignisreichen Lebens und von den Zeiten geprägt, von denen er erzählte. Und zwar in einem höheren Ausmaß als bei anderen Filmemachern, die ihre Erfahrungen verarbeiten, indem sie Geschichten davon erzählen. Žilnik erzählt Geschichten nicht nur von, sondern mit seinen Erfahrungen, Interventionen und Reflexionen. Seine Karriere erstreckt sich über ein halbes Jahrhundert und mehrere Systeme: das blockfreie Jugoslawien, ein sozialistischer, föderaler Staat mit einem charismatischen Staatschef in Marschall Tito und einer Elite in jedem regionalen System von Mazedonien bis Slowenien (das staatliche Fernsehen ist überall ein Teil dieser Elite); die Bundesrepublik Deutschland (auch geläufig als Westdeutschland) nach 1968 und vor 1977, eine Demokratie unter dem Druck linker Terroristinnen und Terroristen und in der Versuchung, darauf mit Mitteln des Ausnahmezustands zu reagieren (in der Bundesrepublik wurde Žilnik als Gastarbeiter empfangen, während er sich als dissidenter Intellektueller im Exil verstand); der scheiternde Staat Jugoslawien nach 1991 in seinem kriegerischen Zerfall in frühere Teilstaaten (und Teile dieser Teilstaaten); und schließlich die Europäische Union in ihren Phasen der Osterweiterung. Südosteuropa (geläufiger: der Balkan) befindet sich nun in einer strategisch wichtigen und verletzlichen Position an den Außengrenzen eines zunehmend umstrittenen geeinten Raums mit definierten Freiheiten. Aufgrund von territorialen Prinzipien und der Aufrechterhaltung einer regelbasierten Ordnung müssen diese Freiheiten Menschen von außerhalb der EU gewährt oder verweigert werden,

auf Grundlage von zunehmend umstrittenen Regelwerken wie der Genfer Konvention.

Žilnik kam 1942 in einem von der Gestapo betriebenen Konzentrationslager im besetzten Serbien zur Welt. Das nationalsozialistische Deutschland war damals auf dem Höhepunkt seiner Expansion. Es sagt viel über die Unwägbarkeiten des Historischen, dass Žilnik aus seiner Position just außerhalb der heutigen Europäischen Union der europäische Filmemacher par excellence werden konnte. Seine politischen und ästhetischen Strategien wurden dabei von den Neuen Wellen geprägt, die es in fast allen europäischen Nachkriegsgesellschaften gab: in Italien in den 1940er und 1950er Jahren (der Neorealismus mit seiner Hinwendung zu Erzählungen über einfache Leute), in Frankreich in den 1960er Jahren (die Nouvelle Vague mit ihren unterschiedlichen Ausprägungen eines Kinos, das zugleich die Pop- und Massenkultur und die Hochmoderne in sich zu vereinen versuchte); in Westdeutschland vor allem in den 1970er Jahren (der Neue Deutsche Film mit seinem Zwiespalt zwischen Romantik und Experiment). Bei Žilnik wichen die filmhistorischen Inspirationen aber zunehmend einem Pragmatismus, der aus den Begegnungen mit den Menschen in seinen Filmen erwuchs. Menschen wie Merlin, Franja Handrla (aus seinem frühen *Der schwarze Film*, 1971), Bora Joksimović (*Die Komödie und Tragödie von Bora Joksimović*, 1977), und der kosovarische Rom Kenedi Hasani (aus der *Kenedi*-Trilogie, 2003–2007) sind typische Beispiele für Žilnik-Protagonistinnen und -Protagonisten. Im Rückblick auf seine außergewöhnliche Karriere sind, trotz all der epochalen Umbrüche, von denen diese Karriere markiert ist, viele überraschende Kontinuitäten zu erkennen. Sein Ansatz wirkt immer spielerisch, folgt aber einem einfachen Grundsatz: Er möchte die Geschichte von unten sehen.

Wir können mit Franja Handrla beginnen, einem Mann, der 1971 in Belgrad auf der Straße lebte. Er wurde zur Hauptfigur in Žilniks *Der schwarze Film*. „Ich schlafe schlecht. Ich esse schlecht. Ich kann mich nie wohlfühlen", sagt er. „Niemand gibt mir etwas." Das ändert sich, als er auf Žilnik trifft, der nicht nur Handrla, sondern fünf weitere Obdachlose mit zu sich nach Hause nimmt. Die Wohnung hat keine fünfzig Quadratmeter. Žilniks Ehefrau schläft auf einer Matratze im Wohnzimmer, sie wird abrupt geweckt und muss zu den Kindern in das andere Zimmer übersiedeln. Žilnik möchte den Armen helfen, er möchte aber auch einen Film machen. Die Männer bringen einen durchdringenden Gestank in die Wohnung. Sie stellen eine Herausforderung für die Gesellschaft dar. Wie kann ein System, das sich als Arbeiterstaat ausgibt, Menschen wie Franja so vollständig übersehen? Žilnik spricht in *Der schwarze Film* als Anwalt (er studierte Rechtswissenschaften, bevor er sich dem Film zuwandte), als Intellektueller, als Künstler.

Am nächsten Morgen geht er auf die Straße, um Menschen zu fragen, was man für jemanden wie Franja tun könnte. Sein Tun wirkt spontan, aber es hat eine grundsätzliche Dimension: In einer sozialistischen

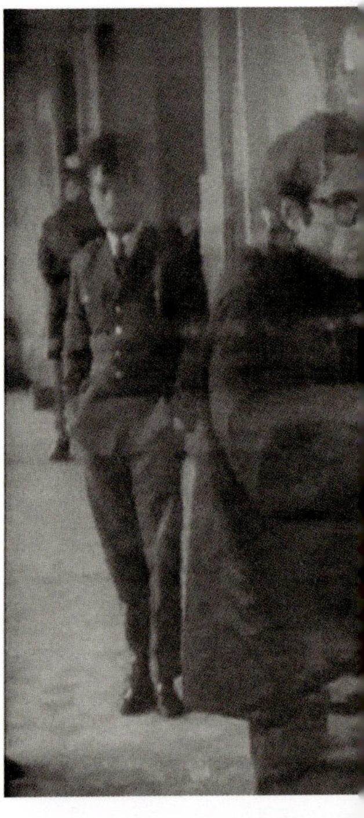

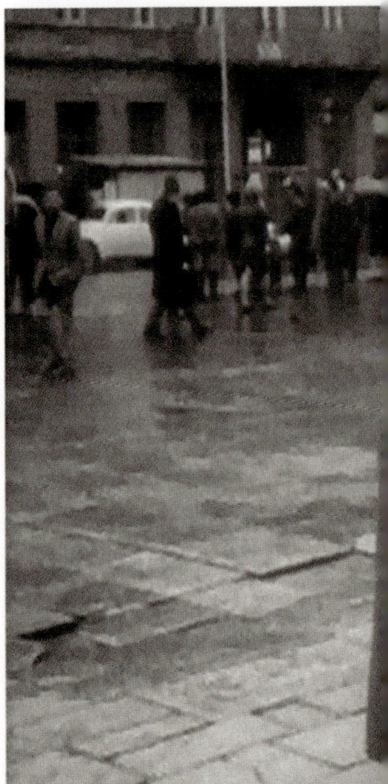

Der schwarze Film
(Standbilder), 1971

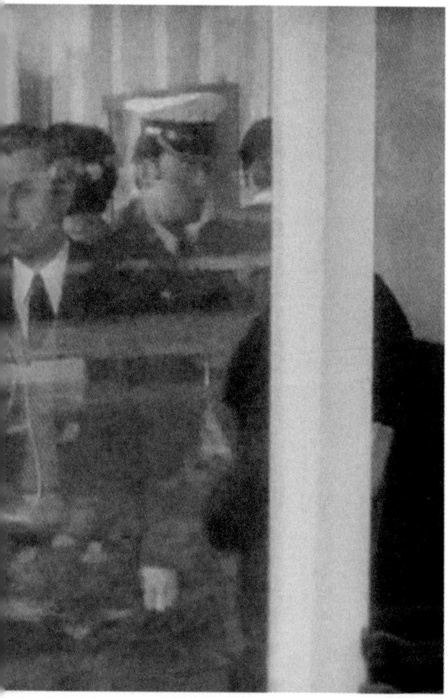
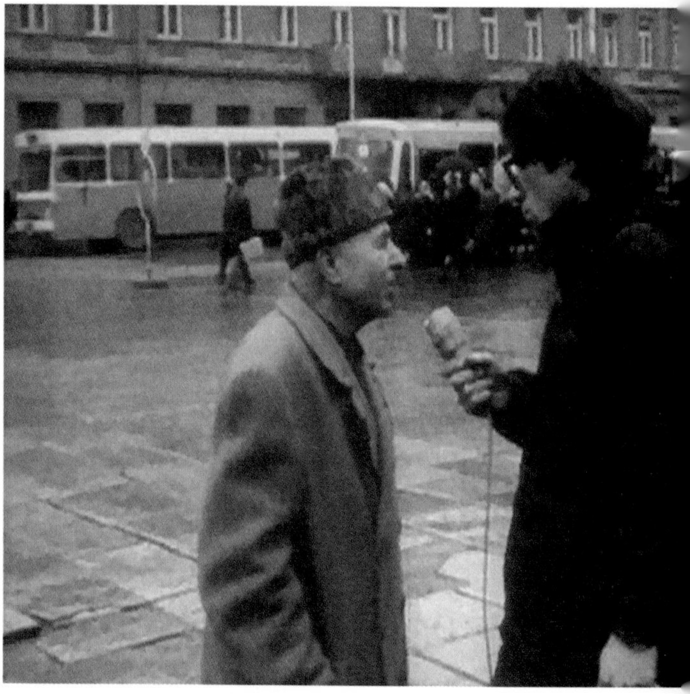
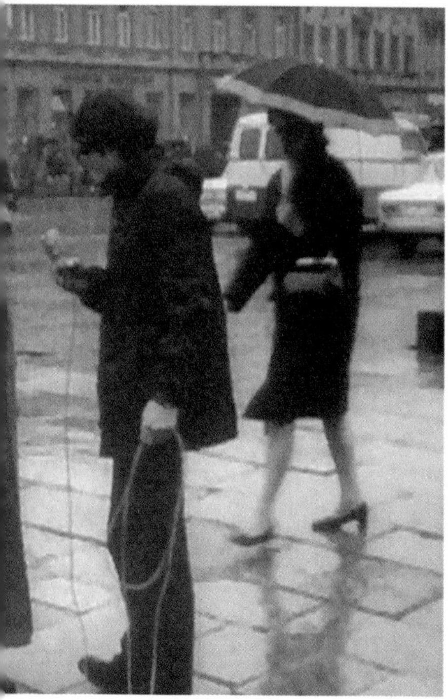
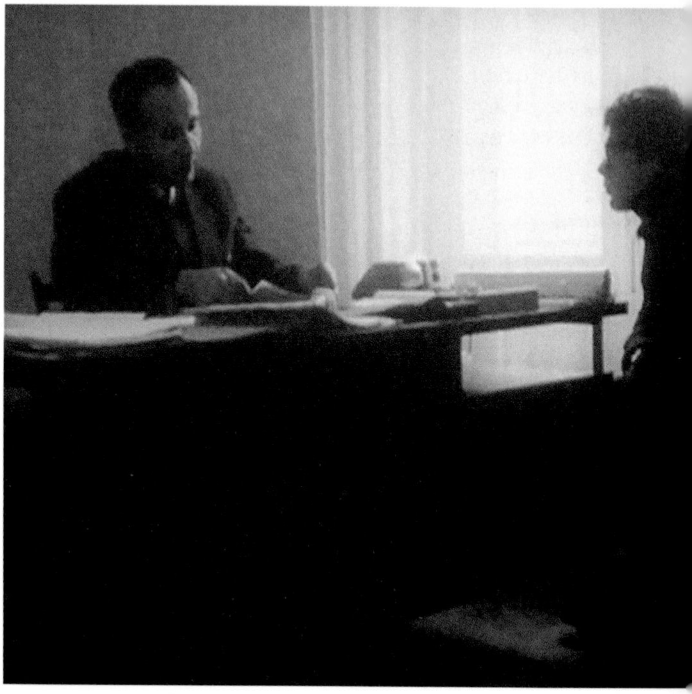

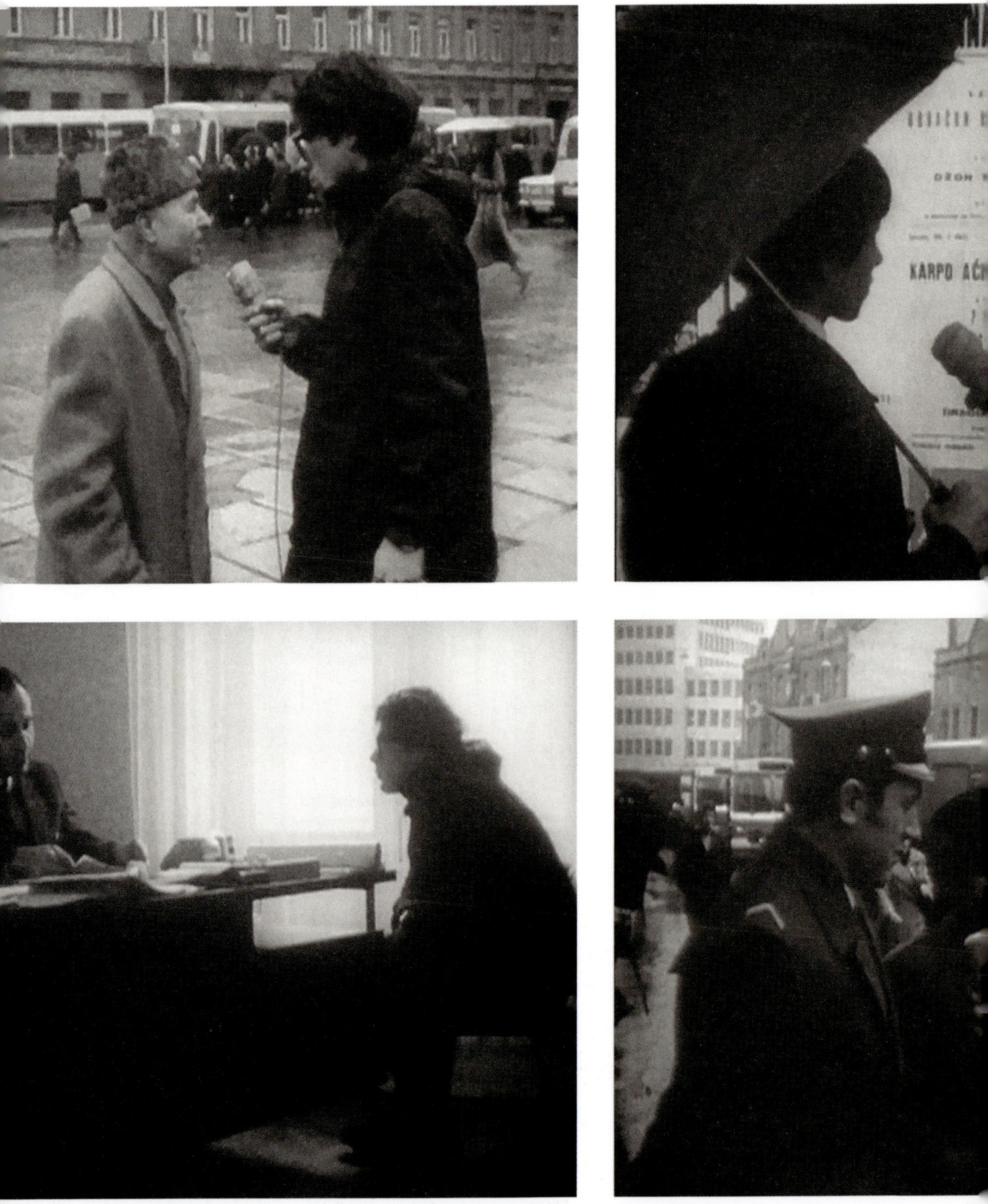

Der schwarze Film (Standbilder), 1971

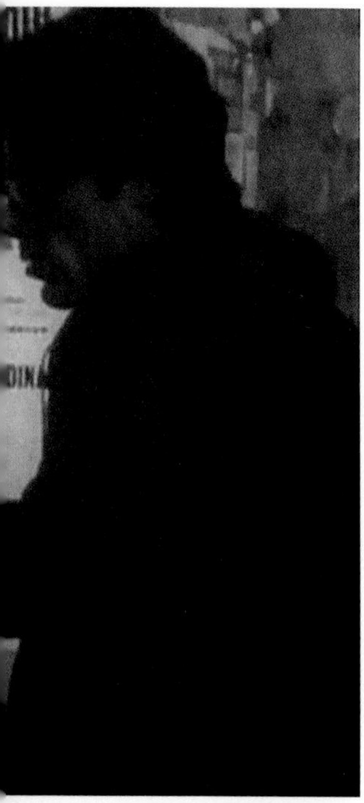

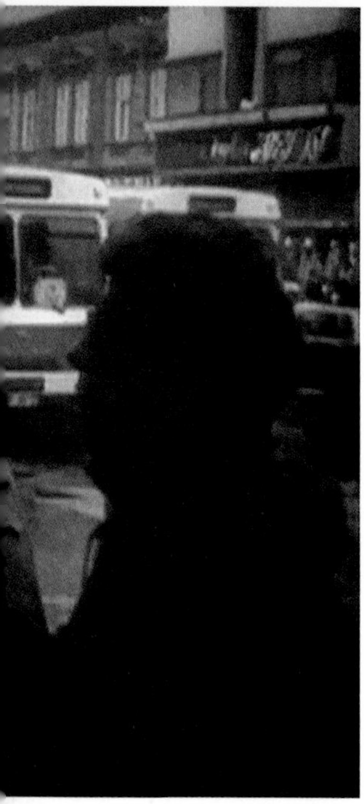

Gesellschaft sollte es keine Lücken geben, in denen ein zivilgesellschaftliches Engagement wie das von Žilnik notwendig wird, denn für alle sozialen Angelegenheiten sollte eigentlich Sorge getragen sein. Žilnik legt mit *Der schwarze Film* einen blinden Fleck frei: Das nackte Leben (mit diesem Begriff beschreibt die politische Theorie ein Leben außerhalb von Institutionalität und Investitur) bemerkt nur der Künstler. Mit der Wohnung, so klein sie de facto ist, wird Žilnik als privilegiertes Subjekt in Jugoslawien ausgewiesen. Mit der skandalösen Performativität von *Der schwarze Film* riskiert er nicht nur seine Privilegien, sondern seine ganze berufliche Existenz als Filmemacher.

Die Wurzeln seines Engagements lassen sich in dem Spielfilm *Frühe Werke* (1969) leicht erkennen. Žilniks Generation stand für Veränderungen. Für Žilnik, als Angehörigem einer sozialistischen Gesellschaft, wurde nicht so sehr der Pariser Mai 1968 zu einer Schlüsselerfahrung als der Prager Frühling und dessen Niederschlagung. Die Reformbewegung in der Tschechoslowakei hatte auch einen starken künstlerischen Flügel. Filmemacherinnen wie Věra Chytilová oder Filmemacher wie Evald Schorm standen an der ästhetischen (utopischen) Spitze der progressiven Bemühungen. Jugoslawien ging durch einen ähnlichen Verlauf: Auf Ansätze zu einer Liberalisierung folgte eine Verstärkung des ideologischen Zugriffs. In *Frühe Werke* sieht man junge Menschen, die in ein Dorf kommen, um unter den Bedingungen provinzieller Rückständigkeit den Kommunismus aufzubauen. Sie verstehen sich nach dem Bild typischer Helden aus sowjetischen Propagandafilmen und der politischen Ideen des Maoismus. Aber ihre Erfahrungen erschüttern ihre Annahmen: Die Vorstellungen vom Fortschritt bleiben buchstäblich in schlammigen Straßen stecken. Mit ihrer Mode und ihrem persönlichen Stilwillen würden diese jungen Leute auch in Jean-Luc Godards *La chinoise* (1967) passen, einem prototypischen Film über die Generation von 1968 in Westeuropa. Aber in Frankreich kamen die engagierten Linksintellektuellen niemals in Regionen, die so *profonde* waren wie die Dörfer, in die Žilnik für *Frühe Werke* ging.

Das System des staatlichen Fernsehens, in dem Žilnik arbeitete, gab ihm im Anschluss gewisse Freiheiten, die auch mit einem allgemeineren Trend in den europäischen Anstalten zu tun hatte: Reformorientiertes, mediales *nation building* stand in vielen Ländern um 1970 auf der Tagesordnung. Fernsehanstalten wie der ORF (Österreichischer Rundfunk) oder die RAI (Radiotelevisione Italiana) waren in diesen Jahren Institutionen, in denen sich Bemühungen um Kritik und Didaktik mit Unterhaltungsansprüchen verbanden. Damit konnte Žilnik eine Menge anfangen.

Sein Kurzfilm *Aufstand in Jazak* (1973) ist ein exzellentes Beispiel für seine Strategie einer Subversion durch Affirmation: In vielerlei Hinsicht sieht er wie ein Propagandafilm über den Partisanenkrieg gegen den Faschismus in den Jahren zwischen 1941 und 1945 aus. Die Menschen aus dem Dorf Jazak (gelegen zwischen Novi Sad und

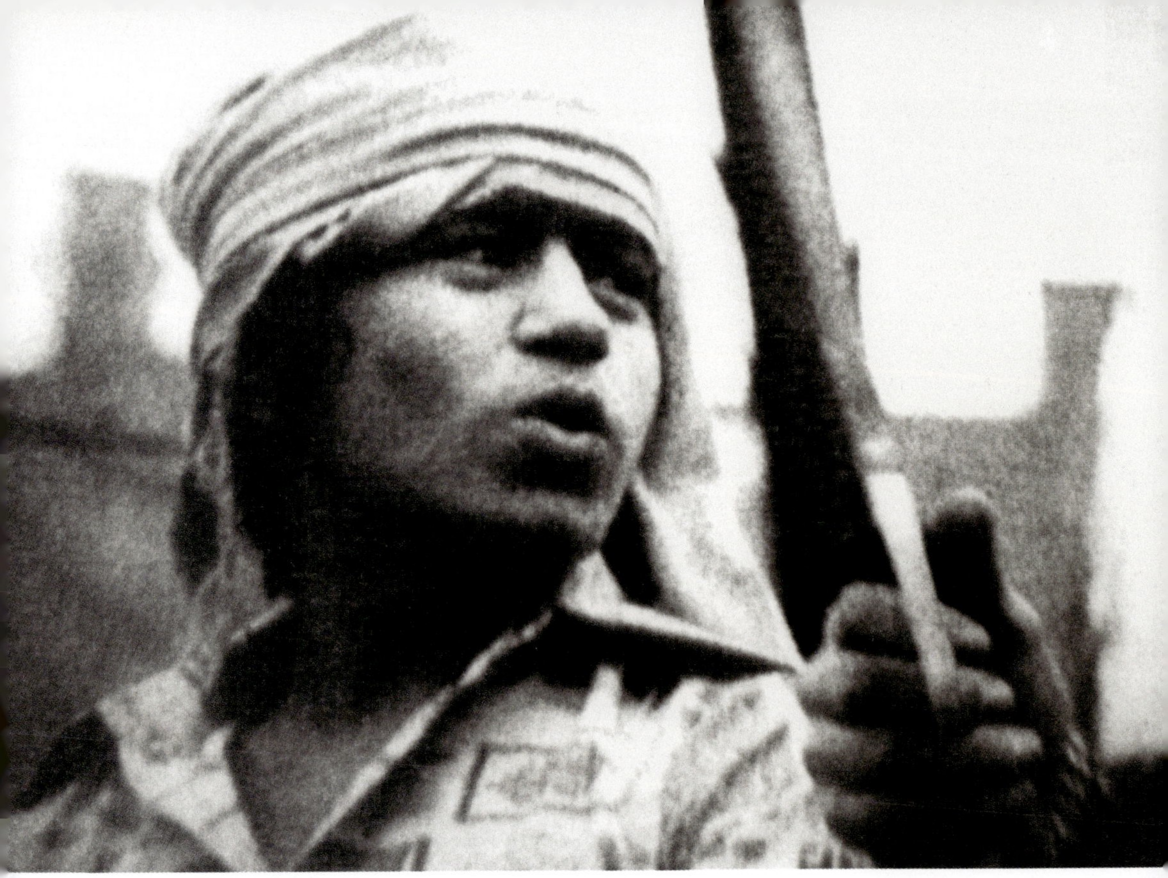

Mitrovica, in der Region Vojvodina) erinnern sich an die Zeit des Widerstands gegen die Besatzung („Schnaps für die Verwundeten", „wir leisteten den Eid im Jahr 1941"). Der Krieg dieser Menschen war der Gründungsmythos des sozialistischen Jugoslawiens. Žilnik stand also vollständig im Einklang mit der offiziellen Geschichtsschreibung. Aber der Enthusiasmus der Menschen scheint ein bisschen zu weit zu gehen. Dazu kommt die verspielte Regie: Žilnik scheint Zeitzeugnisse manchmal richtiggehend im Vorbeigehen oder im Vorbeifahren einzusammeln, die Menschen stehen vor ihren Häusern aufgereiht. Žilnik nimmt ihnen die Parade ab und überführt die Erinnerungen in kleine Reenactments. Gegen Ende des Films reden die Leute davon, wie sie die Ankunft der Roten Armee mit Kozara-Tänzen feierten, und Žilnik filmt dazu einen Ferguson-Traktor, der auch einen ausgelassenen Tanz aufführt. In einer Zeit, in der die Kulturbürokratie in Jugoslawien zunehmend übellauniger wurde, traf dieser Enthusiasmus die Zensur an einem wunden Punkt. Žilnik galt nun als unzuverlässig. Mit seinem nächsten Projekt *Freiheit oder Comicstrip* (1972) bekam er Schwierigkeiten. Es wurde schließlich nie realisiert. Er entschloss sich, das Land zu verlassen, und ging nach Westdeutschland.

Paradies. Eine imperialistische Tragikomödie (Produktionsfoto), 1976
FOTO: ANDREJ POPOVIĆ.

Das große Thema für die weitere Karriere von Žilnik ist seit seiner eigenen Auswanderung vorgegeben: Migration und die vielfältigen Gesellschaften, die daraus hervorgehen. In dem kurzen

Paradies. Eine imperialistische Tragikomödie

Bundesrepublik Deutschland • 1976 • 90 min. • 16 mm • Farbfilm

Ein multinationaler Konzern und seine Eigentümerin, Judit Angst, befinden sich in finanziellen Schwierigkeiten. Die Chefin beschließt daraufhin, eine Gruppe junger Anarchistinnen und Anarchisten anzuheuern, um sich zum Schein von ihnen entführen zu lassen. Nach einigen Wochen in Gefangenschaft will Angst dann die angebliche Entführung nutzen, um in der Öffentlichkeit den Niedergang ihrer Firma zu rechtfertigen und zugleich als Kämpferin gegen Zerstörung und Chaos Statur zu gewinnen. Der Film wurde direkt von der Entführung des konservativen West-Berliner Politikers Peter Lorenz im Jahr 1975 inspiriert. Lorenz verbrachte damals fünf Tage als Gefangener der terroristischen „Bewegung 2. Juni". Er wurde erst freigelassen, nachdem die Regierung die Bedingungen der Entführer erfüllt hatte.

Der Film wurde von Žilnik als eine große Produktion mit einem Budget von 250 000 D-Mark geplant. Er hatte bereits verschiedene Drehorte in München inspiziert und mit prominenten Schauspielerinnen und Schauspielern wie Hanna Schygulla und Rainer Werner Fassbinder verhandelt. Aber die Stimmung in der Stadt war wegen des Terrorismus und der wachsenden Bedeutung der Roten Armee Fraktion (RAF) äußerst angespannt. Auf Grund der politischen Entwicklung entzog das Bayerische Fernsehen dem Film jegliche finanzielle Unterstützung. Nachdem Žilnik sowohl seine staatliche Förderung als auch seinen Produzenten für die Zusammenarbeit mit dem Fernsehen verloren hatte, entschloss er sich, den Film in einer abgespeckten Version zu drehen. Sein Budget war bis auf 60 000 D-Mark geschrumpft, die ihm einige Sponsoren zuvor schon fest zugesagt hatten. Damit drehte er nun zusammen mit einem kleinen Team, das mit Begeisterung bei der Sache war. Darunter beispielweise seine Kostümbildnerin Gisela Siebauer, die auch die weibliche Hauptrolle spielte. Während er seinen Film im Filmverlag der Autoren schnitt, wurde er bereits von Kollegen gewarnt, dass der Film ihn in Schwierigkeiten bringen würde.

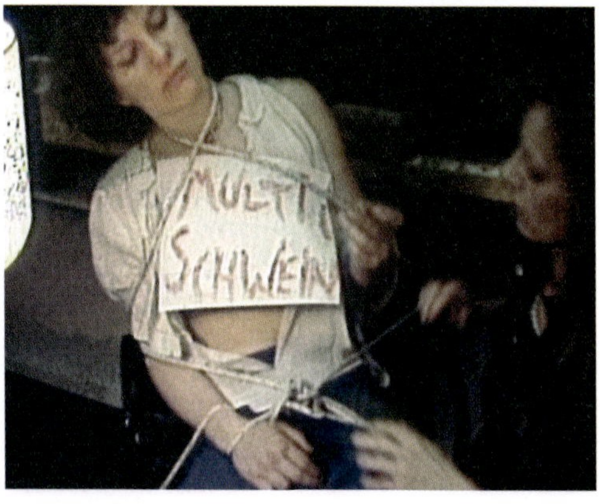

Die Premiere von *Paradies* fand im Münchener Werkstattkino statt. Obwohl er vom Publikum begeistert aufgenommen wurde, musste Žilnik erleben, dass die Polizei am nächsten Tag erschien und anordnete, den Film aus dem Kinoprogramm zu nehmen. Um zu erfahren, wie der Film von einem größeren Publikum aufgenommen würde, entschloss sich Žilnik, ihn einer Versammlung prominenter Filmkritiker vorzuführen, die für die ARD in Frankfurt tätig waren. Nachdem sie den Film gesehen hatten, empfahlen sie ihm, ihn niemandem zu zeigen. Als Žilnik nach München zurückkehrte wurde er fast im selben Augenblick von der Polizei aufgesucht. Sie fanden nichts bei ihm, was ihn mit Terrorismus in Verbindung brachte, aber sie entdeckten einige Quittungen, die deutlich machten, dass Gelder für den Film in bar geflossen waren. Daraufhin wurde ihm Steuerbetrug vorgeworfen. Er und sein Kameramann Andrej Popović wurden festgenommen, und man brachte sie mitten in der Nacht zum Polizeipräsidium. Žilnik rief Alexander Kluge um Hilfe an, der zu der Zeit Geschäftsführer des Filmverlags der Autoren war und außerdem Rechtsanwalt. Kluge verhandelte mit der Polizei, die Anklage fallen und Žilnik und Popović frei zu lassen – unter der Bedingung, dass diese das Land verlassen würden. Man gab ihnen zwölf Stunden, um ihre Sachen zu packen. Danach begleitete die Polizei sie zur österreichischen Grenze. Es gab für sie indes nie eine offizielle Ausweisung noch ein Verbot der Wiedereinreise. ●

Paradies. Eine imperialistische Tragikomödie (Standbild), 1976

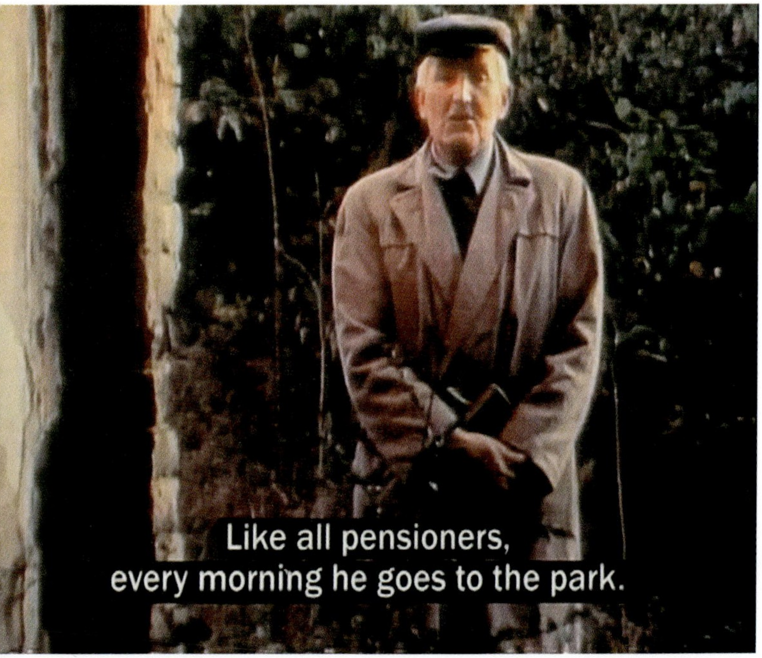

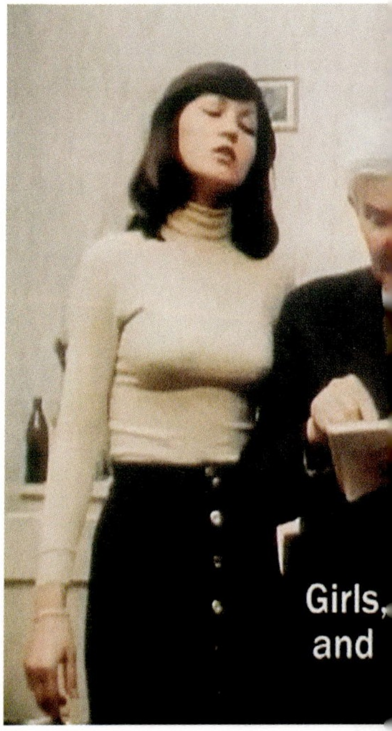

Dokumentarfilm *Inventur – Metzstraße 11* (1975) stellt er die Bewohnerinnen und Bewohner eines Mietshauses in der Metzstraße 11 in München vor. Die Kamera steht im Treppenhaus, und alle Bewohnerinnen und Bewohner wurden dazu eingeladen, die Treppe herab zu kommen, und sich im Vorbeigehen kurz vorzustellen. Sie sprechen ein gebrochenes Deutsch oder ihre Muttersprache, sie verraten ihren Aufenthaltsstatus (Seit wie vielen Jahren im Land?), erwähnen ihre Arbeit oder ihre Ausbildung und ihre soziale Situation („für mich schlecht", sagt die Frau eines gewissen Genaro). Nur zwei Frauen haben die Muttersprache Deutsch: eine lebt der niedrigen Miete wegen in dem Haus, die andere ist arbeitslos. Das letzte Wort hat der Hausmeister. Er lebt seit vierzig Jahren in dem Gebäude: „Ich bin mit allen Hauseinwohnern zufrieden."

Die Komödie und Tragödie von Bora Joksimović (Standbilder), 1977

Der Film zeigt einen Ausschnitt aus der Gesellschaft der Bundesrepublik in den mittleren 1970er Jahren. Der Neue Deutsche Film wurde damals gerade auf diese Realitäten aufmerksam. *Angst essen Seele auf* von Rainer Werner Fassbinder kam 1973 heraus, und sein Einfluss auf Žilniks Arbeit in dieser Zeit ist offensichtlich. Aber der weitere Weg brachte markante Unterschiede: Fassbinder interessierte sich zunehmend für Genrefragen vor dem Hintergrund einer Wirkungsästhetik, die er im amerikanischen Kino realisiert sah; Žilnik hingegen hielt daran fest, Genrekonventionen zu unterwandern.

In Bayern kam er in Kontakt mit einer alternativen Szene, die gemeinschaftliches Leben und politisches Engagement verband. Die Folkband Sparifankal sang eine der Hymnen dieser Zeit: „Des Land is nimma sche zum Lebm" („Es ist nicht mehr schön,

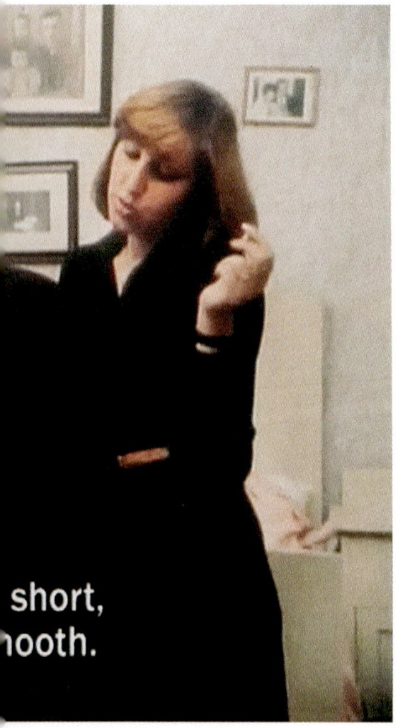

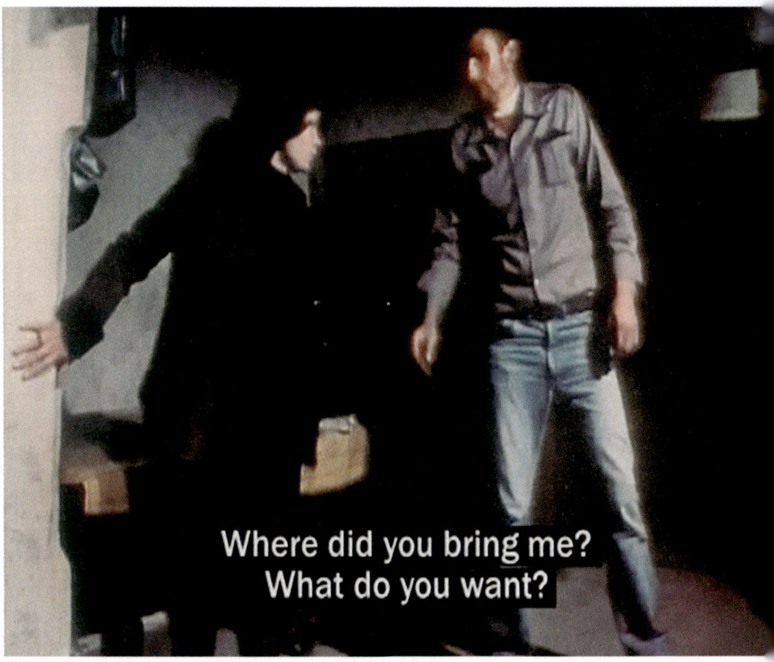

in diesem Land zu leben“). Der einstündige Film *Paradies. Eine imperialistische Tragikomödie* (1976) ist Žilniks zentrale Arbeit aus seiner Zeit in Deutschland. Sein Ansatz war militant und spielerisch zugleich. Bis heute hält er auf seiner Webseite an einer verschwörungstheoretischen Version der Ereignisse fest, auf die er sich mit der zentralen Erzählung des Films bezog: Er hält die Entführung des konservativen Politikers Peter Lorenz in Berlin im Februar 1975 für „fake“. Tatsächlich handelte es sich aber um eine Tat der „Bewegung 2. Juni“ (der Name verweist auf das Datum des Todes des Studenten Benno Ohnesorg 1967, der die Proteste und revolutionäre Bewegung von 1968 in Westdeutschland und West-Berlin hervorrief). Die Entführung, von der Žilnik in *Paradies* erzählt, ist hingegen wirklich nur eingefädelt: Eine Frau namens Angst gibt sie in Auftrag, weil sie den Konkurs ihrer Firma provozieren möchte. Sie will daraus illegale Profite lukrieren. Zur Ausführung ihrer Intrige engagiert Frau Angst einige Radikale, und auch der Film wird von Minute zu Minute radikaler. *Paradies* sieht deutlich nach einem Kollektivprojekt aus: Der Film ist voll von widersprüchlichen Ideen und Strategien, ein kinematographisches Happening, und zugleich ein subvertierter Thriller in der Weise, in der Godard verschiedentlich Kolportage und Trivialromane zum Ausgangspunkt für Bearbeitungen genommen hat (man könnte vor allem an *Made in U.S.A.*, 1966, denken). Im Zentrum der in *Paradies* ebenfalls enthaltenen Analyse der politischen Ökonomie Westdeutschlands in dieser Zeit steht wieder der Einfluss der Arbeitsmigration auf das lokale kapitalistische System – Žilnik spielt darauf mit einer polemischen Szene an, die an Selektionsprozesse in einer anderen Zeit der deutschen Geschichte erinnert.

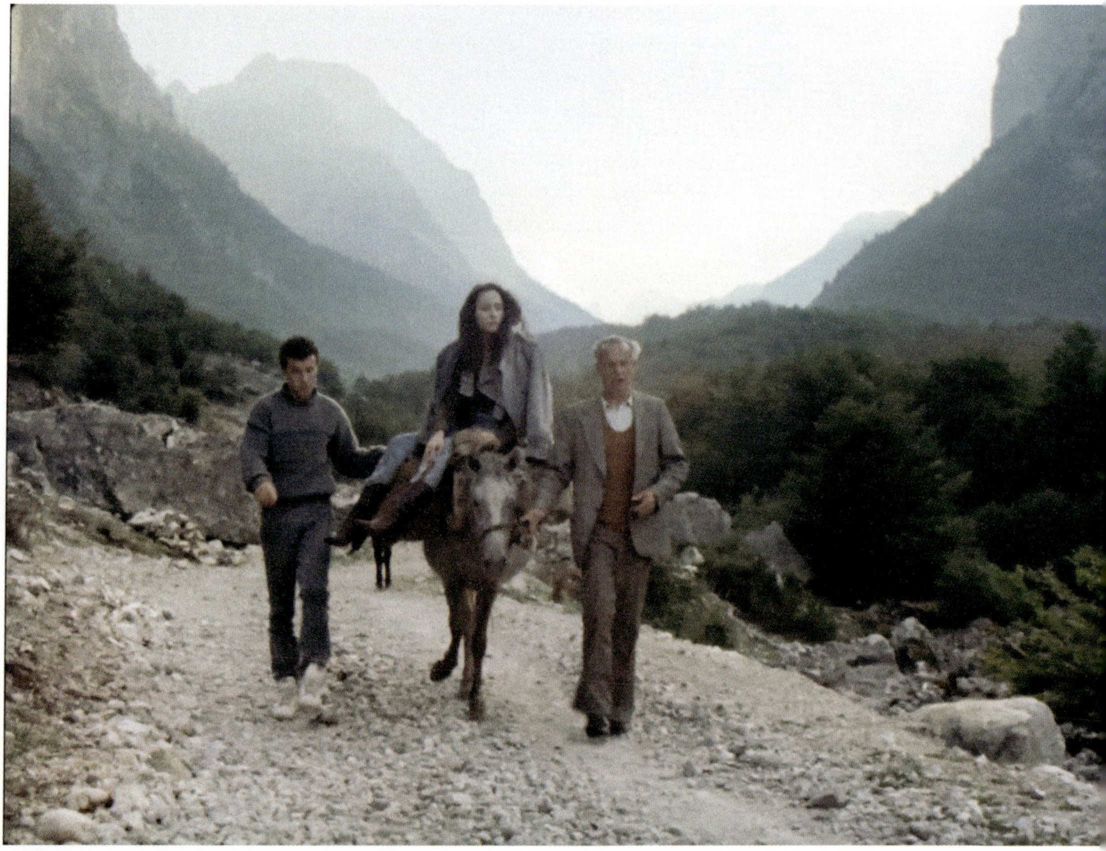

Škeljzen Uljević und Ivana Žigon in *Brooklyn-Gusinje* (Standbild), 1988

1977 war Žilnik wieder in Jugoslawien, und er arbeitet wieder für das Fernsehen. Sein Porträtfilm über einen Theaterangestellten im Ruhestand, *Die Komödie und Tragödie von Bora Joksimović*, ist paradigmatisch für seine künftige Arbeitsweise mit Protagonisten. Im Theater war Bora nicht mit künstlerischen Aufgabe befasst – er war Heizer. Heimlich hat er aber immer geschrieben: Drehbücher, vor allem für Fernsehspiele. Žilnik nimmt zwei dieser Geschichten und inszeniert sie. Allerdings kann man keineswegs von orthodoxen Realisierungen sprechen. Vielmehr sucht er im Leben des Autors selbst nach den Geschichten, die Joksimović erfunden hat. Eine Geschichte ist eine Komödie, die andere eine Tragödie. Beide sind stark von sexuellen Fantasien durchwirkt. Man könnte leicht den Eindruck gewinnen, dass Žilnik sich über die amateurhaften Geschichten von Bora lustig macht. Aber das Gegenteil ist der Fall: Bora ist der erste in einer langen Reihe von Žilnik-Figuren, die als typische Antihelden erscheinen, und die als Medien und Stellvertreter für Gesellschaften dienen, die Žilnik durch ihre Außenseiter und seltsamen Vögel zu entziffern versucht.

Ein gutes Beispiel für die Fernseharbeiten von Žilnik in den späten 1980er Jahren ist *Brooklyn-Gusinje* (1988), eine Produktion von TV Beograd. Es handelt sich um einen weitgehend konventionellen

Fernsehfilm. Die Hauptdarstellerin Ivana Žigon spielt eine Figur, die ihren eigenen Vornamen trägt. Ivana wird in einem kleinen Textilbetrieb (einem Sweatshop) in Novi Pazar entdeckt. Ein Wirt namens Seljo sucht nach Personal für sein Cafe. Er ist aus Gusinje, einer Stadt in Montenegro unweit der Grenze zu Albanien. Die junge Frau lässt sich also auf das Wagnis einer beträchtlichen Umstellung ein. Žilnik verdeutlicht dies in einer Szene, in der Seljo und Ivana auf der Fahrt nach Gusinje einmal Halt machen. Sie betreten eine Schulklasse, und anhand der dort aushängenden Landkarte demonstriert Seljo, wohin die Reise geht. Die einheimische Bevölkerung in Gusinje ist albanisch, und Ivana muss deren Sprache lernen – das beinhaltet auch bestimmte Umgangsformen im Gasthaus. Sie trifft in Gusinje auch einen jungen Mann, der aus Brooklyn, Vereinigte Staaten, zu Besuch ist: Škeljzen würde gern mit einem Pontiac herumfahren, aber es gibt nur einen Volkswagen Polo zu leihen. Er ist einer von vielen Migranten in Žilniks Werk, ein Vorgänger vor allem von Kenedi Hasani. *Brooklyn–Gusinje* ist im strengen Sinn kein Dokudrama, sondern ein fiktionaler Fernsehfilm. Aber dokumentarisches Interesse ist dem Film unmittelbar eingeschrieben. Žilnik bringt die weibliche Hauptfigur in eine Welt, die er dann in Entsprechung zu ihren Erfahrungen zeigt. Viele Szenen haben eine kulturanthropologische Dimension, besonders deutlich wird dies bei einer Art Rede, in der ein Mann über die Pflichten von Frauen und Männern doziert. Škeljzen und sein älterer Bruder Bećir kommen zwar aus dieser Welt, stehen ihr aber nun wie Fremde gegenüber – sie sind auf eine ironische Weise zu Kulturwissenschaftlern durch Erfahrungsdifferenz geworden. *Brooklyn–Gusinje* ist öffentlich-rechtliches oder nationales Fernsehen in maßgeblicher Ausprägung: Das jugoslawische Publikum wird hier mit sich selbst in Gestalt einer seiner Stämme konfrontiert. Die Unterschiede zwischen den Bevölkerungsgruppen, aus denen das Land besteht, werden erkennbar, indem ein Mädchen von nebenan mit Einheimischen konfrontiert wird, die ihr wie Ureinwohner (Indigene) erscheinen können. Gleichzeitig sind alle denkbaren Mythologien von Ursprünglichkeit bereits durch Auswanderung aufgebrochen. Die Heimkehrer aus Amerika verändern die lokalen ökonomischen und sozialen Sphären. Jugoslawien hat immer Arbeitskräfte exportiert, und während der Zeit des real existierenden Sozialismus war das Land nicht zuletzt dadurch auch immer offener für Einflüsse von außen als die so weit wie möglich geschlossenen Gesellschaften des von der Sowjetunion dominierten Ostblocks.

Žilnik blieb schließlich kaum etwas anderes übrig, als die internen Nationalismen in Jugoslawien mit den Essentialismen zusammenzubringen, die von der neoliberalen Globalisierung hervorgebracht werden. Es ist bezeichnend, dass einer seiner bekanntesten Protagonisten ein Rom ist, also jener Nationalität in Europa angehört, die im Wesentlichen eine Transnationalität ist. Kenedi stammt aus der Stadt Mitrovica, die damals noch serbisch war und nun zu dem unabhängigen (aber von der Staatengemeinschaft nicht einhellig anerkannten) Staat Kosovo gehört. Žilnik traf Kenedi in Belgrad, als er eine Familie begleitete, die aus Deutschland abgeschoben

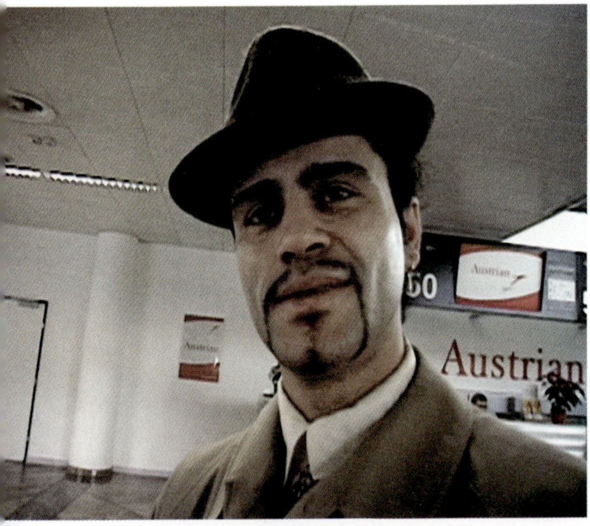

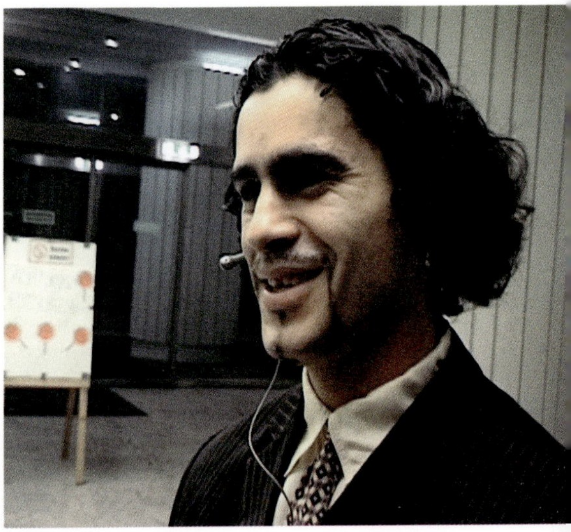

Kenedi Hasani in *Kenedi, verloren und gefunden* (Standbilder), 2005

worden war und in Serbien vor einer ungewissen Zukunft stand. Kenedi ist ein Mann ganz nach Žilniks Geschmack: ein Schwerenöter, der ständig am Organisieren ist und hofft, dass eine Kleinigkeit für ihn herausspringt. Für einen Dokumentarfilmer ist Kenedi ein ideales Medium: In jeder Hinsicht greift Kenedi in die Wirklichkeit ein, und darum geht es Žilnik auch. Er will nicht bloß beobachten. Er will sich einmischen, will sich in Verhältnisse verwickeln lassen. Er möchte die Wirklichkeit aus der Perspektive eines Freundes zeigen. Solidarität und Freundschaft sind wesentliche Bedingungen von Žilniks dokumentarischen Filmen in seiner späteren Phase. Er würde niemals die unsichtbare Fliege an der Wand sein wollen, mit der man bildhaft ein strikt observierendes Kino in Verbindung bringt (das berühmteste Beispiel dafür ist Frederick Wiseman). Er hält sich dabei aber persönlich zurück, und kommt so auch nicht in die Nähe heutiger bewusst subjektiv erzählter Dokumentarfilme in der Manier von Nick Broomfield und anderen.

Die Filme von Žilnik entscheiden sich also meistens schon daran, dass er eine dieser Trickster-Figuren findet, die nicht nur sich selbst spielen, sondern die auch Moderatoren in den Filmen sind. Sie machen Erfahrungen, und stellen diese zugleich auch schon für das Publikum dar. Auch in kollektiven Situationen beschäftigt er diese Figuren mit der Kamera, während er sie beobachtet und inszeniert: In *Die Alte Schule des Kapitalismus* (2009) schloss er sich einem Arbeitskampf in Serbien an, in *Wanderlust* (1998) zeigte er die Abenteuer eines pensionierten Italieners, der auf der Suche nach einer Ehefrau nach dem Ende des Kommunismus die Landschaften Osteuropas bereist. Besonders markant wird Žilniks Methode in *Tito zum zweiten Mal unter den Serben* (1994), denn in dieser politischen Komödie über eine Geschichte, die nicht vergeht, legt der Filmemacher sein Konzept der Performativität ganz deutlich offen: ein Mann, der wie der legendäre Staatschef Tito aussieht, taucht

auf öffentlichen Plätzen im ehemaligen Jugoslawien auf und löst alle möglichen Reaktionen aus. Es liegt nahe, hier noch einmal an *Der schwarze Film* zu denken, wo Žilnik selbst der Mann war, der an öffentlichen Orten auf spielerische Weise unbequeme Fragen stellte.

Die Strategien in Žilniks Werk haben sich im Lauf der Jahre signifikant verschoben. Das hat viel mit den Systemen zu tun, in denen er arbeitete: Das staatliche Fernsehen ließ allmählich stärker idiosynkratische Arbeitsweisen zu, aber von 1970 bis 1990 war es noch möglich, auch hinter der Kamera eine im besten Sinn wiedererkennbare Figur zu werden, ohne selbst ausdrücklich nach vorne treten zu müssen. Sein Humor, sein revolutionärer Witz und sein tiefes Mitgefühl spiegeln sich in den Figuren, die er vor die Kamera holt. Die Identifikationen zwischen Regisseur und Protagonisten spiegeln die möglichen Formen des Engagements für das Publikum. Auf diese Weise hat Žilnik mit seinem umfangreichen Werk so etwas wie eine Integrationsfigur für die grundlegenden Gegensätze des Kinos geschaffen: Wirklichkeit und zweite Wirklichkeit und die Position des Beobachters innerhalb oder außerhalb dieses Gegensatzes lassen diesen als de facto nicht gegensätzlich erkennbar werden. Eher handelt es sich um Schichten derselben Wirklichkeit. Auch nach mehr als fünfzig Filmen wird das Werk von Žilnik unterschätzt. Aber die Anerkennung wächst, dass es nicht viele Filmemacherinnen und -macher gibt, die ein größeres Recht verdient haben, von Menschen im weitesten Sinn dieses großen Wortes zu sprechen, als Želimir Žilnik. ★

ÜBERSETZUNG AUS DEM ENGLISCHEN VON BERT REBHANDL.

Bert Rebhandl studierte Germanistik, Theologie und Philosophie in Wien und Berlin. Er arbeitet als freier Journalist, Autor und Übersetzer in Berlin und schreibt als Filmkritiker für die Frankfurter Allgemeine Zeitung, Der Standard (Wien), tip (Berlin) und andere Publikationen. Rebhandl ist Mitherausgeber der Vierteljahresschrift CARGO Film Medien Kultur (www.cargo-film.de). Er hat Bücher über Orson Welles, den Western, *Seinfeld* und zuletzt über *Der dritte Mann* geschrieben. Auf seiner Website (BRO198.net) veröffentlicht er weitere Texte mit Bezug zum Film.

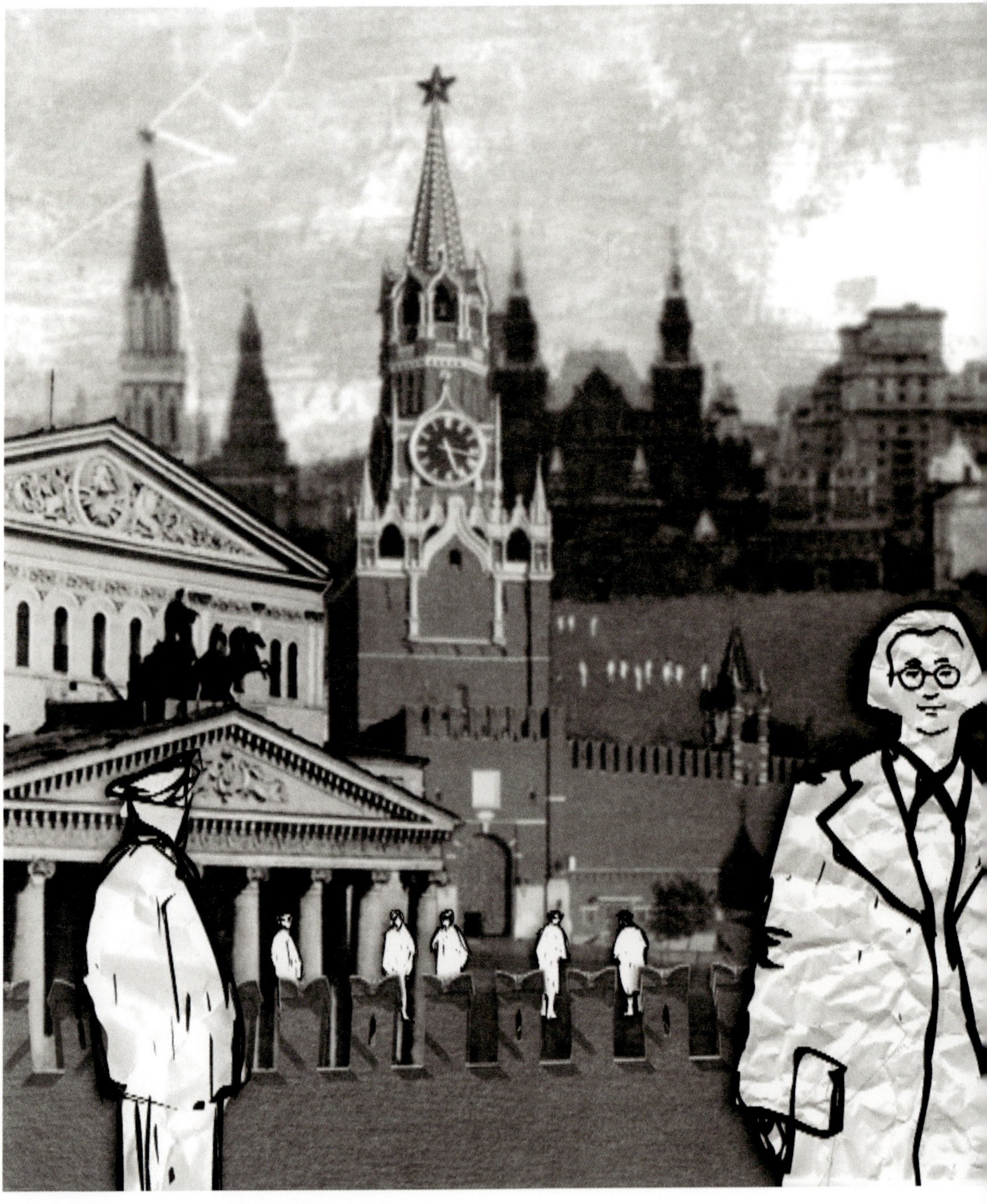

Eine Frau – ein Jahrhundert (Standbild), 2011

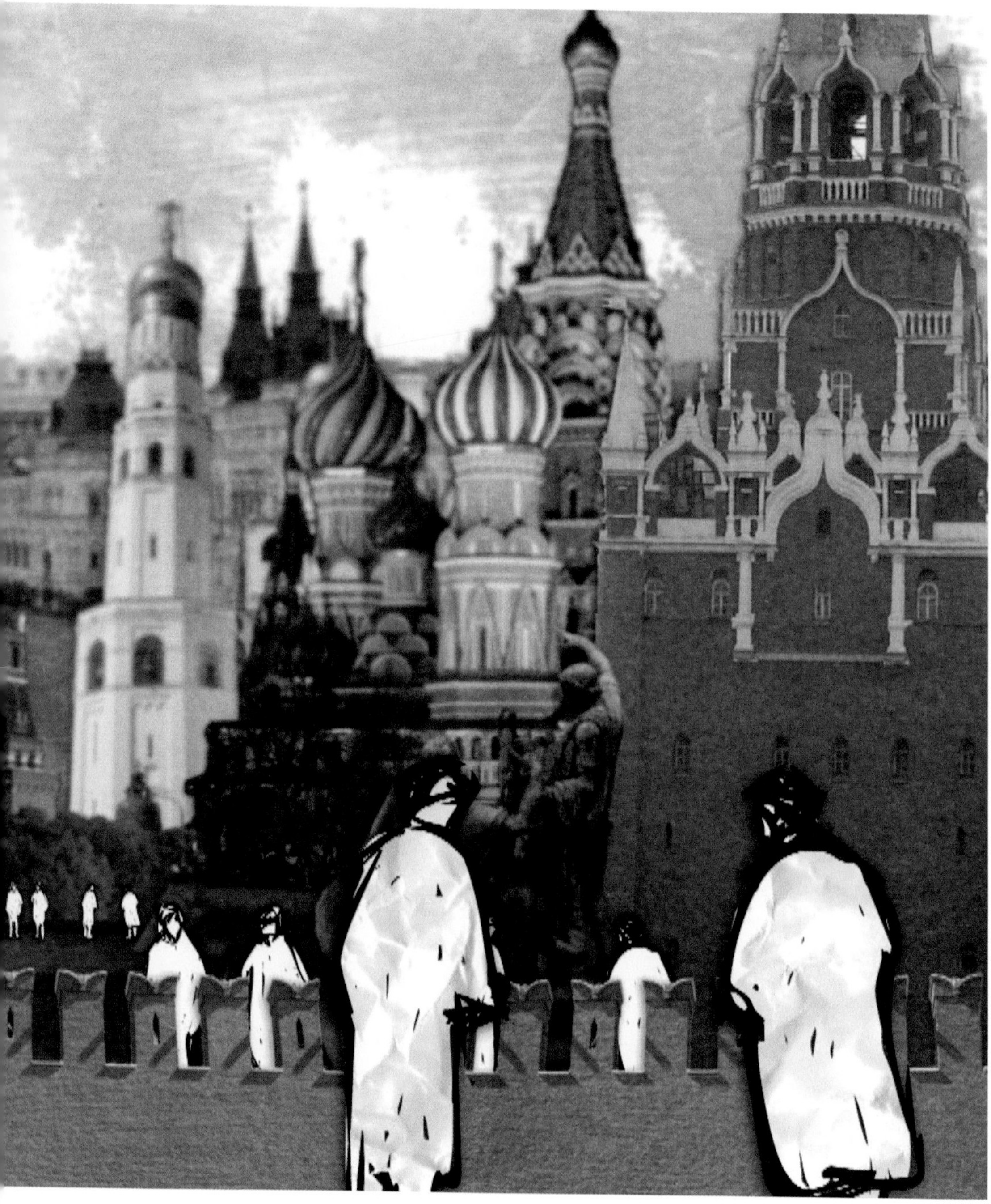

In der heutigen „postideologischen" Welt nach dem Ende des Kalten Krieges sind Marxisten allerdings eine Seltenheit. In einer historischen Realität, die von einer fast vollständigen Diskreditierung der „Utopie" des kommunistischen Internationalismus und vom machtvollen Aufkommen der angeblich viel „natürlicheren", partikularistischen Formen der Identitätspolitik gekennzeichnet ist – von denen insbesondere verschiedene ethnische Essenzialismen um sich greifen –, ist Želimir Žilnik einer der wenigen verbliebenen Vertreter des marxistischen Films. Dies liegt nicht daran, dass sein Werk stur den Kurs eines radikalen, ästhetisch-politischen Programms verfolgen würde, das in den 1960er Jahren aufgestellt wurde. Zum einen war der didaktische Marxismus im Film (wie er durch die Gruppe Dsiga Wertow bekannt wurde) nie ein Merkmal von Žilniks filmischer Praxis. Seine Filme stellen bis heute eine gelungene Praxis dar, weil sie sich in all ihren Erscheinungsformen, immer noch genauso leidenschaftlich engagiert wie vor vierzig Jahren, einer vollständigen Entmystifizierung der Produktionsprozesse widmen; dies gilt für die Filmproduktion ebenso wie für gesellschaftspolitische Aktivitäten. Wenn man die Dynamiken der Produktion verdeutlicht, lassen sich ideologische Täuschungen – seien diese stalinistisch, liberal-demokratisch oder ethnonationalistisch – leichter aufdecken. Dadurch werden auch Vorstellungen von Identität und Community zwangsläufig einer kritischen Neubewertung unterzogen.

—Pavle Levi, in: Pavle Levi und Želimir Žilnik, „Europe's Internal Exiles: Sound, Image, and Performance of Identity in Želimir Žilnik's Films", in: Roland Hsu (Hg.), *Ethnic Europe: Mobility, Identity, and Conflict in a Globalized World* (Stanford, CA: Stanford University Press 2010), S. 114 f.

Die übliche kulturelle Logik, mit der das Schaffen zahlreicher Künstlerinnen und Künstler, die im sozialistischen Jugoslawien arbeiteten, häufig dargestellt wurde, folgt einem einfachen Schema: Es gab das offizielle ideologische Mantra, das eine dogmatische, opportunistische Kultur hervorbrachte, und es gab eine rebellische Opposition gegen diese kulturelle Dumpfheit, die sich in einem „dissidenten“ politischen und künstlerischen Handeln zeigte. Diese beiden Positionen werden meistens als bruchlos und frei von inneren Widersprüchen präsentiert: Auf der einen Seite herrschen politischer Opportunismus, Machthunger, ideologische Dienstbarkeit, kulturelle Einförmigkeit etc., während es auf der anderen Seite einen Mann gibt (die dissidente Figur ist fast immer männlich), der unter diesen Verhältnissen leidet, einen Mann, der unermüdlich eine kreative Distanz zu diesen Verhältnissen wahrt, der aber zugleich eine öffentliche Person und kein heimlicher Abtrünniger ist.

Einige der „offiziellsten“ Kulturprodukte der Sozialistischen Föderativen Republik Jugoslawien (SFRJ) beharrten auf ihrer „künstlerischen Autonomie“ und darauf, eine gewisse politische und ästhetische Distanz zur unmittelbaren Sichtbarkeit der Ideologie und zum Vorbild der modernistischen jugoslawischen Kunst herzustellen, insbesondere zum erfolgreichen Trend der abstrakten Malerei und Skulptur der 1960er und 1970er Jahre. Andererseits waren einige Künstler, die als „dissident“ galten, ein integraler Bestandteil der Kulturpolitik der SFRJ. Ihre Projekte wurden auf die eine oder andere Weise durch offizielle Kanäle finanziert (da es keine anderen Kanäle gab, durch die man ambitionierte Kulturprojekte realisieren konnte); und dies waren die Projekte, mit denen sich die SFRJ international als ein offenes, freidenkerisches Land darstellen konnte, etc.

Innerhalb dieser ideologischen Dichotomie nahm Želimir Žilnik eine ganz einzigartige Position ein.

—Branislav Dimitrijević, „Behind Scepticism Lies the Fire of a Revolutionary!“, in: *For an Idea – Against the Status Quo: Analysis and Systematization of Želimir Žilnik's Artistic Practice* (Novi Sad: New Media Center_kuda.org, Playground produkcija 2009), S. 136 f.

Als der Film in die Kinos kam, wurde er einerseits von der neuen internationalen Filmszene, die sich damals entwickelte, gefeiert, während er andererseits auf der lokalen Ebene Tumulte und Skandale auslöste. Es war ein glücklicher Zufall, dass das internationale Publikum damals anfing, sich sehr für jugoslawische Filmproduktionen zu interessieren. So kaufte beispielsweise das deutsche Fernsehen in jenem Jahr zehn – oder vielleicht sogar fünfzehn – Filme aus dieser Region, um sie in seinen Programmen auszustrahlen.

Mein Film fiel einem deutschen Filmkritiker der ARD auf, die beschloss, ihn zu kaufen, und mit diesem einen Ankauf amortisierten sich die ganzen Investitionskosten. Die Produktion kostete uns damals ungefähr 3 500 D-Mark, und der gesamte Gewinn, der über diesen Betrag hinausging, wurde zu unserem Honorar.

—Želimir Žilnik im Gespräch mit Dubravka Sekulić, Gal Kirn und Žiga Testen, in: Gal Kirn, Dubravka Sekulić und Žiga Testen (Hg.), *Surfing the Black: Yugoslav Black Wave Cinema and Its Transgressive Moments* (Maastricht: Jan van Eyck Academie 2012), S. 67.

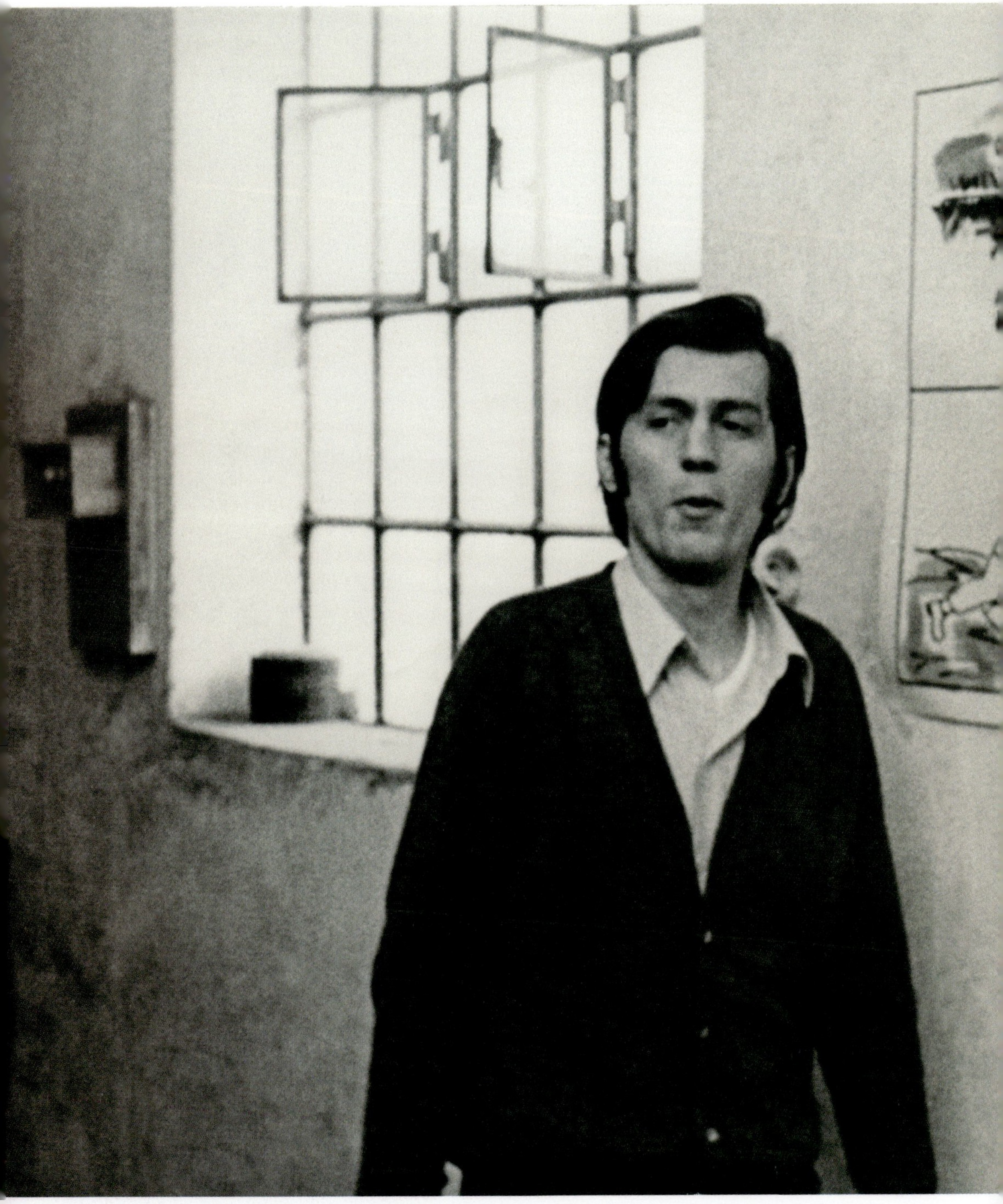

Bogdan Tirnanić in *Frühe Werke* (Standbild), 1969

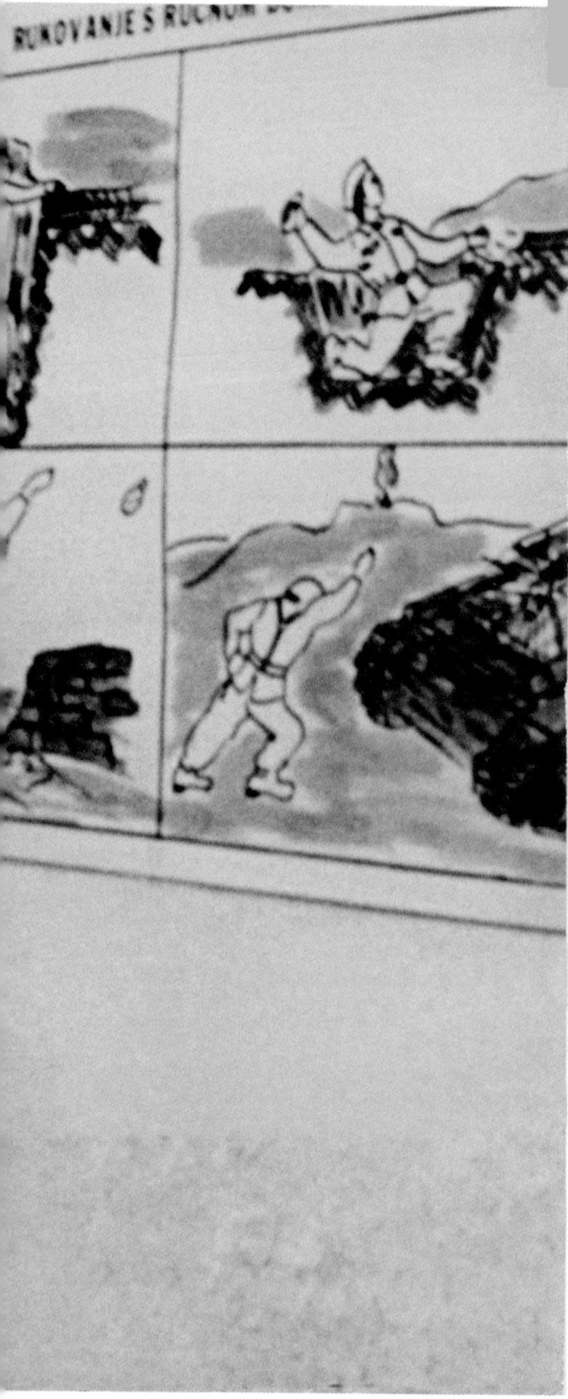

Frühe Werke (Rani radovi)

Jugoslawien • 1969 • 87 min. • 35 mm • Schwarzweißfilm

In allegorischer Weise erzählt *Frühe Werke* die Geschichte junger Menschen, die im Juni 1968 an Studentendemonstrationen in Belgrad teilnahmen. Der Film enthält, wie sein Vorspann deutlich macht, „zusätzliche Dialoge von Karl Marx und Friedrich Engels". Drei junge Männer und eine junge Frau, Jugoslava, wollen der alltäglichen, kleinbürgerlichen Routine die Stirn bieten. Inspiriert von den Schriften des jungen Marx, wollen sie „die Welt verändern". Sie gehen aufs Land und in die Fabriken, um „die Menschen wachzurütteln" und um sie zu ermutigen, für ihre Emanzipation und für ein menschenwürdiges Leben zu kämpfen. Auf dem Land lernen sie Traditionalismus und Elend kennen, aber auch ihre eigenen Grenzen, Schwächen, Unvollkommenheiten und ihre Eifersucht. Sie werden eingesperrt. Aus Enttäuschung über die nicht zustande gekommene Revolution beschließen die drei jungen Männer, Jugoslava als Zeugin ihrer Ohnmacht auszuschalten. Sie erschießen sie, bedecken ihren Körper mit der Fahne der kommunistischen Partei und verbrennen sie. Die schwarze Rauchsäule, die gen Himmel steigt, ist alles, was von ihren Revolutionsanstrengungen übrig bleibt.

Frühe Werke war Žilniks erster Spielfilm. Er wurde von Jugoslawiens größter Produktionsgesellschaft hergestellt, der Avala Film in Belgrad und von der Neoplanta Film in Novi Sad koproduziert. Der Film passierte Anfang März 1969 das Prüfkomitee und hatte Premieren in Belgrad, Zagreb, Ljubljana und Skopje. Nachdem er drei Monate lang mit Erfolg in Kinos in ganz Jugoslawien gezeigt worden war, gab es Polemiken in den Medien. Da der Film eine Einladung zu den Internationalen Filmfestspielen Berlin erhalten hatte, bestellte man Žilnik in das Büro des Direktors der Avala Film. Am Abend zuvor war der Film dem Präsidenten der Republik gezeigt worden. Angeblich hatte Josip Broz Tito die Vorführung unterbrechen lassen und gefragt: „Was wollen diese Verrückten eigentlich?" Nun sollte Žilnik bei der Avala Film eine Erklärung unterschreiben, dass der Film noch nicht fertig geschnitten sei. Er weigerte sich und wandte ein, dass sowohl die Filmschaffenden als auch das Publikum diese Lüge durchschauen würden. Noch

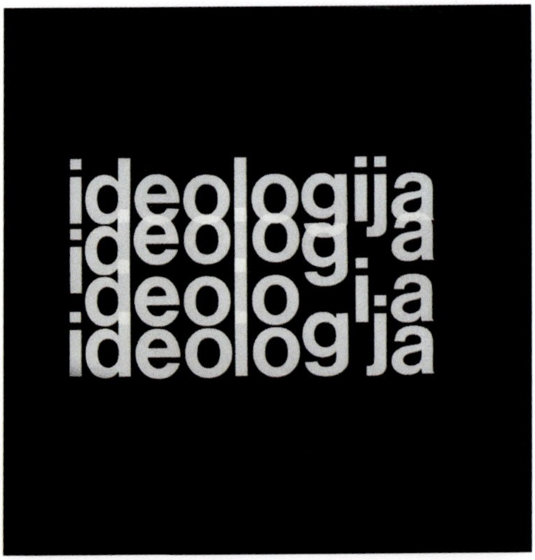

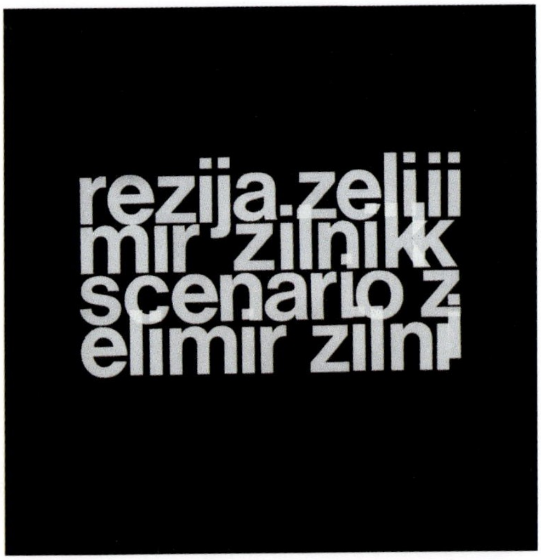

Frühe Werke (Titelsequenz, Gestaltung: Slobodan Mašić), 1969

am selben Tag beschlagnahmte man alle Kopien des Films und erließ eine Verfügung, die die öffentliche Vorführung von *Frühe Werke* untersagte. Einige Tage später begann die Gerichtsverhandlung. Da Žilnik Jura studiert hatte, verteidigte er sich und seinen Film vor Gericht selbst. Im Urteil wurde die Anklage des Staatsanwaltes in allen Punkten zurückgewiesen, und eine Woche später wurde der Film auf den Internationalen Filmfestspielen Berlin gezeigt, wo er den Goldenen Bären für den besten Film sowie den „Preis der jungen Generation" erhielt. Im selben Jahr erhielt der Film zudem mehrere Auszeichnungen auf dem Filmfestival in Pula.

Der Film führte zu großen Kontroversen im politischen Establishment Jugoslawiens, vor allem wegen seiner symbolischen Referenzen, aber auch wegen ziemlich deutlicher Verweise auf die Besetzung der Tschechoslowakei durch sowjetische Panzer im August 1968 sowie wegen seiner Darstellung der Manipulation und Verfolgung der Aktivistinnen und Aktivisten unter den Studierenden, die die Proteste im Belgrad im Juni 1968 organisiert hatten. Als Folge initiierte das Parteigremium in Novi Sad eine ideologische Kampagne gegen den Film unter dem Vorwand, er sei anarchistisch. Žilnik wurde vorgeworfen, er stände „unter dem Einfluss von Trotzki und Rudi Dutschke". Man stieß ihn aus der kommunistischen Partei Jugoslawiens aus. Der Film wurde aus dem Verleih des Landes genommen, aber zugleich durch die staatliche Yugoslavia Film in mehr als dreißig Länder auf der ganzen Welt exportiert. Als *Frühe Werke* das nächste Mal gezeigt wurde, war das fast zwanzig Jahre später, 1987, im staatlichen jugoslawischen Fernsehen.

Der Film *Frühe Werke* wurde in ganz Jugoslawien in vielen unterschiedlichen Medien, von Tageszeitungen bis hin zu Publikums- und Fachzeitschriften, ausführlich diskutiert. In vielen der Beiträge wurde auch Žilniks abschließende Argumentation bei seiner Verteidigung vor Gericht veröffentlicht:

„Der Staatsanwalt versucht zu beweisen, dass der Film *Frühe Werke* gegen die Politik des Landes verstößt. Er mystifiziert den Inhalt des Films und seine Protagonisten und stellt den Film so dar, als dokumentiere er ein bestimmtes Ereignis, um dann zu behaupten, dass dieses Ereignis sich nicht so zugetragen habe, wie es im Film gezeigt wird. Der Staatsanwalt hat das Medium des Spielfilms nicht einmal im Ansatz begriffen. Er will nicht verstehen, dass der einzig mögliche Verstoß eines Filmes in seinem künstlerischen Scheitern besteht. Und sollte es sich bei *Frühe Werke* wirklich um einen schlechten Film handeln, dann ist es nicht Sache des Staatsanwalts, dies zu beweisen.

Alle Aktionen des Staatsanwalts – der Antrag eines zeitweiligen Verbots (des Films), die völlig

unzureichenden Argumente, die Ablehnung von Beweisen – haben im Grunde überhaupt nichts mit meinem Film zu tun, sondern sie betreffen unser reales Leben. Es geht hier um politische Aktionen, über die wir ernsthaft nachdenken sollten. Durch sein Handeln entwürdigt der Staatsanwalt grundsätzlich – ich möchte nicht sagen alle gegenwärtigen Formen von sozialen Beziehungen, was er von meinem Film *Frühe Werke* behauptet – ich möchte es spezifischer sagen: Er entwürdigt in gefährlicher Weise das fortschrittliche und undogmatische Prinzip der Eigenverantwortung in unseren sozialen Beziehungen. Indem er so verfährt, glorifiziert, stützt und fördert er andere Formen ‚moderner Prinzipien' in unserer Gesellschaft: solche, die bürokratisch, dogmatisch und gegen Eigenverantwortung sind. Mit einem solchen Handeln versucht er Folgendes für das reale Leben zu beweisen, was jedoch nicht für meinen Film gilt: dass diejenigen Mächte, die in unserem Land Eigenverantwortung praktizieren, unverantwortliche Wirrköpfe sind; dass wir ‚zur Eigenverantwortung noch nicht fähig sind'; dass gesellschaftliche Mächte, Filmschaffende und Politiker eingeschlossen, nicht über soziale Anliegen nachdenken sollten und dass nicht sie, sondern die Staatsmacht sich darum zu kümmern habe. Das ist es, was uns der Staatsanwalt zu sagen versucht, wenn er diesen Film verbieten lassen möchte, vier Monate nachdem er schon Teil des regulären Filmprogramms war und von kompetenten, eigenverantwortlich handelnden Gremien und staatlichen Behörden geprüft und zugelassen wurde.

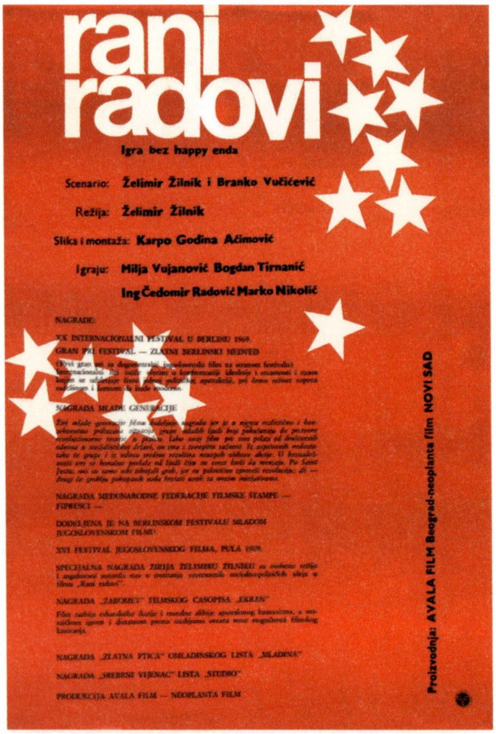

Frühe Werke (Poster, Gestaltung: Slobodan Mašić), 1969

Darüber hinaus versucht der Staatsanwalt zu beweisen, dass die Informationsmedien dieses Landes vorzugsweise unverantwortlich handeln, zudem inkompetent sind und ‚dass die Dinge auch hier wieder in Ordnung gebracht werden müssten'. Er bezweifelt, dass Grundsätze der Freiheit und Verantwortung für die Presse von Wert sind. Er ignoriert die Tatsache, dass dieser Film von fünfzehn Nachrichtenmedien, drei von ihnen Gremien der Sozialistischen Allianz des werktätigen Volkes Jugoslawiens und zwei Gremien des Bundes der sozialistischen Jugend Jugoslawiens positiv bewertet wurde. Er glaubt, dass diese Medien durch den Staat kontrolliert werden sollten. Drittens bezweifelt der Staatsanwalt das internationale Ansehen Jugoslawiens. Er behauptet, dass wenn ein seiner Meinung nach schlechter jugoslawischer Film im Ausland gezeigt wird, die Welt dann diesen Film sofort mit Jugoslawien und seiner Politik gleichsetzt und unser Land darunter zu leiden hat. Der Staatsanwalt kennt ganz offensichtlich nicht die Reichweite eines Films, und er will nicht verstehen, dass seine dogmatische Politik, die auf keinerlei vernünftigen Argumenten gründet, für das Ansehen unseres Landes weitaus gefährlicher ist als jeder Film." •

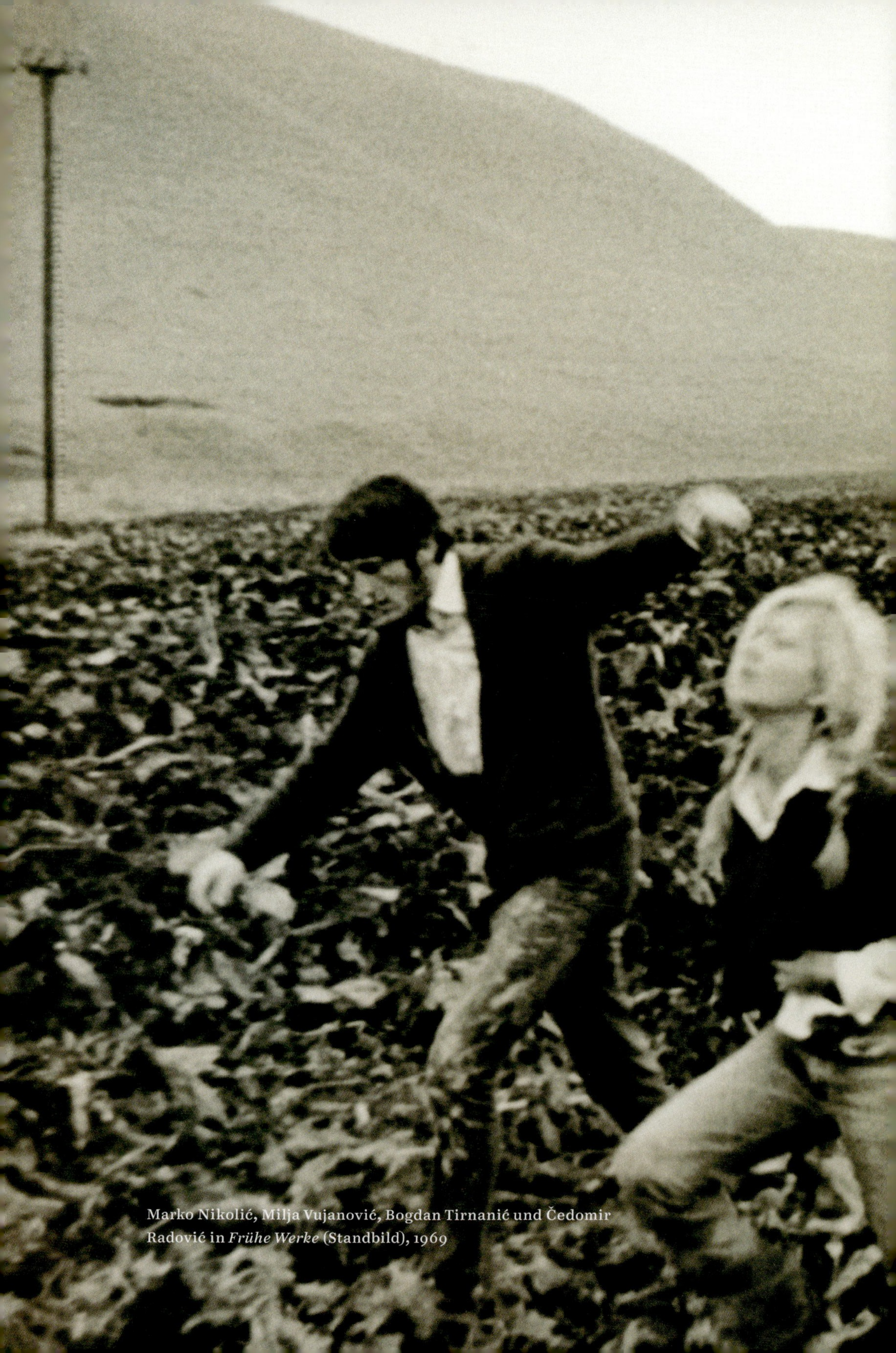

Marko Nikolić, Milja Vujanović, Bogdan Tirnanić und Čedomir Radović in *Frühe Werke* (Standbild), 1969

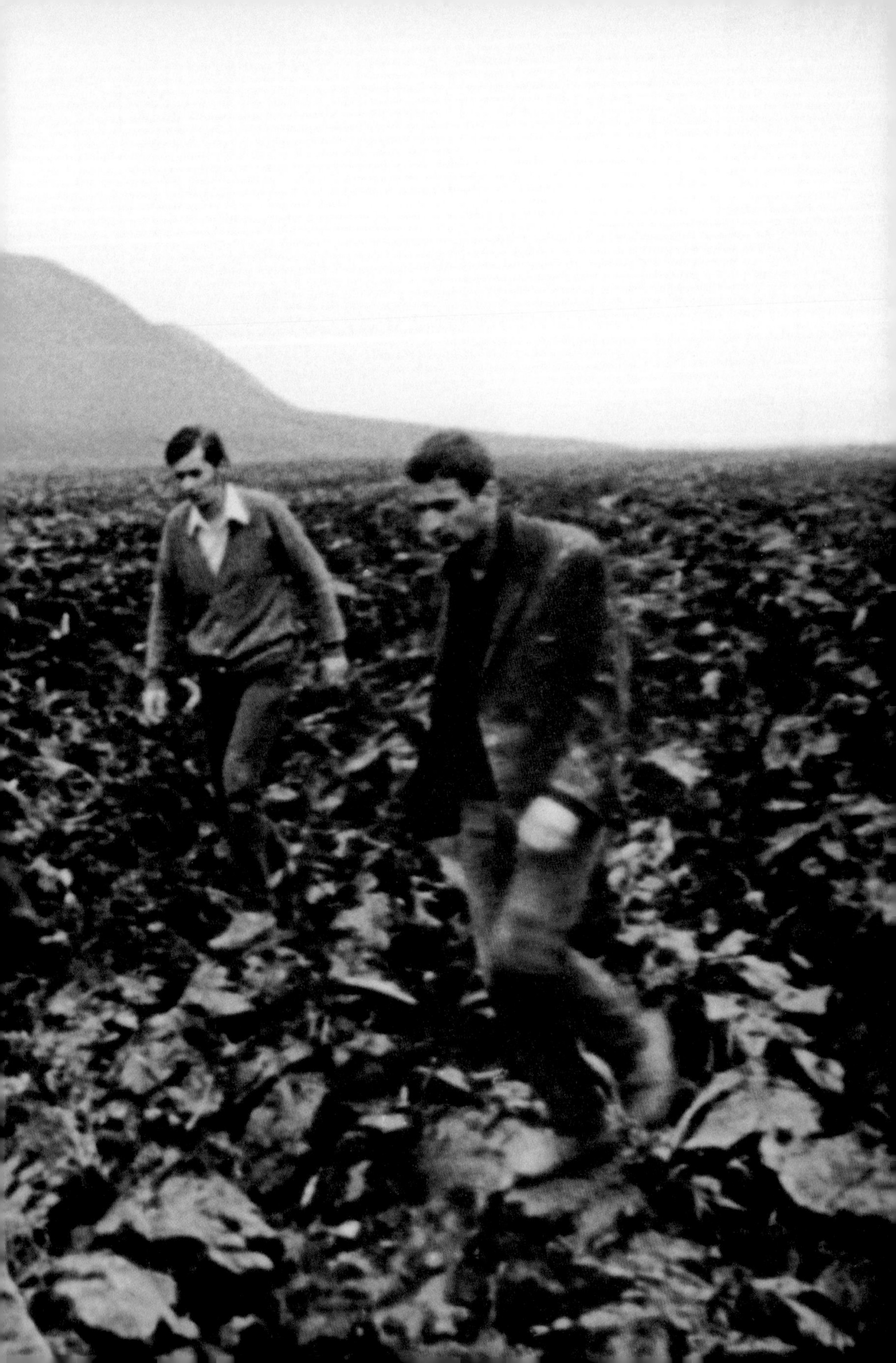

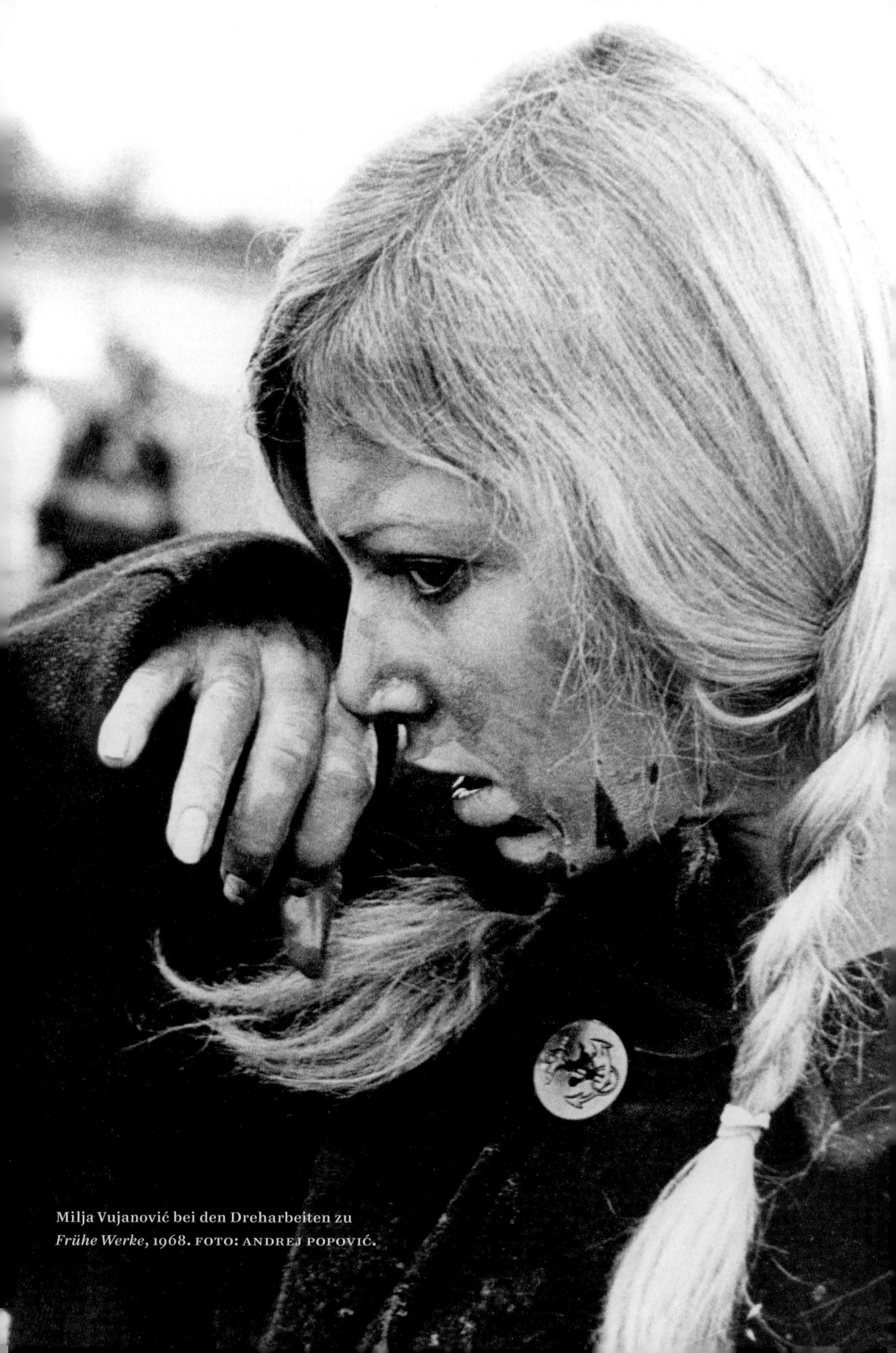

Milja Vujanović bei den Dreharbeiten zu *Frühe Werke*, 1968. FOTO: ANDREJ POPOVIĆ.

BORIS BUDEN

Shoot It Black! Eine Einführung zu Želimir Žilnik

It's not easy facing up when your whole world is black.
—The Rolling Stones, *Paint it Black*, 1966

Želimir Žilnik gilt als einer der prominentesten Vertreter der Schwarzen Welle, einer Richtung im jugoslawischen Film, die aus politischen und wirtschaftlichen Liberalisierungen im Land in den 1960er und 1970er Jahren hervorging. In der kurzen Geschichte Jugoslawiens stellt die Schwarze Welle einen kulturellen Höhepunkt dar.[01] Aber was bedeutet es konkret, ein Protagonist in dieser kulturellen Geschichte aus der kommunistischen Vergangenheit zu sein? Was ist mit schwarz eigentlich gemeint, wenn man von einer Schwarzen Welle spricht? Ich will mit dieser einfachen Frage beginnen.

Der Zeitungsartikel aus dem Jahr 1969, in dem der Begriff Schwarze Welle zum ersten Mal auftauchte, beginnt mit einer merkwürdigen Perspektive.[02] Der Autor blickt aus der Zukunft auf die Wirklichkeit Jugoslawiens. De facto wären wir damit in unserer heutigen Gegenwart. Diese Zukunft wird seiner Meinung nach nicht in der Lage sein, „unser wahres Bild" zu finden. Das authentische Bild der jugoslawischen Gesellschaft dieser Zeit findet sich nämlich nicht in den „vergilbten Jahrgängen der jeweiligen Tagespresse". Diese „Informationsebene wird in Vergessenheit geraten, abgelegt in den Archiven und Computerhirnen". Stattdessen findet man das wahre Bild in der Kunst dieser Zeit. Die Zukunft, so behauptet der Autor, wird nicht denen glauben, die die tatsächliche Wirklichkeit erlebt haben, sondern „der verdichteten und suggestiven künstlerischen

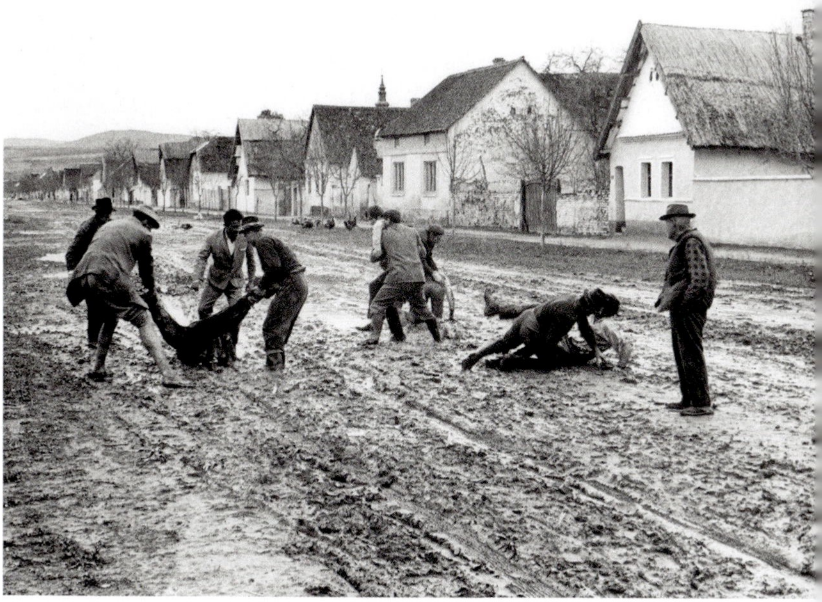

Frühe Werke (Produktionsfoto), 1968. FOTO: ANDREJ POPOVIĆ.

01
Die Autoren der Schwarzen Welle widersetzten sich den Normen und Idealen einer optimistischen, selbstbeweihräuchernden offiziellen Kultur und beleuchteten die dunklen Seiten der sozialistischen Gesellschaft. Sie ließen sich dabei vom italienischen Neorealismus und verschiedenen weiteren Neuen Wellen im europäischen Kino inspirieren. Vor allem zielten sie auf die ideologisch unterdrückte kapitalistische Wahrheit, die mit der Einführung einer Marktwirtschaft einherging. Sie brachte verheerende Auswirkungen mit sich: Arbeitslosigkeit, massive Wanderungsbewegungen von Arbeitern innerhalb des Landes wie über die Staatsgrenzen hinweg, Armut und Verbrechen. Neben Žilnik waren die bekanntesten Filmemacher Živojin Pavlović, Bato Čengić, Dušan Makavejev und Aleksandar Petrović.

02
Vladimir Jovičić, „‚Crni val' u našem filmu", *Borba*, 3. August 1969, S. 17–24; Übersetzung: Boris Buden und Bert Rebhandl.

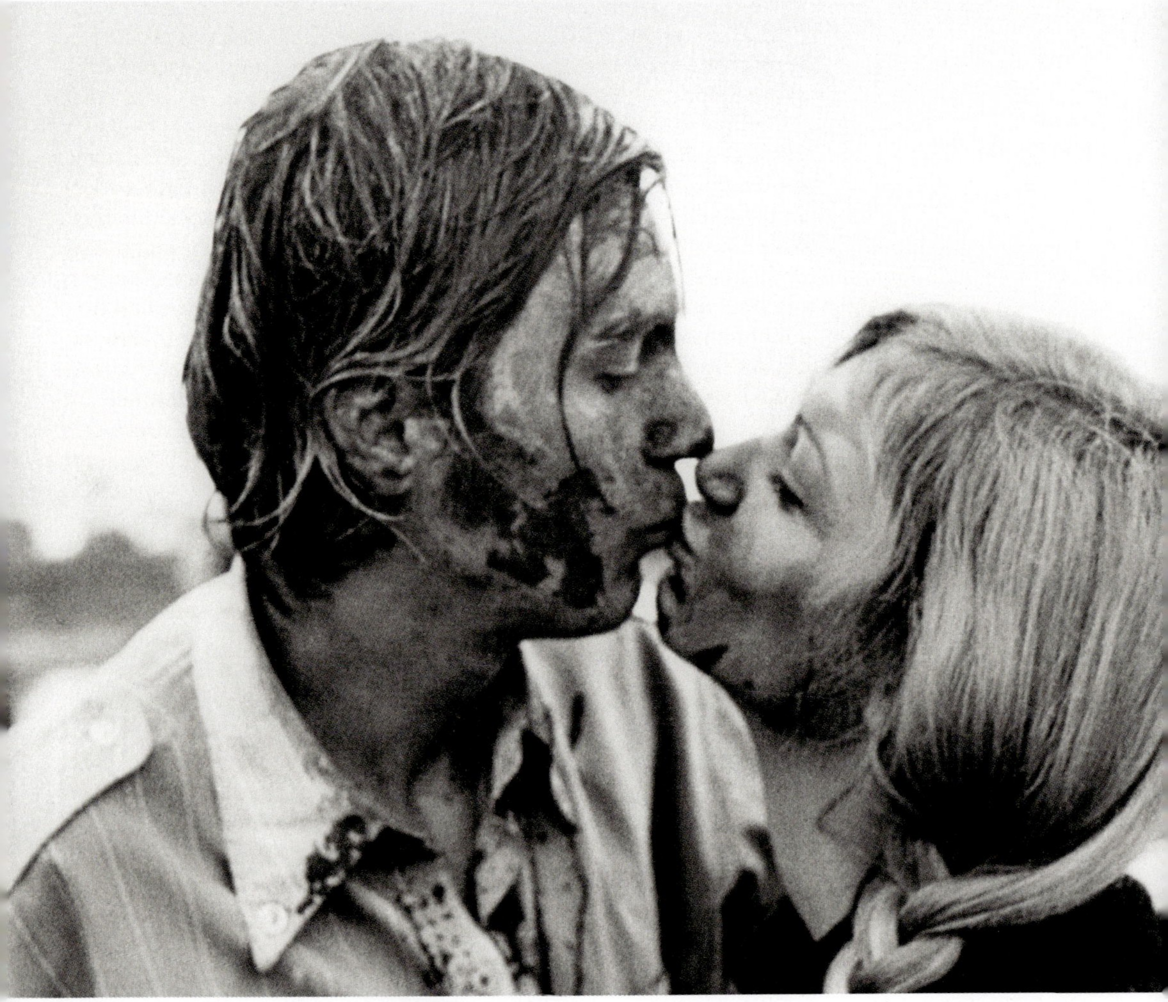

Geschichte und dem Bild, die diese Realität hervorgebracht haben".[03] Darin liegt für ihn der Grund, dass die Zukunft ein schwarzes Bild von der jugoslawischen Gesellschaft der 1960er und 1970er Jahre haben werde – denn die jugoslawische Kunst, vor allem der jugoslawische Film, male diese Gesellschaft schwarz.

Ist das nicht interessant? In einer Gesellschaft mit kommunistischer Herrschaft würde man doch erwarten, dass die Stimme der Partei auch die Stimme der Geschichte selbst ist – was auf *Borba,* die Zeitung, in der dieser Artikel erschien, auch zweifellos zutraf.[04] Und nun zittert diese Zeitung vor der Geschichte und erwartet bang das Urteil der Zukunft. Was wird die Zukunft von uns denken? Das ist keine der Fragen, die doch eigentlich den Lauf der Geschichte kennen sollten und die ihre Herrschaft genau aus dieser Zukunft ableiten. Zudem konnte kein Gesetz des historischen Materialismus, keine noch so undogmatische und schöpferisch aufgeklärte marxistische Auffassung der Kunst, diesem Überbauphänomen, die Macht

03
Ibid., S. 17.

04
Aus diesem Grund erwähne ich den Namen des Autors dieses Artikels nicht ausdrücklich im Text. Wer er genau war, ist von zweitrangigem Interesse, denn seine persönliche und öffentliche Meinung wurde damals sofort als Meinung der Partei selbst verstanden.

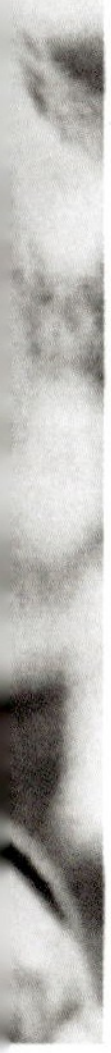

Bogdan Tirnanić und Milja Vujanović bei den Dreharbeiten zu *Frühe Werke*, 1968. FOTO: ANDREJ POPOVIĆ.

verleihen, das einzige „wahre Bild“ der Gesellschaft abzugeben und schließlich sogar selbst das letzte Wort über die Geschichte zu haben. Genau das wäre aber die Logik, auf der das Argument gegen die Filmemacher der Schwarzen Welle beruht. Der Kritiker in *Borba* wirft ihnen Verrat vor. Aber was sollen sie verraten haben? Nicht in erster Linie die Wirklichkeit. Der Vorwurf geht nicht so sehr dahin, dass sie die Wirklichkeit in ihren Filmen nicht getreulich wiedergegeben hätten – sie also schwärzer gezeichnet haben, als sie tatsächlich ist. Ihr eigentliches Verbrechen besteht darin, dass sie die Gesellschaft, der sie angehören, falsch darstellen. Wenn der Kritiker also von einem „wahren Bild unserer Gesellschaft“ schreibt, geht es ihm nicht so sehr um die Wahrheit, also um eine realistische Repräsentation des sozialen Lebens, sondern um das Bild der Gesellschaft. Das bereitet ihm Sorgen. Er beklagt sich, dass sich die Gesellschaft in den Filmen der Schwarzen Welle „in Lumpen kleidet, bevor sie Bilder von sich macht“. Er meint damit offensichtlich nicht, dass sie jegliche Kleidung ablegen und sich in ihrer vollen Nacktheit so zeigen sollte, wie sie wirklich ist.

Die Akzentverschiebung von der Wahrheit zum Bild wirkt geringfügig, hat aber weitreichende Konsequenzen. Der wirkliche Konflikt zwischen dem Kritiker und den Verrätern findet nicht dort statt, wo wir ihn üblicherweise aus unserer postkommunistischen Perspektive hinprojizieren: zwischen der kommunistischen Ideologie auf der einen Seite und der Autonomie der Kunst auf der anderen. Der Fall der jugoslawischen Schwarzen Welle ist keiner zwischen ideologisch verbohrten kommunistischen Apparatschiks, die freiheitsliebende Künstler dem Dogma des (Sozialistischen) Realismus zu unterwerfen versuchen. Dem Kritiker geht es gar nicht um die sozialistische Sache – das wäre der geläufige Diskurs über die soziale Funktion der Kunst, über ihre programmatische Rolle beim Aufbau einer neuen Gesellschaft, über ihre erzieherischen Pflichten beispielweise in der Verbreitung von Optimismus. Die klassischen Argumente für einen Sozialistischen Realismus fehlen in diesem polemischen Text vollständig.[05] Der Pessimismus, dessen er (und durch ihn spricht in diesem Fall die Partei) die Filmemacher der Schwarzen Welle bezichtigt, ist nicht deswegen problematisch, weil er zu Defätismus führt und damit die fortschrittlichen Kräfte entwaffnet. Das Problem ist, dass er ein unvorteilhaftes Bild der jugoslawischen Gesellschaft zeichnet. Darin liegt das ganze Drama: wie die Gesellschaft sich dem Anderen gegenüber darstellt, dem Anderen im Ausland und dem Anderen in der Zukunft. Den Autoren der Schwarzen Welle wird ausdrücklich vorgeworfen, dass sie „die Nation und die Gesellschaft lächerlich machen, um damit billigen und kurzfristigen Ruhm in der Welt zu erlangen“. In den Augen des Kritikers haben sie sich dem Modegeschmack des internationalen Markts unterworfen. Darin liegt ihr Verschulden.

Natürlich braucht er auch Autoritäten, um seine Kritik zu stützen. Er greift dabei aber nicht auf Marx, Engels oder Lenin zurück, oder auf einen jugoslawischen Marxisten oder einen der führenden Par-

05 Der Autor distanziert sich sogar von allen Konzepten einer „erzieherischen“ Funktion von Kunst. Für ihn ist es eine „altmodische Didaktik, Kunst irgendwelche funktionalen Merkmale zu verleihen“. Die Idee, dass ein Kunstwerk eine Art Botschaft enthalten sollte, wischt er beiseite. Das wäre für ihn Schdanowismus, die Parteidoktrin zu Kunst und Kultur, die in der Sowjetunion von dem ZK-Sekretär Andrei Schdanow im Jahr 1946 entwickelt wurde. Er schreibt sogar ganz offen, dass er durchaus Verständnis für die Schwärze des jugoslawischen Films dieser Periode haben könnte, wenn sie im Rahmen der „Kunst um der Kunst willen“ bleiben würden. Jovičić, op. cit., S. 9.

teiintellektuellen. Er beruft sich auf Bosley Crowther, den legendären Filmkritiker der *New York Times*, der zu diesem Zeitpunkt Art Director bei Columbia Pictures war. In einem Interview mit einer jugoslawischen Zeitschrift hatte Crowther gesagt:

> „Ihr Jugoslawen … ihr seid so lebendig … ihr wisst, wie man Frauen anschaut, ihr könnt aus vollem Herzen lachen, ihr seid offen, es gibt eine ursprüngliche Lebensfreude in euch. Warum sind dann eure Filme so bitter, so dunkel? Was ist die Wahrheit? Ihr, wie ich euch erlebt habe, oder wie ihr euch in euren Filmen präsentiert? … Oder ist das in euren Filmen alles ein vorübergehender, modischer Pessimismus, den eure Autoren, mit einer gewissen Verzögerung, aus dem Ausland übernommen haben?“[06]

Hier haben wir also eine offizielle Parteiposition zu Fragen der Kultur, und diese übernimmt ihre Argumente aus einer Identifikation mit einem westlich-orientalistischen Blick, der Jugoslawien als ein exotisches Reich authentischer Lebensfreude und natürlicher Vitalität ausmalt.

Noch tiefgreifender stellt sich die Frage der Repräsentation aus der Perspektive der Zukunft und in der Beziehung zur Nachwelt. Auch hier geht es um das Bild der Gesellschaft, das in den Werken der Kunst weiterbestehen wird. Der Kritiker der *Borba* schreibt von einem „Bild von uns, das der Zukunft hinterlassen“ wird. Es ist ihm wichtig, dass uns diese „Form der Anerkennung“ nicht gleichgültig sein sollte. Denn wenn die Kunst dieses Bild nun schwarzmalt, dann wird auch die Zukunft ein schwarzes Bild von uns haben.

Aus einer heutigen Perspektive legt sich dementsprechend für uns nahe, dass wir unweigerlich unsere postkommunistische Perspektive ablegen müssen, wenn wir wirklich verstehen wollen, was das Schwarze war, das einem Großteil der jugoslawischen Filmproduktion gegen Ende der 1960er Jahre zugeschrieben wurde. Nicht nur wegen all dieser unerträglichen Klischees über die kommunistische Vergangenheit (deren tatsächlicher ideologischer Effekt nicht so sehr darin lag, die Utopie der Vergangenheit zu verdunkeln, sondern die gegenwärtige von liberaler Demokratie und Kapitalismus als den einzigen Aus- und Lösungsweg aus der Weltgeschichte leuchtend auszumalen). Es gibt noch einen weiteren, besseren Grund: Der Begriff der Schwarzen Welle stammt selbst aus dieser postkommunistischen Perspektive.

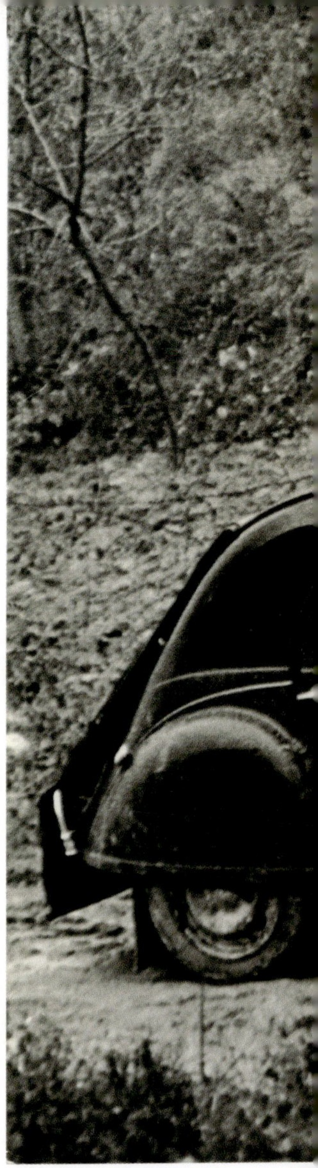

Die Schwarze Welle ist offensichtlich eine Idee, die aus einem Kampf stammt, und impliziert eine bestimmte Instrumentalisierung der Kunst in diesem Kampf. Aber welcher Kampf? Nicht der für eine bessere Gesellschaft – zum Beispiel eine gerechte, klassenlose, kurz gesagt: eine kommunistische Gesellschaft? Wir haben es hier eindeutig nicht mit einer Geschichte über eine Kunst zu tun, die ungerechtfertigterweise in einen sozialen Kampf verwickelt wird. Aus der

06
Ibid., S. 20.

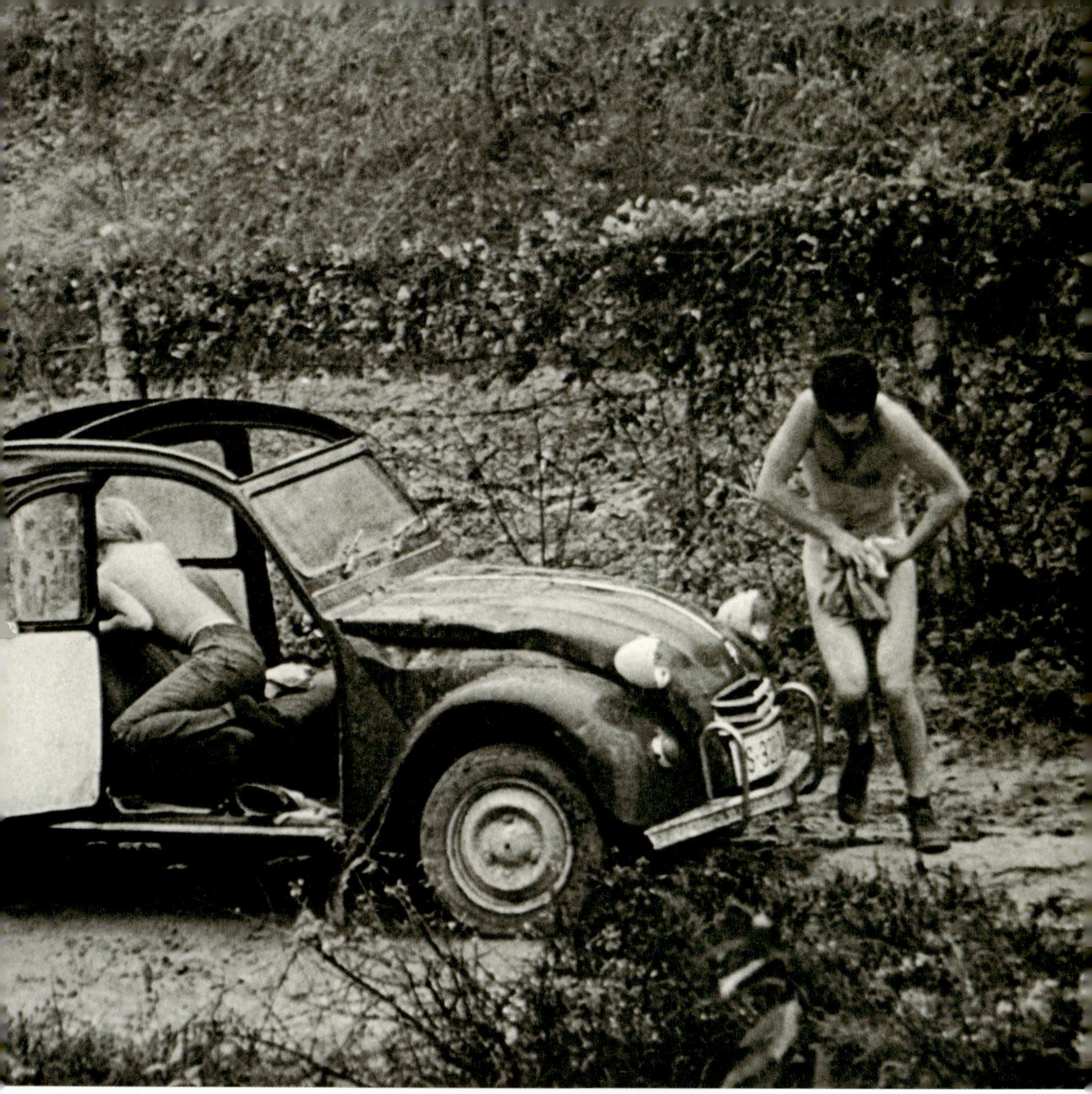

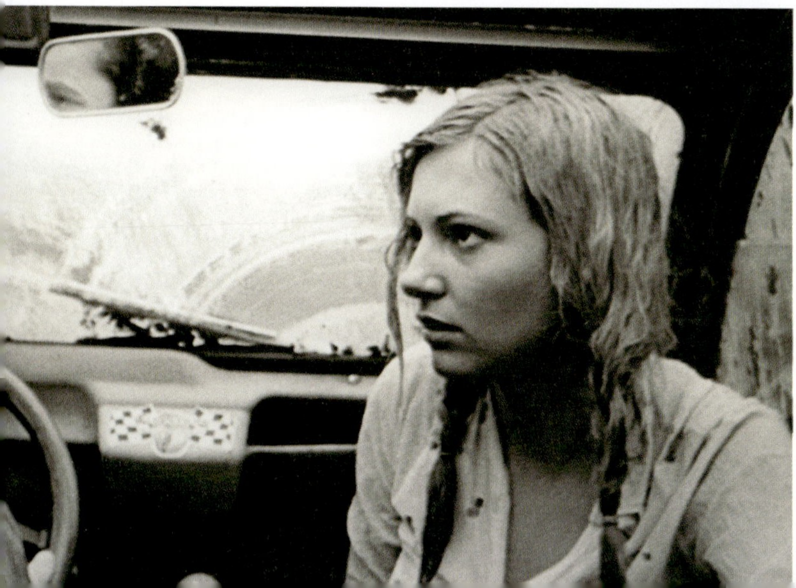

Frühe Werke (Produktionsfotos), 1968. FOTOS: ANDREJ POPOVIĆ.

Oben: Milja Vujanović und Marko Nikolić

Unten: Milja Vujanović

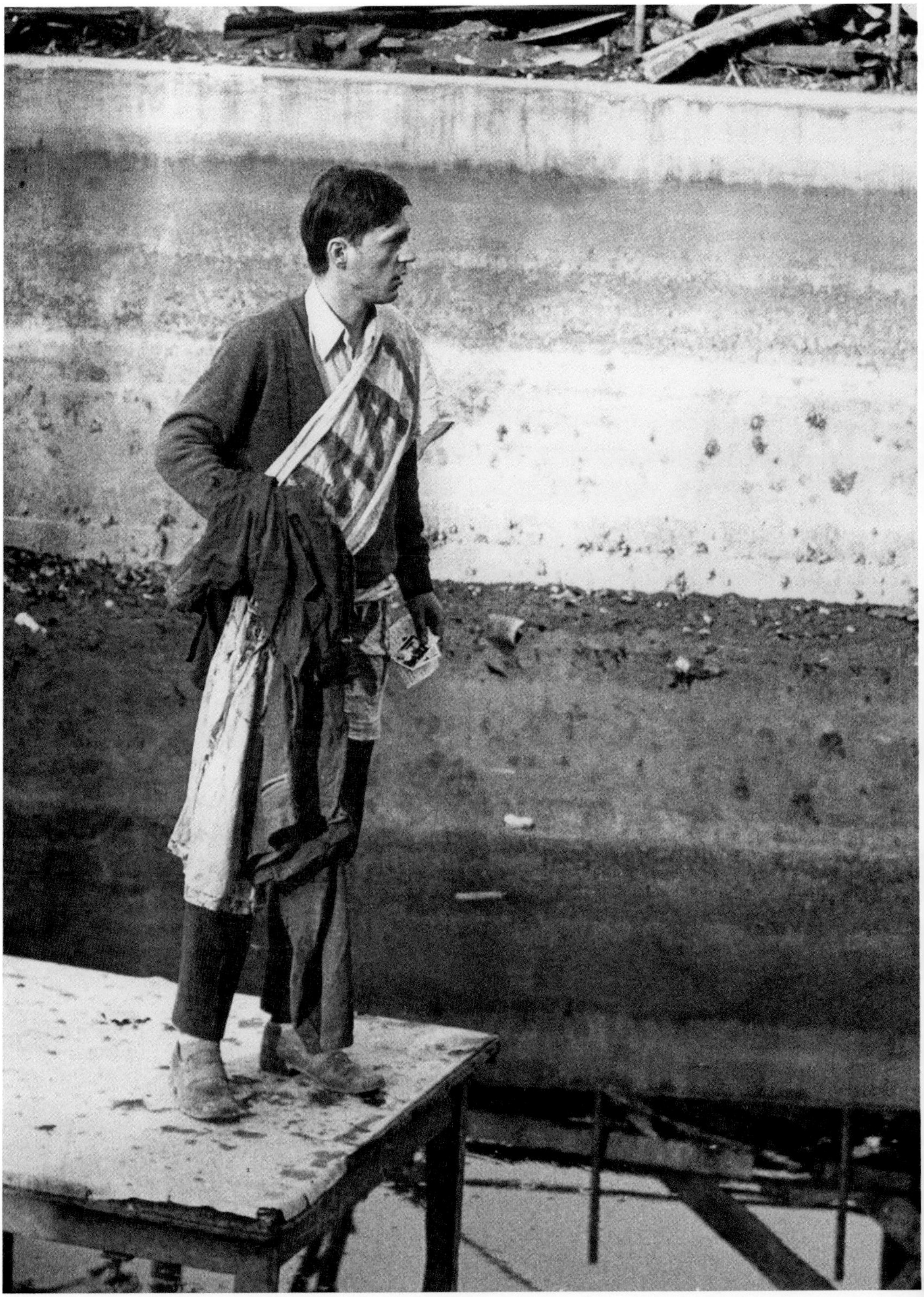

Bogdan Tirnanić bei den Dreharbeiten zu *Frühe Werke*, 1968. FOTO: ANDREJ POPOVIĆ.

Sicht des Kritikers, der den Slogan Schwarze Welle eingeführt hat, war der soziale Kampf schon beendet, genauer gesagt: die sozialen Gründe für den Kampf waren obsolet geworden. Und doch ging der Kampf weiter, aber in einer anderen Form, auf einem anderen Feld und mit einem anderen Ziel. Nun war es der Kampf um Anerkennung, und der wurde ausschließlich auf dem Feld der Kultur ausgefochten. In diesem Kampf ging es nun um eines: Identität.

So paradox es klingen mag: Die Position, von der aus die Stimme der Partei ihr *J'accuse* gegen die Filmemacher der Schwarzen Welle erhob, war die Position einer Gesellschaft, die schon tot war – eine Gesellschaft, die ihr ganzes utopisches Potential erschöpft und die Grenzen ihrer künftigen Ausdehnung an sozialer Gerechtigkeit und allgemeiner sozialer Prosperität erreicht hatte. Es war eine Gesellschaft, die ihrem historischen Ende ins Auge blickte, eine Gesellschaft ohne irgendeine Zukunft. Sie konnte sich buchstäblich nicht in der Zukunft sehen, oder genauer gesagt, sie konnte dort nur ein entfremdetes Bild von sich sehen, ein Bild, das sich die Kunst in den Filmen der Schwarzen Welle schon angeeignet hatte. Das ist der Grund, warum unser Verständnis der Schwarzen Welle nicht auf ein postkommunistisches Klischee von einer Kunst reduziert werden kann, die mit der Gesellschaft um ihre Freiheit kämpft. Im Gegenteil ist es die Gesellschaft selbst, die mit der Kunst um das wahre Bild von sich selbst ringt, eine Gesellschaft in einem letzten Kampf um ihr kulturelles Überleben. Indem sie diesen Kampf 1969 eröffneten, erwiesen sich die kommunistischen Kritiker der Schwarzen Welle ausgerechnet als Postkommunisten, und zwar lange vor all den Demokraten, die später an ihre Stelle treten sollten. Sie wussten nur zu gut, dass sie nicht mehr über die Geschichte verfügen konnten, aber sie waren immer noch in der Lage, ihre Entwicklung abzusehen. Und indem sie sich so ausschließlich mit der Frage kultureller Repräsentationen befassten, hatten sie auch schon diesen berüchtigten cultural turn vollzogen, den man später als eines der wichtigsten Charakteristika der Postmoderne zuschreiben sollte. Die jugoslawischen Kommunisten dieser Zeit sahen die Gesellschaft, für die sie zuständig waren, aus dem Blickwinkel ihres kulturellen Nachlebens.

Politisch wurde die Partei natürlich weiterhin mit ihrer historischen Mission identifiziert: radikale Veränderung der Gesellschaft zum Besseren. Und sie sah sich auch in der Lage, dieses Ziel zu erreichen. Aber das betraf – in den Begriffen Lacans – nur die imaginäre Ebene ihrer Identifikation. In dieser Sichtweise identifizierten sich die jugoslawischen Kommunisten mit dem Idealbild von sich selbst, mit ihrem Ideal-Ich. Gleichzeitig identifizierten sie sich, auf einer symbolischen Ebene, mit dem Blick der Geschichte selbst – also: mit ihrem Ich-Ideal. Sie sahen dabei die Gesellschaft, die sie aufgebaut hatten, nur in einer kulturellen Übersetzung, die sich gänzlich ihrer Kontrolle entzog. Sie herrschten über die Gesellschaft, aber nur in einem Reich des Imaginären. Symbolisch hatten sie die Gesellschaft schon an die Kultur verloren. Im Jahr 1969 bestand die Herausforderung für die Partei nicht mehr darin, eine neue, bessere Gesellschaft

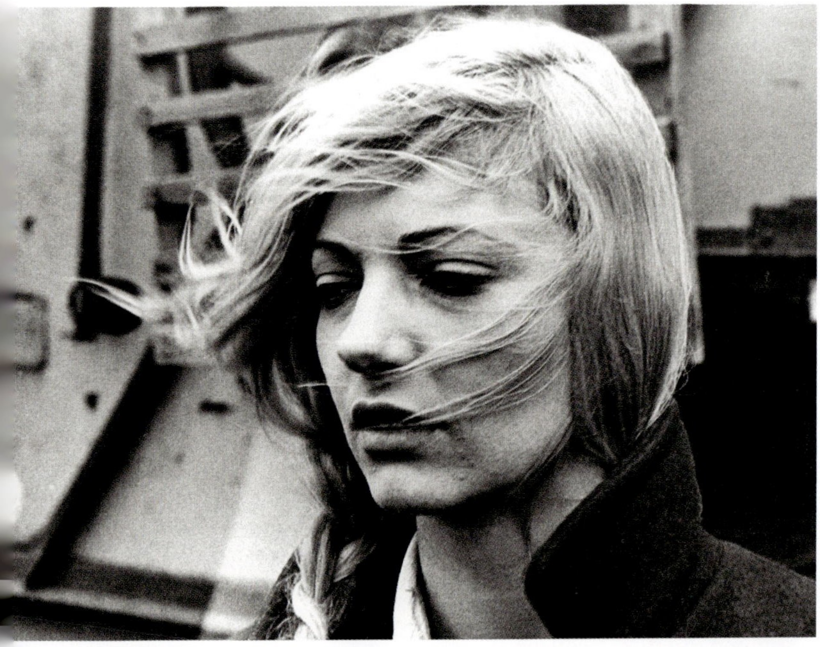

Milja Vujanović bei den Dreharbeiten zu *Frühe Werke*, 1968. FOTO: ANDREJ POPOVIĆ.

aufzubauen, sondern stattdessen die tote Gesellschaft angemessen zu repräsentieren. Ein wahres Bild der sozialen Realität schien noch möglich, aber nur in einer vorweggenommenen kulturellen Rückschau. Damit ist auch eine Veränderung innerhalb des Realismus bezeichnet: von seiner sozial vorausschauenden Dimension (das Konzept des Sozialistischen Realismus im Dienst einer Gesellschaft als utopisches Projekt) zu einem kulturell retrospektiven Realismus. Letzteres ist um nichts weniger ideologisch dogmatisch als Ersteres. Das Dogma hat nur einen neuen Namen. Er lautet nun kulturelles Gedächtnis – die einzige Form, in der soziale Erfahrung für uns heute zugänglich ist, natürlich rückblickend. Die Partei wusste das schon 1969.

Nun könnten wir wahrscheinlich die Frage beantworten, mit der wir begonnen haben: Worauf bezieht sich das Schwarz in dem Begriff einer Schwarzen Welle im jugoslawischen Kino? Es bezieht sich in erster Linie auf das Ende der Gesellschaft, auf die Erfahrung des Abgrunds, der sich an diesem Ende öffnet, auf diese bodenlose Kontingenz, der man nach einem sozialen Experiment begegnet – oder, genauer gesagt, nachdem sich das menschliche Experimentieren mit dem Sozialen historisch erschöpft hat. Es ist die Schwärze, die jegliches utopische Leuchten absorbiert hat. Der Weg der Gesellschaft in die Zukunft liegt nun im Dunkeln. In einer subjektiven Dimension ist es die Dunkelheit der Angst, die uns erfüllt, wenn wir existenziell die Endlichkeit der Gesellschaft begreifen, wenn wir also die Möglichkeit ihrer totalen Abwesenheit zu erahnen beginnen. Kurz gesagt: wir sprechen hier von einer sozialen Angst in ihrer ontologischen Dimension.[07] Am besten findet man das in den Worten eines der berühmtesten Schauspieler der jugoslawischen

07 Im Sinne von Heideggers Angst, die ein Subjekt das Sein zum Tode der Gesellschaft erfahren lässt.

08 Bekim Fehmiu, zit. n. Jovičić, op. cit., S. 20.

09 Mit der neuen Verfassung von 1974 wurde Multikulturalismus zur offiziellen Ideologie des jugoslawi-

Schwarzen Welle ausgedrückt: Bekim Fehmiu, der auch in europäischen und in Hollywood-Produktionen mitwirkte. In dem Artikel in *Borba* wird Fehmiu folgendermaßen zitiert: „Uns ging es nie besser, und doch ist alles schwarz vor unseren Augen."[08]

Zur Besänftigung dieser Angst und zur Beruhigung dieser Ambivalenz wurde ein Fetisch eingeführt: der Fetisch kultureller Identität. Im Zusammenhang des politischen Konzepts der Souveränität wurde daraus auch nationale Identität. Zu dieser Zeit – gegen Ende der 1960er und Anfang der 1970er Jahre in Jugoslawien – vollzog sich ein grundlegender Wandel in der Art und Weise, wie die Kommunisten ihre Herrschaft legitimierten. Das Narrativ des Klassenkampfs wurde weitgehend aufgegeben. Die Partei begriff sich nicht länger als Avantgarde einer universalen Geschichte, die auf ihr klassenloses Ende im Kommunismus zulief. Stattdessen begann sie ihre Herrschaft im Zusammenhang der Geschichte einer bestimmten Nation zu legitimieren. Sie identifizierte sich als politische Elite, die, nachdem sie schließlich das Ziel nationaler Befreiung und voller nationaler Souveränität erreicht hatte, die (national verstandene) Gesellschaft in einen Fortschritt unter den vorgegebenen historischen Bedingungen einer sozialistisch regulierten Marktwirtschaft und einer offenen Teilnahme an internationaler Realpolitik und am globalen Kapitalismus führte. Zugespitzt: Die kommunistischen Führer dieser Ära versuchten nicht, die Gesellschaft an eine kommunistische Utopie anzupassen. Sie passten umgekehrt die kommunistische Utopie an eine Gesellschaft an, die sich nun vollständig mit ihrer Nation identifizierte. Damit verändert sich natürlich die Situation an der sogenannten kulturellen Front grundlegend. Die Grabenkämpfe der Kommunisten gegen die traditionelle bürgerliche Kultur waren zu Ende. Sie setzten der Schaffung essentialistischer Identitäten der jugoslawischen Völker (Serben, Kroaten, Slowenen, Bosnier, Mazedonier, Montenegriner, Albaner etc.) nichts mehr entgegen. Alles lief nun auf einen Nichtangriffspakt hinaus: „Ihr lasst uns die Politik, wir lassen euch die nationale Kultur." (Ein paar Ausnahmen wurden klar definiert.) Sie stärkten damit ihre identitäre, also ihre nationale Legitimation. Um weiter im Sattel zu bleiben, mussten sie auf ein frisches Pferd setzen: Identitätspolitik. Und auf diesem ritten sie dann blindlings in die Katastrophe der 1990er Jahre.[09]

Zusammenfassend: Identität oder, in einem etwas weiteren Sinn, kulturelle Identifikation konnte von nun an eine Perspektive eines Lebens nach dem Ende der Gesellschaft eröffnen. Kein Wunder, dass fast alle händeringend danach griffen. Aber eben nicht alle. Einige wollten lieber nicht.

Der Prominenteste unter denen, die mit weit geöffneten Augen – und Objektiven – in die Dunkelheit am Ende der Gesellschaft blickten, war und ist bis heute Želimir Žilnik. Sein gesamtes filmisches Werk, das sich über fast ein halbes Jahrhundert erstreckt, stellt den radikalsten und konsistentesten Ausdruck dieser Schwärze dar. Darüber hinaus ist Žilnik der einzige von den Filmemachern der Schwarzen

schen Staates. Der Diskurs über soziale Gerechtigkeit verschwand dabei nicht einfach aus der jugoslawischen Politik. Er wurde in eine neue Sprache der Identitätspolitik übersetzt, die in der politischen Öffentlichkeit dominierte – allerdings nicht als eine innersoziale Angelegenheit, sondern vielmehr als eine inter-nationale. Die Frage (un)gerechter Umverteilung wird nun nicht in Hinsicht auf die Beziehung einer Klasse der Gesellschaft zu einer anderen gestellt, sondern einer Republik – einer Nation – der jugoslawischen (Kon)Föderation zu einer anderen. Das ist deutlich eine postsozialistische Wende, wie Nancy Fraser sie in *Die halbierte Gerechtigkeit. Schlüsselbegriffe des postindustriellen Sozialstaats* (Frankfurt am Main 1997, S. 11) definiert hat: Diese zeigt eine Verschiebung weg „von einem sozialistisch geprägten Repertoire politischer Vorstellungen, in dem das Hauptproblem der Gerechtigkeit die Umverteilung ist" hin zu „einem ‚postsozialistisch' geprägten Repertoire politischer Vorstellungen, in dem das Hauptproblem der Gerechtigkeit die Anerkennung ist."

Welle, der ausdrücklich auf die offiziellen Vorwürfe einging: „Sie werfen mir vor, dass ich schwarze Filme mache. Dann mache ich eben welche." 1971 drehte er einen Dokumentarfilm, den er ganz buchstäblich *Der schwarze Film* nannte.[10] Žilnik nahm sechs obdachlose Menschen von der Straße mit nach Hause. Er wollte nicht nur die Wärme in der Wohnung mit ihnen teilen (es war Mitte Januar), sondern er wollte sie auch dazu bringen, aktiv an einem Film über ihr Problem mitzuarbeiten. (Dieses Prinzip wurde bestimmend für Žilniks Form des Dokudramas: Er erlaubt seinen Amateurschauspielern, um die es in der Geschichte des Films geht, bewusst, sich an der Herstellung zu beteiligen, anders gesagt: er lässt sie sich selbst spielen.)[11] Am nächsten Tag ging er mit der Kamera in Novi Sad auf die Straße und befragte die Menschen nach Lösungsmöglichkeiten für die Probleme der Obdachlosen in der Stadt. Weder die Passanten noch die Amtsträger haben eine Antwort. Der Filmemacher selbst hat auch keine Lösung, denn diese Menschen können nicht auf Dauer in seiner Wohnung bleiben. Dazu „stinken" sie auch zu sehr, wie er einmal im Film sagt. Der Film endet damit, dass Žilnik sie auffordert, die Wohnung zu verlassen. Ihr Problem ließ sich nicht lösen, und das Filmmaterial geht auch zu Ende.

Noch einmal: Was ist an *Der schwarze Film* schwarz? Die abgebildete Wirklichkeit? Das Versagen der Kommunisten bei der Lösung sozialer Probleme? Der offenkundige Spalt zwischen einem utopischen Versprechen und der Realität? Nein! Es ist der Film selbst, die Idee der Kunst als solcher, vor allem der Filmkunst, die den Anspruch erhebt, die soziale Wirklichkeit zu verändern – das ist wirklich schwarz in *Der schwarze Film*. Es beginnt schon damit, dass der Autor in die Kamera sagt: „Ich habe diesen Film vor zwei Jahren gemacht, aber

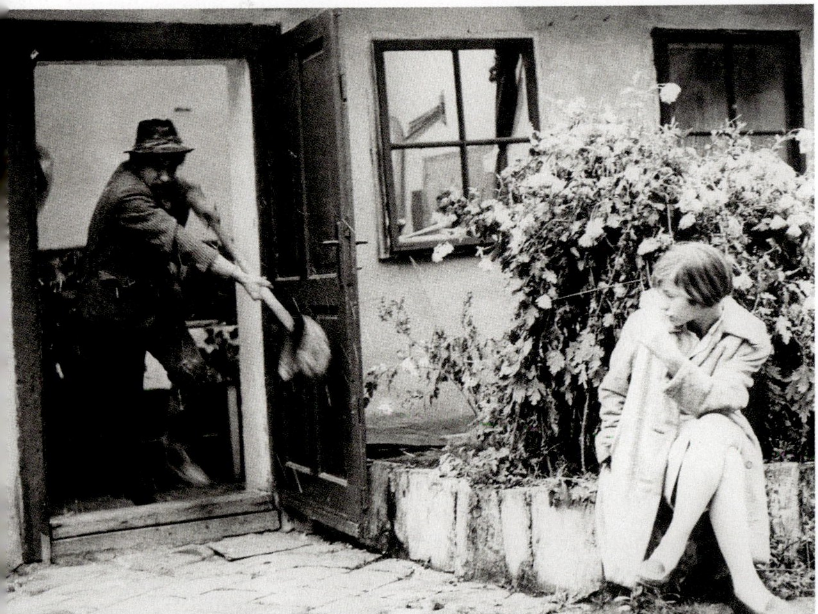

Slobodan Aligrudić und Piroška Čapko bei den Dreharbeiten zu *Frühe Werke*, 1968. FOTO: ANDREJ POPOVIĆ.

10 *Der schwarze Film* war Teil des von Alexander Horwath kuratierten Filmprogramms bei der documenta 12.

11 „Ich tue gegenüber den Menschen, mit denen ich drehe, nicht so, als würde ich keinen Film drehen. Im Gegenteil. Ich helfe ihnen, ihre eigene Situation zu erkennen, und ihre Position darin zum Ausdruck zu bringen, und zwar so effizient wie möglich. Und sie helfen mir dabei, in der bestmöglichen Weise einen Film über sie zu machen." Želimir Žilnik, „My Films are Optimistic", Interview mit Valdislav Urban, in: *Dnevni*, 14. April 1968; zit. nach: Dominika Prejdová, „Socially Engaged Cinema According to Želimir Žilnik", in: Branislav Dimitrijević et al., *For an Idea – Against the Status Quo*, Novi Sad 2009, S. 164; aus dem Englischen übersetzt von Bert Rebhandl.

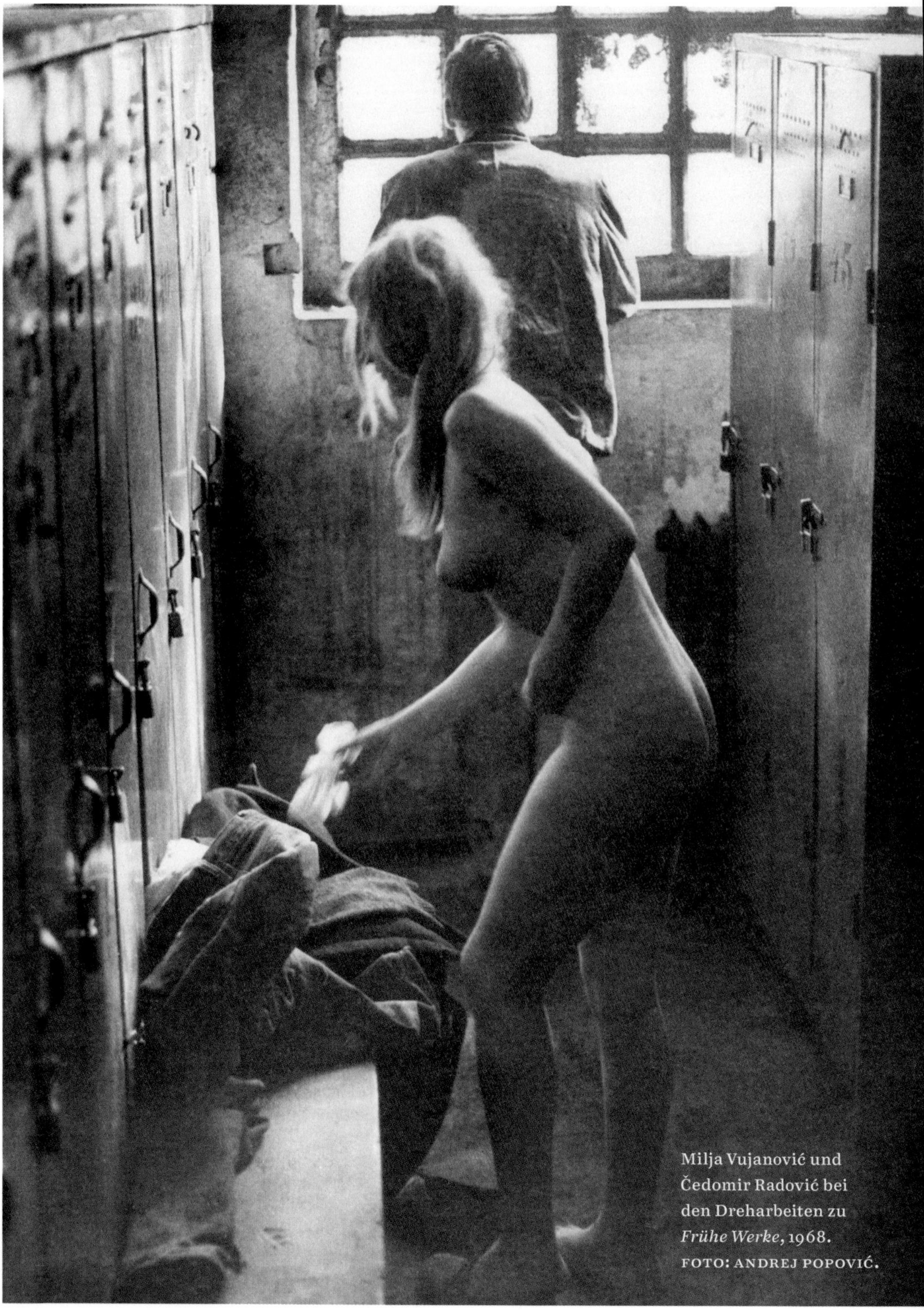

Milja Vujanović und Čedomir Radović bei den Dreharbeiten zu *Frühe Werke*, 1968. FOTO: ANDREJ POPOVIĆ.

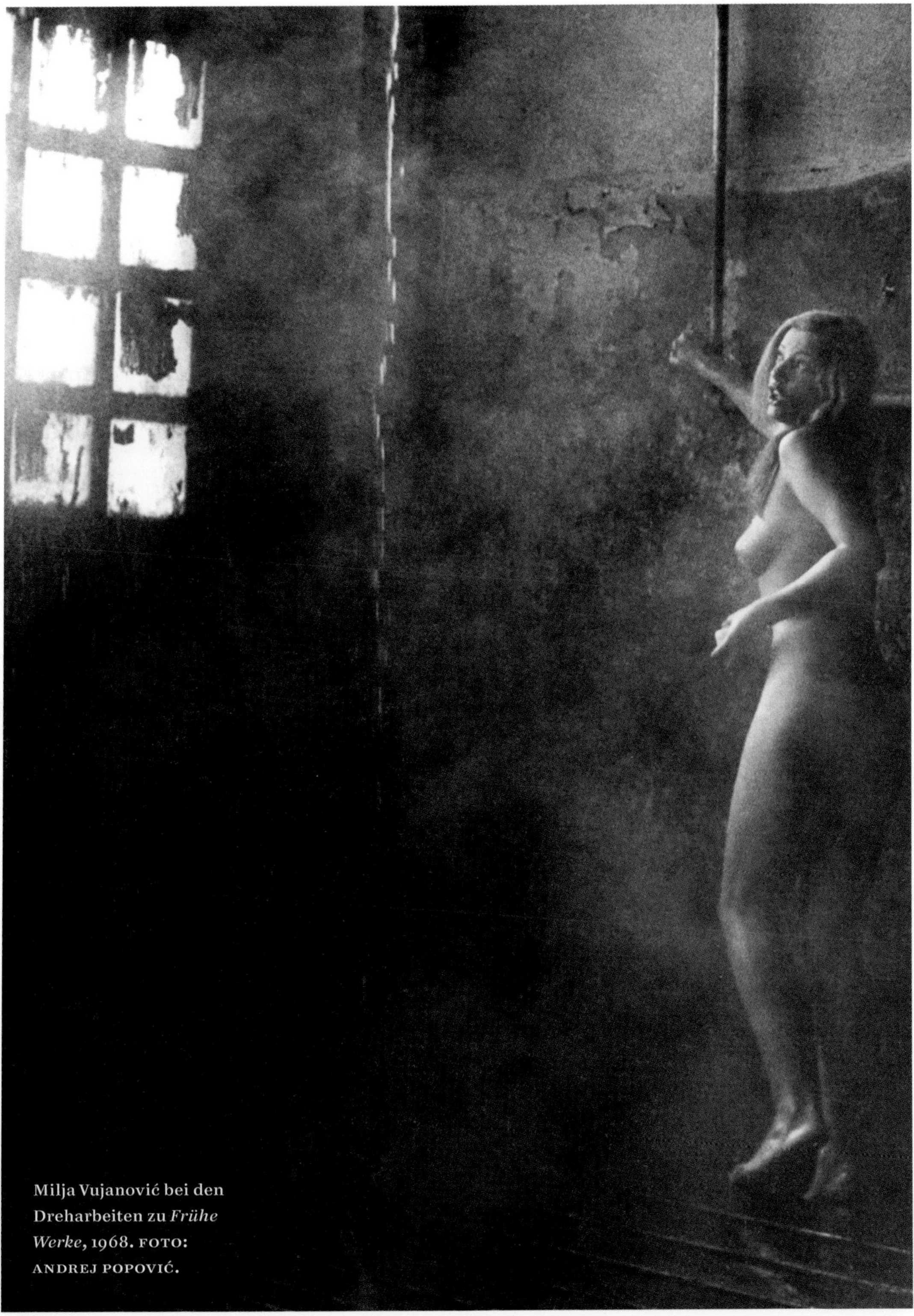

Milja Vujanović bei den Dreharbeiten zu *Frühe Werke*, 1968. FOTO: ANDREJ POPOVIĆ.

12 Želimir Žilnik, „Dieses Festival ist ein Friedhof. Manifest zum 18. Festival des jugoslawischen Kurzfilms in Belgrad 1971“, in: Will Wehling (Hg.), XVII. Westdeutsche Kurzfilmtage Oberhausen, Oberhausen 1971, S. 24–25.

13 Želimir Žilnik, zit. nach: Heinz Klunker, „Soziale Experimente“, in: Wehling, op. cit., S. 23.

14 Želimir Žilnik, „Dieses Festival ist ein Friedhof“, in: op. cit., S. 24.

15 Vgl. Želimir Žilnik, in: Heinz Klunker, op. cit., S. 23.

16 Ibid. In einem Bericht vom Festival in Belgrad kritisiert der genannte Autor Heinz Klunker Žilnik dafür, die Situation „zu schwarz“ zu sehen, und die Freiheit zu unterschätzen, die Filmemachern in Jugoslawien eingeräumt wird. Žilnik setze diese gewonnene Freiheit mit „purer Selbstgefälligkeit“ gleich. Heinz Klunker, „Eifer und Eifersucht. Leute, Filme und Politik in Belgrad“, in:

solche Menschen (Obdachlose) sind immer noch da.“ Der Film ist eine radikal aufrichtige, selbstreflexive Kritik der Idee und der Praxis des sogenannten sozial engagierten Kinos. Žilnik überlegt in aller Offenheit, ob *Der schwarze Film* nicht als sein Grab zu betrachten wäre. In einem Manifest aus Anlass des Kurz- und Dokumentarfilmfestivals in Belgrad im Jahr 1971, auf dem *Der schwarze Film* Premiere hatte, bezeichnet er das ganze Festival als einen „Friedhof“.[12] Schwarz bezieht sich hier auf das „Elend eines abstrakten Humanismus“[13] und des „sogenannten engagierten Films […], der sich als die herrschende Mode unserer seit je bürgerlich verfaßten Kinematographie erweist“[14]; es bezieht sich auf seinen falschen Avantgardismus, seine soziale Demagogie und linke Phraseologie; auf seinen Missbrauch sozial deklassierter Menschen für filmische Zwecke; die Ausbeutung sozialer Not durch die Filmemacher; etc.[15] Noch wichtiger: Schwarz bezieht sich nicht im geringsten auf einen Mangel an Freiheit. Aus der heutigen postkommunistischen Perspektive wird dieser Mangel üblicherweise als die schlimmste Schwärze der kommunistischen Vergangenheit dargestellt. In dem Manifest aus dem Jahr 1971 hielt Žilnik ausdrücklich fest: „Sie ließen uns unsere Freiheit. Wir wurden frei, aber unwirksam.“[16]

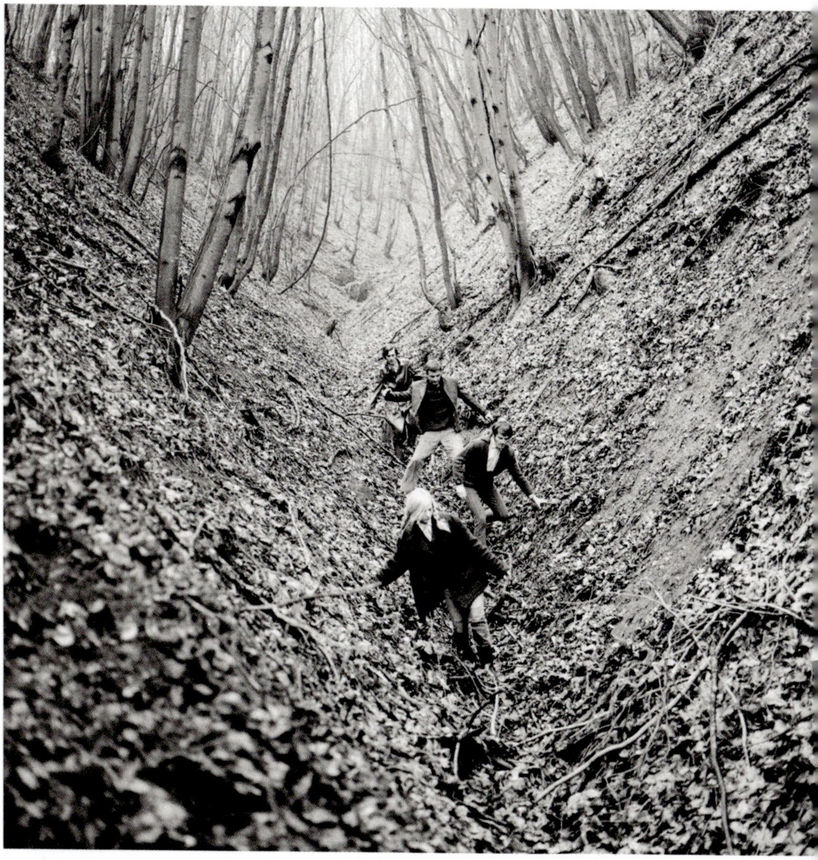

Frühe Werke (Produktionsfoto), 1968. FOTO: ANDREJ POPOVIĆ.

Für Žilnik kann ein Film niemals eine Lösung für soziales Elend sein. Das gilt in einem weiteren Sinn auch für die Kultur im Allgemeinen, ganz gleich, wie frei von totalitärer Unterdrückung sie ist. Für ihn ist das emanzipatorische Versprechen der Kultur ein Bluff. Er macht sich über die Autoren der sozial engagierten Filme des Jahrgangs 1971 lustig, und wirft ihnen vor, sie suchten, „einen möglichst malerischen Elenden [...], der sich bereit erklärt, vor der Kamera überzeugend zu leiden".[17] Žilnik trifft damit auch schon den liberalen Inklusivismus, der zwanzig Jahre später den Kulturproduzierenden der neuen (und alten) Demokratien seinen normativen Dogmatismus vorschreiben sollte. Wir kennen dieses Bild nur zu gut: jemand entdeckt irgendwo am Rand der Gesellschaft ausgeschlossene Menschen, arme, subalterne Geschöpfe ohne Gesicht und ohne Stimme. Zum Glück ist ein Künstler in der Nähe, der ihnen dabei hilft, ein Gesicht und eine Stimme zu bekommen. Ist doch wunderbar: Eine böse Gesellschaft schafft Exklusion, eine gute Kunst kann dann inklusiv wirken. Das alles in dem guten Glauben, dass das sozial Marginalisierte immerzu kulturell ins Zentrum gerückt werden kann – von den dunklen Rändern der Gesellschaft ans Licht, und damit in die Transparenz der öffentlichen Sphäre. Der Rest ist demokratische Routine: Eine wohlmeinende Zivilgesellschaft, die mit dem Leiden der Armen und Ausgeschlossenen sympathisiert, macht aus der sozialen Dunkelheit eine politische Sache; und sobald Parteipolitik ins Spiel kommt, nach einer politischen Lösung gesucht und schließlich eine gefunden wird, wird ein Gesetz geändert, und eine Demokratie wird wiedergeboren. Sie ist nun inklusiver als jemals zuvor.

Ohne mich, antwortete Žilnik schon 1971. Sein ganzes Leben lang hat er mit verschiedensten sogenannten marginalisierten Menschen gearbeitet – Straßenkinder, Arbeitslose, Wohnungslose, Transvestiten, illegale Migrantinnen und Migranten, Roma und Romnija, etc. Er weiß nur zu gut, was es mit ihrer Schwärze auf sich hat. Sie verweist darauf, dass die Gesellschaft als Gesellschaft abwesend ist, und was Politik, und sei sie noch so demokratisch, nicht repräsentieren kann: eine Schwärze, die mit zunehmender Geschwindigkeit das Licht verschluckt, um das wir uns historisch versammelt haben. ★

Deutsches Allgemeines Sonntagsblatt, Nr. 13, 28. März 1971, S. 6.

17
Želimir Žilnik, „Dieses Festival ist ein Friedhof", in: op. cit., S. 24.

Boris Buden ist Autor und Kulturkritiker mit Sitz in Berlin. Er promovierte in Kulturtheorie an der Humboldt-Universität zu Berlin. In den 1990er Jahren war er Redakteur der Zeitschrift *Arkzin* in Zagreb. Seine Essays und Artikel behandeln Themen aus der Philosophie, Politik, Kultur- und Kunstkritik. Er hat an zahlreichen Konferenzen und Kunstprojekten in West- und Osteuropa, Asien und den USA teilgenommen, unter anderem an der Documenta11 in Kassel. Buden ist Permanent Fellow des European Institute for Progressive Cultural Policies in Wien. Er lehrte Kulturtheorie an der Fakultät für Kunst und Gestaltung der Bauhaus-Universität Weimar. Buden ist Mitherausgeber und Autor mehrerer Bücher, darunter *Der Schacht von Babel* (2004), *Zone des Übergangs* (2009) und *Transition to Nowhere* (2019).

ÜBERSETZUNG AUS DEM ENGLISCHEN VON BERT REBHANDL.

ERSCHIENEN IN ENGLISCHER SPRACHE IN: *Afterall: A Journal of Art, Context and Enquiry*, Nr. 25, Herbst/Winter 2010, University of Chicago Press S. 38–47.

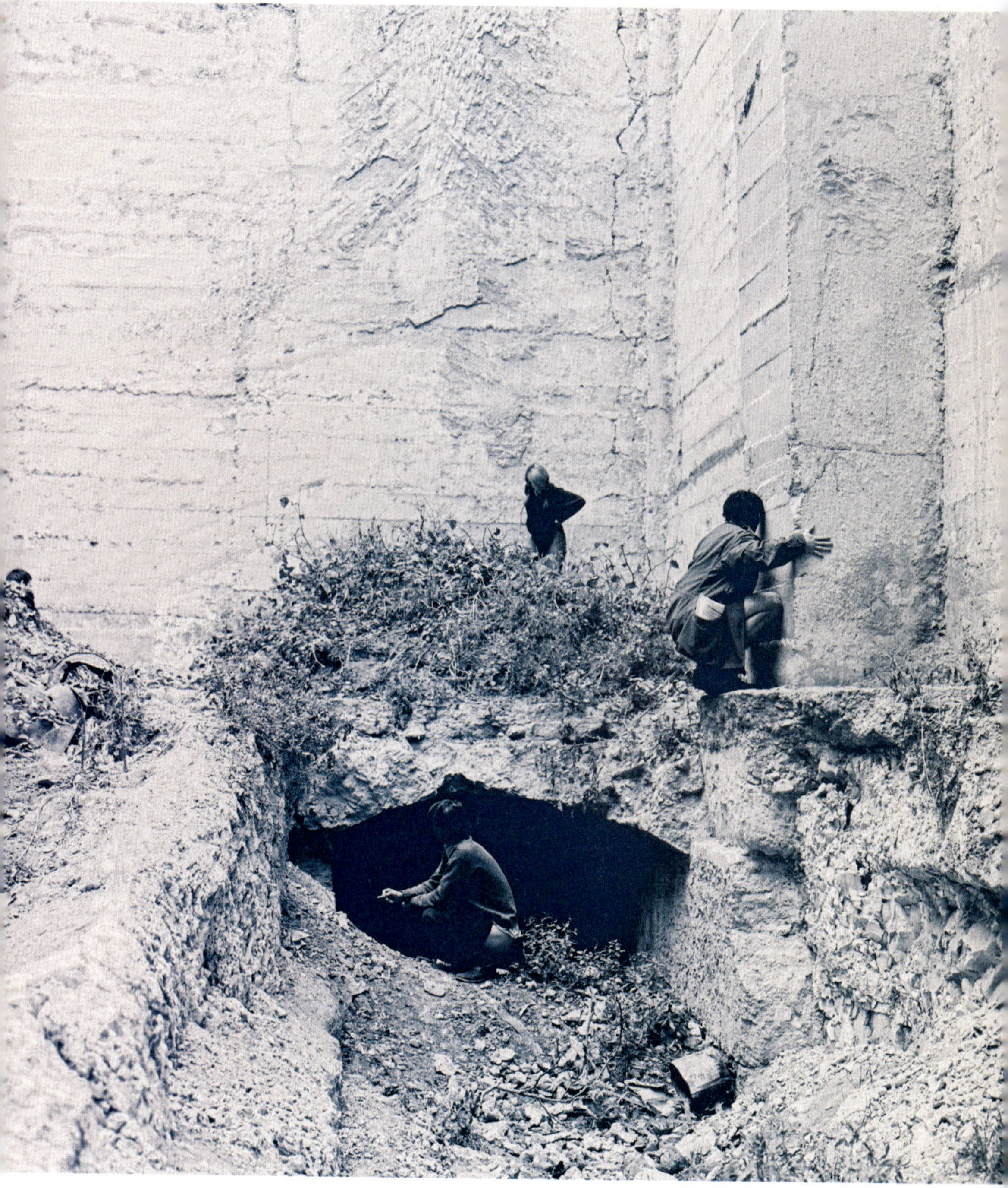

Čedomir Radović, Milja Vujanović, Marko Nikolić und Bogdan Tirnanić bei den Dreharbeiten zu *Frühe Werke* (Produktionsfoto), 1968.
FOTO: ANDREJ POPOVIĆ.

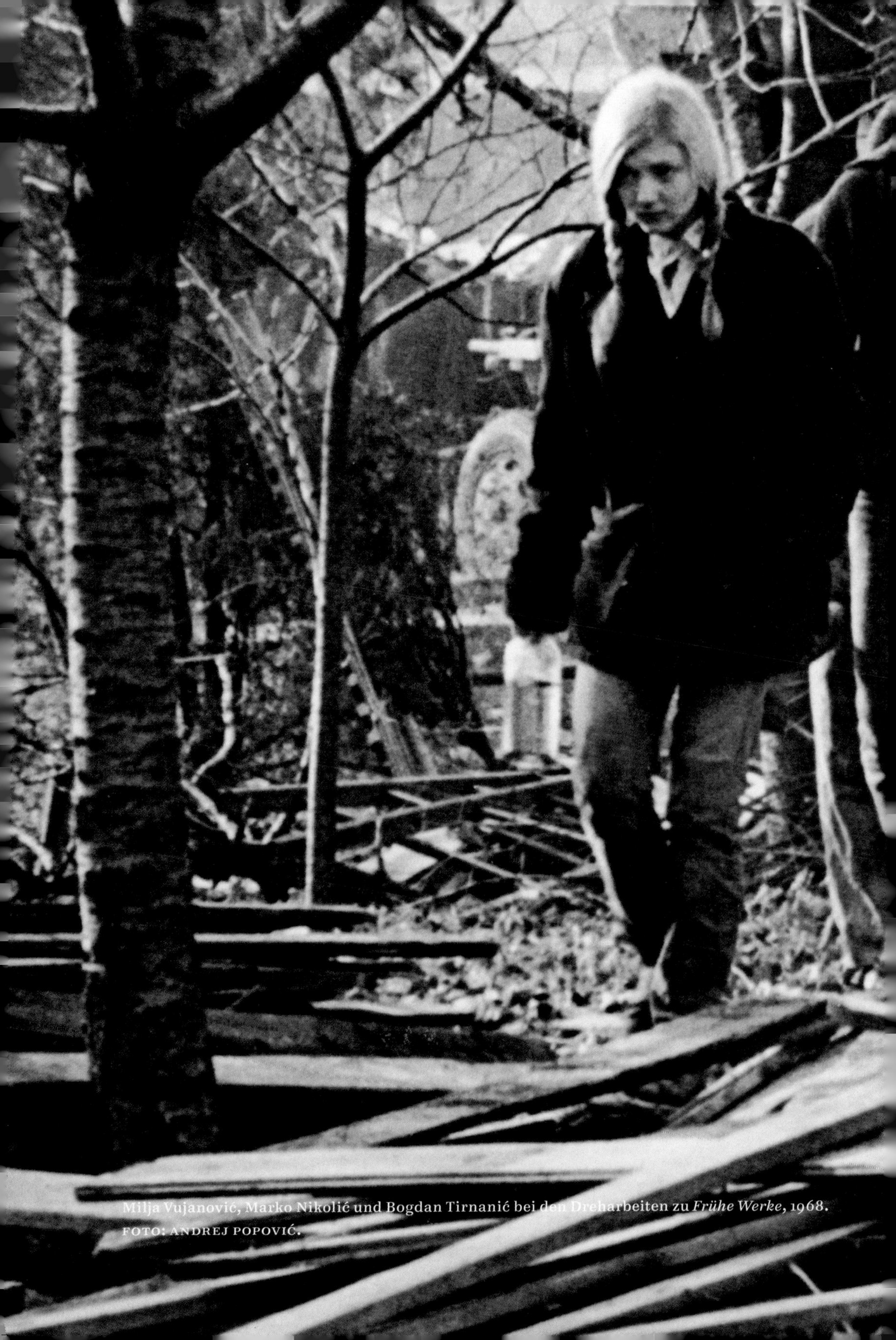

Milja Vujanović, Marko Nikolić und Bogdan Tirnanić bei den Dreharbeiten zu *Frühe Werke*, 1968.
FOTO: ANDREJ POPOVIĆ.

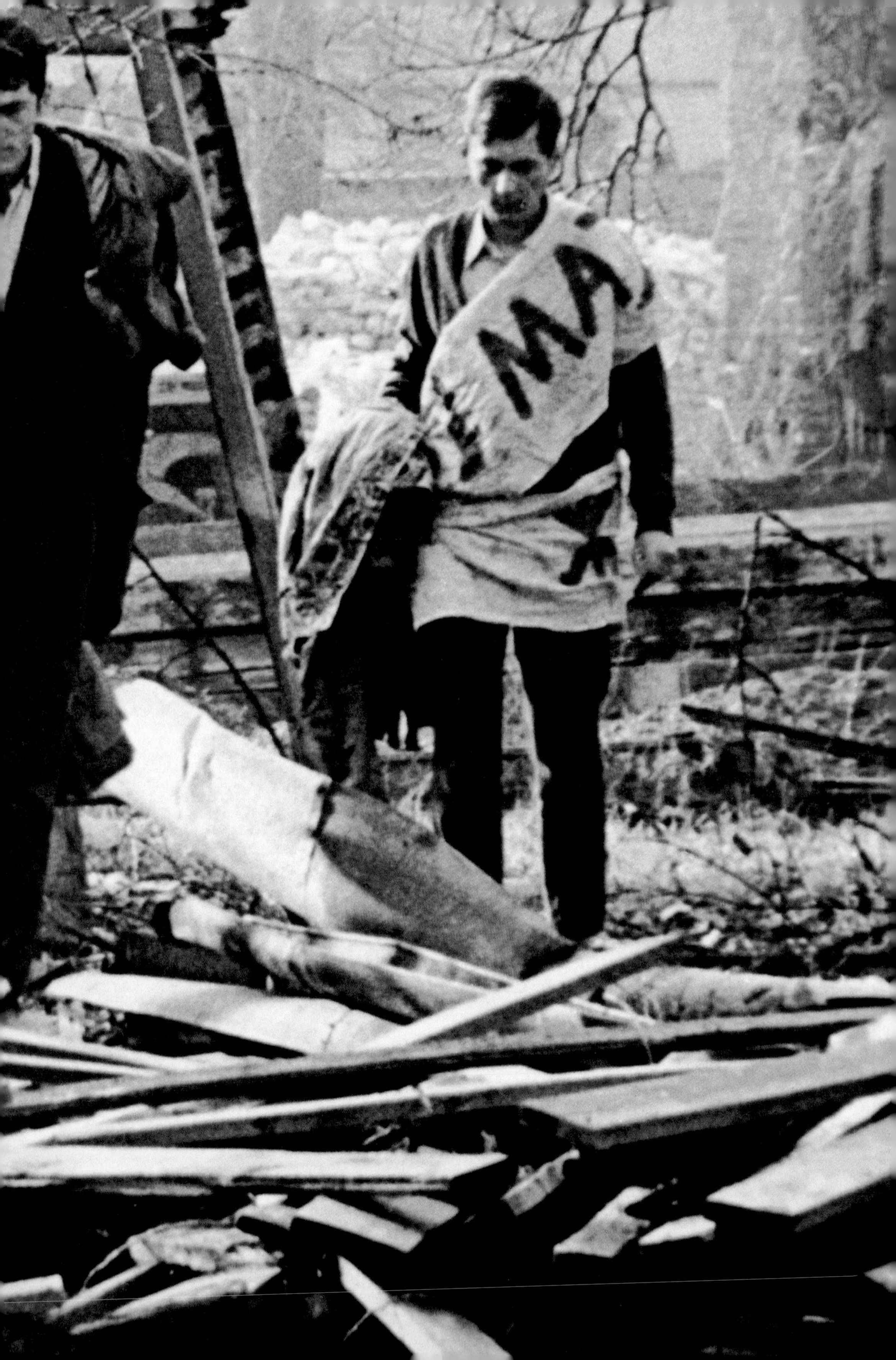

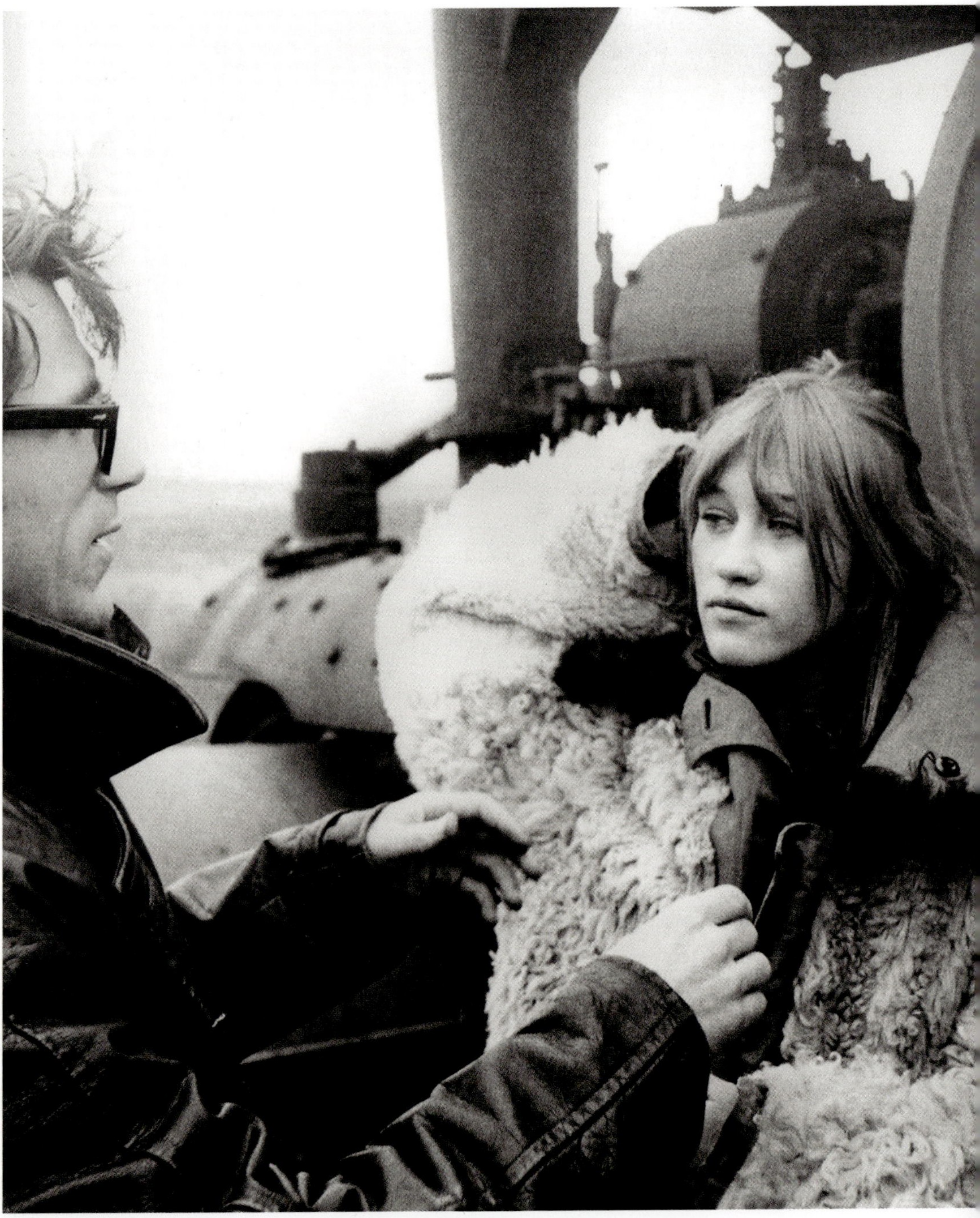

Želimir Žilnik, Alenka Zdešar und Dragana Đurić bei den Dreharbeiten zu *Freiheit oder Comicstrip*, 1971.
FOTOS: ANDREJ POPOVIĆ.

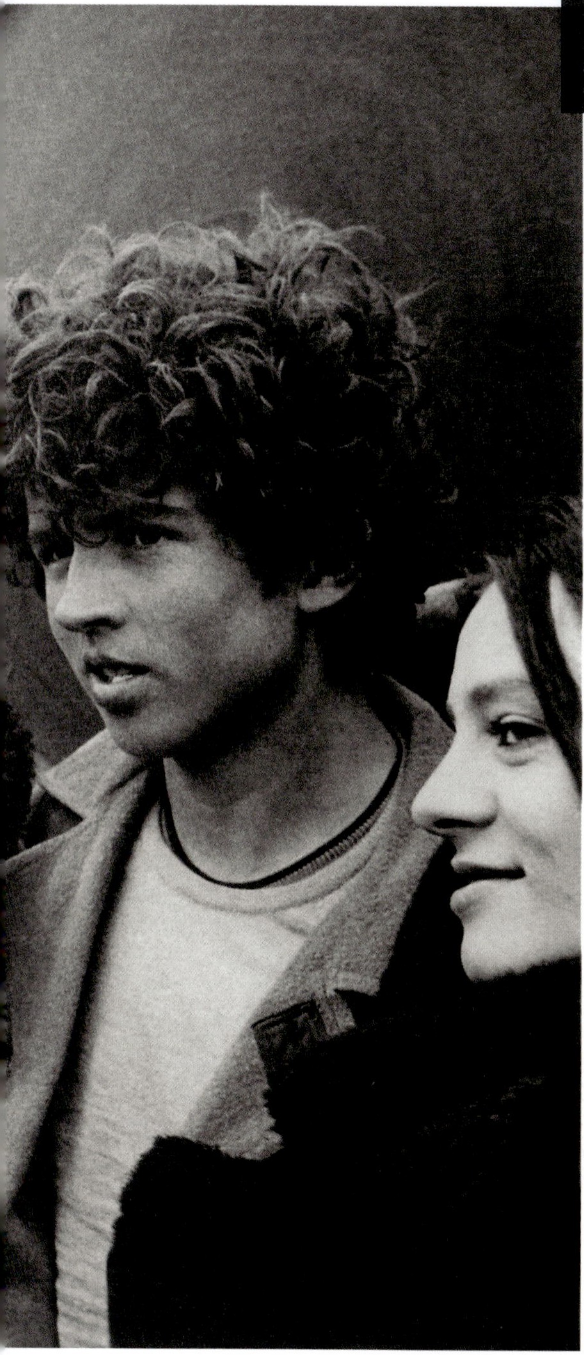

Freiheit oder Comicstrip (Sloboda ili strip)

Jugoslawien • 1972 • unvollendet • 35 mm • Farbfilm

Mit Hilfe der Geschichte von Svetozar, eines erfolgreichen, selbstständigen Kaufmanns aus der Vojvodina, und seiner Kinder, die er aus Ehen in verschiedenen jugoslawischen Städten hat, Zagreb, Belgrad, Ljubljana und Skopje, erzählt der Film die turbulenten politischen Ereignisse im Sommer 1971. Der Film enthält Dokumentarfilmaufnahmen von den Ereignissen in Zagreb, als eine Welle nationalen Erwachens durch die Stadt ging. Er zeigt die Ankunft junger Politikerinnen und Politiker, die an der Spitze der studentischen Organisationen sind. Weiterhin zeigt er die Pro-Mao-Demonstrationen der Studierenden in Ljubljana und Belgrad und die leidenschaftlichen Diskussionen für und gegen Veränderungen der jugoslawischen Verfassung.

Nach erhitzten Diskussionen über Žilniks *Frühe Werke*, der 1969 in die Kinos kam, und Dušan Makavejevs *WR-Mysterien des Organismus*, 1971 in den Kinos, sowie Angriffen auf beide Filme wegen ihres Anarchismus und angeblichen Antikommunismus, wurde Svetozar Udovički, der Direktor der Produktionsgesellschaft Neoplanta Film, von seinem Posten entlassen. Der neue Direktor verlangte von Žilnik, dass er aus *Freiheit oder Comicstrip* alle Originalaufnahmen der Ereignisse in Zagreb und Ljubljana herausnehmen sollte, die zu der Zeit Gegenstand einer polizeilichen Untersuchung waren, und außerdem alle „Teile mit unannehmbaren politischen Anspielungen". Der Film sollte auf dem Filmfestival von Pula seine Premiere feiern. Aber nachdem Žilnik sich geweigert hatte, die entsprechenden Schnitte vorzunehmen, wurde die Bearbeitung des Films 1972 gestoppt und danach nie wieder aufgenommen. Erst kürzlich wurde ein Teil eines ungeschnittenen Negativs des Films gefunden, von dem der Originalton fehlte. Žilnik überprüft derzeit (2019) die Möglichkeit, eine rekonstruierte Version zu erstellen. •

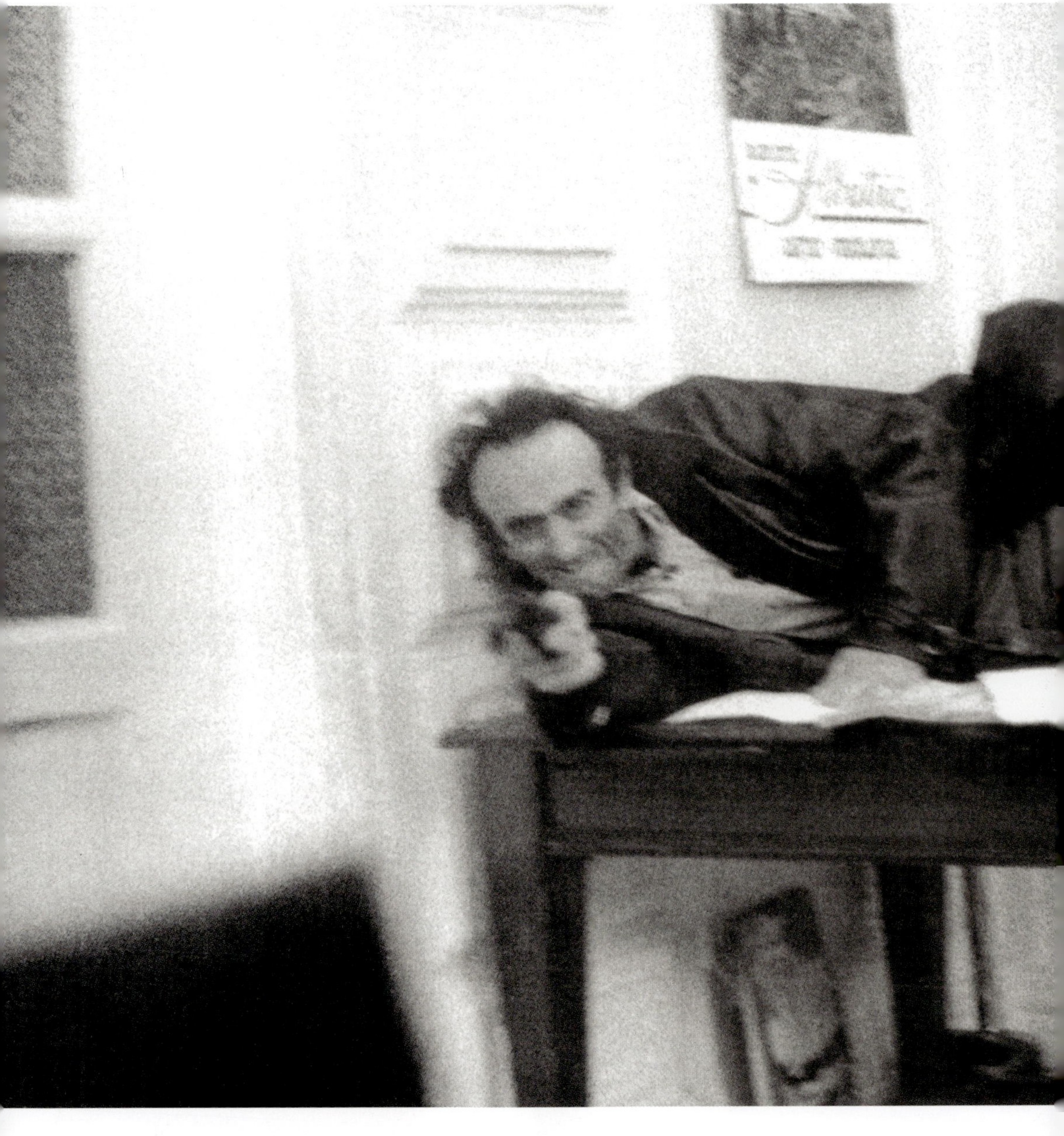

Freiheit oder Comicstrip (Produktionsfotos), 1971.
FOTOS: ANDREJ POPOVIĆ.
Links: Ilija Bašić
Rechts oben: Dragana Đurić
Rechts mitte: Milja Vujanović
Rechts unten: Dragana Đurić und Alenka Zdešar

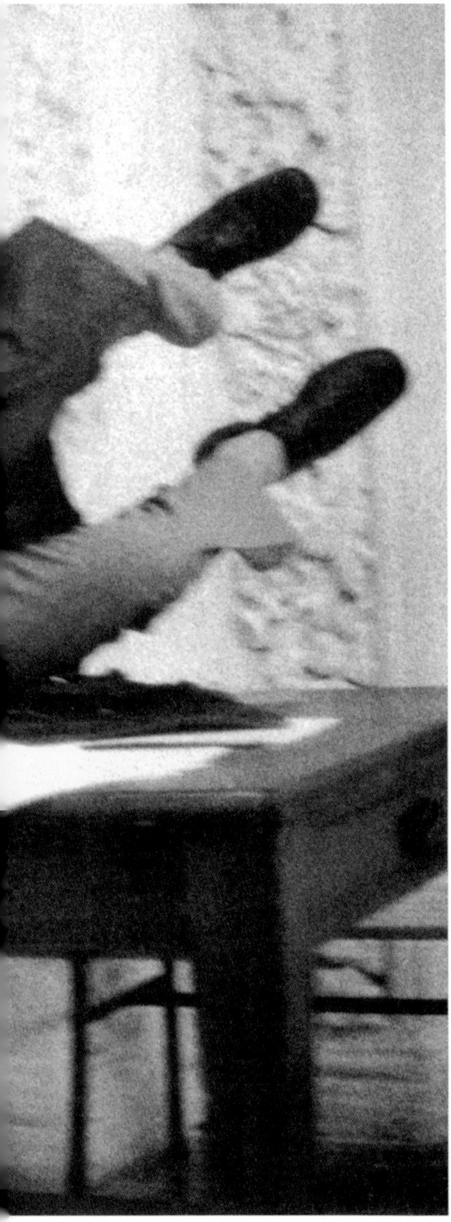

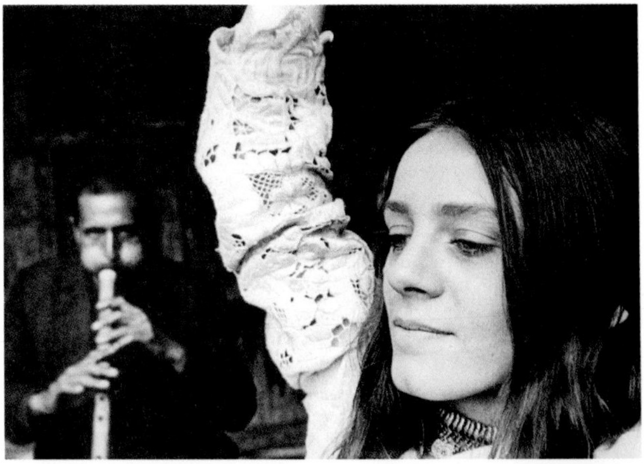

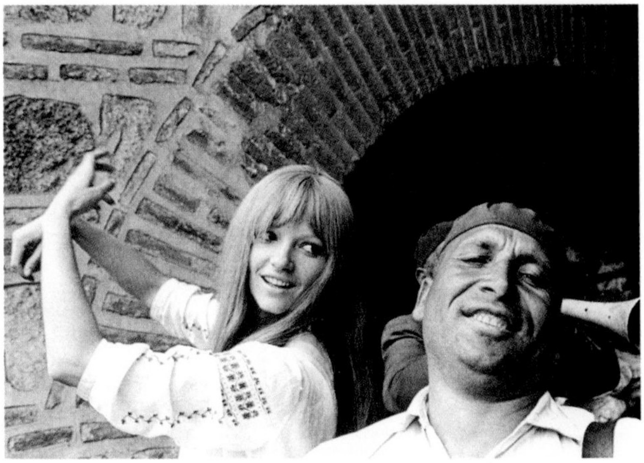

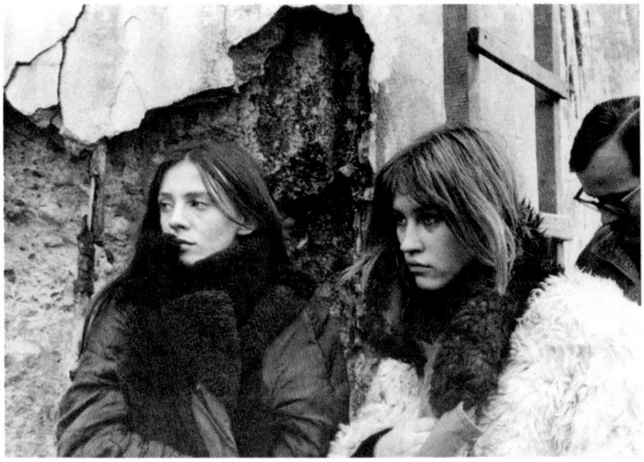

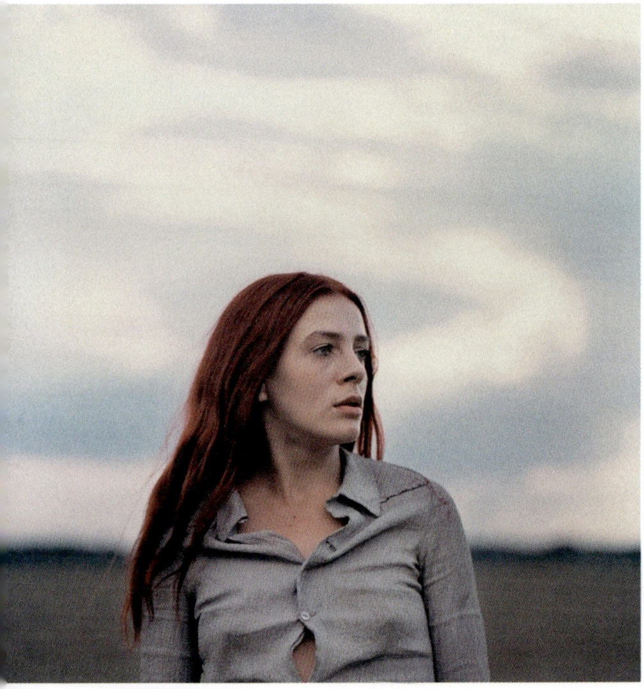

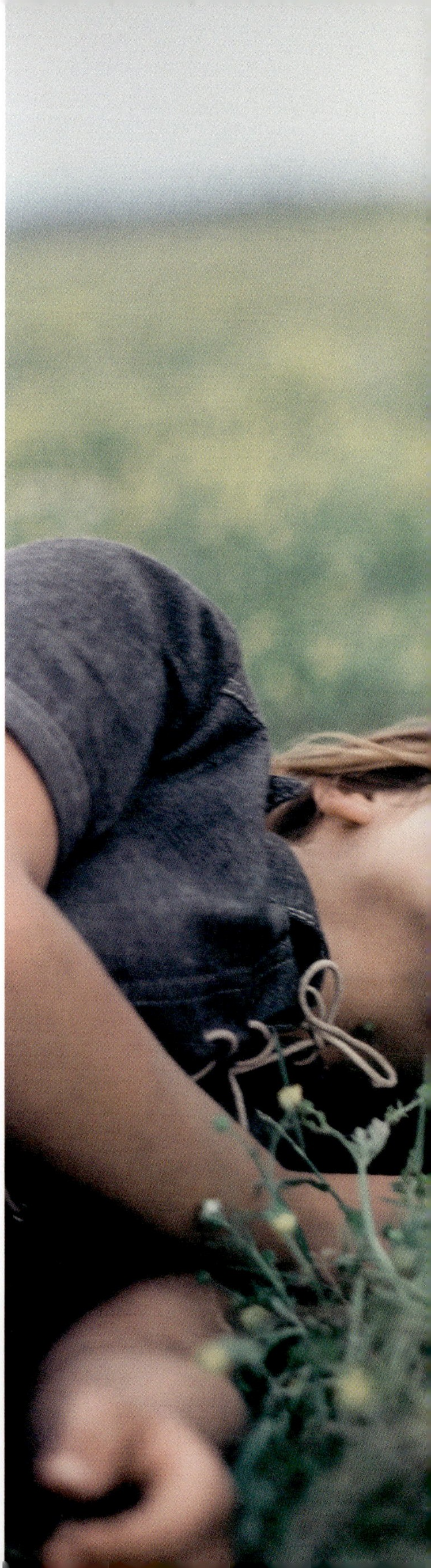

Freiheit oder Comicstrip
(Produktionsfotos), 1971.
FOTOS: ANDREJ POPOVIĆ.
Links: Dragana Đurić
Rechts: Alenka Zdešar, Čeda Radović
und Dragana Đurić

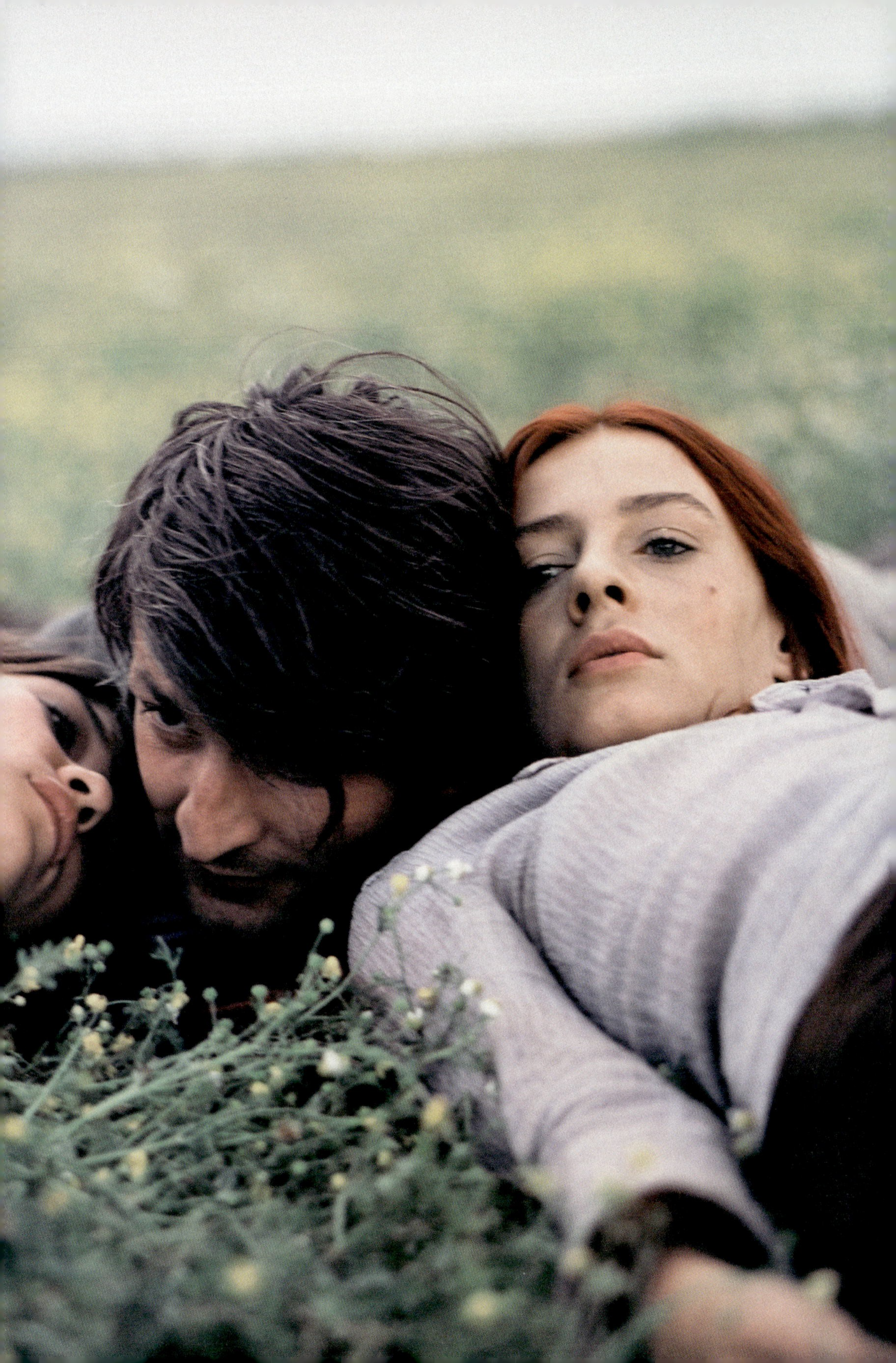

Žilnik hat es immer geschafft, auf einen blinden Fleck der Ideologie oder auf ein höchst umstrittenes Symptom für die Unfähigkeit einer Ideologie hinzuweisen, die vermeintlich im Einklang [mit] ihren erklärten Prinzipien funktioniert.

—Branislav Dimitrijević, „Behind Scepticism Lies the Fire of a Revolutionary!", in: *For an Idea – Against the Status Quo: Analysis and Systematization of Želimir Žilnik's Artistic Practice* (Novi Sad: New Media Center_kuda.org, Playground produkcija 2009), S. 145.

Jeder Film, den Želimir Žilnik gemacht hat, ist eine Übung darin, wie Menschen ein neues, authentisches Kollektiv gründen und ein Versuch, dieses Kollektiv so tief wie möglich im bestehenden gesellschaftlichen Gefüge zu verankern. Dies ist letztlich der Grund, warum diese Filme gleichzeitig fiktiv und dokumentarisch sind und schwerlich etwas anderes sein können: Ihre Protagonistinnen und Protagonisten schauspielern immer, ob sie nun (in dokumentarischen Reenactments) sich selbst darstellen oder jemand anderen (als Figuren, die im Rahmen der gespielten Handlung vorgegeben sind). Žilniks filmische Subjekte sind die ungelernten Kräfte und Facharbeiter einer (stets) kommenden Film-Kommune.

—Pavle Levi, in: Pavle Levi und Želimir Žilnik, „Europe's Internal Exiles: Sound, Image, and Performance of Identity in Želimir Žilnik's Films", in: Roland Hsu (Hg.), *Ethnic Europe: Mobility, Identity, and Conflict in a Globalized World* (Stanford, CA: Stanford University Press 2010), S. 122.

In einem Moment sprechen wir über Krieger und gewonnene Kriege, und schon im nächsten Moment werden diese Menschen beschuldigt, Mitglieder paramilitärischer Verbände und die neuen Profiteure zu sein. Manche Leute sind in einem Moment im Parlament und in einem anderen Moment Opfer von Bandenkriegen in Belgrad. Wir erleben die Kriminalisierung der gesamten Szene, die Vernichtung des ganzen Wertesystems, obwohl ein neues System noch nicht aufgebaut worden ist. Diese Personengruppen sind einerseits marginalisiert, und andererseits in einer Situation, in der sie den Pulsschlag der Gesellschaft fühlen können.

Als ich diesen Film [*Marble Ass*] machte und mit Prostituierten und Transvestiten sprach, habe ich erfahren, dass sie manchmal zwei oder drei Monate in einem Hyatt lebten und in Superluxus-Autos herumfuhren. Sie bewegten sich in dem Teil der Gesellschaft, der sich sicher fühlt. Mit den Kriegern ist es genauso. In den Zeitungen stehen Dokumente, die zeigen, dass viele der sogenannten Freischärler, die dem „Ruf der Nation" folgten, in Wirklichkeit Verbindungen zum Innenministerium und zur Polizei, zu sozialen Organisationen und Stadtverwaltungen hatten. Sie sind auf organisierte Weise in den Krieg gezogen. Ich will damit sagen, dass der Film, den wir gemacht haben, nicht weit von der Haupttendenz des Lebens entfernt ist, das wir alle durchmachen. Und dass das Leben selbst ein unglaublich anstrengender Balanceakt zwischen Krieg und Frieden ist: von der Tatsache, dass wir in einem Moment Feinde und im nächsten mit der ganzen Welt befreundet sind, über die Angst, wohin wir gehen sollen, wenn die Bombardierungen anfangen, bis zu der aktuellen Euphorie, die dadurch ausgelöst wird, dass wir unsere Fußballspieler auf internationaler Ebene spielen sehen.

—Želimir Žilnik, Interview, „Contributions for a Biography", in: *Ekran 2000*, Nr. 2, 1995

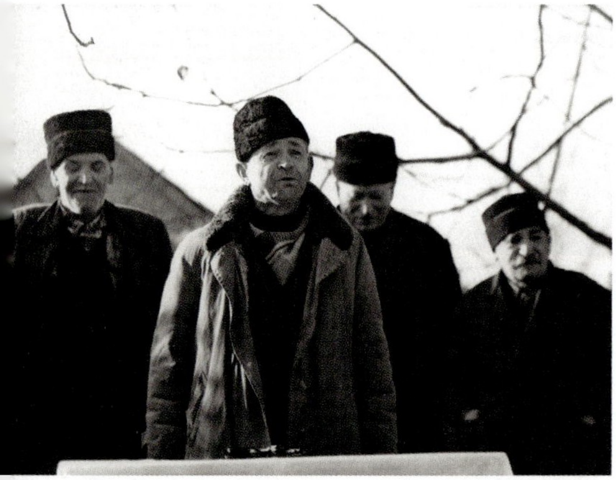

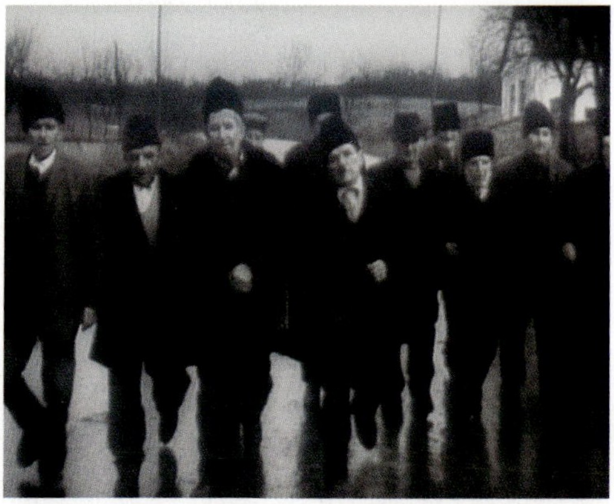

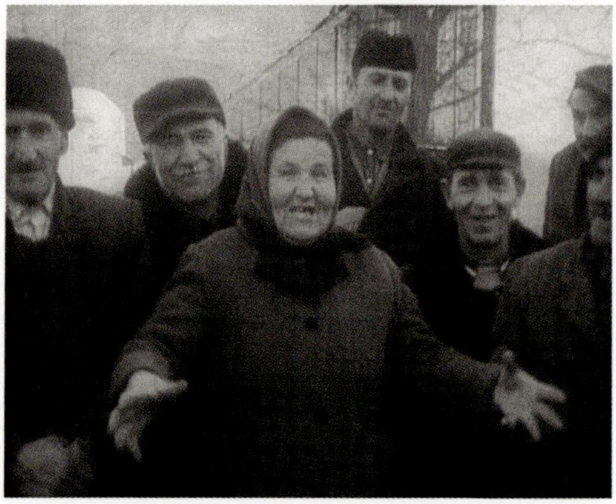

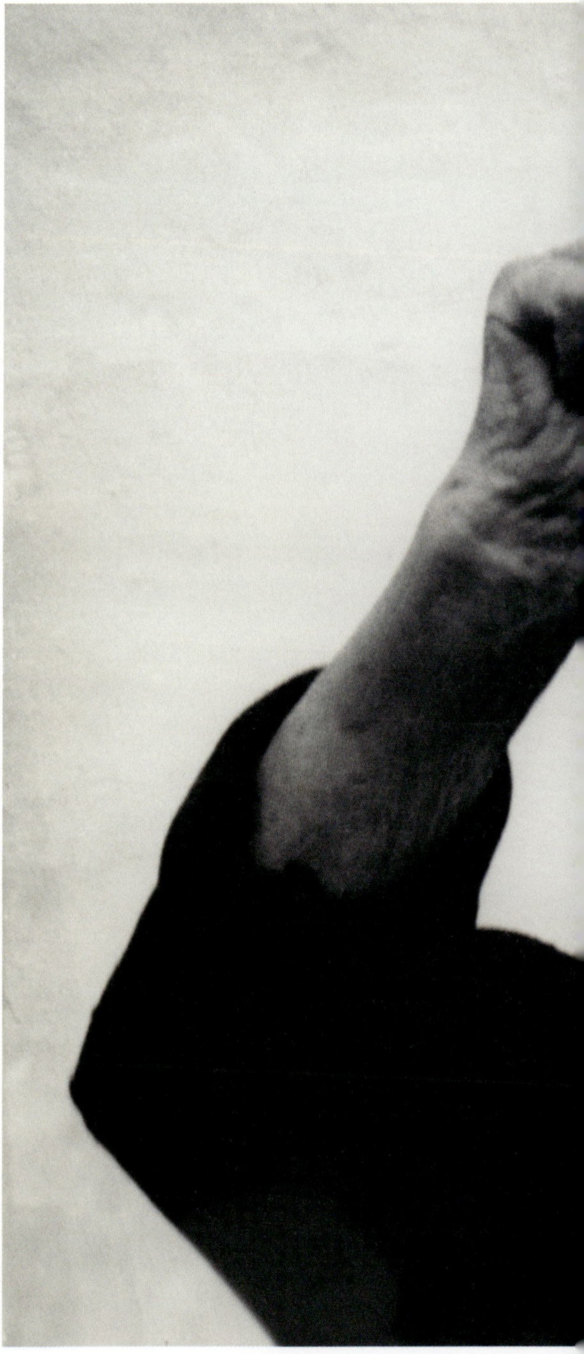

Aufstand in Jazak (Produktionsfotos), 1972.
FOTOS: MILIVOJE MILIVOJEVIĆ.

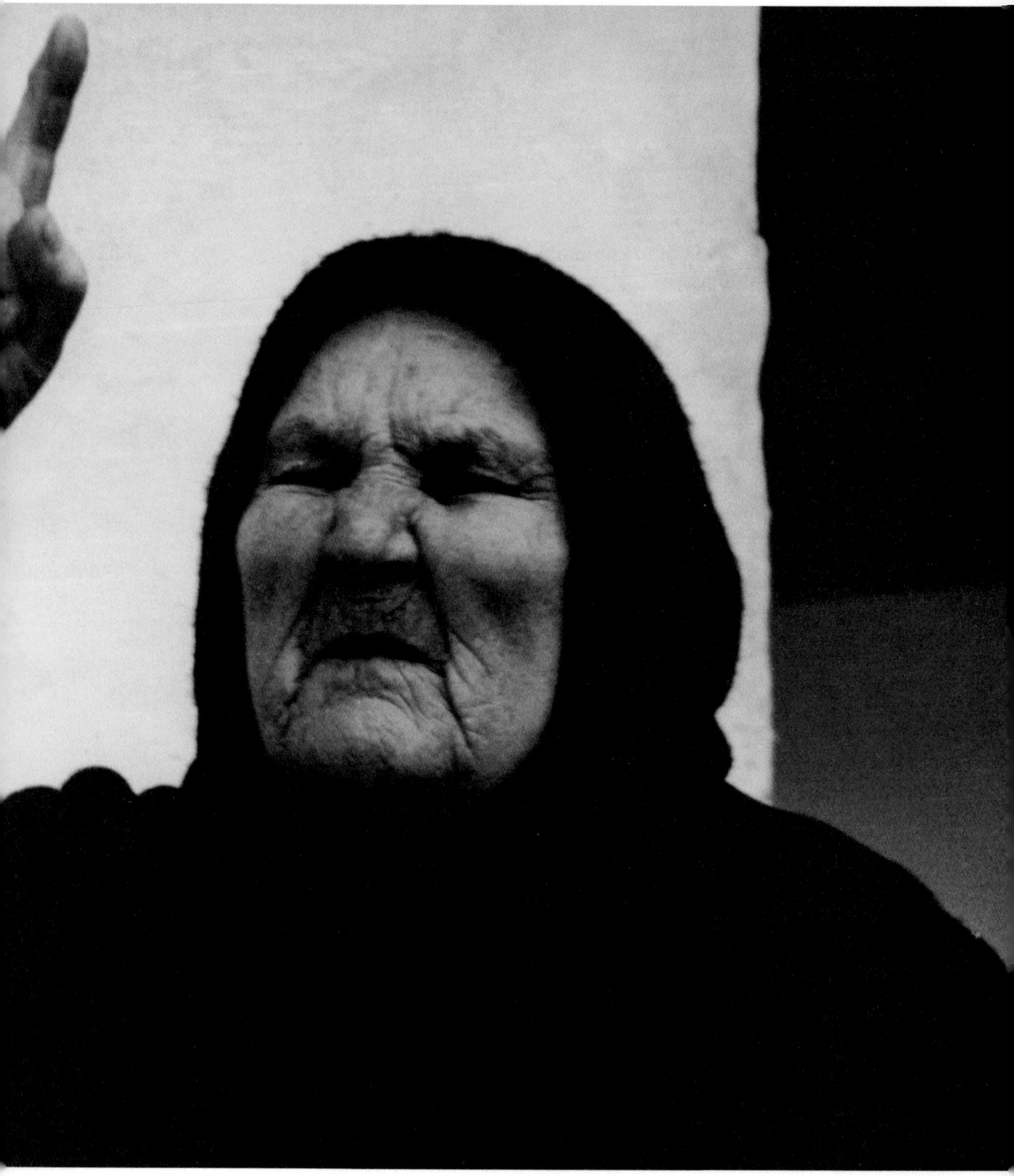

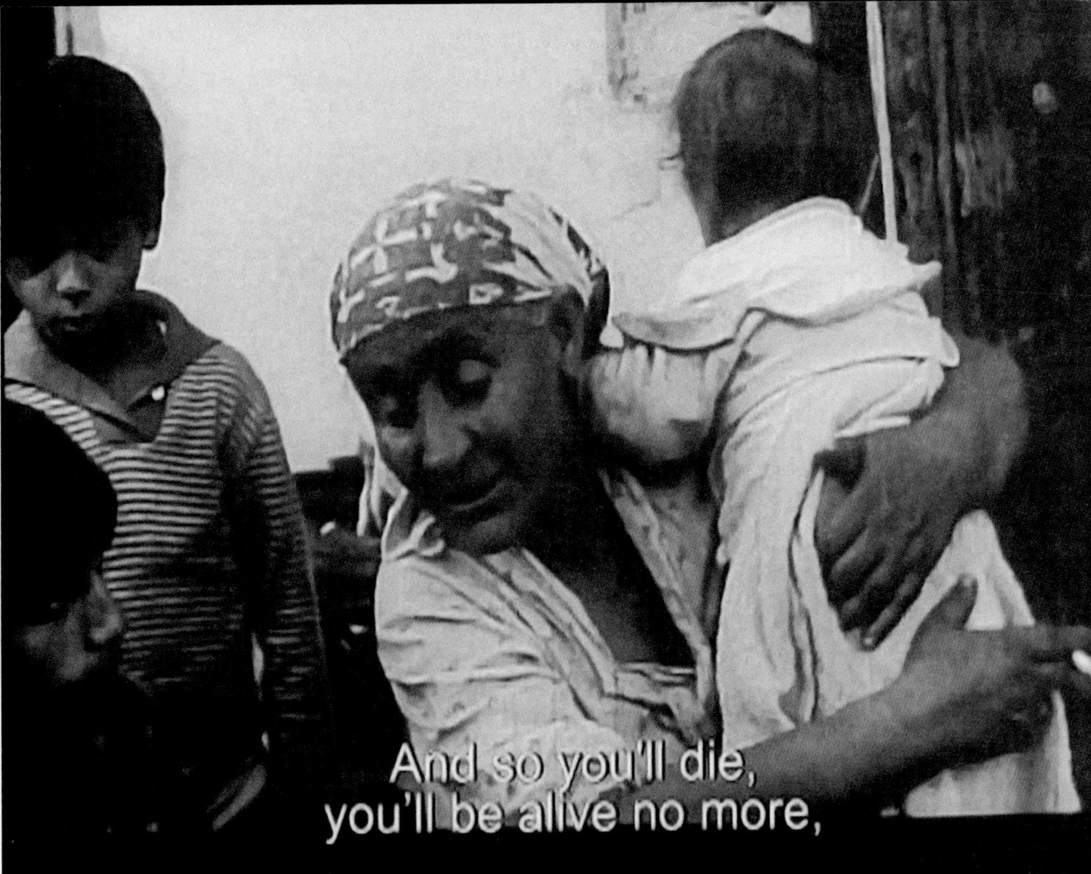
And so you'll die,
you'll be alive no more,

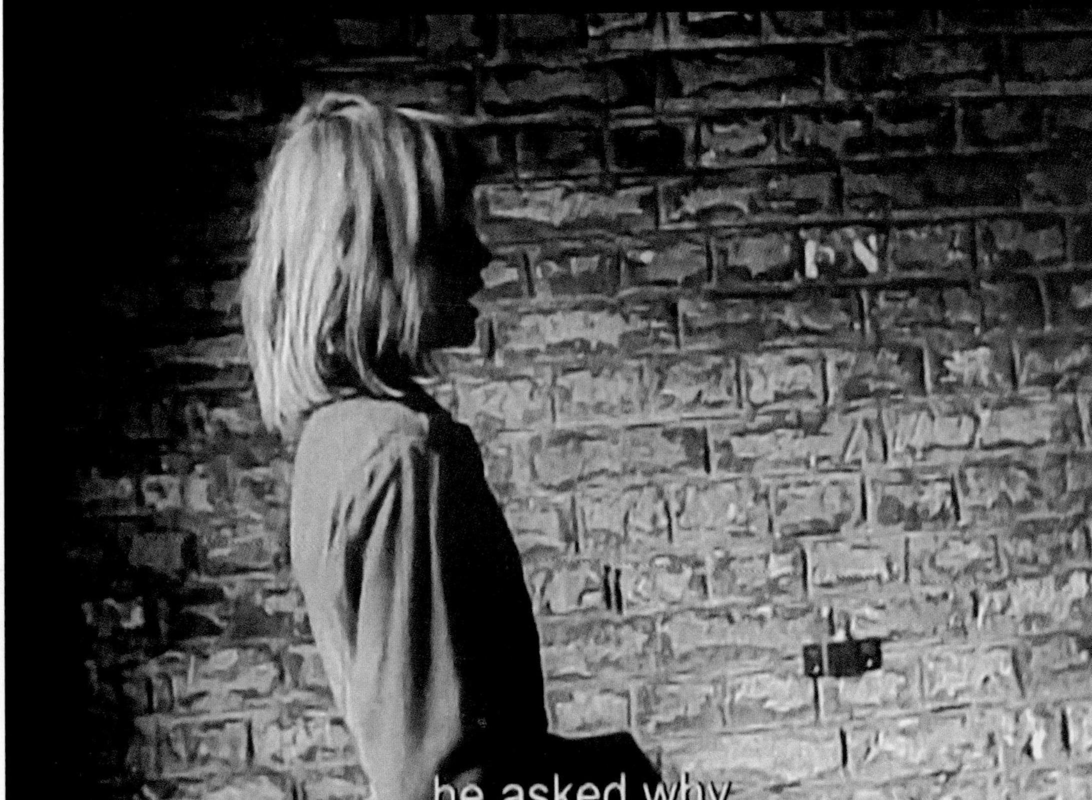
he asked why
I hadn't come back.

DIJANA JELAČA

Double Binds: Die Politik von Gender und Sexualität in den Filmen von Želimir Žilnik

Seit seinen frühesten Arbeiten hat Želimir Žilnik auf ebenso beharrliche wie provozierende Weise die Politik von Gender und Sexualität erforscht. Eine eher konventionelle, an Epochen orientierte Herangehensweise an Žilniks Werk würde die Filme, die während der Bewegung des Neuen Jugoslawischen Films entstanden (die ungefähr von 1962 bis 1972 dauerte), vom Rest seines Œuvres trennen, oder sie würde zwischen seinen jugoslawischen und seinen postjugoslawischen Filmen unterscheiden. Dieser Essay hingegen wird veranschaulichen, wie Žilniks Werk – über historische, gesellschaftliche, geografische und kulturelle Grenzen hinweg – eine beständige und leidenschaftliche Aufmerksamkeit für die sich überschneidenden politischen Bereiche von Klasse, Identität, Gender-Performativität und Performance widerspiegelt. Denn Žilniks Interesse gilt stets den politischen Dimensionen von Gender und Sexualität, und zwar besonders insofern, als sie mit gesellschaftlichen und kulturellen Fragen der spezifischen Orte und Zeiten zusammenhängen, in denen seine Filme entstanden.

Schon in Žilniks frühem dokumentarischen Kurzfilm *Kleine Pioniere* (1968) kündigt sich sein lebenslanges Interesse an gesellschaftlichen Außenseiterinnen und Außenseitern an – Individuen und Gruppen an den Rändern der Gesellschaft, die systematisch diskriminiert und oft vollständig unsichtbar gemacht werden. In *Kleine Pioniere* verleiht Žilnik armen, obdachlosen Kindern, von denen die meisten Roma sind, Sichtbarkeit und eine Stimme. Während die Kamera Kinder zeigt, einige von ihnen mit Handicaps, die in verlassenen, zerstörten Häusern herumlaufen, geben ihre Stimmen aus dem Off ein oft schockierendes Zeugnis ihres Alltags – von den Bagatelldelikten, die sie begehen, bis zur Polizeigewalt, die sie häufig erfahren. Schon der Titel des Films, *Kleine Pioniere*, ist eine offene, provokative politische Intervention. Er zitiert die erste Zeile eines populären Liedes über jugoslawische Kinder als kleine Pioniere: sie sind ehrenhaft, anständig, gesund und gehorsam – eine richtige Armee des sozialistischen Staates. Die Kinder in Žilniks Dokumentarfilm bilden das andere Ende des Spektrums der sozialistischen Jugend Jugoslawiens, die in dem Kinderlied überhöht wird. Indem Žilnik das Lied und seine offenkundigen Implikationen über die jugoslawische Jugend mit schonungslosen Bildern von Armut, Vernachlässigung und mutiger Entschlossenheit kontrastiert, die die Kinder im Film erleben und verkörpern, macht er auf ebenso provozierende wie aufschlussreiche Weise auf etwas aufmerksam, das die offizielle Ideologie Jugoslawiens – eine Gesellschaft, deren Mitglieder, und vor allem deren Kinder, unbeirrbar anständig und vorbildhaft sein sollen – ansonsten ausblendet oder bewusst übersieht.

Kleine Pioniere, wir sind eine Armee, wir sprießen wie grünes Gras (Standbilder), 1968

Doch der Film schreckt nicht davor zurück, die schockierenden Lebensbedingungen der ruppigen Straßenkinder zu zeigen, die von dem vorherrschenden Bild jugoslawischer Kinder als unschuldigen, hart arbeitenden Pionieren meilenweit entfernt sind. Während sie nach und nach ihre Geschichten erzählen, zeigt sich ein unverkennbares Muster: Geschichten unerwünschter sexueller Annäherungsversu-

che und unterschwelliger Androhungen sexueller Gewalt, die die Mädchen in Begegnungen mit erwachsenen Männern häufig erleben, werden von einigen aus dem Off detailliert und mit erschreckender Sachlichkeit beschrieben. Tatsächlich widmen sich die letzten Minuten des Films (die vom ersten Teil durch den Zwischentitel *Sledeća Epizoda, Das nächste Kapitel*, getrennt sind) ausschließlich diesem Thema: Zunächst erzählt ein junger Mann, dass er oft Sex mit Mädchen habe, die manchmal freiwillig mitmachen und manchmal nicht. Er behauptet, dass er einige von ihnen dazu zwingen müsse und dass er dies „mit ein paar leichten Schlägen und solchen Sachen" tue. Während er spricht, schwenkt die Kamera zu einigen anderen jungen Männern hinüber, die zusammen herumstehen und sich lachend unterhalten. Die Aussage des jungen Mannes wird abrupt unterbrochen durch eine Einstellung, die ein junges Mädchen im Profil zeigt; sie erzählt, dass ihr ein Fremder Geld für Sex angeboten habe. Sie akzeptiert das Angebot erst, nachdem es ihr gelungen ist, den Betrag zu verdoppeln. Auch ihre Erzählung wird unterbrochen, diesmal von einem anderen Mädchen, das von einem sexuellen Übergriff spricht, bei dem ihm ein Mann ein Messer an den Hals hielt, um es zu vergewaltigen. An dieser Stelle tritt Žilnik interessanterweise selbst auf. Während man den erschütternden Bericht aus dem Off hört, sieht man den Regisseur, der dem Mädchen gegenübersteht und der Kamera das Action-Zeichen gibt (ABB. 1).

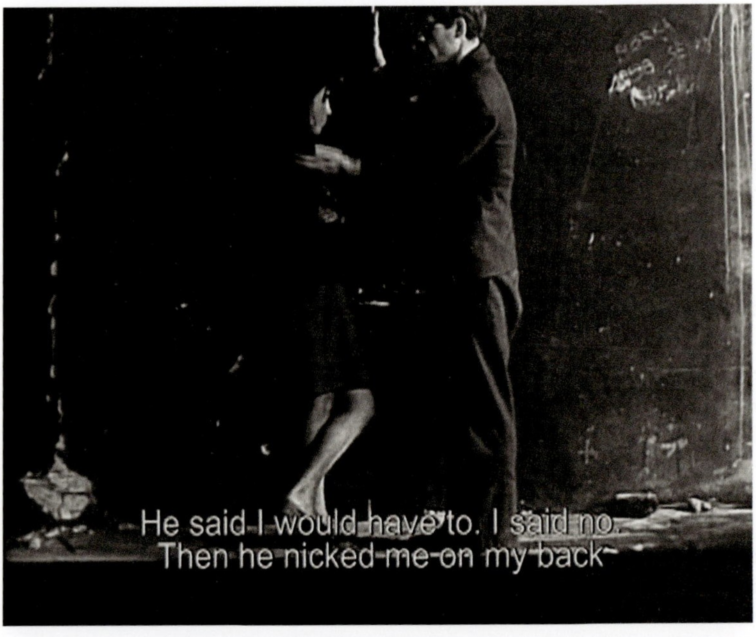

ABB. 1: Der Filmemacher und seine Darstellerin. *Kleine Pioniere*, (Standbild), 1968.

Dadurch, dass Žilnik in diesem entscheidenden Moment selbst auftritt – indem er zeigt, wie er Regie führt –, lenkt er die Aufmerksamkeit ebenso auf die Anwesenheit der Kamera wie auf seine eigene Präsenz: Ein erwachsener Mann, der ein junges Mädchen filmt, während sie detailliert über einen traumatischen Übergriff durch einen ande-

ren Mann spricht. Indem Žilnik sich selbst und seine Regiearbeit sichtbar macht, erkennt er das Machtgefälle an, das – vor allem im Hinblick auf Alter und Geschlecht – die Politik der Repräsentation in diesem Film prägt. Auf diese Einstellung folgt ein Schwarzbild, während der Off-Kommentar weiterläuft: Das Mädchen berichtet, dass es von seinem Angreifer gewarnt wurde, niemandem davon zu erzählen. Es habe erwidert, dass es niemandem diese Geschichte erzählen würde, der dümmer sei als er, sondern nur jemandem, der klüger sei. Auch hier wird direkt auf die Präsenz der Apparatur des Geschichtenerzählens – die Kamera, den Filmemacher und die Filmcrew – hingewiesen, denn die nahtlose Wiedergabe eines Erfahrungsberichts, die üblicherweise darauf abzielt, die Anwesenheit dieser Apparatur unsichtbar zu machen, wird unterbrochen. Anschließend sehen wir noch einmal das Action-Zeichen vor dem Gesicht des Mädchens, während seine Stimme aus dem Off erzählt, dass der Mann, der es vergewaltigte, ihm nun drohe, es umzubringen, dies jedoch „noch nicht in die Tat umgesetzt" habe. Seine Geschichte endet mit diesem zermürbenden Unterton einer im Raum stehenden Bedrohung. Die letzte Einstellung des Films zeigt ein anderes Mädchen; es informiert uns, dass es noch nicht achtzehn ist und noch keinen Sex mit Männern hatte, aber glaubt, dass dies „eine schöne Sache" sei. Dieser Schlusssatz bildet einen weiteren Kontrapunkt, der das Narrativ von Mädchenalter, Sexualität und Handlungsmacht noch vielschichtiger und komplexer macht; denn er weigert sich, die Mädchen ausschließlich im Kontext von Gewalt, Opferrolle, Prekarität und Bedrohung darzustellen. Dennoch sind diese Mädchen zweifellos verletzlich. Selbst innerhalb der grundsätzlich prekären Bevölkerungsgruppe armer, obdachloser Kinder gibt es unterschiedliche Grade von Vulnerabilität, und die Mädchen scheinen am unteren Ende dieser Hierarchie zu stehen. Sie befinden sich in einem Double Bind und sind doppelt benachteiligt: Sie sind nicht nur verletzlich, weil sie arm und daher gesellschaftlich geächtet sind, sondern auch, weil sie Mädchen sind.

Eines der Mädchen aus *Kleine Pioniere*, Piroška „Pirika" Čapko, wirkte auch in Žilniks erstem Spielfilm *Frühe Werke* (1969) mit und bildet dadurch ein intertextuelles Bindeglied zwischen seinen Filmen sowie zwischen dem Dokumentarischen und dem Fiktionalen. In *Frühe Werke* spielt es eine jüngere Schwester der weiblichen Hauptfigur, Jugoslava. Žilniks organische Zusammenarbeit mit Laiendarstellerinnen und -darstellern umfasst das gesamte Spektrum vom Spielfilm bis zur Dokumentation, und so wirkte Čapko auch an seinen jüngeren Arbeiten, den Dokumentarfilmen *Pirika im Film* (2013) und *Unter den Menschen: Leben & Schauspiel* (2018) mit. Letzterer entstand als Auftragsarbeit anlässlich seiner Ausstellung im Edith-Russ-Haus für Medienkunst mit dem treffenden Titel *Shadow Citizens*; für diese Produktion lud Žilnik zahlreiche Beteiligte seiner früheren Filme ein, von ihrer Zusammenarbeit mit dem Regisseur zu berichten. In Žilniks mittlerweile legendärem *Frühe Werke* bildet die Gender-Politik wiederum einen wichtigen Subtext und, wie ich behaupten möchte, einen entscheidenden Aspekt der im Film

formulierten Gesellschaftskritik. Einer der ersten Sätze Jugoslavas, einer jungen Frau aus der armen Arbeiterklasse, lautet: „Ich verstehe, warum mein Vater meine Mama schlägt. Er ist nach der Arbeit selbst ganz erschlagen." Anders gesagt, perpetuiert der Vater zu Hause die Gewalt, die er in der Welt draußen aufgrund seiner fehlenden Handlungsmacht als gesellschaftlicher Akteur erlebt. In diesen ersten Szenen sehen wir mehrfach, wie Jugoslavas betrunkener Vater aus dem schlammigen Boden eine Sickergrube mit der Schaufel aushebt. Die prekären sozialen Verhältnisse, welche die genderspezifische und häusliche Gewalt fördern und verstetigen, stehen also gleich zu Beginn im Vordergrund des Films und sind offenkundig eine wichtige Motivation für Jugoslava, zusammen mit ihren drei männlichen Gefährten eine Revolution anzustiften. In den Szenen, die in den Zwischentiteln als Politisches Theater bezeichnet werden, zitieren oder lesen die vier Jugendlichen oft aus dem *Kommunistischen Manifest* von Karl Marx und Friedrich Engels, wie auch aus Marx' *Kapital* (tatsächlich werden, neben Žilnik und Branko Vučićević, auch Marx and Engels als Drehbuchautoren genannt). Doch die Aufführungen dieses Theaters finden nicht jenseits des Alltags statt, sondern werden vielmehr zu Aufführungen von Politik im Alltag.

Als Jugoslavas Vater eines Tages wieder einmal betrunken von der Arbeit zurückkehrt, kommt es zwischen ihm, seiner Frau und Jugoslava zu einer körperlichen Auseinandersetzung. Dies bringt Jugoslava zu der Feststellung: „In diesem Haus herrscht der Feudalismus", und sie erklärt ihrer Familie, dass diese sie nie mehr wiedersehen werde. Im Weggehen hält sie vor dem Haus kurz an und lässt ihre jüngere Schwester (das weiter oben erwähnte Mädchen aus *Kleine Pioniere*) in einen Apfel beißen (ABB. 2) – eine symbolische Geste, die den Versuch der älteren Schwester würdigt, der zurückbleibenden jüngeren Wissen, aber auch Stärke und

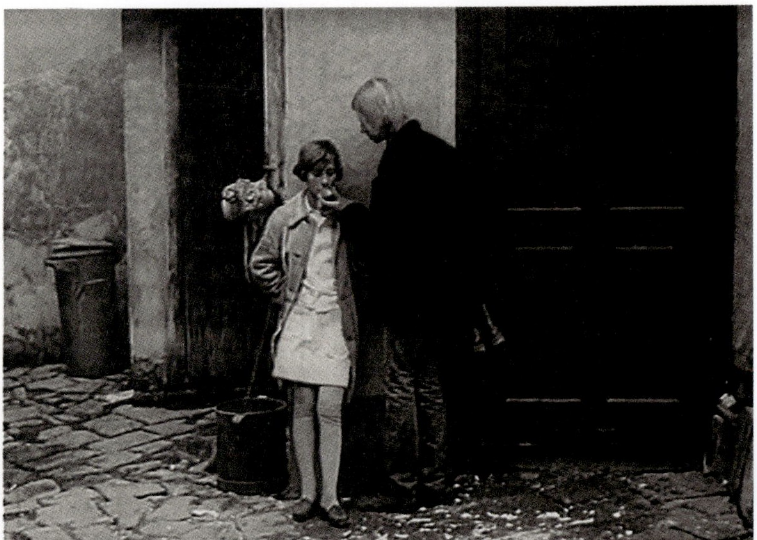

ABB. 2: Jugoslava (Milja Vujanović) lässt ihre jüngere Schwester (Pirika Čapko) einen Bissen von ihrem Apfel nehmen. *Frühe Werke* (Standbild), 1969.

Widerstandskraft zu vermitteln. Erneut findet die prekäre Situation von Mädchen kritische Aufmerksamkeit und wird für Jugoslava zum entscheidenden Auslöser ihres politischen Handelns.

Zusammen mit ihren männlichen Gefährten begibt sich Jugoslava auf eine Reise durch das ländliche Serbien, um eine sozialistische Revolution zu propagieren. Die Beziehung zu ihren Freunden ist häufig von sexuellen Spannungen, aber auch von zunehmenden Gewaltandrohungen geprägt. So verspottet sie einen der Männer nach ihrer ersten sexuellen Begegnung mit ihm, weil er nicht sofort wieder Sex haben kann; als Reaktion darauf richtet er eine Waffe auf sie, während man (diesmal noch imaginäre) Schüsse hört. In dieser gespielten Erschießung deutet sich die drohende genderspezifische Gewalt an, die am Ende des Films auf dramatische Weise real werden wird.

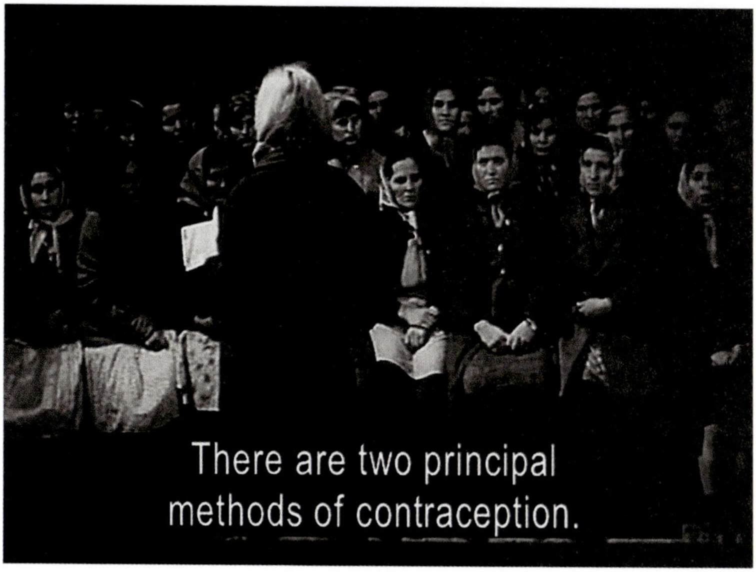

ABB. 3: Jugoslava spricht vor einer Gruppe von Landfrauen. *Frühe Werke* (Standbild), 1969.

In einer bemerkenswerten Szene, in der die Gruppe ihre revolutionären Ideen auf dem Land verbreitet, sieht man, wie Jugoslava einen Workshop für die Dorfbewohnerinnen abhält, um sie über die besten Verhütungsmethoden aufzuklären (ABB. 3). Die Frauen, sämtlich Laiendarstellerinnen, stellen verschiedene Fragen, von den gesundheitlichen Auswirkungen der Abstinenz bis zur wirksamsten Verhütungsmethode. In ihrem Vortrag zitiert Jugoslava einen revolutionären Gedanken der linken Ikone des Feminismus, Clara Zetkin, nämlich, dass Revolutionen nur stattfinden können, „wenn der Familienvater aufhört, sich wie ein Dienstherr, ein Aristokrat und ein Besitzer aufzuführen, während eine Frau wie ein Proletarier ausgebeutet wird. Frauen können aus ihrer Unterdrückung nur durch eine Veränderung der Beschäftigungsverhältnisse und durch die Abschaffung der monogamen Familie befreit werden.“ Damit formuliert Jugoslava eine sehr zugespitzte Kritik des real existierenden

Sozialismus: Obwohl das Proletariat in sozialistischen Systemen nominell die Macht hat und dort Gleichberechtigung herrscht, stehen die Frauen aufgrund der fortbestehenden patriarchalischen Geschlechterordnung weiterhin unter der autokratischen Herrschaft der Männer. Eine echte Revolution kann daher nur stattfinden, wenn diese Hierarchie der Geschlechter abgeschafft wird – und das bedeutet, dass auch die monogame Familie abgeschafft werden muss. Überdies sollte das Recht der Frau, keine Kinder zu bekommen und nicht mit ungewollter reproduktiver und häuslicher Arbeit belastet zu werden, als legitime Forderung anerkannt werden. Dass sich Jugoslava hier an eine Gruppe am unteren Ende der gesellschaftlichen Hierarchie – an ungebildete Landfrauen – wendet, macht ihre Kritik umso treffender. Diese Frauen erleben, ebenso wie die armen Mädchen in *Kleine Pioniere*, Prekarität als Double Bind. Auch hier überschneiden sich Gender- und Klassenzugehörigkeit und geben einen kritischen Einblick in die ungleiche Verteilung gesellschaftlicher Handlungsmacht im sozialistischen Jugoslawien. Auf diese Szene folgen, mit einem Sinn für Komik, männliche Stimmen, die ausrufen: „Es lebe der 8. März, der Internationale Frauentag!“, in Jugoslawien ein weithin begangener Feiertag, an dem Frauenrechte allerdings oft nur nominell anerkannt wurden.

In ihrem Vortrag vor den Frauen fügt Jugoslava hinzu, dass „die technologische Revolution, der wir entgegengehen“, schließlich zur vollständigen Emanzipation der Frau führen werde. In einer späteren Szene, die diese Behauptung über die technologische Entwicklung wieder aufgreift, erklärt Jugoslava mit einer gewissen Bitterkeit: „Eine Waschmaschine hätte meine Mutter mehr befreit als das Wahlrecht.“ Im Verlauf des gesamten Films werden die unbeschwerteren und satirischen Momente oft abrupt von Szenen brutaler Gewalt unterbrochen, wie zum Beispiel, als eine Gruppe von Dorfbewohnern, die offenkundig von den Predigten der jungen Revolutionäre genug haben, Jugoslava und ihre Freunde attackiert. Die hartnäckigen Angriffe richten sich besonders gegen Jugoslava, die von zwei Männern zur Seite gezogen und gewaltsam entkleidet wird. An dieser Stelle, die unmissverständlich auf eine Vergewaltigung hindeutet, endet die Szene abrupt. Dieser Überfall scheint das Ende des Films anzukündigen: Die gescheiterte Revolution der vier jungen Leute gipfelt darin, dass sich ihre militärische Guerilla-Ausbildung, die sich durch den Film hindurchzieht, gegen Jugoslavas Körper richtet. Angesichts der zunehmenden Desillusionierung durch ihr revolutionäres Projekt und der wachsenden Spannungen zwischen Jugoslava und ihren männlichen Gefährten verlässt die junge Frau die Gruppe und kehrt nach Hause zurück. Doch die drei Männer suchen sie in ihrem Haus auf, entführen sie auf ein Feld, reißen ihr die Kleider vom Leib, erschießen sie und verbrennen ihren Körper. Das einzige sichtbare Ergebnis ihrer revolutionären Sache scheint das beinahe rituelle Opfer einer Frau zu sein; zum einen, weil sie diese Sache vermeintlich verraten hat, und zum anderen, weil die aufgestauten gesellschaftlichen Frustrationen letztlich wieder in erschreckendster Weise am Körper einer Frau ausgelassen werden.

Frühe Werke erhebt eine schwere Anklage gegen Jugoslawiens halbe Revolution und liefert eine aufschlussreiche Untersuchung der Gender-Politik dieses (gescheiterten) Projekts, indem er das Double Bind aufdeckt, das vordergründig die Gleichberechtigung der Geschlechter propagiert, zugleich aber die Herrschaft des Patriarchats aufrechterhält. Jugoslavas Tod am Ende des Films verkörpert daher treffend ihre Worte vom Anfang des Films, dass es ohne die Abschaffung des Patriarchats keine erfolgreiche sozialistische Revolution geben werde.

Es gilt anzumerken, dass sich Žilniks ausgeprägtes Interesse an der (fehlenden) gesellschaftlichen Handlungsmacht von Frauen, das sein gesamtes Werk kennzeichnet, meistens auf Arbeiterinnen und arme Frauen richtet: von den bereits erwähnten *Kleine Pioniere* und *Frühe Werke* bis zu seinem Dokumentarfilm *Die Frauen kommen* (1972), der eine Gruppe von in Westdeutschland tätigen Gastarbeiterinnen begleitet, die in den Ferien zu ihren Familien in Jugoslawien zurückkehren. Weitere bedeutende Beispiele sind *Vera und Eržika* (1981), ein Fernsehfilm über zwei langjährige Textilarbeiterinnen (einem der gängigsten Berufe für Frauen aus der Arbeiterklasse in Jugoslawien), und die Fernsehserie *Heiße Löhne* (1987), die sich unter anderem mit dem Alltag von weiblichen Reinigungskräften beschäftigt. Ein weiteres wichtiges Beispiel für die Auseinandersetzung des Regisseurs mit Communities der Arbeiterklasse ist sein Fernsehfilm *Brooklyn-Gusinje* (1988), der die Erfahrungen der jungen Kellnerin Ivana schildert, die seit Kurzem in einer Kleinstadt an der jugoslawisch-albanischen Grenze lebt. Ivana lernt Škeljzen kennen, einen jungen Mann, der aus dieser Gegend kommt, aber mittlerweile in Brooklyn in den Vereinigten Staaten lebt. Žilniks Film beschäftigt sich, wie viele seiner Arbeiten, mit Formen von Arbeitsmigration, sei es innerhalb des Landes (Ivana gibt ihre Arbeit als Schneiderin in Prizren für einen besser bezahlten Job als Kellnerin in Gusinje auf) oder international (viele Einwohnerinnen und Einwohner von Gusinje wollen, ebenso wie Škeljzen, auf ihrer Suche nach besseren Möglichkeiten das Land verlassen). Als unangepasste, ein wenig naive junge Frau muss Ivana oft auf lokale Traditionen hingewiesen werden, doch ihre Naivität steht ihrer pointierten Kritik am Patriarchat nicht im Wege. So fragt sie in einer Szene, in der sie Škeljzens Verwandte in deren Haus in Albanien besucht, den Gastgeber, was die Frauen in seiner Familie tun. Auf seine lange Aufzählung weiblicher Pflichten wie Hausarbeit und Kindererziehung erwidert sie: „Und was tut dann ihr Männer?" Ivana und ihre befreundete Kollegin Goca sind eigensinnige, unabhängige junge Frauen, denen zunehmend bewusst wird, dass sie in konservative, patriarchalische Milieus nicht gut hineinpassen. Als Goca kurz vor ihrer Heirat mit einem Einheimischen Bedenken kommen, flüchten die beiden Frauen von Gocas Hochzeitsfeier, wobei ihnen ein freundlicher Fremder hilft – ein gehörloser Mann, der die deutlichste feministische Botschaft des Films ausspricht: „Frauen müssen dieselben Rechte haben wie Männer, damit nicht nur die Männer privilegiert sind." Žilnik

behandelt Gender-Politik oft vor dem Hintergrund von allgemeinen Lebensverhältnissen des Arbeitermilieus, spanungsgeladenen Grenzregionen und transnationalen, vor allem ökonomisch begründeten Migrationsbewegungen.

Im Hinblick auf queere Themen und nicht heteronormative Herangehensweisen stellt Žilniks Film *Marble Ass* (1995) eine extrem provokative Behandlung der Politik von Gender und Sexualität dar, die sich hier besonders im Verhältnis zur imaginierten heteronormativen Gesundheit eines kollektiven ethno-national(istisch)en Körpers artikuliert. Der Film handelt von Trans-Sexarbeitenden, die inmitten und zugleich am Rande der glühend nationalistischen Kriegstreiberei im Serbien der 1990er Jahre leben. Wie ich an anderer Stelle ausgeführt habe, ist *Marble Ass* eine prägnante oppositionelle Beobachtung und ein subversives Statement dazu,

> „wie manche Körper zu ungeeignet sind, um in einen ethnonationalistischen Diskurs interpelliert zu werden: Die beiden Trans-Prostituierten, die am Rande der Gesellschaft leben, sind buchstäblich zu queer, und ihre Leben und ihre Gestaltung von Zeit und Ort sind zu unkonventionell, um in eine kollektive ethno-nationale Subjektivität aufgenommen zu werden, die sich durch die von ihr ausgeübte Gewalt als gesund konstituiert."[01]

Der Film ist ein einzigartiges Beispiel für ein regionales queeres und Trans-Kino, da er in enger Zusammenarbeit mit seinen Trans-Protagonistinnen Merlinka[02] und Sanela entstand, zwei Laien, die im Film eine Version ihrer selbst spielen. Wie die meisten nichtdokumentarischen Werke Žilniks entspricht *Marble Ass* eher einem Dokudrama als einem reinen Spielfilm, wodurch er umso provokativer wirkt, da Fakten und Fiktion nie eindeutig voneinander abgegrenzt werden.

Der Film ist singulär, denn er ist bis heute der vielleicht einzige regionale (postjugoslawische) Film, der nicht nur inhaltlich queer ist, wobei solche Filme üblicherweise die bedauerliche Lage lokaler LGBTQ-Communities aus dem Blickwinkel heterosexueller Cisgender-Filmemacherinnen und -macher sowie Schauspielerinnen und Schauspieler schildern, wie etwa *Fine Dead Girls* (2002) und *Go West* (2005). *Marble Ass* bietet hingegen eine durchgängig stimmige Vorstellung dessen, was der queere Theoretiker Jack Halberstam in einem anderen Zusammenhang als queere Zeit und queeren Ort theoretisch reflektiert hat.[03] Dies gelingt dem Film, indem er „die für gewöhnlich marginalisierte Sichtweise queerer Zeitlichkeit und Räumlichkeit"[04] in den Mittelpunkt stellt und sich weigert, die Erfahrungen der Trans-Protagonistinnen anders zu vermitteln als aus dem Blickwinkel queerer Zeitlichkeit und Räumlichkeit. Überdies „beharrt der Film darauf, dass queere Körper nicht vollständig in eine Ideologie des normativen, gewaltsamen ethnisch-nationalen Körper hineingerufen (interpelliert) werden können, sodass die beiden

01 Dijana Jelača, *Dislocated Screen Memory: Narrating Trauma in Post-Yugoslav Cinema*, New York 2016, S. 116; übersetzt aus dem Englischen von Barbara Hess.

02 Merlinka ist die weibliche Form des Namens Merlin, oft als Kosename (Anm. der Herausgeberinnen)

03 J. Jack Halberstam, *In a Queer Time and Place: Transgender Bodies, Subcultural Lives*, New York 2005.

04 Jelača, op. cit., S. 118.

05
Ibid., S. 118 f.

06
Merlinka arbeitete lange mit Žilnik zusammen und wirkte vor *Marble Ass* auch in *Guten Morgen, Belgrad* (1986) und in *Schöne Frauen gehen durch die Stadt* (1986) mit.

Trans-Protagonistinnen in ihrem eigenen, scheinbar parallelen Universum leben, das jedoch trotzdem durch seine Nähe zum normativen, gewaltsamen Nationalismus bestimmt ist, der die Realität des sie umgebenden Krieges ausmacht."[05] Erneut verwischt die Politik der verkörperten Erfahrung die Grenzen zwischen Fakten und Fiktion, denn die Trans-Protagonistinnen des Films sind keine Cisgender-Schauspieler oder -Schauspielerinnen, die Trans-Charaktere spielen, sondern Personen, deren Erfahrungen jenseits der Grenzen des Films sehr stark das widerspiegeln, was im Film selbst passiert. Diese umfassende Realität geriet 2003 tragischerweise noch stärker ins Blickfeld, als einer der Protagonisten, Vjeran Miladinović Merlinka, brutal ermordet wurde.[06]

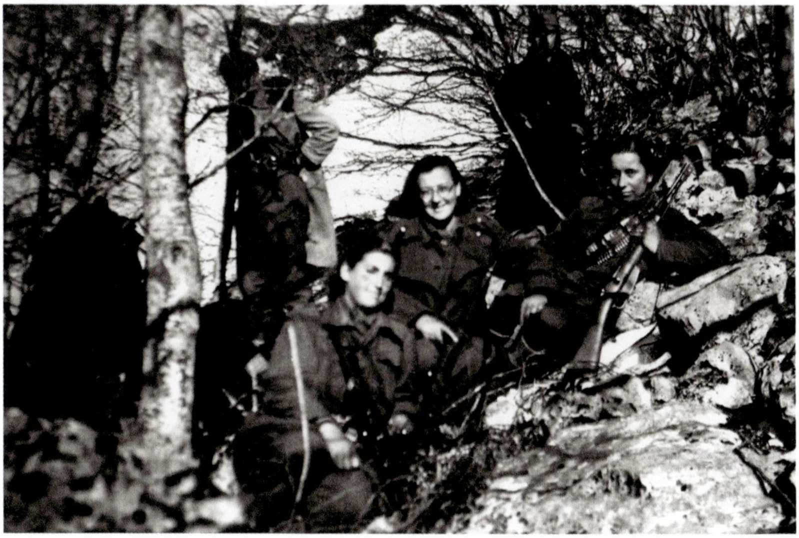

ABB. 4: Dragica Vitolović Srzentić mit ihrer weiblichen Guerillatruppe während des Zweiten Weltkriegs. *Eine Frau-ein Jahrhundert*, (Standbild), 2011.

An den Schluss dieser Beschäftigung mit Žilniks kontinuierlichem und immer höchst engagiertem Interesse an der politischen Dimension von Gender möchte ich den Dokumentarfilm *Eine Frau-ein Jahrhundert* (2011) über Dragica Vitolović Srzentić (ABB. 4) stellen, eine Frau, die zum Zeitpunkt der Dreharbeiten fast hundert Jahre alt war. Vitolović Srzentić war in den 1930er Jahren eine sozialistische Revolutionärin und schrieb unter anderem für die progressive Frauenzeitschrift *Žena danas* (*Die Frau heute*, 1936). Während des Zweiten Weltkriegs nahm sie auch am revolutionären, antifaschistischen Kampf teil, der auch als Volksbefreiungskampf (NOB) bezeichnet wird, und nach dem Krieg war sie diejenige, die Josef Stalin 1948 das historische Nein des Präsidenten Josip Broz Titos überbrachte. Damit markierte sie den berühmt-berüchtigten Moment, in dem sich die Wege der beiden Anführer trennten und Jugoslawiens Emanzipation von der Sowjetunion sowie die Entwicklung seiner singulären Form des Marktsozialismus begann. Während Vitolović Srzentić im Film ihre fast hundertjährige Geschichte erzählt, werden ihre Archivaufnahmen oft von Blockbuchstaben unterbrochen, die langsam die Namen prominenter Männer buchstabieren, die ihre

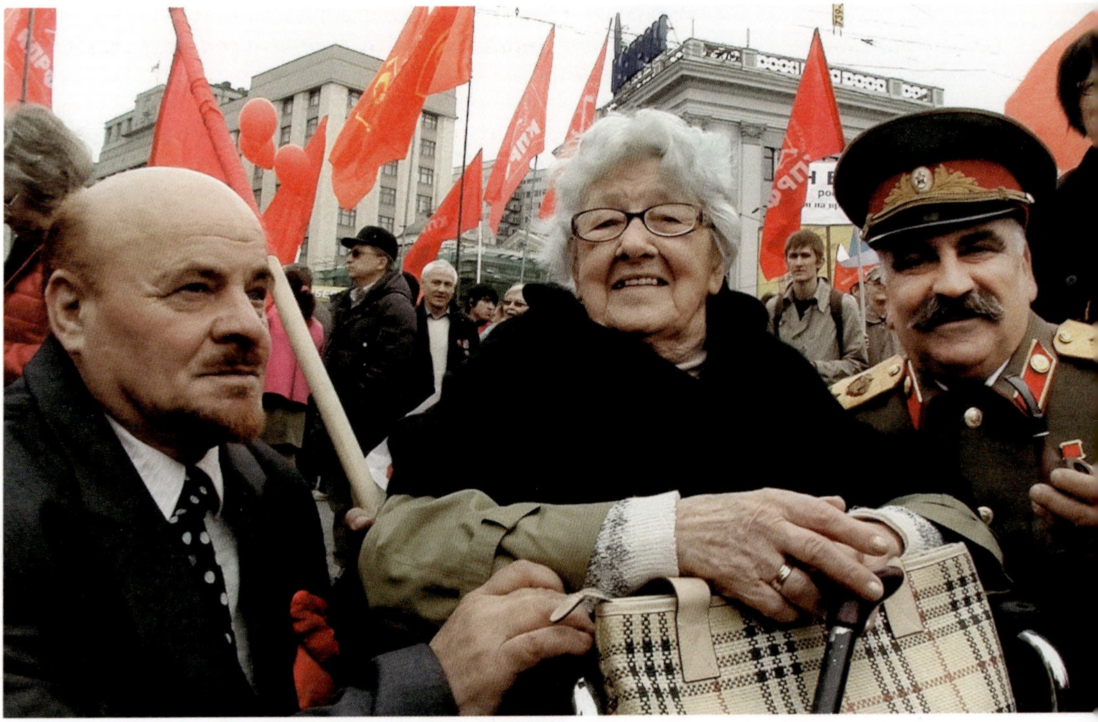

Zeitgenossen, engen Freunde und/oder Kooperationspartner waren: Diese reichen von Familienmitgliedern – ihrem Bruder Viktor Vitolović und ihrem Ehemann Vojo Srzentić – bis zu bekannten Figuren des jugoslawischen Sozialismus wie Otokar Keršovani, Miroslav Krleža, Veselin Masleša, Moše Pijade, Jaša Prodanović, Bora Prodanović und Tito selbst. All diese männlichen Namen sind fest in die Geschichte Jugoslawiens eingeschrieben, während der von Vitolović Srzentić relativ unbekannt geblieben ist. Somit inszeniert Žilniks Dokumentarfilm eine Intervention: Es sind nicht die männlichen Namen, die Vitolović Srzentićs Geschichte unterbrechen, sondern im Gegenteil: Ihre Geschichte unterbricht die überwiegend männlich dominierte Geschichte des sozialistischen Jugoslawiens und des revolutionären, antifaschistischen Kampfs im Zweiten Weltkriegs, indem der Name und die Lebenserfahrungen einer Frau darin eingefügt werden. *Eine Frau – ein Jahrhundert* veranschaulicht, wie sehr Žilniks Aufmerksamkeit für die genderspezifische Dynamik großer und kleiner historischer Ereignisse sein gesamtes reiches und vielgestaltiges Filmschaffen prägt.

Eine Frau – ein Jahrhundert (Standbild), 2011.

Mit einer erneuten Aneignung von Marx' berühmter Erklärung, „Die Philosophen haben die Welt nur verschieden interpretiert; es kommt aber darauf an, sie zu verändern",[07] behauptet der Filmwissenschaftler Pavle Levi, Žilniks Programm sei

> „im Wesentlichen eine Version von Karl Marx' *11. These zu Feuerbach*, übertragen auf das Gebiet der filmischen

07
Karl Marx, zit. nach: Pavle Levi, *Jolted Images: Unbound Analytic*, Amsterdam 2017, S. 87.

Praxis: *Die Filmemacher haben die Welt nur verschieden reproduziert* (repräsentiert); *es kommt aber darauf an, sie zu produzieren.*“[08]

Dieses Fazit beruht auf Levis folgender treffender Behauptung:

> „[Žilnik ist] fest überzeugt davon, dass die Aufgabe der Kamera nicht darin besteht, einfach die existierende Wirklichkeit abzubilden, sondern dass sie danach streben sollte, das Darzustellende in ihrem Inneren zu erzeugen; sie sollte im gesellschaftlichen Gefüge eine Vielzahl erwünschter und unerwarteter Bewegungen, Wendungen und Brüche bewirken (Filmen als Negation des Status quo) und sollte diejenigen, die gefilmt werden, dazu inspirieren, neuartige, oft improvisierte und temporäre Bündnisse zu schmieden (durch die Bildproduktion beschleunigte Emanzipation).“[09]

Welche Themen oder gesellschaftlichen Fragen, einschließlich der Fragen von Gender und Sexualität, Želimir Žilniks Filme auch behandeln: Sie sind nie kalkulierte politische Erklärungen, sondern vielmehr kooperative Begegnungen und oftmals spontane Vorführungen neuer gesellschaftlicher Möglichkeiten, die etwas an den bestehenden Verhältnissen erkennbar machen, das bis dahin unsichtbar war. ★

08 Levi, op. cit., S. 87. Hervorhebung im Original; übersetzt aus dem Englischen von Barbara Hess.

09 Ibid., S. 87.

ÜBERSETZUNG AUS DEM ENGLISCHEN VON BARBARA HESS.

Dijana Jelača ist Filmwissenschaftlerin und lehrt am Film Department des Brooklyn College und an der Feirstein Graduate School of Cinema, New York. Zu ihren Forschungsgebieten gehören feministische Filmwissenschaften, transnationaler Film, posthumane Herangehensweisen an Gender und Sexualität sowie südslawische Filmkulturen. Jelačas jüngste Veröffentlichung ist das Überblickswerk *Film Feminisms: A Global Introduction* (Routledge 2019, mit Kristin Lené Hole). Sie ist Autorin von *Dislocated Screen Memory: Narrating Trauma in Post-Yugoslav Cinema* (Palgrave 2016) und Mitherausgeberin von *The Routledge Companion to Cinema and Gender* (Routledge 2017), *The Cultural Life of Capitalism in Yugoslavia* (Palgrave 2017) und *The Future of (Post)Socialism* (SUNY Press 2018). Jelačas Essays erschienen unter anderem in *Camera Obscura, Signs, Feminist Media Studies* und *Jump Cut.*

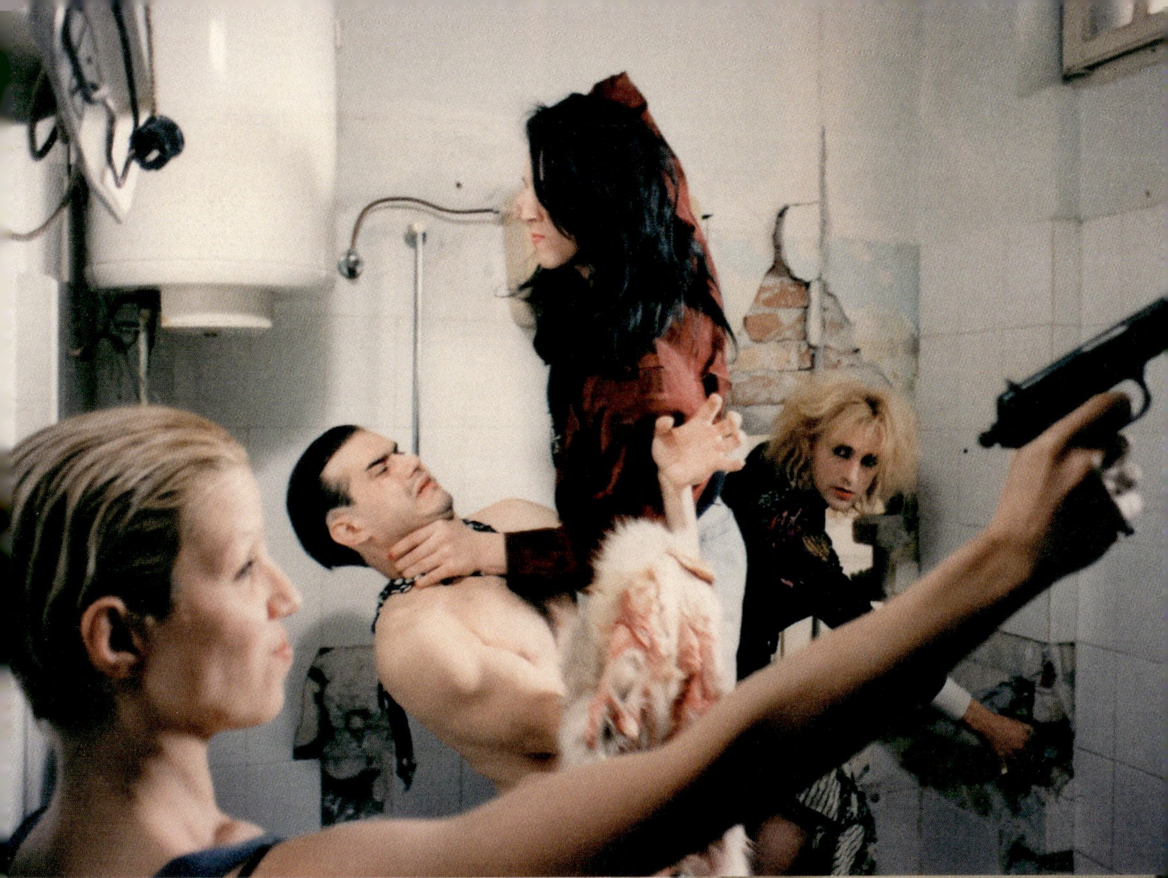

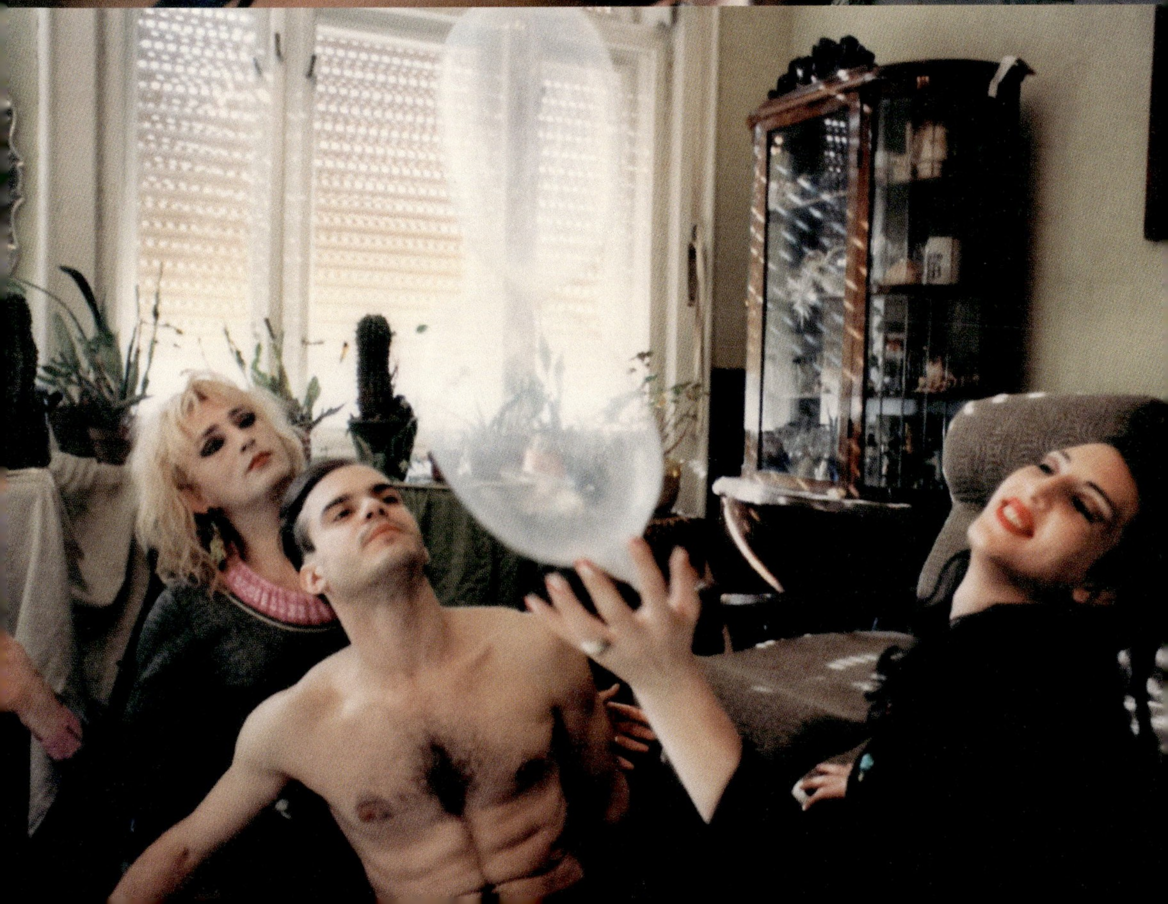

Marble Ass

Bundesrepublik Jugoslawien • 1995 • 87 min. • Betacam, auf 35 mm kopiert • Farbfilm

Merlin hilft mit, den Balkan zu befrieden, indem sie zahllose serbische Männer austrickst. Dabei agiert sie wie ein Blitzableiter, der Belgrad beschützt. Sie beruhigt gewalttätige Nachtschwärmer, angeberische Großkotze, sich elend fühlende Einzelgänger, geile junge Burschen, und sie beschützt kleine Mädchen, wehrlose Mütter und hilflose alte Frauen. Denn wenn auch noch Waffen im Spiel sind, führt solch entfesselte Energie am Ende leicht zu Blutvergießen. Merlin kühlt das heiße Blut gewalttätiger Männer mit ihrer Liebe. Džoni (Johnny) dagegen kommt gerade aus dem Krieg zurück und in seiner Heimatstadt Belgrad an. Seine Motive sind ganz ähnlich wie die von Merlin. Auch er möchte heißes Blut kühlen. Aber er tut das, indem er mit Revolverkugeln und Messerstichen in den menschlichen Körper fährt und ihn auf diese Weise öffnet. *Marble Ass* ist eine filmische Abhandlung über die unterschiedlichen Methoden, Konflikte zu lösen. Wie die von Merlin und Džoni.

Den nur halbfiktionalen Charakter von Merlin spielt der Schauspieler Vjeran Miladinović, der zuvor schon in einigen Filmen Žilniks aufgetreten war. Eine zufällige Begegnung mit ihm hat zu diesem Film geführt. Vjeran/Merlin hat Žilnik mit den Transsexuellen-Bars und -Lokalen von Belgrad bekannt gemacht. Dort lernt er mitten im Krieg eine Gesellschaft von Gleichen kennen, die ihm höchst normal erscheint. Der Film wurde mit den Einnahmen von *Tito zum zweiten Mal unter den Serben* finanziert. Er war sehr erfolgreich, erhielt 1995 bei den Internationalen Filmfestspielen Berlin den Teddy Award und wurde auf LGBT-Filmfestivals auf der ganzen Welt gezeigt. ●

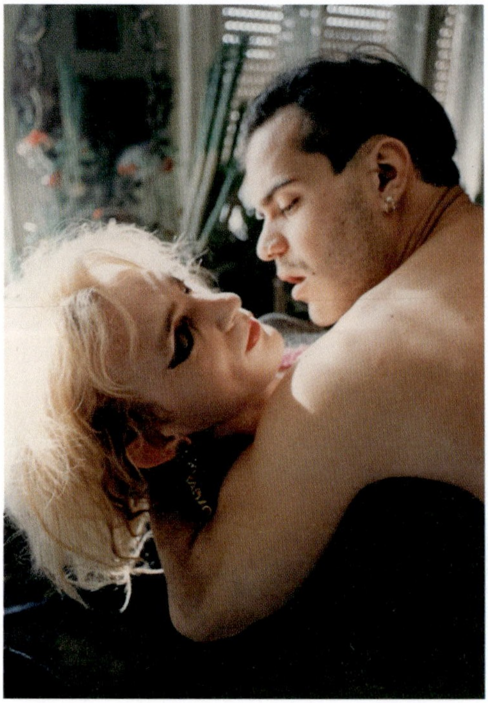

Vjeran Miladinović und Nenad Racković bei den Dreharbeiten zu *Marble Ass*, 1995.
FOTO: MIODRAG MILOŠEVIĆ.

Marble Ass (Produktionsfotos), 1995.
FOTOS: MIODRAG MILOŠEVIĆ.

Links oben: Suzana Zlatković, Nenad Racković, Nenad Milenković und Vjeran Miladinović

Links unten: Vjeran Miladinović, Nenad Racković und Nenad Milenković

Ein Regisseur, der auch Drehbücher schreibt – und ich bin ein solcher Fall –, erlebt seinen Film wie eine Art Entbindung. Und bei einer Entbindung versucht man, die schlechten Seiten zu verbergen, obwohl sie sichtbar sind – aber der Mensch kann nicht vor sich selbst davonlaufen. Ich habe vor langer Zeit angefangen, Filme zu machen, und mir ist klar geworden, dass dies die einzige Kunst ist, in die das Leben selbst stückweise eingeht. Alles, was ich gemacht habe, hat nie versucht, der Mainstream-Ästhetik zu folgen; das war für mich nebensächlich. Ich habe vielmehr immer versucht, das, was mir in meinem Leben zu dem Zeitpunkt wichtig war, als der Film gemacht wurde, darin festzuhalten. Alles, was ich gemacht habe, ob Dokumentar- oder Spielfilme, war bei seiner Entstehung eine Art Happening. Das ist etwas, was ich als Herausforderung empfinde, und nicht die bloße Nachahmung der Realität durch „die Realisierung des Texts“.

—Želimir Žilnik, unbetiteltes Interview, in: *Reporter*, August 1986

Der schwarze Film zeigt, dass die sich selbst rechtfertigende und eigennützige Position des humanistischen Mitleids, die für Linksliberale charakteristisch ist, auf grundlegende Weise in die Irre führt.

—Branislav Dimitrijević, „Concrete Analysis of Concrete Situations: Marxist Education According to Želimir Žilnik“, in: *Afterall*, Herbst/Winter 2010, S. 55.

Žilniks Filme [...] beruhen auf dem Prozess, auf der Reihe von Beziehungen, durch die ein Film entsteht und die hier bereits als ein direkter, lohnender Eingriff in den gesellschaftlichen Bereich aufgefasst werden. Bei dieser Art des Films ist der Akt des Filmens selbst mindestens so wichtig wie der (fertiggestellte) Film. Der künstlerischen/filmischen Praxis wird die Aura einer privilegierten kreativen Tätigkeit entzogen, sodass sie zu einer gewöhnlichen Arbeitssituation wird. Man kann sich Žilniks Filme gewissermaßen als eine Chronik vorstellen, die eine Gruppe von Werktätigen – der Regisseur, die Darstellenden, die Crew – von ihren versuchsweisen Übungen in gesellschaftlicher und kultureller Produktivität an der Basis hinterlassen hat. Es handelt sich um „Filme-als-Dokumente" ihrer eigenen Herstellung, die in erster Linie als Selbstzweck angelegt ist: als entdinglichtes kollektives Engagement für eine „sinnhafte menschliche Aktivität".

In Žilniks Fall (noch mehr als im Fall anderer Autorinnen und Autoren des Neuen Films, einschließlich [Dušan] Makavejevs) entwirft der „Film-als-Praxis" das Filmemachen entschieden als eine Art Spiel. Jedes neue Projekt fungiert als eine weitere Runde eines experimentellen sozialen Spiels. Ein Problem wird vorgestellt, eine Situation wird geschaffen, und dann wird der Prozess des Filmens in Gang gesetzt. Das Filmemachen funktioniert gleichzeitig 1.) als Anreiz, um vorliegende Probleme zu lösen, 2.) als Übung, um eine neue subkulturelle Zelle/Formation zu bilden, und 3.) als Reflexion darüber, was möglicherweise im oder durch den Produktionsprozess erreicht worden ist. Selbst wenn also mit dem Ende der Dreharbeiten die behandelten Probleme noch nicht gelöst sein sollten, wäre allein der Entstehungsprozess des Films bereits eine lohnenswerte Übung in gesellschaftlichem Aktivismus.

—Pavle Levi, in: Pavle Levi und Želimir Žilnik, „Europe's Internal Exiles: Sound, Image, and Performance of Identity in Želimir Žilnik's Films", in: Roland Hsu (Hg.), *Ethnic Europe: Mobility, Identity, and Conflict in a Globalized World* (Stanford, CA: Stanford University Press 2010), S. 117.

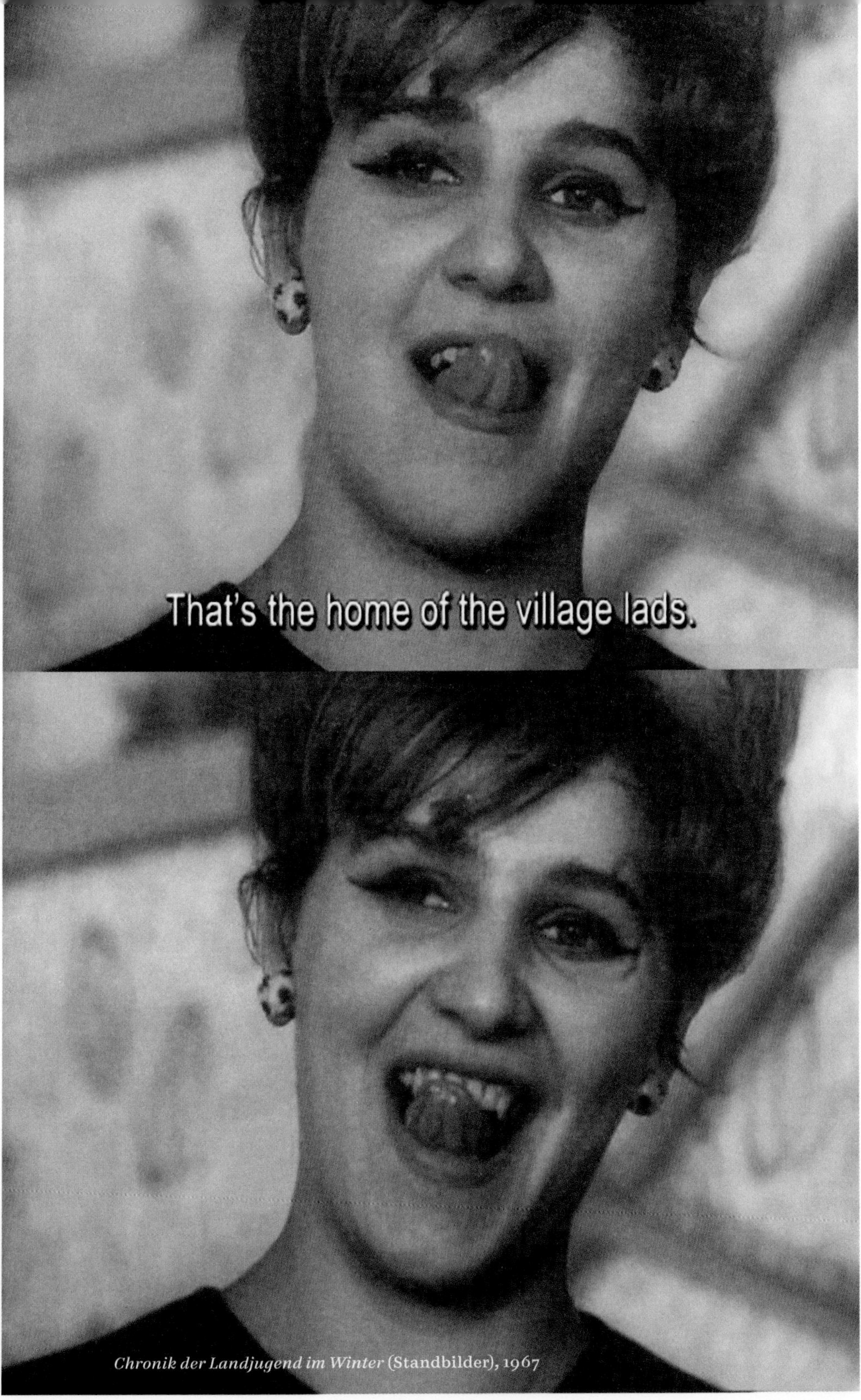

Chronik der Landjugend im Winter (Standbilder), 1967

ANA JANEVSKI

Das Tanzparadox. Über Bewegung, Tanz und Körper in Želimir Žilniks Filmen

Die Kamera bewegt sich vom unteren rechten Bildrand nach oben, sie nimmt die Gesichter und Posen einer Gruppe in den Blick: Menschen, ältere und jüngere, lehnen an einer Mauer oder bilden davor eine Reihe. Die meisten schauen in die Kamera, lächelnd oder ernsthaft, einige der Beteiligten richten ihren Blick auf etwas außerhalb des Bildes. Sie wiegen kaum merklich ihre Körper. Die Musik im Hintergrund, eine experimentelle Rockmusik, lässt erkennen, dass die Szene in einem Tanzlokal stattfindet. Die Kamera zoomt den Frontmann der Band heran. Er singt: „Hey Jelo Jeleno / tritt nicht auf das gemähte Heu" (*Oj Jelo Jelena / ne gazi seno košeno*). Dann fokussiert die Kamera eine Gruppe tanzender junger Leute, umgeben von einer zuschauenden Menge. Ihre Körper bewegen und verrenken sich ausgelassen zum Rhythmus der Musik. Wenn wir diese Szene isolieren würden, sähen wir eine Gruppe junger Menschen, die irgendwann in den 1960er Jahren zu Rockmusik tanzt und an der nichts weiter besonders ist. Die Kamera kehrt noch einmal zum Sänger und dann wieder zu den Tanzenden zurück. Sie zoomt die Beine heran, die sich drehen und beugen. Plötzlich, ein kaum wahrnehmbarer Moment – die Rockmusik verschiebt sich allmählich zu Volksmusik und die zeitgenössische Choreographie verwandelt sich in einen Volkstanz: *Kolo*.[01]

Das ist eine Szene aus Želimir Žilniks frühem Film *Chronik der Landjugend im Winter* (1967). Der Film wurde in Dörfern im Umland von Novi Sad gedreht und widmet sich dem Freizeitverhalten junger Menschen auf dem Land. So legt es jedenfalls der Titel am Anfang nahe: Kultur- und Unterhaltungsleben in der Vojvodina. Der Film zeigt einige von Žilniks inzwischen bestens bekannten Innovationen und experimentellen Verfahrensweisen, angefangen mit seinem „fiktionalen Dokumentarismus oder dokumentarischen Fiktionalismus"[02]. Dazu gehört das Arbeiten mit nichtprofessionellen Darstellerinnen und Darstellern, die direkte Reaktion der Protagonisten auf das Kameraauge und ein Verzicht auf die Unterscheidung gespielt und spontan. Die Protagonisten, die in Žilniks Filmen zu sehen sind, sind nicht nur Amateurdarstellerinnen und -darsteller, sondern auch Außenseiter – unsichtbare, unterdrückte, und unterrepräsentierte (oder unangemessen repräsentierte) Mitglieder der Gesellschaft, oder, wie es der Titel der Ausstellung gut auf den Punkt bringt: *Shadow Citizens*. Žilnik zeigt sie ohne Voreingenommenheit. Er urteilt nicht über sie. In einer zeitgenössischen Kritik von *Chronik der Landjugend im Winter* hieß es:

> „Žilnik geht sein Thema unprätentiös an, ohne im Voraus eine Hypothese aufzustellen, so dass dieses Thema uns, trotz seiner authentischen Gruseligkeit, auch durch die Erkenntnis verblüfft, dass wir bis dahin nicht wussten, dass es solche Oasen der Trostlosigkeit und der geistigen Armut in den Bereichen unseres Seins gibt, wie jene, wo junge Männer einer sonst reichen Region sich die Langeweile damit vertreiben, sich Bierflaschen gegenseitig am Kopf zu zerschlagen."[03]

01 Kolo (Kreis oder Rad) ist ein südslawischer traditioneller Tanz, bei dem Menschen einander an den Händen halten (idealerweise in einem Kreis, daher der Name).

02 Branislav Dimitrijević, „Behind Scepticism Lies the Fire of a Revolutionary!", www.zilnikzelimir.net/essay/behind-scepticism-lies-fire-revolutionary-1; übersetzt aus dem Englischen von Bert Rebhandl.

03 Bogdan Tirnanić, „Njihov prvi film (Ili: šta su pokazali debitanti 14. festivala)", in: *Film-novosti*, 29. 03. 1967, o. S.; dieses und folgende Zitate aus dem Serbischen übersetzt von Boris Buden.

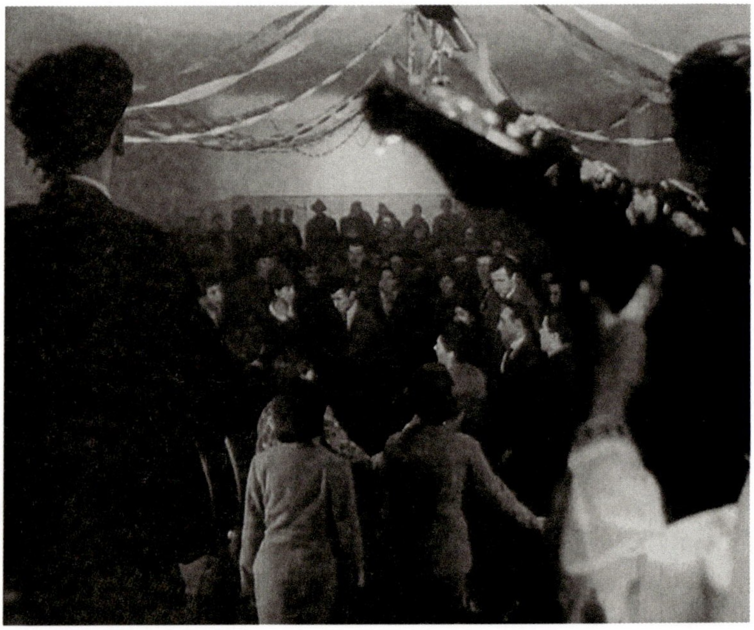

Chronik der Landjugend im Winter (Standbilder), 1967

Nachkriegs-Jugoslawien berief sich auf einen emanzipatorischen Sozialismus, eine Ideologie, in der die Zukunft vermeintlich in der Hand der jungen Generation liegt. Von Beginn seiner Karriere an hat Žilnik auf die Widersprüche und Versäumnisse des jugoslawischen Sozialismus und seiner offiziellen Diskurse hingewiesen. Seine enthüllende Darstellung der sinnlosen, prosaischen und unkultivierten Freizeitgestaltung kann damit beinahe als ein subversiver Akt gelesen werden.[04]

Ich würde mich gern auf einige Aspekte von Žilniks Filmen konzentrieren, die in den vielen Erörterungen seines Werks noch nicht diskutiert wurden, und zwar seine Betrachtungen und Analysen von Bewegung, Sprache, Musik und der Anordnung von Körpern in Bezug auf die widersprüchlichen, komplexen und vielschichtigen Aspekte des jugoslawischen Sozialismus und seiner sozialen Dynamiken.

Žilnik interessiert sich für die Jugendkultur und für den Generationenwechsel, der in den 1960er Jahren stattfand, als eine junge Generation ohne direkte Erfahrung mit dem antifaschistischen Kampf die Szene betrat. In *Chronik der Landjugend im Winter* beklagt sich deswegen die ältere Generation darüber, dass es heute keine Disziplin mehr gibt und dass die jungen Leute tun, was sie wollen. Es war auch eine Zeit, in der der Einfluss von populären Genres aus dem Westen (vor allem amerikanische und europäische Popmusik) stark mit der Öffnung des Landes zum Westen einherging. Die Auswirkungen auf die etablierte lokale kulturelle Produktion waren naheliegend. Die Rockmusik, die zu Beginn dieses Aufsatzes erwähnt wird, ist eine lokale Abwandlung des westlichen Popmusik-Idioms. Die Verbindung und das Überlappen lokaler Tradition und interna-

04
Der Film wurde für das 14. Debütantenfilmfestival in Belgrad im Jahr 1967 ausgewählt. Er lief nicht im offiziellen Wettbewerb, sondern als Teil einer Informationsschau. Die Mitglieder der Jury gaben zu, sie wären unangenehm beeindruckt „von einem Aspekt unseres Gesellschaftslebens, den wir bislang nicht kannten und der uns, auch dadurch, dass er in diesem Film so überraschend und in seiner ganzen Komplexität auftaucht, bloß durch seine Existenz, absolut bezwingt.“ Tirnanić, „Njihov prvi film“.

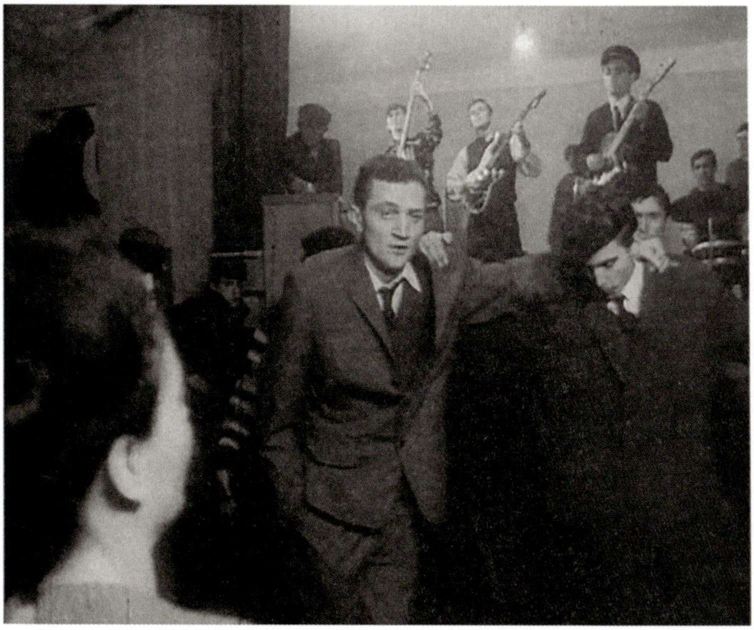

05
Ana Hofman, „Questioning Socialist Folklorization: The Beltinci Folklore Festival in the Slovenian Borderland of Prekmurje“, in: Eckehard Pistrick, Nicola Scaldaferri, Gretel Schwörer (Hg.), *Audiovisual Media and Identity Issues in Southeastern Europe*, Newcastle upon Tyne 2011, S. 238; übersetzt aus dem Englischen von Bert Rebhandl.

tionaler Einflüsse ergaben ein besonders interessantes Beispiel eines Hybrids mit herausstechendem Symbolismus. Die Körper, die zu Rockmusik tanzen, stellen eine Affirmation einer sozialen Veränderung dar, einen Punkt, an dem Modernisierung auf eine traditionelle Form von Sozialisation trifft. Die sozialistische Kulturpolitik bestand auf einer Modernisierung der Massenkultur. Sozialistische Folklore wiederum war eine ideologische Kategorie, die von den Autoritäten verwendet wurde, um der Modernisierung ein Forum zu geben. Sie diente als Fassade, die ein glückliches Leben auf dem Land in Wohlstand zeigen und zugleich die Realität der Armut des bäuerlichen Lebens verbergen sollte. Sozialistische Folklore wurde darüber hinaus als „ein vorrangiges Instrument im Prozess des Aufbaus einer supranationalen Identität“ gesehen.[05]

Žilnik konzentriert sich nicht auf das Repertoire von Amateurensembles oder von bekannten Sängern und Sängerinnen; er wendet sich stattdessen den Menschen und ihren Geschichten zu, die normalerweise vergessen und marginalisiert werden. In *Chronik der Landjugend im Winter* beobachtet er, wie diese zwei Momente – Rock und Folklore – im Alltag und in der volkstümlichen Kultur vorkommen. Die doppelte Natur der tanzenden Jugend in der Vojvodina steht nicht so sehr für eine Dualität oder ein Aufeinanderprallen des Urbanen mit dem Ruralen als für die parallele Koexistenz der beiden. Das eine schließt das andere nicht aus, weder im normalen Leben noch in der Politik und den popkulturellen Aktivitäten in Jugoslawien.

Miroslav Krleža, ein kroatischer Schriftsteller und eine prominente intellektuelle Figur im sozialistischen Jugoslawien, schrieb über die Modernisierung Jugoslawiens im Jahr 1979, dass Josip Broz Titos‘

Sozialismus zum kulturellen Reichtum und zur Entwicklung der jugoslawischen Nation im Verlauf der vergangenen dreißig Jahre mehr beigetragen habe als die ganzen 150 Jahre davor. „Dieses Tempo der kulturellen Entwicklung", so setzt er fort, „lässt sich mit jenem gar nicht vergleichen!" Er glaubte allerdings auch, dass Jugoslawien nicht ins dritte Jahrtausend gehen könne, ohne sich von seinen nationalistischen Mythen zu emanzipieren:

> „Die Partei wurde am Anfang durch den Bauernaufstand überwältigt, dem sie sich angeschlossen hat, um das große und komplizierte Werk zu vollenden, indem sie die Masse in die eigene Richtung umgesteuert hat. Immer noch aber ist *Kozaračko kolo*[06] das Symbol von all dem geblieben. Doch wir müssen weiter. *Kozaračko kolo* sollte der Vergangenheit überlassen werden."[07]

Die Position von Žilnik hingegen scheint nicht so energisch wie die von Krleža zu sein. Er beobachtet stattdessen ganz einfach die Symptome der Ohnmacht der Parteiideologie. Die tanzende Jugend in *Chronik der Landjugend im Winter* stellt eine Herausforderung für das ideologische Ziel dar, ein festes, statisches Konzept und eine Lesart sozialistischer Kultur zu schaffen. Die jungen Männer und Frauen, die sowohl Rock wie Kolo verkörpern, repräsentieren das Paradox, das nicht nur in der sozialistischen Kulturpolitik, sondern

06
Volkstanz, vgl. Fußnote 01 in diesem Text (Anm. der Redaktion)

07
Miroslav Krleža, zitiert nach: Damir Pilić, „Tito očima Krleže", unveröffentlicht.

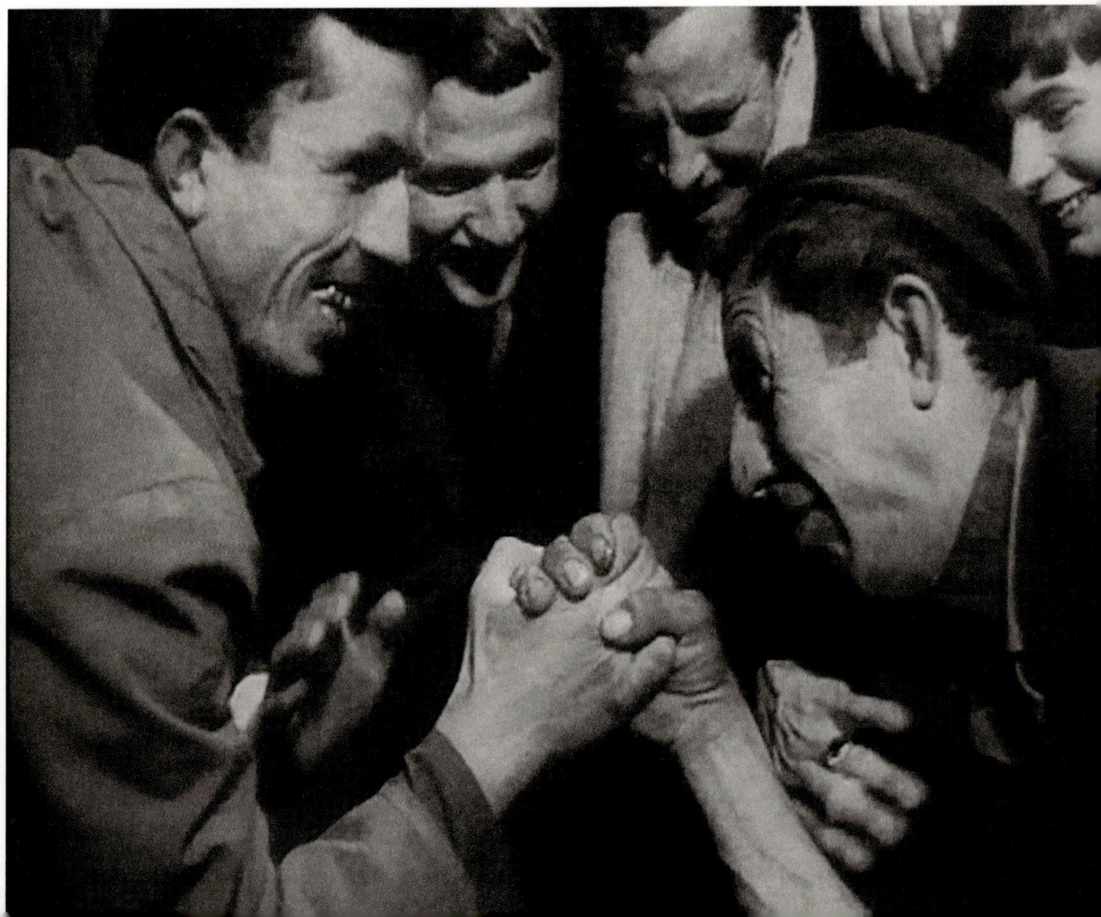

Chronik der Landjugend im Winter (Standbild), 1967

in einem allgemeineren Sinn in sozialistischen Gesellschaften zu verzeichnen war. Dieses Paradox bildet einen wichtigen Aspekt in Žilniks gesamtem Werk. Der Kunsthistoriker Branislav Dimitrijević fasst es in seiner Analyse von Žilniks Werk so zusammen:

> „Von einem Paradox kann man in verschiedener Hinsicht sprechen. Es lässt sich definieren als eine vermeintlich zutreffende Behauptung oder eine Gruppe von Behauptungen, die zu einem Widerspruch oder zu einer Situation führen, die der Intuition widerspricht; oder es kann ein offensichtlicher Widerspruch sein, der eine nicht-duale Wahrheit zum Ausdruck bringt. Im Begriff des Paradoxes liegt ein effektives Mittel, nicht nur jedes statische Argument zu dekonstruieren, sondern auch ein Verfahren, das keine einfache Zurückweisung eines der relevanten Blickpunkte erlaubt, sondern eine Synthese oder eine Kombination der gegensätzlichen Behauptungen erfordert.“[08]

Paradoxes ist auch in Žilniks Beziehung zur dominanten Ideologie erkennbar. Nachdem er wegen seiner anarcho-liberalen Ansichten aus der Partei ausgeschlossen worden war, beschäftigte Žilnik sich weiter mit der Komplexität des Marxismus in einem sozialistischen Jugoslawien. Er blieb selbst ein Linker.[09] Es lag nicht in seiner Absicht, die sozialistische Realität zu kritisieren, sondern den sozialistischen Diskurs kritisch zu bereichern.[10] Als der scharfe Beobachter, der er ist, entging ihm nicht, dass Bewegung, Körperdynamiken und Popkultur diese Kritikalität enthielten.

Wenn man Žilniks Beschäftigung mit menschlicher Gestalt und Bewegung im Sinn einer Anthropologie des Körpers entschlüsseln möchte, findet man bei Michel Foucaults Begriff der Biomacht ein hilfreiches Werkzeug. Biomacht sieht im Körper einen Ort der Unterwerfung; das Konzept hebt hervor, wie Individuen in ihre eigene Unterdrückung eingebunden werden. Tägliche Körperpraktiken und Gewohnheiten spielen dabei eine wesentliche Rolle. Foucault zufolge wird Macht nicht von oben ausgeübt, sondern kommt vielmehr von unten. Das heißt, wir sind alle „Träger der Macht“, denn Macht „ist in Diskurse und Normen eingebettet, die Teil von kleinteiligen Praktiken, Gewohnheiten und Interaktionen unseres täglichen Lebens sind“.[11] Macht ist damit überall: Sie ist etwas, „was sich von unzähligen Punkten aus und im Spiel ungleicher und beweglicher Beziehungen vollzieht.“[12] Körperliche Disziplinartechniken, die Zeit, Raum und tägliche Praktiken in einer Gesellschaft organisieren, werden in Schulen, Gefängnissen, Spitälern und Betrieben institutionalisiert und auch individuell durch selbstregulierendes Verhalten internalisiert. Žilnik wählt Schattenbürger als Protagonistinnen und Protagonisten und fokussiert damit auf undisziplinierte Körper, auf den Teil der Bevölkerung, der nicht institutionalisiert oder selbstregulierend ist. Diese Menschen tanzen, singen, bewegen und ertüchtigen sich auf ihre eigene Weise.

08
Dimitrijević, op. cit.

09
„Die Tragödie des Bundes der Kommunisten liegt darin, dass die wichtigsten Posten mit Menschen besetzt wurden, die offensichtlich von Familienkomplexen heimgesucht werden und päpstlicher als der Papst sein wollen“, verkündete Žilnik, als er nach einem Streit über die Neoplanta Filmproduktion aus der Partei ausgeschlossen wurde. S. Boris Buden, Želimir Žilnik, *Uvod u prošlost*, hg. v. kuda.org, Novi Sad 2013, S. 88, www.kuda.org/sites/default/files/Uvod u proslost_web.pdf.

10
Dimitrijević, op. cit.

11
Jen Pylypa, „Power and Bodily Practice. Applying the Work of Foucault to an Anthropology of the Body“, in: *Arizona Anthropologist*, Bd. 13, 1998, S. 23. Aus dem Englischen von Bert Rebhandl.

12
Michel Foucault, *Sexualität und Wahrheit, Bd. 1: Der Wille zum Wissen*, übersetzt von Ulrich Raulff und Walter Seitter, Frankfurt am Main 1983, S. 94.

In *Kleine Pioniere* (1968)[13] zeigt Žilnik vernachlässigte Kinder, die sich selbst überlassen sind und sich mit Taschendiebstahl, Betteln und anderen illegalen Aktivitäten über Wasser halten. Diese Kinder sind das genaue Gegenteil des Bildes von den glücklichen und unbeschwerten jungen sozialistischen Pionierinnen und Pionieren, das von der jugoslawischen Regierung verbreitet wurde. Žilniks Film legt keine pädagogische oder moralisierende Haltung an den Tag. Eine der ersten Szenen zeigt ein Mädchen, das an der Mauer eines verfallenen Gebäudes steht und singt. Der Text des Lieds erzählt von einer jungen Frau, die vor ihrer Hochzeit verlassen wird. Das Mädchen ist eigentlich zu jung für diese Geschichte. Die Kamera folgt den Kindern auf ihren täglichen Abenteuern, dazu erzählen sie aus dem Off in einem Voiceover von Situationen, die sie erlebt haben: Diebstähle, Prostitution, Misshandlung. Žilnik zeigt sie ständig in Bewegung, vor allem an unbeachteten Orten in der Stadt. Sie sind immer in der Gruppe, sie singen, heulen, schreien, flüstern, sie erzeugen Geräusche mit allem, was ihnen unterkommt, sie rauchen und werfen Steine. Und dann werden wir wieder zu einem Tanzlokal gebracht. Hier hören wir keine Musik, sondern einen der jungen Protagonisten, der von seinen Abenteuern erzählt, während eine Gruppe von jungen Leuten in der Nähe ihre Körper in wiedererkennbaren Rock-Bewegungen verrenkt. Inmitten dieser tanzenden Vertreterinnen und Vertreter einer progressiven jugoslawischen Jugend rauchen und reden die kleinen Pioniere, sie tanzen und klatschen rhythmisch ihre Hände auf die Bühne. Mit *Kleine Pioniere* fängt Žilnik also ein weiteres soziales Paradox der Zeit ein, und damit die widersprüchliche Natur der offiziellen Kulturpolitik. Nach der Vorführung auf dem 15. Jugoslawischen Dokumentar- und Kurzfilmfestival sahen sich einige Filmkritiker veranlasst, Žilnik das Talent zu bescheinigen, die obskursten und verborgensten Teile der jugoslawischen Gesellschaft ans Licht zu bringen. Er selbst formulierte es so:

> „Ich rede von den Dingen, die in der Tat ernstzunehmende soziale Kämpfe sind und zwar nicht in einem quasi subversiven, sondern vielmehr in einem polyvalenten Sinn. Ich bin der Meinung, dass ein pathetisches Verhältnis zum Thema nie aufrichtig sein kann. Deshalb halte ich ein humoristisches Verhältnis zum Leben für viel wichtiger."[14]

Er erwähnt seine Bewunderung für die Filme des tschechischen Regisseurs Miloš Forman und seiner scheinbar leichten Motive, hinter denen sich eine Dunkelheit verbirgt, die das Publikum entweder freilegen kann oder nicht. Diese Dunkelheit ist vielleicht eine Grundannahme in Žilniks *Der schwarze Film* (1971) und steht auch hinter der Idee von Schwärze, die ihn und seine Gefährten seit den 1970er Jahren begleiteten: nun als Vorwurf, dass ihre Filme die jugoslawische Gesellschaft schwarz und negativ zeichneten.[15]

Für Žilnik liefern dokumentarische Filme und Kultur kein Heilmittel gegen soziales Elend. Er bezweifelt die emanzipatorische Macht von

13 Eine Beschreibung des Films findet sich in dem Essay von Dijana Jelača auf Seite 97 in diesem Buch.

14 Želimir Žilnik, zit. nach: „Nova filmska nada", *Filmske novosti*, September 1967.

15 Gemeinsam mit anderen Filmemachern, darunter Dušan Makavejev und Živojin Pavlović, kritisierte Žilnik in seinen Filmen offen die Entfremdung des sozialistischen Menschen. Sie hoben Klassen- und soziale Widersprüche im sozialistischen Jugoslawien dieser Zeit hervor. In der Folge einer ideologischen Kampagne, die von dem kulturpolitischen Establishment ausging, wurden diese Filme unter dem Begriff Schwarze Welle bekannt. Der Artikel, der den Begriff etablierte, erschien 1969 in der Zeitung *Borba*. Ein Journalist befand, dass die Schwarze Welle im jugoslawischen Kino „eine systematische Entstellung der Gegenwart" zeige, in der alles durch eine monochromatische Linse gesehen werde. Die Themen seien „obskur und ergäben unangemessene An-

sichten und Bilder von Gewalt, moralischer Verkommenheit, Elend, Liederlichkeit und Trivialität". Siehe Vladimir Jovičić, „,Crni val' u našem filmu", *Borba*, 3. August 1969.

16
Želimir Žilnik, zit. nach: Stefan Vuković, „Notes on Paradigms in Experimental Film in Socialist Yugoslavia", in: *This is All Film! Experimental Film in Yugoslavia 1951–1991*, hg. v. Bojana Piškur, Ana Janevski, Jurij Meden und Stefan Vuković, Ljubljana 2010, S. 53.

17
What, How & for Whom/WHW, „Želimir Žilnik, Shadow Citizens", www.zilnikzelimir.net/project/zelimir-zilnik-shadow-citizens.

Kultur. Gegen Ende von *Kleine Pioniere* beginnen die Kinder einander zu beleidigen. Sie klingen vulgär und ziemlich erwachsen, während im Hintergrund ein kleiner Junge in einen Karton schlägt und ein Mädchen, das zuvor von seinen sexualisierten Begegnungen mit älteren Männern erzählt hat, tanzt und ihren Körper sinnlich bewegt. Sie sind beide losgelöst von der Gruppe und voneinander, aber sie bilden eine Einheit. Žilnik filmt nicht die Vitalität oder Energie der jungen Körper; er zeigt sie eher als Symptome der Realitäten, die aus der Ohnmacht der sozialistischen Ideologie geboren werden. Das alltägliche Leben geht in all seiner Dunkelheit weiter. Žilnik entwickelte seine filmischen Praktiken in den Cineclubs von Novi Sad. Er beschreibt, wie ein Do-it-yourself-Zugang zu seiner Befähigung beitrug, sich in seinem Werk solch subversiven Themen zu widmen:

> „Von Anfang an war ich dazu gezwungen, alle Methoden der Amateurfilmbewegung einzusetzen. Die Umgebung des Amateurfilms erlaubt es mir, mich aus den administrativen Labyrinthen zu befreien, die den einzigen Weg darstellten, Geld für einen Film zu bekommen. Es war eine Form von Freiheit."[16]

Couragierter Amateurismus ist in Žilniks Filmen ein hervorstechendes Merkmal. Er dient als Konzept und als Methode, und die Ausstellung *Shadow Citizens* ging besonders auf „unterschiedliche Facetten der Potentiale von Schattenbürgern ein, wie auch auf den Druck, dem der untergründige Amateurismus in emanzipatorischer Politik und künstlerischer Produktion unterlag."[17]

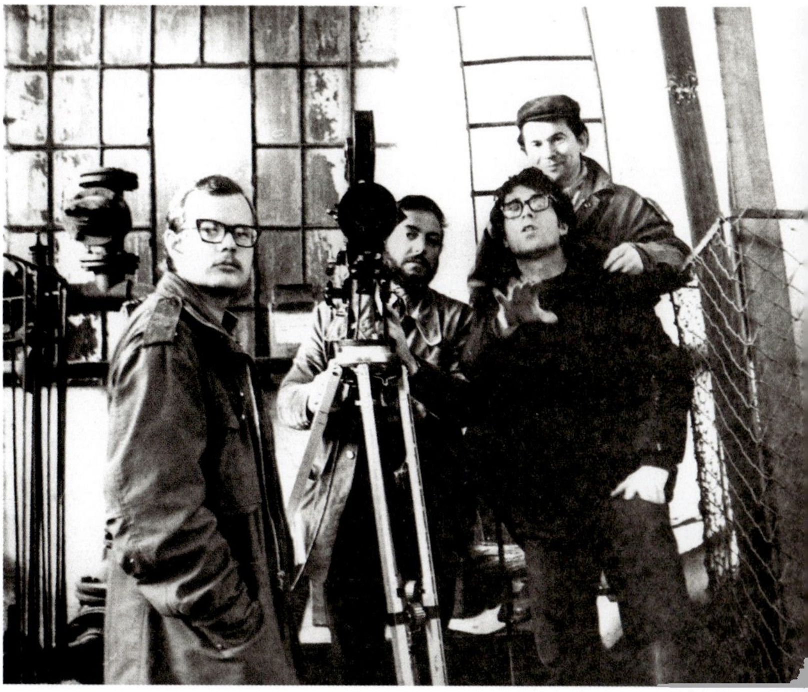

Dušan Ninkov, Karpo Godina, Želimir Žilnik und Ivan Čirković bei den Dreharbeiten zu *Freiheit oder Comicstrip*, 1972. FOTO: ANDREJ POPOVIĆ.

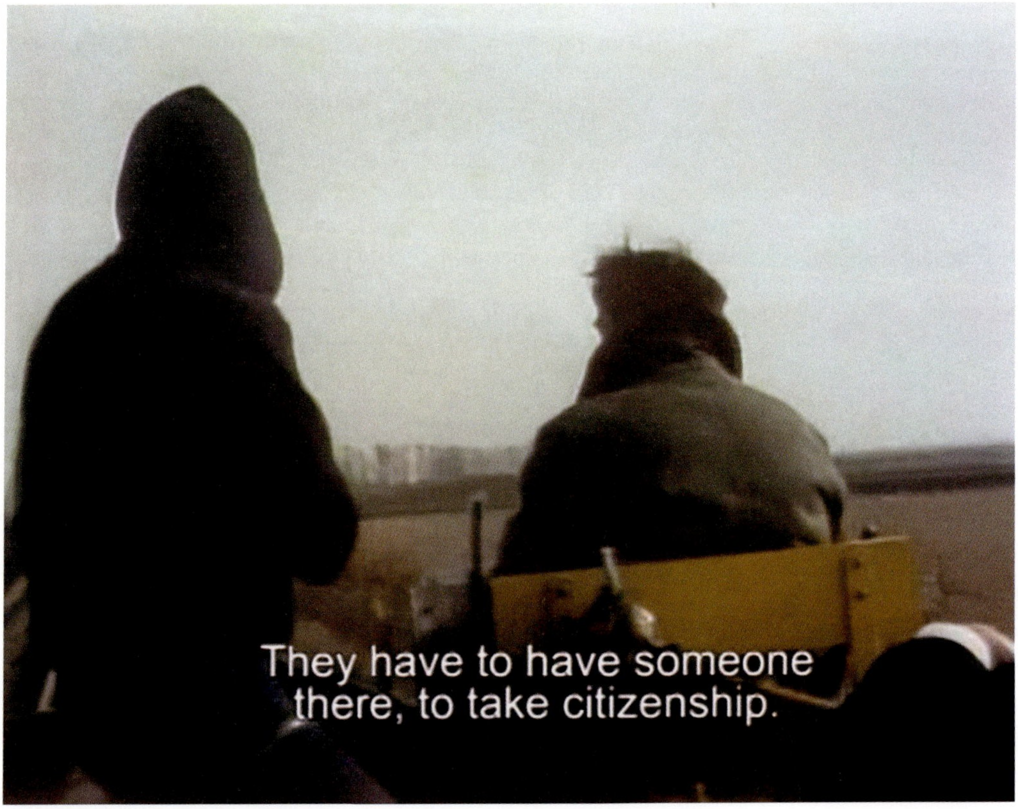

Das erste Trimester von Pavle Hromiš (Standbilder), 1983

In den 1970er Jahren verließ Žilnik Jugoslawien und ging nach Westdeutschland. Er realisierte dort mehrere Filme, die sich mit lokaler Politik beschäftigten. Insbesondere fing er Momente ein, die mit dem zunehmenden Terrorismus zu tun hatten. Er beschäftigte sich aber auch mit der soziopolitischen Position von Gastarbeiterinnen und Gastarbeitern. Bald musste er Deutschland jedoch aus politischen Gründen wieder verlassen und kehrte nach Jugoslawien zurück, wo er als nächstes eine Reihe von Fernseh- und Spielfilmen machte. In seinen frühen Filmen ging es um das komplexe Zusammenspiel von Ideologie, Bewegung, Musik und Praktik. In seinen Filmen seit den frühen 1980ern richtete er die Aufmerksamkeit auf die zunehmenden sozialen Konflikte im Land. Die Figur des Gastarbeiters wurde für ihn dabei entscheidend. Die Anthropologinnen Tanja Petrović und Ana Hofman beschreiben die soziale Situation von Gastarbeitern in Jugoslawien und anderen Ländern Mitte des 20. Jahrhunderts:

> „Das kulturalisierte Bild eines Gastarbeiters als eines bizarren, grotesken Individuums, dessen kultureller Geschmack von Kitsch und Eklektizismus charakterisiert ist, passt weder in die akzeptierbare kulturelle Norm des Landes, das er oder sie verlassen hat, noch in die des Ankunftslands. Es bestimmt aber sowohl die Populärkultur wie die akademische Diskussion. Das schwierige Leben und die harte Arbeit

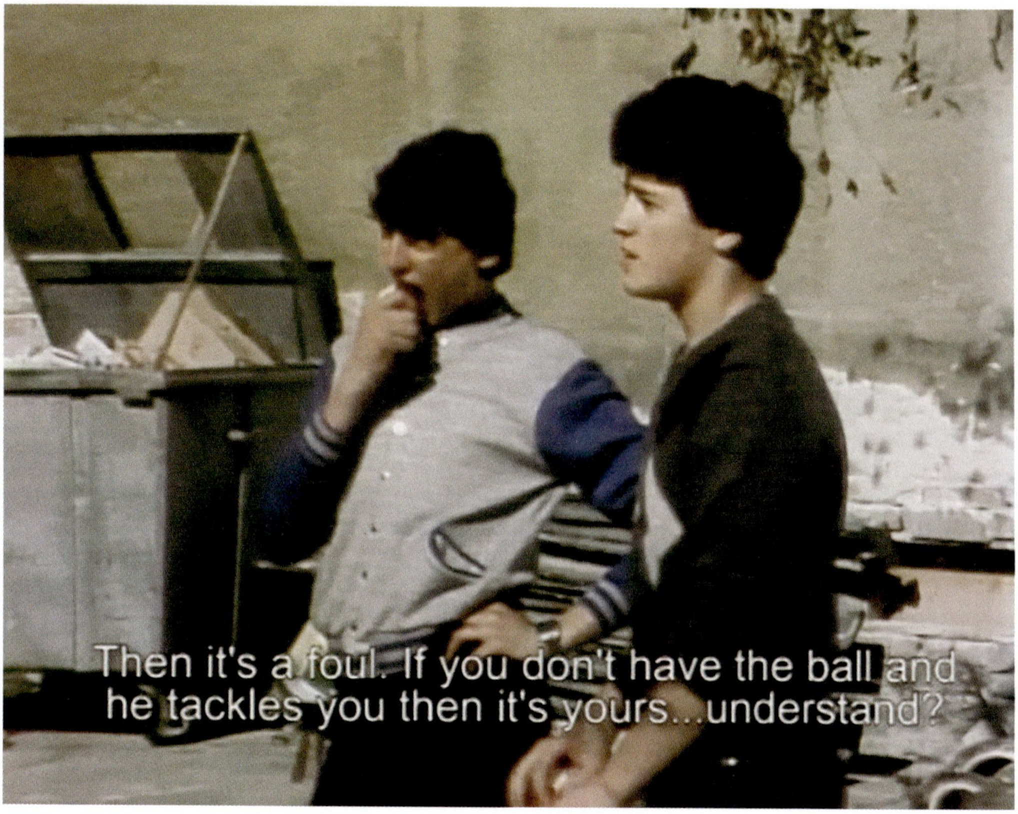

der Migranten, ihre Ängste in Folge der Trennung von ihren Kindern und Familien und andere existenzielle und psychologische Aspekte ihrer Arbeit und ihres Lebens werden nur selten in all ihrer Komplexität angesprochen."[18]

Junge Menschen standen in dieser Zeit einmal mehr im Mittelpunkt von Žilniks Interesse. Der Fernsehfilm *Das erste Trimester von Pavle Hromiš* (1983) gibt ein berührendes und genaues Porträt des Teenagers Pavle Hromiš. Er kehrt nach Jugoslawien zurück, während seine Eltern in Deutschland bleiben, um dort zu arbeiten. Žilnik begleitet Pavle bei seiner Integration in die jugoslawische Gesellschaft der 1980er Jahre. Pavle ist 15 Jahre alt, er hat elf Jahre in Deutschland gelebt, und soll nun bei seiner Großmutter in einem Dorf in der Nähe von Novi Sad leben. Žilnik dokumentiert auch hier einen Generationenkonflikt, in diesem Fall zwischen Großmutter und Enkelsohn. Pavle zieht daraus eine Konsequenz und entscheidet sich, während des Besuchs der Mittelschule in ein Schülerheim zu ziehen.

In der Schule lernt er neue Freunde kennen. Sie haben vergleichbare Erfahrungen gemacht. Pavle und seine Freunde wirken wie verloren zwischen zwei Identitäten. Es ist sehr bewegend und lebendig, wie sie vor der Kamera eingehende Vergleiche anstellen zwischen Ländern, in denen sie gelebt haben. Ein Teenager spricht davon, dass Österrei-

18 Tanja Petrović und Ana Hofman, „Rethinking Class in Socialist Yugoslavia: Labor, Body, and Moral Economy", in: Dijana Jelača, Maša Kolanović, Danijela Lugarić (Hg.), *The Cultural Life of Capitalist Yugoslavia*, Baskingstoke 2017, S. 71; übersetzt aus dem Englischen von Bert Rebhandl.

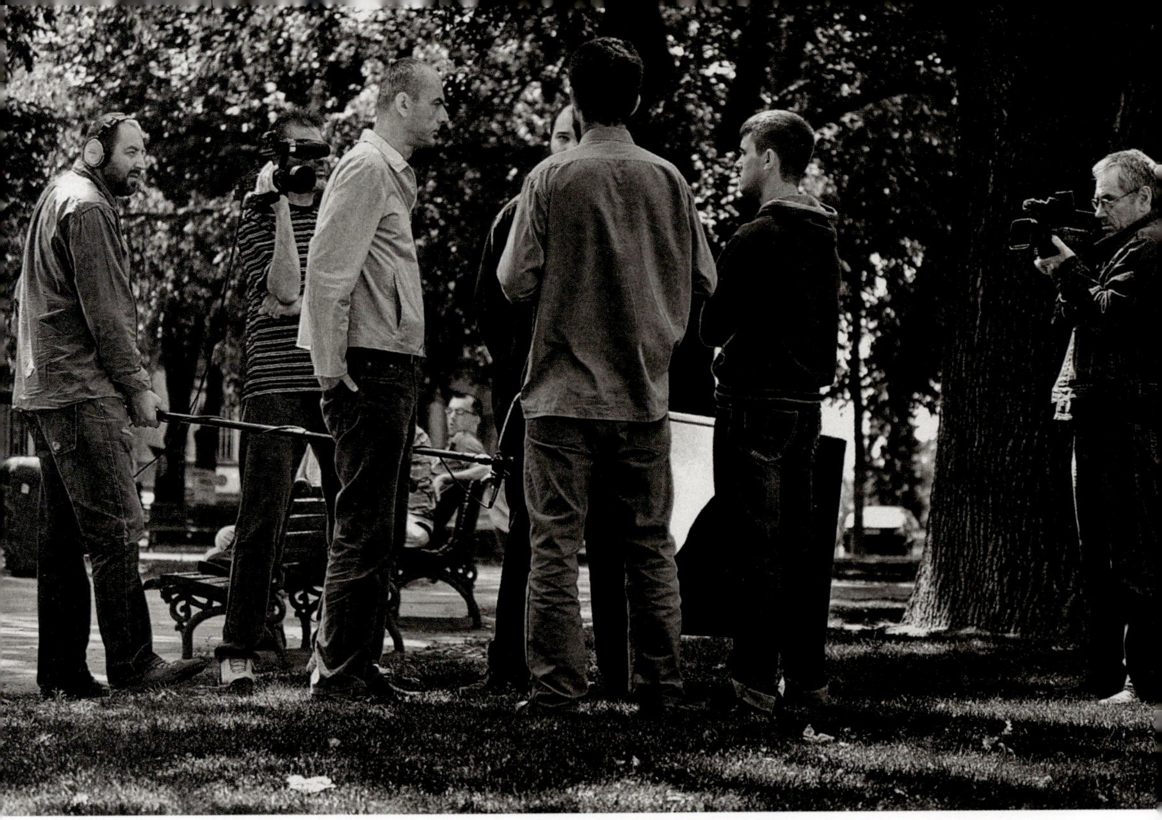

cher keinen Respekt vor Türken und Jugoslawen haben. Ein anderer Junge erzählt davon, dass er aus einer Geschichtsstunde in Russland verwiesen wurde, weil er Zweifel an der Tatsache angemeldet habe, dass die Rote Armee Jugoslawien befreit hat. Ihre Geschichten sind auch voller Überraschungen. Ein Mädchen behauptet auf Niederländisch, dass die Menschen in den Niederlanden respektvoller und altruistischer erscheinen als die Menschen in Jugoslawien. Verschiedene Geschichten wechseln sich mit Pavles Erzählung ab. Er spricht über die begrenzten Möglichkeiten, die er in Deutschland bei seinem Versuch hatte, einen angesehenen Beruf zu ergreifen. Alles schien ihm einen Weg als einfachem Arbeiter vorzuzeichnen. Zu seinem Voiceover ist eine Szene zu sehen, die ihn und seine Klassenkameraden beim Sport zeigt. Sie trainieren eine Form von Martial arts. Sie sind alle ständig in Bewegung, egal ob man sie in einer Turnstunde in der Schule sieht oder ob sie an anderen Stellen Laufen, Wirbeln, Fallen. Manchmal hängen sie auch einfach nur auf dem Dach eines Gebäudes oder an einer Uferpromenade ab. In anderen Momenten des Films fängt Žilnik Pavle allein in Bewegung ein, dann eilt oder springt er von einem Waggon zum anderen, wie in einem Action-Film. Auch hier steht die kinetische Metapher für instabile soziale Dynamiken. Žilnik bleibt gleichermaßen aufmerksam für die maßgebliche Rolle der Popkultur. Zum Beispiel bereitet die Gruppe eine Schultheateraufführung vor, und ein Mädchen singt ein Volkslied. Ihre Kumpel buhen sie sofort aus. Die jugoslawische Kultur in den 1980er Jahren war in mancherlei Hinsicht progressiv und verwestlicht. Volkstümliches wurde deswegen nicht mehr akzeptiert.

Dragan Kolarić, Miodrag Milošević, Branimir Stojanović Trša, Ratibor Trivunac, Zoran Paroški, Milan Paroški und Želimir Žilnik bei den Dreharbeiten zu *Die Alte Schule des Kapitalismus*, 2009

Diese Einstellung äußert sich auch in dem Gespräch, in dem Pavle und seine Freunde sich über Musik unterhalten. Sie kommen auf Disco, Funk, Heavy Metal und andere Genres zu sprechen, Bands wie Depeche Mode oder Simple Minds werden erwähnt. Žilnik zeigt aber auch die Underground-Musikszene von Novi Sad. Bei einem Konzert treten alternative und New Wave-Bands wie Obojeni Program und Boye auf.

Die Teenager in *Das erste Trimester von Pavle Hromiš* sind verloren zwischen zwei sozioökonomischen Systemen. Die Tatsache geht ausdrücklich aus einer hitzigen Diskussion unter den Studierenden hervor: Sie sprechen über das Pro und Kontra von Sozialismus und Kapitalismus. Die meisten von ihnen halten den Sozialismus immer noch für fairer und für das System mit der größeren Sicherheit (nicht allen geht es nur um Geld); wenn der jugoslawische Sozialismus allerdings auf der Führung durch seine Jugend beruht, dann zeigt das System in genau dem Moment, in dem die Jugend daran Zweifel hegt, erste Anzeichen von Schwäche. Pavle beginnt sich schließlich für das Leben beim Militär zu interessieren. Es gefällt ihm, weil es Ordnung und Sicherheit gibt. Es hilft ihm, die Ungewissheit in seinem Leben zu bekämpfen. Die letzte Szene des Films zeigt ein geläufiges militärisches Ritual: das Bett machen und die einheitliche Kleidung anziehen. Žilnik unterlegt diese neue Anpassung an das Soldatenleben mit einer Punknummer von Gang of Four. Zwar wird der Körper schließlich diszipliniert, aber Punk und jugoslawischer Sozialismus bestehen weiter nebeneinander in einem Paradox, das erst durch die endgültige Auflösung des Systems aufgehoben wird.

The good life was so elusive
Handouts, they got me down
I had to regain my confidence
So I got into camouflage
The girls they love to see you shoot
I love a man in a uniform[19] ★

19 Gang of Four, „I Love a Man in Uniform“, Songs of the Free, EMI, 1982. Gang of Four spielten im Rahmen der Musikbiennale 1981 in Zagreb. Siehe „Entertainment: Gang of Four, live in Zagreb, 1981“, *Dangerous Minds*, 20. August 2014, https://dangerousminds.net/comments/entertainment_gang_of_four_live_in_zagreb_1981.

ÜBERSETZUNG AUS DEM ENGLISCHEN VON BERT REBHANDL.

Ana Janevski ist Kuratorin am Department of Media and Performance Art des Museum of Modern Art, New York. Zuletzt organisierte sie dort 2018/19 (mit Thomas Lax und Martha Joseph) die Ausstellung Judson Dance Theater: *The Work Is Never Done.* Sie kooperierte mit zahlreichen Choreografinnen und Choreografen sowie Künstlerinnen und Künstlern wie Anne Teresa De Keersmaeker, Jérôme Bel, Yvonne Rainer, Rabih Mroué, Boris Charmatz und dem Musée de la danse, Simone Forti, Martha Rosler, Ralph Lemon und Trajal Harrell. Von 2007 bis 2011 war sie Kuratorin am Museum of Modern Art in Warsaw, wo sie neben vielen anderen Projekten die umfangreiche Ausstellung *As Soon as I Open My Eyes I See a Film* über experimentelle Filme und Kunst im Jugoslawien der 1960er und 1970er Jahre kuratierte; sie ist außerdem Herausgeberin der gleichnamigen Begleitpublikation zur Ausstellung. 2010 war Janevski Co-Kuratorin der ersten umfassenden Ausstellung über den Experimentalfilm in Jugoslawien, *This Is All Film! Experimental Film in Yugoslavia 1951–1991,* am Museum of Modern Art in Ljubljana.

Das Leben durch das Leben verlieren

Zelimir Zilniks „Gastarbeiter-Oper" in Novi Sad: „antideutsch"?

BELGRAD. Dem Spektakel folgte Spektakuläres: Im 80 Kilometer entfernten Novi Sad, so hörte man in Belgrad, werde ein Theaterstück gespielt, dem die lokale Kritik anarchistische Tendenzen nachsage. Diplomaten aus der bundesdeutschen Botschaft, die zur Premiere angereist waren, kehrten empört von ihrem Ausflug in die Metropole zurück: da werde ein antideutsches Machwerk offensichtlich zu einem Publikumserfolg, Gefahr sei im Verzuge, Protest zu erwägen.

Zelimir Žilnik, in der Bundesrepublik nicht nur durch seinen Spielfilm „Frühe Werke" (Goldener Bär Berlin 1969, später im Fernsehen gesendet) bekanntgeworden, sondern vor allem durch seine Kurzfilme, wie „Studentenstreik", „Der schwarze Film" oder „Aufstand in Jasak", die über Oberhausen fast alle ins TV-Programm gelangten — Žilnik hat das Thema seiner im Ausland arbeitenden Landsleute über Jahre hinweg verfolgt. Er nannte sie die wirklichen positiven Helden unserer Zeit. Wenn da ein arbeitsloser Häusler aus einem Dorf der Vojvodina ins Weite zieht, um etwa in Stuttgart auf dem Bau zu arbeiten, dann sei das ein Abenteuer, vergleichbar mit den Entdeckungsreisen von Kolumbus oder Amundsen.

Als die Arbeitsbedingungen sich für den Intellektuellen Žilnik, Jurist und Filmemacher, in Jugoslawien immer mehr verschlechterten, ging auch er 1974 als „Gastarbeiter" in die Bundesrepublik. Žilnik drehte in München Kurzfilme, denen man ihren knappen Etat kaum ansah, etwa „Unter Denkmalschutz", „Abschied", „Der Antrag", „Inventur," und die im Milieu der ausgebeuteten Gastarbeiter, der Unterdrückten, Angepaßten und Aufbegehrenden angesiedelt waren.

In dieser bundesdeutschen Zeit entstand der Spielfilm „Das Paradies", in dem auf dem Hintergrund der Baader-Meinhof-Hysterie die Geschichte eines vorgetäuschten Kidnapping (eine pleite gegangene Unternehmerin sucht so ihre Krise zu meistern) erzählt wird, zwischen Naivität und Raffinement, Pornographie und Bayern, bedenkenlos und frech; beinahe selbstverständlich verschloß sich der Markt solcher Zumutung.

In dieser Zeit arbeitete der Emigrant auf Widerruf, der immer wieder in seine Heimat zurückkehrte, auch an einem Projekt über jene Bürger zweiter Klasse aus Italien und Jugoslawien, aus Spanien und der Türkei, die hierzulande „Gastarbeiter" heißen, eine Art musikalisch-theatralischer Revue mit politisch-moralischer Brisanz, gespielt von einem national gemischten Ensemble. Eine Kooperation mit den Münchener Kammerspielen scheiterte, auch sonst gab es unüberwindbare Hindernisse.

Als sich die kulturpolitische Situation in Jugoslawien entspannte, kehrte Žilnik zurück. Nun konnte er sein Projekt, allerdings in der Zusammenarbeit mit dem Komponisten Predrag Vranešević und dem heimischen Ensemble in Novi Sad grundlegend verändert, endlich realisieren. Am 24. Januar dieses Jahres war die Premiere der „Gastarbeiter-Oper" von Žilnik und Vranešević, inszeniert von Žilnik. „Freude über ein verdorrtes Korn" überschrieb die Lokalzeitung ihren kritischen, polemisch eingefärbten Bericht; das Publikum drängte sich nach Karten.

Žilnik treibt Verhaltensforschung auf dem Theater. Eigentlich erzählt er keine Story, sondern setzt seine Figuren verschiedenen Situationen aus, veranstaltet mit ihnen ein soziales Experiment. Dabei gehen seine Thesen ganz in theatralischen Formen auf. Es beginnt mit dokumentarischem Theater: Drei Frauen, eine hat ihren Mann verloren, die andere ist ohne Job und die dritte auf Abenteuer aus, beschreiben mit Ironie und schwarzem Humor ihr Dasein, aus dem sie gemeinsam ausbrechen. Sie geraten in die schillernde Konsumwelt des Westens, probieren nicht nur neue Kleider, sondern auch neue Haltungen.

Die rührend-komischen Wirkungen werden ausgelöst durch zeremonielle Formen von Brecht und Ionescu bis zur Wagner-Parodie. Wenn die Frauen
das unerbittliche Räderwerk der mod
nen Industrie geraten, wo Befehl u
Gehorsam exerziert werden, schlägt
Geschehen in eine Rock-Oper um, u
Chaplins „Moderne Zeiten" laden
Assoziation ein.

Doch den drei Heldinnen gelingt
Anpassung ans Fließbandleben nicht,
werden von der Arbeit gejagt, verfal
in Katzenjammer und überdenken i
Lage in einer Art Melodrama. Als
auf ein zerstrittenes Kapitalisten-E
paar treffen, beschimpfen sie erst
Frau, schlagen sich dann aber soli
risch gegen den Patriarchen auf i
Seite. Das letzte Bild zeigt die Frau
nun westlich ummontiert, bei
Heimreise an der Grenze. Eine Vis
vom Müll-Europa wird konfrontiert
pervertierter Folklore, die ihres vol
tümlichen Charakters ganz entkle
wurde, zur leeren Euphorie in frem
Sprache heruntergekommen. Die E
fremdung hat sie nun auch in der H
mat eingeholt, das bitterböse St
endet mit einem Aufschrei, „Rosema
Baby" von Polanski zitierend: Wäc
da ein Kind im Bauch heran oder
Geschwür? Europa begräbt sich
Müll, die Frauen singen am Schl
„Durch das Leben verlieren wir
selbst . . ." Die sich vom Müll nähr
wehren sich verzweifelt gegen den M
Am Ende ist eine große Unruhe
ihnen.

Žilniks „Gastarbeiter-Oper" bedi
sich aus dem Steinbruch der Kultur
schichte, hier werden souverän Vers
stücke zu einer Collage montiert,
über Emotionen und Aggressio
soziale und ökonomische Einsich
transportiert. Die Musik, die ebe
schmarotzt, kommentiert und sch
die Verhaltensweisen. Hinter Satire u
Polemik, Parodie und Ironie wird e
verzweifelte Menschlichkeit sicht
eine Parteinahme für die Frauen,
nicht nur als Arbeitskräfte, also ges
schaftlich, ausgebeutet werden, sond
auch als Frauen, also existentiell.
allein reagieren menschlich, die Män
sind die Bosse, mehr Symbole, Plak
der Herrschaft, als wirkliche Geg
spieler. Darin steckt die Gefahr
Mythologisierung, und es mag die
feministische Zug gewesen sein, der
einige scheu gewordene Bürokra
gleich Anarchismus vermuten ließ.
gibt in diesem Stück deutsche Spra
brocken (der Autor hat diese Spra
gelernt in München, nicht Schwedi
zum Beispiel, aber sie ist austausch
ein Kunstmittel), es gibt Brechts Ho
Wessel-Parodie (ja, auf deutsch: „
Metzger ruft, die Augen fest geschl
sen . . .") und es gibt schwarz-weiß-g
dene (nicht: schwarz-rot-goldene) K
ten, wenn der Mensch da als Ware m
braucht wird: „Ich muß mich imr
selbst anbieten, aber ich bekomme
den gerechten Preis!"

Aber dieses mit bitterer Schokol
überzogene schwarze Stück ist g
ohne nationalistische Töne (was
Vielvölkerstaat Jugoslawien ohne
nur schwer zu bewerkstelligen wä
und natürlich auch nicht etwa deuts
feindlich. Wenn westdeutsche Diplo
ten, die überdies den Collage-Charak
der „Gastarbeiter-Oper" übersahen,
ren unverhüllte antikapitalistische T
denz mit einer antideutschen Stimm
verwechseln, dann müssen sie das sc
auf die eigene Kappe nehmen. Sachv
stand, politischen wie ästhetischen, k
nen sie für sich jedenfalls nicht in A
spruch nehmen.

Nach einer Schrecksekunde, die

AUS DER PRESSE:
Frankfurter Rundschau, 16. März 1977, über Die Gastarbeiter-Oper.

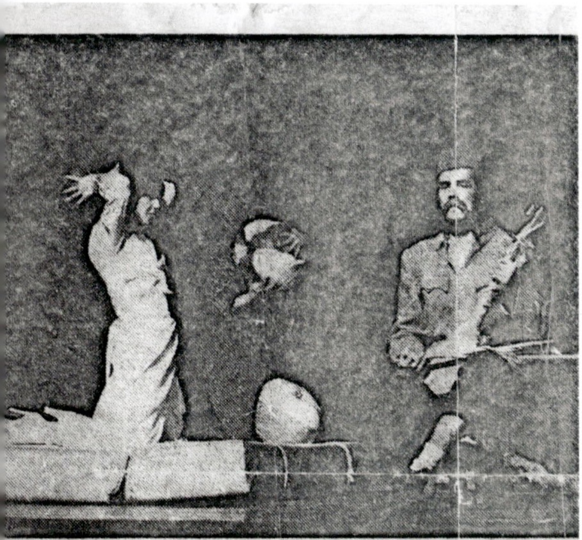

:zene aus dem „Gastarbeiter“-Musical von Zelimir Zilnik, das in Jugosla
e macht. Siehe unseren Bericht. Foto: Klu

Die Gastarbeiter-Oper (Gastarbajter opera)

Jugoslawien • 1977 • Theaterstück

Das erste Projekt, das Žilnik nach seiner Rückkehr aus Westdeutschland in Angriff nahm, war dieses Theaterstück, das auf der Experimentalbühne des Serbischen Nationaltheaters in Novi Sad aufgeführt wurde. Es ist ein Singstück in fünf Aufzügen und folgt verschiedenen jugoslawischen Frauen vom Lande, die als Gastarbeiterinnen nach Westdeutschland gehen. Dort begegnen sie neuen Arbeitsbedingungen, einer neuen Kultur und einer neuen Sprache. Während die jüngeren Frauen in der Lage sind, sich anzupassen, erleben die älteren Frauen Deutschland als Schock und Konflikt. Nach einer gewissen Zeit entschließt sich die ganze Gruppe, nach Jugoslawien zurückzukehren. Als sie die Grenze erreichen, und bevor sie sie noch überquert haben, stirbt die Hauptprotagonistin.

Das Stück war beides: kritisch und populär. Und es war ein Erfolg. Es wurde mehr als 80 Mal aufgeführt und gewann Preise bei verschiedenen Festivals. Aber einige Monate nach der Premiere beklagte sich der bundesdeutsche Kulturattaché in einem förmlichen Brief über das Stück, das er gesehen hatte: es enthalte das Horst-Wessel-Lied der Nazis, was er als antideutsche Provokation empfand. Daher forderte er dazu auf, das Stück aus dem Spielplan des Theaters zu nehmen. Als Antwort sandte ihm das Theater eine Höraufnahme zu, aus der hervorging, dass es sich bei dem Lied um eine Parodie von Bertolt Brecht handelte, in der sich der Dichter über das Nazi-Lied lustig macht und die Verse zu einem „Das Kalb marschiert“ verändert sind. Als Folge des Streits schrieben mehrere deutsche Zeitungen über das Stück, und es gab auch einen Bericht darüber im deutschen Fernsehen. •

VRIJ NEDERLAND 13 Juli 1996

MARBLE ASS

De travestiehelden van cineast Želimir Žilnik

AB VAN IEPEREN ■ *In het voormalige Joegoslavië zoekt iedereen nu een nieuwe identiteit. Travestieten doen dat vitaal en inventief, zegt Želimir Žilnik. Daarom koos hij hun scene als uitgangspunt voor zijn inmiddels veelgeprezen film 'Marble Ass'. Daarmee kreeg hij tot zijn verbazing eindelijk eens géén last in zijn land. Dat is nieuw voor de filmmaker, die wordt achtervolgd door verbanning en filmverboden. Žilnik over het leven als gokspel.*

In de late jaren zestig was er opeens een reeks films uit Oost-Europa die de aandacht trok. Ze kwamen vooral uit Tsjechoslowakije, Hongarije en Joegoslavië. Tijdens een kortstondige politieke luwte hadden jonge regisseurs de kans gegrepen om maatschappijkritische of juist provocerend onbekommerde films te maken. Zeer geprezen was *Rani Radovi* (*Early Works*) van de jeugdige Joegoslaaf Želimir Žilnik, over de *rebels without a cause* in zijn land. Anders dan de meesten van zijn collega's maakte Žilnik later geen carrière in het Westen met veel gelikte films, maar ook van filmactiviteit in eigen land werd weinig vernomen en niets geëxporteerd.

Tot hij vorig jaar op de festivals van Berlijn en Moskou *Marble Ass* presenteerde, een stilistisch ongepolijste en inhoudelijk verbazende film over de relatie tussen seks en oorlog. In Nederland werd *Marble Ass* onlangs vertoond op de Roze Filmdagen. De film geeft veel aandacht aan twee Servische prostitués in travestie, Merlyn en Salena (gespeeld door mannen die in werkelijkheid hetzelfde vak hebben). Hun betaalde gunsten werken als bliksemafleider voor agressieve frustraties in een geruïneerde samenleving. Ze geven geen seks, maar wel loyale zorg aan ex-soldaat Johnny die, psychisch verminkt door zijn oorlogservaringen, op een onafwendbaar fataal einde afstevent.

Žilnik, een aantrekkelijke en verrassend jeugdige vijftiger, blijkt een even bevlogen spreker als filmer te zijn. Hij onderbreekt zijn betoog regelmatig met vragen als: 'Interesseert het je wel?' of 'Wil je dit eigenlijk wel horen?' Jawel.

U was zevenentwintig toen uw eerste speelfilm grote waardering en verspreiding kreeg. Het leek alsof u een minstens zo grote reputatie te wachten stond als sommige succesvolle landgenoten.

'*Rani Radovi* is verkocht aan vijftig landen en heeft grote internationale prijzen gekregen, maar in eigen land kreeg ik enorme problemen. Eerst werd hij in beslag genomen, wat leidde tot een nogal geruchtmakend proces waarbij ik zelf optrad als verdediger van de film. Van de rechter mocht hij in de bioscoop, maar officieus werd vertoning nog steeds onmogelijk gemaakt door de partij. In die film werden zin en betekenis van revolutie betrekkelijk gesteld: of zoiets ooit kán leiden tot uiteindelijk geluk. Daarmee raak je de kern van elke samenleving die wordt gedicteerd door een partijprogramma. Mijn volgende film kreeg een algeheel verbod toen hij nog in de montage was. Er was toen – 1969, 1971 – niet alleen ideologische kritiek op mij, er was een hetze tegen álle jonge filmers: Makavejev, Pavlovic, Petrovic en anderen. Ze zeiden dat we uitsluitend nihilistische films maakten – de Zwarte Golf – en antisocialistisch waren. Terwijl sommige van de films ook in eigen land succes hadden en in het buitenland mooie publiciteit betekenden voor de liberale openheid van Tito's regime. Heel naïef dachten wij zelf ook dat we daar uitdrukking aan gaven. Maar in werkelijkheid was er al een neostalinistische bureaucratische dictatuur die iedereen de mond wilde snoeren. Filmers kregen geen subsidie meer. Als je na bijna dertig jaar terugkijkt, zie je dat niemand die periode goed te boven is gekomen. Dusan Makavejev en Aleksandar Petrovic moesten naar Parijs uitwijken en hebben elders nooit meer films gemaakt die zo goed waren als toen. Ik ben naar Duitsland gegaan waar mijn film een Gouden Beer had gekregen. Jonge collega's die zijn gebleven, belandden in de gevangenis.'

U hebt toch geen Duitse carrière gemaakt.

'Toen ik er kwam, begonnen Fassbinder, Herzog en Kluge succes te krijgen, er was veel staatssteun voor de nationale cinema. Ik dacht dat ik me in een gunstig klimaat bevond, tot ik na een paar maanden de hysterie rondom de Rote Armee Fraktion merkte, die akelig veel leek op wat ik had ervaren in mijn land. Alle vragen over wat de welvaartsstaat aanrichtte in natuur en milieu, de gecomputeriseerde beheersing van de arbeidersklasse, hoe provocerend en destructief ook gebracht – je schiet niks op met een warenhuis in brand steken – kwamen op een moment dat Duitsland op een kruising stond. Sinds de oorlog had het steeds open gestaan voor andere culturen, maar in de jaren zeventig kwam de vraag of die ontwikkeling naar een multiculturele democratie moest worden doorgezet, of dat er moest worden teruggegrepen naar een traditioneel nationalisme. Door die identiteitstwijfels voelde de staat zich buitenproportioneel bedreigd door de acties van in feite zo'n kleine groep.

Op het televisiejournaal zag ik hoe de politie een huis omsingelde waarin Raf-leden waren ondergedoken en iedereen die buiten kwam zonder meer neerschoot. Die beelden deden me denken aan de openbare executies in de vorige eeuw. Ik heb toen een documentair essay gemaakt: *Öffentliche Hinrichtung*, met de strekking dat wat politie, staat en televisie nu deden daarvan een moderne versie was, met dezelfde opzet het volk te intimideren. De film werd voorgelegd aan de Bewertungsstelle om een vertoningspredikaat. Ik kreeg een brief: de commissie voor freiwillige Selbstkontrolle heeft uw film technisch ondermaats bevonden en we vrezen dat u als buitenlander onvoldoende inzicht hebt in wat er in dit land gebeurt.

Verbolgen over de afwijzing besloot ik een stap verder te gaan en maakte met gratis medewerking van de crew een speelfilm: *Das Paradies*. Criminele ondernemers huren in het aangezicht van een bankroet veronderstelde terroristen om zich te laten kidnappen. Na een paar weken brengen ze hun gijzelnemers om, zodat ze naar buiten kunnen treden als overwinnaars van de anarchie die hun firma had willen saboteren. Mijn bron van inspiratie was een ultrarechtse parlementariër die gegijzeld was geweest en later steeds pochte dat een goede Duitsers altijd sterker blijkt dan het vuilis. Vlak voor de première werd Andreas Bader geliquideerd; echt niemand in Duitsland geloofde in zijn zelfmoord. De toevallige parallel met mijn filmverhaal leidde tot een fiks schandaal. De politie viel bij me binnen. Ze dachten dat ik connecties had met de terroristen – wat niet zo was – en hoewel ze niets vonden, moest ik het land uit. De film mocht ook twintig jaar lang niet worden vertoond. Binnen een paar jaar was ik tot twee maal toe banneling geworden en vier keer getroffen door filmverboden.'

U moest weer terug naar Joegoslavië.

'Ik dook daar onder in het theater. Het is curieus, je zou denken dat toneel bij uitstek officieel was en dienstbaar aan de staat, maar misschien juist daarom werd ik veel minder in de gaten gehouden. Ik had zelfs behoorlijk veel succes. Tot *Gastarbeiter Oper*, in 1977, een eigen stuk waarin ik songs van Brecht en Weill had gebruikt. Ook een parodie die Brecht had gemaakt op het nazistische Horst Wesellied. De voorstelling werd erg gewaardeerd, maar de Duitse ambassade protesteerde. Ze dachten dat het mijn tekst was en eisten stopzetting van de opvoeringen. Omdat de staat belang hechtte aan een goede relatie met Duitsland kreeg ik een werkverbod in het theater. Filmsubsidie kon ik ook niet krijgen, ik zat echt op de bodem van de put. Ik was begin dertig, dacht: ik moet opnieuw beginnen. Ik ging lezen over mensen die in hun pogingen om iets voor de samenleving te betekenen op non-actief waren gezet. Ik las hoe Isaak Babel naar Maxim Gorki was gegaan om advies. Gorki had hem gezegd: ga onder het volk.

Dat leek me een goede raad, dat ging ik doen. Ik maakte documentaires over het leven van alledag, een soort immense kroniek van in totaal vijftien films voor de televisie. Ze waren heel succesvol – ook op televisiefestivals waarvan de filmwereld geen weet heeft – en volgens mij zijn sommige daarvan het beste wat ik heb gedaan.'

Voor iemand die steeds last had van censuur en bureaucratie, lijkt bij de televisie gaan werken, vragen om moeilijkheden.

'Zelf had ik ook weinig soepelheid van de televisie verwacht, maar televisie vreet programma's die altijd vrij simpel zijn geproduceerd, met minder fasen waarop de staat vat kan krijgen. Ik mocht in alle vrijheid en in een ontspannen sfeer programma's maken, omdat ze dachten dat ze bij uitzending nog konden knippen, toevoegen of veranderen wat hun ideologisch niet aanstond. Het interessante is dat dat nooit is gebeurd, terwijl ik soms kritischer was dan in de bioscoopfilms waarmee ik last had gekregen. Ik heb een dramatisch portret gefilmd van kinderen van teruggekeerde gastarbeiders, die onbeholpen waren in hun moedertaal omdat die alleen thuis in de keuken was gesproken, terwijl ze op school en straat de vreemde taal wel goed hadden geleerd. Al zijn ze nog zo begaafd, terug op de Joegoslavische scholen worden zij geminacht en geweerd als achterlijke boeren. Ze worden kansloos gemaakt in plaats dat ze worden beschouwd als mogelijke bruggenbouwers naar de rest van de wereld.

Voor die films heb ik tien jaar lang door Joegoslavië gereisd en gezien hoe riskant en zelfdestructief de maatschappij functioneerde. Dus was ik – helaas! – niet al te verbaasd toen alles uit elkaar barstte, al was er ook genoeg ervaring en kracht waarmee het land zich wél had kunnen ontwikkelen tot een echte democratie. Tito's socialisme heeft een immense bureaucratie gecreëerd. Niet alleen de overheid, maar ook bij industrieën in de steden. Het land telde miljoenen klerken, was verdeeld in velerlei hiërarchieën met alle parasitisme van dien. Boeren en ongeschoolde arbeiders waren daarvan uitgesloten, zodat de spanning tussen platteland en stad steeds meer groeide.'

U noemde wat met Joegoslavië is gebeurd een Oedipus-tragedie.

'Na Tito's dood deden zich drie fenomenen voor. Ten eerste die bijna middeleeuwse oorlog tussen zijn opvolgers: zonen die in de schaduw van een autoritaire vader hadden gestaan en eigen feodale staten gingen formeren ter bescherming van status en eigenbelang en eindelijk zelf een greep waagden naar de roem. Ten tweede trilde niet alleen het socialisme op zijn grondvesten, maar ook de kerk, wat de identiteitscrises vergrootte. Alle bureaucraten waren doodsbang voor de gevolgen van verandering en bekeerden zich tot het nationalisme, dat niet zou leiden tot analyse van het verleden. Het was verbijsterend om te zien hoe miljoenen communisten zich op [illegible] profi-

58 VRIJ NEDERLAND 13 juli 1996

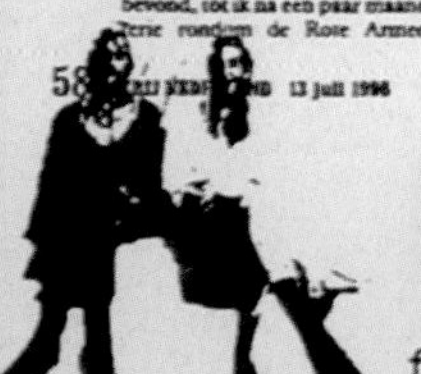

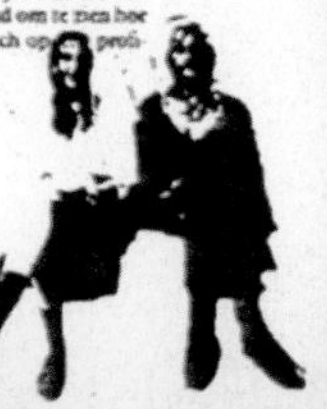

MARBLE ASS

film by Želimir Žilnik

AUS DER PRESSE: *Vrij Nederland*, 13. Juli 1996, über *Marble Ass*.

Ich habe meinen ersten Film nach der „Riskier-es-Methode“ gemacht. Ich habe die gesamte Crew aus Leuten zusammengestellt, die bereit waren, ohne Vorauszahlung zu arbeiten. Filme, die als „sichere“ Investition galten, mussten ein fertiges Drehbuch und einen Drehplan haben, um wirklich in Produktion zu gehen, und dann wurde ein Budget bereitgestellt. Ich hatte kein Budget, und ich hatte auch kein detailliertes Drehbuch und konnte auch keines haben, deshalb hatte ich beschlossen, zu improvisieren.

—Želimir Žilnik im Gespräch mit Dubravka Sekulić, Gal Kirn und Žiga Testen, in: Gal Kirn, Dubravka Sekulić und Žiga Testen (Hg.), *Surfing the Black: Yugoslav Black Wave Cinema and Its Transgressive Moments* (Maastricht: Jan van Eyck Academie 2012), S. 67.

Žilnik beschränkte seine Herangehensweise nicht auf eine gewisse humanistische Empathie mit den Benachteiligten, sondern erforschte die Unvorhersagbarkeit der politischen und gesellschaftlichen Rolle dieser Gruppe. Seine Vorgehensweise ist frei von Sentimentalität, aber er hat (im Unterschied zur Modernisierung-von-oben, was die Tendenz der Kulturpolitik war) ein Verständnis für eine bestimmte Kreativität-von-unten, die Žilnik beobachtet und später in seine Filme, vor allem die Fernsehproduktionen der 1980er Jahre, einbezieht.

—Branislav Dimitrijević, „Behind Scepticism Lies the Fire of a Revolutionary!“, in: *For an Idea – Against the Status Quo: Analysis and Systematization of Želimir Žilnik's Artistic Practice* (Novi Sad: New Media Center_kuda.org, Playground produkcija 2009), S. 144 f.

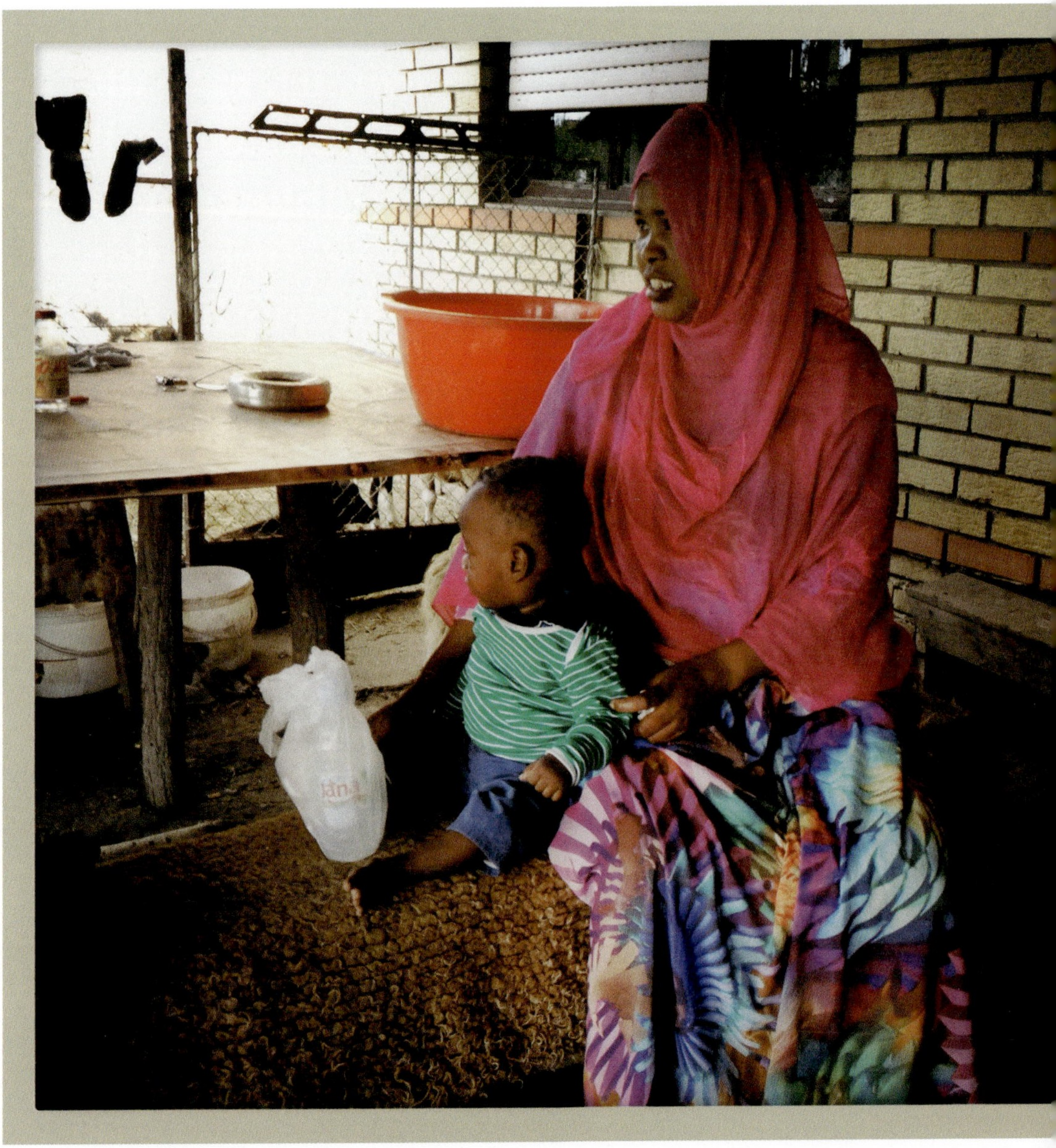

Destination_Serbistan (Produktionsfoto), 2015.
FOTO: ORFEAS SKUTELIS.

GREG DE CUIR JR

Schwarzerde

Präskript

Kohlenstoff wurde oft als König der Elemente bezeichnet. Es handelt sich um ein nichtmetallisches Element in der 14. Gruppe des Periodensystems mit der Ordnungszahl 6, einem Schmelzpunkt von 3 550 °C (6 420 °F) und einem Siedepunkt von 4 827 °C (8 721 °F). Im Jahr 1961 wurde das Isotop Kohlenstoff-12 ausgewählt, um Sauerstoff als die Maßeinheit zu ersetzen, nach der die atomare Masse aller anderen Elemente gemessen wird. Kohlenstoff ist, wie es sich für einen guten Anführer gehört, ein lehrreiches Vorbild für seinesgleichen. Dank eines ihm kollektiv zugeschriebenen Rechts regiert er auf eine Art und Weise, die die Gemeinschaft stärkt, der er zugleich dient und angehört.

Kohlenstoff ist König, weil er mehr chemische Verbindungen aufweist als alle anderen Elemente zusammen. Außerdem ist er mit einer Masse von knapp neunzehn Prozent, nach Sauerstoff, das zweithäufigste Element im menschlichen Körper. Tatsächlich gehört Kohlenstoff zu den wenigen Elementen, die seit der Antike bekannt sind. Im 19. Jahrhundert vermutete man, dass die meisten bekannten Kohlenstoffverbindungen aus lebenden Organismen stammen. Elementarer Kohlenstoff kommt hingegen in mehreren Erscheinungsformen vor, von denen jede ihre eigenen physikalischen Eigenschaften und besonderen Anwendungsbereiche hat.

Humus besteht zu etwa sechzig Prozent aus Kohlenstoff. Humus ist eine tote, stark zerkleinerte organische Substanz im Boden, die durch die mikrobielle Zersetzung von pflanzlichen und tierischen Substanzen entsteht. Obwohl es sich um eine tote Substanz handelt, dient sie dem Leben. Während des Zersetzungsprozesses transformieren sich ihre Bestandteile zu Bausteinen, die von Pflanzen aufgenommen werden können. Daher wird Humus von Landwirten und Gärtnern geschätzt. Seine Farbigkeit reicht von braun bis schwarz. Man könnte die Hypothese wagen, dass Humus umso nährstoffreicher und wertvoller ist, je dunkler seine Farbe ist, doch diese Annahme bedürfte einer weiteren wissenschaftlichen Begründung.[01]

Schwarzerde enthält einen hohen Humus-Anteil, der von vier bis sechzehn Prozent reicht und Schwarzerde zu einem sehr fruchtbaren Weideland macht, das hohe landwirtschaftliche Erträge erbringen kann. Im 19. Jahrhundert waren Legenden über die sagenhafte Fruchtbarkeit der Schwarzerde und die Leichtigkeit, mit der man sie bewirtschaften konnte, weit verbreitet. Sie wurde als ein besonderer Boden beschrieben und ist bis heute immer noch eine Art Wunder, auch wenn wir ihre Eigenschaften und Werte mithilfe wissenschaftlicher Tatsachen erklären können.

Weltweit gibt es nur zwei Schwarzerde-Gürtel, und einer von ihnen ist die eurasische Steppe. Die Erforschung dieser sagenumwobenen natürlichen Substanz begann in einem prägenden Entwicklungsstadium der Bodenwissenschaft. Die Identifikation und Klassifizierung

01 Die Angaben zu Kohlenstoff und Humus stammen von der Website britannica.com.

der Schwarzerde, auch Tschernosem genannt, im Jahr 1883, wird überwiegend dem russischen Geologen und Geografen Wassili Dokutschajew zugeschrieben. Dokutschajew betrachtete das Erdreich als „einen natürlichen Körper, der seine eigene Entstehungs- und Entwicklungsgeschichte hat, einen Körper, in dem komplexe und vielgestaltige Prozesse stattfinden."[02] Tatsächlich gilt Dokutschajew allgemein als Begründer der Bodenwissenschaft, was zum großen Teil seiner visionären, anthropomorphisierenden Auffassung des Bodens geschuldet ist. Doch es gab einen anderen Wissenschaftler, der Dokutschajew vorausging und dessen Arbeit den Grundstein für spätere Erkenntnisse legte.

Der Österreicher Franz Josef Ruprecht erhielt Anfang des 19. Jahrhunderts eine Einladung nach Russland, um dort an einem Botanischen Museum zu arbeiten. Es dauerte nicht lange, bis die Eurasische Steppe mit ihrer fantastischen Erde seine Aufmerksamkeit fand. Im Jahr 1866 verfasste Ruprecht einen einflussreichen Artikel mit dem Titel *Über den Ursprung und die wissenschaftliche Bedeutung des Tschernosjom oder Schwarzerde Russlands. Geobotanische Untersuchungen*. Dieser Text ist nicht nur bedeutsam, weil er bahnbrechende Leistungen beschrieb, sondern auch, weil er den Begriff geobotanisch einführte. Der Titel des Artikels belegt zudem, dass die Bezeichnung Tschernosjom oder Tschernosem bereits zirkulierte – vielleicht sogar lange, bevor Ruprecht sie in Umlauf brachte. Sie wird gemeinhin von Bauern, Landwirten und anderen verwendet worden sein, die den Boden bearbeiteten und von der großen Nähe zu ihm geprägt waren – denn das russische Kompositum chernozem bedeutet einfach schwarzer Ackerboden oder, wie wir metaphorischer und abstrakter sagen, schwarze Erde.

★

Die Eröffnungseinstellung von *Destination_Serbistan* (2015) zeigt, wie das strömende Flutwasser Ablagerungen und andere Überreste wegschwemmt. Der Schauplatz ist Südosteuropa, wo es 2014, ausgelöst durch die stärksten Niederschläge in dieser Region seit einhundertzwanzig Jahren, zu starken Überschwemmungen kam. Genauer gesagt, ist der Schauplatz die Serbische Republik, und die beiden Männer, die auf das vorbeiströmende Wasser hinuntersehen und es erstaunt betrachten, scheinen Reisende zu sein.

Die Bewegung der Blockfreien Staaten wurde formell 1961 in Belgrad gegründet, das damals zur Sozialistischen Republik Serbien innerhalb der Sozialistischen Föderativen Republik Jugoslawien gehörte. Die Staaten, die sich dieser Bewegung anschlossen, waren geopolitisch mit keiner der beiden damals dominierenden Mächte – den Vereinigten Staaten von Amerika und der Union der Sozialistischen Sowjetrepubliken – verbündet. Man könnte die Bewegung der Blockfreien als eine De-facto-Gipfelkonferenz bezeichnen, die die Staaten des Globalen Südens verband und dadurch die Mehrheit von People of Color auf der Welt zusammenschloss. Mehrere afrikanische Länder gehörten zu den Gründungsmitgliedern der

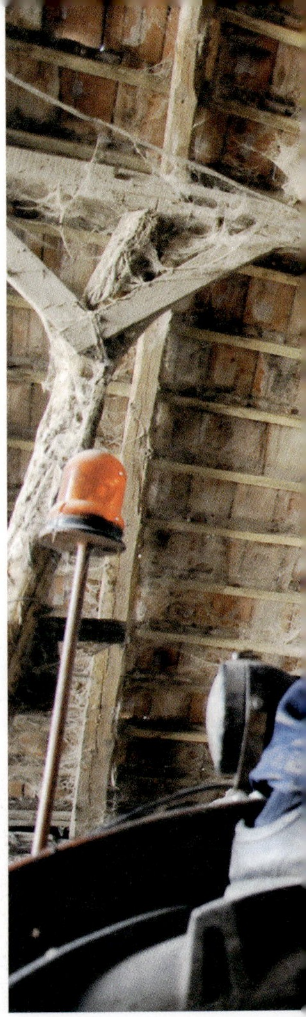

02
N. A. Krasilnikov, „Soil Microorganisms and Higher Plants", Moskau 1958, https://soilandhealth.org/wp-content/uploads/01aglibrary/010112.krasilnikov.pdf; übersetzt aus dem Englischen von Barbara Hess.

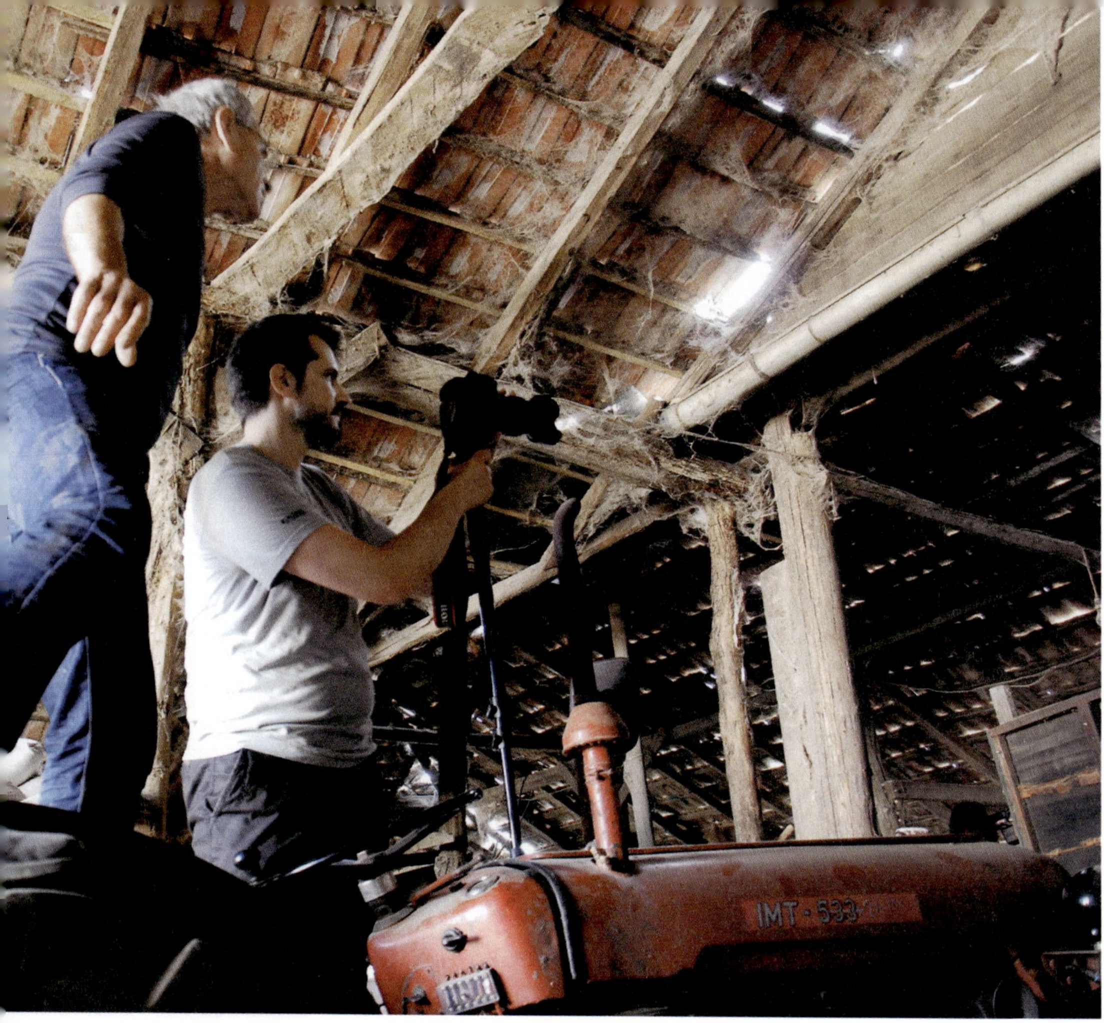

Želimir Žilnik und Orfeas Skutelis bei den Dreharbeiten zu *Destination_Serbistan*, 2015. FOTO: LEON ŠURBANOVIĆ.

Blockfreien-Bewegung, und bis auf zwei Ausnahmen sind alle afrikanischen Nationen derzeit dort organisiert. Der jugoslawische Präsident Josip Broz Tito hatte immer eine gewisse Affinität zu Afrika verspürt. Als echter politischer Abtrünniger war Tito nur selten auf offiziellen Staatsbesuchen in den USA oder der UdSSR. Doch er wurde von zahlreichen afrikanischen Ländern eingeladen, bereiste den Kontinent ausgiebig, und stets wurde ihm dort der rote Teppich ausgerollt. Zu den ursprünglichen Prinzipien der Blockfreien-Bewegung gehörten gegenseitiger Respekt, Gleichheit und friedliche Koexistenz. Obwohl diese Grundsätze bis heute gelten, werden sie nicht immer in die Praxis umgesetzt, insbesondere nicht auf dem Gebiet des früheren Jugoslawiens, vom Rest Europas ganz zu schweigen.

Auch der Künstler Želimir Žilnik, der während des Aufstiegs Jugoslawiens aufwuchs, wurde durch die frühen 1960er Jahre geprägt. In praktischer Hinsicht bedeutete dies, dass er genügend Zeit hatte, um Jura zu studieren und gleichzeitig als Hauptorganisator des Kulturzentrums Tribüne der Jugend in seiner Heimatstadt Novi Sad zu arbeiten. Während dieser parallelen Aktivitäten entwickelte er

ein Interesse für Filmkunst, engagierte sich im Kino Klub Novi Sad und begann, nonkonformistische kurze Amateurfilme zu drehen, was ihm bald die Gelegenheit gab, professionelle Filme zu machen. Ein weiterer Vorzug der Blockfreien-Bewegung waren verbesserte Möglichkeiten für Bürgerinnen und Bürger anderer Nationen, das sozialistische Jugoslawien zu bereisen, was auch den freieren Austausch von Gedanken und Kulturen förderte. Es war für Žilnik nichts Ungewöhnliches, mit Studierenden aus ganz Afrika und aus anderen blockfreien Staaten zusammenzutreffen. Daher wurde seine Einstellung frühzeitig von politischen Idealen geprägt, die das Andere wertschätzten und die gerade aufgrund von engen Kontakten und interkulturellen Netzwerken der gegenseitigen Unterstützung und des Austauschs gediehen. Diese kulturelle Wertvorstellung stand nicht nur im Zentrum der Identität des sozialistischen Jugoslawiens, sondern lässt sich in dieser Region weit zurückverfolgen in die Zeit vor den beiden Jugoslawiens des 20. Jahrhunderts: vom 19. Jahrhundert über das Habsburger und das Ottomanische Reich bis ins 6. Jahrhundert, als verschiedene slawische Stämme in die Pannonische Tiefebene einwanderten. Diese war um die Zeit von Christi Geburt eine Provinz des Römischen Reiches und wurde nach Pan, dem Gott der Natur, benannt.

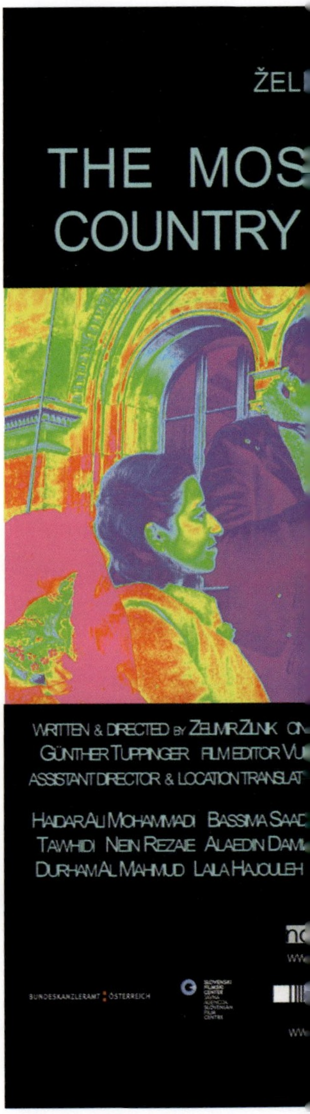

Das schönste Land der Welt (Poster, Gestaltung: Peter Roehsler), 2018

Die beiden Männer, die in *Destination_Serbistan* auf der Brücke über dem aufgewühlten Wasser stehen, sind afrikanische Migranten, die zu verstehen versuchen, was diese Fluten für die Lebensperspektiven in Serbien – für sie ebenso wie für die Bürgerinnen und Bürger dieses Staates – bedeuten. Man könnte diese bildhafte Symbolik für unsensibel halten, da die Migration nach Europa oft auf grausame Weise als Welle, Schwarm oder Flut bezeichnet wird – Begriffe, die an Katastrophen biblischen Ausmaßes denken lassen. Doch Žilnik kehrt diese Symbolik der Strafe um und nutzt sie stattdessen als Symbol für etwas, das ihn in seiner gesamten Laufbahn beschäftigt hat: kollektive Arbeit. Um genauer zu sein, interkulturelle, transnationale Arbeit. Der folgende Abschnitt des Films zeigt in einer langen wortlosen Sequenz die Arbeit, die dazu dient, die von der Überflutung beschädigten Häuser zu retten und die Trümmer zu beseitigen, damit der Wiederaufbau beginnen kann. Einer der beiden Afrikaner auf der Brücke, Lee – einer der Protagonisten, die wir durch den gesamten Film begleiten werden –, ist dabei zu sehen, wie er an dieser Arbeit teilnimmt, gemeinsam mit seinen Kollegen, darunter Serben sowie Migranten aus Afrika und dem Nahen Osten.

Bleiben wir einen Moment bei dieser frühen Sequenz und erfreuen uns an der Vision, die sich dort zeigt. Sie erinnert an das Goldene Zeitalter der Blockfreien-Bewegung, das zugleich die Hochphase der Mythologisierung kollektiver Arbeit war. Wir sehen zugleich eine Momentaufnahme davon, wie ein modernes Europa funktionieren könnte und vielleicht funktionieren muss: Verschiedene People of Color, Ethnien, Nationen und Glaubensvorstellungen verbünden sich, um eine neue, menschlichere Gesellschaft aufzubauen, eine bessere Gesellschaft, die auf gegenseitiger Unterstützung beruht;

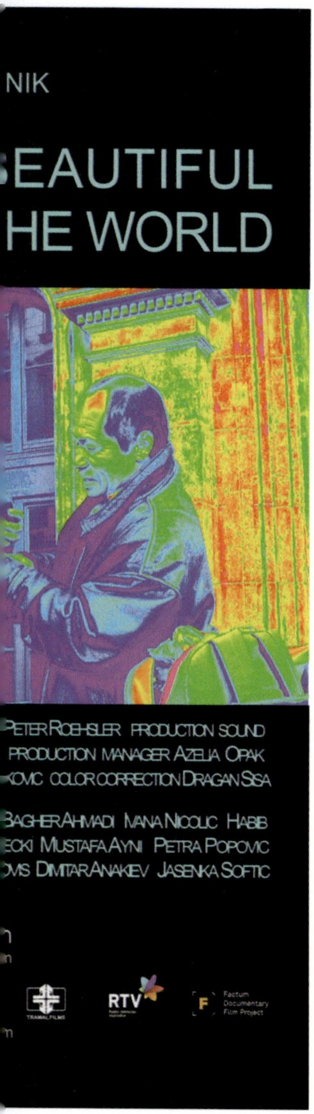

einer Unterstützung, die man vor über fünfzig Jahren in Belgrad vereinbarte, als das Prinzip der Blockfreiheit als politische Praxis zum ersten Mal gestärkt wurde. Diese Sequenz könnte eine der utopischsten in Žilniks Werk sein. Doch wie so viele andere in seinem Œuvre wird sie ohne jede ästhetische oder emotionale Übertreibung behandelt. Sie wird vielmehr zu einer Tatsache, einer rationalen Schlussfolgerung. Sie zeigt, wie die Welt funktionieren sollte – und wie sie vielleicht sogar einmal funktioniert hat. Zweifellos hat Žilniks Welt – für kurze Zeit – auf diese Weise funktioniert. Sein Kino funktioniert auf diese Weise, weil er Teile seiner früheren Welt und alles, wofür sie stand, in sich trägt. Auch wenn ihn die Welt mehr als einmal enttäuscht haben sollte, ist er ein Künstler, der seinen Glauben nie verloren hat. Vielleicht ist es gerade das, was ihn überhaupt erst zum Künstler macht.

In den vergangenen fünf Jahren gab es nicht wenige Kunstwerke, darunter auch Filme und Videos, die sich mit der Situation von Migrantinnen und Migranten in Europa auseinandergesetzt haben. Manche dieser Arbeiten bringen ihren Macherinnen und Machern Auszeichnungen und andere Formen von kulturellem Kapital ein. Manche haben große Budgets und reizvolle Effekte, die die Aufmerksamkeit entweder auf die Meisterschaft der Filmschaffenden oder auf die Beharrlichkeit ihres engagierten Standpunkts lenken. Doch nur wenige können einen Film wie *Destination_Serbistan* machen, in dem Migranten im Mittelpunkt stehen und an einer Überschreitung der Grenze zwischen Spiel- und Dokumentarfilm beteiligt sind, die zugleich eine Überschreitung von Herrschaftsprinzipien und eine Überschreitung des Mythos vom allein schaffenden, genialischen Auteur ist. Die für Žilniks Arbeit charakteristische Großzügigkeit zeigt sich darin, wie er die Reisenden, die sich auf der Balkanroute bewegen, und diejenigen, denen sie unterwegs begegnen, darstellt. Žilniks Verhältnis zu seinen Protagonisten und sein Verhältnis zu den ethischen Fallstricken des Genres wird in der Schlusssequenz seines Films erkennbar, in der wir auch die helfende Hand des Regisseurs sehen.

Über die Frage nach dem Zusammenhang zwischen der Ethik des Dokumentarfilms und seinen interventionistischen Möglichkeiten ist schon viel Tinte geflossen. Die Debatte darüber, ob Regisseure hinter der Kamera hervortreten sollten, um sich in das Leben ihrer Protagonisten einzumischen, ist immer noch relevant und ungelöst. Eine solche Einmischung ist für gewöhnlich dann gefragt, wenn dieses Leben an einem Scheideweg steht und gute Taten Mangelware sind, sodass die Filmemacher und -macherinnen die Konstruktion einer nahtlosen Repräsentation aufbrechen. Für Žilnik ist diese Frage entscheidend. Er hat immer interveniert. Für diejenigen, die nicht selbst an vorderster Front agieren und denen ihre Arbeit wichtiger ist als das menschliche Material, das sie dazu brauchen, ist die Diskussion über eine moralische Haltung ein Luxusproblem. Žilnik nähert sich ihr aus der entgegengesetzten Richtung. Kurz vor dem Ende von *Destination_Serbistan*, als Lee und sein Begleiter auf

dieser Reise, Stanley, kurz vor der ungarischen Grenze angekommen sind – das heißt, an der Grenze zur Europäischen Union, die das Ziel der meisten ist –, begegnen sie einer Gruppe von Migrantinnen und Migranten aus dem Nahen Osten, die in einem verlassenen Gebäude Schutz suchen. Sie sind tagelang auf der tückischen Balkanroute unterwegs gewesen, und einer von ihnen hat wunde Füße, die ihn nicht weitertragen werden. Das ist ein schwer erträglicher Anblick und in gewisser Weise auch der Höhepunkt des Films. Nachdem die beiden Protagonisten ein paar ermutigende Worte an sie gerichtet haben, kommt ein Mitglied des Produktionsteams ins Bild und reicht ihnen eine Salbe, die helfen soll, die wunden Füße des Reisenden zu heilen. Diese beiläufige Geste hat eine enorme Bedeutung für den Film und seine Gesamtwirkung, seine implizite Argumentation. Es ist ein Moment, der ganz beiläufig daherkommt, der nicht gespielt ist, um eine dramatische oder reflexive Wirkung zu entfalten. Aber es ist eine der bedeutsamsten Gesten des zeitgenössischen europäischen Films. Wegen dieser Hand sollte man sich an Žilnik erinnern. Vielleicht ist es sogar seine eigene.

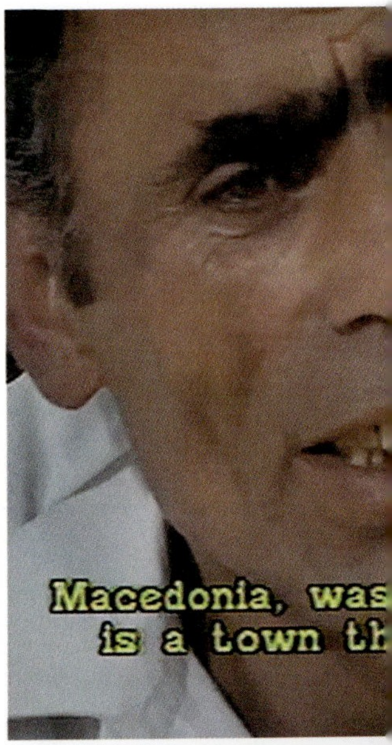

Der Film endet mit einer Einstellung, in der Stanley in der Ferne verschwindet, in Richtung der ungarischen Grenze und in eine ungewisse Zukunft in der Europäischen Union. Der Fernsehfilm *Schwarz und weiß* (1990) beginnt umgekehrt: Ein Mann aus Afrika, Reuben, fährt per Anhalter auf der Autobahn nach Serbien, genauer gesagt nach Novi Sad, wo er früher einmal studiert hat und wo er eine Freundin zurückließ. Ein unmittelbares Ergebnis der Blockfreien-Bewegung war, dass zahlreiche junge Menschen aus dem Globalen Süden nach Jugoslawien gingen, um dort zu studieren. Reuben ist ein Beispiel für diese Studierenden, und Žilnik interessiert sich hier dafür, zu untersuchen, wie er in eine Gesellschaft reintegriert wird, die er einmal kannte, die sich jedoch Ende der 1980er Jahre, als er zuletzt in Serbien lebte, in etwas anderes verwandelte.

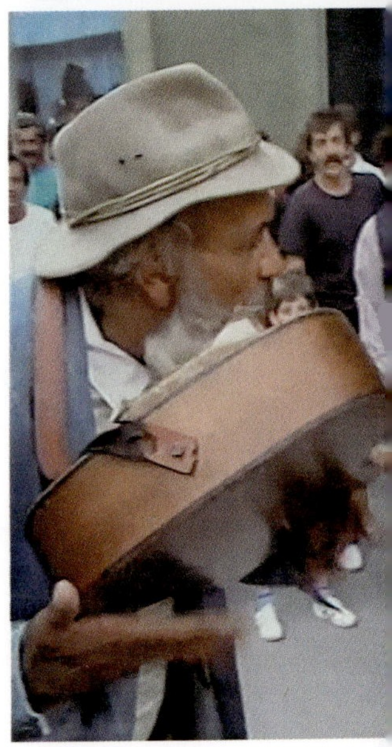

Schwarz und weiß (Standbilder), 1990
Unten rechts: Reuben Oyeyle

Schwarz und weiß enthält eine Szene, in der Reuben eine Roma-Familie besucht und sich mit ihren Mitgliedern über ihren Hintergrund unterhält. Sie erwähnen, dass sie Wurzeln in Ägypten haben und dass Präsident Gamal Abdel Nasser einmal Präsident Tito gefragt haben soll, ob alle Ägypter in ihr Ursprungsland zurückgeschickt werden sollten. Titos Antwort lautete nein, denn, wie die Familie im Film feststellt, die Roma seien sein schönstes und bestes Volk. Es ist fraglich, ob diese Anekdote wahr ist und ob Tito wirklich so viel Respekt an den Tag legte. Trotzdem ist diese Geschichte vielsagend, wie so oft, wenn es um Übertreibungen geht. Es gibt eine Legende, einen Mythos, eine Tradition der interkulturellen Toleranz, die in Jugoslawien und insbesondere in der Region von Novi Sad herrschte. Die Menschen spürten diese Ideologie, verließen sich auf sie und nutzten sie sogar als moralische und emotionale Unterstützung. Man stelle sich ein europäisches Land vor, in dem Minderheiten heute wirklich das Gefühl hätten, dass die Verantwortlichen sie niemals im Stich lassen würden, dass sie das Salz dieses besonderen Stücks Erde wären und dass sie innerhalb der Grenzen dieser Nation immer

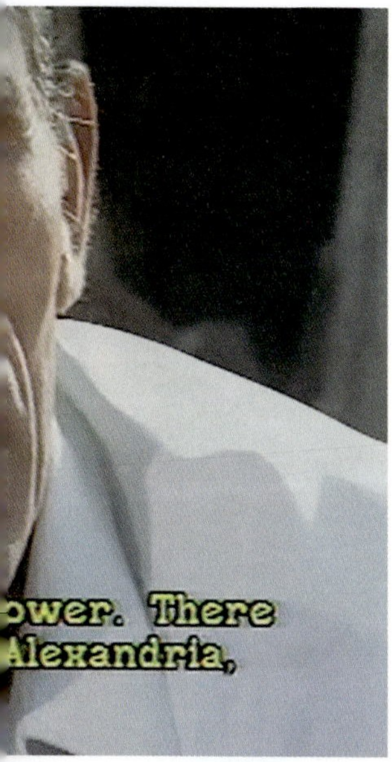

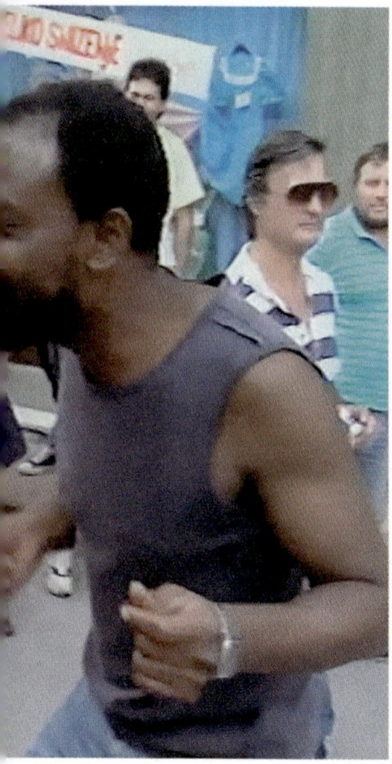

ein Zuhause hätten. Das Ironische an dieser Situation ist, dass dieses Gefühl auf dem Gebiet des ehemaligen Jugoslawiens, auf dem einmal zahlreiche Ethnien zusammenlebten, heute stärker geschwunden ist als in anderen europäischen Nationen, die eine solche Bewegung von ethnischen Gruppen und ein Wiederausgleichen der nationalen Demografie nie erfahren haben. Selbstverständlich haben auch wirtschaftliche Gründe und politische Veränderungen zu diesem gesellschaftlichen Strukturwandel beitragen, doch rückblickend können wir das sozialistische Jugoslawien schon als ein Exempel für die beste Sammlung von Nationen und Ethnien hochhalten.

Auch die kurze Parabel über Ägypten, Stämme im Exil und den Wunsch, Menschen zurückzuholen und sie zur Rückkehr zu drängen, hat etwas Biblisches. Die Menschen in *Schwarz und weiß* sind nicht verwurzelt. Reuben ist immer auf Reisen. Auch Reubens serbischer Freund Saša ist aus London nach Novi Sad zurückgekehrt, ist jedoch am Ende des Films erneut unterwegs. Sašas Vater, Steve, gibt sein Haus auf und verbringt die meiste Zeit auf einem salaš, einem Gehöft, wo er versucht, wieder ein Gefühl dafür zu bekommen, wer er ist. Milena, Reubens Freundin, darf das Haus nicht mehr verlassen, nachdem ihr Vater herausgefunden hat, dass sie in einer Beziehung mit einem Afrikaner lebt. Auch der obdachlose Musiker, den Reuben und Saša schlafend unter Steves Fenster finden, führt ein nichtsesshaftes Leben.

Salz war in biblischer Zeit eine äußerst wichtige Substanz und eines der bedeutendsten Symbole. Salz machte den Boden fruchtbar und wurde auch als Währung verwendet. Die Vorstellung, dass Menschen das Salz der Erde sind, lässt sich bis in das Neue Testament zurückverfolgen; dort heißt es in der Einheitsübersetzung des Evangeliums nach Matthäus (Mt 5, 13): „Ihr seid das Salz der Erde. Wenn das Salz seinen Geschmack verliert, womit kann man es wieder salzig machen? Es taugt zu nichts mehr, außer weggeworfen und von den Leuten zertreten zu werden." Das kann als Warnung verstanden werden: Verliert nicht die Würze, die Vielfalt, die wunderbaren Eigenheiten der Männer und Frauen, sonst geht etwas Elementares und Grundlegendes verloren. Dies ist die subtextuelle Botschaft von Reubens Anwesenheit in Novi Sad und zugleich die Botschaft von Žilniks Film, ein warnendes Beispiel für die Region und darüber hinaus, ebenso wie die Verse aus der Offenbarung des Johannes, die Sašas Freund ihm und Reuben vorträgt.

Žilnik plädiert in *Schwarz und weiß* nicht nur implizit dafür, die Gesellschaft durch kulturellen Austausch und gute Kontakte zu verbessern, sondern er macht aus dem Film ein Genre-Pastiche. *Schwarz und weiß* beginnt und endet unterwegs, und seine Protagonisten sind immer auf der Durchreise. Es wird das Genre des Roadmovies evoziert, in dem die Charaktere einen vorbestimmten Weg verfolgen müssen, ihr Ziel jedoch nie erreichen. Der Film enthält auch Elemente des romantischen Melodrams, in dessen Zentrum eine verbotene Liebe steht und in dem sich die ganze Welt gegen die beiden Liebenden

verschworen zu haben scheint. Dann ist da noch der Western mit seinen fernab der Städte gelegenen Schauplätzen, Pferden, Farmen und Schießereien. Auch die Filmmusik kann als Pastiche oder Melange betrachtet werden: Afrikanische Rhythmen verbinden sich mit afroamerikanischen Spirituals, die Reuben und seine Kollegen vortragen. Steve spielt mit seiner Band Heavy Metal, und auch die Rockmusik seiner Jugend spielt eine Rolle. Und dann sind da noch die ikonischen Melodien von Ennio Morricone, der die Filmmusik für die berühmten Western von Sergio Leone komponierte. Aus all dem entsteht eine Welt, in der sich verschiedene Kulturen mischen und sich gegenseitig bereichern.

Sašas eingangs erwähnter Freund, der nach einem sündigen Leben religiös wird, spricht über die Endzeit, die letzten Tage und das Feuer, das dann vom Himmel fallen wird. Später im Film bringt Reuben dem obdachlosen Musiker den Gospelsong *When the Saints Go Marching In* bei, ein altes Spiritual mit Bibelzitaten aus der Apokalypse, das davon spricht, dass die Sterne vom Himmel fallen werden und der Mond vom Blutvergießen rot werden wird. Dies sind ganz unverhohlene Warnungen an die Figuren des Films, deren Welt aufgrund von Korruption, Intoleranz und anderer tödlicher Missetaten außer Kontrolle gerät. Dies ist nicht das berühmte, freundliche Novi Sad, sondern eine Region, die von einer Art Fieber befallen ist. Wenn wir dem Song *Paranoid* nachgehen, der den Film wie ein Leitmotiv strukturiert, bekommt man vielleicht einen besseren Eindruck von dem Leid, das die Region heimgesucht hat. Steve probt mit seiner provisorischen Band ständig diesen Titel der Gruppe Black Sabbath. Die Lyrics erzählen von einem Gefühl der Unzufriedenheit, dem Wunsch nach innerer Ruhe, von der Blindheit für das wahre Glück und davon, dass es zu spät sei, um das Leben zu genießen. Der Bandname Black Sabbath erinnert an den Titel von Žilniks Film, hat aber auch biblische Konnotationen. Der Sabbat dient dem Gottesdienst und ist ein Tag, an dem die Arbeit ruht. Die Band dachte bei ihrer Namensfindung allerdings vermutlich eher an den Hexensabbat, ein mitternächtliches Treffen von Hexen. Sašas Freund fürchtet diese Teufelsanbetung, die für ihn das Anbrechen der letzten Tage ankündigt – und er liegt mit seiner Vorhersage nicht ganz falsch, da sich Novi Sad tatsächlich für alle Protagonistinnen und Protagonisten des Films als ein unhaltbares Vorhaben erweist.

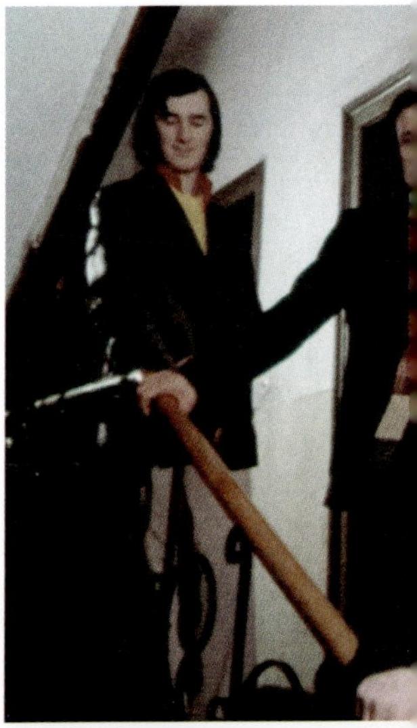

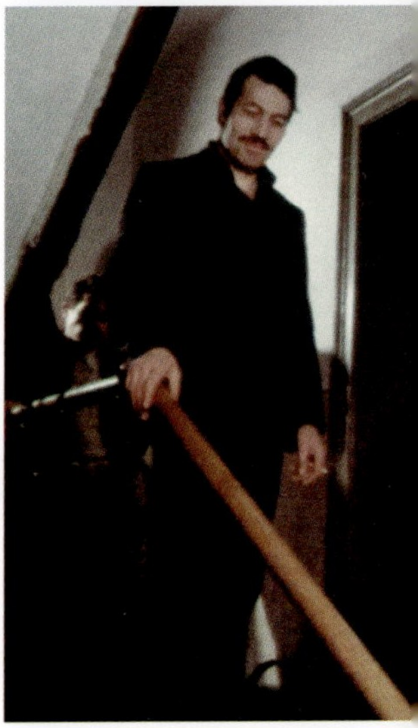

Inventur – Metzstraße 11 (Standbilder), 1975

In der Art und Weise, wie Grenzen behandelt werden und wie der Internationalismus Vorrang erhält, sind sich *Schwarz und weiß* und *Destination_Serbistan* sehr ähnlich. Grenzen müssen überschritten werden, auch wenn die Aussichten, auf der anderen Seite das Glück zu finden, in *Schwarz und weiß* gedämpft sind. *Destination_Serbistan* vermittelt die Vorstellung, dass die Grenzen, die man unterwegs unversehens überschreitet, zu Verhältnissen führen können, die gastfreundlicher sind als diejenigen, die am Ziel der Reise herrschen. Internationalistische Perspektiven sind in *Schwarz und weiß* eine Quelle von Paranoia. Als Saša seinem Vater erzählt, dass er in London als DJ arbeiten kann, lacht Steve ihn aus und erklärt ihn für

verrückt. Als Reuben Saša den Wert seines Universitätsabschlusses erklärt und behauptet, dass er – vor allem, weil er mehrere Sprachen spricht – überall Arbeit finden könne, tut Saša das mit einem Lachen ab und sagt ihm, dass er verrückt sei. Die Menschen sind paranoid angesichts der Grenzen, die sie überschreiten – aber sie wissen, dass sie sie überschreiten müssen oder verkümmern werden, wo sie sind. Die Migranten und Migrantinnen in *Destination_Serbistan* sind hinsichtlich der Grenzen, die sie überschreiten, viel idealistischer, obwohl sie mit Repressionen seitens der Polizei und mit Hass konfrontiert sind und an ihren Zielorten nur sehr geringe Chancen haben. Ihr Glaube, dass sie auf der anderen Seite etwas Besseres erwartet, treibt sie an. Žilnik hat diese Eigenschaft von Reisenden immer aufmerksam beobachtet und in bewegten Bildern entsprechend dargestellt. Die internationalistische Einstellung seiner Filme ist von einer humanistischen Einstellung nicht zu trennen. Nicht Schwarz oder Weiß, sondern Schwarz und Weiß.

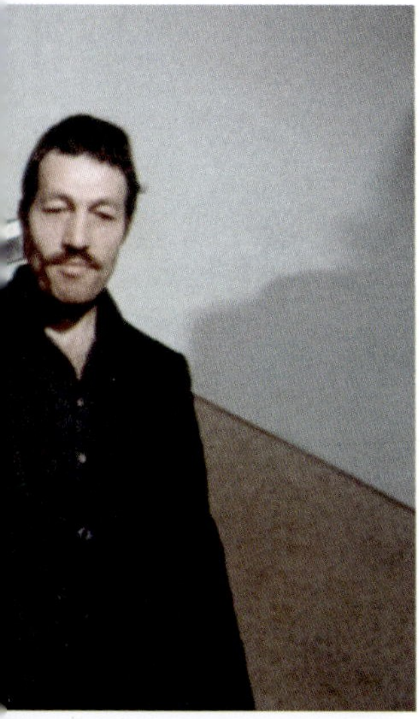

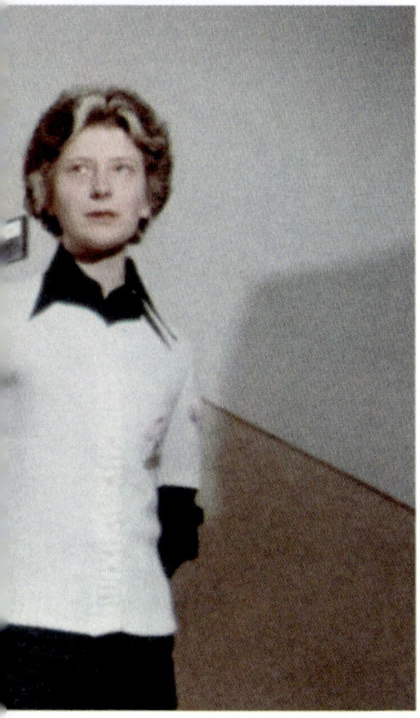

In München gibt es einen Stadtbezirk, der sich aus zwei Stadtteilen zusammensetzt: Au und Haidhausen. Dieser Stadtbezirk war ursprünglich eine einfache Wohngegend für Arbeiter und Tagelöhner. In Au-Haidhausen liegt das Franzosenviertel, das so heißt, weil dort zahlreiche Straßennamen auf die Orte siegreicher Schlachten im Deutsch-Französischen Krieg von 1870/71 verweisen. In diesem Stadtteil liegt die Metzstraße 11.

Der Film *Inventur – Metzstraße 11* (1975) ist tatsächlich eine Inventur: eine Aufnahme der Bewohnerinnen und Bewohner des Hauses Metzstraße 11. *Inventur – Metzstraße 11* ist ein kurzes, strukturelles, minimalistisches Dokumentarfilm-Experiment, für das Žilnik seine 16 mm-Kamera in einer festen Position auf einem Treppenabsatz platzierte und alle Bewohnerinnen und Bewohner des Gebäudes einlud, die Treppe hinunterzugehen, kurz anzuhalten, sich selbst und ihre Lebensumstände vorzustellen und dann weiter treppab zu gehen. Diese Katalogisierung ist bedeutsam, weil die meisten Bewohner des Gebäudes sogenannte Gastarbeiter sind, die aus ganz Europa kamen, um zum westdeutschen Bruttoinlandsprodukt beizutragen und etwas Geld zu verdienen, das sie ihren erweiterten Familien daheim schicken.[03] Sie sind Italiener, Griechen, Türken und Jugoslawen. Sie kommen aus dem Süden oder Südosten Europas, und viele von ihnen sprechen davon, dass sie nicht genug Geld verdienen oder dass es für sie schwierig ist, sich an das Leben in Westdeutschland anzupassen. Man könnte diese Situation, in der es keinen gegenseitigen Respekt oder bedeutenden kulturellen Austausch gibt, sondern in der es nur ums Geldverdienen geht, als das Gegenteil der Blockfreien-Bewegung betrachten.

03 Die einzigen Ausnahmen – neben dem Hausmeister – sind zwei junge Frauen mit offensichtlich deutscher Muttersprache, von denen sich eine als Sekretärin vorstellt, die in dem Haus wohnt, weil sie wenig verdient und das Apartment günstig ist.

Ich habe an anderer Stelle geschrieben, dass Žilnik die Kamera nicht wie einen Pinsel verwendet, um etwas zu verzieren, sondern sie eher wie ein Skalpell einsetzt, um etwas herauszuschneiden und es zu untersuchen. Diese Ästhetik der Gesellschaftsanalyse ist in *Inventur – Metzstraße 11* deutlich erkennbar. Oberflächlich betrachtet,

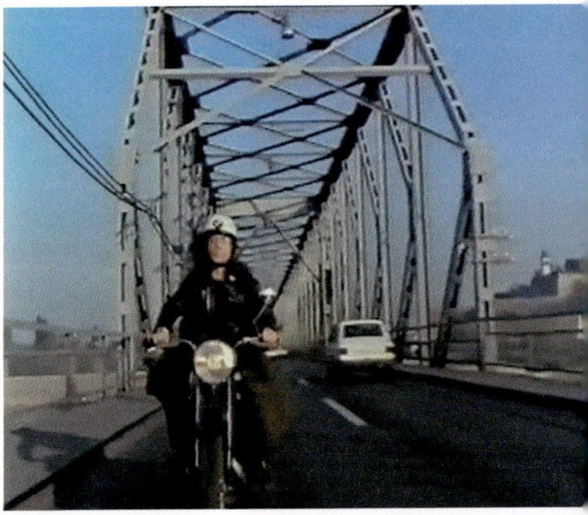

Oldtimer (Standbilder), 1989

hat der Film etwas Kaltes und Chirurgisches, das durch die streng formale Kameraposition betont wird. Doch seine Gesamtwirkung ist ein emotionales und sehr menschliches Plädoyer für soziale Aufstiegsmöglichkeiten, bessere Arbeits- und Lebensbedingungen und die Emanzipation der internationalen Arbeiterklasse.

Es gilt festzuhalten, dass Žilnik seinen Kamerablick an Arbeitern und Arbeiterinnen schult, die gemeinhin als europäische Andere oder als Minderheiten gelten und denen oft vorgehalten wird, reiche, entwickelte Gesellschaften und deren Ressourcen zu plündern. Žilnik hat immer für die Marginalisierten Partei ergriffen, für diejenigen, die als Ausgestoßene an den Rändern leben. Wie Präsident Tito gegenüber Präsident Nasser erklärte, sind das die besten Leute, die er nicht im Stich lassen werde. Žilnik beweist hier auch seine Solidarität und seine Affinität zum gesamten kulturellen Spektrum der Welt, für das Zusammenleben mit Menschen, die andere Hintergründe, andere Erfahrungen und andere Weltanschauungen haben. Er weiß, dass diese elementare Mischung das Salz, die Würze der Erde ist, und dass alles andere ein gefährliches Experiment mit abscheulichen gesellschaftlichen Manipulationen ist.

Inventur – Metzstraße 11 ist zudem beispielhaft für Žilniks internationalistische künstlerische Methode: Er überschreitet mit seiner Kamera Grenzen, um Befreiungskämpfe zu unterstützen und an ihnen teilzunehmen. In Westdeutschland hat Žilnik eine Reihe von Filmen gedreht, die schnell zu unmittelbaren Auseinandersetzungen mit dem Staat führten. Die Filme waren schonungslos kritisch und immer darauf angelegt, Ungerechtigkeiten aufzudecken – nicht anders als die Art von Filmen, die er zuvor im sozialistischen Jugoslawien und später im postsozialistischen Jugoslawien machte. Man könnte sich vorstellen, einen Film wie *Inventur – Metzstraße 11* tatsächlich alle paar Jahre zu drehen, als wiederholten Versuch, davon Rechenschaft abzulegen, wie man mit seinen Nachbarinnen und Nachbarn umgeht, wie die Wirtschaft für Menschen in den prekärsten Verhältnissen funktioniert oder nicht funktioniert, und wie

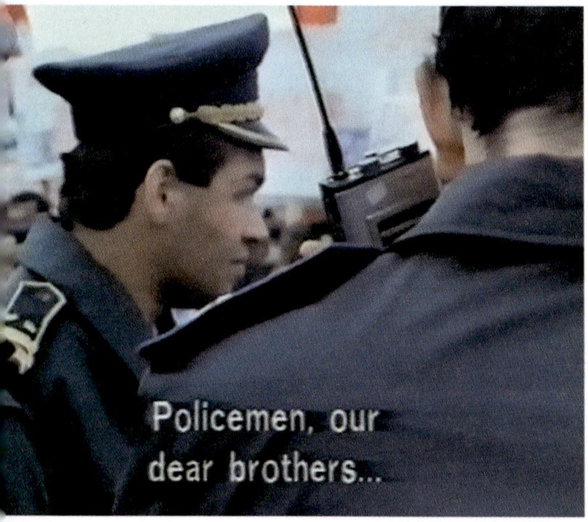

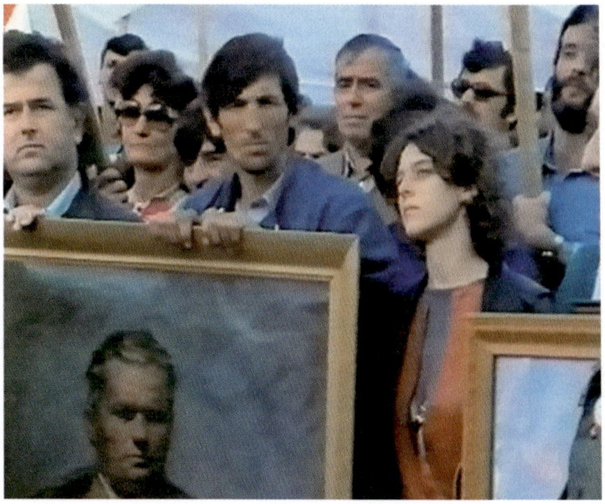

Menschen leben, wenn sie auf der Suche nach einer annehmbaren Existenz Grenzen überqueren.

Die Geschichte und die Zusammenhänge dessen, was als strukturell-materialistischer Film bezeichnet wird, wurden bislang innerhalb der engen Grenzen von Westeuropa und Nordamerika betrachtet. Für Filme, die im Verhältnis zu diesen Kinomächten blockfrei sind, hat der Kanon wenig Raum gelassen. Der Kanon folgt dem Belieben dieser Mächte und wurde oft als Waffe eingesetzt. Die Kraft der formalen Strenge von *Inventur – Metzstraße 11* beruht zum großen Teil darauf, dass der Film an einer strukturalistischen Ästhetik festhält. Jean-Luc Godard hat Kamerafahrten einmal als eine Frage der Moral bezeichnet. Žilniks wichtigstes moralisches Anliegen ist es, die Kamera so aufzustellen, dass die Welt um sie herum und durch sie hindurchgehen kann. Er verzichtet auf Kamerafahrten und ermöglicht stattdessen den Menschen, die Bewegung im Verhältnis zur Apparatur selbst zu erzeugen. Im strukturellen Film nimmt die Kamera oft eine nichtmoralische Haltung oder einen unpolitischen Blickwinkel ein. Žilnik politisiert hier das Experimentelle, weil er weiß, dass eine Inventur mehr als eine reglose Bestandsaufnahme ist. Es geht um das Leben von Menschen, und ihre wesentlichen Eigenschaften sollten bewahrt werden, deshalb muss die Kamera ein Zeugnis von ihnen geben. Žilniks Film ist nicht neutral, sondern interventionistisch. Seine Drehorte sind sorgfältig ausgewählt und angemessen ins Bild gesetzt. Der Strukturalismus, den Žilnik evoziert und analysiert, ist die Struktur der Gesellschaft, die Struktur eines Gebäudes, die Architektur sozialer Beziehungen. Die Form folgt der Funktion, und das Material, mit dem er arbeitet, sind die Leute, die Seelen der unterschiedlichsten Menschen. Die alten Regisseure der klassischen Ära sagten gerne, dass es nichts Schöneres und Geheimnisvolleres, nichts Wichtigeres gebe, als eine Kamera auf das Gesicht eines Menschen zu richten. Sie hatten recht, aber sie suchten oft nur nach einem bestimmten Gesicht, das eine bestimmte Erfahrung widerspiegeln und die Erwartungen eines bestimmten Publikums bedienen sollte. Žilnik hingegen macht eine Bestandsaufnahme

des gesamten Spektrums von Gesichtern, die mit ihrer Vielfalt und ihrer Fähigkeit, sich untereinander zu verbinden, die Schönheit und das Wunderbare der Welt ausmachen. Ohne diese Gesichter gibt es keine Welt. Und ein Regisseur, der kein offenes Auge für sie hat, der nicht die Welt für sie öffnet, ist kein Regisseur.

Im 21. Jahrhundert, über vierzig Jahre nach der Entstehung von Žilniks Film, ist die Metzstraße voller trendiger Cafés und Restaurants. Sie ist eine weitere Wohngegend, die immer teurer wird, in einem immer teureren München. Es ist kaum vorstellbar, dass hier noch „Gastarbeiter" leben. In ihrer unmittelbaren Nachbarschaft liegt der Max-Weber-Platz. Der Gründervater der Soziologie schrieb einmal: „Der Kapitalismus kann den praktischen Vertreter des undisziplinierten ‚liberum arbitrium' als Arbeiter nicht brauchen, so wenig er, wie wir schon von Franklin lernen konnten, den in seiner äußern Gebarung schlechthin skrupellosen Geschäftsmann brauchen kann."[04] Das ist wohl wahr, doch der postmoderne Kapitalismus ist eine ganz andere Sache.

★

Postskriptum

Die Vojvodina ist eine autonome Provinz im Norden der Republik Serbien. Sie erstreckt sich über eine Fläche von 21 506 km² und ist damit größer als Montenegro oder die Republik Slowenien. 75 Prozent dieser Fläche, das heißt 1 628 000 Hektar, sind kultivierbares Land. Tatsächlich besitzt die Vojvodina aufgrund des hohen Anteils von Schwarzerde, die die Pannonische Tiefebene bedeckt, die fruchtbarsten Böden Europas.[05]

Dank dieser ungewöhnlich fruchtbaren Böden hat die Vojvodina während ihrer gesamten Geschichte Migranten angezogen. Tatsächlich bildet diese Provinz aufgrund ihrer Lage und geografischen Struktur eine natürliche Brücke zwischen Mitteleuropa, der Balkanhalbinsel und dem Nahen Osten. Dadurch, und bedingt durch ihre nationale Struktur, stellt die Vojvodina ein besonderes ethnisches Phänomen dar, das in der Geschichte des Kontinents vielleicht einzigartig ist. Zum Zeitpunkt des Zensus von 2002 wurden in der Vojvodina 2 031 992 Menschen registriert. Mehr als 150 Jahre lang war dort keine ethnische Gruppe in der Mehrheit, und erst in den zurückliegenden wenigen Jahrzehnten – nur durch den Zustrom von Geflüchteten, als Nebenprodukt von Krieg und Intoleranz – haben sich die Serben zur größten Bevölkerungsgruppe der Provinz entwickelt.

Jahrhundertelang waren die Amtssprachen in der Vojvodina Serbisch, Deutsch, Kroatisch, Ungarisch, Rumänisch, Ruthenisch und andere. Es heißt, dass die Lebendigkeit dieser Provinz auf ihrer Offenheit für ein inklusives Umfeld beruht, in dem Ethnien und Religionen zu polyvalenten Normen verschmelzen. Diese tief verwurzelte Mentalität der Toleranz und der Wertschätzung von Unterschieden entstand in den vielen Jahren des Zusammenlebens. Aber das allein ist es nicht; es gibt noch etwas anderes, möglicherweise etwas auf einer

04
Max Weber, *Die protestantische Ethik und der Geist des Kapitalismus.* Vollständige Ausgabe, hg. von Dirk Kaesler, 3. Auflage, München 2010 [1905], S. 81.

05
Dragomir Jankov, Vojvodina. *The Ruination of a Region.* Data and Facts, Novi Sad 2005.

elementaren Ebene Unbestimmbares, das die Vojvodina zu einem einzigartigen Ort macht.

Man glaubt auch, dass die Vojvodina eher ein politisches Konzept als eine geografische Bezeichnung ist. Dieses Konzept könnte als Prototyp des Prinzips der Blockfreien angesehen werden, ja sogar als ein Prototyp der verschiedenen Jugoslawiens, die existiert haben; doch während diese Jugoslawiens zerfallen sind, besteht die Vojvodina immer noch. Vielleicht symbolisiert der Name ihrer Hauptstadt – Novi Sad, Neusatz, Neoplanta oder New Seed – dieses latente politische Potenzial.

Alle Botaniker wissen, dass „eine Spezies fernab von ihrem Ursprungsort leben und sich vermehren kann."[06] Auch Anthropologen wissen das. Soziologen wissen, dass Ethnien und Nationen manchmal fern von ihren Wurzeln gedeihen müssen. Und Politologen wissen, dass diese besonderen Fälle und ihre Hintergründe die Lokomotiven der Geschichte sind. Künstler sollten und müssen wissen, dass die spirituellen und physischen Bewegungen von Ethnien und Kulturen eine Stärke sind und die Möglichkeit bieten, die Welt zum Besseren zu verändern; sie sind eine Methode, um unsere Mitmenschen wirklich kennenzulernen, das heißt, sie wirklich so zu akzeptieren, wie sie sind, und sich vielleicht sogar für sie einzusetzen, wenn es sonst niemand tut. Man könnte die These aufstellen, dass das besondere politische Konzept, das den Geist der Vojvodina ausmacht, es der autonomen Provinz ermöglicht, Künstler und Künstlerinnen auszubilden, die ein entsprechendes politisches Bewusstsein aufweisen. Es täte Europa gut, wenn es mehr von diesen ästhetischen Phänotypen und ihren Arbeiten gäbe – wenn sie sich nur so leicht und zahlreich entwickeln könnten wie das Leben der Pflanzen in der eurasischen Steppe.

> „Diese Körper haben immer ihren eigenen besonderen Ursprung; sie sind immer und überall das Ergebnis der gesamten Aktivitäten des Grundgesteins, der lebenden und unbelebten Organismen (Pflanzen ebenso wie Tiere), des Klimas, des Alters des Landes und der Topografie der Umgebung."
> —Wassili Dokutschajew[07] ★

ÜBERSETZUNG AUS DEM ENGLISCHEN VON BARBARA HESS.

Greg de Cuir Jr organisierte Programme an zahlreichen Institutionen, darunter an der National Gallery of Art, Washington DC; Institute of Contemporary Arts, London; National Museum of African American History and Culture, Washington DC; Palais des Beaux-Arts, Brüssel; Los Angeles Filmforum; Locarno Film Festival; Flaherty Film Seminar, New York; Internationale Kurzfilmtage Oberhausen; Museum of Modern Art in Warsaw; Museum of Contemporary Art Vojvodina, Novi Sad und Alternative Film/Video, Belgrad. De Cuir ist Managing Editor der Zeitschrift *NECSUS* und Herausgeber der Schriftenreihe *Eastern European Screen Cultures*, die beide bei Amsterdam University Press erscheinen. Seine Texte entstanden im Auftrag des Centre Pompidou in Paris und des Institute of Contemporary Arts in London und erschienen in *Cineaste*, *Jump Cut*, *Millennium Film Journal*, *ARTMargins* und anderen Publikationen.

06
Anastasia A. Fedotova, „The Origins of the Russian Chernozem (Black Earth): Franz Joseph Ruprecht's ‚Geo-botanical Researches into the Chernozem' of 1866", in: *Environment and History*, Jg. 16, Nr. 3, August 2010, S. 271–293.

07
Wassili Dokutschajew, *Collected Works*, Bd. 2, Moskau/Leningrad 1949, S. 260; übersetzt aus dem Englischen von Barbara Hess.

Kenedi se vraća kući (Kenedi kehrt nach Hause zurück)

Serbien und Montenegro • 2003 • 75 min. • DV auf 35 mm kopiert

Der Film erzählt die Geschichte von Jugoslawinnen und Jugoslawen, die ihr Land während des Kriegs verließen und mehr als zehn Jahre lang als Flüchtlinge oder im Asyl in Westeuropa lebten. In der zweiten Hälfte des Jahres 2002 sandten verschiedene Länder der Europäischen Union viele dieser Menschen mit ihren Familien zurück nach Serbien und Montenegro, weil sie glaubten, es gebe für sie keinen Grund mehr, länger zu bleiben. Die Abwicklung der Rückkehr vollzog sich üblicherweise sehr streng. Die Familien wurden nachts zusammengeführt, zum Flughafen gefahren und mit dem ersten Flugzeug nach Belgrad geschickt. Um die Dramatik der Sache noch zu steigern: Die Mehrzahl der Kinder, die in den entsprechenden Ländern der EU geboren worden waren, sprach deren jeweilige Sprache besser als ihre Muttersprache. Und da diese Familien bei ihrem urspünglichen Weggang alles verkauft hatten, was sie besaßen, fanden sie in ihrer Heimat eine Situation vor, in der ein normales Leben praktisch unmöglich war.

Kenedi kehrt nach Hause zurück folgt zwei Freunden, Kenedi und Denis, wie auch der Familie Ibinci aus Kostolac, während der ersten Tage, nachdem sie am Belgrader Flughafen angekommen sind. Wir sehen, wie sie sich um eine Unterkunft bemühen und nach Bekannten und Familienangehörigen fahnden. Kenedi begibt sich nach Kosovska Mitrovica, wo seine Familie einmal ein Haus besaß, das er aber nun nicht mehr betreten darf. Der Film konzentriert sich auf die Lage der Roma als dem verletzlichsten Teil aller Rückkehrenden.

Die Produktion des Films begann mit einer Untersuchung der Lage der Kinder, die in Deutschland geboren wurden oder dort aufwuchsen und nun unter Zwang zurück nach Serbien gebracht wurden. Žilnik filmte die Kinder dabei, wie sie Grußbotschaften an ihre ehemaligen Klassenkameradinnen und Klassenkameraden sandten. Wenn solche Sequenzen bei Diskussionen und Gesprächsforen öffentlich gezeigt wurden, führten sie regelmäßig zu öffentlicher Empörung. Die deutschen Behörden kontaktierten Žilnik, und dabei kam heraus, dass die deutsche Regierung der serbischen Regierung für jede Familie zum Neuanfang in ihrer Heimat Geld überwiesen hatte, das indes nie bei den Familien angekommen war. Žilnik erhielt keine Erlaubnis, die Rückkehrenden am Flughafen zu filmen. Als er in Rahmen eines Castings nach jemandem suchte, der deutsch, serbisch und die Sprache der Roma sprach, lernte er Kenedi kennen, der so tun konnte, als sei er am Flughafen, um dort seine Familie zu empfangen.

Zur selben Zeit trat die deutsche Partei der Grünen an Žilnik heran. Sie hatte fünf Parlamentarier nach Serbien geschickt, die untersuchen sollten, wo die unterschlagenen Gelder für die Rückkehrenden geblieben waren. Als sie die zur Rückkehr gezwungenen Familien aufsuchten und sahen, in welch elenden Umständen sie lebten, baten sie Žilnik, einen abendfüllenden Film darüber zu drehen, den man dann in deutschen Kinos zeigen wollte. Die Grünen waren der Meinung, dass gute Schüler und Studierende nicht gezwungen werden sollten, Deutschland zu verlassen, da das Land qualifizierte Arbeitskräfte brauche. Sie bezahlten die Produktionsfirma Terra House dafür, eine 35 mm-Kopie des Films herzustellen. Der Film trat dann seine Reise durch Kinos in Nordrhein-Westfalen, Hessen und Berlin an. Wo immer er gezeigt

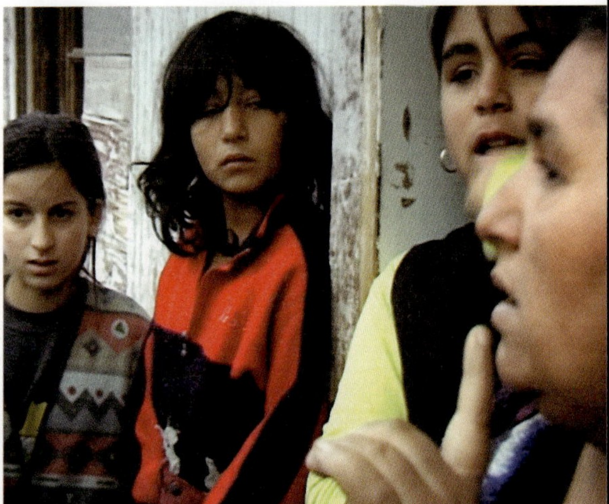

Kenedi kehrt nach Hause zurück (Standbilder), 2003

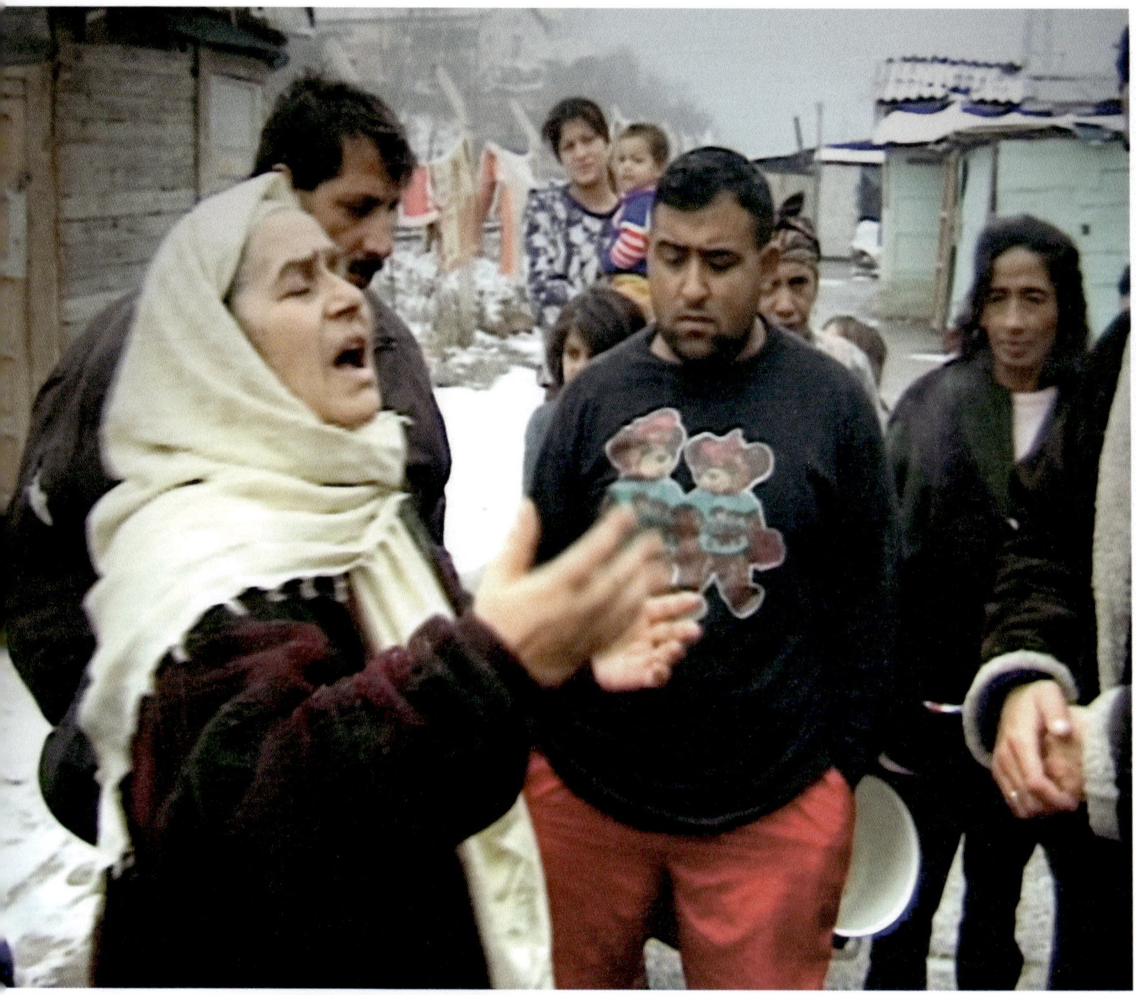

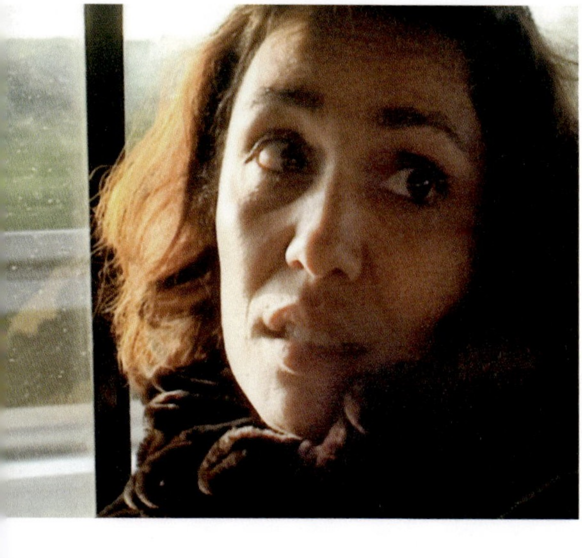

wurde, sorgte er für heftige Diskussionen. Und am Ende sorgte er dafür, dass manche Städte die Abschiebung junger Menschen völlig stoppten. Der Film wurde außerdem in Länderparlamenten und im Europäischen Parlament sowie beim Asylpolitischen Forum in Deutschland diskutiert. Der Film gewann Auszeichnungen bei Filmfestivals in Herceg Novi und in Novi Sad. Später drehte Žilnik zwei weitere Filme mit Kenedi. ●

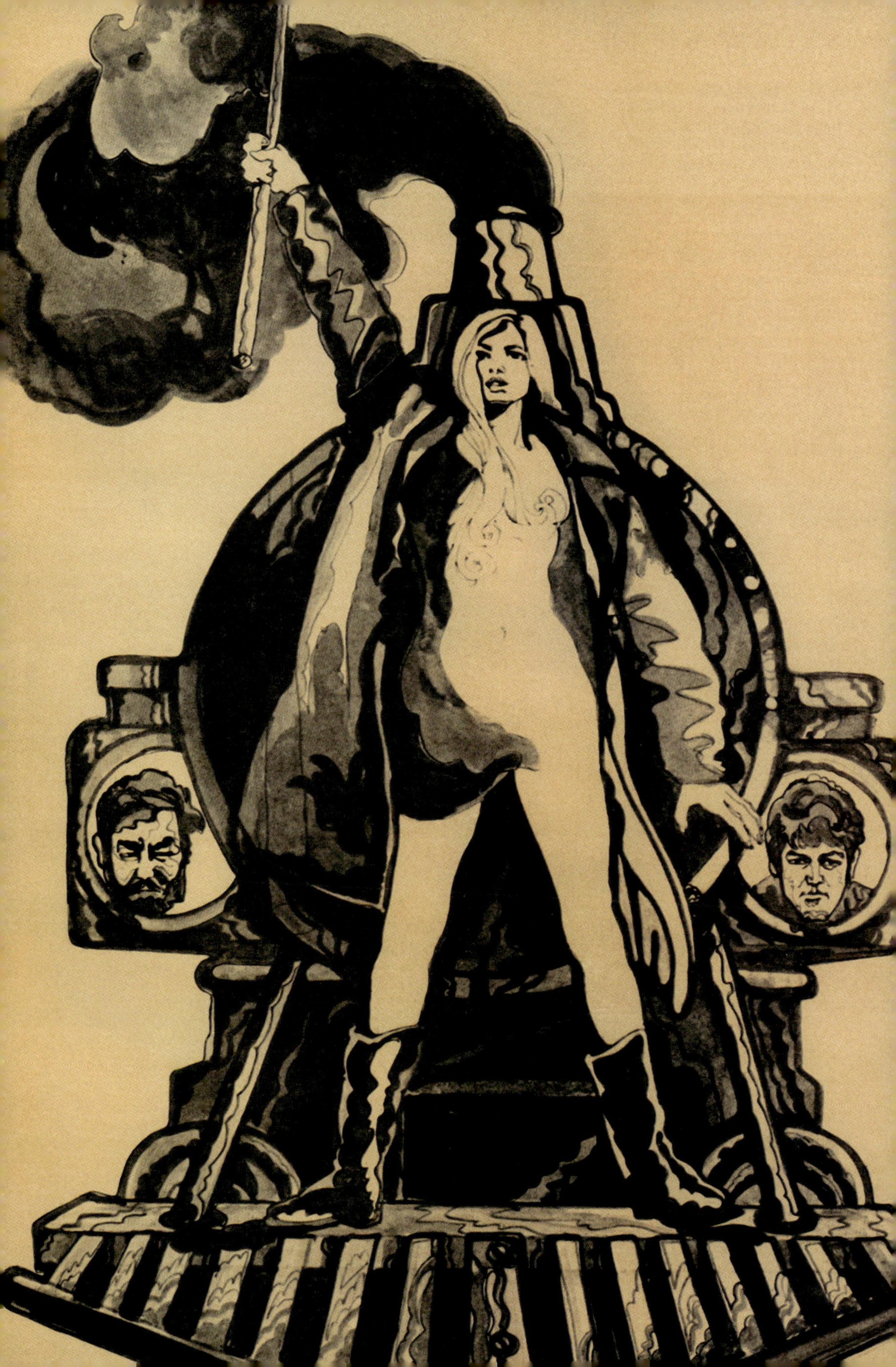

Žilniks experimentelle Einstellung war ein Versuch, über einfache Widersprüche (die sich üblicherweise in der Dichotomie zwischen dem „Offiziellen" und dem „Dissidenten" zeigten) hinauszugehen. Er folgte vielmehr der Logik der „materialistischen Dialektik" – um diesen umgekehrten, ursprünglich von Engels verwendeten Begriff zu nehmen, der angemessener erscheint als der durch den Stalinismus pervertierte „dialektische Materialismus"; mithilfe dieser Logik entdeckte er symptomatische Oppositionen in materiellen Praktiken, durch die letztere in Bewegung versetzt werden können, anstatt sie in ihren idealistischen Widersprüchen zu belassen.

—Branislav Dimitrijević, „Concrete Analysis of Concrete Situations: Marxist Education According to Želimir Žilnik", in: *Afterall,* Herbst/Winter 2010, S. 51.

žž: Ich glaube, dass das grundlegende Merkmal des sogenannten öffentlichen Engagements, von dem Sie sprechen, in Wirklichkeit darin besteht, chamäleonhaft zu sein. Leute segeln unter falschen Flaggen, sie präsentieren ihre Frühwerke unter Vortäuschung falscher Tatsachen, arbeiten einfach immer weiter und treiben unsere unglücklichen Menschen in den Wahnsinn. Es macht mich krank, wenn ich die Leute sehe, die bis vor Kurzem, bis vor zwei Jahren, die Fahne des Nationalismus geschwenkt haben und die wir als die Hauptschuldigen ansehen können, die Hass und Faschismus verbreitet haben, und die jetzt versuchen, uns alle zum Narren zu halten – als ob wir nicht wüssten, dass es auch ihr Fehler war, die Bestie aus dem Käfig zu lassen. In unserer Öffentlichkeit wird, wie es in den letzten Jahrzehnten üblich war, viel geprahlt und wenig auf die eigene Arbeit hingewiesen. Ich glaube, dass unsere sogenannte Öffentlichkeit ein großer Zirkus ist und selbstverständlich ein Horror, der dem Zirkus und dem Horror des offiziellen Faschismus gleicht.

[INTERVIEWER]: Sehen Sie keine Option, der Sie sich möglicherweise anschließen könnten?

žž: Nun, ich sehe zum Beispiel die Menschenrechtsbewegung. Aber ich beschäftige mich ohnehin mit nichts anderem als den Menschenrechten. Ob im Film oder beim Fernsehen – die Erfahrung, wieder auf jede erdenkliche Weise behindert zu werden. Alles, was ich gemacht habe, war entweder nicht sozialistisch genug oder nicht serbisch genug oder nicht blockfrei genug oder zu blockfrei …

—Želimir Žilnik, Interview, „These Are Only Old Movies", in: *Nezavisni vojvođanski građanski list,* 15. Januar 1993

Frühe Werke, Illustration Kevin Peter, Grove Press International Film Festival Book, 1969

Želimir Žilnik (geb. 1942, lebt und arbeitet in Novi Sad, Serbien) ist Autor und Regisseur zahlreicher Spiel- und Dokumentarfilme. Seine Filme beschäftigten sich von Anfang an mit aktuellen Problemen und zeigten gesellschaftliche, politische und ökonomische Ansichten des Alltags (*Chronik der Landjugend im Winter* [1967], *Kleine Pioniere* [1968], *Die Arbeitslosen* [1968], *Der Studentenstreik* [1969], *Der schwarze Film* [1971], *Aufstand in Jazak* [1973]).

Im Mittelpunkt von Žilniks erstem Spielfilm, *Frühe Werke* (1969), der im gleichen Jahr auf der Berlinale mit dem Goldenen Bären und in Pula mit vier Preisen ausgezeichnet wurde, standen die Studentenproteste von 1968 und die Unruhen, die auf die Besetzung der Tschechoslowakei folgten.

Während der Arbeit an seinem zweiten Spielfilm, *Freiheit oder Comicstrip* (1972, produziert von Neoplanta Film, unvollendet), geriet Žilnik in Konflikt mit der Zensur in Jugoslawien. Mitte der 1970er Jahre lebte er in Westdeutschland und realisierte dort als freier Regisseur mehrere Dokumentarfilme und einen Spielfilm, *Paradies. Eine imperialistische Tragikomödie* (1976). Diese Filme gehören zu den ersten, die sich mit ausländischen Arbeitskräften – den sogenannten „Gastarbeitern" – in Westdeutschland beschäftigten, und werden bis heute im Rahmen von Retrospektiven und Symposien gezeigt.

Nach seiner Rückkehr nach Jugoslawien Ende der 1970er Jahre arbeitete Žilnik als Regisseur zahlreicher Fernsehfilme und Dokudramen für TV Belgrade und TV Novi Sad (u. a. *Die Krankheit und Gesundung des Buda Brakus* [1980], *Vera und Eržika* [1981], *Dragoljub und Bogdan: Elektrizität* [1982], *Das erste Trimester von Pavle Hromiš* [1983], *Stanimir geht in die Stadt* [1984], *Guten Morgen, Belgrad* [1985], *Heiße Löhne* [1987], *Brooklyn-Gusinje* [1988], *Oldtimer* [1989], *Schwarz und weiß* [1990]).

Bis zum Ende der 1980er Jahre entstanden Žilniks Filme innerhalb einer kooperativen Produktionsstruktur von Film und Fernsehen, wobei jedes seiner Werke auf die wachsenden Spannungen und die drohenden politischen und gesellschaftlichen Veränderungen hindeutete, die das Land treffen sollten: *Die zweite Generation* (1984), *Schöne Frauen gehen durch die Stadt* (1986) und *So wurde Eisen gehärtet* (1988).

In den 1990er Jahren wandte sich Žilnik der unabhängigen Film- und Medienproduktion zu und beschäftigte sich in einer Reihe von Spiel- und Dokumentarfilmen mit den katastrophalen Ereignissen auf dem Balkan (*Tito zum zweiten Mal unter den Serben* [1994], *Marble Ass* [1995], *Die Fesseln sprengen* [1996], *Wanderlust* [1998]). 1995 wurde *Marble Ass* auf der Berlinale mit dem renommierten Teddy Award ausgezeichnet.

Im Mittelpunkt von Žilniks jüngsten Filmen, von *Fortress Europe* (2000) bis *Destination_Serbistan* (2015) und *Das schönste Land der*

Welt (2018), stehen der Zusammenbruch des Wertesystems mittel-, ost- und südosteuropäischer Länder nach der „Transition" und die Probleme von Flucht und Migration, die mit den neuen Verhältnissen im erweiterten Europa einhergingen.

Želimir Žilniks Filme wurden auf nationalen und internationalen Filmfestivals mit zahlreichen Preisen ausgezeichnet. In jüngerer Zeit fanden umfangreiche Retrospektiven seines filmischen Werks statt, unter anderem im Centre Pompidou, Paris 2019; Cinemateca Argentina, Buenos Aires 2018; Mar del Plata International Film Festival, 2017; Anthology Film Archives, New York 2017; Harvard Film Archive, Cambridge, MA 2017; Ankara International Film Festival, 2016; Doclisboa, Lissabon 2015; Arsenal, Berlin 2015; Cinusp, São Paulo 2014; Thessaloniki International Film Festival, 2014.

Seit 2010 wurden seine Filme auch in den Programmen von Galerien, Museen und anderen Kunstinstitutionen gezeigt, darunter die documenta, Kassel; Venedig-Biennale; Institute of Contemporary Arts, London; mumok – Museum Moderner Kunst Stiftung Ludwig Wien; MACBA – Museu d'Art Contemporani de Barcelona; Museo Universitario Arte Contemporaneo, Mexico City; Museo Nacional Centro de Arte Reina Sofía, Madrid.

In jüngster Zeit, 2018/19, wurden Žilniks Filme und Videoinstallationen unter anderem in Programmen folgender Institutionen gezeigt: Museum of Modern Art (MoMA), New York; Renaissance Society, Chicago; National Gallery of Art, Washington DC; Flaherty Seminar, New York; Edith-Russ-Haus für Medienkunst, Oldenburg; Lentos Kunstmuseum, Linz; MMK – Museum für Moderne Kunst Frankfurt; Deutsches Historisches Museum, Berlin; Arsenal – Institut für Film und Videokunst, Berlin; Galleria Nazionale d'Arte Moderna e Contemporanea, Rom.

Neben seiner unablässigen Arbeit als Filmemacher und Produzent ist Žilnik auch auf dem Gebiet der Ausbildung tätig: Seit 1997 war er Mentor und Executive Producer in zahlreichen internationalen Workshops in Europa und den USA. ★

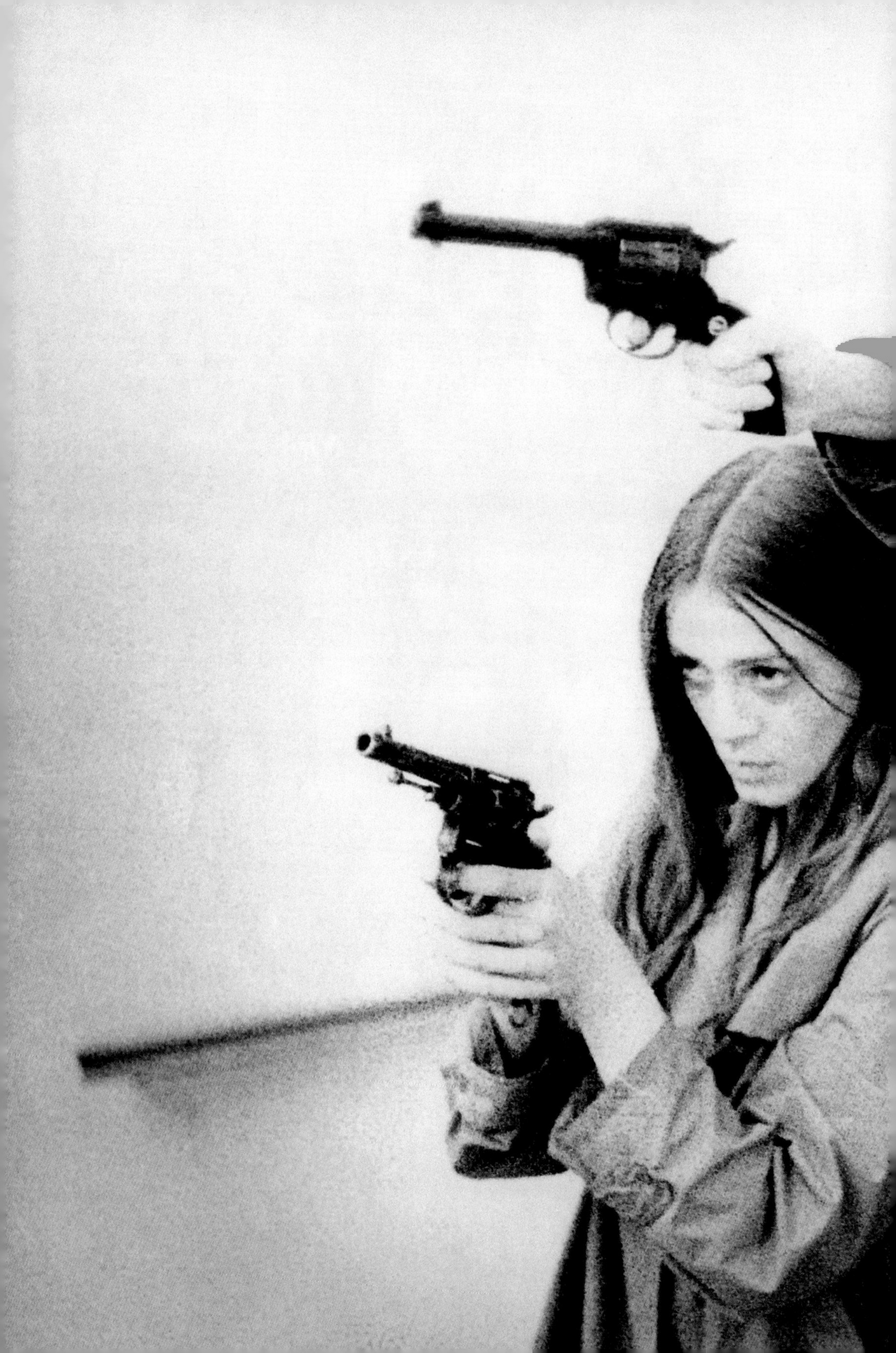

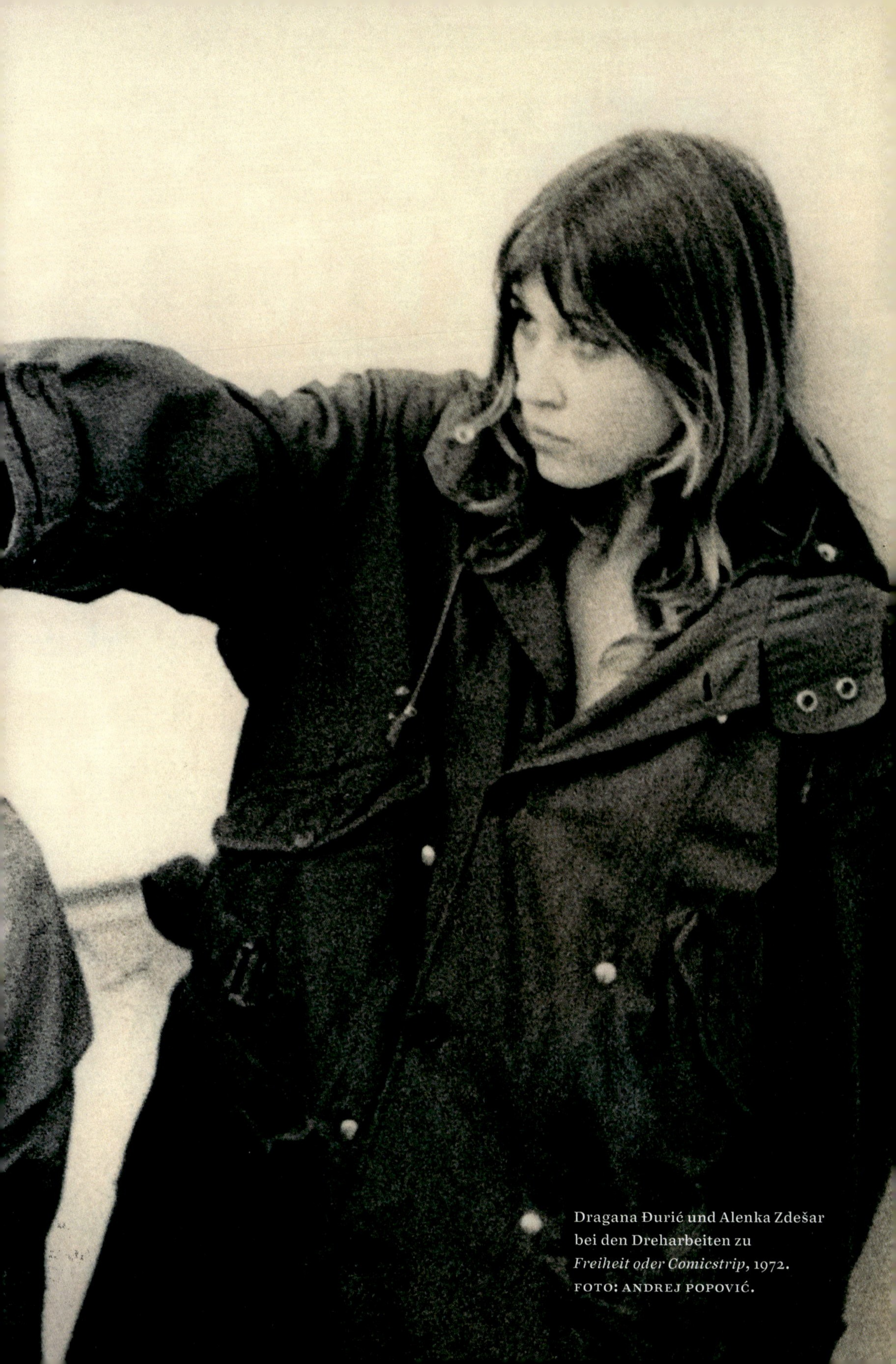

Dragana Đurić und Alenka Zdešar bei den Dreharbeiten zu *Freiheit oder Comicstrip*, 1972. FOTO: ANDREJ POPOVIĆ.

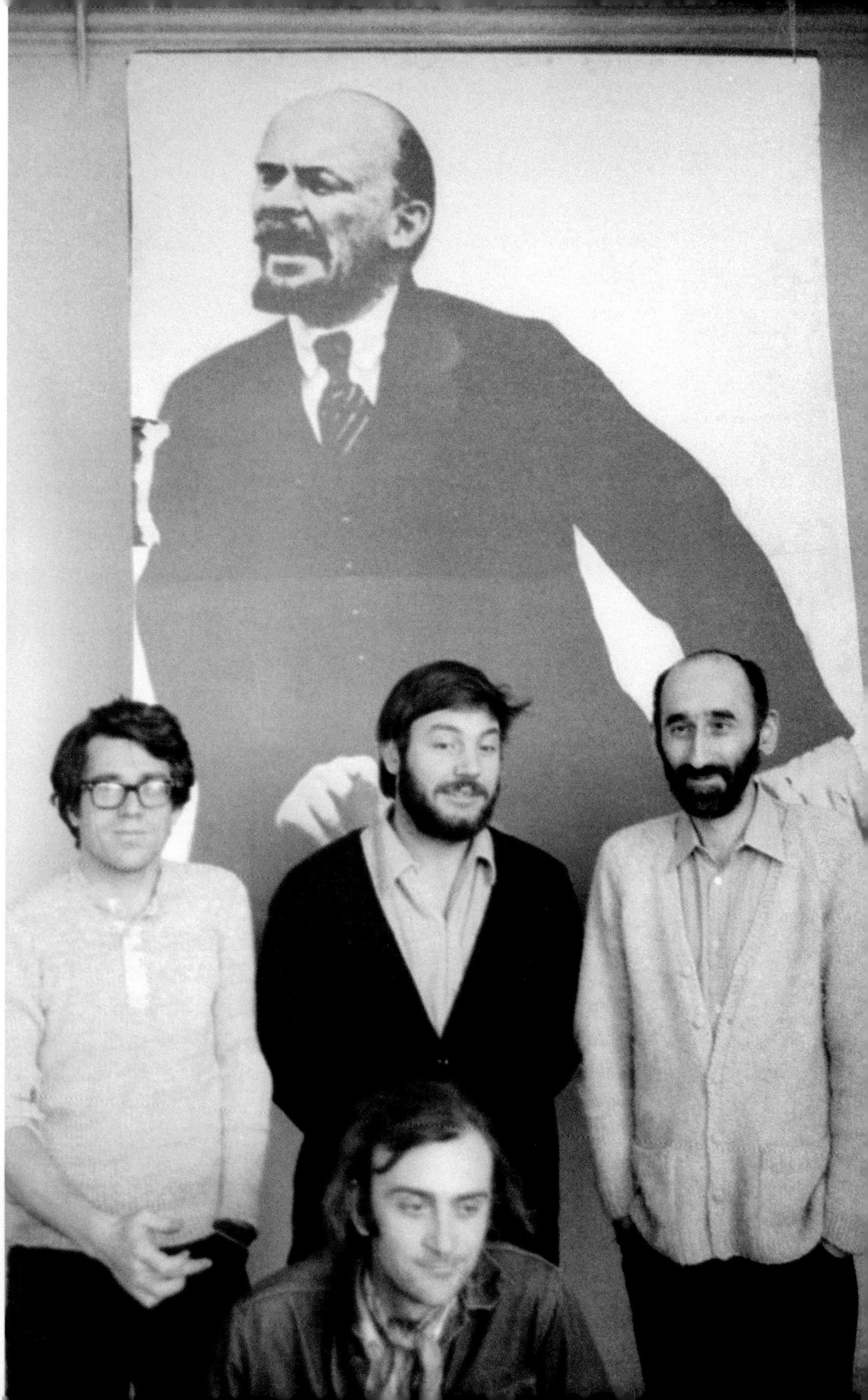

Um 1965, als ich anfing, mit Avala Film zusammenzuarbeiten, befand sich das jugoslawische System in einem Prozess, in dem es versuchte, seinen Unterschied zur Sowjetunion zu beweisen. Damals wurde die Organisationsstruktur der Selbstverwaltung, die es bis dahin nur in der Industrie gegeben hatte, auch in der Kulturpolitik eingeführt. Das System der Selbstverwaltung war im Prozess des Wiederaufbaus und der Industrialisierung des Landes extrem erfolgreich gewesen, und dieser Erfolg gab uns eine entscheidende Energie.

Die Werktätigen, die Teil dieses Systems waren, empfanden sich wirklich als Mitbesitzende der Fabriken; sie dachten, dass sie die Entscheidungen der Führungsebene tatsächlich beeinflussen könnten. Aber wir Filmemacher waren in Wirklichkeit Teil des freien Marktes, denn wir waren nicht angestellt. Wir standen eher außerhalb als innerhalb des Systems. Wir sahen, dass alle Vorzüge des Systems – ein sicherer, fester Job, gute Renten, das Recht auf Wohnung, [was hieß, dass] Werktätige eine Wohnung in einer Neubausiedlung und einen Dauermietvertrag bekamen – das revolutionäre Potenzial der Werktätigen verringerten und sie zu sozialistischen Kleinbürgern machten. Die Veränderungen des Landes, die wir Jahr für Jahr beobachteten, waren enorm. Und daraus zogen wir unsere Inspiration.

—Želimir Žilnik im Gespräch mit Dubravka Sekulić, Gal Kirn und Žiga Testen, in: Gal Kirn, Dubravka Sekulić und Žiga Testen (Hg.), *Surfing the Black: Yugoslav Black Wave Cinema and Its Transgressive Moments* (Maastricht: Jan van Eyck Academie 2012), S. 60–62.

Želimir Žilnik, Karpo Godina, Branko Vučićević und Branko Andrić Andrla (vorne) bei den Dreharbeiten zu *Freiheit oder Comicstrip*, 1972. FOTO: ANDREJ POPOVIĆ.

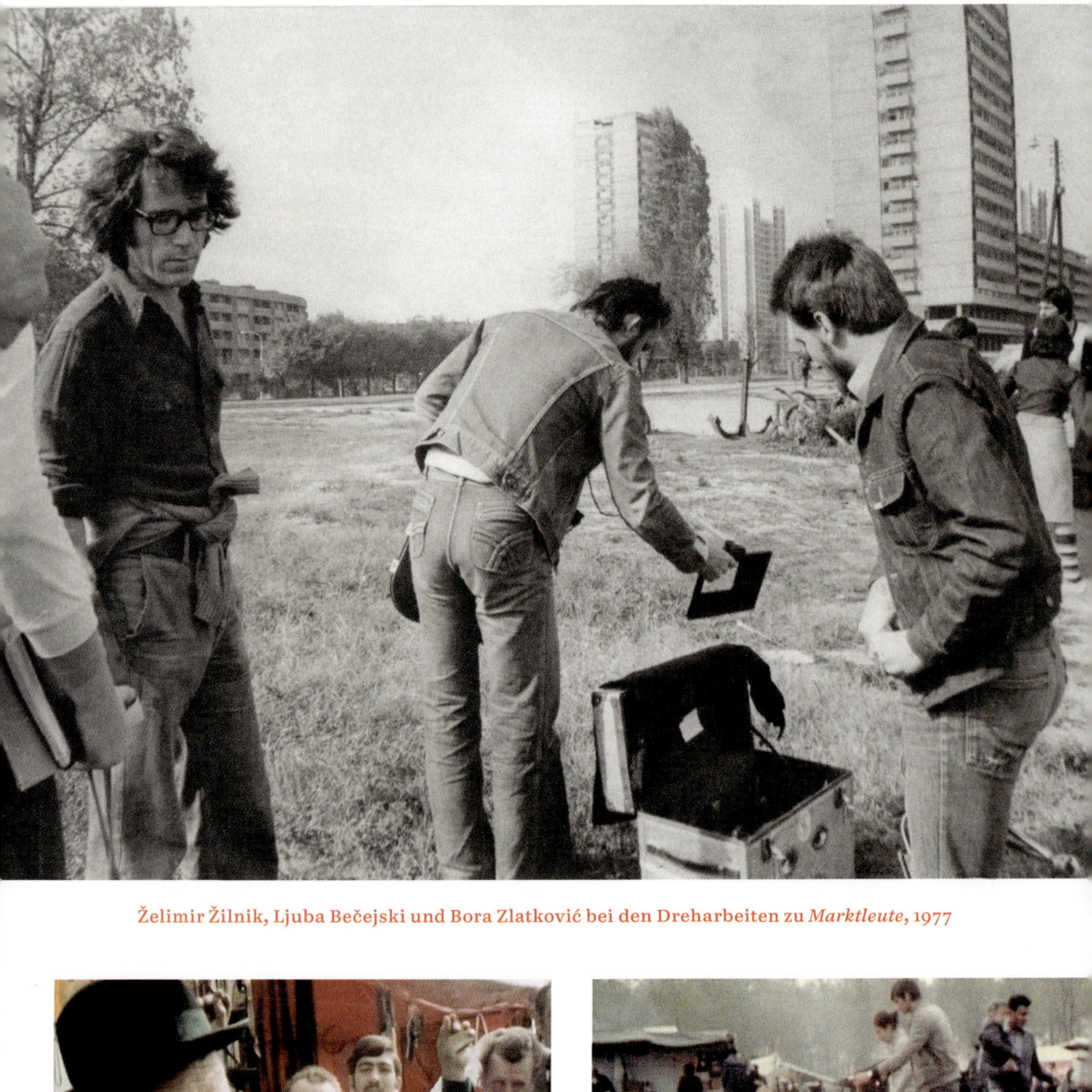

Želimir Žilnik, Ljuba Bečejski und Bora Zlatković bei den Dreharbeiten zu *Marktleute*, 1977

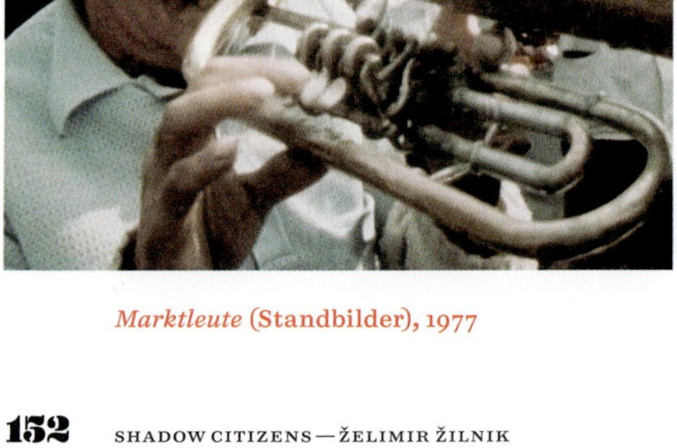

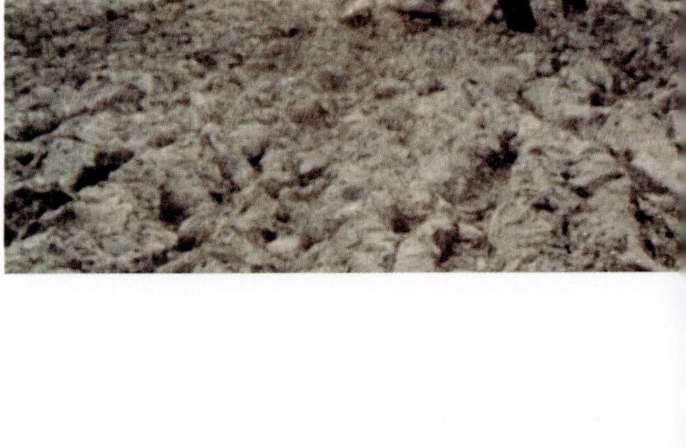

Marktleute (Standbilder), 1977

Das Fernsehen ist a priori frei von den Mystifikationen der Filmarbeit. Hier [in Jugoslawien] beruht ein Teil der Mystifikation des Films darauf, dass die Menschen auf den Film abfärben. Jeder Ziegelstein ist fünf Mal bedeutungsvoller und teurer, wenn er in einem Film bewegt wird. Beim Fernsehen wird viel Geld ausgegeben – Arbeit wird realistischer bewertet. Wenn wir über den Film sprechen, sprechen wir über den Markt, den Preis, Waren und Umsätze, obwohl von den rund dreißig Filmen, die jedes Jahr produziert werden, nur zwei oder drei einen Teil der Kosten wieder einspielen. Wenn man nur einigermaßen wirtschaftlich denken würde, müssten die übrigen Produzenten Pleite gehen. Für einen so kleinen Markt sollte folgendes Gesetz gelten: finanzielle Bescheidenheit, Kooperation mit dem Fernsehen und außergewöhnliche Investitionen nur, nachdem man mögliche kommerzielle Effekte nachgewiesen hat. Stattdessen sitzen hier Dutzende von Filmemachern und warten auf Hollywood-Spektakel!

Das Fernsehen hat eine normalere Beziehung zum Leben. [...] TV Novi Sad hat fünfzig großartige Kameras, dreißig Schnittplätze, und diese technische Grundlage ist hundert oder tausend Mal stärker als die eine Kamera bei Neoplanta, um die sich Hunderte von Mystifikationen ranken. Das Fernsehen ist zur Kunst der breitesten Massen geworden und es hat auch angefangen, sich mit der Populärkultur zu beschäftigen. Als ich Gelegenheit hatte, für das Fernsehen zu arbeiten, habe ich das in dem Bewusstsein seiner Möglichkeiten getan, und ich habe versucht, an einigen Aspekten seiner Macht teilzuhaben. Ein Mensch, der für das Fernsehen arbeitet, fühlt sich normal. Er weiß, dass alles, was normal und gut ist, schon im Fernsehen gezeigt worden ist und alleine die Tatsache, dass er selbst spricht, bedeutet, dass er ein integrierter Mensch ist. Das Fernsehen hat die Möglichkeit, ständig den Grundwert unserer Gesellschaft zu untersuchen: die Vielfalt.

—Želimir Žilnik, Interview, „Getting a Film Made Is Getting a Mandate“, in: *TV Novosti*, 14. Mai 1982

Filmografie

1967

Žurnal o omladini na selu, zimi
Chronik der Landjugend im Winter
15 min
35 mm
Neoplanta film

1968

Pioniri maleni mi smo vojska prava, svakog dana ničemo ko zelena trava
Kleine Pioniere, wir sind eine Armee, wir sprießen wie grünes Gras
18 min
35 mm
Neoplanta film

Nezaposleni ljudi
Die Arbeitslosen
13 min
35 mm
Neoplanta film

1969

Lipanjska gibanja
Der Studentenstreik
10 min
35 mm
Neoplanta film

Rani radovi
Frühe Werke
87 min
35 mm
Avala film, Neoplanta film

1971

Crni film
Der schwarze Film
14 min
16 mm ➡ 35 mm
Neoplanta film

1972

Žene dolaze
Die Frauen kommen
12 min
16 mm
Neoplanta film

Sloboda ili strip
Freiheit oder Comicstrip
unvollendet
35 mm & 16 mm
Neoplanta film

1973

Ustanak u Jasku
Aufstand in Jazak
18 min
35 mm
Panfilm

1974

Antrag
Antrag
10 min
16 mm ➡ 35 mm
Vlada Majic Filmproduktion KG

Öffentliche Hinrichtung
Öffentliche Hinrichtung
9 min
35 mm
Vlada Majic Filmproduktion KG

1975

Ich weiß nicht, was soll es bedeuten
Ich weiß nicht, was soll es bedeuten
9 min
35 mm
Vlada Majic Filmproduktion KG

Abschied
Abschied
9 min
16 mm
Vlada Majic Filmproduktion KG

Inventur – Metzstraße 11
Inventur – Metzstraße 11
9 min
16 mm
Alligator Film

Unter Denkmalschutz
Unter Denkmalschutz
11 min
16 mm
Alligator Film

Hausordnung
Hausordnung
12 min
35 mm
Vlada Majic Filmproduktion KG

1976
Paradies. Eine imperialistische Tragikomödie
Paradies. Eine imperialistische Tragikomödie
90 min
16 mm
Alligator Film

1977
Placmajstori
Marktleute
29 min
16 mm
TV Novi Sad

Komedija i tragedija Bore Joksimovića
Die Komödie und Tragödie von Bora Joksimović
30 min
16 mm
TV Novi Sad

1978
Naše zvezde sa ekrana duševna su naša hrana
Unsere Fernsehstars sind unsere geistige Nahrung
10 min
35 mm
TV Novi Sad

Sedam mađarskih balada
Sieben ungarische Balladen
30 min
16 mm
TV Novi Sad

1979
Dobrovoljci
Freiwillige
30 min
16 mm
TV Novi Sad

1980
Bolest i ozdravljenje Bude Brakusa
Die Krankheit und Gesundung des Buda Brakus
98 min
16 mm
TV Novi Sad

1981
Vera i Eržika
Vera und Eržika
75 min
16 mm
TV Novi Sad

1982
Dragoljub i Bogdan: struja
Dragoljub und Bogdan: Elektrizität
85 min
16 mm
TV Beograd

1983
Prvo tromesečje Pavla Hromiša
Das erste Trimester von Pavle Hromiš
87 min
16 mm
TV Novi Sad

1984
Druga generacija
Die zweite Generation
87 min
16 mm ➜ 35 mm
Art film, TV Novi Sad

Stanimir silazi u grad
Stanimir geht in die Stadt
75 min
16 mm
TV Beograd

1985
Beograde dobro jutro
Guten Morgen, Belgrad
57 min
16 mm
TV Beograd

1986
Lijepe žene prolaze kroz grad
Schöne Frauen gehen durch die Stadt
103 min
35 mm
Art film

Posrnule ovčice
Strauchelnde Schafe
46 min
Betacam
TV Novi Sad

1987
Vruće plate
Heiße Löhne
103 min
Betacam
TV Novi Sad

1988
Bruklin – Gusinje
Brooklyn–Gusinje
87 min
16 mm
TV Beograd

Tako se kalio čelik
So wurde Eisen gehärtet
101 min
35 mm
Terra film

1989
Stara mašina
Oldtimer
81 min
16 mm
TV Ljubljana

1990
Crno i belo
Schwarz und weiß
58 min
Betacam
TV Novi Sad

1993
Silos Dunav, Vukovar
Getreidesilo Donau, Vukovar
1 min
35 mm
Terra film

1994
Tito po drugi put među Srbima
Tito zum zweiten Mal unter den Serben
43 min
Betacam
B92

1995
Marble Ass
Marble Ass
84 min
Betacam ➡ 35 mm
B92

1996
Do jaja
Die Fesseln sprengen
12 min
Betacam
B92

1997
Za Ellu
Für Ella
10 min
Betacam
Terra film

1998
Kud plovi ovaj brod
Wanderlust
91 min
Betacam ➡ 35 mm
Teresianum b.t., VP Kregar, Terra film, Kvadrat, TV Crna Gora

2000
Trdnjava Evropa
Festung Europa
80 min
Betacam
Low Budget Production, RTV Slovenia

Cosmo Girls
Cosmo Girls
27 min
Betacam
Teresianum b.t.

2002
EXIT ujutru
EXIT am Morgen
12 min
Betacam
Terra film, Radio 021

2003
Kenedi se vraća kući
Kenedi kehrt nach Hause zurück
75 min
DV ➡ 35 mm
Terra film, Multiradio

2005
Evropa preko plota
Europa nebenan
61 min
DV
Terra film

Gde je dve godine bio Kenedi
Kenedi, verloren und gefunden
26 min
DV
Terra film

2006
Dunavska sapunska opera
Seife in der Donau-Oper
70 min
DV
Terra film

2007
Kenedi se ženi
Kenedi heiratet
80 min
DV ➡ 35 mm
Terra film, Jet Company VKTV

2009
Stara škola kapitalizma
Die Alte Schule des Kapitalismus
122 min
DV & HD ➡ 35 mm
Playground produkcija

2011
Jedna žena – jedan vek
Eine Frau – ein Jahrhundert
110 min
HD
Playground produkcija

2013
Pirika na filmu
Pirika im Film
54 min
HD
Playground produkcija

2014
Naš čovek u Gabonu
Unser Mann in Gabun
66 min
HD
Žilnik produkcija

2015
Destinacija_Serbistan
Destination_Serbistan
94 min
HD ➡ DCP
Playground produkcija

2018
Among the People: Life & Acting
Unter den Menschen: Leben & Schauspiel
83 min
HD
Žilnik produkcija, Edith-Russ-Haus für Medienkunst

The Most Beautiful Country in the World
Das schönste Land der Welt
101 min
HD ➡ DCP
nanookfilm, Tramal Films, Factum, RTV Vojvodina

2019
Où en êtes-vous, Želimir Žilnik?
Wo stehen Sie heute, Želimir Žilnik?
20 min
HD ➡ DCP
Playground produkcija, Centre Pompidou

ANMERKUNG DER HERAUSGEBERINNEN: Die Schreibweise der deutschen Titelübersetzungen folgt, soweit vorhanden, den historischen Verleihtiteln.

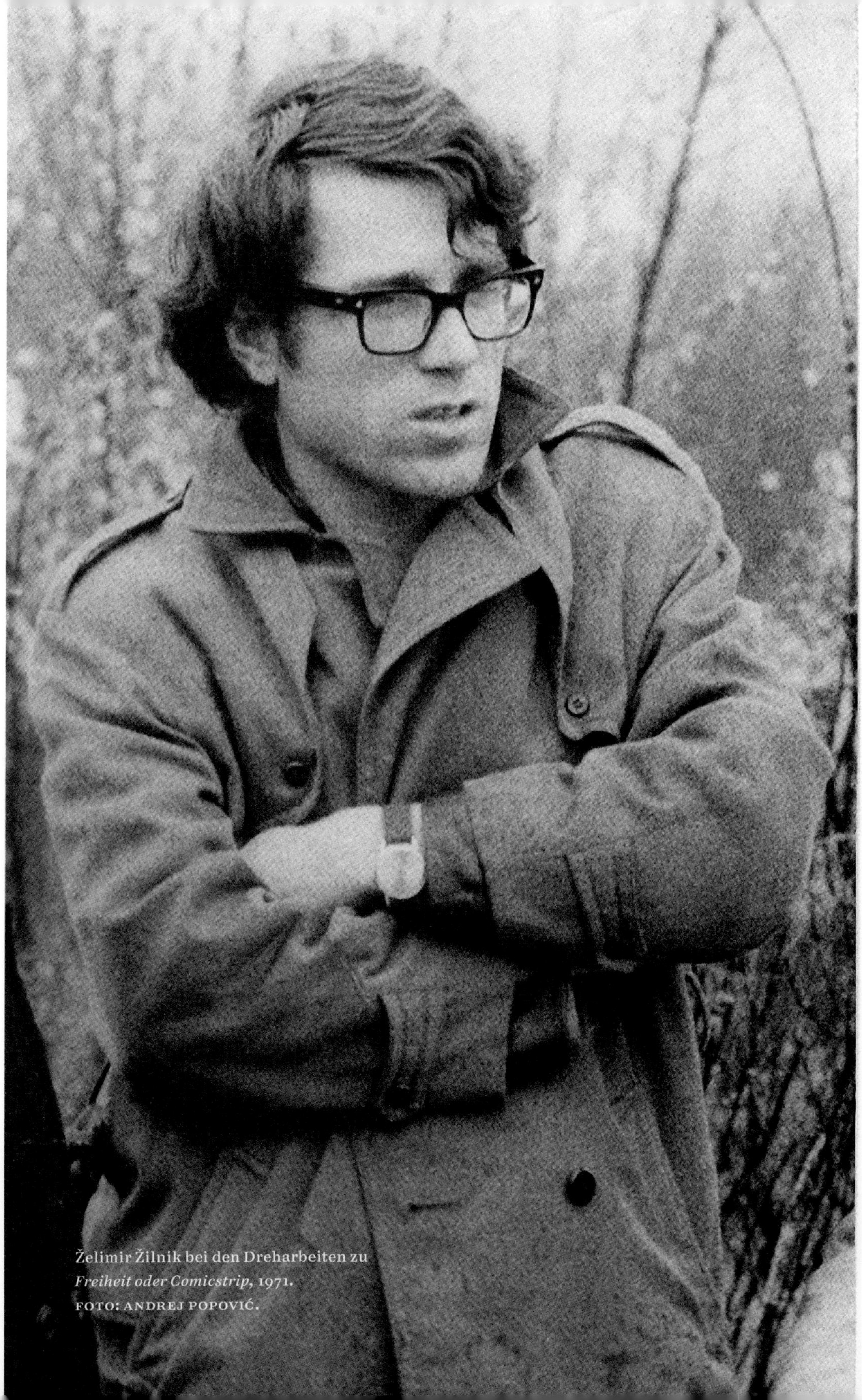

Želimir Žilnik bei den Dreharbeiten zu *Freiheit oder Comicstrip*, 1971.
FOTO: ANDREJ POPOVIĆ.

In einer Angelegenheit war unsere Obrigkeit, die wir üblicherweise für inkompetent halten, äußerst erfolgreich – in dem Vorhaben, das Blut der Nationalitäten auf dem Gebiet Ex-Jugoslawiens zu vergießen. Aus meiner Sicht war der Hass künstlich geschürt, und dieser Prozess hat schon Jahre begonnen, bevor der Krieg ausbrach. Wir haben die Schrecken des Spätfaschismus durchlebt, als man in einer kriegerischen Anstrengung, die von den [verschiedenen] Stammesältesten angeführt wurde, Nationalstaaten gründete. Tatsächlich ist es so, dass ich nur, wenn ich nach Kroatien komme, die Sprache sprechen kann, die Sie verstehen, so wie Sie meine Filme verstehen. Diese Nationen haben so viel gemeinsam, dass sogar Liebe und Hass an gewisse Familienstreitigkeiten erinnern, die sehr brutal sein können.

—Želimir Žilnik, Interview, „From Early Works to Late Wars“, in: *Zarez*, 7. April 2000

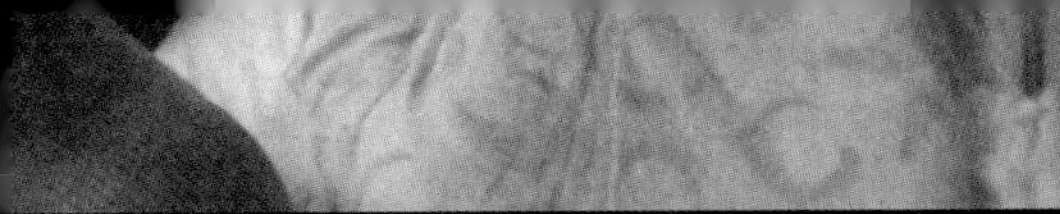

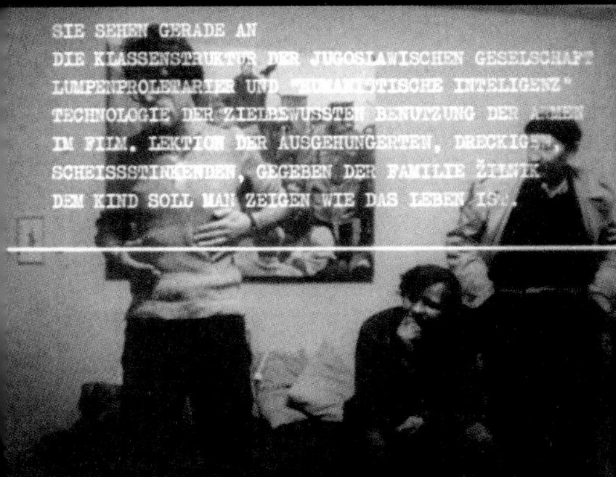

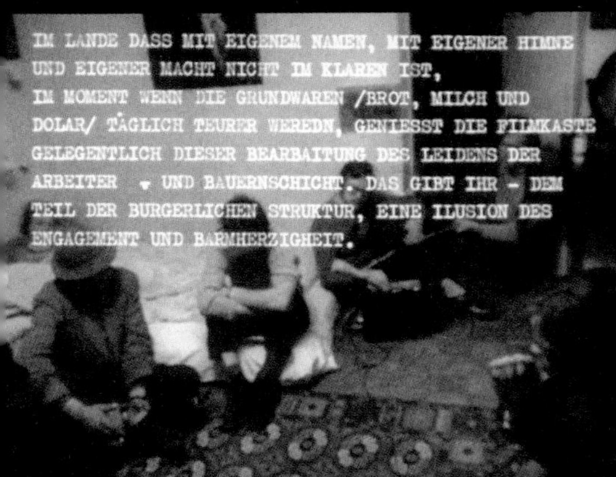

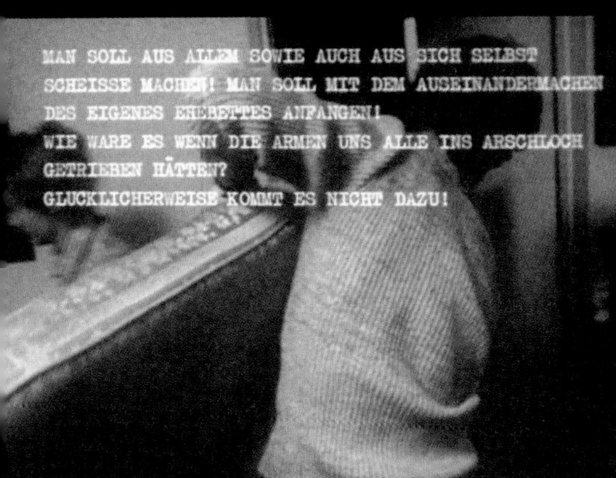

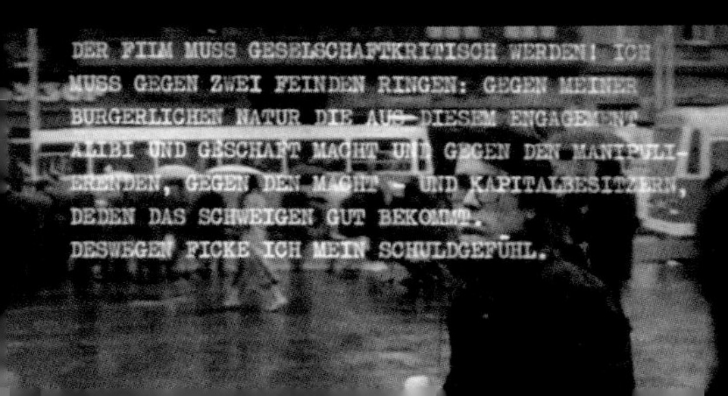

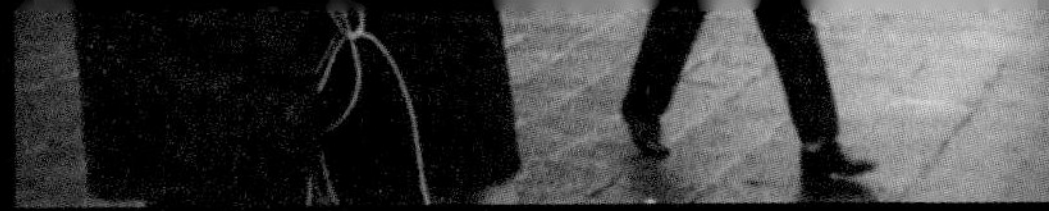

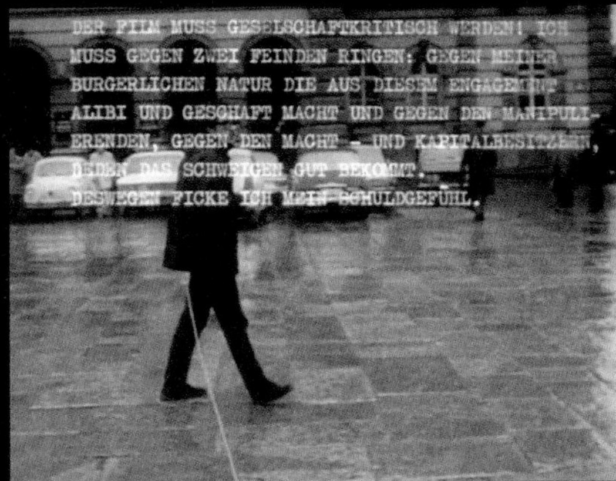

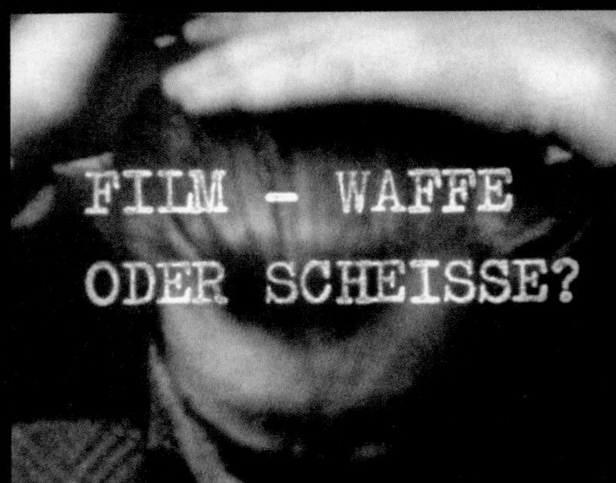

DER FIIM MUSS GESELSCHAFTKRITISCH WERDEN! ICH
MUSS GEGEN ZWEI FEINDEN RINGEN: GEGEN MEINER
BURGERLICHEN NATUR DIE AUS DIESEM ENGAGEMENT
ALIBI UND GESCHAFT MACHT UND GEGEN DEN MANIPULI-
ERENDEN, GEGEN DEN MACHT - UND KAPITALBESITZERN,
DEDEN DAS SCHWEIGEN GUT BEKOMMT.
DESWEGEN FICKE ICH MEIN SCHULDGEFÜHL.

DER FIIM MUSS GESELSCHAFTKRITISCH WERDEN! ICH
MUSS GEGEN ZWEI FEINDEN RINGEN: GEGEN MEINER
BURGERLICHEN NATUR DIE AUS DIESEM ENGAGEMENT
ALIBI UND GESCHAFT MACHT UND GEGEN DEN MANIPULI-
ERENDEN, GEGEN DEN MACHT - UND KAPITALBESITZERN,
DEDEN DAS SCHWEIGEN GUT BEKOMMT.
DESWEGEN FICKE ICH MEIN SCHULDGEFÜHL.

Manifest des Schwarzen Films

1971 wurde Žilnik zu den Internationalen Kurzfilmtagen Oberhausen eingeladen, konnte aber nicht anwesend sein. Da er mit Publikum und Presse nicht persönlich sprechen konnte, schrieb er, auf Serbokroatisch, ein Manifest. Die ursprüngliche, nicht von einem Muttersprachler angefertigte deutsche Übersetzung dieses Manifests wurde auf die Kopie des Filmes eingebrannt. Diese Filmkopie wurde nur in Oberhausen gezeigt und war in dieser Form bis zur Ausstellung im Edith-Russ-Haus nirgendwo anders zu sehen. Die in diesem Buch gedruckten Standfotos stammen aus dieser Kopie. Der deutsche Text ist eine neue, genauere Übersetzung von Milica Vlajković aus dem serbokroatischen Originalmanifest.

Der schwarze Film (Standbilder), 1971

1. **Was Sie gerade sehen, ist die Klassenstruktur der jugoslawischen Gesellschaft, Lumpenproletariat und „humanistische Intelligenz"; die Instrumentalisierung der Armen zu filmischen Zwecken.**
   Eine Lektion über die Hungrigen, Schmutzigen und Stinkenden für die Familie Žilnik.
   Dem Kind sollte man zeigen, wie das Leben wirklich ist.

2. **In einem Land, das sich seines Namens, seiner Hymne und seiner Regierung nicht ganz sicher ist; in einem Moment, in dem sich die Grundbedürfnisse (Brot, Milch und Dollars) täglich verteuern, genießt die Filmkaste narzisstisch die „Erforschung" des Arbeiter- und Bauernelends.**
   Das erlaubt ihr – als einem Teil der staatsbürgerlichen, die Gesellschaft manipulierenden Klasse – eine Illusion des Engagements und Barmherzigkeit.

3. **Man soll alles in Stücke hauen, auch sich selbst.**
   Am besten beginnt man mit dem eigenen Ehebett!
   Wie wäre es, wenn uns die Armen in den Arsch treten würden?
   Glücklicherweise kommt es nicht dazu.

4. **Dennoch muss ich weiter sozialkritische Filme machen. Denn ich muss gegen zwei Feinde kämpfen: Gegen meine eigene kleinbürgerliche Natur, die aus meinem Engagement ein Alibi und ein Geschäft macht; und gegen die Manipulatoren und Machthaber, die von meinem Schweigen profitieren würden.**
   Deshalb scheiß' ich auf mein Schuldgefühl.

5. **FILM – WAFFE ODER SCHWACHSINN?**

6. **Siehe noch einmal Punkt 4.**

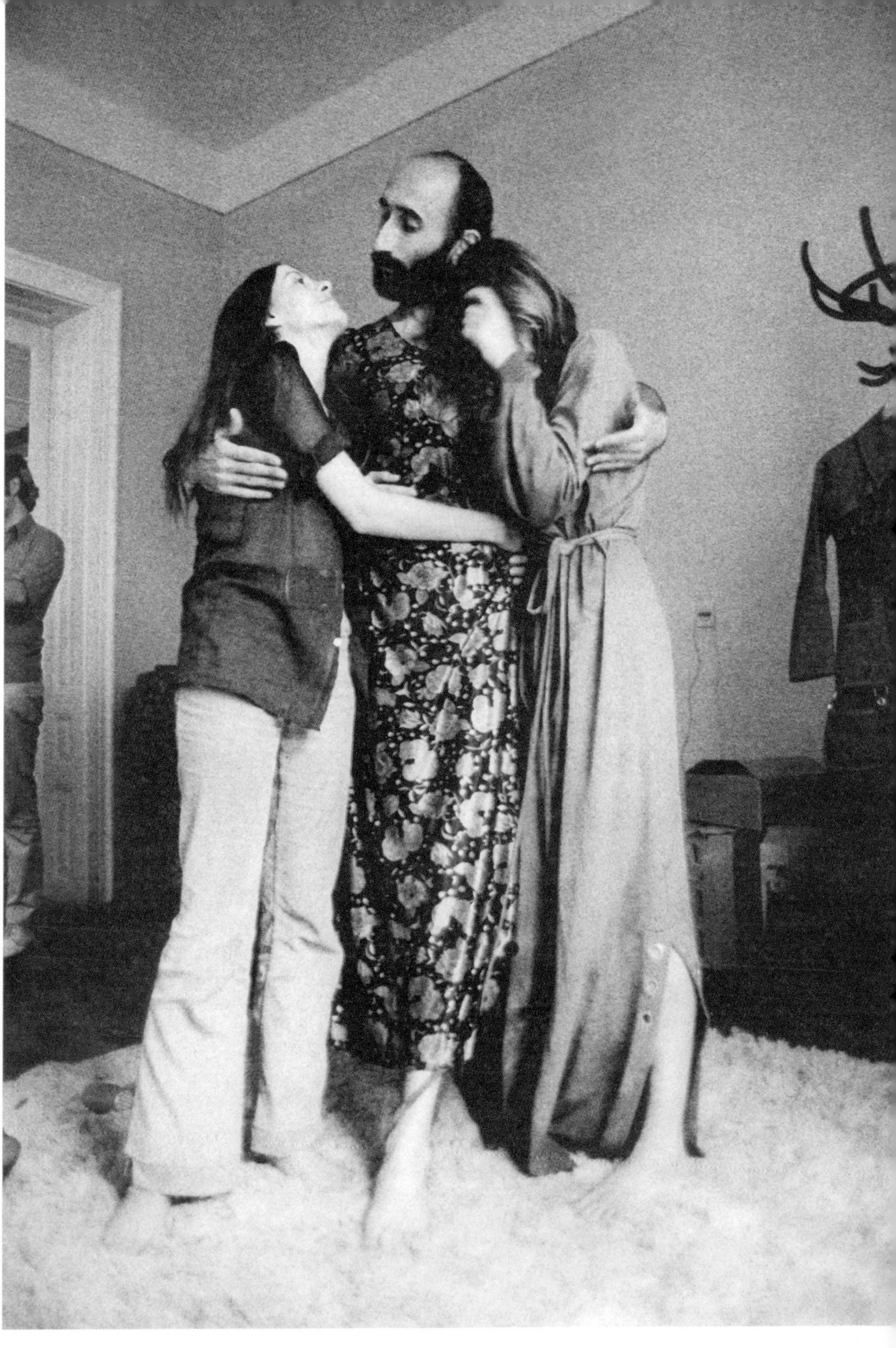

Edit Molnár ist Kuratorin und lebt zurzeit in Deutschland. Sie erwarb einen MA in Kunstgeschichte und Kunsttheorie an der Eötvös-Lóránd-Universität Budapest. Von 2000 bis 2005 war sie Direktorin der Studio Gallery, Budapest, dem nichtkommerziellen Ausstellungsraum der Studio of Young Artists Association; von 2005 bis 2007 war sie Kuratorin an der Műcsarnok | Kunsthalle in Budapest, von 2007 bis 2009 Leiterin der unabhängigen, nichtkommerziellen Institution Contemporary Image Collective mit Sitz in Kairo. Seit 2015 leitet sie, zusammen mit Marcel Schwierin, das Edith-Russ-Haus für Medienkunst in Oldenburg.

Marcel Schwierin ist Kurator, Filmemacher und Mitbegründer der Werkleitz Biennale in Halle, der Experimentalfilm-Datenbank cinovid und des Filmfestivals Arab Shorts in Kairo. Zu seinen Filmen gehören unter anderem *Die Bilder* (Experimentalfilm, 1994) und *Ewige Schönheit* (Dokumentarfilm, 2003). Er kuratierte unter anderem regelmäßig für die Werkleitz Biennale, das Goethe-Institut und die Internationalen Kurzfilmtage Oberhausen. Von 2010 bis 2015 war er Kurator für Film und Video der transmediale in Berlin. Seit 2015 leitet er, zusammen mit Edit Molnár, das Edith-Russ-Haus für Medienkunst in Oldenburg.

What, How & for Whom/WHW ist ein kuratorisches Kollektiv, das 1999 in Zagreb gegründet wurde. Mitglieder sind die Kuratorinnen Ivet Ćurlin, Ana Dević, Nataša Ilić und Sabina Sabolović sowie der Designer und Publizist Dejan Kršić. WHW organisierte ein breites Spektrum von Produktions-, Ausstellungs- und Publikationsprojekten und leitet seit 2003 die städtische Galerija Nova in Zagreb. Seit der ersten Ausstellung *What, How & for Whom, on the occasion of the 152nd anniversary of the Communist Manifesto,* die 2000 in Zagreb stattfand, hat WHW zahlreiche internationale Projekte kuratiert, darunter in jüngerer Zeit *Everything we see could also be otherwise* (*My sweet little lamb*), das mit Kathrin Rhomberg kuratiert wurde und 2016/17 an verschiedenen Orten in Zagreb zu sehen war, sowie die 2nd Industrial Art Biennial 2018, die unter dem Titel *On the Shoulders of Fallen Giants* an verschiedenen Standorten in den kroatischen Städten Rijeka, Pula, Labin, Raša und Vodnjan stattfand. 2018 gründete WHW ein neues internationales Studienprogramm für junge Künstlerinnen und Künstler, die WHW Akademija mit Sitz in Zagreb. Im März 2019 wurden drei Mitglieder von WHW – Ivet Ćurlin, Nataša Ilić und Sabina Sabolović – als Künstlerische Leitung der Kunsthalle Wien berufen. Als Kollektiv arbeitet WHW weiterhin in Zagreb, wo die Aktivitäten von Ana Dević koordiniert werden. ★

Dragana Đurić, Branko Vučićević und Alenka Zdešar bei den Dreharbeiten zu *Freiheit oder Comicstrip*, 1971.
FOTO: ANDREJ POPOVIĆ.

Verbote und Gerichtsverfahren, diese kleinkarierten Zurechtweisungen, sind nicht nur chirurgische Operationen, mit denen Bücher oder Filme auf den Müllhaufen geworfen werden, und das war es. Im Gegenteil: Verbote und Gerichtsverfahren, das sind Anreize – das ist ein Konzept, ein Wegweiser für eine Praxis, die versucht, nicht verklagt oder verboten zu werden. Wenn man das kritische Denken vor Gericht stellt, ist das zugleich ein Verfahren, mit dem man das Feld düngt, auf dem Karrierismus, Rückgratlosigkeit und Trägheit wie Unkraut in die Höhe schießen – das ist trivial und allgemein bekannt. Die Ästhetik eines geschlossenen Mundes ist wie eine Honigfalle. Jede noch so kleine Repression wird Befürworter finden, die angeblich von ihr verängstigt sind und die sich für alle möglichen mutlosen Leidenschaften rechtfertigen. Wenn es also wirklich Filme gäbe, die von Feinden gemacht werden, bekämen wir nur zu bald die endgültige Antwort auf die Frage, welche Art Film von „einem Freund“ gemacht wird.

—Želimir Žilnik, Interview, „Film Cannot Stand Head Transplantation“, in: *Telegram*, 15. September 1972

Schon seit dem Moment der Refeudalisierung des Staates Mitte der 1970er Jahre, als die lokalen Eliten anfingen, sich so viel wie möglich unter den Nagel zu reißen und gleichzeitig ihre eigenen Kriterien aufstellten, war offensichtlich, was auf uns zukommen würde. Die Zügel wurden gestrafft, die Spannungen nahmen zu, und es gab zwei mögliche Resultate: entweder eine Welle der Öffnung, Demokratisierung und Freiheit oder etwas, das am Ende nur zu einer Herrschaft nationaler Eliten führen kann, die sich gegenseitig die Kehle durchschneiden. Das war mir klar, aber der Film *Schöne Frauen gehen durch die Stadt* **war relativ erfolglos. Wahrscheinlich kursierte das Gerücht: „Žilnik ist verrückt geworden! Er hat einen Dachschaden!" … Und jetzt, wo sich diese grauenhafte Wunde geöffnet hat, wo das, was geschehen ist, geschehen ist, wo hunderttausende Leichen und Millionen Vertriebener hinter uns liegen, wo wir Zeugen einer furchtbaren Zerstörung sind – werden die Dinge durchschaubarer. Diese gegenseitige Zerstörung konnte nicht allein von den Politikern bewirkt werden.**

—Želimir Žilnik, Interview, „Contributions for a Biography", in: *Ekran 2000,* Nr. 2, 1995

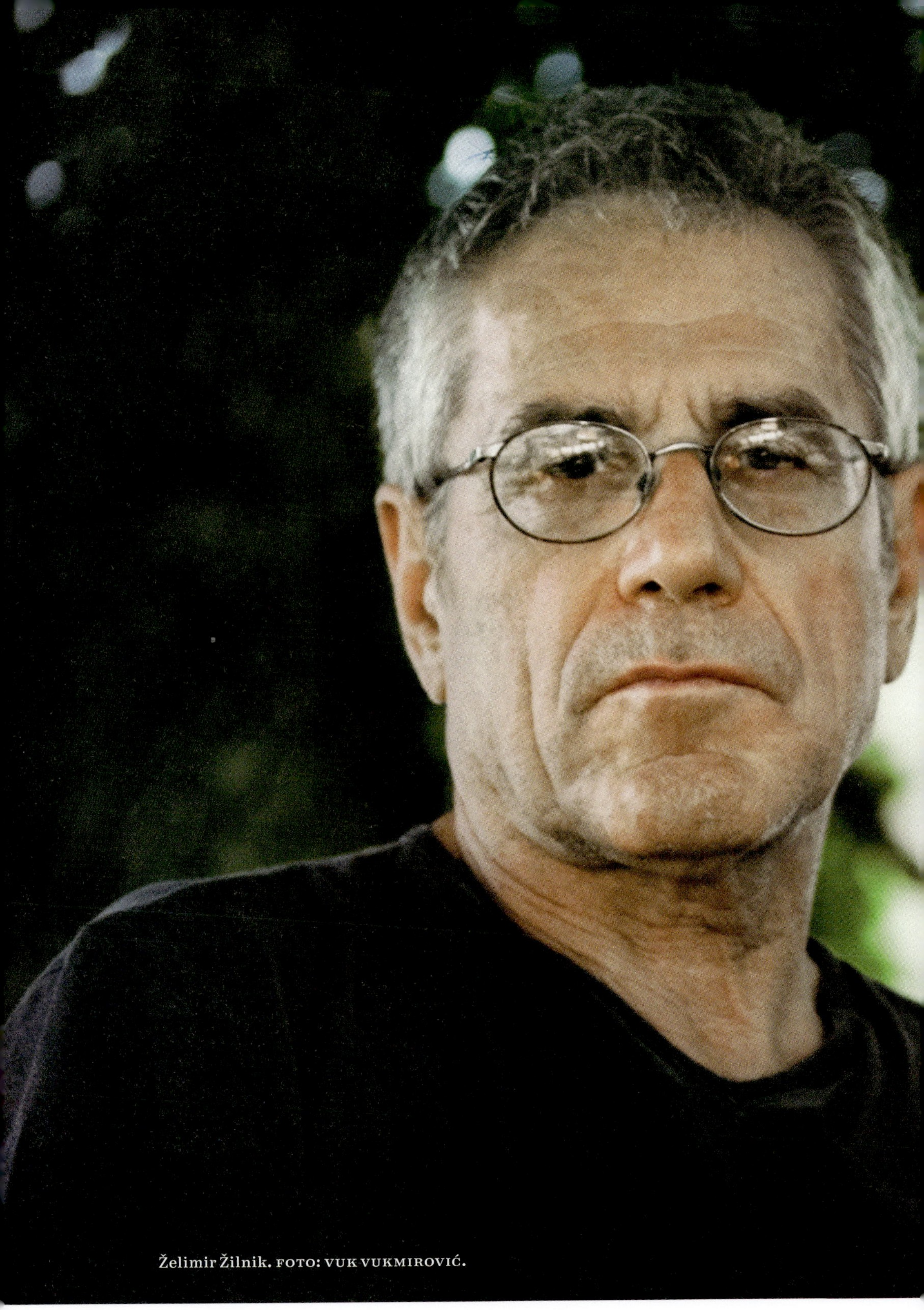

Želimir Žilnik. FOTO: VUK VUKMIROVIĆ.

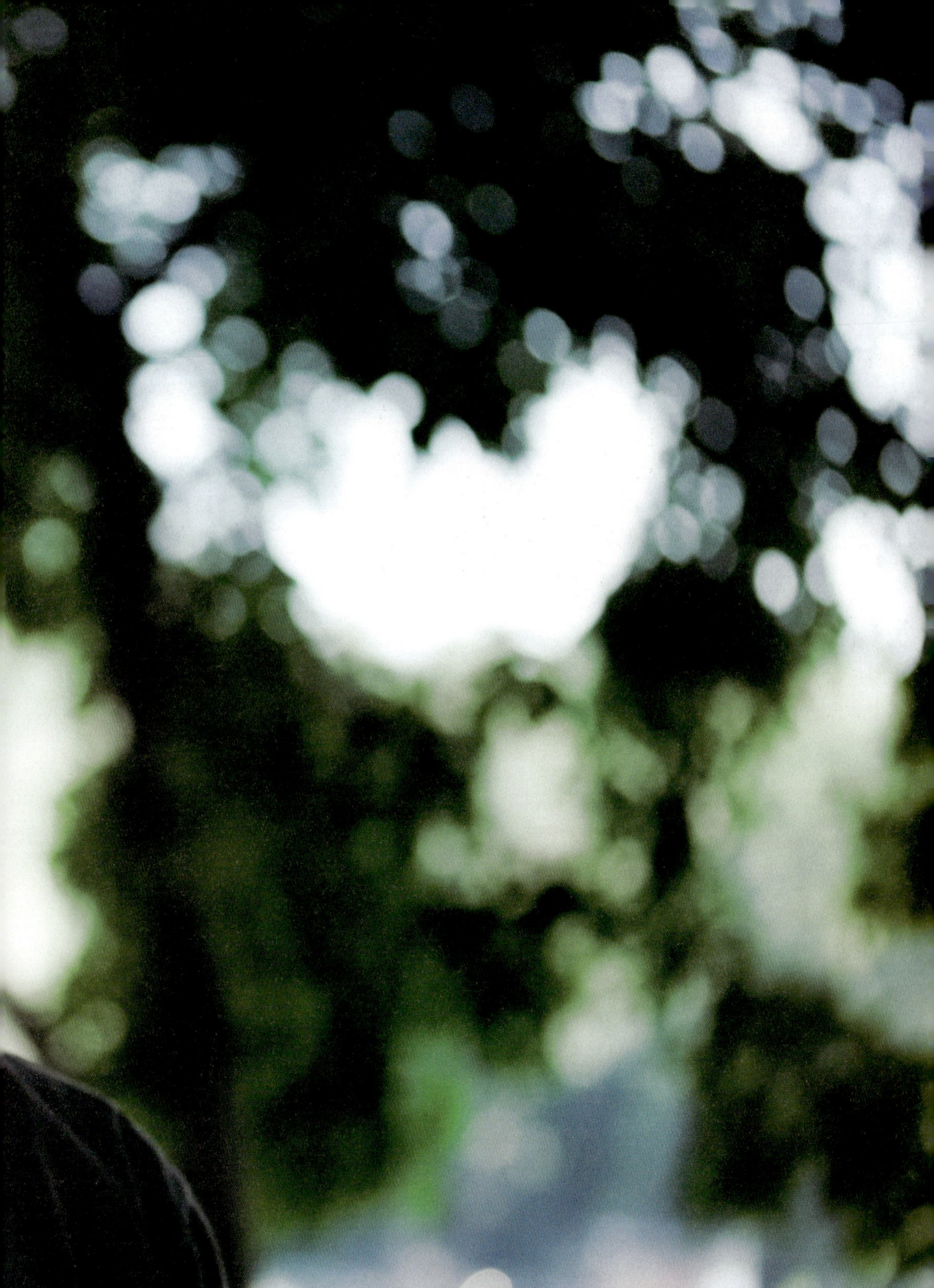

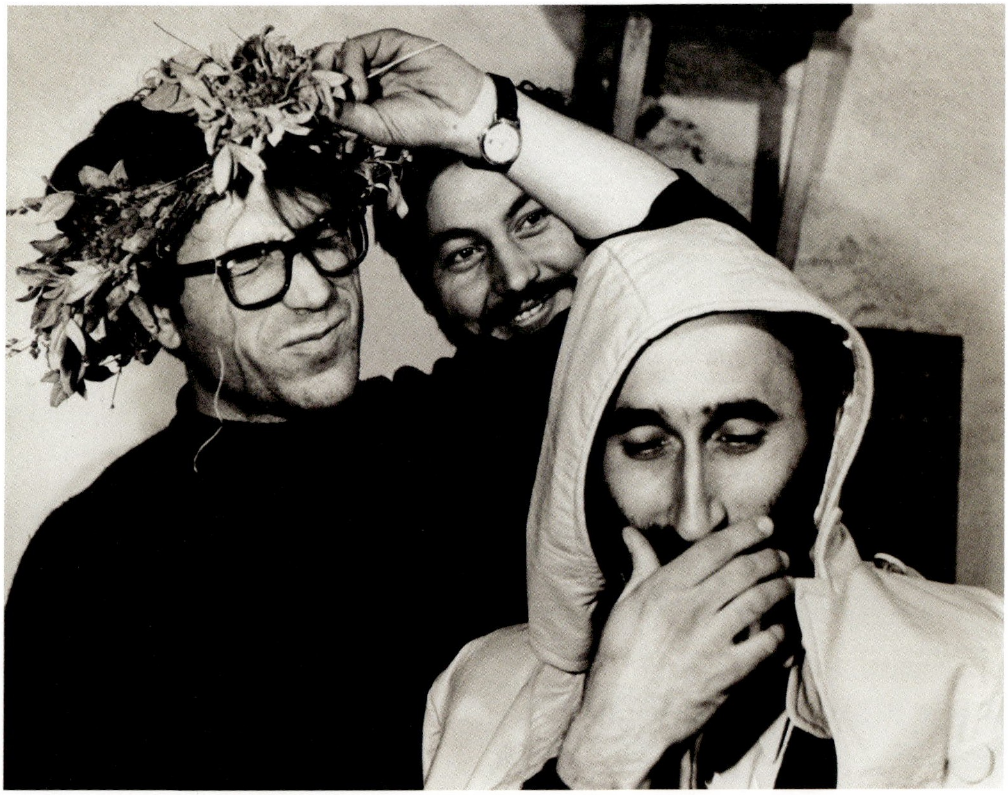

LEFT TO RIGHT Želimir Žilnik, Karpo Godina, and Branko Vučićević on the set of *Early Works*, 1968.

VON LINKS NACH RECHTS Želimir Žilnik, Karpo Godina und Branko Vučićević bei den Dreharbeiten zu *Frühe Werke*, 1968. PHOTO/FOTO: ANDREJ POPOVIĆ.

Thank you / Danke an

Afterall (Ana Bilbao, Charles Esche) • Boris Buden • Jasna Čagalj • Branislav Dimitrijević • Human Rights Film Festival (ZAGREB) • International Short Film Festival Oberhausen • Kino Tuškanac • Gal Kirn • Ana Kovačić • kuda.org • Pavle Levi • Jurij Meden • Petar Milat • Zoran Pantelić • Ivan Ramljak • Ana Šeba • Dubravka Sekulić • Borka Stojić • Žiga Testen.

We are grateful to the production houses that helped to make Želimir Žilnik's films, as well as to all the authors and collaborators who have contributed to this book.

Our utmost gratitude goes to Sarita Matijević and Želimir Žilnik, without whose openness, support, and infectious enthusiasm neither the exhibitions in Oldenburg and Zagreb nor this volume would have been possible. ●

Wir bedanken uns bei den Produktionsfirmen, die Želimir Žilniks Filme ermöglicht haben, sowie bei allen Autorinnen und Autoren, Mitarbeiterinnen und Mitarbeitern, die zu diesem Buch beigetragen haben.

Unser größter Dank gilt Sarita Matijević und Želimir Žilnik, ohne deren Aufgeschlossenheit, Unterstützung und ansteckenden Enthusiasmus weder die Ausstellung in Oldenburg und Zagreb noch dieses Buch möglich gewesen wären. ●

oni koji revoluciju
izvedu tek. doppla
samo kopaju.sebi grob
sen zist

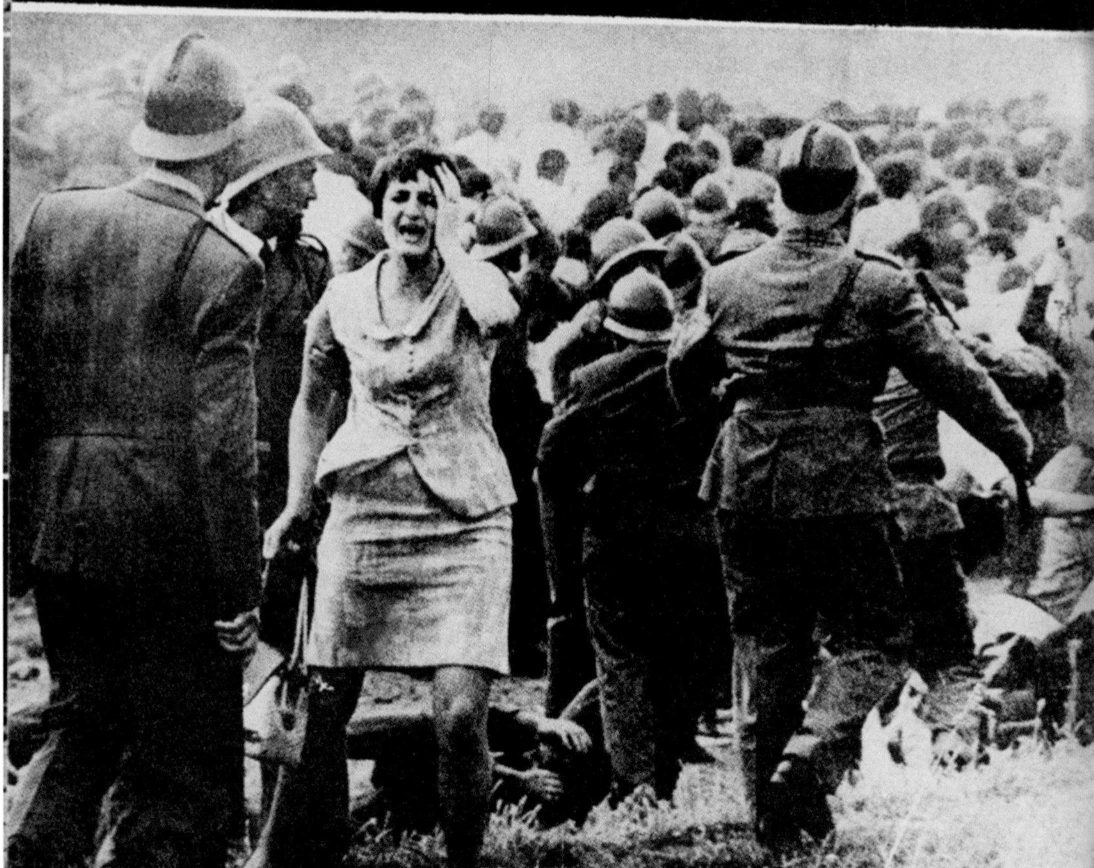

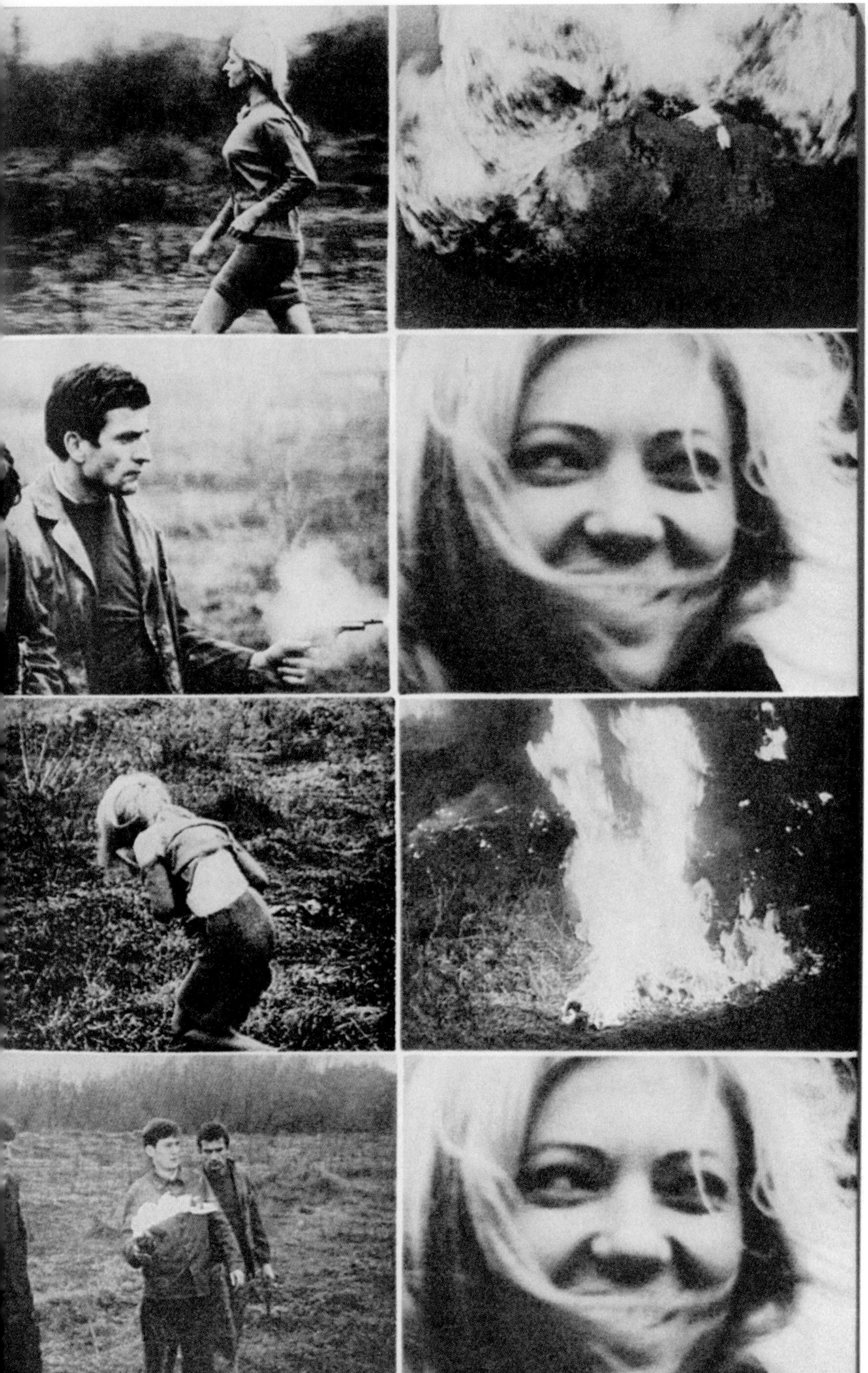

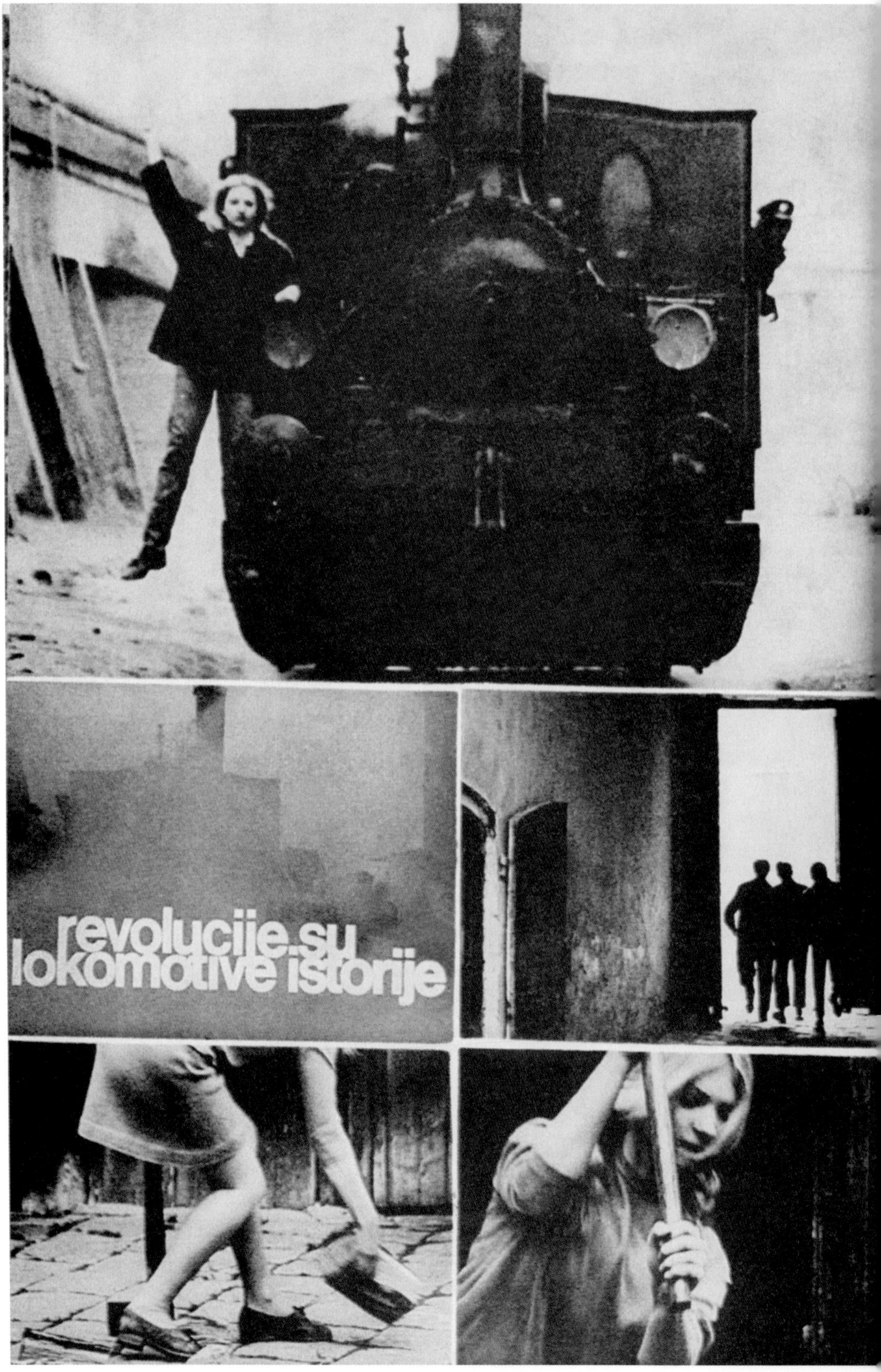
revolucije su
lokomotive istorije

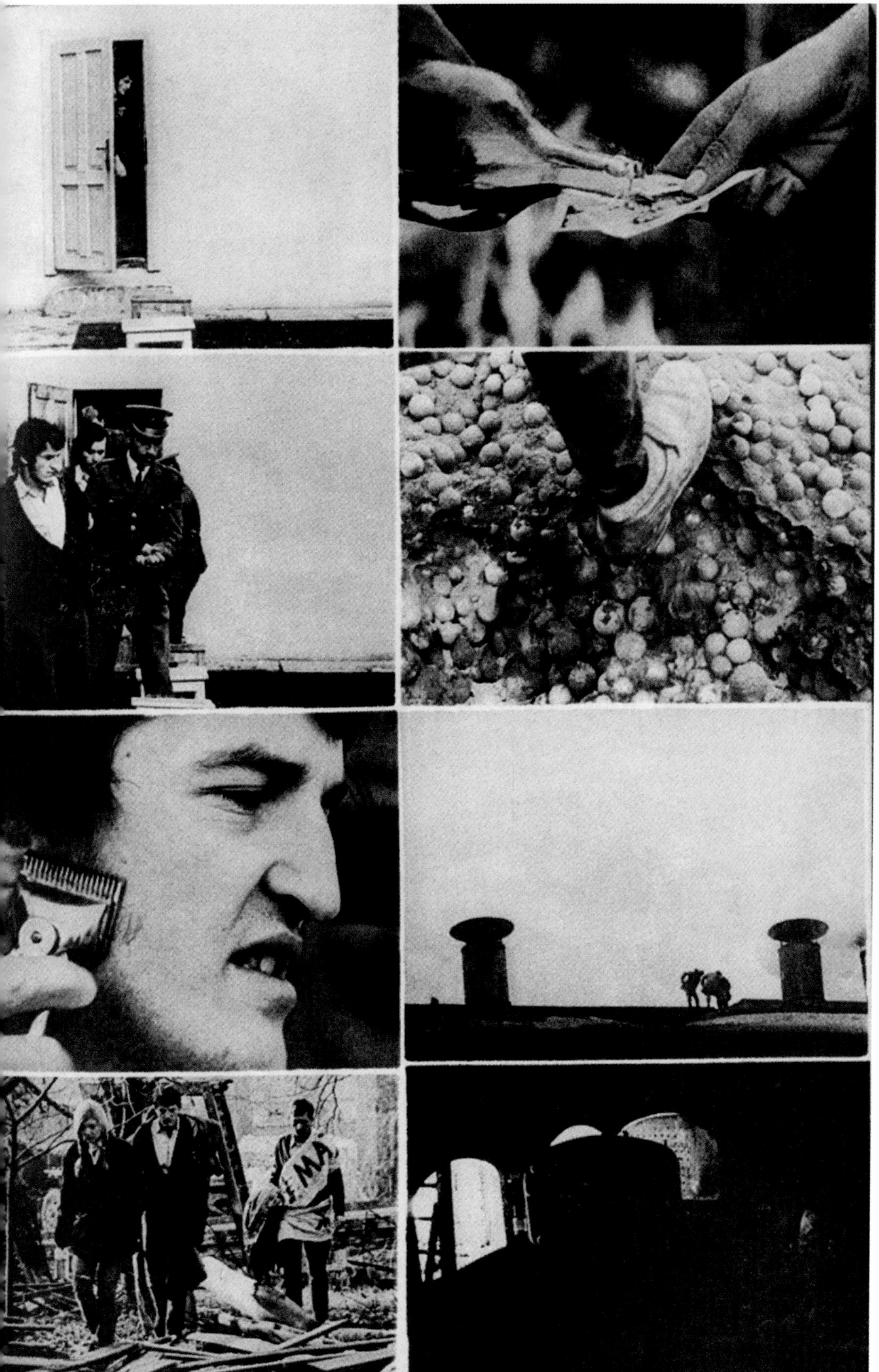

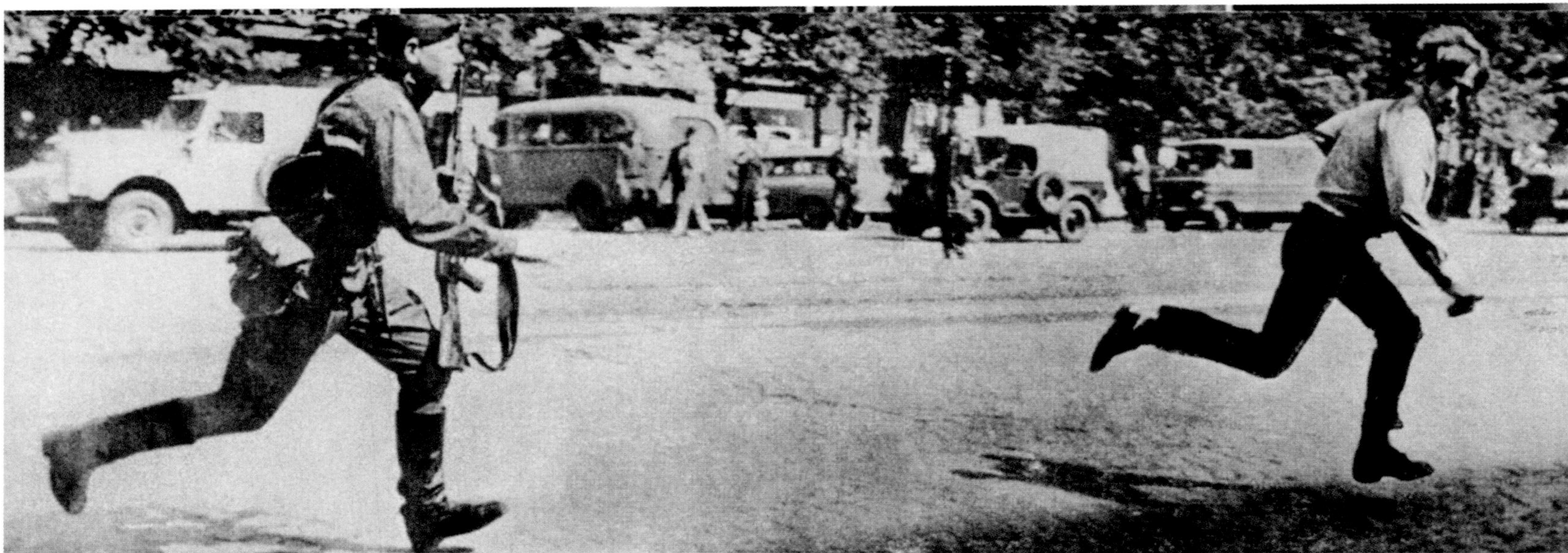

… leur gouvernement. Les beatniks se montrent les plus intrépides. Ici, un soldat russe se lance à la poursuite d'un manifestant qui l'a nargué. Souvent ces courses se sont terminées

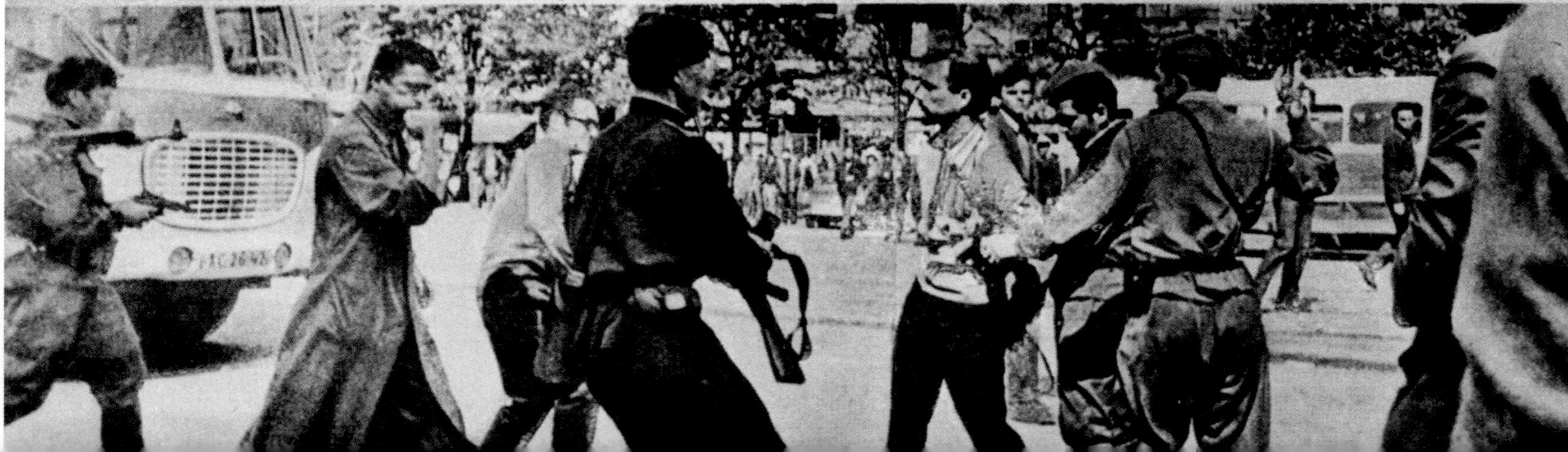

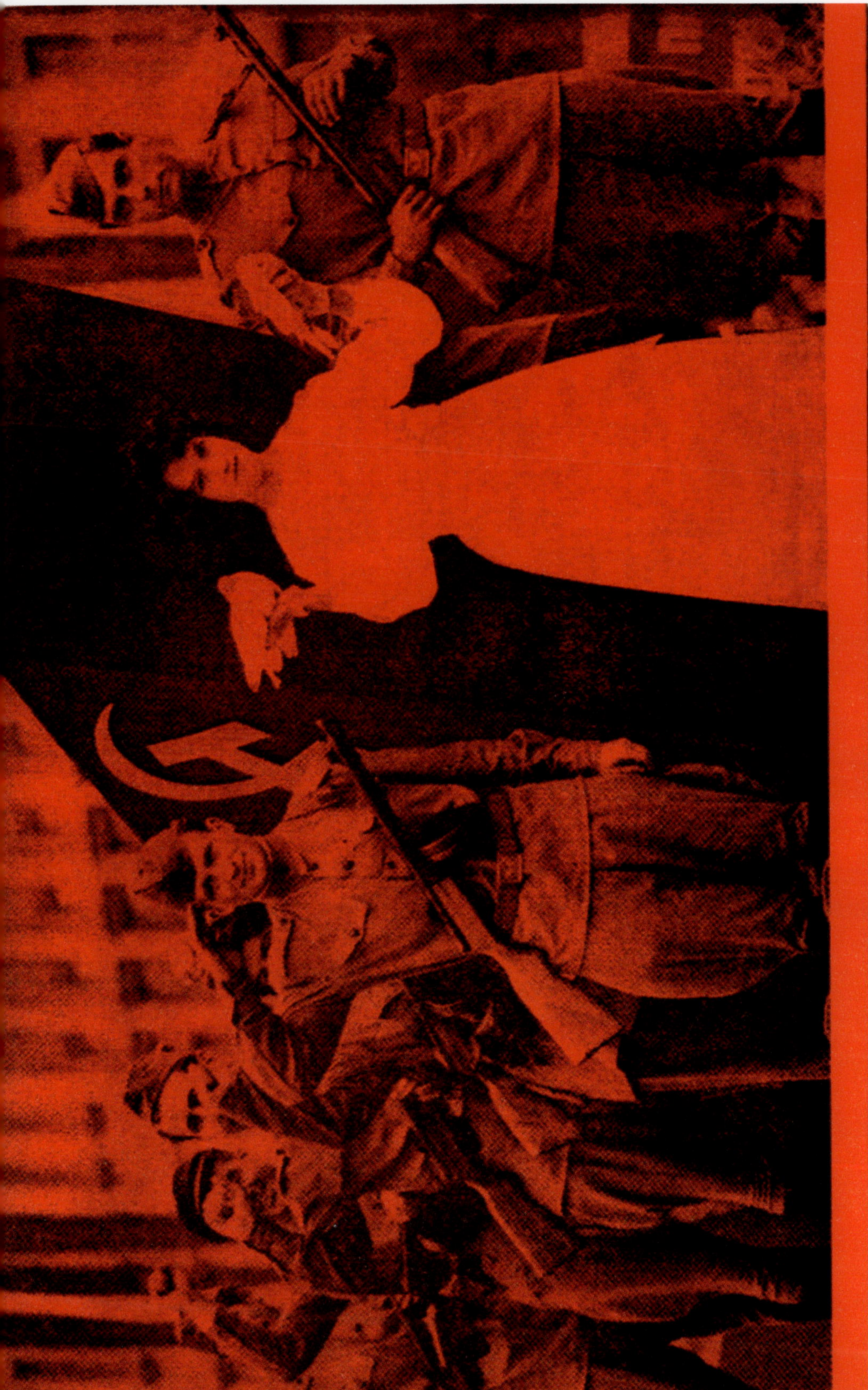

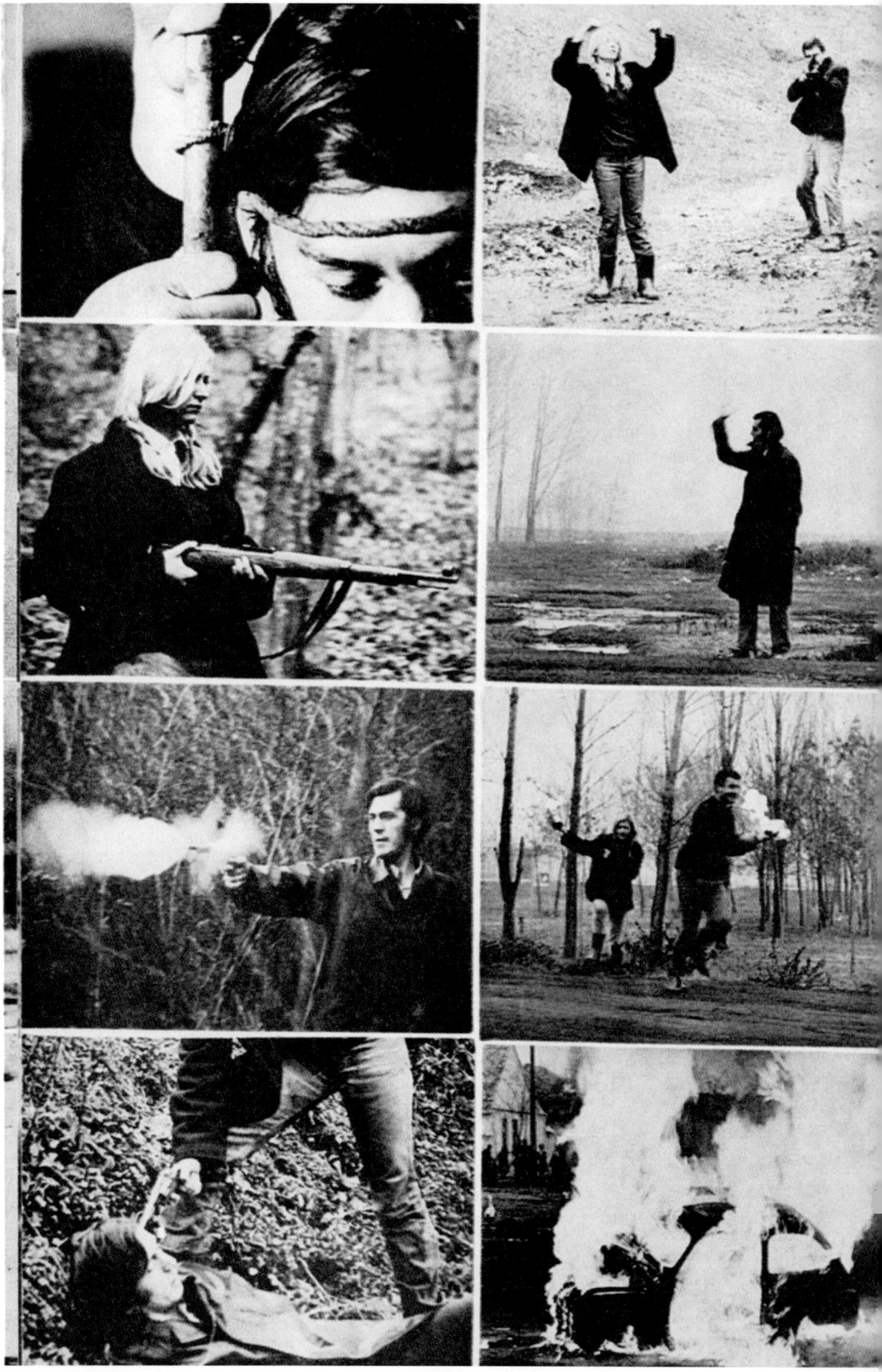

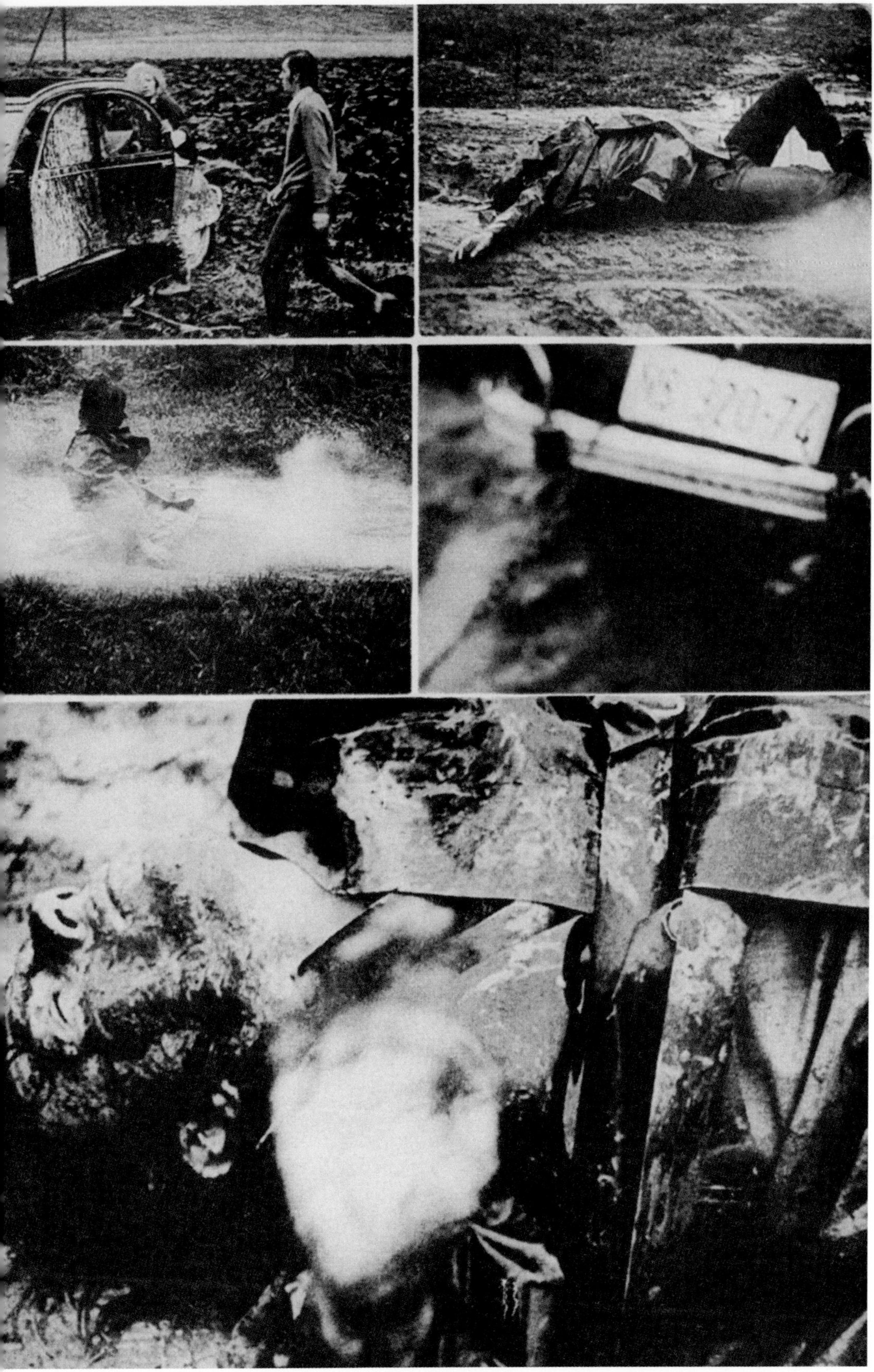

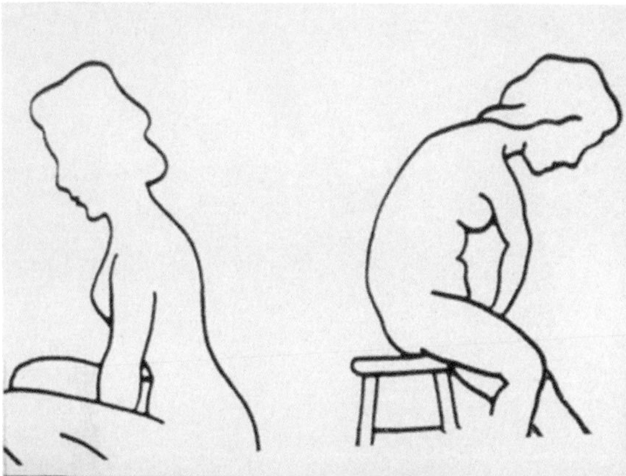
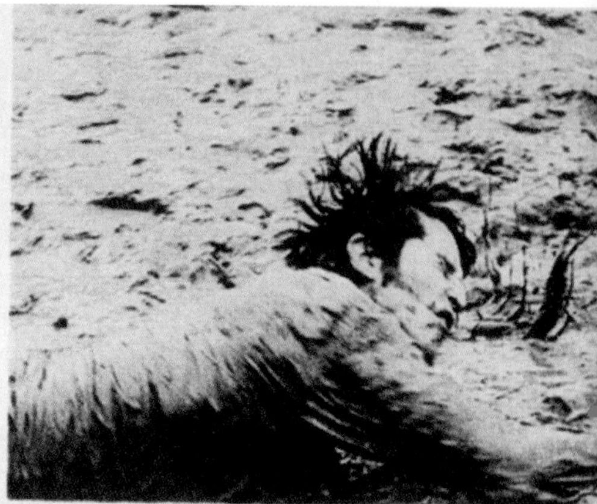
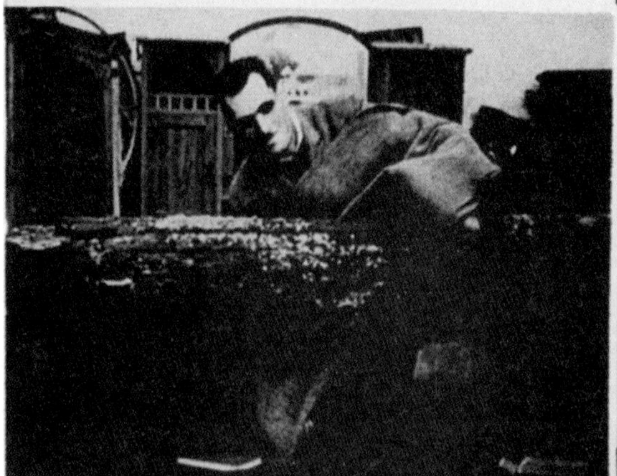
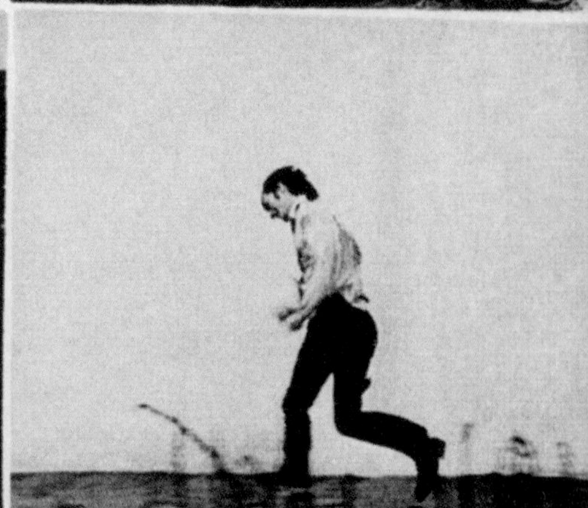
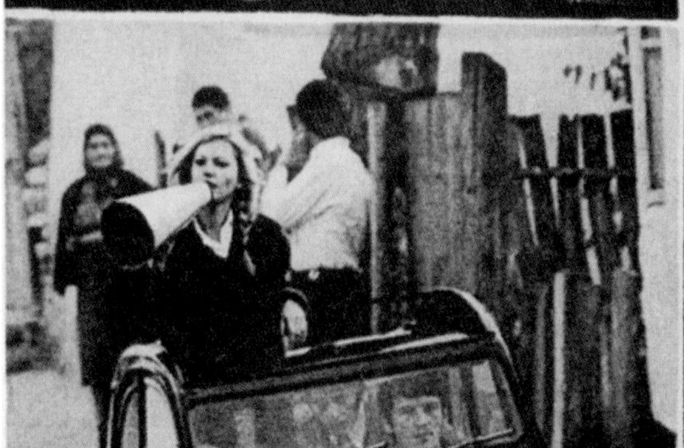
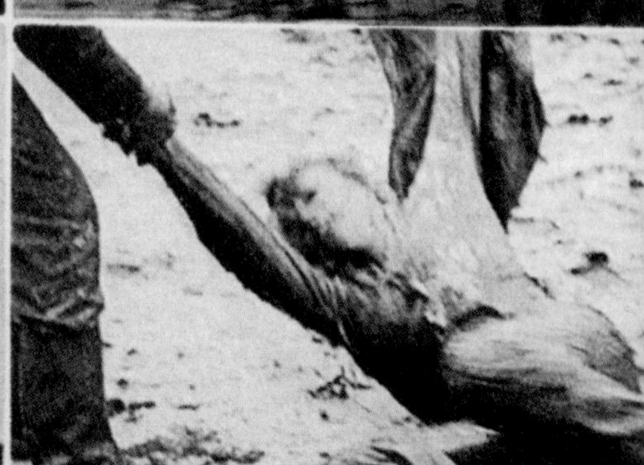
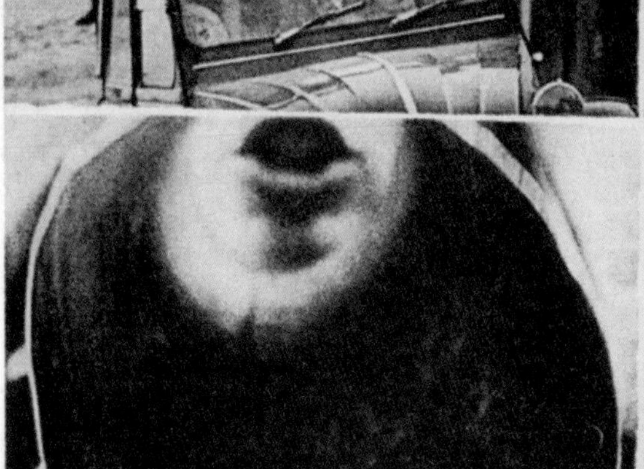
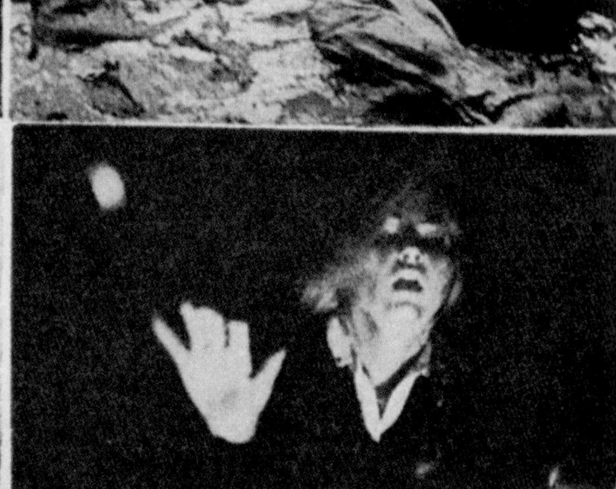

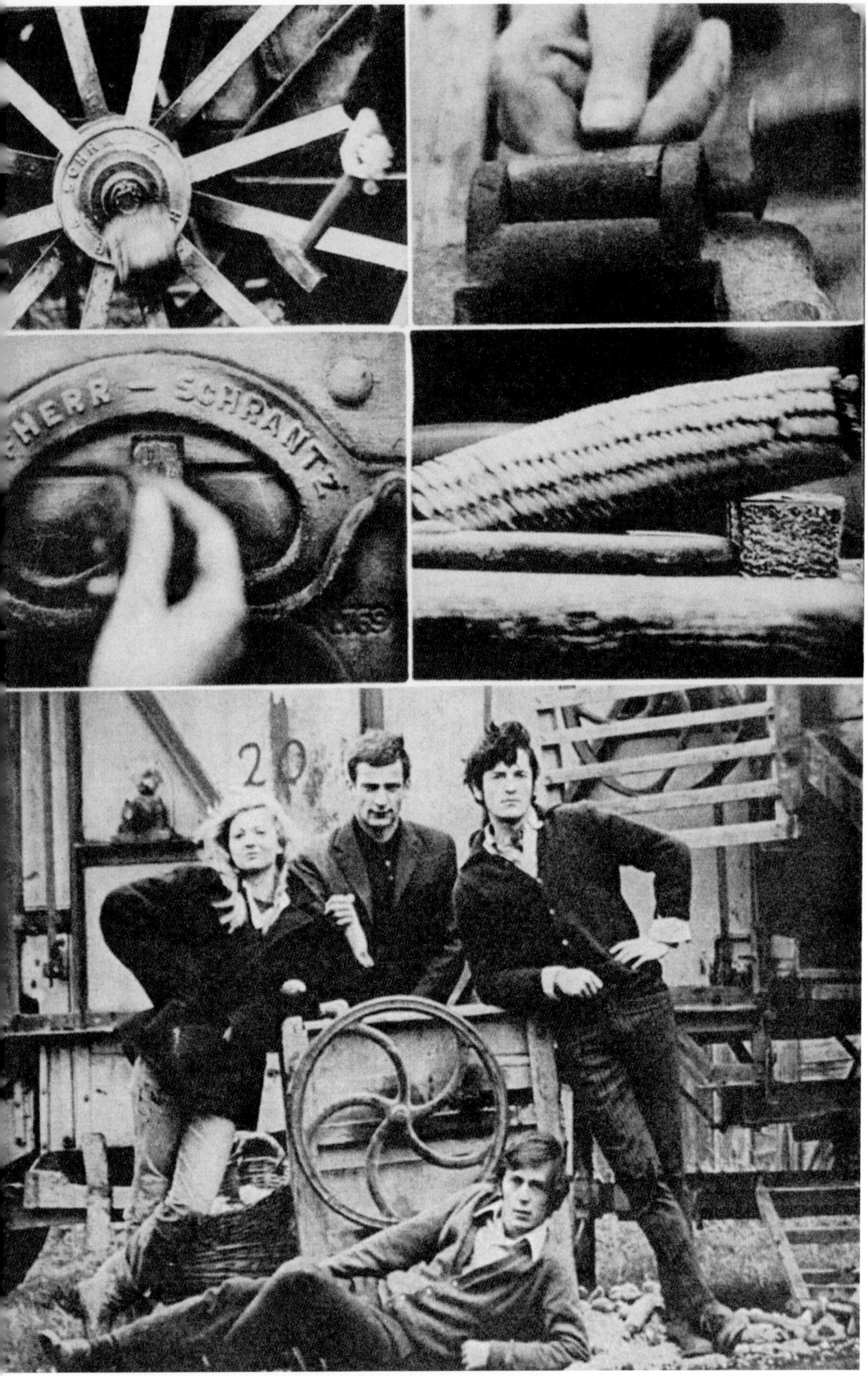
HERR — SCHRANTZ
20

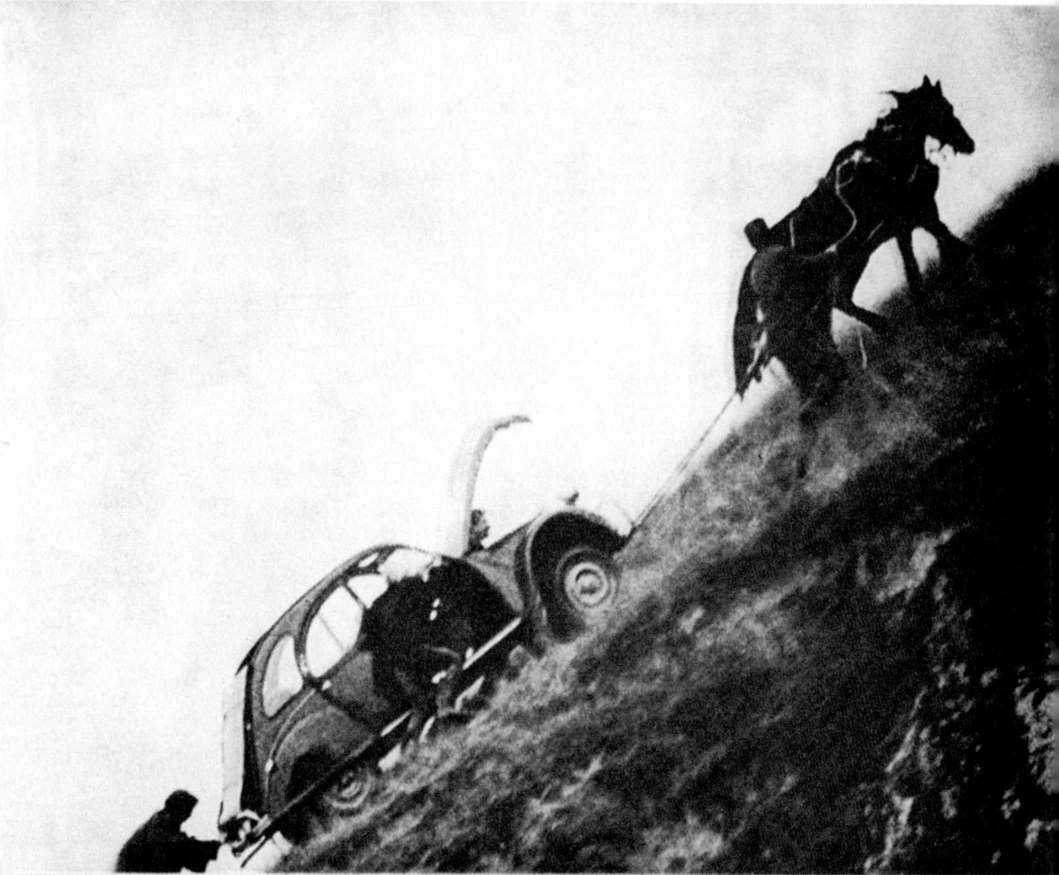

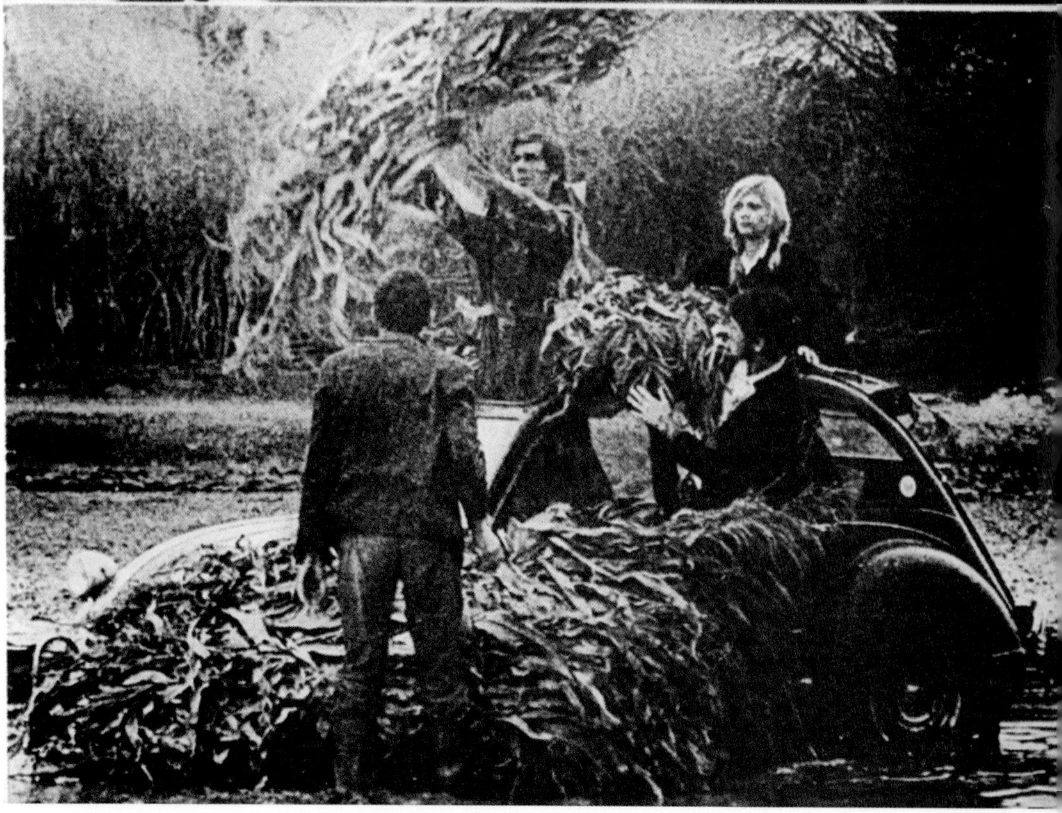

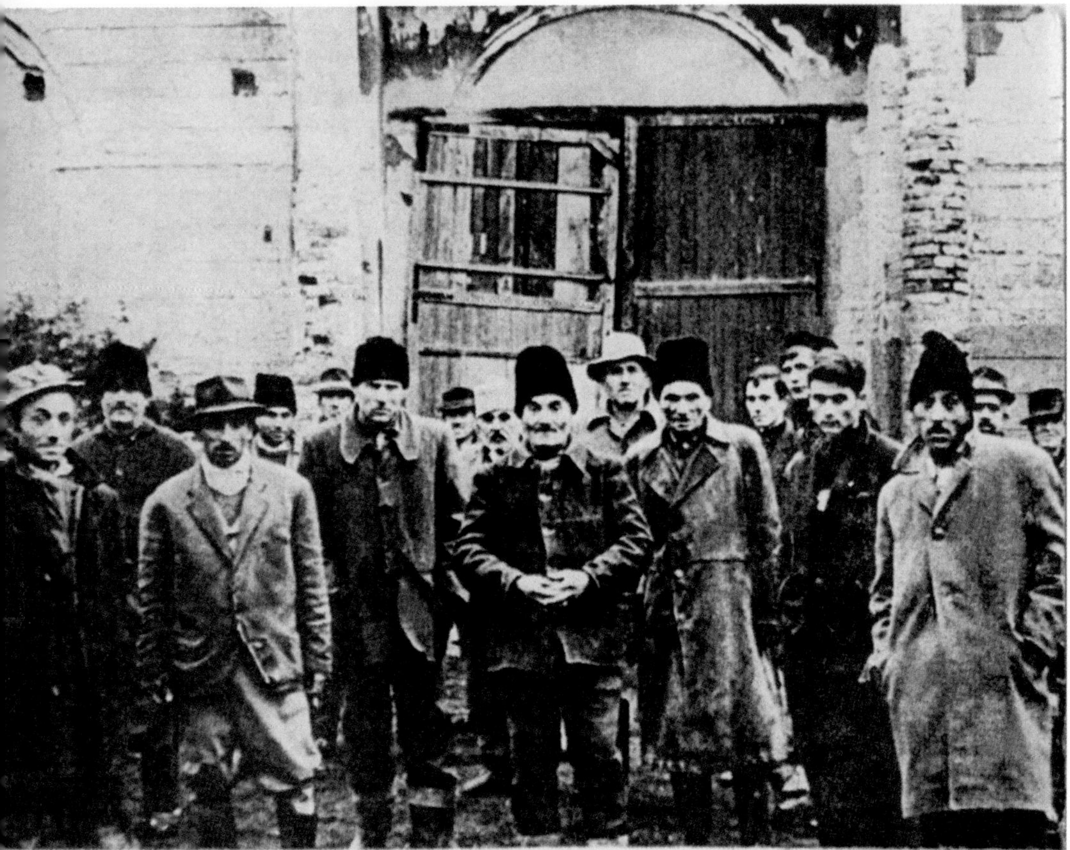

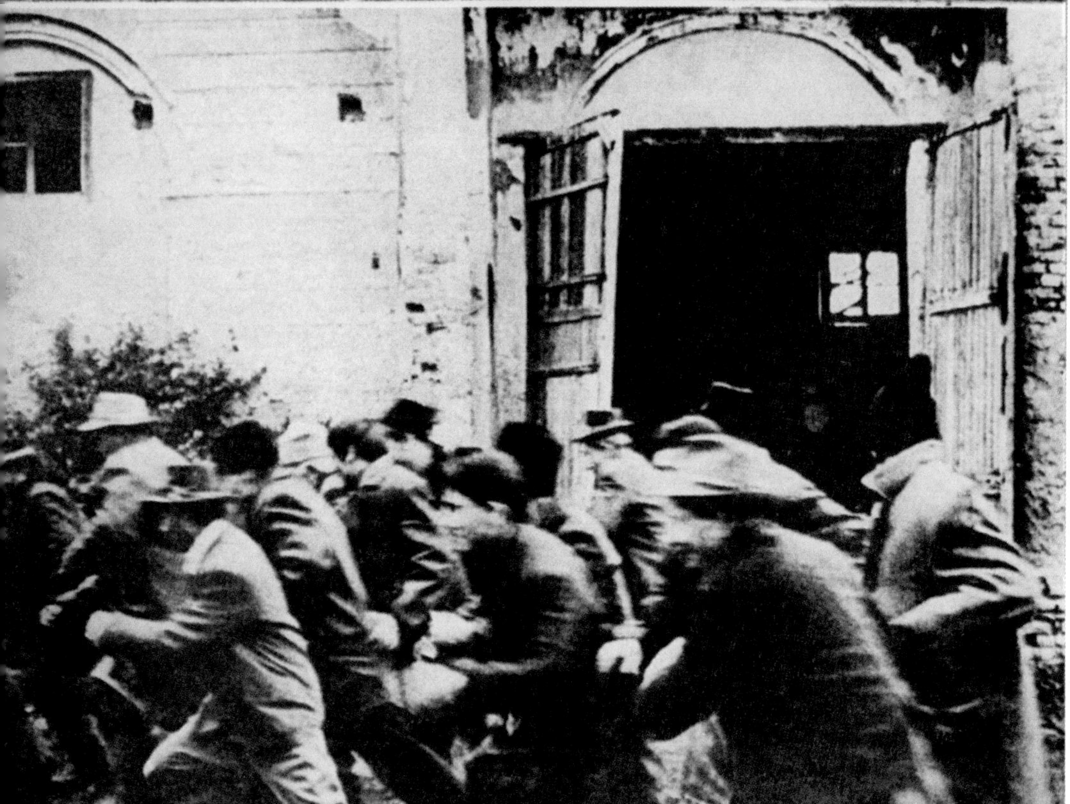

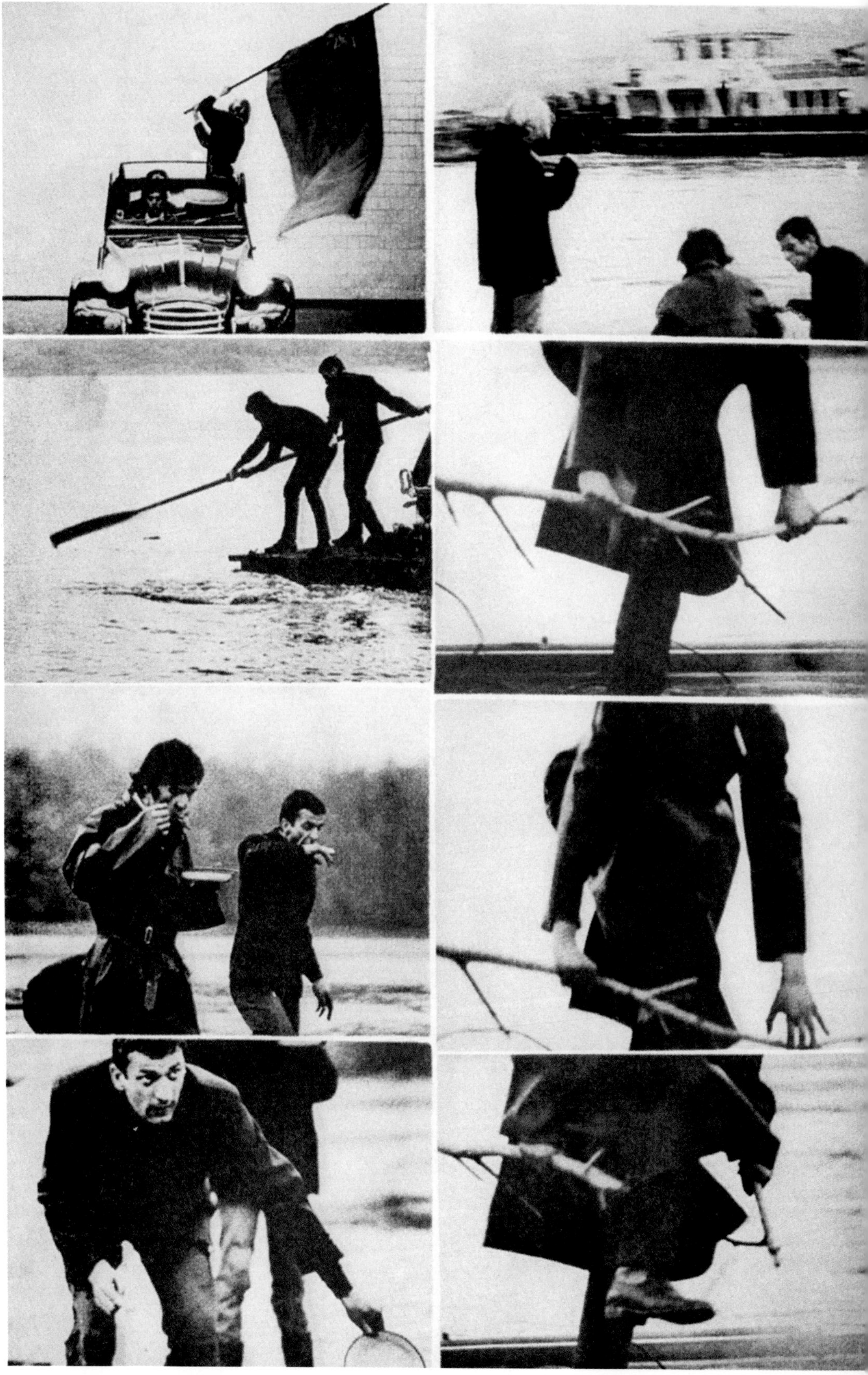